# THE HILL AND BEYOND

# THE HILL AND BEYOND

## CHILDREN'S TELEVISION DRAMA – AN ENCYCLOPEDIA

Alistair D. McGown & Mark J. Docherty

 Publishing

First published in 2003 by the
British Film Institute
21 Stephen Street, London W1T 1LN

The British Film Institute promotes greater
understanding of, and access to, film and moving
image culture in the UK.

Type design and layout by Alistair D. McGown
Printed in Malta by Interprint

British Library Cataloguing-in-Publication Data
A catalogue record for this book is available
from the British Library
ISBN 0–85170–879–x (pbk)
ISBN 0–85170–878–1 (hbk)

# Contents

# Acknowledgments

Thanks are due to the following fellow enthusiasts for their various brands of advice and assistance, obtainable immediately: Tony Achatz, Alan Barnes, Alan Bissett, Paul Cornell, David Darlington, Robert Dick, Clayton Hickman, Gareth Humphreys, Gerard Johnson, Graham Kibble-White, Jack Kibble-White, Ian Potter, Jim Sangster, David Savage and many more good fellows everywhere. Thank you also to Chris Barlas and Leonard White.

Our appreciation also extends to all staff of the BFI and Scottish Screen with particular thanks due to Tom Cabot, Kathleen Dickson, Alan Docherty (no relation), Annie Docherty (no relation either!), Sarah Prosser, Olwen Terris and especially our publisher Andrew Lockett for seeing some kind of promise in the original proposal way back when.

Most very special thanks are reserved for Paul Moore, telly addict, computer technician and getaway driver, whose enthusiasm never flagged whenever ours threatened to do so.

# Preface

The children's serial has its own rules, properties and mythology –
some written, some understood through long custom ...

**S**o wrote Shaun Sutton in 1982. Sutton had been a writer, producer, director and even reluctant actor in the earliest days of children's drama at the BBC in the 1950s. He and the other members of the children's department had to try, virtually by guesswork, to ascertain the kind of stories that could be told for youngsters.

Its conflicts must be boisterous rather than violent, sex is holding
hands, bad language is out. The strand has always been a sort of moral
touchstone for those who guard the young viewer (sometimes
unnecessarily) against the harms of television.

The children's audience has long been seen as a vulnerable one – as well as second guessing what the audience will enjoy, the makers of children's drama have also had to struggle with questions of taste and suitability. Despite this protective approach, which pervaded the BBC in the 50s and 60s, various breakthrough approaches were employed, particularly in the early 70s, until children's television drama grew to encompass all kinds of stories beyond literary adaptation of the classics and wholesome adventure stories. Sutton summed up his view of children's drama:

It requires a simplicity of storyline and presentation, avoiding the
oblique. Complicated personal relationships, Freudian obsessions and
the darker side of human nature are better left out.

We would beg to differ and so too would many of the writers and producers who have fashioned children's television drama in just such shapes and directions since the 1970s. The last three decades of the 20th century have witnessed the maturity of the subgenre and the delivery of ever more complex and contentious programming, true to its audience. Children's drama has been a hotbed for controversy, particularly realistic contemporary series like Grange Hill and Byker Grove, though none of the complaints ever come from the children but from their parents. Younger viewers who don't appreciate a programme will quickly become restless and ultimately switch off their television sets and go and do something less boring instead. They are the ultimate arbiters and perhaps television's most demanding audience.

Looking back at children's television without recourse to nostalgia is a very difficult thing to do. Certainly, in our fortunate position of having been able to view many of our childhood favourites again, we have found ourselves admittedly disappointed by revisiting some programmes, but on the other hand we have been glad to be surprised and delighted by others more sophisticated than we ever remembered them. All the programmes you loved ought to be here but, having done our best to look at them through objective, adult eyes, we can hopefully leave the reminiscing in the mind of the individual reader while presenting a considered overview of the development of children's drama programming in Britain.

*Dr Alistair D. McGown & Mark J. Docherty*

# Introduction

The aim for this book is, fairly obviously, to cover in at least some level of detail every British-made live action children's drama shown on television in the fifty years covering 1950 to 2000. While this may seem relatively straightforward at first, there are several issues of definition to be considered.

'British-made' means that a series has been made by British-based production companies, be they the BBC, an ITV franchise-holder or, in more recent years, an independent programme-maker. The picture has become clouded, particularly with the onset of global television since the 1990s, by co-production deals where several countries have contributed expertise or cash to the enterprise. In these cases we have had to make a value judgment as to whether the British component is of enough note to merit inclusion. For example, while almost a dozen companies are credited in the 1990s version of *The Famous Five*, several ITV franchises held executive status and the series was filmed in Britain by mostly British crews with British actors. The 1995 series *Moonacre* was a pan-European aggregate filmed overseas – but with a British screenwriter adapting a British novel, and with several leads played by English and Welsh actors, it was thought worthy of inclusion.

Obviously this rule means no imports – series made in other countries and later purchased for screening on British television. British television, particularly since the advent of the commercial channels, has long relied on imported programming, particularly from America, and the children's arena is no exception. By excluding imported dramas we hope to be able to construct a cogent mass of like material which shows just what British programme-makers have thought suitable for children over these fifty years. The rule also, of course, fits in with the tenets of the *British* Film Institute. So no *Red Hand Gang*, *Littlest Hobo* or *Goosebumps* we're afraid nor, perhaps more disappointingly, will there be coverage of *Belle and Sebastian*, *White Horses* and their kin from Europe. Some imports of importance will be mentioned in passing (after all, it was the long-running Dutch version of *Heidi* which made most impact with viewers down the years in comparison with various BBC serial adaptations).

The hardest definition of course concerns 'children's drama'. What is it? Well, fairly obviously, it is drama made for children. That suggests a two-part concept. Let's take drama first. 'Drama' is fiction; that at least should be obvious. 'Sitcom' is fiction too though – containing a storyline populated with characters. What drama has but sitcom does not is, perhaps, emotional realism. Actions mean consequences, sometimes painful, sometimes less so, but always with a lesson learned and the character changed by the experience. Sitcom will tend towards rebooting each week with the status quo and all character development reversed (*Only Fools and Horses*, for one, is an exception but hopefully proves the rule).

The 1980s comedy drama *Seaview* definitely counts as 'drama' when it comes down to emotional realism, despite comic scrapes going on around it; adventure serials on the other hand rarely contain emotional depth but at least when someone gets hit it hurts. Various entries on the fringes are included for illustration more than anything – the *Marmalade Atkins* series, with its satirical barbs, has more to say about many aspects of British life than any number of *Famous Fives*, for example, and *Worzel Gummidge* is a very humanist series. *Rentaghost* is not included, nor *Pardon My Genie*, we're afraid, nor many of their later over-the-top anti-realist panto progeny (*Graham's Gang*; *Gruey*; *Simon and the Witch*; *Galloping Galaxies*; *Watt on Earth*; *Uncle Jack* and so on). Comedy drama is a term much bandied around children's television today but, on examination, the balance now swings far more in the favour of the comedic and silly, so fun series such as *Barmy Aunt Boomerang*, *Big Kids*, *The Worst Witch* and the like are all excluded from more 'serious' examination.

So much for 'drama', but what about its possessive, 'children's drama'? Drama belonging to children? Drama made for children? Drama viewed and enjoyed by children? Each of these is slightly different in emphasis. Technically speaking, the programmes contained within this book were, on the whole, made by defined, appointed children's departments within the production companies or commissioned from an external supplier by them. In addition, it's a children's programme if it airs between the designated 'children's hours' on weekday afternoons (the actual timeslots have shifted and adapted over the years although in practice are still overseen by children's departments). One historical complication was the wresting away of drama productions from the BBC Children's Department in 1962 and the entire department's politically motivated closure between 1964 and 1967. (This meant, for example, we were inclined not to include one of the programmes most popular with children in the 1960s, 1970s and 1980s – *Doctor Who*, first aired in 1963. A wealth of printed material discussing the good Doctor's exploits is readily available elsewhere, an infinitesimal proportion of it written by ourselves.)

Where this simple definition begins to weaken is on the weekends. With a family audience reckoned to be watching on Saturday and Sunday teatimes, many programmes aired at that time are produced by 'adult' departments for consumption by the family. Now the definition of 'children's' becomes harder to capture. These programmes are no longer made exclusively for children but are expected to appeal to them, therefore certain elements may be included to hold their attention alongside the other members of the family. What we have attempted to do is ascertain those occasions where the content aimed at children reaches a significant level and thus is/was more likely to hold their interest.

This value judgment is particularly important when it comes to assessing the so-called 'Sunday Classic'. A staple of BBC Sunday teatime schedules in the 1960s and 1970s and later annexed with a freer hand by the ITV companies, the serial adaptations of period literary works were thought to be nominally – although we would contend inaccurately – for children, even if they included the weighty notions of such works as *Vanity Fair*, *The Old Curiosity Shop*,

*David Copperfield* or *A Tale of Two Cities* (now more likely to be remade with vast budgets and aired in peak time for more appreciative adult viewers). Even 1981's accurate adaptation of *Gulliver in Lilliput* concentrates far more on Swift's political asides than corny 'little people' antics and so is not included here.

The BBC of the 1950s and early 1960s was almost obsessed with period drama made 'For the Children' (as the umbrella title indicated) but we would contend that many serials were made '*at* the children' with little understanding of what engages younger audiences. To cover many of these serials would, we believe, detract from the central thrust of this book, which is to recall the history of children's fiction on television. A good indicator is whether a series includes child leads central to the storyline; so preference is given to the likes of *The Silver Sword*, *Huckleberry Finn* or *The Swish of the Curtain* as recognisably television drama for children.

Additionally, we admit that the entries included here covering the 1950s and 1960s are only intended to act as a representative overview of those decades' output. In the 1950s, many dramas went out live with minimal film inserts and so were never recorded. By the early 1960s, telerecordings could be made by pointing a specially adapted film camera at a flat screen monitor of the live or taped transmission, and by the late 1960s, videotaped broadcasts were kept. Sadly though, many of the copies retained on both of these formats were later destroyed in the mass junkings of the late 1960s and early 1970s. The lack of available viewing material from this era – effectively rendered pre-history by both technological limitations and lack of foresight – makes it difficult for us to assess and critique productions of this era and so by necessity has limited coverage to a minimum.

Several children's productions would later be remade in the colour era and earlier versions are referenced at the appropriate points in the text (in entries such as those for 1975's *The Secret Garden*, 1998's *Children of the New Forest* etc.). The best-recalled or most popular versions of oft-remade series will be given preference in the chronological entries presented here so that, for example, all versions of *Just William* are included in 1977, the year of LWT's very successful adaptation, in preference to the junked BBC stories of the 1960s or the less successful remake of the mid-1990s. This grouped approach is intended to avoid repetition and encourage comparison.

With the ground rules for inclusion agreed, next came another vexing issue – that of assigning relative importance and resulting level of coverage for the accepted series and serials. There were three main criteria: popularity, longevity and quality.

Popularity means how well received it was by its audience on initial transmission. Ratings indicators help to measure that response while available merchandise is something of an epiphenomenon that helps second it. How well remembered something is today by those that watched first time round also counts as a valid measure on this score.

Longevity is fairly self-explanatory, but is perhaps the weakest of our three criteria. Longevity can act as a second measure of popularity – demand from viewers sustained the run – but arguably one instalment of *Dramarama* can have had more impact on viewers than ten years of *Children's Ward*, say.

This leads to measures of quality. Well-made productions, adaptations of well-known works of children's fiction or by noted writers and groundbreaking or controversial works were all considered to possess this 'quality'. Being subjective, this is the hardest criterion to justify and quantify but hopefully the qualitative assessments made in our entries will go some way to matching the reader's own tastes.

The level of coverage also extends to determining how much additional programme data accompanies each entry. Each includes, as a minimum, the production company, number of episodes made and broadcast information. Note that all programmes included here as made by the BBC have been shown on BBC1 except otherwise indicated as 'BBC2' (for the likes of *Maggie* and *Tucker's Luck* or Sunday morning same-week repeats of BBC1 shows). For ITV series the franchise-holder that produced a programme is given at the top of the data section. Franchise shake-ups and non-renewals are indicated where relevant.

We have given Main Cast for all entries, taking in the most important characters in the plot and some notable guest stars. Writers, directors, producers and designers will always be given, although note that for 1950s BBC productions the producer was also often the director (and sometimes even the writer) but this was not always explicitly stated and we have not attempted to redefine these roles in modern contexts. When viewing material has been unavailable, details are as given in *Radio Times* or *TV Times* and sometimes, due to error or lack of space in these source publications, certain details have been missed out.

Quirks of history also play their part – we have been unable to include at least one series that fulfilled our selection criteria because of an unfortunate lack of reliable information. *Emerald Soup* was a Blyton-like seven-part adventure serial from ABC. Apparently long junked, it aired Saturdays from 9/11/63 – 21/12/63 (quite possibly against the first episodes of *Doctor Who*), had a lead cast of three or so plucky youngsters and may well have been about jewel thieves. We just can't say much else for certain – it seems that the nascent BFI simply ran short of money towards the end of 1963 and cancelled its subscription to *TV Times* for the last quarter of the year! The rarity of early 1960s copies of the publication have meant a few gaps and on this occasion *Emerald Soup* is sadly off the menu.

Strikes beset both *TV Times* and *Radio Times* on several occasions in the 1970s and have led to omissions here. Such things are unfortunate but, as they used to say on television, 'We hope it won't spoil your enjoyment too much.' What is more sad to note is that as the number of television channels has increased, the amount of space available to such listings magazines has dramatically decreased. Children's programmes have fared worse than most, with programme data often inconsistently presented or absent altogether. Our data for many 1990s series is far more incomplete than we would like (*Grange Hill* and *Byker Grove* directors, for example, are largely missing) and much has been gleaned from our own video collections and secondary sources such as novelisations and contemporary magazine articles. Ironically it can be far easier to research a series from 1973 than one from 1993 due to these limitations.

Since there are many types of programmes there is not a consistent, rigid format for the accompanying data but hopefully what we have presented here best matches the kind of programme under scrutiny, given the ever-present limitations of space, be it a one-off four-part serial or a soap which has run for twenty years.

As well as cast, crew and transmission information we have also listed very relevant tie-ins. While these do not stretch to which series had Easter eggs produced as spin-off merchandise (*Grange Hill* and *Worzel Gummidge* both did, if you must know) we try to give details, wherever possible, of tie-in novels since these are a reasonably easily accessible way of revisiting a programme that isn't currently showing on television. When we say tie-ins we are referring to one of two things. Novelisations are adaptations of a previously screened teleplay (i.e. the TV series came first) while tie-ins of a novel (a previously published literary work) are defined by us to be a new edition of a book which utilises photographic material from the recent or forthcoming television production on its cover. Since it is easier to prove that something does exist than it does not (as any theologist will tell you) we have been tentative in ruling out conclusively the non-existence of many tie-ins. Novelisations are easier to disprove but rare one-off tie-in novels are harder to refute. If a tie-in is thought conclusively not to exist, the tie-in data is absent altogether; if it is unproven then status is recorded as not known. Should there be any further editions of this book, details from anyone else's collections would be appreciated. Note that tie-in novelisations are very rarely reprinted beyond the life of the television programme but can usually be found today in the UK's larger reference libraries.

Very importantly, we have given indication as to commercial video availability of the series discussed. We have strived to be as accurate as possible with our information although there may be one or two omissions with regards to US releases. Please note that although we may now live in a global village thanks to the internet, any purchases of video and DVD material from the United States may be subject to duty imposed by HM Customs and are made at your own risk! We are sure that many of you will be dismayed to learn that many titles listed here are deleted but possibly even more amazed to learn that some tapes were released at all. The distribution of videotapes to the high street has been notoriously poor for several titles we list here. As a result many are now collector's items – even a more widely available example such as the BBC's 1991 version of *Tom's Midnight Garden*, last in the shops in 1996, can sell for more than £50 second-hand.

While the BFI's own archive (via the National Film and Television Archive at Berkamsted) is open to bona fide researchers and industry professionals by appointment, it may be more worthwhile for those wishing to see their favourite series again to write to video companies such as Network and Contender. The smaller, more dedicated companies are usually fairly open to correspondence and suggestion as to future releases. DVD does seem to have renewed the enthusiasm of the video companies for releasing archive television – recent releases have included such children's material as *The Tomorrow People*, *Chocky* and *Children of the Stones*. Readers might also try writing to TV stations such as CBBC, UK Gold and Granada Plus to suggest repeats. It would be nice to think that, as well as cataloguing the heritage of children's drama television, this book might indirectly help to get some of it back on our screens for us – and our children, of course – to enjoy.

# 1950s & 60s

Children's television in Britain began on 7 July 1946, one month after the post-war service resumed transmission, with a strand called *For the Children*. At this time there was of course just one channel, the BBC, and fewer than 25,000 television receivers in and around the London area. *For the Children* was a regular one-hour package of programmes for Sunday afternoon intended for children and a natural successor to radio's *Children's Hour* which had run since 1922. *For the Children*, and its better-remembered successor *Watch With Mother* (on air from 1953), largely consisted of presentation to camera and very cheaply made but extremely popular string puppet series such as *Muffin the Mule*, *Andy Pandy*, *The Flower Pot Men* and *The Woodentops*.

*For the Children* was overseen by television's Head of Talks, Mary Adams, and she was keen to expand the service. Adams had grand ambitions. She wanted the children's service to reflect and replicate the variety of adult television and include 'plays, how-to-series, storytelling, a collectors' corner, pets, travel, outside broadcasts from museums and factories, informational films, quizzes and encyclopaedia programmes'. Certainly these lofty aims would not be achieved in her time in nominal charge of children's programming. What Adams had done was state a goal and, while the phrase might not have been coined at this time, her intentions mark the first call for a 'service in miniature'.

Of Adams' wishlist, 'plays' or drama was probably the least likely genre to come to the screen at this time. Rehearsed drama of any reasonable length made for children was not possible given the small finances and facilities available to those working at the Alexandra Palace Studios.

The opening of a new transmitter at Sutton Coldfield, serving the English Midlands, on 17 December 1949 meant an expansion in the television service and increased revenues from licence fees. For children's television the time had come – in 1950 new posts in children's television were advertised and seven staff appointed. There was now for the first time a dedicated department given the task of producing programmes aimed at a young audience. The year 1951 saw Children's Television take up residence at Studio H Lime Grove. Virtually all programmes came from here, largely live (with some telecine inserts played in as broadcast) until the availability of video recording in 1958. The facilities, although rudimentary, were in place. Still, in 1950 the two acting heads of Children's Programmes – Richmond Postgate and then Cecil Madden (Madden was in place for eight months) – both called for delays to the expansion of the children's service, fearing their staff were not ready.

It was Madden who oversaw what is thought to be the very first drama serial made for children – *Little Women* – in December 1950 and the first telling of *The Railway Children* in early 1951. Come May 1951, and Madden's work was extended by the permanent

**Above:** E. Nesbit's *The Railway Children* was adapted for television several times in the 1950s and 60s by the BBC. The 1957 version made the cover of *Radio Times*.

appointment of Freda Lingstrom. By 1951 the department had already begun to see itself as performing a role of little status but great responsibility. From this ethos came a tendency towards didacticism and an emphasis on education and improvement. The 'schoolmarmy' epithet would come to describe readily the work of the department in the early 50s. Some have called it a 'patrician' regime but given its predominance of women staff it should more correctly be thought of as a maternal institution. You would be hard pushed to find a woman working anywhere outside of presentation or secretarial in the BBC of 1951, yet of the eight staff of Children's Programmes appointed in 1950, women outnumbered their male counterparts five to three. It would seem that looking after children was indeed considered a woman's job, even in television. As the years progressed, a considerable number of women would shape television for children at times when they were scarcely visible in the industry as a whole.

Freda Lingstrom was a woman with a strong voice for the department and was certainly vocal when it came to airing her own beliefs for the service. Among her pet dislikes were 'Americanised' fare, especially filmed Westerns, and the hardline antipathy towards American imports would come to typify the service under Lingstrom and ultimately lead to its near demise. More surprising, and greatly influencing the character of children's drama on the BBC at this time, was Lingstrom's dislike of the very English works of Enid Blyton.

If Lingstrom's reign was maternal she was perhaps an overprotective mother. For all her enthusiasm as Head, and the undoubted consolidation of the output, little change can be seen to have been wrought in the five years she oversaw the department. Dramas took their cue from Madden, coming from recognised 'classic' sources and including *The Secret Garden* and *Five Children and It*. A rare hint at anything approaching modernity came with the trivial, home counties escapades of soap family *The Appleyards*. Live action comedy featured the perennially popular Billy Bunter. Most drama at this time was under the direct auspices of Shaun Sutton, who either wrote, directed, produced or even acted in almost every drama production under Lingstrom. It was quite a grounding – Sutton went on to become BBC Head of Drama Serials in 1966 and overall BBC Head of Drama between 1969 and 1981.

Output in Lingstrom's era amounted to almost an hour each day of the week and at this time there was the 'Toddler's Truce'. BBC television would close down for one hour after 'children's hour', obviously considering it a broadcaster's responsibility to allow parents to get the children to bed. From this we can see that 'children's programmes' were largely aimed at younger children.

The Toddler's Truce and many more of the BBC's now established conventions would soon be swept away with the coming of ITV. With the new competition, ratings crashed through the floor in all parts of the BBC, falling to 70:30 in ITV's favour among two-channel households and sometimes as far as 80:20. Children's programmes were no exception. ITV had won the kids over with series aimed at the whole family, made-in-studio action film series such as *The Adventures of Robin Hood* (1955), *The Adventures of Sir Lancelot* (1956) and *The Buccaneer* (1956). In terms of outlook these film series offered honest-to-goodness escapist thrills without the edifying didacticism of the BBC. ITV was what children 'wanted' even if it wasn't what they 'needed' and in fact had not been made specifically for them alone. Though the budgets were small by current standards they far outstripped anything the BBC was willing to offer at the time. ITV had invested quite heavily in these productions and shot them on film with an eye on overseas sales. The BBC was still making live broadcasts of children's dramas at the time, shown once and lost forever. The telerecording process of filming studio output from an adapted monitor was at an experimental stage by the mid-50s and recordings often failed (the earliest surviving examples are thought to be fragments of the second episode of a Sunday Classic serial, *Robin Hood*, made in 1953 and starring Patrick Troughton). Videotape was developed by Ampex in 1957 and did not become available in studio at the BBC until 1958. Even so, tape was too expensive to retain and would be reused wherever possible.

In 1956 Owen Reed became Head of the Children's Department at the BBC, with former *Children's Hour* radio presenter Ursula Eason as his deputy. Reed's primary remit seems to have been purely and simply to stop the ratings rot. Although this may well have been intended as a bargain of necessity and purely a stopgap measure, the face of children's programmes on the BBC was changed forever when Reed was allowed to buy in imported series such as *Champion the Wonder Horse* and *Whirlybirds* from America (both of which still aired almost thirty years later in the school holidays). These offered the same sort of open-air filmed action as Robin and his fellow swashbucklers did on ITV. You could say they were hackneyed but, putting prejudice aside, in terms of execution they were far ahead of what the BBC had to offer up to that time.

Interestingly Reed made reference to his outgoing predecessor's work, recognising that you could cater for 'the oldest [age group] with *Jane Eyre* or whatever you want to do'. The classics, then, still had their place. Reed saw the home-grown drama serials (still almost exclusively classic adaptations) as providing the bridge between child and adult viewing. This reaffirms the notion that the classics were never really made *for* children. They were made *at* them in Lingstrom's time and for them to enjoy *with the family* in Reed's time. Television drama in the 50s then, it could be said, was never made for children to enjoy as their own programmes. The function of the drama as bridge between exclusively child and exclusively adult audiences became more pronounced in 1957 when the Toddler's Truce was abandoned. ITV had lobbied the hardest for its removal, claiming it was costing them advertising revenue, and eventually the BBC capitulated. This placed 'children's' drama in a difficult position thematically and also meant undue pressure for it to perform in the ratings.

Family shows are difficult to define, usually leading the observer to point to timeslots above all else, but at this time the BBC family serial could be defined as one which needed to earn the adult approval, making the classics ideal fodder. ITV family drama series meanwhile offered safe, clean *escapist* thrills that everyone could enjoy and relax in front of. In both cases parental approval

**Above:** in the 1950s the majority of children's drama was period fare but by the 1960s both BBC and ITV were producing series and serials set in the present day. *Quick Before They Catch Us*, set in 1966 London, was perhaps the most fashion-conscious of these.

amounted to discerning that the programme was not likely to corrupt children, but in the case of the BBC classics output, some amount of worthiness or educational aspect was also prescribed.

By the late 50s, children's television on the BBC was still underfunded, with drama its most expensive commodity. Still, Reed had ambitious plans for the drama output of his department and saw that tastes were changing. Speaking in 1958, he said: 'BBC Children's Television has drawn its strength from the classics ... but the really compulsive series [in terms of drawing viewers] are speed and space and adventure.' Reed felt these new demands were being encouraged by Saturday morning cinema-going, where reels of 1930s film serials still played, among them *Flash Gordon*, *Buck Rogers*, *King of the Rocket Men* and their ilk. Taking note of ITV's recipe for success, Reed was the first at the BBC to suggest the Corporation engage in production of children's film series for the worldwide market. This would have drawn the BBC into an almost purely commercial arena and as such was an idea years ahead of its time. Reed's ideas were ignored.

The year 1960 was a turning point for the BBC Children's Programmes department. There were now twelve producers, where a few years earlier there had been eight, and total output was up. As Shaun Sutton remembered several years later, children's drama and its need for outdoors adventure had done much to break new ground in television location filming, ahead of the rest of the BBC Drama output as a whole.

The base on which to establish and grow the service may have seemed well in place by 1960 but the year also saw the onset of a crisis for the department. Questions were raised about the ghettoising of 'Children's Television'; did on-screen continuity and titling referring directly to children's programmes chase away those children who didn't see themselves as children? This became a particularly hot topic when audience research revealed that many children of eight to ten and upwards enjoyed 'adult' crime thrillers on TV – this age group was seen as the bulk of the children's drama audience. If the title of 'Children's Television' was agreed to be off-putting and so dropped, might the department itself go too?

In 1960 Sir Hugh Carleton Greene (Graham Greene's brother) became Director General of the BBC and ushered in a new and exciting era at the Corporation in an attempt to woo audiences back from ITV. Greene was determined to shake things up and to that end appointed Stuart Hood as Controller of Television with Donald Baverstock as his assistant. Apocryphally, Hood saw the BBC output he was inheriting as being 'too bloody middle class'. Hood was Scottish and Baverstock Welsh so it was maybe to be expected that 1962 saw the beginning of the likes of the markedly less home counties *Steptoe and Son* and *Z Cars*, reflecting the lives of a wider cross-section of the television audience.

Children's programmes were very much a part of what Hood hated: a self-satisfied ghetto both culturally and in terms of the viewing figures, embodying for him the 'negative side of Reithism'. Early on he warned that period drama's days were numbered.

Hood's biggest step was to 'steal' drama and light entertainment from the control of the children's department and place it in the hands of the programme-makers in the relevant adult departments.

While it might have seemed a good move to wrest these genres from this supposedly rather reactionary bunch, could it really be seen as good for the development of television for children? As had been the case when the Toddler's Truce was done away with, this development highlighted the dangers of middle-ground family drama that had to satisfy the needs and sensibilities of children and adults. Problems in both subject matter and tone arose; a 1962 production of *Oliver Twist* made by the Serials Department was criticised by Owen Reed for being potentially disturbing. Drama for children could perhaps be revolutionised by these new figures but there remained the possibility that the cause of programmes made exclusively for children and addressing their own needs and desires could be forgotten. Early examples of tougher, more adult fare airing in recognised children's slots included the World War II action dramas *The Long Way Home* (24/4/60 – 5/6/60) and *The Last Man Out* (6/10/62 – 10/11/62).

One huge success to come out of this 'family' policy was *Doctor Who*. When the series began in November 1963, the Children's Department did not control drama serials and that control was never passed on in the twenty-six years that followed. The series seemed almost to have been born on the words of Owen Reed, delivering the 'speed and space and adventure' he had called for long before. *Doctor Who* was devised by Sydney Newman, a commercially minded but never brash Canadian who had helped develop the science fiction adventure *Pathfinders* at ABC (the ITV weekend franchise-holders for the Midlands and North). *Doctor Who* seemed an attempt to directly rival that long-running series.

In 1964 the axe fell. Stuart Hood killed the Children's Department off completely, merging it with 'Women's Programmes' (responsible for undemanding housewife fare) to create 'Family Programmes'. Thus there was an enforced hiatus in the development of children's drama at the BBC and the loss of any central strategy. The classic serials still persisted, usually shown on Sundays, but with this strand now forced to jostle for position and timeslots with all manners of (adult) drama, it seems to have been low down the priority list. Among the few successes of the period from 1964 to 1968 were *Quick Before They Catch Us* – delivering rigorously pop-styled, more classless, swinging action – and a very lively and fairly lavish *Railway Children*, finally getting the costume drama out into the fresh air.

By comparison, drama for children from ITV was flourishing in the mid-60s. The weekday children's slot had a later start time than the BBC, usually at 4.50p.m. and running until 5.55p.m. Programmes invariably included imported American film series (*Flipper*, *The Littlest Hobo*, *The Forest Rangers*) and studio 'presentational' magazine programmes. The latter included both networked efforts such as *The Five O'Clock Club* and some regional opt-outs like Scottish Television's *Cartoon Cavalcade* and a number of local variants of *Romper Room*.

Significantly, ITV was investing more and more in home-grown drama by the mid-60s, definitely gaining the upper hand over the BBC with a host of popular series. London's Rediffusion ruled the roost at this time, providing the bulk of children's drama for the network. This was to be expected, since Rediffusion was the

**Above:** a thriller series made for children but set in a stylised adult world was *Orlando*. This tie-in annual was produced for the 1967 Christmas market.

provider of London weekday programming and thus the biggest, richest franchise-holder (channels like Grampian, Border and Westward only opened in 1961 and provided little more than news and local interest magazine programming). More surprising was that at this time, and for at least another decade, the second biggest provider of children's drama was Southern, the small station serving the south coast of England. The network output of this franchise outside of the children's market was negligible.

The ready currency of both Rediffusion and Southern was the 'adventure serial'. While this catch-all title might be thought to cover all manner of styles, at this time it almost always meant kids in anoraks on bikes, accompanied by a dog or two, roaming the countryside in search of smugglers and bank robbers and usually finding them in ready supply! Fifteen years earlier Freda Lingstrom had all but banned the works of Enid Blyton from the screen but now all manner of ersatz *Famous Five* wannabes crowded ITV. *Smuggler's Cove*, *The Barnstormers*, *New Forest Rustlers* and *Mystery Hall* were all pure variants of this Blytonesque subgenre, with *The Master* and *Sierra Nine* adding science fiction concepts into the cops and robbers mix. *Orlando* and, later, *Freewheelers* tried a different tack by disposing of the kids on bikes to instead offer cut-down versions of the action-adventure series enjoyed by parents which their little ones might not be allowed up late enough to watch (*The Avengers*, *The Saint*, *The Champions* and so on).

There seemed a never-ending supply of these series at a time of relative inactivity by the BBC. With the Children's Department stripped of its drama content, it could only offer storytelling in its purest sense via the narrator and illustrations approach of *Jackanory*, which began in 1965. Anna Home tried introducing live drama sequences into *Jackanory* with the likes of *Children of Green Knowe* (1966), *Bookshop on the Quay* (1968) and *The Warden's Niece* (1968). Small units would shoot silent film footage under adverse conditions and these would be narrated by a storyteller in studio. *The Witch's Daughter* (1968) was a breakthrough in that it included recorded sound. Underfunded and makeshift these sequences might have been, but they displayed ambition.

By the late 60s ITV regions even scandalously dared to tackle the BBC's stock-in-trade, the period drama, albeit as a more exciting hybrid of historic settings and modern action, unshackled by the textbook origins that held the BBC classics. Series in this vein included *Tom Grattan's War* and *The Flaxton Boys* from Yorkshire and *Sexton Blake* from Rediffusion (later Thames). No doubt about it, it was the ITV regions (chiefly Rediffusion, Southern and Yorkshire) who ruled the roost with regard to children's drama in the latter half of the 60s. LWT even had a dedicated Children's Department from its inception in 1967 although this did not last long. The BBC meanwhile seemed to have no reply.

Of course the adventure serials were all a little one-dimensional but nonetheless reflected the imaginations of the audience and, to an extent, their surroundings. What children's drama needed by the end of the 60s was perhaps to dig a little deeper, to tap into the emotions of the audience as well as their imaginations and thirst for excitement.

What the genre also needed was more concerted effort from the BBC, whose hands were still tied by Stuart Hood's decision of 1964. The most positive move came in 1967 as Doreen Stephens left as Head of Family Programmes to join the nascent LWT (she would later become head of the ITV Network Children's Programmes Committee). 'Children's Programmes' was finally reinstated that year as a department, with Monica Sims in charge.

Change would not come overnight however – the department was as notoriously underfunded as before. With a considerable proportion of airtime given over to cheaply imported cartoons, there were criticisms from some quarters. Infamously, Sims replied:

> American cartoons whether comedy like *Deputy Dawg* and *Tom and Jerry* or adventures like *Journey to the Centre of the Earth* or *Marine Boy* [*sic* – it was actually Japanese in origin] always attract a very high proportion of satisfied child viewers even though their parents may sometimes object to the use of American material or to the fact that the programmes are not informative or uplifting. My own view is that such comedy cartoons are first-class entertainment and are so expensive to make that we could never afford to make our own.

Despite this spirited defence it would be foolish to think that this was what Sims really wanted for the child audience. Expense was also the bottom line when it came to drama output. The majority of programmes on the BBC at this time were foreign imports, though being European in origin it was probably hoped that these would not be considered as 'crass' as American fare. Most notable series included *Belle and Sebastian*, *The Flashing Blade*, *Robinson Crusoe* from France, the German *Tales From Europe* and Yugoslavia's *White Horses*. These buys and their subsequent adaptation were the preserve of department member Peggy Miller. The BBC itself could simply not afford to make its own drama in the late 60s.

Nonetheless Sims was the first of the modern Children's Department heads and oversaw the slow changeover for the BBC at the end of the decade that would usher in a challenging golden era of children's television and drama on both channels.

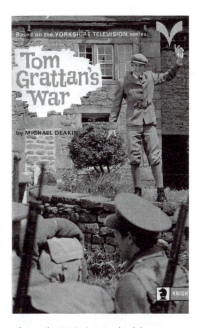

**Above:** the TV tie-in paperback became a mainstay of children's publishing in the 1970s and 80s. The first examples began to appear in the late 1960s, including this novelisation of Yorkshire Television's *Tom Grattan's War*, published by Knight Books in 1969.

## Little Women

It all began here with the famous story of the March girls Jo, Meg, Beth and Amy in mid-nineteenth-century New England. With their father away fighting in the American Civil War, this was their story.

This was the first serialised work to be shown on British television, deviating from the standard single play or recital format and transmitted live to only the South of England and the Midlands. The fledgling Children's Department had just recruited its first staff a few short months earlier and this was the first drama to be made for children under its *For the Children* banner. Would it be unfair to suggest that 'At the Children' might have been a more accurate reflection of programme policy at this time?

*Little Women* very much sets the genre pattern for the first half of the decade at the BBC, before the advent of commercial television. An eighty-year-old book handed down through the generations was what the next generation deserved. It seems that no-one had thought to ask what they might *like*. The production was a straight retelling of a RADA stage adaptation, minimally reworked to fit the episodic serial format, demonstrating how far television had yet to go to develop its own broadcasting identity.

The book was adapted again in the two-channel television era by the BBC and this remake (transmitted 13/4/58 –18/5/58) has been retained by the BBC archives as telerecorded film prints. One of Alcott's sequel's, *Jo's Boys*, about the March family setting up an orphanage, was adapted soon thereafter as a seven-episode serial (8/2/59 – 22/3/59).

**BBC**
**6 episodes** ('A Merry Christmas'; 'The Laurence Boy'; 'The Palace Beautiful'; 'The Telegram'; 'Dark Days'; 'Pleasant Meadows')
(b&w)
**Broadcast:** Tuesdays 12/12/50 – 23/1/51

**Main Cast:** Jane Hardie (Jo March), Sheila Shand Gibbs (Meg March), Nora Gaussen (Beth March), Susan Stephen (Amy March), Barbara Everest (Mrs March), Arthur Ridley (Mr March)

Based on the novel by Louisa M. Alcott (first publication 1868)
**Adapted by** Winifred Oughton, Brenda R. Thompson

**Designers:** Stephen Taylor, Lawrence Broadhouse
**Producer:** Pamela Brown

## Puck of Pook's Hill

The first hints at fantasy television for children, although with history lessons integral to the piece. Adapted from Rudyard Kipling's story, this trip through the ages occurs when two children, Dan and Una, magically summon up Shakespeare's sprite character Puck, having just acted in a performance of *A Midsummer Night's Dream*. Puck is really Robin Goodfellow, the spirit of Old England, and he shows the children how the Sussex land where they live has come to be shaped down the centuries. Their furthest journey sees them travel back to the time of the Romans.

Halfway through the serial's broadcast, the Holme Moss transmitter for the North West of England opened, meaning that Puck acted as an introduction – albeit a slightly jumbled one – to children's drama for another part of the country.

The notion of time travel as history classroom would be continued in *The Silver Swan* the following year.

**BBC**
**6 episodes** ('Weland's Sword'; 'Young Men at the Manor'; 'Old Men at Pevensey'; 'A Centurion of the Thirtieth'; 'On the Great Wall'; 'Winged Hats')
(b&w)
**Broadcast:** Tuesdays 25/9/51 – 30/10/51 South England and Midlands (Holme Moss transmitter for the North West of England officially opened 12/10/51, meaning that episodes 4 to 6 could be seen in that area. It is possible that earlier episodes may have been seen in test transmissions)

**Main Cast:** Georgie Wood (Puck), Carole Lorimer (Una), Barry Macgregor (Dan)
Others in order of appearance: Archie Duncan (Weland), John Wyse (Sir Richard), John Springett (Hugh), Stanley van Beers (De Aquila), Basil Dignam (Maximus)

Based on the novel by Rudyard Kipling (first UK publication 1906)
**Adapted by** Vere Shepstone

**Designer:** Lawrence Broadhouse
**Producer:** Matthew Forsyth

## Stranger From Space

A Martian boy, Bilaphodorous, crash-lands on Earth to be befriended by English youngster Ian Spencer. *Stranger From Space* probably counts as the first science fiction thriller ever made for British television, predating even the adventures of Bernard Quatermass.

The serial was shown as part of the children's hour Saturday strand *Whirligig* with Hazel Adair (later the creator of *Compact* and *Crossroads*) and Ronald Marriott (a children's producer at Rediffusion by the 60s) writing their scripts apparently based on suggestions sent in by young viewers. The fortnightly broadcast pattern allowed time for viewers' letters and ideas to be incorporated into subsequent episodes. Production standards would have been basic and the live episodes were thought to have run considerably shorter than the standard twenty-five minute duration of most serials.

A second, shorter sequel run had radio's Man in Black, Valentine Dyall, cast as a Martian villain.

The accent seems to have been on honest adventure – compare this with *Space School*, 1956's semi-educational science fiction serial, and it becomes apparent that this entertaining thriller may have been made in a time before more stringent directives on children's drama could be issued.

**BBC**
**2 seasons**
(b&w)

**Written by** Hazel Adair and Ronald Marriott
**Producer** for *Whirligig*: Michael Westmore

**Season One**

**11 episodes** ('Crash Landing'; 'On the Run'; 'Come to the Fair'; 'The Trap'; 'The House on Reigate Downs'; 'The Intruders'; 'Lost Energy'; 'The New Forest'; 'Journey Through Space'; 'Journey Through Space'*; 'The Prisoner')
* Episodes 10 and 11 are listed in *Radio Times*, presumably in error, as having the same title
**Broadcast:** Saturdays fortnightly 20/10/51 – 22/3/52 (South England, Midlands and North West only – episode 11 available in Central Scotland)

**Main Cast:** Brian Smith (Ian Spencer), Michael Newell (Bilaphodorous), Richard Pearson (Professor Watkins), John Gabriel (John Armitage), Betty Woolfe (Mrs Spencer), Isabel George (Pamela Vernon), Bruce Beeby (Delpho)

**Season Two**

**6 episodes** ('Message From Mars'; 'Return Journey'; 'The Cage'; 'Trouble in the Air'; 'Total Eclipse'; 'The Battle of Power')
**Broadcast:** Saturdays fortnightly 11/10/52 – 13/12/52

**Main Cast:** Brian Smith (Ian Spencer), Michael Newell (Bilaphodorous), John Gabriel (John Armitage), Peter Hawkins (Petrio), Valentine Dyall (Gorgol)

## The Appleyards

The earliest days of television soap opera and *The Appleyards* were the very first British nuclear family to allow us into their home. Episodes went out live (with a second performance the following Sunday) and the theme music was also played in live off a 78rpm record. *The Appleyards* made it to the screen two years before *The Grove Family* – Britain's first true soap as it went out in an unbroken run. The Appleyards' 'adventures' were aired in contained series, some only six episodes long.

The family consisted of Mr and Mrs Appleyard and their four children, the teenage John and Janet and little Tommy and Margaret. Long before the infamous cast changes of 80s soaps such as *Dallas*, *The Appleyards* too underwent some personnel alterations and most of these happened in order to keep the children at believable ages in what was after all a children's series. What little evidence there is suggests that the family lived notoriously twee, mundane and uneventful lives.

The series ended in 1957 but was revived for one Christmas reunion special in 1960, written and produced by the Children's Department's Kevin Sheldon.

**BBC**
**69 episodes**
(b&w)

First episode Thursday 2/10/52 'Meet the Family'

**8 seasons** (2/10/52 – 9/4/53; 13/6/53 – 19/12/53; 9/10/54 – 18/12/54; 2/4/55 – 7/8/55; 24/9/55 – 30/12/55; 7/4/56 – 13/7/56; 17/11/56 – 26/1/57; 16/3/57 – 20/4/57) and one Christmas special 24/12/60

**Main Cast:** Frederick Piper* (Mr Appleyard), Constance Fraser (Mrs Appleyard), David Edwards (John), Maureen Davis** (Janet), Derek Rowe (Tom), Patricia Wilson*** (Margaret)

* Later replaced by Douglas Muir
** Later replaced by Tessa Clarke
*** Later replaced by Carole Oliver and Pat Fryer

**Written initially** by Philip Burton
**Theme Music:** 'Looking Around' – library piece by Colin Smith
**Designer Season One:** Richard Wilmot
**Producer Season One:** Naomi Capon

## Huckleberry Finn

The perennial tales of two boys whose antics light up the sleepy town of St Petersburg in America's Deep South in the middle of the 19th century were first tackled in 1952 with the adaptation of *Huckleberry Finn*. The story sees Finn and his buddy Tom Sawyer take a journey down the Mississippi River after fleeing with their escaped slave friend Jim. While full of incident and mischief, the journey is a leisurely one which the makers felt would probably have lasted the same seven weeks as the serial itself. St Petersburg to Illinois to Jackson's Island, St Louis and onto Hicksville – although, since this was 1950s BBC, it was considered a big deal even to have shot-establishing location film on the Norfolk Broads.

It was the next decade before Mark Twain's other novel was serialised. *The Adventures of Tom Sawyer* was an episodic piece in print before coming to television so it comfortably fitted the seven-part format. Tom and Huck looked for grave robbers, staged Tom's own funeral and looked for hidden loot over the weeks.

Two American boys were found to play the leads after a trawl of American air force bases in England, meaning there were few problems with accents. Much of the shooting took place in the wide open spaces of the BBC's Ealing film studios, marking one of the earliest departures from the confines of Lime Grove.

Young BBC viewers in the early 80s enjoyed a long-form adaptation of the two books, a Canadian/West German import under the title *Huckleberry Finn and his Friends*, made in 1979.

### *Huckleberry Finn* (1952)
**BBC**
**7 episodes** ('The Widow Douglas's'; 'Jackson's Island'; 'Life on the Mississippi'; 'The Rightful King of France?'; 'The Wilks' Fortune'; 'The Auction'; 'Back to the River')
(b&w)
**Broadcast:** Tuesdays 4/11/52 – 16/12/52 South England, Midlands, North West England, Central Scotland, West England and South Wales

**Main Cast:** Colin Campbell (Huckleberry Finn), Jeremy Spenser (Tom Sawyer), Orlando Martins (Jim), Kenneth Connor ('Pap' Finn)

Based on the novel by Mark Twain (first publication 1884)
**Adapted by** W. S. Merwin

**Designer:** Stephen Taylor
**Producer:** Vivian Milroy
**Assistant Producer:** Shaun Sutton

*The Adventures of Tom Sawyer* (1960)
**BBC**
**7 episodes** ('Clever Tom'; 'A Cure for Warts'; 'The Saving of Muff Potter'; 'Gone But Not Forgotten'; 'Noble Tom'; 'Buried Treasure'; 'Lost and Found')
**Broadcast:** Sundays 24/7/60 – 4/9/60

**Main Cast:** Fred Smith (Tom Sawyer), Mark Strotheide (Huckleberry Finn), Betty Hardy (Aunt Polly), Lorna Henderson (Mary), Lindsay Scott-Patton (Sid), Janina Faye (Becky Thatcher), John Bennett (Injun Joe), Deering Wells (Judge Thatcher), Barbara Cavan (Widow Douglas)

Based on the novel by Mark Twain (first publication 1876)
**Adapted by** Cecil Edwin 'Bunny' Webber

**Music** played and sung by Peggy Seegar
**Designer:** Archie Clark
**Producer:** Dorothea Brooking

## The Silver Swan

An important milestone, this is thought to be the very first children's serial written for television and not adapted from a literary source. The central idea of a violin handed down through the generations came from BBC children's producer John Hunter Blair one day, suggested to Rex Tucker in the Lime Grove canteen. C. E. Webber developed the script and the ideas of time travel to present what was perhaps the most interesting and different drama idea yet produced for children. 'Although this serial is "about" the adventures of an old violin in the past,' wrote Tucker in *Radio Times*, 'it has a quality of romance and wonder which we hope will come across to children through the excitement of the stories themselves.'

Lucy visits her aunt, a housekeeper to Lady Gresham in the old mansion of Gresham Hall. The music room there holds a special fascination for Lucy. The wall is decorated with portraits of the Gresham family line and many include the family crest of the Silver Swan within them. Lucy notices a violin sitting in the room; picking it up, she sees the back of it is also decorated with the Silver Swan. She realises too that the violin is pictured in the portrait of Francis, a Gresham from the time of Queen Elizabeth I. Next discovering a piece of music called 'The Silver Swan' in the room, she sits down at the piano to play and is transported into 1558.

Lucy's adventures take her through the ages to meet the Gresham lineage, beginning with a tale of Franco–Italian skullduggery at Elizabeth's court. Further trips had Lucy meet a Royalist who became fiddler to Oliver Cromwell, see how the violin saved a Gresham from being press-ganged into service on a boat at Bristol, discover the 'lost' violin unearthed in Vienna in 1850, visit Belgium at the time of the Great War and join the Resistance in the occupied France of 1942.

It was undoubtedly a very *Look and Learn*-styled semi-educational serial but one which was bound to entertain also. The imaginative linking device between the tales may well have owed something to the then contemporary *The Lion, the Witch and the Wardrobe* (even the name Lucy suggests C. E. Webber possessed a familiarity with C. S. Lewis's works).

Although the scripting may have been innovative, conditions at Lime Grove were as before. Department producer Shaun Sutton acted in every episode, each time

in a different part. He appeared as Bartholomew Read, a soldier, an innkeeper, Hans Wehrli, a farmer and a Gestapo officer across the six-week run! The small part of Lord Henriques in episode one was played by a young actor called Peter Cushing, which perhaps best demonstrates how long ago this was.

Rex Tucker and 'Bunny' Webber would both go on to take a hand in creating *Doctor Who* ten years later and something of its genesis is clearly visible in *The Silver Swan*.

**BBC**
**6 episodes** ('Francis'; 'Roger'; 'Timothy'; 'Gerald'; 'John'; 'Elsa') (b&w)
**Broadcast:** Tuesdays 30/12/52 – 3/2/53

**Main Cast:** Carole Maybank (Lucy), Violet Lamb (Housekeeper), Robert Irving (Francis Gresham/Timothy Gresham), Randal Herley (Gerald Gresham/John Gresham), Peggy Livesey (Elsa Gresham)

**Written by** C. E. Webber

**Musical direction:** John Hunter Blair
**Designer:** John Cooper
**Producer:** Rex Tucker
**Assistant Producer:** Shaun Sutton

## Seven Little Australians

Long before the heightened goings on of *Neighbours*, a rather more sedate soap told of life in Australia. This period adaptation focused on the lives of the Woolcot family of seven children living outside Sydney in the 1890s. Everyday 'adventures' of little consequence followed.

Shaun Sutton yet again played small parts in the serial. The sixth episode was put back to make way for the live coverage of the Queen's Coronation on 2 June 1953 so it's interesting to speculate that the final part of the serial aired the following Saturday probably introduced children's drama to many, as television ownership increased in the UK.

An Australian company made a colour television series based on the books in the mid-70s.

**BBC**
**6 episodes** ('Introducing Them'; 'A Day in Town'; 'Up in the Loft'; 'Nell Moves in Society'; 'The Forest Picnic'; 6 n/k) (b&w)
**Broadcast:** Tuesdays 28/4/53 – 26/5/53 and Saturday 6/6/53

**Main Cast:** Sheila Shand Gibbs (Esther Woolcot), Gerald Case (Capt Woolcot), Margaret Anderson (Meg), Barry McGregor (Pip), Adele Long (Nell), Pixie Murphy (Judy), Barry Knight (Bunny), Gillian Gale (Poppet), Ann Mallory (Bridget)

Based on the books *Seven Little Australians* and *The Family At Misrule* by Ethel S. Turner (original publication 1894 and c.1900, Ward, Lock & Co)
**Adapted by** Pamela Brown

**Assistant Producer:** Shaun Sutton
**Producer:** Pamela Brown

## The Treasure Seekers

*The Treasure Seekers* is a story of hope, where adversity and poverty are beaten back by family togetherness and love. The Bastable family were once rich but now hover on the brink of financial ruin and the six Bastable children turn to treasure seeking in a desperate effort to save the family home. All of the children have their own ideas about where possible treasure may lie but with the demands of the creditors growing and their father toiling away on his latest invention, time is running out.

First adapted for children's television in 1953 by Dorothea Brooking, her narrative had the running theme of the children working towards rescuing their family from its predicament, but with each episode as a self-contained story in its own right, concentrating on a different idea for finding treasure. 'As each adventure is complete in itself perhaps music and dancing lessons, Brownies and other important engagements will not prove such an interruption to the thread of the story,' Brooking commented.

The production in 1961, once again produced and adapted by Dorothea Brooking, incorporated a small amount of film locations and also saw novelist Noel Streatfeild play the part of the poet Mrs Leslie. The story was adapted again by the BBC, this time in colour, in 1982. Most recently it was remade as a slick TV movie feature by Tetra for ITV with overseas markets in mind.

All adaptations based on the novel by E. Nesbit (first UK publication 1899)

### The Story of the Treasure Seekers (1953)
**BBC**
**6 episodes** ('Digging for Treasure'; 'The Poet and the Editor'; 'Being Bandits and Noel's Princess'; 'The "G. B." and Lord Tottenham'; 'The Robber and the Burglar'; 'Lo! The Poor Indian')
(b&w)
**Broadcast:** Tuesdays 14/7/53 – 18/8/53

**Main Cast:** Wilfrid Downing (Oswald), Isla Richardson (Dora), Ernest Downing (Dicky), Caroline Denzil (Alice), Anthony Lang (Noel), Sonny Doran (HO), Oliver Burt (father), Damaris Hayman (Eliza)

**Adapted by** Dorothea Brooking

**Designer:** Richard Henry
**Producer:** Dorothea Brooking

### The Treasure Seekers: being the adventures of the Bastable children in search of a fortune (1961)
**BBC**
**6 episodes** ('The Council of Ways and Means'; 'Good Hunting'; 'Held to Ransom'; 'The Deadly Peril'; 'The Golden Nectar'; 'Lo! The Poor Indian')
(b&w)
**Broadcast:** Sundays 19/2/61 – 26/3/61

**Main Cast:** Anthony Klonda (Oswald), Hilary Wyce (Dora), Jonathan Collins (Dicky), Richard Williams (Noel), Sarah O'Connor (Alice), Mark Mileham (H. O.), Philip Latham (Mr Bastable), Patricia Fryer (Eliza)

**Adapted by** Dorothea Brooking

**Designer:** Susan Spence
**Producer:** Dorothea Brooking

### The Story of the Treasure Seekers (1982)
**BBC**
**6 episodes**
(colour)
**Broadcast:** Wednesdays 6/1/82 – 10/2/82

**Main Cast:** Simon Hill (Oswald), Lucinda Edmonds (Dora), Christopher Reilly (Dicky), Jeremy Dimmick (Noel), Jayn Rosamond (Alice), Timothy Stark (H. O.), David Quilter (Mr Bastable), Pauline Quirke (Eliza)

**Adapted by** Julia Jones
**Designer:** Barrie Dobbins
**Producer:** Paul Stone
**Director:** Roger Singleton-Murray

**Tie-in publications:** paperback edition published by Armada, 1982

### The Treasure Seekers (1996)
**Tetra Films for Carlton in association with PBS** (ITV transmission)
**Feature length TV movie**
(colour)
**Broadcast:** 25/12/96

**Main Cast:** Nicholas Farrell (Bastable), James Wilby (Carlise), Gina McKee (Mary Leslie), Ian Richardson (Haig), Peter Capaldi (Jellicoe), Nigel Davenport (Blackstock), John Sessions (Mr Redman), Donald Sinden (Old Wincott), Camilla Power (Dora Bastable)

**Adapted by** Juliet May
**Producer:** Alan Horrox
**Director:** Juliet May

**Video:** released in UK as a 97-minute compilation by Carlton 15/9/97; US release as two-tape set by Questar; released as Region 1 DVD in US only 25/7/00

## Thames Tug
### A tale of London's river

Jimmy Spurgeon is a schoolboy who finds himself in a strange world he knows nothing of when he accidentally ends up lost in London with nowhere to stay. He is found and befriended by the streetwise Toughy Wren. Toughy is rather less well-off than Jimmy, as his ragged clothes attest. His dad, Ted, is an old salt who scrounges a living beachcombing among the quays and wharves down river. Sister Sally has a slightly better job, working in the dockside office of a tug company. With all those cargoes coming and going every day, it's not long before Jimmy and the Wrens, accompanied by Bill the handyman, soon uncover some shady dealings by the quayside.

Another star of the serial was *Trojan*, a diesel tug that worked the waterways of the Thames and led Jimmy and Toughy into adventure.

An early experiment in extensive use of filmed location work (credited to the Television Film Unit), a similar trick would be attempted by the rejuvenated Children's Department in 1975, in the same dockland settings and using a similar plot, with *Sam and the River*.

### Thames Tug
**BBC**
**6 episodes** ('Half a Pound'; 'Jimmy and the Joker'; 'Cross Purposes'; 'The Gent and the Joker'; 'Uncle John Enjoys the Joke'; 'Ebb and Flow')
(b&w)
**Broadcast:** Tuesdays 25/8/53 – 29/9/53

**Main Cast:** Sean Barrett (Jimmy Spurgeon), Timothy Reynolds (Toughy Wren), Ray Jackson (Bill Rawlings), Glenda Davies (Sally Wren), Douglas Blackwell (Smythe), Christopher Hodge (Huggins)

**Written by** C. E. Webber

**Designer:** Richard Henry
**Producer:** Rex Tucker
**Assistant Producer/Director:** Shaun Sutton

## Heidi

*Heidi* tells the tale of a young orphan girl taken to live high in the Swiss Alps with her cantankerous old grandfather, who shuns the mountain community and lives a solitary existence in a remote bothy. At first Heidi has difficulty communicating with the old man and finds him gruff and lacking in affection. In a short time they become firm friends and Heidi even manages to get her grandfather to start talking to the villagers. She also makes friends with the mountain boy, Goat Peter, and the two roam happy as Peter herds the goats.

Heidi's happiness is curtailed when her Aunt Dete decides that the girl should be take to Frankfurt, where she will be a companion to the crippled girl, Clara. Heidi finds Frankfurt a noisy, flat city and the household is governed intensely by the foreboding Fraulein Rottenmeier. Heidi is made to stand on ceremony at all times and, regardless of her growing friendship with Clara, she cannot adjust to the strange customs of such a civilised house. When Heidi's health subsequently declines, it is felt that she should return to the Alps, where her delighted grandfather awaits her.

*Heidi* was dramatised on three occasions by the BBC, a reflection of its popularity with the younger generation of the time. More interesting perhaps was the adaptation of *Heidi Grows Up*, a sequel to Spyri's novel written by Charles Tritten, broadcast in 1954 just a year after the BBC's first adaptation of the original novel. The story follows Heidi through boarding school and her coming of age.

Inevitably it is the most recent TV production, the lengthy Dutch version by Strengholt (not German as many believe), dubbed and aired by the BBC in 1981, which is the most vividly remembered of all the adaptations.

All adaptations of *Heidi* based on the novel by Johanna Spyri (first UK publication 1880)
*Heidi Grows Up* based on the novel by Charles Tritten (first UK publication 1938, Whitman)

### Heidi (1953)
**BBC**
**6 episodes** ('Up the Mountain'; 'Two Visitors'; 'Away From Grandfather'; 'Another Grandmother'; 'Home Again'; 'Happy Ending')
(b&w)
**Broadcast:** Tuesdays 6/10/53 – 10/11/53

**Main Cast:** Julia Lockwood (Heidi), Lance Secretan (Peter), Roger Maxwell (Grandfather), Totti Truman-Taylor (Fraulein Rottenmeier), Charles Hodgson (Sebastian), Hilary Rennie (Clara), Dorothy Primrose (Narrator)

**Adapted by** Joy Harington
**Designer:** Michael Yates
**Producer:** Joy Harington

### Heidi Grows Up (1954)
**BBC**
**6 episodes** ('Boarding School'; 'Home Again'; 'Fire on the Mountain'; 'Chel'; 'The Secret of the Cave'; 'Heidi and Peter')
(b&w)
**Broadcast:** Tuesdays 28/9/54 – 2/11/54

**Main Cast:** Julia Lockwood (Heidi), Roger Maxwell (Grandfather), William Simons (Peter)

**Adapted by** Joy Harington
**Designer:** Donald Horne

### Heidi (1959)
**BBC**
**6 episodes** ('Up the Mountain'; 'Two Visitors'; 'Away From Grandfather'; 'Another Grandmother'; 'Home Again'; 'Happy Ending')
(b&w)
**Broadcast:** Tuesdays 19/5/59 – 23/6/59

**Main Cast:** Sara O'Connor (Heidi), Colin Spaull (Peter), Mark Digham (Grandfather), Nan Braunton (Fraulein Rottenmeier), Charles Hodgson (Sebastian), Lesley Judd (Clara)

**Adapted by** Joy Harington
**Designer:** Susan Spence

### Heidi (1974)
**BBC**
**6 episodes**
(colour)
**Broadcast:** Sundays 20/10/74 – 24/11/74

**Main Cast:** Emma Blake (Heidi), Nicholas Lyndhurst (Peter), Hans Meyer (Grandfather), June Jago (Fraulein Rottenmeier), Barry Lowe (Sebastian), Chloe Franks (Clara)

**Translated by** Marion Edwards
**Dramatised by** Martin Worth
**Script Editor:** Alistair Bell
**Designer:** David Spode
**Producer:** John McRae
**Director:** June Wyndham-Davies

**Tie-in publications:** n/k

## The Rose and the Ring

The panto season had come early to the BBC with this 'fireside' fairy story. Two neighbouring countries, Paflagonia and Crim-Tartary, are visited by a fairy who lives somewhere between them. Fairy Blackstick presents a ring to the Queen of Paflagonia and a rose to the Queen of Crim-Tartary, but when both parties are rather off-hand and slow to thank her, she wishes misfortune on both of them. The comedic results that ensued were played out no doubt more than adequately by a cast of established and up-and-coming actors.

**BBC**
**3 episodes**
(b&w)
**Broadcast:** Tuesdays 24/11/53 – 8/12/53

**Main Cast:** Jacqueline Hill (Fairy Blackstick), Kenneth Connor (Mr Gruffanuff), Joan Benham (Mrs Gruffanuff), John Ruddock (King of Paflagonia), Muriel George (Queen), David McCallum (Giglio), Patrick Cargill (Glumboso), Timothy Bateson (HRH Prince Bulbo), Eugene Leahy (King Padella), Peter Coke (Narrator)

From the story by W. M. Thackeray
**Adapted by** Stanley Haynes

**Designer:** Stephen Taylor
**Producer:** Stanley Haynes

## A Castle and Sixpence

A sort of modern-day E. Nesbit tale, with a family of children finding adventure. The Martingale family are left a castle in the will of an elderly relative. When they move in they find dear old Miss Button, the housekeeper, a whole host of cats and, odder still, a boy called Christopher Sixpence. What is *he* doing there?

The Martingale children's exciting new life exploring the castle may soon come to an end should Mr Neatsfoot have his way. The eccentric poet who lives in the nearby village lays claim to the castle and plots to have them thrown out.

**BBC**
**6 episodes** (n/k; 'Ragged Knights'; 'A Job for the Dungeon'; 'Who is Christopher Sixpence?'; 'The Triumph of Mr Neatsfoot'; 'The Riches That Remain')
(b&w)
**Broadcast:** Tuesdays 5/1/54 – 9/2/54

**Main Cast:** William Simons (Christopher Sixpence), Cicely Walper (Mrs Martingale), Wilfrid Downing (Nicholas), Elizabeth Saunders (Petronella), Caroline Denzil (Dinah), Colin Gibson (Benjamin), Evelyn Moore (Miss Button), Tony van Bridge (Mr Neatsfoot)

Based on the novel by Margaret J. Baker (first UK publication n/k)
**Adapted by** Dorothea Brooking

**Designer:** John Clements
**Producer:** Dorothea Brooking

## The Cabin in the Clearing

Given Freda Lingstrom's dislike for the Western as Americanised fare, this home-produced tale can only have got through by the back door somehow as the period story of a resourceful frontier family under threat. The Sutherlands find themselves under siege in their log cabin in the Ohio wilderness when the recently united Miami and Shawnee Indians begin attacking white settlers. Help from the authorities is many miles away but – luckily for Silas Sutherland, his wife and young daughter – their good friend Brayton Ripley is hidden out in the woods. Ripley is accompanied by Mul-Keep-Mo, an Indian whose life he once saved. As the Red Indians attempt to smoke the Sutherlands out, Ripley and Mo plan to rescue the family.

Department producer Shaun Sutton was once again in the cast, but this time in a lead role – as Sutton would later admit, financial limitations often led to bad casting. It's rather harder to find reasons why the distinctly non-Native-American features of Ewen Solon were chosen to play the Indian lead. Tony van Bridge meanwhile had been the villain just the previous week in *A Castle and Sixpence*.

The serial was later remade in 1959, with three of the original version's cast reprising their roles.

*The Cabin in the Clearing* (1954)
**BBC**
**5 episodes** ('Friends and Foes'; 'Besieged'; 'Ordeal by Fire'; 'A Desperate Plan'; 'The Break-Out')
(b&w)
**Broadcast:** Tuesdays 16/2/54 – 16/3/54

**Main Cast:** Shaun Sutton (Silas Sutherland), Peggy Mount (Polly Sutherland), Ann Hanslip (Alice), Charles Swain (Scipio), Derek Aylward (Brayton Ripley), Tony van Bridge (Simon Kenton), Ewen Solon (Mul-Keep-Mo), Carl Overing (Haw-Hu-Da)

Based on the novel by Edward Sylvester Ellis (first UK publication n/k)
**Adapted by** Felix Felton and Susan Ashman

**Designer:** Richard Henry
**Producer:** Rex Tucker

*The Cabin in the Clearing* (1959)
**BBC**
**5 episodes** ('Friends and Foes'; 'Besieged'; 'Ordeal by Fire'; 'A Desperate Plan'; 'The Break-Out')
(b&w)
**Broadcast:** Sundays 14/1/59 – 1/2/59

**Main Cast:** Thomas Heathcote (Silas Sutherland), Brenda Dunrich (Polly Sutherland), Ann Hanslip (Alice), Joseph Layode (Scipio), Derek Aylward (Brayton Ripley), Patrick Troughton (Simon Kenton), Ewen Solon (Mul-Keep-Mo), John Woodnutt (Haw-Hu-Da)

**Adapted by** Felix Felton and Susan Ashman (same script as first version)

**Designer:** Richard Henry
**Producer:** Rex Tucker
**Director:** Patrick Dowling

19

## The Windmill Family

Another summery – and twee – adventure from Pamela Brown. When the Channing family learn that nasty Uncle Porteous plans to make them sell their windmill home and thus move into town 'to live more sensibly organised lives' it seems all is lost. Then fate lends a hand when young Colin Channing discovers 'Puffin' at the mill. Puffin is the nickname of young Prince Suresh of Ranistan – his father has recently abdicated the throne of the Oriental state and Puffin is to be crowned king. Puffin wishes to have one last fishing holiday before his work as king begins.

The Ranistan government believe the young heir has been kidnapped and offer a reward – Puffin suggests that if Colin and his sister Kate can hide him here at the windmill and allow him to enjoy his fishing in peace then they may claim the reward: Puffin's weight in gold. Since this would secure the family's windmill home, they agree to hide Puffin in the loft. They must keep Puffin away from both the Ranistan government and enemy agents to safeguard their reward.

**BBC**
**5 episodes** ('Puffin'; 'Robinson Minor'; 'Raju Singh'; 'Celia'; 'The Magicali Brothers')
(b&w)
**Broadcast:** Tuesdays 11/5/54 – 8/6/54

**Main Cast:** Diana Day (Kate), Glyn Dearman (Colin), Norah Gorsen (Celia), Clement Lister (Mr Channing), Barbara Cochran (Mrs Channing), Ronald Moody (Puffin)

**Written by** Pamela Brown

**Designer:** Richard Henry
**Producer:** Pamela Brown

**Tie-in publications:** novelisation by Pamela Brown published by Nelson, 1954

## The Gordon Honour

Very much taking its cue from the earlier *The Silver Swan*, although without the forerunner's fantasy trappings, this was an educational journey through the ages as seen through the eyes of one particular family. The linking device was a valuable candlestick with fourteen branches, the symbol of the Gordon family honour. Each hundred years of its life another branch has been added to the candlestick by the incumbent Gordon generation, providing that honour has not been besmirched by greed or dishonesty. The original candle was won by a courtier of King Arthur, having saved the King's life.

Through time the Gordons have had to guard the candlestick against the Fitzwilliams, a jealous family line. Each adventure in time would pit another ancestral Gordon against Fitzwilliam. The first story told of how the stick was won from King Arthur, with subsequent adventures set at the time of King Richard and the Crusades, the invention of the cannon, the genesis of the Spanish Armada, the English Civil War and the Indian Mutiny. Barry Letts, Paul Whitsun-Jones and the aptly named Bruce Gordon – all principal players from the Children's Department's 'repertory cast' – acted out several parts down the generations.

The latter run (of only six episodes rather than the seven

you might have expected if the candle is to have fourteen branches) was up against the fledgling ITV companies and it is interesting to note how the sequel focused less on history textbook sources and managed to slip in several crowd-pleasing Wild West adventures.

**BBC**
**2 seasons**
(b&w)

**Season One**
**7 episodes** ('King Arthur's Candlestick'; 'The Crusader's Candlestick'; 'The Gunpowder Candlestick'; 'The Sea Captain's Candlestick'; 'The Cavalier's Candlestick'; 'The Mutiny Candlestick'; 'The Secret Agent's Candlestick')
**Broadcast:** Tuesdays 5/7/55 – 16/8/55

**Main Cast:** Bruce Gordon (Lord Freddie Gordon/The Varlet/Sir Rufus/Sir Phineas/Walter/Sir Roger/Private Lord Albert Gordon), Colin Douglas (Sir James Fitzwilliam/Sir Guy/Sir Hubert/Colonel Fitzwilliam/Sergeant Fitzwilliam), Barry Letts (Ronald Fitzwilliam/Rollo/Sir Malthus/Sir Thomas/Sir Jeremy/Corporal Fitzwilliam/Major Fitzwilliam), Paul Whitsun-Jones (Admiral the Duke of Tyburne/Captain Sir Francis Gordon), Sheila Shand Gibbs (Poppy the maid/Rowena the kitchen wench), Richard Wordsworth (King Arthur), Robert Raikes (King Richard)

**Written by** Shaun Sutton

**Designer:** Stephen Taylor
**Producer:** Shaun Sutton

**Season Two**
*The Gordon Honour: the further adventures of a candlestick*
**6 episodes** ('The Prisoner's Candlestick'; 'The Potato Candlestick'; 'The Red Indian Candlestick'; 'The Twins' Candlestick'; 'The Wild West Candlestick'; 'The Diving-Bell Candlestick')
**Broadcast:** Fridays 13/1/56 – 23/3/56 (shown fortnightly)

**Main Cast:** Bruce Gordon (parts include Lord Freddie Gordon/Jonathan/Philip/Sir Joshua/Lord 'Beau'/Lord Clarence/Lord Algy/Lord George), Paul Whitsun-Jones (parts include Admiral the Duke of Tyburne/Sir Francis Gordon/Commodore the Duke of Tyburne), Colin Douglas (parts include Sir James Fitzwilliam/Sir Bardolph/Sir Clive/Black Jack), Barry Letts (parts include Ronald Fitzwilliam/Piers/Ronnie/Sir Maurice/Seth/Sir Lucius), Penelope Bartley (Poppy/Meg/Mary/Virginia), Michael Allinson (Henry V), Peggy Thorpe-Bates (Queen Elizabeth I), Peter Bull (Chief Sitting Bull), Arthur Lowe (Tim Rafferty)

**Written by** Shaun Sutton

**Designers:** Richard Henry (episode 1), Donald Horne (2–4) (eps 5 and 6 not given)
**Producer:** Shaun Sutton

## The Blakes

Jim, head of the Blake family, loses his factory job in a Herefordshire town and grows disenchanted with living in rented accommodation. Don't be misled into thinking this was some kind of hard-hitting examination into redundancy and the family however. Jim Blake reckoned that if the family could return south to his Sussex birthplace, everything would be all right, and to this end he bought an old bus, turned it into a home on wheels and named it Ellenjean.

Jim and his wife Ellen, his eldest son Bill, his daughter Jean and little Micky pack into the bus and enjoy all manner of undeniably twee 'adventures' en route, meeting gypsies and imagined burglars in four less than high octane episodes. The publicity line in *Radio Times* best sums up its outlook: 'The cast will also include a cat, a sheep dog and a horse who does not mind being shut up in a pantry.' The book on which this serial was based was written by a husband and wife couple, Daphne and Douglas Holmes, who claimed to have made a similar bus journey themselves. The book was adapted by Muriel Levy for radio and it was Levy who brought it to television.

**BBC**
**4 episodes**
(b&w)
**Broadcast:** Sundays 2/10/55 – 23/10/55

**Main Cast:** Betty Woolfe (Ellen Blake), Robert Raglan (Jim Blake), Anneke Willys (Jean Blake), Martyn Anderson (Bill Blake), Douglas Hankin (Micky Blake)

Based on the novel by 'Alison Wright' (first UK publication 1952, Dent)
**Adapted by** Muriel Levy

**Designer:** Claude Whatham
**Producer:** Pamela Brown

## Space School

*'Imagine going to school in a space suit ... living with your mother and father in a colony of 400 or so engineers, scientists and space pilots in a great wheel silently turning 1,075 miles above the surface of the earth ...'*

It may well have been about a space school but this serial also acted as a lesson in science and then current theories about space travel, postulating a possible future amid never-knowingly-too-thrilling space adventures. The three tweely named Winter children – Wallace, Winifred (or 'Winnie' as she's known) and Wilfred – live with their mother on the space station Earth Satellite One while their father is on a survey mission to study the moons of Mars.

Between classes at space school the Winters become friendly with the various people who live and work in the colony. There's the ace pilot Space Commodore Sterling, hot-headed Irish daredevil O'Rorke, Cockney navigator 'Tubby' Thompson and Sam Scroop, the 'trapper of the spaceways' and cook on the Commodore's ship. On the fringes is ace newshawk for the Interplanetary Television Commission, Humphrey Soames.

Most exciting for those viewers craving 'space, speed and adventure', in programme head Owen Reed's words, would have been the satellite and other hardware such as 'space tankers darting noiselessly from planet to planet'. These were credited as having been 'built' by John Ryan but since Ryan was the man behind the adventures of animated cardboard pirate Captain Pugwash his effects might well have tended towards the two-dimensional.

*Space School* remains notable as another step away from the period adaptation but it's also indicative of the BBC attitudes of the time – *Flash Gordon*-styled unabashed adventure was still clearly regarded as too frivolous.

**BBC**
**4 episodes**
(b&w)
**Broadcast:** Sundays 8/1/56 – 29/1/56

**Main Cast:** Michael Maguire (Wallace Winter), Ann Cooke (Winnie Winter), Meurig Jones (Wifred Winter), Maud Long (Mrs Winter), Julie Webb (Miss Osborne), John Stuart (Commodore Sir Hugh Sterling), Matthew Lane (Michael O'Rorke), Donald McCorkindale (Tubby Thompson), Neil McCallum (Sam Scroop), David Drummond (Humphrey Soames), Anthony Toller (Captain of the School), Shay Gorman (The Stranger)

**Written by** Gordon Ford

**Designer:** Gordon Roland
**Producer:** Kevin Sheldon

## The Watch Tower

In this one-off half-hour teleplay, two children living in 1940 Britain discover a crash-landed German pilot hiding out behind enemy lines in an old ruined castle tower which also houses an unexploded bomb.

*The Watch Tower* is one of the earliest surviving examples of children's drama television and at first glance this archive document seems a risible piece of the most reactionary rhetoric. This appears to be a tale of tea at the vicarage in a sickly sweet England of white fence posts whose peace is shattered by the arrival of a nasty Jerry. You'd be mistaken, however, to take at face value such lines of dialogue as 'The Germans started it. They always start wars,' delivered in such a matter-of-fact way as to sound like they have come from Harry Enfield's Mr Cholmondley-Warner films. As the play progresses it becomes clear that these lines are used to mirror the more vengeful attitudes of post-war Britons – these feelings are being condemned not condoned.

Clearly a new, tolerant liberalism is at work here in what must have seemed an almost treasonable tract at the time. On meeting the German pilot the two children, Jo and Paul, discover their belligerence fading as they realise that he is a man not unlike their own fighter pilot father. Their growing belief that he is 'not such a bad chap, really' is given further credence when, at risk to himself, the pilot joins forces with the children's friend Mr Bradley to help save the pair from the ticking bomb they uncover in the castle ruins.

In contemporary context *The Watch Tower* was possibly among the more dynamic BBC output of the time. The cramped sets are complemented by a decent amount of filmed inserts which appear to have been played live into the transmission at the appropriate points. The fledgling BBC special effects 'department' of Jack Kine and Bernard    21

Wilkie even provided a fairly spectacular explosion on film for the UXB. The acting is of the less naturalistic school prevalent at the time and it's also worth noting the casting of a 'child' lead (Margaret Barton) who appears to be the wrong side of twenty.

The whys and wherefores of the well-meaning ideology and treatise on the futility of war are beyond the focus of this book (were the German troops not cowards rather than brave men, for acquiescing to a government that was clearly persecuting the Polish Jews?), but nonetheless *The Watch Tower* must be recognised as a work whose intent to forge a new British mindset at such a historically malleable time was clear. The final rationing limits were being lifted and Britain was beginning to rebuild not only its cities but also its national identity. Thus the piece stands as a bona fide act of television subversion. It's worth noting that the play's central tenets are identical to those of the much later novel and television serial *The Machine Gunners*, published and aired in far less fractious times.

**BBC**
**1 episode**
(b&w)
**Broadcast:** 13/11/56

**Main Cast:** Margaret Barton (Joanna), Nigel Anthony (Paul), Barry Letts (The German), Paul Whitsun-Jones (Mr Bradley), Christine Russell (Mrs Fraser), Garth Adams (PC Wheatland)

**Written by** Shaun Sutton

**Designer:** Eileen Diss
**Producer:** Shaun Sutton

**Above:** in *The Silver Sword* Edek Balicki (Melvyn Hayes) and his family flee Nazi oppression in wartime Poland.

## The Silver Sword

When the Nazis invade Poland, Warsaw schoolmaster Joseph Balicki and his wife Magrit are separated from their three children and imprisoned in German slave camps. When their house is blown up, Ruth, Edek and Bronia take up residence in a ruined cellar before moving onto the countryside beyond. When Joseph escapes from the camp, he returns to Warsaw to find the family gone. Before he leaves for Switzerland, where he and his wife agreed they would meet should they survive the war, he encounters an orphan boy called Jan. He gives Jan a paperknife in the shape of a sword and asks the boy, should he meet the children, to tell them to head for Switzerland. Jan later finds the children and together they set off for Switzerland in search of the parents.

Adapted for television just a year after its publication and little more than ten years since the end of the war, *The Silver Sword* dispenses with the approach one might expect of war-based drama. Rather than focusing on complicated issues like the ethics of war, or reiterating how nasty the Jerries were, the narrative concentrates instead on the children's epic journey across Europe.

As a tale of adventure the novel works well but the BBC's first adaptation struggles to realise the images suggested in the book. The viewer is seldom made to feel that the children are suffering any great hardship. Their stay in the cellar beneath the ruined house would surely have been one of dark squalor, yet they seem to live in comparative comfort. The way in which Edek puts food on the table is also trivialised. In a scene not included in the novel we see Edek throwing a stone at a German soldier, who then proceeds to chase Edek in circles in a comedic fashion around the outside of a bakery. Each time Edek passes the bread stall he takes another loaf of bread.

Production limitations meant that the children's efforts to gain access to Switzerland by crossing Lake Constance in a small boat had to be omitted from the adaptation. The novel details a fierce storm in which the children are caught and almost drowned. The adaptation, unable to recreate this on screen, instead had a witness to the incident recall everything that had happened as dialogue.

*The Silver Sword* was incredibly exciting in its time, so much so that members of the public were still writing to the BBC requesting another screening more than ten years after its broadcast. Instead of repeating the serial, the BBC replied by adapting the series again, this time in colour. Transmitted late in 1971 and trailed in *Radio Times* as early as October 1970, the production incorporated a greater amount of location work, with filming taking place in Wales and also in Leeds, where a demolition site was used effectively to represent battle-scarred Warsaw.

Instead of complicating issues by involving children on the rights and wrongs of war, it engaged them in an entertaining, no-strings-attached adventure story.

Based on the novel by Ian Serraillier (first UK publication 1956, Jonathan Cape)

***The Silver Sword* (1957)**
**BBC**
**7 episodes** ('Escape from the Nazis'; 'Escape from Prison'; 'Burning of the City'; 'Return of Edek'; 'Jan in Trouble'; 'Escape from Bavaria'; 'The Last Lap')
(b&w)
**Broadcast:** Sundays 24/11/57 – 5/1/58

**Main Cast:** Pat Pleasance (Ruth Balicki), Melvyn Hayes (Edek Balicki), Ingrid Sylvester (Bronia Balicki), Frazer Hines (Jan), Barry Letts (Joseph Balicki), Gwen Watford (Magrit Balicki)

**Adapted by** C. E. Webber
**Designer:** Lawrence Broadhouse
**Producer:** Shaun Sutton

**Tie-in publications:** short story in the *BBC Children's Annual 1959* (edited by Ursula Eason)

***The Silver Sword* (1971)**
**BBC**
**8 episodes**
(colour)
**Broadcast:** Sundays 22/8/71 – 30/10/71

**Main Cast:** Joanna Shelley (Ruth Balicki), Rufus Frampton (Edek Balicki), Cherrald Butterfield (Bronia Balicki), Simon Turner (Jan), Philip Brack (Joseph Balicki), Elizabeth Burger (Magrit Balicki)

**Adapted by** Alexander Baron

**Designer:** Peter Brachacki
**Producer:** John McRae
**Director:** Joan Craft

**Tie-in publications:** n/k

## Run to Earth

The contemporary adventure thriller moved out of the home counties for this serial with a more regional flavour. Two adventurous Glasgow boys discover they have a new neighbour, Captain Gaunt. Gaunt is an American naval officer who has come to Glasgow seeking a former member of his crew from an ill-fated mission off American shores ten years earlier. Gaunt's daughter Lindy befriends the boys and enlists their help in tracking down the seaman who disobeyed Gaunt's orders and caused a collision that foggy night. As might be expected, their hunt takes some unexpected twists.

It's not presently known whether the serial was shot on location in Glasgow and on the Clyde (episode four was set in the Clyde coastal town of Dunoon) but, if it were, this would have represented the longest journey made by the Children's Department up to that point. Even intending a provincial setting as far-flung as Glasgow was an innovation of sorts nonetheless.

**BBC**
**5 episodes** ('Strange Neighbours'; 'Aunt Alexa'; 'Captain Gaunt's Secret'; 'Discovery at Dunoon'; 'Ninian McHarg')
(b&w)
**Broadcast:** Tuesdays 7/2/58 – 11/3/58

**Main Cast:** Andrew Irvine (Archie Almond), Frazer Hines (Mick Fairbairn), Shandra Walden (Lindy Gaunt), Michael Balfour (Captain Gaunt), James Cairncross (Mr Fairbairn), Katharine Page (Mrs Fairbairn), Hope Jackman (Mrs Ferguson), Barbara Cavan (Mrs Almond), Tim Hudson (Mr Almond) Edna Petrie (Aunt Alexa), Joe Greig (Lucky)

From the novel by Elisabeth Kyle (first UK publication 1958, publisher n/k – London)

**Designer:** Lawrence Broadhouse
**Producer:** David Goddard

## Captain Moonlight – Man of Mystery

Several years before *Doctor Who* became a Saturday teatime institution, younger viewers could follow the escapades of Captain Moonlight. A comedy thriller with a limited run, this was way ahead of its time. A pre-modern piece of post-modernism, it told the tale of a bespectacled, rather nerdy radio actor called Tony who played a famous radio character, in the *Dick Barton* mould, called Captain Moonlight. The international man of mystery would travel the world battling spy rings and the like, while plain old Tony rather disliked the thought of physical violence. But when he and his friends are threatened by a group of gangsters (rendered as very cartoonish spivs), Tony decides to draw on the experience of his character to 'become' Captain Moonlight.

While played for laughs, it was undoubtedly a very sophisticated piece for its time. Among all the cross-media playfulness this TV series was, ironically, a sure indicator of the drawing power that radio still held in 1958.

**BBC**
**2 seasons**
(b&w)

**Season One**
**6 episodes** ('The Letter'; 'Captain Moonlight Hits Out'; 'The Secret of the Record Shop'; 'Head Office'; episode 5 n/k; 'Business as Unusual')
**Broadcast:** Saturdays 22/3/58 – 26/4/58

**Main Cast:** Jeremy White (Tony/Captain Moonlight), Lorraine Peters (Alice), Leonard Jefferey (Jimmy Bell), Anthony Bate (Forrest), Donald Masters (Ken), Terry Baker (Les)

**Written by** Kevin Sheldon

**Designer:** Gordon Foster
**Producer:** Kevin Sheldon

**Season Two**
**6 episodes** (no titles given)
**Broadcast:** Saturdays 12/3/60 – 16/4/60 (this season was not shown in Scotland, where a regional sports round-up programme replaced it)

## The Dangerous Game

Perhaps the most elusive children's drama serial of all – with no episodes in the archive and virtually no contemporary publicity material having yet to come to light all that is known for certain is that this was the story of two young boys caught up in espionage.

Clues suggest that it may have concerned a race to possess a very special chess set sold at auction which contains certain secret information – but then again it might not! A mystery inside a mystery then. Worthy of a mention nonetheless as an indicator of the continuing shift away from historical adventure towards contemporary tales of cops, robbers and secret agents.

**BBC**
**4 episodes** ('Pawns in the Game'; 'Red to Move'; 'Knight in Danger'; 'Checkmate')
(b&w)
**Broadcast:** Tuesdays 13/5/58 – 3/6/58

**Main Cast:** Gerald Andersen (Henderson), Shaw Taylor (Marco), Patrick Ellis (Joe Hunter), Anthony Wilson (Pete Hunter), Tim Hudson (Major Seton), Colin Douglas (George Clayton), Betty Cooper (Mrs Hunter), Joe Greig (Purvis), Patrick Troughton (Philip Baker), Patrick Cargill (Mr Goldman), Bryan Kendrick (Max Brett)

**Written by** David Carr

**Designer:** Marilyn Roberts
**Producer:** David Goddard

## Queen's Champion
### Loyalty and treason on the eve of the Armada
An interesting development in BBC children's drama by becoming the first long-form historical serial to be specially written for television as an ersatz 'literary classic' by Shaun Sutton. Also influential was the success of the adaptation of Ian Serraillier's *The Silver Sword* earlier in the year. As in the Serraillier tale, a keepsake becomes a symbol of personal freedom. In this case the 'Queen's Champion' is a golden statuette of a knight in armour passed on through the generations to the eldest son of the aristocratic Penlynden family. Only through his adventure in Elizabethan England does fourteen-year-old Roger Penlynden truly earn his right to the Champion.

The adventure begins on the eve of the battle of the Armada on 20 July 1588 (the first episode of the serial also went out on 20 July 370 years later) and sees Roger and his friend Toby, the scullery boy, discover fifth columnists and a Spanish plot to kill the Queen.

The cast contained many names who would go onto become well-known in years to come and once again drew upon Shaun Sutton's favoured 'repertory' cast. Of note was the casting of Peggy Thorpe-Bates as the Queen, a role she had played two years earlier in Sutton's 'time travelling' adventure *The Gordon Honour*.

The serial was telerecorded in its entirety and repeated the following summer, though only the first episode now exists in the BBC archive.

**BBC**
**8 episodes** ('The Betrayal'; 'The Escape from Penlynden'; 'The Outlaws'; 'The Rescue'; 'The Trap'; 'The Eve of the Armada'; 'The Edge of Defeat'; 'The Return to Penlynden')
(b&w)
**Broadcast:** Sundays 20/7/58 – 7/9/58

**Main Cast:** Michael Anderson (Roger Penlynden), Frazer Hines (Toby), Patrick Cargill (Master Fidian), Roger Delgado (Don Jose), Peggy Thorpe-Bates (Queen Elizabeth I), Terry Baker (Hal), John Woodnutt (Master Allan), Paul Whitsun-Jones (Rumble), Colin Douglas (Ralph), William Devlin (Sir Henry Penlynden), Barry Letts (Sir Thomas Wycherly), Jane Asher

(Mary Brandon), Michael Brennan (John Brandon), Nigel Arkwright (Barthlomew), Patrick Troughton (Don Alonzo), Desmond Llewellyn (Lord Bretherton)

**Written by** Shaun Sutton

**Designer:** Eileen Diss
**Producer:** Shaun Sutton

**Tie-in publications:** novelisation by Shaun Sutton published in hardback by Edward Arnold, 1961

## Ask For King Billy
Not a period tale of the house of Hanover, but a modern-day detective drama with an obscure connection to King William. This seems a direct response to the audience research finding that children liked to watch adult programmes rather than those specifically made for them: an ersatz adult thriller for the tinies. Gone were the resourceful kids who usually populated these things, replaced by the stoic Gordon Stewart, a down-at-heel private detective on the verge of going broke until one day a mysterious client appears with a job for him.

The job is not without its hazards, however, and soon Stewart finds himself wanted for a murder he didn't commit. He makes his way to Hull to investigate the case, with the police and three shady figures in tow. Just who are the Man in Black, the Little Man and the Tall Man?

'King Billy' is a golden statue of the historical figure which stands in the market square in Hull. The statue marks the centre of a smuggling ring – Hull has been known as a hive of activity in contraband since the days of sailing ships and moonshine. Warrens of secret tunnels are thought to weave their way across the town – are some of them still in use in 1959? Something fishy is going on and it's up to Stewart to find out what and clear his name.

What might have appeared a radically adult tale of gumshoes and murder was, beneath the surface, just another smuggling tale, albeit a slightly more credible one than the Blyton-style adventures prevalent at the time.

**BBC**
**5 episodes**
(b&w)
**Broadcast:** Tuesdays 3/11/59 – 1/12/59

**Main Cast:** Donald Churchill (Gordon Stewart), Gillian Barber (Connie), Philip Ray (The Client), Peter Bull (Man in Black), Wolfe Morris (Little Man), Peter Thomas (Tall Man), Anthony Woodruff (Alan Brookes), Ronnie Reeves (Garage Man)

Based on the novel by Henry Treece (first UK publication 1955, Faber and Faber)
**Adapted by** C. E. Webber

**Designer:** Susan Spence
**Producer:** Tony Halfpenny

## Biggles

The adventures of air ace Inspector James Bigglesworth had thrilled generations of schoolboys before he came to TV courtesy of the nascent North West England broadcaster. The format of the famous *Biggles* books had changed over the years to reflect public tastes and international affairs.

This 1960 TV series used the then current template which had a post-war Biggles leaving the RAF to join the CID, heading up a crack unit of aviator troubleshooters solving crimes all over the globe (even if corners of the world as far-flung as South America, Monte Carlo, the West Indies and Egypt were recreated in the Manchester studios). Most of these crimes had Biggles' old enemy Von Stalhein behind them as it turned out. Although Biggles was now a flying policeman, many stories harked back to World War II for their plots. Young boys – and no doubt their dads – were hooked by the after-tea serial which went twice weekly part way through its run and later aired overseas in countries including Australia.

Ginger actor John Leyton became a hugely successful pop star for a few years on the back of the fame the series brought him, but most notable of all its cast and crew was one of its minor writers – Tony Warren was developing *Coronation Street* for Granada while working on *Biggles*. William Roache was chosen for the part of Ken Barlow after Warren saw the actor in an episode of this series.

**Granada**
**44 episodes**
(b&w)

**Main Cast:** Nevil Whiting (Biggles), David Drummond (Lord Bertram Lissie), John Leyton (Ginger Hebblethwaite), Carl Duering (Erich Von Stalhein)

Adapted from the novels of Captain W. E. Johns

**Producers:** Harry Elton (1–29), Kitty Black (30–44)

Nominally the series was a collection of episodic serials, although less detailed published listings have made it difficult to delineate between them with 100 per cent certainty

### Story 1
**3 episodes** (Fridays 6.30p.m. 1/4/60 – 15/4/60)
Biggles investigates a £100,000 jewel theft
**Adapted by** H. V. Kershaw
**Designer:** Denis Parkin
**Director:** Stuart Latham

### Story 2
**5 episodes** (22/4/60 – 20/5/60)
Biggles travels to the North Pole and Eskimo Island
**Adapted by** Alick Hayes
**Designer:** Denis Parkin
**Director:** Christopher McMaster

### Story 3
**5 episodes** (27/5/60 – 24/6/60)
Is Von Stalhein behind aircraft wreckage found in the North Sea?
**Adapted by** H. V. Kershaw
**Designer:** Denis Parkin
**Director:** Stuart Latham

The series then went twice weekly, shown on Wednesdays and Fridays 7p.m. on ITV

### Story 4
'Amazon Adventure' (29/6/60)
**Adapted by** H. V. Kershaw
**Designer:** Denis Parkin
**Director:** Stuart Latham

### Story 5
**6 episodes** (1/7/60 – 20/7/60)
A trip to Monte Carlo and a disappearing Crown Prince
**Adapted by** Thomas Clarke
**Designer:** Denis Parkin
**Director:** Douglas Hurn

### Story 6
**9 episodes** (22/7/60 – 19/8/60)
'Mystery Island': Biggles searches for the blueprints of an anti-radar device thought to have been developed by the Germans at the end of the war and now held by Von Stalhein
**Adapted by** H. V. Kershaw (1, 4–9), Tony Warren (2–3)
**Designer:** Denis Parkin
**Directors:** Christopher McMaster (2–9), Eric Price (1)

### Story 7
**3 episodes** (24/8/60 – 31/8/60)
'Biggles at World's End': two botanists lost in Tierra del Fuego lead to hidden treasure
**Adapted by** Rex Howard Arundel
**Designer:** Denis Parkin
**Director:** Derek Bennett

### Story 8
**6 episodes** (2/9/60 – 21/9/60)
'Biggles Springs the Lock': the disappearance of stores of ammunition leads to a plot by Von Stalhein to blow up the Panama Canal
**Written by** H. V. Kershaw
**Designers:** Roy Stonehouse (1–3), Denis Parkin (4–6)
**Directors:** Derek Bennett (1), Christopher McMaster (2–3), Eric Price (4–6)

### Story 9
**3 episodes** (23/9/60 – 30/9/60)
'Biggles in the East': the intrepid flier tackles pearl thieves
**Written by** Edward Luckarift
**Designer:** Denis Parkin
**Director:** David Main

### Story 10
**3 episodes** (5/10/60 – 12/10/60)
'Biggles on the Nile': Biggles tries to find Jasmine Day, a British movie star missing in the lands of ancient Egypt
**Written by** H. V. Kershaw
**Designer:** Denis Parkin
**Director:** Christopher McMaster

## The Pen of My Aunt

'A gay, light-hearted adventure which is not to be taken too seriously' was how *Radio Times* described this six-part contemporary comedy thriller. Set in 1960 Paris, unsurprisingly the production team journeyed no further than Chelsea for its location shoot, going to great lengths to create a French street scene. Cars drove on the 'wrong' 25 side of the road, street signs were provided by the design department, a coiffured poodle was a key prop and passers-by were requested to 'walk with a French accent'.

The action concerned two conspicuously middle-class English children residing in a Paris hotel with their tutor Mr Ash. One rainy day, stuck in the hotel, the Harper children are looking down the back of an armchair for a few loose francs when they discover something far more exciting (contemporary publicity material doesn't say what, but it's a safe bet that it was a pen of special significance!). Their discovery causes all sorts of consternation among the rather oddball residents of the hotel. They include Perichon, a bumbling hotel detective, and the over-the-top prima donna Madame Blitskaya. The children's adventure also involves their old friend Miss Merrell, the puppet collector, and her 'friend' Mr Jinks – a huge toy rabbit! Whether Mr Jinks actually talked and took part in the adventure is not known but it would be nice to think that he did.

**BBC**
**6 episodes** ('It Always Rains on Sundays'; 'Wild Goose Chase'; 'Hiders and Finders'; 'Lucky Dip'; 'Pack and Follow'; 'Winner Takes All')
(b&w)
**Broadcast:** Tuesdays 12/4/60 – 17/5/60

**Main Cast:** Hilary Wyce (Susan Harper), Jonothan Bergman (Dennis Harper), Joan Hart (Anna Merrell), Eric Dodson (Mr Ash), Michael Hitchman (Perichon), Nicolette Bernard (Madame Blitskaya), David Grey (Kapra), Maurice Colbourne (General Upperton)

**Written by** Eric Allen

**Music** for flute and percussion composed and played by Lionel Solomon and James Blades
**Accordionist:** Henry Krein
**Designer:** Richard Wilmot
**Producer:** Barbara Hammond

## Pathfinders

Broadcast as a self-contained drama serial, *Target Luna* would turn out to be the forerunner to ABC's successful *Pathfinders* trilogy. The action starts in a rocket station situated on an island off the coast of Scotland (with location scenes actually shot at the Essex coast and surrounding countryside). Professor Wedgwood is joined for the Easter holidays by his three children, Valerie, Geoffrey and Jimmy. The scientists on the island plan to send the first manned rocket around the moon but the project goes wrong when the pilot falls ill and young Jimmy finds himself accidentally launched into space.

*Pathfinders* followed just a few months later and went on to comprise three stories: *Pathfinders in Space*, *Pathfinders to Mars* and *Pathfinders to Venus*. Predating the *Lost in Space* format of a family embarking on a series of adventures in space, the *Pathfinders* series saw Jimmy and Hamlet the hamster return to space, this time accompanied by Jimmy's siblings and father.

In *Pathfinders in Space* a team of lunar explorers led by Wedgwood (now played by Peter Williams) overcome many obstacles to land on the surface of the moon. Unfortunately the supply rocket has landed some distance

from the main ship and, while Wedgwood starts his long journey towards it, the others discover an alien spaceship and the remains of its occupant. When one of their rockets is destroyed by meteorites, Wedgwood plans to return to Earth using the alien craft.

The following two stories used basically the same set-up as the first but introduced some new characters to cover cast changes. With Jimmy unable to travel due to a broken arm, the Professor's eldest son Geoffrey pilots the rocket. Reporter Conway Henderson is joined by his niece. The daring venture to the red planet is jeopardised when crew member Professor Hawkins turns out to be an impostor – actually a fanatical writer of science fiction called Harcourt Brown, who is determined to prove that there is life on Mars. Before long, a hostage situation ensues.

Having successfully regained control of the mission, the crew are returning to Earth when they intercept a distress call from an American pilot situated on Venus. When they land, the crew find that the pilot's spaceship has been ransacked and they are soon attacked by carnivorous plants and primitive ape creatures.

*Pathfinders* was broadcast as part of ITV's Sunday Family Hour, appealing just as much to adults as it did children at a time when Yuri Gagarin was still over a year away from being the first man in space. Canadian producer Sydney Newman brought a more Americanised slant to the otherwise British production, particularly evident in the character of Professor Meadows who possesses a prominent mid-Atlantic accent. Whether this was an attempt to promote international sales or inject a higher level of bravado drama is open to debate. The latter would appear to be just as likely, with many of the actors frantically delivering their lines in raised voices.

The majority of the series was recorded on videotape and special effects were satisfactorily achieved with the limited resources of the time. Actors could be made to look like they were spacewalking by lying on podiums draped in black velvet positioned in front of a black backdrop. The actors were then recorded from unusual angles, giving the impression of weightlessness.

Sydney Newman consolidated the success of *Pathfinders* with *Plateau of Fear*, a children's adventure serial set in a nuclear power station high in the Andes. Although Gerald Flood and Stewart Guidotti, who had both appeared in *Pathfinders*, starred in this new series, it was in no way a continuation of the *Pathfinders* story and both played new parts.

Flood and Guidotti would appear in two further serials similar in style to the *Pathfinders* trilogy but differing in one major way. *City Beneath the Sea* and *Secret Beneath the Sea*, as the titles suggest, switch the action from 'outer' to 'inner' space. Submarines and ocean cities, rather than spaceships, became the setting for further intrigue and adventure.

Detailed below are four series linked by character, cast and plot, generally known as the *Pathfinders* series

**ABC**
(b&w)

### Target Luna
**6 episodes** ('The Rocket Station'; 'Countdown'; 'The Strange Illness'; 'Storm in Space'; 'The Solar Flare'; 'The Falling Star')
**Broadcast:** Sundays 24/4/60 – 29/5/60

**Main Cast:** David Markham (Professor Wedgwood),
John Cairney (Ian Murray), Frank Finlay (Mr Henderson),
Michael Craze (Geoffrey Wedgwood), Michael Hammond
(Jimmy Wedgwood), Sylvia Davies (Valerie Wedgwood)

**Written by** Malcolm Hulke and Eric Paice
**Designer:** David Gillespie
**Producer:** Sydney Newman
**Director:** Adrian Brown

*Pathfinders in Space*
**7 episodes** ('Convoy to the Moon'; 'Spaceship from Nowhere';
'Luna Bridgehead'; 'The Man in the Moon'; 'The World of Lost
Toys'; 'Disaster on the Moon'; 'Rescue in Space')
**Broadcast:** Sundays 11/9/60 – 23/10/60

**Main Cast:** Peter Williams (Professor Wedgwood), Harold
Goldblatt (Dr O'Connell), Gerald Flood (Conway Henderson),
Stewart Guidotti (Geoff Wedgwood), Richard Dean (Jimmy
Wedgwood), Gillian Ferguson (Valerie Wedgwood), Pamela
Barney (Professor Mary Meadows)

**Written by** Malcolm Hulke and Eric Paice
**Designers:** Tom Spalding (1, 3–7), David Gillespie (1 and 2)
**Producer:** Sydney Newman
**Director:** Guy Verney

*Pathfinders to Mars*
**6 episodes** ('The Impostor'; 'Sabotage in Space'; 'The
Hostage'; 'Lichens!'; 'Zero Hour on the Red Planet'; 'Falling
into the Sun')
**Broadcast:** Sundays 11/12/60 – 15/1/61

**Main Cast:** George Colouris (The Imposter/Harcourt Brown*),
Gerald Flood (Conway Henderson), Stewart Guidotti (Geoff
Wedgwood), Hester Cameron (Margaret Henderson), Pamela
Barney (Professor Mary Meadows)
*Credited as 'The Imposter' for episodes 1 and 2, Harcourt
Brown thereafter

**Written by** Malcolm Hulke and Eric Paice
**Designer:** David Gillespie
**Producer:** Sydney Newman
**Director:** Guy Verney

*Pathfinders to Venus*
**8 episodes** ('SOS from Venus'; 'Into the Poison Cloud';
'The Living Planet'; 'The Creature'; 'The Venus People';
'The City'; 'The Valley of the Monsters'; 'Planet on Fire')
**Broadcast:** Sundays 5/3/61 – 23/4/61

**Main Cast:** George Colouris (Harcourt Brown), Gerald Flood
(Conway Henderson), Graydon Gould (Captain Wilson),
Stewart Guidotti (Geoff Wedgwood), Hester Cameron
(Margaret Henderson), Pamela Barney (Professor Mary
Meadows)

**Written by** Malcolm Hulke and Eric Paice
**Designers:** David Gillespie (all), Douglas James (6–8)
**Producer:** Sydney Newman
**Directors:** Guy Verney (1–5, 7), Reginald Collin (6, 8)

The following are spin-off vehicles for stars of *Pathfinders*,
telling the adventures of Mark Bannerman and Peter Blake

**ABC**
**3 seasons**
(b&w)

*Plateau of Fear*
**6 episodes** ('Terror at Potencia One'; 'Menace in the Night';
'Cavern of Death'; 'The Growing Peril'; 'The Invisible Shield';
'Slam-Down')
**Broadcast:** Sundays 24/9/61 – 29/10/61

**Main Cast:** Gerald Flood (Mark Bannerman), Stewart Guidotti
(Peter Blake), John Barron (Dr Miguel Aranda), Jan Miller
(Dr Susan Fraser)

**Written by** Malcolm Stuart Fellows and Sutherland Ross
**Music:** Clive Rogers
**Designers:** Roger King and James Douglas
**Producer:** Guy Verney
**Director:** Kim Mills

*City Beneath the Sea*
**7 episodes** ('The Pirates'; 'Escape to Aegira'; 'Tide of Evil';
'Cellar of Fear'; 'Power to Destroy'; 'Operation Grand Design';
'Three Hours to Doomsday')
**Broadcast:** Saturdays 17/11/62 – 29/12/62 part networked

**Main Cast:** Gerald Flood (Mark Bannerman), Stewart Guidotti
(Peter Blake), Caroline Blakiston (Dr Ann Boyd), Haydn Jones
(Prof Westfield), Aubrey Morris (Prof Ludwig Ziebrecken)

**Written by** John Lucarotti
**Producer:** Guy Verney
**Director:** Kim Mills

*Secret Beneath the Sea*
**6 episodes** ('The Mysterious Metal'; 'Voyage Into Danger';
'Sabotage'; 'The X-Layer'; 'Take-Over'; 'The Death Trap')
**Broadcast:** Saturdays 16/2/63 – 23/3/63

**Main Cast:** Gerald Flood (Mark Bannerman), Stewart Guidotti
(Peter Blake), Peter Williams (Capt Payne), Richard Colemann
(Dr Deraad), Ingrid Sylvester (Janet Slayton), Delena Kidd
(Dr Ellen), Robert James (Prof Gordon), David Spenser
(Prof Soobiah)

**Written by** John Lucarotti
**Producer:** Guy Verney
**Director:** Kim Mills

## Sheep's Clothing
Writer A. R. Rawlinson described his serial as 'plainly and
simply an adventure story' and few would disagree. Pretty
teenager Petra and fair-haired, blue-eyed boy Derek solve
mysterious goings-on hidden beneath the surface of a
sleepy, picturesque village in the South of England. A
signpost pointing to nowhere sparks the adventure for the
two kids. The kindly village constable seems ill-equipped
to deal with events, so they are forced to take matters into
their own hands.

A fair amount of location filming was vital to achieve the desired open air, pastoral feel of this contemporary if sedate piece.

**BBC**
**4 episodes**
(b&w)
**Broadcast:** Sundays 18/9/60 – 9/10/60

**Main Cast:** Leonard Cracknell (Derek Orr), Katy Wild (Petra Carew), Derek Smee (Lorning), Noel Howlett (Ulrich Panssand), Arthur Lowe (Mudor), Clare Wyton (Almoner), Denise Coffey (Stumpy), John Dunbar (Bleeker), Vivien Lacey (Eulalie Svensen), Suzanne Gibbs (Susan), Andrew Irvine (Dan), Jack Rodney (Morgan), Hazel Douglas (Mrs Morgan), Frank Siemen (Village Constable)

**Written by** A. R. Rawlinson based on his own book *Sheep's Clothing* (first UK publication 1929, publisher n/k)

**Designer:** Frederick Knapman
**Producer:** David Goddard

## Paradise Walk

Something of a forgotten landmark this serial, which saw the Sunday afternoon costume drama slot handed over to one of the first contemporary urban adventures made for children. West Indian boy Sammy comes to live with his Uncle Joshua and Aunt Jubilee in a big English city. His naive excitement at having arrived in this country means he all too easily gets involved with the unscrupulous Joe Cartwright who works beside his uncle in the garage. Ted Collis, the garage owner's stepson, is meanwhile caught up in vandalism. Events escalate until Joe gets shot and killed at the story's close.

Set in the poorer parts of a recognisable city (and with some location filming included to bolster the on-screen credibility) this story would have been very hard-hitting in its day, the drama unfolding as if it were on most viewers' doorsteps. *Paradise Walk* looked set to take BBC children's drama into a new era, being very different from most output up to that time and predating the arrival of Stuart Hood as BBC controller, but its realism was not really followed through until the 70s. If utilising the setting of a big city in 1961 was a real step forward then the casting of a West Indian in the lead role must have seemed nothing short of revolutionary at the time, albeit that the cast of ethnic characters was written from a white, educated, middle-class viewpoint.

**BBC**
**4 episodes** ('Gathering Storm'; 'Nothing But Trouble'; 'Suspicion of Robbery'; 'Brink of Disaster')
(b&w)
**Broadcast:** Sundays 15/1/61 – 5/2/61

**Main Cast:** Dudley Hunt (Sammy), Errol John (Joshua Brown), Gladys Taylor (Aunt Jubilee), Nigel Arkwright (Old Hornpipe), George A. Cooper (Mr Collis), Murray Melvin (Ted Collis), James Sharkey (Joe Cartwright)

**Written by** Shaun Sutton

**Designer:** Frederick Knapman
**Producer:** Shaun Sutton

## Strange Concealments
### An adventure in seven clues

An early TV airing for a soon-to-be familiar plot of a hunt for family treasure (see also *Treasure Over the Water* and several others). When wealthy stage manager Edmund Blundell died in 1811 he set up a cryptic treasure hunt in the hope that his feuding sons would make up their differences in order to seek their inheritance. The sons never did resolve their differences and the treasure has lain unclaimed for a century and a half. Now it is 1962 and Kate and Boyd George, two of Blundell's descendants, arrive in England from America armed with the first clue.

It was hoped that viewers at home would try to solve the mystery for themselves ahead of the George family. The riddle was based upon a quote from Shakespeare's *As You Like It*, Act Two, Scene One:

Sweet are the uses of adversity
Which like the toad, ugly and venomous
Wears yet a precious jewel in his head
And this our life, exempt from public haunt
Finds tongues in trees, books in the running brooks
Sermons in stones, and good in every thing

**ATV**
**7 episodes** ('The Clue in the Lockets'; 'A Precious Jewel'; 'Tongues in Trees'; 'Books in the Running Brooks'; 'Sermons in Stones'; 'The Uses of Adversity'; 'And Good in Everything')
(b&w)
**Broadcast:** Saturdays 29/9/62 – 10/11/62

**Written by** Michael Bancroft

**Main Cast:** Barbara Clegg (Kate George), Robin Walker (Boyd George), Frederick Jaeger (David Stimpson), Victor Platt (John Harmer), Henry Soskin (Ambrose Lemmon), Clare Asher (Victoria Lemmon)

**Designer:** Eric Sheddon
**Producer:** Cecil Petty

## Badger's Bend
### The animal hotel

If the old adage that you should never work with children and animals is true then it must have been a brave crew who worked on this serial which combined both each week.

Initially this was the story of young Tim Cordon who had moved to the countryside to discover an interest in the care of animals. Befriending local vet Mr Francis and his assistant Sheila, Tim was given some convalescing hamsters to look after and soon hit upon the idea of setting himself up as an animal hotel. Cats and dogs, badgers, kestrels, buzzards, ponies, monkeys, a naughty goat and even a cheetah all passed through its doors. Sometimes the series was played for laughs with animal high jinks all round but sometimes there was sad news and the odd case of animal cruelty to deal with.

Tim befriended local girl Betsy Alder, and it was Betsy who would become the series lead as it progressed through various cast changes. For the second series Betsy travelled to Alemouth where she met Oliver, nicknamed Ocky. Later, returning to Badger's Bend, she was joined by local lad Dave Banks.

Informative as it was fun or dramatic, factual wildlife accuracy came courtesy of the series consultants, Grahame Dangerfield and the British Veterinary Association. Much ad-libbing ensued when the live animals brought unscheduled chaos to the studios.

**Associated Rediffusion**
**2 seasons**
(b&w)

**Main Cast:** Malcolm Patton (Tim Cordon – Season 1), Gay Emma (Betsy Alder), James Ward (Mr Francis), Rosemary Nicholls (Sheila Dicken – Season 1), Kenneth Nash (Oliver 'Ocky' Crossley – Season 2), Hugh Janes (Dave Banks), Jean Alexander (Mrs Alder), Philip Newman (Mr Alder – Season 1), Michael Beint (Mr Alder – Season 2), Geoffrey Russell (Mr Cordon), Pamela Pitchford (Mrs Cordon)

**Season 1**
**17 episodes**
**Broadcast:** Fridays 4/1/63 – 26/4/63

**Written by** Suzanne Gibbs from a story by John Rhodes
**Designers:** John Hurst (1–14), John Clarke (15–17)
**Directors:** Adrian Brown (1–13), Eric Croall (14–17)

**Season 2**
**21 episodes**
**Broadcast:** Tuesdays 1/10/63 – 25/2/64 (episodes 14–21 were billed in *TV Times* as a new series but since there was no transmission break it is confusing to use that term here)

**Writers include:** Jeremy Kingston and Suzanne Gibbs (14–21)
**Designers include:** Jim Nicolson
**Directors include:** Marc Miller and Bob Gray (14–21)

## Sierra Nine

Watchdog organisation Sierra Nine has the responsibility of monitoring potential threats to the scientific equilibrium of Earth. At the head of this mini-taskforce is eccentric but highly gifted scientist Sir Willoughby Dodd, and help is at hand from his two young assistants, Peter Chance and Anna Parsons, who embark on dangerous and exciting missions.

Travelling to the Middle East, they must locate the maverick scientist, 'The Baron', and disable the microwave radio device that he is using to hypnotise research workers. When prominent nuclear physicist Sir Hugo Petersham's minute atomic warhead is stolen while in transit, Anna and Peter desperately try and track it down before it explodes. They then travel to a monastery in France to investigate a potion that apparently enables people to defy the aging process. Finally, the team find themselves in a second battle with 'The Baron', who has succeeded in stealing a new deadly weapon.

The series was developed after ITV's Head of Children's Television, John Rhodes, contacted Peter Hayes and Marc Miller, proposing a new approach on science fiction or a

'*Sexton Blake* of science'. Similar ideas would later be used as the basis of 70s adult drama *Doomwatch*, although that series took a more pronounced pro-environmental standpoint, popular at that time.

**Associated Rediffusion**
**1 season** (4 stories)
'The Brain Machine' (4 eps); 'The Man Who Shook the World' (3 eps); 'The Elixir of Life' (2 eps); 'The Q-Radiation' (4 eps) (b&w)
**Broadcast:** Tuesdays 7/5/63 – 30/7/63

**Main Cast:** Max Kirby (Sir Willoughby Dodd), David Sumner (Dr Peter Chance), Deborah Stanford (Anna Parsons), Harold Kasket (The Baron – Stories 1 and 4)

**Written by** Peter Hayes

**Designers:** Bernard Goodwin (Story 1), Duncan Cameron (Story 2), Andrew Drummond (Story 3), Ken Jones (Story 4)
**Director:** Marc Miller

## Smuggler's Cove
### Adventures in Cornwall

A soon-to-be archetypal story of holidaymaking kids getting tangled up in nocturnal crimes by the coast. Patricia, a teenager with a love of horses, and her brother Beetle arrive at the cove for their summer holiday, befriend local lad Tim and investigate the mystery of Uncle Jem's empty lobster pots – is the shady Mr Tregellet behind it? Smugglers were once again at large in this Blytonesque tale.

Location work for the serial was based in the seaside fishing harbour town of Looe in Cornwall.

**Associated Rediffusion**
**6 episodes** ('Sailor's Warning'; 'The Moonlight Folk'; 'Frog in Deep Water'; 'A Sign of the Hand'; 'Clue in Camera'; 'Beetle in a Hole')
(b&w)
**Broadcast:** Tuesdays 6/8/63 – 10/9/63

**Main Cast:** Frazer Hines (Tim), Billy Hamon (Beetle), Ingrid Sylvester (Patricia), Anthony Sagar (Uncle Jem), John Dearth (Tregellet), Annette Kerr (Miss Bond), Nigel Jenkins (Melvin)

**Written by** Jean McConnell

**Designer:** John Plant
**Director:** Richard West

## The Barnstormers

Five bored teenagers decide 'let's do the show right here' and form their own theatre group, The Tudor Players. Searching for a suitable stage they chance upon an old abandoned water mill. It's rumoured a pirate once lived in the mill and hid his treasure there. When the children begin to explore the mill it turns out to be a maze of hidden passageways and trapdoors. Their search is disturbed by the arrival in the village of a property developer who has also heard the legends of the treasure and is determined to buy the mill.

29

The lost treasure plot is mixed with an equally familiar tale of stage-struck youngsters *á la The Swish of the Curtain* – the latter strand takes over in the final episode when The Tudor Players finally put on their show. This episode alone was written by cast member Henry Soskin. Also among the cast was a post-*Just William*, pre-*Sweeney* Dennis Waterman.

**Associated Rediffusion**
**11 episodes** ('Mystery at the Mill'; 'Philip'; 'The Lost Treasure'; 'Enter a Stranger'; 'The Trap'; 'Camberley's Guest'; 'The Spanish Casket'; 'A Door to Nowhere'; 'Rusty in Danger'; 'Old Alexander's Secret'; 'Play Making With the Barnstormers')
(b&w)
**Broadcast:** Tuesdays 3/3/64 – 19/5/64

**Main Cast:** Dennis Waterman (Mike), Peter Hempson (Philip), Gerald Rowland (Rusty), Patricia Wilson (Sarah), John Pike (Alan)

**Written by** Joy Thwaites (episode 11 by Henry Soskin)

**Designer:** Bernard Goodwin
**Director:** Marc Miller

# Mike

The light-hearted adventures of a freckle-faced tyke. Thirteen-year-old Mike Willis fancies himself as a young inventor and uses his dad's garage as a laboratory. His first wacky idea is to invent black whitewash, seeing it as a much needed commodity for the building trade. Helping Mike in his schemes are his long-suffering tomboy sister, Kate, and his three friends Pete, Alfie and Joey.

Ginger-haired lead Denis Gilmore was something of a child star before coming to *Mike*. He was known all over the country as the impish boy who reminded his mother, 'Don't forget the fruit gums, mum,' in a series of TV adverts and he replaced Dennis Waterman as the lead in the second of the BBC's *Just William* series in 1963.

**Rediffusion**
**13 episodes** (Episode 1: 'A Black Wash-out'; 13: 'The Big Beat Contest')
(b&w)
**Broadcast:** Tuesdays 29/9/64 – 22/12/64

**Main Cast:** Denis Gilmore (Mike), Laurie Heath (Pete), Leslie Hart (Alfie), Billy Hamon (Joey), Deborah Cranston (Kate), Sheila Shand Gibbs (Mum), Geoffrey Matthews (Dad)

**Written by** Dickens Crouch

**Designers include:** Sylva Nadolny (1), John Plant (13)
**Directors include:** Bob Gray

**Tie-in publications:** cover of *TV Times* for week 10/10/64 – 16/10/64

# Orlando

If research at the time showed that children preferred 'adult' action series to those programmes specifically intended for them – macho little boys might be expected to answer a questionnaire this way – then *Orlando* must be seen as a direct answer to their stated tastes. *Orlando* was a spin-off from the prime-time adult thriller *Crane*. The Associated Rediffusion series had starred Patrick Allen in the title role as a hard-headed businessman who quit London for glamour and adventure living the life of a smuggler in Morocco. In February 1965 the series ended but Crane's trusted assistant and friend Orlando O'Connor returned just a few months later in his own series aimed at a much younger audience.

The wily old Irishman had been educated at the school of hard knocks, growing up in various children's homes and later joining the foreign legion. A rogue with a heart of gold, his time with Crane was spent smuggling cigarettes and booze (but never drugs) and occasionally helping out the authorities at those times when it took a crook to catch a crook.

The *Orlando* series opened with the man himself having returned to England and running a boatyard called Drake's Landing, with Crane having quit Morocco and moved on elsewhere. Orlando was now accompanied on a series of one-off episodic adventures by two kids, Long John and Triss. Orlando's boatyard soon fell into debt (no doubt he was spending too much of his time solving crimes to fix any boats) and so for the second season he picked up his famous woolly hat and moved to the London docks to look for work and his old friend Tony. When he arrived he found that Tony was dead, murdered. In trying to find out what has happened to his friend, Orlando falls in with two teenage detectives who have inherited their uncle's agency. Steve and Jenny Morgan were in their late teens (although the actors who played them were in their early twenties). The three formed a new partnership, with Steve taking on the strong-arm stuff and Jenny wearing nice trouser suits (as one publicity line put it, 'Jenny throws a feint and Steve throws punches').

In 1966, probably the most popular TV series with children were the way-out and wacky action series *Batman* and *The Man from UNCLE* (*The Avengers* and its ilk generally didn't go out until after 9p.m. in the evenings) and from Season Two onwards *Orlando* tended to provide a home-grown variant on these campy adventures (even going as far as to steal the '... and the ... Affair' *UNCLE*-style of titling for its last few stories). Gadgets were the in-thing and Orlando was not immune – his life was often saved by the magical powers of his talisman, the Gizzmo. The stories, like those of *UNCLE*, became more and more irreverent as O'Connor and friends travelled the high seas finding adventure. In 'Orlando and the Frightened Clown' the gang met such luminaries of the musical stage as Dolly Mintwhacker and Percy Poopdeck, while Clive Dunn guested. The less said about 'The Fifi Affair' and Serge Trowzerzoff, the better perhaps. Among the diamond smugglers and the like that Orlando encountered most weeks his arch-enemy was Moosh, his evil doppelganger played, naturally, by Sam Kydd.

**Facing page:** Orlando O'Connor (Sam Kydd, right) and his assistants Jenny (Judy Robinson, left) and Steve (David Munro, second from left) take care of another pair of hoodlums.

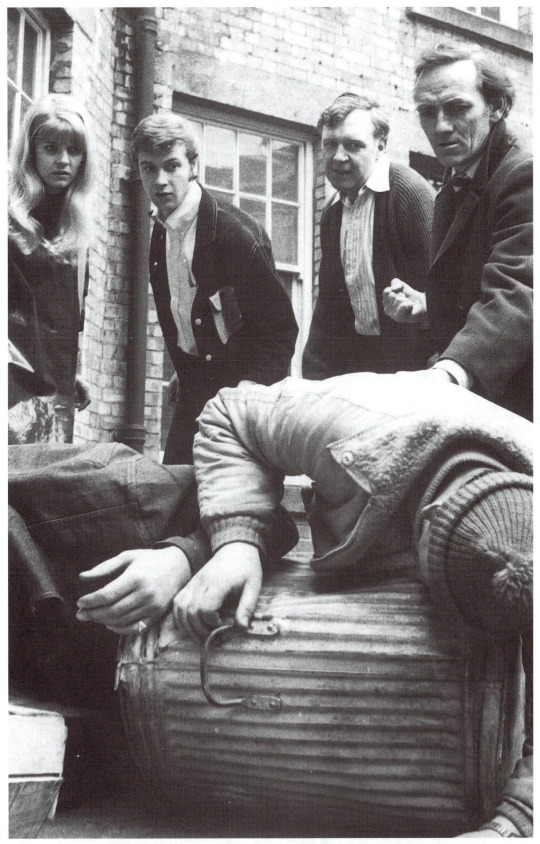

The series' popularity was reflected in the weekly picture strip which ran in *TV Comic* for several years, even if the rights budget never stretched to include Jenny alongside her brother Steve. *Orlando* was a long-running series – indeed its continuous fifty-one-episode run for Season Two is a record in children's television drama – but the irony was that this meant the series was considered factory-line product and thus expendable. Only a handful of episodes have survived out of seventy-five produced.

**Rediffusion**
**3 seasons**
(b&w)

**Season One**
**13 episodes** ('The Silver Spoon'; 'Orlando Tells a Story'; 'A Ring of Dogs'; 'Humpty-Dumpty'; 'Mask of Fear'; 'The Black Snake'; 'Ding-Dong Bell'; 'Flight to Calais'; 'A Load of Bilge Water'; 'The New People'; 'Skinny'; 'A Code for Life'; 'The Gold-Plated Football')
**Broadcast:** Tuesdays 13/4/65 – 6/7/65

**Written by** David Butler (1 and 6), David Weir (2 and 9), Ludovic Peters (3 and 12), David Wilde (4), Larry Forrester (5 and 11), Julia Durell (7), Reed de Rouen (8 and 13), Len Herwood (10)
**Script Editor:** Denis Butler
**Designer:** Andrew Drummond
**Directors:** Hugh Munro (all except 8, 10), John Rhodes (8, 10)

**Main Cast:** Sam Kydd (Orlando O'Connor), Gregory Phillips (Long John Turner), Margo Andrew (Triss Fenton), Archie Duncan (Captain Dan), Clifton Jones (Nelson), Clifford Earl (Sgt Prothero)

**Season Two**
*A series of adventures and escapades*
**9 stories/51 episodes**
**Broadcast:** Tuesdays 5/4/66 – 28/3/67 (shown Wednesdays in some ITV regions during this run)

**Regular Cast:** Sam Kydd (Orlando O'Connor), David Munro (Steve Morgan), Judy Robinson (Jenny Morgan)
**Producer:** Ronald Marriott

**Story 1**
**'A Slight Case of Pilfering'** by David A. Yallop
**7 episodes** ('Packet of Trouble'; 'A Man Called Burton'; 'The Achilles Heel'; 'Check'; 'The Cookie Begins to Crumble'; 'Rainbow Day'; 'Follow the Leader')
**Broadcast:** 5/4/66 – 24/5/66 (no broadcast 3/5/66 due to budget coverage)
**Designer:** Nicholas Ferguson
**Director:** Adrian Cooper

**Story 2**
**'Orlando and the Cemetery Walkers'** by Paddy Manning O'Brine
**6 episodes** ('The Cemetery Walkers'; 'A Body in the Basin'; 'The Plot Thickens'; 'Maiden Voyage'; 'Break Out'; 'The Tables Turned')
**Broadcast:** 31/5/66 – 5/7/66
**Designer:** Nicholas Ferguson
**Director:** Ronald Marriott

**Story 3**
**'The Gizzmo's Revenge'** by Len Herwood
**5 episodes** ('High Jinks and Old Junk'; 'Royalty Moves In'; 'Lady-in-Waiting'; 'Corpse Diplomatic'; 'Sink or Swim')
**Broadcast:** 12/7/66 – 9/8/66
**Designer:** Nicholas Ferguson
**Director:** Adrian Cooper

**Story 4**
**'Now you see it – Now you don't'** by David A. Yallop
**6 episodes** ('That was no lady – that was the Man from M.I.N.C.E.'; 'Shuffle the Pack and up pops the joker'; 'A Funny Thing Happened To Me On My Way To The Prison'; 'And For My Next Trick'; 'The Spies That Went Into The Cold'; 'Don't go down the mine chaps, it's bursting at the seams')
**Broadcast:** 16/8/66 – 20/9/66
**Designer:** Nicholas Ferguson
**Director:** Fred Sadoff

**Story 5**
**'Dangerous Waters'** by Ivor Jay
**6 episodes** ('Clue to a Clue'; 'Skin Deep'; 'Rhyme – But No Reason'; 'Victory in Sight'; 'Find the Lady'; 'All in the Book')
**Broadcast:** 27/9/66 – 1/11/66
**Designer:** Nicholas Ferguson
**Director:** Bryan Shiner

**Story 6**
**'Orlando and a Man Called Moosh'**
by Paddy Manning O'Brine
**5 episodes** ('Has Anyone Seen Fred Kebab?'; 'Come With Me to the Casbah'; 'A Man Called Moosh'; 'Only a Camel Loves a Camel'; 'Hubble, Bubble, Double Trouble')
**Broadcast:** 8/11/66 – 6/12/66
**Designer:** Andrew Drummond
**Director:** Adrian Cooper

**Story 7**
**'Stealers Keepers'** by Ivor Jay
**5 episodes** ('Storm Warning'; 'Wake Up Screaming'; 'A Peeping Tom and a Shoe'; 'Assassin Airborne'; 'In At the Death')
**Broadcast:** 13/12/66 – 10/1/67
**Designer:** Andrew Drummond
**Director:** Fred Sadoff

**Story 8**
**'Orlando and the Frightened Clown'** by Dino Irlandese
from an original story by David Fisher
**6 episodes** ('Beginners Please'; 'The Show Must Go On'; 'Clown on a Bike'; 'An Apple a Day...'; 'Send for Fred Pinwad'; 'Curtain Up')
**Broadcast:** 17/1/67 – 21/2/67
**Designer:** Andrew Drummond
**Director:** Adrian Cooper

**Story 9**
**'Irish Stew'** by Len Herwood
**5 episodes** ('A Tune in the Night'; 'The Stew Thickens'; 'Masks Over Masks'; 'A Bit of a Dance'; 'Pincer Movement')
**Broadcast:** 28/2/67 – 28/3/67
**Designer:** Andrew Drummond
**Director:** Adrian Cooper

**Season Three**
**3 stories/12 episodes**
**Broadcast:** Mondays 25/3/68 – 10/6/68

**Regular Cast:** Sam Kydd (Orlando O'Connor), Arthur White (Shish Kebab)
**Producer:** Ronald Marriott

**Story 1**
**'Orlando and the Return of Moosh'**
by Paddy Manning O'Brine
**4 episodes** ('Beau Geste and All That'; 'When Did You Last See Your Father?'; 'Don't Look Now, There's a Djellebah Behind You'; 'Where was Moosh When the Light Went Out?')
**Broadcast:** 25/3/68 – 15/4/68
**Designer:** Sylva Nadolny
**Director:** Adrian Cooper

**Story 2**
**'Orlando and the Up the Jungle Affair'**
by Paddy Manning O'Brine
**4 episodes** ('Lady Tapwater Turns It On'; 'Who's Afraid of Piranha Fish?'; 'Me Tarzan – Up a Gum Tree'; 'Let's All Be Hairy Together')
**Broadcast:** 22/4/68 – 17/5/68
**Designer:** Andrew Drummond
**Director:** Nicholas Ferguson

**Story 3**
**'Orlando and the Fifi Affair'** by Paddy Manning O'Brine
**4 episodes** ('Où est Fifi le Bon Bon?'; 'Aimez Vous Serge Trowzerzoff?'; 'Comment Allez Are You Up?'; 'Au Revoir But Not Goodbye')
**Broadcast:** 20/5/68 – 10/6/68
**Designer:** Andrew Drummond
**Director:** Adrian Cooper

**Tie-in publications:** *Orlando Annual 1968* written by Roger N. Cook and illustrated by Patrick Nevin, published by TV Publications, 1967

## Object Z

Two astronomers discover that an unidentified object is travelling through space at great speed and on a collision course with Earth. The opposing superpowers on Earth must combine their forces and work together towards developing a rocket which will enable them to eliminate the object before it reaches Earth and causes a global catastrophe. Could it be possible that the object isn't a natural phenomenon and is in fact created by aliens? Or is it all a complex hoax designed to bring the nations of Earth together in the hope of establishing global peace?

*Object Z* was initially written by Chris McMaster with an adult audience in mind but he elected to adapt it for younger viewers at a time when ITV were looking for ideas for children's dramas.

The series was originally recorded on videotape and primarily studio-bound, using stock footage film inserts whenever the interior of a bustling tracking station was required. It clearly owes much, both in terms of production style and narrative, to earlier science fiction series like *Quatermass* and *The Trollenberg Terror* with its stiff upper lip scientists facing global disaster.

The series was followed up by a sequel, *Object Z Returns*. Scientists discover that three more objects are travelling in formation towards Earth. Professor Ramsay, jailed after his earlier hoax for world peace, is freed to try and establish what's happening. This time it's no joke – as the aliens land in Earth's oceans and the world begins to freeze, it may well be that he's too late to stop them.

**Rediffusion**
**2 seasons**
(b&w)

**Main Cast:** Ralph Nossek (Professor Ramsay), Trevor Bannister (Peter Barry), Celia Bannerman (Diana Winters – Season One), Margaret Neale (June Challis), Toni Gilpin (Terry – Season Two), Denys Peek (Robert Duncan), William Abney (Ian Murray, Home Secretary), Julian Somers (Sir John Chandos, Prime Minister)

**Season One: Object Z**
**6 episodes** ('The Meteor'; 'The World in Fear'; 'Flight from Danger'; 'The Aliens'; 'Too Late'; 'The Solution')
**Broadcast:** Tuesdays 19/10/65 – 23/11/65

**Season Two: Object Z Returns**
**6 episodes** ('The Voice from Space'; 'The Machine'; 'The Monsters'; 'The Menace from the Depths'; 'The Big Freeze'; 'The Eleventh Hour')
**Broadcast:** Tuesdays 22/2/66 – 29/3/66

**Written by** Christopher McMaster

**Designer:** Andrew Drummond
**Producer/Director:** Daphne Shadwell

## The Master

This serial marked the beginning of fifteen years of children's drama from the Southern region, finally offering competition after Associated Rediffusion's near monopoly of the genre on commercial television. Producer John Braybon asked his children Gail and Tony to give him their recommendations and, after making their way through nearly a hundred books, they finally selected *The Master* by *The Sword in the Stone* author T. H. White.

*The Master* plunged two standard brother and sister adventurers (and of course their dog, Jokey) into a rather more macabre than usual tale. The Master was an emaciated 150-year-old master criminal bent on world domination. His Bond-like plot was to hold the world to ransom with his high-powered laser ray, all from his labyrinthine base on the storm-lashed island of Rockall, 500 miles out in the Atlantic, where our young heroes Judy and Nicky land while on a sailing expedition. Conveniently for the kids, Squadron Leader Frinton also drops in and helps them to battle against The Master and his scientist lackey Totty McTurk (a typically manic performance from John Laurie). Matters are complicated further when The Master realises that, like himself, Nicky has telepathic powers and so the mastermind plans to groom the boy to become his successor. The serial showed some sophistication by confronting young Nicky with a dilemma; it becomes clear that the only way to defeat The Master is to kill him and Nicky must wrestle with his conscience for the good of humanity. The quandary and 33

**Above:** Judy (Adrienne Poster), Nicky (Paul Guess) and Squadron Leader Frinton (George Baker) plot to thwart the evil plans of *The Master*.

the adventure is resolved, however, when The Master has a fatal accident.

Paul Guess as Nicky had his blonde hair dyed black to match that of his 'sister', sixteen-year-old Adrienne Poster playing twelve as Judy. A year or so later, as Adrienne Posta, she would be one of the darlings of the Swinging 60s British movie scene.

*The Master* was a key entry in the development of the genre, costing a whacking £6,000 an episode, trailed in colour in *TV Times* and garnering extremely high ratings. It was a pivotal piece without a doubt, not just because it marked Southern's entry into this field but also because it added a dash of sci-fi to the Blyton-derived formula.

**Southern**
**6 episodes** ('The Yellow Hands'; 'Totty McTurk'; 'Behind the Antlers'; 'The Squadron Leader'; 'World of Disbelief'; 'Death by Misadventure')
(b&w)
**Broadcast:** Tuesdays 11/1/66 – 15/2/66

**Main Cast:** Olaf Pooley (The Master), John Laurie (Totty McTurk), Paul Guess (Nicky), Adrienne Poster (Judy), George Baker (Squadron Leader Frinton), Terence Soall (Chinaman), Richard Vernon (Father)

Based on the novel by T. H. White (first UK publication 1957, Jonathan Cape)
**Adapted by** Rosemary Hill

**Designer:** John Dilly
**Producer:** John Braybon
**Directors:** John Frankau and John Braybon

**Tie-in publications:** not known – edition published by Blackie, 1967, may be a tie-in

## Quick Before They Catch Us

Blyton brought bang up to date was the essence of this mod mystery series for older kids. A gang of three teenagers stumbled improbably into way-out mysteries in the Swinging London of 1966. Each of the trio had a special skill that would help to crack the case. The youngest of the three, the elfin Kate, was working in Mr Lane's cafe while she waited to go to art school. The money was obviously spent on the latest fashions from the King's Road judging by her wardrobe of Lennon caps and PVC dresses. Kate's drawing talents came in handy if there was an identikit picture required and her photographic memory often came into play. Johnny was a technology student and this allowed him to whip up electronic whirligigs at the drop of a hat, from walkie-talkies to surveillance equipment. Bookish Mark was the son of a well-known photographer and he was following in his father's footsteps. The bespectacled nerd of the three, he was the brains of the outfit.

There were no smugglers' caves for these three investigators though, as they patrolled the mean streets of Carnaby and bedsit land. The accent, as the title suggests, was on pace and the gang enjoyed a series of adventures in the snappier four-part format. Their first case saw Kate threatened with eviction from her digs by a crooked estate agent moving tenants out as part of a seedy scam. The second case, 'Mark of Distinction', had them on the trail of stolen stamps. 'Season of the Skylark' moved out of London for a few weeks to enjoy a holiday at the seaside (which could surely only have meant Brighton for these coffee-bar types?). Story Four, 'The Tungsten Ring', had Mark attacked when he accidentally photographed the theft of a new gadget down by the docks. The final adventure had the group becoming a pop trio for the opening of a new nightclub and stumbling across an art fraud in the process. This never happened to the Famous Five.

An outrageously fashionable piece of fluff – only *Adam Adamant Lives!* and *The Avengers* could be more 1966 – it was possibly the only children's series to have a theme song performed by a Brian Epstein-managed group. Paddy, Klaus and Gibson (Klaus was Klaus Voorman who drew the sleeve to The Beatles' *Revolver* LP) failed to have a hit with the theme, possibly since they split up as the TV series went to air.

**BBC**
**20 episodes/5 stories**
(b&w)
**Broadcast:** Saturdays 7/5/66 – 24/9/66 (no broadcast 2/7/66 due to cricket coverage)

**Main Cast:** Teddy Green (Johnny Martin), Pamela Franklin (Kate), David Griffin (Mark Dennison), Colin Bell (Don), Colin Douglas (Andrew Lane)

**Theme song** written by Monty Norman, perfomed by Paddy, Klaus and Gibson
**Series Producer:** William Sterling

**Story One**
**'Power of Three'** by N. J. Crisp
**4 episodes** (7/5/66 – 28/5/66)
**Designer:** Malcom Middleton
**Director:** Richard Martin

**Story Two**
**'Mark of Distinction'** by George F. Kerr
**4 episodes** (4/6/66 – 25/6/66)
**Designer:** Malcom Middleton
**Director:** Derek Martinus

**Story Three**
**'Season of the Skylark'** by Jack Trevor Story
**4 episodes** (9/7/66 – 30/7/66)
**Designer:** Barry Newbery
**Director:** Morris Barry

**Story Four**
**'The Tungsten Ring'** by Margot Bennett
**4 episodes** (6/8/66 – 27/8/66)
**Designer:** Peter Kindred
**Director:** Paddy Russell

**Story Five**
**'The Weasel Goes Pop'** by John Gray
**4 episodes** (3/9/66 – 24/9/66)
**Designer:** Oliver Bayldon
**Director:** James Cellan Jones

**Tie-in publications:** *Radio Times* cover for 7/5/66 –
15/5/1966 edition

## The New Forest Rustlers

Two brother and sister pairs of bike-riding, pony-loving youngsters are on their school holidays in the New Forest when they stumble across a gang of international crooks hiding out in the abandoned old Ridgeway House, planning to steal a painting. This being the 60s, boys Bill and Freddy were all for investigating while Fiona and Pat were more interested in ponies and ice-skating.

The storyline was as you might expect; there was a disbelieving police inspector, single-prop planes buzzing curiously over the forest, a cute foal to be rescued. The only bit of weirdness involved singer Anita Harris (in her acting debut) as 'a mysterious ice-skater' who appeared to be in league with the smuggling crooks.

To have brought Blyton's *Famous Five* to the screen at this or any other time would have involved lengthy rights negotiations and the Blyton Foundation has always demanded close approval. Besides, if ITV could screen a serial as clearly derivative of the Blyton formula as this and get away with it, then why should they bother?

**Southern**
**6 episodes** ('The House in the Trees'; 'The Secret of Ridgeway House'; 'Enter the Law'; 'Trouble Among Thieves'; 'Operation Stampede'; 'The Round Up')
(b&w)
**Broadcast:** Thursdays 29/9/66 – 3/11/66

**Main Cast:** Paul Guess (Bill Deverill), Michael Sarson (Freddy Guise), Gina Clow (Fiona Guise), Daphne Foreman (Patricia Deverill), Anita Harris (Maureen), Ronan O'Casey (Chief), Reginald Marsh (Inspector Foster)

Based on the novels *A New Forest Adventure* and *The New Forest Smugglers* by Stephen Mogridge (first UK publications 1953 and 1958, Nelson)

**Adapted by** Stephen Mogridge
**Script Consultant:** John Gray

**Designer:** John Dilly
**Directors:** John Braybon (1 and 2) and Ian Curteis (3–6)

## Look and Read

These educational serials broadcast for schools are so fondly if inaccurately remembered as bona fide dramas that it would have been remiss not to include at least some of them here. The purpose of each serial (usually ten parts long) was to spin an exciting yarn, around which could be based various reading lessons. The actual drama segments only amounted to about six minutes out of each episode's eighteen minute or so runtime. The rest of the programme usually consisted of the bizarre, floating orange golfball-print head Wordy (few children actually guessed what he was supposed to be) introducing a variety of word-based activities and songs between two parts of the drama. What was left then was essentially a thin collection of cliffhangers but these were generally so brilliantly constructed that most who watched in the classroom as an eight or nine year old child can still recall their favourites. Drama-wise there was no room for characterisation or subtlety, just runabout action (the 70s adventures were almost all filmed on location) and, of course, some English lessons shoehorned into the storyline.

The first story to be told was the ten-part *Bob and Carol Look for Treasure*, whose title is self-explanatory (9/1/67 – 13/3/67). Made in black and white, it had something of a limited shelf life, while later colour productions would be repeated for up to a decade. Possibly the best known of all the productions, screened several times in twenty years, was *The Boy from Space*, a science fiction tale of a lost alien boy discovered by two children, who name him Peep-Peep. A sinister Thin Man (John Woodnutt) tries to capture the boy and his new friends while holding the boy's father prisoner. Much use was made of mirror-writing – the alien boy writes like this, having learned English from a reversed see-through carrier bag! The drama footage was reused in a revised version nine years later, which was narrated by the two children, now grown-up.

The same kind of revision happened with *Sky Hunter*, a tale of peregrine falcon egg smuggling. In the 90s the existing drama segments were re-edited into new linking material featuring the show's original young leads, now playing adults working for the Royal Society for the Protection of Birds (RSPB). The story was basically one of reversed expectation – the shady guy lurking with intent turned out to be a goodie from the RSPB and the kindly old Mr Trim (Geoffrey Bayldon) from the antique shop was a nasty old egg thief.

Another popular fantasy entry was *Dark Towers*, a creepy mystery tale about the down on his luck Lord Dark (David Collings) falling prey to some crooked antique dealers. His son Edward (Gary Russell, ex-*Famous Five*) and a young girl Tracy (Juliet Waley, ex-*Carrie's War*) help him, solving various word puzzles along the way, as does the ghost of the Dark Knight, come to aid Dark Towers in its hour of need. The serial was scary enough to cause more nervous members of Britain's classrooms to ask to be excused.

*Badger Girl* was very similar to the earlier *Sky Hunter* and was a story about a very town-minded Cockney girl (Paula Millbank, later of *Running Scared*) learning the ways of the country and helping foil some pony rustlers. Her nickname

35

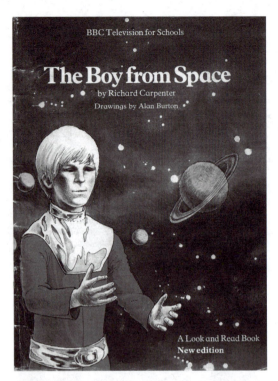

BBC Television for Schools

## The Boy from Space
by Richard Carpenter
Drawings by Alan Burton

A Look and Read Book
New edition

**Above:** school pupils watching *Look and Read* received workbooks of the current story, a brief form of illustrated novelisation in pamphlet format. Most of these workbooks were retained by the schools themselves and later binned – few have survived. The book shown here is for the revised *Boy from Space*, shown several times in the early 1980s.

*Sky Hunter*
**Written by** Leonard Kingston
**Producer:** Roger Tonge
**Broadcast:** Tuesdays 19/9/78 – 28/11/78 and *Sky Hunter II* from 14/1/92 – 24/3/92

*Dark Towers*
**Written by** Andrew Davies
**Producer:** Sue Weeks '
**Broadcast:** Tuesdays 22/9/81 – 1/12/81

*Badger Girl*
**Written by** Andrew Davies
**Producer:** Susan Paton
**Broadcast:** Tuesdays 18/9/84 – 27/11/84 (*Look and Read* shown on BBC2 from now on)

*Geordie Racer*
**Written by** Christopher Russell
**Producer:** Sue Weeks
**Broadcast:** Tuesdays 12/1/88 – 22/3/88

*Through the Dragon's Eye*
**Written by** Christopher and Christine Russell
**Producer:** Sue Weeks
**Broadcast:** Tuesdays 19/9/89 – 20/11/89

Note: the above is only a partial listing of the best-recalled serials

**Tie-in publications:** story workbooks and teachers' reference materials were published by the BBC for each story. Novelisations of *Sky Hunter* and *Through the Dragon's Eye* were also published during the 90s.

came about because of her two-tone dyed hair. This entry was notable for having Wordy's studio co-host actually appear in the drama segments, which had not happened since the black and white days. Another child with animal friends was the central hero of *Geordie Racer*, a sort of *Kes* with pigeons. Pigeon-racer Spuggy Hilton finds strange messages attached to carrier pigeons and uncovers a plan by a gang of crooks to go on a burgling spree while the Great North Run is taking place.

The series ended the 80s with another fantasy entry, the rather brash and colourful eight-parter *Through the Dragon's Eye* which had a group of children (among them Simon Fenton, who grew up to live in *Century Falls*) solving word and map-reading puzzles to help Gorwen the friendly dragon defeat the evil Charwen (David Collings) and retain the Veetarod, the source of his power.

The series continued to be made into the early 90s after providing a welcome distraction from real schoolwork for millions of schoolkids. Episodes are still being repeated at the time of writing.

### The Boy from Space
**Written by** Richard Carpenter
**Producer:** Maddalena Fagandini
**Series Producer:** Claire Chovil
**Broadcast:** Tuesday mornings 21/9/71 – 30/11/71 and revised version from 15/1/80 – 25/3/80 on BBC1

## Danger Island

While on holiday with his parents in the Mediterranean, twelve-year-old Nicholas Johnston gets himself into some serious trouble when he overhears two men plotting the assassination of their country's leader. From that moment forward, Nicholas realises that he is in grave danger. Unsure of who he can trust, Nicholas goes on the run.

Well-known husband and wife comedy team Eric Barker and Pearl Hackney took the opportunity to work together again in this adventure drama, this time playing straight roles. Hackney was Nicholas' mother and Barker played the president whose life Nicholas must somehow save.

The gunboat in *Danger Island* was Southern's high-powered, jet-engine boat *Southerner*, usually used for outside news broadcasts, which had been given a makeover for its appearance in the drama.

### Southern
**6 episodes** ('The Conspirators'; 'The Holiday Continues'; 'Help Wanted'; 'Captured'; 'The Assassin'; 'All At Sea') (b&w)
**Broadcast:** Thursdays 6/7/67 – 10/8/67

**Main Cast:** Mervyn Joseph (Nicholas), Pearl Hackney (Mother), Eric Barker (President)

**Written by** John Gray

**Music:** Ron Grainer
**Designer:** John Dilly
**Director:** John Braybon

## Send Foster

The *Redstone Chronicle*'s junior reporter is eighteen-year-old Johnny Foster. His editor sends him out on a number of assignments which Johnny expects to be boring but end up being more than he bargained for. Along the way he becomes involved with a variety of people and situations, learning more about himself and life.

The plot is an interesting mix of serious and light-hearted storylines. Early on in his career Johnny is forced to question his conscience and think about how he will feel when writing stories that have the potential to adversely affect other people's lives. Issues of race are addressed when Johnny discovers that a colour bar is operating in the local area. Ultimately, Johnny learns the hard way what he can and cannot do as a journalist when he takes issue with a local councillor.

Slightly less taxing is Johnny's venture into the local pop scene when he finds himself involved in a competition for best group. He also finds himself surprised by the power of the pen when some tough words about the local amateur dramatic society come back to haunt him.

Hayward Morse, son of British actor Barry Morse, played Johnny and had to learn to drive for the part.

George Markstein's format was briefly revived as a one-off pilot episode for *Dramarama* in 1984 as 'Snoop!'

**Rediffusion**
**12 episodes** ('Hole in the Road'; 'Once a Thief…'; 'Family Likeness'; 'Henry Wasn't There'; 'I'm Not Coloured – I'm Black'; 'The Peg'; 'The Drama Critic'; 'Which Wedding Were You At'; 'The Accident'; 'Off the Record'; 'Just Read That Back To Me, Young Man'; 'Unprofessional Conduct')
(b&w)
**Broadcast:** Thursdays/Fridays* 6/7/67 – 22/9/67
* Only episode 1 transmitted on a Thursday; changed to Fridays thereafter

**Main Cast:** Hayward Morse (Johnny Foster), Polly James (Susan), Patrick Newell (Arthur Harding)

**Written by** George Markstein (1, 6, 10, 12), Victor Pemberton (2), Anne De Gale (3), Mike Watts (4, 5, 8, 9), Geoffrey Hughes (7), Max Oberman (11)

**Designers:** Andrew Drummond (1, 4, 6, 8, 10), John Plant (2, 7, 9, 11, 12), Sylva Nadolny (3), John Plant (5)
**Producer:** Geoffrey Hughes
**Directors:** Geoffrey Hughes (1), William G. Stewart (2, 7, 9), Fred Sadoff (3), Ronald Marriott (4), Adrian Cooper (5, 8), Nicholas Ferguson (6, 11), Hugh Munro (10), Don Gale (12)

**Above:** Edmund (Edward McMurray) encounters the White Witch of Narnia (Elizabeth Wallace) in ABC's 1967 adaptation of *The Lion, The Witch and the Wardrobe*.

## The Lion, The Witch and the Wardrobe

Initially intended as a small-scale *Jackanory*-style presentation with just a narrator and illustrations, this production grew and grew – along with its budget – to become a fairly ambitious live action Sunday serial. Much of this seems to have been due to the involvement of Ian Mackenzie from ABC's religious programmes department. Aware of the Christian allegory at the heart of C. S. Lewis's famous novel, he helped to persuade programme chiefs to up the budget until it reached a very workable £1,000–£1,200 per twenty-minute episode. Mackenzie was credited as the serial's Religious Advisor.

It's the technical aspects of the serial that are particularly noteworthy, and the adaptation acts as a case study on how an epic can be staged with relatively meagre resources. The production team even brought in sheets from home to provide snow-covered hills, while several features of the set came second-hand from *The Max Bygraves Show* in the studio next door.

The overwhelming impression is of watching a theatre production on television. The designer goes for a delightfully stylised look which doesn't try to ape reality too closely, preferring instead to suggest an impression of the land of Narnia. The handover from the real setting of a contemporary 1967 to the fantastical world beyond the wardrobe was clearly delineated, via a clear split between location film for the Professor's house in the early episodes and studio videotape for Narnia itself.

37

Realising the inhabitants of Narnia was again tackled as might be expected in a stage play. Taking a cue from the novel's original illustrations of the likes of Mr Tumnus, all of the creatures – including Aslan the lion – were played by actors walking on two legs. Certainly this enables the actors to deliver their best, most of them wearing half-masks so that the dialogue in studio could be clearly heard in this 'as live' production. Aslan's baggy costume may look a little like the Cowardly Lion of Oz, or even the Lenny the Lion TV puppet in places, but there is no doubting the power of Bernard Kay's performance which portrays Aslan as sensitive and fierce by turns.

Special effects, the bugbear of the majority of children's dramas with their less than vast budgets, were beyond the means of the team and this is where the narrator came into his own. The Professor who lives in the old house where the children are staying is chosen to tell the story. Sitting by a crackling fireside, usually seen carefully refilling his pipe or perusing his library of dusty tomes, Jack Woolgar tells the tale in hushed tones, leaving the viewer hanging on his every word. As well as being what writer Trevor Preston admitted was a 'way of getting round doing the magic', the narrator also performed another function, covering live costume and prop changes between scenes.

Preston viewed these limitations in a positive way, feeling that it made the child viewers push their imaginations that little bit further. Producer Pamela Lonsdale admitted that while there was no way they could convincingly achieve such concepts as Aslan flying through the sky, the words of C. S. Lewis, as recalled by the Professor, told it all.

**ABC**
**10 episodes** ('What Lucy Found in the Wardrobe'; 'Edmund and the White Witch'; 'Into the Forest'; 'A Day with the Beavers'; 'The Witch's House'; 'Aslan is Coming'; 'Peter's First Battle'; 'The Triumph of the Witch'; 'Deeper Magic From Before the Dawning of Time'; 'The Battle') (b&w)
**Broadcast:** Sundays 9/7/67 – 10/9/67

**Main Cast:** Edward McMurray (Edmund), Paul Waller (Peter), Zuleika Robson (Susan), Elizabeth Crowther (Lucy), Bernard Kay (Aslan), Elizabeth Wallace (White Witch), George Claydon (Dwarf), Jack Woolgar (Professor), Susan Field (Mrs Beaver), Jimmy Gardner (Mr Beaver), Angus Lennie (Tumnus)

Based on the novel by C. S. Lewis (first UK publication 1950, Geoffrey Bles)
**Adapted by** Trevor Preston

**Music:** Paul Lewis
**Design and Costumes:** Neville Green
**Producer/Director:** Pamela Lonsdale (Helen Standage directed episodes 5 and 6)

Also told on
*Jackanory* 24/4/67 – 28/4/67
**5 episodes** ('Lucy Looks Into the Wardrobe'; 'Into the Forest'; 'The Spell Begins to Break'; 'Peter's First Battle'; 'Deeper Magic From Before the Dawn of Time')
**BBC**
(b&w)
**Read by** Marian Diamond

## Sexton Blake

Gentleman detective Sexton Blake first came to life in 1893 in the pages of *The Halfpenny Marvel*, shortly after Sir Arthur Conan Doyle had killed off his famous sleuth, Sherlock Holmes. Referred to as 'the office boy's Holmes', a number of comparisons were drawn between the two detectives. Sexton Blake even lived on Baker Street.

Blake's adventures were certainly less cerebral than those of Holmes. While the latter spent much of his time in quiet contemplation and deduction, Blake was a far more dashing character and enjoyed the rough and tumble involved in fighting various villains and rascals.

The adaptation of *Sexton Blake* for children's television created an amount of frustration for adult fans. One member of the 'grown-up' population commented, 'Here we've been waiting donkey's years for *Sexton Blake* on "tele" and now we find it at 5.25 on Monday evenings, a time when many of us are still at work.' Later seasons were moved to a far more sensible Sunday afternoon slot in many regions.

Blake was joined by two companions for the duration of his adventures. Tinker was his faithful retainer and Pedro, his trusty bloodhound, was played by female Crufts winner Sanguine Saintly.

The BBC Sunday Classics team reintroduced the character to television with a one-off story, *Sexton Blake and The Demon God*, with Jeremy Clyde as the detective (BBC1 10/9/78 – 15/10/78).

**Rediffusion/Thames**
**5 seasons**

**Main Cast:** Laurence Payne (Sexton Blake), Roger Foss (Tinker), Sanguine Saintly (Pedro)

**Season One**
**Rediffusion**
**6 stories/25 episodes** and **1 Christmas Special**
(b&w)
**Broadcast:** Mondays 25/9/67 – 18/3/68
**Producer:** Ronald Marriott

**Story 1**
**'The Find the Lady Affair'** by Max Oberman
**4 episodes** ('The Lady Vanishes'; 'The Lady Has Two Faces'; 'Search for the Lady'; 'The Lady is Found')
**Broadcast:** 25/9/67 – 16/10/67
**Designer:** Andrew Drummond
**Director:** Adrian Cooper

**Story 2**
**'Knave of Diamonds'** by n/k
**5 episodes** ('The Black Star'; 'The White Dove'; 'The Green Demon'; 'The Blue Lily'; 'The Red Waistcoat')
**Broadcast:** 23/10/67 – 20/11/67
**Designer:** Roger Hall
**Director:** Peter Croft

**Story 3**
**'The Great Tong Mystery'** by Max Oberman
**4 episodes** ('Ding Dong Hong Kong'; 'Oranges and Lemons'; 'Here Comes a Candle...'; 'Ding Dong Beat the Gong')
**Broadcast:** 27/11/67 – 18/12/67
**Designer:** Bryan Bagge
**Director:** Adrian Cooper

**Christmas Special**
**Broadcast:** 25/12/67
**'The Vanishing Snowman'** by David Edwards
Strange happenings at Tench Hall challenge Sexton Blake and
Tinker to unravel the mystery of 'The Snowman'
**Director:** Michael Currer-Briggs

**Story 4**
**'House of Masks'** by Peter Ling
**4 episodes** ('The Mask of Murder'; 'The Mask of Fear';
'The Mask of the Demon'; 'The Masks are Off')
**Broadcast:** 1/1/68 – 22/1/68
**Designer:** Roger Hall
**Director:** Peter Croft

**Story 5**
**'The Invicta Ray'** by David Edwards, from an original story by
Gwyn Evans
**4 episodes** ('Enter Mr Mist'; 'Tinker is Dead'; 'Mr Mist Has a
Turn'; 'Scandal in the House')
**Broadcast:** 29/1/68 – 19/2/68
**Designer:** David Catley
**Director:** Ian Fordyce

**Story 6**
**'The Red Swordsman'** by Max Oberman, from an original
story by Robert Murray
**4 episodes** ('The First Matador'; 'The Third Matador';
'The Matador Strikes Again'; 'The Matador Unmasked')
**Broadcast:** 26/2/68 – 18/3/68
**Designer:** Roger Hall
**Director:** Peter Croft


**Season Two**
**Rediffusion**
**1 story only**
(b&w)

**'Sexton Blake v The Organisation'** by Roy Russell
6 episodes ('Blake Meets His Match'; 'The Danger Sign';
'Up Against It'; 'Rendezvous with Death'; 'The Secret of
Hoodoo House'; 'No Escape')
**Broadcast:** Wednesdays 19/6/68 – 24/7/68
**Designer:** David Catley
**Director:** Peter Moffat
**Producer:** Ronald Marriott


**Season Three**
**Thames**
**4 stories/9 episodes**
(b&w)
**Broadcast:** Thursdays 14/11/68 – 13/2/69
**Producer:** Ronald Marriott

**Story 1**
**'The Case of the Gasping Goldfish'** by Max Oberman
**2 episodes** ('Tinker Gets a Bite'; 'Menace for Miranda')
**Broadcast:** 14/11/68 – 21/11/68
**Designer:** Roger Burridge
**Producer:** Ronald Marriott
**Director:** n/k

**Above:** dashing gentleman detective Sexton Blake (Laurence
Payne) keeps a tight leash on faithful bloodhound Pedro and
is accompanied as ever by retainer Tinker (Roger Foss).

**Story 2**
**'The Return of the Scorpion'** by Max Oberman
**2 episodes** ('War of the Tong'; 'An Eye for an Eye')
**Broadcast:** 28/11/68 – 5/12/68
**Designer:** Frank Gillman
**Director:** Ronald Marriott

(From Story 3 the series is dropped from Scottish Television so
we have been unable to give full details for the rest of this
run)

**Story 3**
**'The Great Train Robbery'**
**2 episodes** ('Danger on the Line'; 'Find Mrs Bardell')

**Story 4**
**'The Great Soccer Mystery'**
**3 episodes** ('Death on the Touchline'; 'Snakes Alive';
'Better Late Than Never')

**Season Four**
**Thames**
**5 stories/13 episodes**
(colour in regions where available)
**Broadcast:** Tuesdays 8/10/69 – 30/12/69 (final two episodes shown Wednesdays in most regions)
**Producer:** Ronald Marriott

**Story 1**
**'Captain Nemesis'** by Ivor Jay
**3 episodes** ('Collision Course'; 'Kill Two Birds with One Bomb'; 'Guns Bearing')
**Broadcast:** 8/10/69 – 22/10/69
**Designer:** Sylva Nadolny
**Director:** Daphne Shadwell

**Story 2**
**'Sexton Blake versus The Gangsters'** by Roy Russell
3 episodes ('Doctor Angelo'; 'Killer Fingers'; 'The Battle Before Waterloo')
**Broadcast:** 29/10/69 – 12/11/69
**Designer:** Frank Gillman
**Director:** Ronald Marriott

**Story 3**
**'Sexton Blake and the Frightened Man'** by Len Mariott
**2 episodes** ('Call for Help'; 'Cornered')
**Broadcast:** 19/11/69 – 26/11/69
**Designer:** Frank Gillman
**Director:** Adrian Cooper

**Story 4**
**'Sexton Blake and the Undertaker'** by Max Oberman
**3 episodes** ('Coffin for the Colonel'; 'Lilies for Lancelot'; 'Fair Maid of Astolat')
**Broadcast:** 3/12/69 – 17/12/69
**Designer:** Frank Gillman and Jim Nicholson
**Director:** Adrian Cooper

**Story 5**
**'Sexton Blake and the Toy Family'** by Roy Russell
**2 episodes** ('The Highest Price'; 'The Trump Card')
**Broadcast:** 23/12/69 – 30/12/69
**Designer:** Frank Gillman
**Director:** Adrian Cooper

**Season Five**
**Thames**
**1 story only**
(colour)
**Broadcast:** Wednesdays 9/12/70 – 13/1/71

**'Sexton Blake and the Puff Adder'** by Max Oberman
**6 episodes** ('Forced Landing'; 'Summons to Tea'; 'Blind Alley'; 'The Door in the Wall'; 'Room of Secrets'; 'The Catacombs')
**Designer:** Frank Gillman
**Director:** Adrian Cooper

**Tie-in publications:** *The Valiant Book of Sexton Blake*, reprints of original Blake stories in large format hardback with television photo cover. Published by Fleetway, 1968.

## The Flower of Gloster

Jim Doherty owns a boatyard in North Wales and is due to deliver a new barge, *The Flower of Gloster*, to a customer in London when he breaks his leg. Jim's eldest son, eighteen-year-old Richard, offers to help pilot 'Glossie' along the canals to the capital. His younger sister, thirteen-year-old Elizabeth, decides to come along too, with Richard's friend Annette also joining in. The youngest Doherty, Mike, is left at home but runs away to join the crew nonetheless.

*The Flower of Gloster* was extremely experimental in many ways. It was the first colour drama to be filmed by Granada (with the ITV colour service still two years away) and was semi-improvised, mixing documentary factual features with the plotted storyline. The lead characters were all essentially playing themselves. Along the journey the children stopped off to visit many of the West England Waterway's towns, cities and places of interest such as Woburn Abbey and Stoke Bruene museum. This gave the programme a strange mixture of the didactic and the dramatic. Producer Bill Grundy said, rather oddly, of the serial: 'This is an educational series too, because I have included information about rock formation and fauna in the programmes.'

One suspects the young audience were more interested in the perils encountered by Glossie's crew. One night in the woods near Market Drayton a ghost was thought to be abroad while in Birmingham the barge was ambushed by a gang of very real Brum boys.

Chris McMaster went on to greater success and even more episode titles with exclamation marks as creator of the less sedate *Freewheelers*. Bill Grundy meanwhile went on to kickstart punk rock – and end his own career – when he rather foolishly attempted to cross the Sex Pistols on his live *Today* programme in 1976.

**Granada**
**13 episodes** ('The Accident'; 'The Cut'; 'The Boy'; 'The Girl'; 'Betton Woods'; 'The Dog'; 'Lost!'; 'The City'; 'Life and Death'; 'The Tunnel'; 'The Deadline'; 'The Hitch'; 'Late!')
(colour)
**Broadcast:** Wednesdays 27/9/67 – 20/12/67 (broadcast in b&w)

**Main Cast:** Richard O'Callaghan (Richard Doherty), Annette Robertson (Annette), Elizabeth Doherty (Elizabeth Doherty), Mike Doherty (Mike Doherty), Jim Doherty (Jim Doherty)

**Written by** Chris McMaster

**Music:** John Snow
**Producer:** Bill Grundy
**Director:** Mike Beckham

**Tie-in publications:** novelisation by Bill Grundy published in hardback by Rupert Hart-Davis, 1967

## Mystery Hall

Young Jimmy Brent is spending a holiday at a remote hotel on the Dorset coast when he sees a guest shoot the hotel owner. No-one believes the boy when the 'dead man' later returns unharmed. Soon Jimmy hears about the lost treasure from a sunken Spanish galleon, thought to be hidden in a secret passage underneath the fifteenth-century mansion hotel.

Who can Jimmy trust? Jane, the pretty receptionist? Alex Ramsey, a writer staying at the hotel? Aside from Jimmy's constant canine companion, Solo, the odd odd-job man Zebediah Gast appears to be the boy's only ally.

A boy and his dog, secret passages and hidden treasure – all the elements of the Blyton-influenced serials omnipresent on ITV at the time were present and correct. The final episode of the serial is thought to have been postponed and rescheduled for the following week.

**Southern**
**6 episodes** ('Jimmy Brent'; 'The One That Got Away'; 'The Double Blood Knot'; 'Disturbed Waters'; 'False Bait'; 'Spring Trap')
(b&w)
**Broadcast:** Thursdays 28/9/67 – 9/11/67

**Main Cast:** Mark Colleano (Jimmy Brent), Philip Newman (Zebediah Gast), Alan Wheatley (Alex Ramsey), Hilary Mason (Mrs Thompson), Anthony Woodruff (Mr Blake-Clanton), Shelagh Fraser (Mrs Blake-Clanton), Paddy Glynn (Jane)

**Written by** Donald Tosh

**Music:** Wout Steenhuis
**Designer:** John Dilly
**Director:** John Braybon

## The Flight of the Heron

A rather epic period drama for children, made by Scottish Television at a cost of £60,000. If this outlay seemed steep, the region recouped some of its investment by repeating the drama in a 10.30p.m. evening slot on each day following its transmission for children. This policy rather highlights the notion of drama made for children in the 50s and 60s – if one could be transposed this easily into adult viewing times, what was the real qualitative difference?

This was a story told against the background of the Jacobite Rebellion of 1745. Angus MacMartin, a blind old soothsayer, foresees that the flight of the heron will herald five meetings between a young highland chieftain and an English officer. The prophecy is fulfilled by Ewen Cameron and Captain Windham, two soldiers on different sides who nonetheless come to respect and learn from each other amid action and adventure as the scene is set for the bloody battle of Culloden.

The series was shot in studio (with many props travelling all the way from London) and in locations just feet from where the real events of 1745 had taken place, among them Fort Augustus at the southern end of Loch Ness.

**Scottish**
**8 episodes** ('Capture'; 'Rebellion'; 'Escape'; 'Levee'; 'Retreat'; 'Rescue'; 'Torture'; 'Revenge')
(b&w)
**Broadcast:** Wednesdays 28/2/68 – 17/4/68

**Main Cast:** Ian McCulloch (Ewen Cameron), Jon Laurimore (Captain Keith Windham), Finlay Currie (Angus MacMartin), Sheila Wittingham (Alison Grant), Bill Henderson (Lachlan MacMartin), Robert Docherty (Neil MacMartin), Brown Derby

(Captain Scott), Paul Young (Lt Sharpe), Sophie Stewart (Aunt Margaret), Bruce McKenzie (Prince Charles), Leonard Maguire (Lochiel), Helena Gloag (Lady Easterhall), W. H. D. Joss (Mr Grant), Richard Wilson (Sir Everard Faulkner), Tom Conti (Captain Greening)

Based on the novel by Dorothy Kathleen 'D. K.' Broster (first UK publication 1925, Heinemann)
**Adapted by** Moultrie R. Kelsall

**Music:** Peter Knight
**Designer:** Archie McArthur
**Producer:** Brian Mahoney
**Executive Producer:** Francis Essex

**Tie-in publications:** unconfirmed edition by Peacock Books, 1968

## Freewheelers

'Action is what *Freewheelers* is all about ... the snarl of high-powered engines, the stammer of automatic rifles and the shattering roar of a bomb that has only just missed blowing the Freewheelers sky-high.' The publicity blurb says it all; action was indeed the secret of this long-running series' success and really there's very little to add to that. At a time when much children's television still consisted of studio-bound presentation to camera, *Freewheelers* crashed into the kids' schedules with a bone-jarring impact rarely matched since.

*Freewheelers* was the opportunist adaptation of adult successes for a younger audience often denied the escapist thrills of the ITC spy series by their later timeslots. In

**Above:** the original line-up of *Freewheelers* in their first adventure; (l to r) Chris Kelly (Gregory Phillips), Bill Cowan (Tom Owen) and Terry Driver (Mary Maude).

**Above:** the sixth season team of *Freewheelers*; (l to r) Mike (Adrian Wright), Sue (Wendy Padbury), Colonel Buchan (Ronald Leigh-Hunt) and Steve (Leonard Gregory).

essence it was Bond without the sex or the sadism but retained a fair proportion of the all-important hardware. For five years, fleets of sports cars, jeeps, beach buggies, motor boats, warships, tanks and helicopters roared across the small screen to the delight of the Action Man generation.

Of course, it was never as glossy as the escapades of Bond or *The Avengers* but made a fair fist of it on a fraction of the budget. Chris McMaster oversaw the series for its entire run and some impressive (free)wheeler-dealing by him brought the viewers more bang for their buck. The shooting certainly owed more to pragmatism than artistry and the high-octane location work was couched between slow-moving debriefing talky bits in studio but this was the most dynamic children's series on TV at that time bar none.

*Freewheelers* might never have got off the ground at Southern without one key acquisition. Southern was the only British TV station to own an outside broadcast boat for news gathering. Its yacht *Southerner*, first seen as a 'stunt boat' in the serial *Danger Island*, thus captured countless boat chases down the years for *Freewheelers* and doubled as the villains' own craft in many episodes. Events in the series often seemed predicated on such a catch-as-catch-can basis – if McMaster could get hold of the army on manoeuvres or organise something with the local historical re-enactment society, they would end up in the script. Plotting was usually secondary to the planning of on-screen action set pieces, appearing to be used only to link the stunts together. In later years what happened next usually depended on which European country McMaster had managed to persuade to back the series this time round; in the colour era the series went beyond Cornwall

and the New Forest to take travelogue-styled jaunts to Spain, Sweden and France.

The storylines were, without fail over eight seasons, based on a single plot formula. Bad guy (or maxi-boot-wearing femme fatale in one story) bent on world domination kidnaps top scientist with intention of turning the scientist's new research (hypnotic induction, weather control – usually a raybeam of sorts) to the bad guy's own evil ends. Freewheelers help MI5/6 to stop them on land, air or sea. It was that simple.

The background to the series' formula was that the so-called Freewheelers were a group of teenagers called in on an ad hoc basis by the secret service to help out when official channels failed. The age of the leads was crucial to its success. Traditionally, children's adventure serials had pitted child heroes against grown-up villainy with varying resulting degrees of credibility. With the Freewheelers aged up to around the eighteen–nineteen mark (although the actors were usually in their late twenties) the heroes could compete on level terms, driving fast cars and swapping punches with the baddies, even enjoying the odd half pint of beer. The kids were essentially older-looking children though – there was no hanky panky between them or emotional depth to any of them, just bags of enthusiasm. The good looks of the ever-changing line-ups added definite sex appeal to the show as far as its young fans were concerned however, with pin-up Adrian Wright in particular adding a female constituency to the broadly male fanbase.

Commentators who grew up with the show believe that the series' black and white days constituted its heyday. The monochrome era each week pitted the Freewheelers against their nemesis Von Gelb, a Wagner-loving Nazi war criminal bent on revenge for World War II (Von Gelb was removed from the format when West Germany decided to buy the series). However, the lie of a more serious, edgy drama would appear to be a myth brought about through misplaced nostalgia. Surviving early episodes (the entire first series was recovered in 2000) in fact show it was always the same high-spirited nonsense of careening speedboats and kidnapped scientists.

It's easy to mock now, with its straight-faced heroism and occasionally underfunded histrionics but, make no mistake, *Freewheelers* was a revolutionary and hefty kick up the backside of children's television in its day.

**Southern**
**8 seasons**
(Seasons One to Three in black and white; Seasons Four to Eight made in colour)

**Producer:** Chris McMaster (all eight seasons)

**Season One**
**3 stories/13 episodes**
'Menace': 'The Sleepers'; 'No Smoke'; 'The Camp';
'The Ultimatum'; 'Face to Face'
'Recipe for Danger': 'Too Many Cooks'; 'One Man's Meat';
'Trouble Brewing'; 'Bring to the Boil'
'The Big Freeze': 'Icarus'; 'Valkyrie'; 'Anvil'; 'Gotterdammerung'
**Broadcast:** Thursdays 4/4/68 – 27/6/68

**Regular Cast:** Ronald Leigh-Hunt (Colonel Buchan), Tom Owen (Bill Cowan), Gregory Phillips (Chris Kelly), Mary Maude (Terry Driver), Geoffrey Toone (Von Gelb)
**Writers:** James Hopes (1–5), Barry Busbridge (6–9), Trevor Preston (10–13)
**Directors:** Chris McMaster (1–5 and 10–13), John Braybon (6–9)

**Season Two**
**2 stories/13 episodes**
'The Zander Plot': 'Break Out'; 'Treasure'; 'Master Plan'; 'The Code'; 'The Lighthouse'; 'The Stones'; 'Time Bomb!'; 'Doomsday!'
'The Secret Base': 'The Key'; 'Black Knight'; 'Vulcan'; 'Double Trouble'; 'Damocles!'
**Broadcast:** Wednesdays 20/11/68 – 12/2/69
**Regular Cast:** Ronald Leigh-Hunt (Colonel Buchan), Tom Owen (Bill Cowan), Mary Maude (Terry Driver), Chris Chittell (Nick Carter), Jeanne Moody (Olga Yevchenko), Geoffrey Toone (Von Gelb)
**Writers:** Don Douglas and Keith Miles (1–4), Rick Trader Whitcombe (5, 6, 9, 10), Barry Busbridge (7, 8, 13), Bryan Cooper (11, 12)
**Directors:** Chris McMaster (1, 2, 7, 8, 11–13), Peter Croft (3–6, 9, 10)

**Season Three**
**13 episodes** ('Rammed!'; 'The Banshee'; 'Mined'; 'Trapped'; 'Tanks!'; 'Caged!'; 'The Tower'; 'Triton'; 'Kidnapped'; 'The Voyage'; 'The Island'; 'Blockade'; 'Thunderbolt!')
Nominally this season is two linked stories grouped as episodes 1–7 and 8–13
**Broadcast:** Tuesdays 9/7/69 – 1/10/69
**Regular Cast:** Ronald Leigh-Hunt (Colonel Buchan), Tom Owen (Bill Cowan), Chris Chittell (Nick Carter), Carole Mowlam (Fiona), Geoffrey Toone (Von Gelb)
**Writers:** Chris McMaster (1, 8, 13), John Cannon (2, 4, 7), Barry Busbridge (3, 5, 6), Paul Erickson (9, 10), Keith Miles (11, 12)
**Directors:** Peter Croft (1, 2, 5, 6, 10, 11), Chris McMaster (3, 4, 7–9, 12, 13)

**Season Four**
**13 episodes** ('Not In Jest'; 'A Thing Like Death'; 'Package Deal'; 'Spartika'; 'Merely Players'; 'Agincourt'; 'Microdot'; 'Kythera!'; 'The Dictator'; 'Petrov'; 'Decoy'; 'Firing Squad'; 'Explosion')
**Broadcast:** Wednesdays 29/4/70 – 22/7/70
**Regular Cast:** Ronald Leigh-Hunt (Colonel Buchan), Adrian Wright (Mike Hobbs), Tom Owen (Bill Cowan), Carole Mowlam (Fiona), Valentine Dyall (O'Toole)
**Writers:** Bryan Cooper (1, 3), Rick Trader Whitcombe (2, 4, 5), Chris McMaster (6), Paul Erickson (7–10), Keith Miles (11–13)
**Directors:** Chris McMaster (1–6, 10, 11, 13), Peter Croft (7–9, 12)

**Season Five**
**13 episodes** ('Sniper!'; 'Spin Off'; 'The Mill'; 'Blackmail'; 'Zukov'; 'Russian Roulette'[b]; 'Destruct'[b]; 'Zyton!'[b]; 'Entombed'[b]; 'Roll Up'[b]; 'Booby Trap'; 'Pipeline'; 'The Answer'[b])
Episodes marked 'b' transmitted in b&w due to ITV strike
Nominally this season is two linked stories grouped as episodes 1–7 and 8–13
**Broadcast:** Wednesdays 20/1/71 – 14/4/71

**Regular Cast:** Eric Flynn (Major Graham), Adrian Wright (Mike Hobbs), Wendy Padbury (Sue Craig), John Colcough (Max), Richard Shaw (Ryan), Michael Ripper (Burke)
**Writers:** Richard Montez (1–7), Paul Erickson (8–13)
**Directors:** Peter Croft (1–6), Chris McMaster (7–13)

**Season Six**
**13 episodes** ('Nero'; 'Operation Seagull'; 'Medusa'; 'Mayday'; 'Pirates'; 'The Threat'; 'Doomsday'; 'Black Box'; 'Cypher'; 'The Parcel'; 'The Race'; 'Red Herring'; 'Pay Off')
Nominally this season is two linked stories grouped as episodes 1–7 and 8–13
**Broadcast:** 27/9/71 – 20/12/71 Thames, Southern, ATV and Grampian (1–3 and 13 Mondays; 4–12 Fridays). Rest of ITV network all as Mondays from 27/9/71
**Regular Cast:** Ronald Leigh-Hunt (Colonel Buchan), Adrian Wright (Mike Hobbs), Wendy Padbury (Sue Craig), Leonard Gregory (Steve Walker), Richard Shaw (Ryan), Michael Ripper (Burke)
**Writers:** Paul Erickson (1–7), Richard Montez (8–13)
**Directors:** Chris McMaster (1, 2, 7–13), Dave Heather (3–6)

**Season Seven**
**Co-production Southern/Sveriges Radio (Sweden)**
**13 episodes** ('Traitor!'; 'The Race'; 'Framed!'; 'Vertigo!'; 'The Knot'; 'The War Game'; 'Helga!'; 'Helga!'; 'Midsummer'; 'The Mine'; 'Tricked!'; 'Ares!'; 'Archimedes')
Nominally this season is two linked stories grouped as episodes 1–6 and 8–13 with episode 7 as a handover. NB episodes 7 and 8 were given the same titles in error
**Broadcast:** Mondays 4/9/72 – 27/11/72
**Regular Cast:** Ray Armstrong (Colin Wade), Adrian Wright (Mike Hobbs), Leonard Gregory (Steve Walker), Caroline Ellis (Jill Rowles 1–7), Katarina Granlund (Eva 8–13)
**Writers:** Ralph Wright (1–7), Peter Lover (8–13)
**Directors:** Dave Heather (1, 2, 5, 6), Chris McMaster (3, 4, 7–13)

**Season Eight**
**13 episodes** ('Contact!'; 'Libra!'; 'The Auction'; 'The Third Man!'; 'Rapids!'; 'Darkness at Noon'; 'Double-Cross'; 'Impasse!'; 'The Crypt'; 'Switched!'; 'Break-Up!'; 'The Think Bank'; 'The Hoist!')
**Broadcast:** Mondays 6/8/73 – 5/11/73
**Regular Cast:** Bernard Horsfall (Cunliffe), Martin Neil (Dave), Wendy Padbury (Sue Craig), Robert Gillespie (Naylor), Neil McCarthy (Crouch)
**Writers:** Ralph Wright (1–4, 11–13), David Stevens (5–10)
**Directors:** Chris McMaster (1, 2, 5, 6, 9–13), Bob Leng (3, 4, 7, 8)

**Theme music:** 'Teenage Carnival' by Keith Mansfield (stock)
**Incidental music:** stock, several pieces by Laurie Johnson

**Tie-in publications:** original novels *The Sign of the Beaver* and *The Spy Game* by Alan Fennell, published in paperback by Piccolo, 1972

## The Railway Children

In 1951 Edith Nesbit's story was chosen as one of the very first to be adapted by the BBC. The broadcast was not recorded but its popularity meant the serial was remounted in studio a few months later, now in hour-long episode format. It would be impossible to tell this tale of trains and the great outdoors without recourse to location filming and indeed some outdoor work took place for the original version – these film inserts were retained and reused for the later remount. With no evidence remaining today, it can only be suggested that this would be a very literal adaptation of Nesbit's novel, given that the episode titles are almost all taken directly from the novel's chapter titles. It would be by necessity that when in 1957 the decision came to show the serial again, the whole thing had to be remade from scratch but it stuck closely to Dorothea Brooking's 1951 script, possibly with a little more in the way of location filming. The 1957 broadcast was the first version shown nationwide and was considered enough of an event to earn a *Radio Times* front cover.

Despite the tumultuous events of the next decade the tale persisted and in 1968 was tackled again by the BBC. Since this serial has thankfully survived, some comparison with Nesbit's work can be made. Her story was vaguely autobiographical; Edith Nesbit had enjoyed an 'Eden' of an early childhood in a prosperous middle-class family but the death of her father at 43 and the illness of a sister began a nomadic life for the family. This upbringing is reflected in the sudden lifestyle change of the Waterbury family, who have to move from their Edwardian suburban idyll to an insecure life of poverty in the country when Father is arrested on suspicion of spying. Mrs Waterbury has to try and sell stories and poems to support her family, just as Nesbit herself had done when her husband lost money to a swindling business partner. The book is essentially about how privilege can be no sort of privilege at all, with the children learning far more about life when forced to 'rough it' without servants and expensive toys.

The novel has been criticised, however. There are some unlikely coincidences – when the children rescue a boy lying injured in a railway tunnel he turns out to be the grandson of their friend 'The Old Gentleman'. One of the clearest flaws is the untidiness of some of the plotting. The book sprawls through largely unconnected episodes – including the discovery of a Russian dissident, Mother's illness and the prevention of a disastrous train crash – in between Father's arrest and final return as an innocent man. The 1968 adaptation benefits from its serial nature in this regard, each episode having its own self-contained story and disguising the lack of real narrative build. For its time, this is an excellent production. There's an abundance of location filming, most of it on Yorkshire's Keighley and Worth Valley Preservation Railway. Jenny Agutter is superb as Bobbie, always trying to keep a level head, although the effusive Gillian Bailey (later Billie in *Here Come the Double Deckers!*) as the younger Phyllis almost steals every scene she is in.

With hindsight, however, comparison with the celebrated 1970 film is inevitable – the cinema version has arguably even superseded Nesbit's original text as the definitive telling. The chronology of the film's inception is vague – writer and director Lionel Jefferies recalled that the idea was his daughter's on reading the book, the girl remarking: 'Daddy, this is a lovely thing, surely it should be made into a film.' So whether the 1968 TV adaptation influenced the film is not known but its 1969 TV repeat must surely have had some effect. Jenny Agutter was again cast as Bobbie and the Keighley line was the principal location when shooting took place in Spring 1970.

The TV adaptation was a direct, mechanical transfer of page to small screen but Jefferies imposes his own chosen reading onto the picture. Now the life of poverty is rendered in gloriously nostalgic, idyllic terms. Thus the more sentimental – though undeniably powerful – telling casts a retrospective disappointment over the 1968 serial, one which would not have been there on the original broadcasts. Particularly galling on backward viewing for example is the flat presentation of the tear-jerking 'Oh, my Daddy' reunion scene. There's no slow motion, no figure emerging from the clouds of train steam. Having been made in black and white, the 1968 TV version was made technically obsolete almost instantly with the onset of colour television – allowing the film to go on to dominate holiday television throughout the late 70s. Only a 1986 repeat of Episode 7, as part of the BBC's TV50 celebrations, reminded us that the 1968 serial had ever existed.

'And now, for the second time, Jenny Agutter stars in *The Railway Children*.' Anyone doubting the all-consuming power of the 1970 film should take note of the incorrect continuity announcement that introduced the reasonably lavish 2000 television movie remake. Agutter was indeed among the cast, now playing Mother and having read of her supposed involvement in excited newspaper reports. The Keighley line failed the audition this time and the Bluebell Railway in closer-to-London Sussex stood in.

This was supposedly made to celebrate the thirtieth anniversary of the film version, Carlton executive Jonathan Powell saying: 'It is one of the great classic children's books and we feel the time is right to return to it.' At the time, however, Carlton had also stated their intention to make a name for themselves as producers of global television and it was no doubt expedient to remake a commodity with such marketable worldwide appeal. In the UK, meanwhile, the telemovie was screened at the child-unfriendly hour of 8p.m., clearly aimed more at parents and, with the resulting ten million prime-time viewers, no doubt helping Carlton recoup their investment. Intent aside, this was an excellent adaptation. Largely concentrating on the themes of Nesbit's novel, very much in the more literal style of 1968, it went as far as to underline its class discourse with the expansion of a scene which sees working-class bargees throwing coal at the three children and calling them 'posh bloody kids'. Nonetheless it still found it impossible to resist the thrall of the classic film – Bobbie and her Daddy were reunited in slow motion amid clouds of train steam, pushing the notion of 'remake' to extremes.

Based on the novel by E. Nesbit (first UK publication 1906, Wells Gardner, Darton and Co.)

**1st version (1951)**
**BBC**

**8 episodes** ('The Beginning of Things'; 'Peter's Coal Mine'; 'Illness and a Birthday'; 'Prisoners and Captives'; 'Saviours of the Train'; 'The Pride of Perks and the Terrible Secret'; 'Hound in the Red Jersey'; 'The End of Things') (b&w)
**Broadcast:** Tuesdays 6/2/51 – 27/3/51 5.30–6p.m. (South England and Midlands)

**Main Cast:** Marion Chapman (Bobbie), Carole Lorimer (Phyllis), Michael Croudson (Peter), Jean Anderson (Mother), Michael Harding (Perks), D. A. Clarke-Smith (Old Gentleman)

**Title Music:** Symphonic Dances No. 2 by Grieg
**Designer:** Lawrence Broadhouse
**Writer and Producer:** Dorothea Brooking

**1st version remount (1951)**
**BBC**
**4 episodes** ('The Beginning of Things'; 'The Old Gentleman'; 'Saviours of the Train'; 'The End of Things')
(b&w)

**Broadcast:** 10/7/51 – 31/7/51 5–6p.m. (South England and Midlands)

**Main Cast and Crew:** as original except actor playing Perks was recast

**2nd version (1957)** effectively remount of the original script
**BBC**
**8 episodes** ('The Beginning of Things'; 'Peter's Coal Mine'; 'The Old Gentleman'; 'Prisoners and Captives'; 'Saviours of the Train'; 'The Pride of Perks'; 'Hound in the Red Jersey'; 'The End of Things')
(b&w)
**Broadcast:** Sundays 3/3/57 – 21/4/57 5.20p.m.

**Main Cast:** Anneke Willys (Roberta), Sandra Michaels (Phyllis), Cavan Kendall (Peter), Jean Anderson (Mother), John Richmond (Father), Richard Warner (Perks), Norman Shelley (Old Gentleman), Donald Morley (Station Master), Richard Peters (Jim)

**Designer:** Eileen Diss
**Writer and Producer:** Dorothea Brooking

**Tie-in publications:** *Radio Times* cover 3/3/57 – 9/3/57

**3rd version (1968)**
**BBC**
**7 episodes** ('The Visitors'; 'The Coalminers'; 'The Message'; 'The Foreign Gentleman'; 'The Secret'; 'The Rescue'; 'The Meeting')
(b&w)
**Broadcast:** Sundays 12/5/68 – 23/6/68 5.25–5.50p.m.

**Main Cast:** Jenny Agutter (Bobbie), Neil McDermott (Peter), Gillian Bailey (Phyllis), Ann Castle (Mother), Frederick Treves (Father), Gordon Gostelow (Perks), Joseph O'Connor (Old Gentleman), Brian Hayes (Station Master)

**Dramatised by** Denis Constanduros
**Script Editor:** Michael Voysey

**Title Music:** Symphonic Dances No. 2 by Grieg
**Designer:** Oliver Bayldon
**Associate Producer:** John McRae
**Producer:** Campbell Logan
**Director:** Julia Smith

**Video:** released as a double-pack by DD Video 3/12/01; Region 2 DVD issued 15/7/02

**4th version (2000)**
**A Carlton Production**
**Feature length TV movie**
(colour)
**Broadcast:** Easter Monday 23/4/00 8p.m.

**Main Cast:** Jemima Rooper (Bobbie), Jack Blumenau (Peter), Clare Thomas (Phyllis), Jenny Agutter (Mother), Michael Kitchen (Father), Gregor Fisher (Perks), Clive Russell (Station Master), Sir Richard Attenborough (The Old Gentleman)

**Screenplay:** Simon Nye
**Script Supervisor:** Marissa Gower
**Script Editor:** Philip Shelley

**Music:** Simon Lacey
**Production Designer:** Tim Hutchinson
**Production Executive:** Julie Burner
**Associate Producer:** Freya Pinsent
**Executive Producer:** Jonathan Powell
**Producer:** Charles Elton
**Director:** Catherine Morshead

**Video:** released by Carlton Video, April 2000

## Devil-in-the-Fog

Leon Garfield's Grand Guignol novel of the 18th century was one of ITV's earliest period literary adaptations, even given that Garfield's work was in fact an ersatz piece of faux Dickensania written just two years before this serial came to the screen. His novel had won the Guardian Prize for Children's Fiction in 1967.

George Treet is an affected self-proclaimed genius, part of the Treet family's group of travelling players entertaining in the hostelries of England. Then one night a dark stranger visits the head of the family with an important message. It is time for Mr Treet to reveal to George that the boy is not a Treet after all, but is in fact a nobleman, the son of Baron Dexter. Quite taken by this thought, which explains a lot to him about his regal manner, George journeys to his new family home only to find a cold and inhospitable mansion and a dying father. Worse still, he finds himself tangled up in an old family feud and faces death somewhere out there in the fog.

While *Devil-in-the-Fog* functioned ostensibly as an adventure story, there was also the realisation for George that, while his birthright may have been the noble Dexter seat, his true family were the down-to-earth Treets.

For the serial, the character of George was aged up a good few years from the fourteen-year-old of the novel, while a key location was the moated house, Ightham Mote near Sevenoaks, Kent.

**Rediffusion**
**6 episodes** ('Some are born to greatness…'; 'Some have greatness thrust upon them…'; 'O my prophetic soul: my Uncle!'; 'That one may smile, and smile, and be a villain…'; 'Fair is foul, and foul is fair…'; '…this fell serjeant death…')
(b&w)
**Broadcast:** Mondays 17/6/68 – 22/7/68

**Main Cast:** Nicholas Evans (George Treet), Martin Dempsey (Salathiel Treet), Keith Skinner (Edward Treet), Diana Simpson (Jane Treet), John Moulder-Brown (Hotspur Treet), Verina Greenlaw (Rose Treet), Richard Leech (Sir John Dexter), Gary Watson (Captain Richard Dexter), Stephanie Bidmead (Lady Dexter), Valentine Dyall (The Stranger), Milton Johns (Joseph)

Based on the novel by Leon Garfield (original UK publication 1966, Constable)
**Dramatised by** Stanley Miller

**Designer:** John Emery
**Producer:** Michael Currer-Briggs

**Tie-in publications:** n/k

## The Queen Street Gang

By the late 60s one of the most popular TV shows with kids was the prime-time spy romp *The Man from UNCLE*. Saturday morning cinema meanwhile was based largely around screenings of the Children's Film Foundation features, with all their runabout antics. *The Queen Street Gang* seems a fairly deliberate attempt to combine elements of the two. A Blyton-style gang of resourceful kids were now clad from head to toe in cool denim and solved absurd crimes in a bizarre fantasy world.

Inviting further comparison with *The Famous Five*, gang leader Mini's dad was working on top secret research for the government, placing the kids close to danger and excitement – this had been exactly the function of George's father Quentin Kirrin in the Blyton books.

In the first of two episodic stories Professor Kirrin – sorry – Morris was kidnapped and the Silver Egg stolen. This latest piece of research was intended to hold enough electricity to power the world. The egg and its egghead creator had been taken by four unlikely comic strip hoodlums who could have walked from the pages of *Batman* – or indeed the Adam West TV series. These were the dapper Spitz, the pink-suited, beautiful Auntie Cuthbert (well, it was a pink suit for filming even if the show was made in black and white), the flat-cap thug Greenface and midget Tich. The second story saw Dr Sturgeon's new virus stolen from his lab by a gang of modern-day pirates.

**Thames**
**9 episodes**
(b&w)
**Broadcast:** Thursdays 1/8/68 – 26/9/68

**Main Cast:** The Gang – Michael Feldman (Mini Morris), Anthony Peplow (Speedy), Len Jones (Sniffer), Sebastian Abineri (Big Bill), Elizabeth Crowther (Philippa); Michael Gwynn (Professor Morris), Maureen O'Reilly (Mrs Morris), Lesley Judd (Miss Roberts)

**Written by** Roy Russell
Based on the book *The Case of the Silver Egg* by Desmond Skirrow (first UK publication 1966, The Bodley Head)

**Producer:** Pamela Lonsdale

**Story One**
**'The Supercharged Egg'**
**4 episodes** ('Plans are Hatched'; 'Things Begin to Boil'; 'Scrambling for the Egg'; 'Bringing Home The Bacon')

**With:** Harold Innocent (Spitz), Caroline Blakiston (Auntie Cuthbert), Terence Rigby (Greenface), Norman McGlen (Tich)

**Designer:** Roger Allan
**Director:** Adrian Cooper

**Story Two**
**'The Bug Pirates'**
**5 episodes** ('Into Uncharted Seas'; 'Ahoy! Skull and Crossbones'; 'Into Troubled Waters'; 'The Captain's Treasure'; 'In Davy Jones' Locker')

**With:** Donald Morley (Dr Sturgeon), Godfrey Quigley (Captain Morgan), Marty Cruikshank (Miss Pilkington), David Leland (Franco), Tony Caunter (Luigi)

**Designers:** Norman Garwood (1–3), Tony Borer (4, 5)
**Director:** Nicholas Ferguson

## Tom Grattan's War

Children's fiction has certainly told many stories of young World War II evacuees coming to terms with life in the countryside, but this was slightly different, if only because it was set at the time of the Great War of 1914–18. Tom Grattan's father was fighting in Europe and his mother had been sent to work in a munitions factory. At sixteen, Tom was too young for conscription so his contribution was to work on a farm and help with the nation's food production. The London boy travelled the long journey to the Kirkby's moorland farm in Yorkshire to learn country ways and also found that the war was still being fought in this small corner of England.

While the Somme was thousands of miles away, many German prisoners were being held near Kirkby, working in quarries. Often the prisoners would be attacked by angry locals and Tom found himself questioning both their motives and his own attitudes. Should ill prisoners be cared for? Could Tom help a German to escape?

The series functioned at an adventure level too of course: two bombers planned to blow up a troop train; another tried to attack the prison quarry in retaliation for the death of his son on the battlefield. Tom later had to rescue a rich young Lord kidnapped by two opportunist tinkers; he and his girlfriend Julie themselves had to be sprung from a castle dungeon by their handyman friend Stan at the controls of an early fighter plane. For these concluding episodes, Yorkshire made sure the series went out with a bang. A working Tiger Moth was redressed in 1915 style and flying sequences were filmed from a helicopter, the plane finally coming to earth in a staged crash.

The hero's name was borrowed from a sixty-year-old Yorkshire farmer Tom Gratton, although the series was not his story.

*Tom Grattan's War*
**Yorkshire**
**2 seasons**

**Main Cast:** Michael Howe (Tom Grattan), Sally Adcock (Julie Kirkby), Connie Merigold (Mrs Kirkby), George Malpas (Stan Hobbs), Richard Warner (Narrator)

**Season One**
**13 episodes** ('The Watcher'; 'The Night Intruder'; 'Menace at the Mine'; 'Monster of Steel'; 'The Hero'; 'The Prisoner'; 'The Secret Boat'; 'The Terrible Townsends'; 'The Fire Raisers'; 'Battle at Weaver's Lock'; 'The Hero'; 'The Mysterious Lighthouse'; 'The Wreckers')
(filmed in colour, transmitted in b&w)

**Broadcast:** Wednesdays 21/8/68 – 13/11/68 and Saturdays 24/8/68 – 16/11/68 in various ITV regions

**Written by** David C. Rea and Bernie Cooper (1, 5), David C. Rea (2–4, 6, 7), (8–13 n/k)

**Producer:** David C. Rea
**Executive Producer:** Tony Essex
**Directors:** David C. Rea (1–4, 6, 7), Ronald Eyre (5), (8–13 n/k)

**Tie-in publications:** novelisation by Michael Deakin, published in paperback by Green Knight, 1969

**Season Two**
**13 episodes** ('The Walking Bomb'; 'Blind Man's Buff'; 'Bridge of Death'; 'The Coward'; 'Badge of Fear'; 'Eye for an Eye'; 'Five Minute Fuse'; 'Soldier from Margham'; 'Pedlar's Ransom'; 'Ghost of Hookey Vale'; 'The Inventor'; 'Castle of Terror'; 'Sky Patrol')
(colour)
**Broadcast:** Mondays 6/4/70 – 29/6/70

**Written by** Frank Charles (1–4), Tony Essex (5–8), Audley Southcott (9–13)

**Producer:** Audley Southcott
**Executive Producer:** Tony Essex
**Directors:** Stephen Frears (1–5), Michael Blakstad (6, 7, 9, 10), Ian McFarlane (8), Don Higgins (11–13)

## Adventure Weekly

The escapades of five young budding reporters working on a junior newspaper. Peter, Andy, Tubby, Swot and 'Fred', the female member of the group, deal with a variety of situations, assisting in the capture of post office robbers and dealing with an unexploded bomb.

Unfortunately, the *Adventure Weekly* relies on the use of the *Cliffsea Recorder*'s facilities, a paper that isn't in a healthy financial position. It looks certain that the *Recorder* is going to fail, which will mean an end to the junior paper. Even when the *Recorder* finds a buyer, it transpires that he may not be keen on keeping the *Adventure Weekly*. The children take matters into their own hands, crashing into Lord Huntingford's London office in an attempt to prevent him closing their newspaper.

Having successfully campaigned to save their paper, the children find themselves in the middle of the 'silly season', where stories are very hard to come by. Swot, following up a hunch, arrives at a 'haunted' windmill and stumbles across what could turn out to be the paper's biggest scoop.

**BBC South and West**
**13 episodes** ('Into Print'; 'United Effort'; 'Explosion'; 'Take-Over' (parts 1–3); 'The Great Treasure Hunt'; 'The Dig' (parts 1–3); 'Double Bluff'; 'The Siege'; 'Stop Press')
(b&w)
**Broadcast:** Mondays 30/12/68 – 24/3/69

**Main Cast:** Brent Oldfield (Peter Perkins), Frank Barry (Swot English), Len Jones (Andy Rogers), Ian Ellis (Tubby Taylor), Elizabeth Dear ('Fred' Somers)

**Written by** Shaun Sutton (2, 7, 13), Peter J. Hammond (3), Victor Pemberton (4–6, 8–10, 12), Ian Shurey (11), (episode 1 n/k)

**Designers:** Desmond Chinn (1–7, 11–13), Chris Robilliard (8–10)
**Producer:** John McRae
**Director:** Barry Letts

## The Tingaree Affair

The British state of Tingaree is in considerable trouble. It is threatened by the military dictatorship of neighbouring Caris, which wants to exploit Tingaree's extensive mineral resources. Tingaree's independence talks in London must go ahead unhindered, to protect the state and ensure that it gains its new status without succumbing to Caris. Thus most of the action takes place at the Tingaree High Commission offices in London, with Commissioner Ferrera's son Martin and his chauffeur's fashion-mad daughter Sandy investigating suspicious goings-on to make sure events run smoothly. That may prove difficult, however, with Caris' Freedom Fighters, secret service agents and Drew, the mercenary superspy and master of disguise, all on the prowl. Who is the mysterious tramp hanging around outside the High Commission offices, or the Irish handyman, or the Australian car mechanic? Can they all really be the supersmooth spy with the villa in the South of France?

Sandy and Martin were 'just good friends' according to lead actor Vivienne Cohen: 'Where children are concerned we don't want any complications.' These feelings were mirrored by director Margery Baker, who said, '*Tingaree Affair* doesn't need anything like that.' These comments clearly reflect a period in time where the issue of relationships between teenagers wasn't one for examination on children's television, while clean-cut espionage and action were clearly thought far more suitable.

**Thames**
**7 episodes** ('First Move'; 'Spy'; 'Freedom Fighters'; 'Explosion'; 'Kidnap'; 'Escape'; 'Attack')
(b&w)
**Broadcast:** Wednesdays 21/5/69 – 2/7/69

**Main Cast:** David Ballantyne (Martin Ferrera), Vivienne Cohen (Sandy), Valentine Palmer (Drew), Leon Lissek (Torres), Peter Arne (High Commissioner Ferrera), Lewis Wilson (Andrews), Rita Davies (Mrs Ferrera), Frank Mills (Eddy)

**Written by** Francis Megahy and Bernie Cooper

**Designer:** Frank Gillman
**Producer:** Ronald Marriott
**Director:** Margery Baker

## The Flaxton Boys

Each of this epic period drama's four seasons charts the adventures of a different aristocratic generation of Flaxton boys.

The story opens in 1854 at Flaxton Hall, where young Jonathan Flaxton and his mother have just taken up residence. Standing against the bleak backdrop of the Yorkshire Moors, the house is run-down and eerie, perfect for Jonathan and his friend Archie Weekes to explore. The young Flaxton has battlements to climb and a river full of trout. There's also the ghostly woman in black who stands among the graves. Life becomes more sobering when Jonathan discovers that his father, fighting in the Crimea, is missing in action and a visiting troop of soldiers are threatened by bombers. Three convicts who believe Flaxton Hall to be the hiding place of a great treasure provide some distraction but, with the convicts safely dispatched, no fortune is found and the family situation becomes desperate.

The second season takes the audience to the 1890s. Andrew Flaxton and his friend Peter Weekes try to solve the mystery of Jonathan Flaxton and find the rightful heir to Flaxton Hall. While doing so they play an important role in helping a servant girl escape an unappealing life at Stilgoe Lodge. There they find an important clue to the mystery but become entangled in the conflict between two factions of the Chinese Tong class. Sir Tarquin Stilgoe, frightened that the boys may discover the truth, attempts to burn Flaxton Hall to the ground. Will the children be able to discover the truth behind Jonathan Flaxton's disappearance twelve years previously?

It's 1928 and a young Jonathan Flaxton is bringing school friend William Pickford home to Flaxton Hall for the summer holidays. The boys discover that the vicar is planning to turn the now-derelict Stilgoe Lodge into an orphanage. The boys visit the lodge intent on offering their help but, after hearing a series of mysterious noises, conclude it is haunted. It transpires that the hauntings are more earthly than first expected and someone is trying to prevent the lodge conversion. The boys must discover who is behind the hauntings.

The final season has a 1940s wartime setting. Mathew Flaxton befriends Terry Nichols, an evacuee from London, and the two embroil themselves in adventures involving prisoners of war, spies and machine guns.

*The Flaxton Boys* involved both studio and location work but stands out through being recorded entirely on videotape. The first season started in 1969, years before use of tape for location recording was commonplace.

**Yorkshire
4 seasons**
(colour)

**Season One**
**13 episodes** ('The Deserter'; 'The Dog'; 'The Watcher' (aka 'The Ghost'); 'The Tutor'; 'The Smugglers'; 'The Seafarer'; 'The Patient'; 'The Witches'; 'The Bridge'; 'The Hunt'; 'The Island'; 'The Will'; 'The Return')
**Broadcast:** Sundays 21/9/69 – 14/12/69 (in colour where available)

**Main Cast:** David Smith (Jonathan Flaxton), Penelope Lee (Lucy Flaxton), James Hayter (Nathan), Peter Firth (Archie Weekes), Molly Urquhart (Flora), Richard Gale (Sir Peregrine Stilgoe), Gerry Cowan (Narrator)

**Series originated by** Sid Waddell
**Written by** Sid Waddell (1, 6), Don Houghton (2, 7–13), Barry Cockcroft (4), David Crane (5), (3 n/k)
**Script Editor:** David Crane

**Designer:** Geoffrey Martin
**Producer:** Robert D. Cardona
**Executive Producer:** Jess Yates
**Directors:** Robert D. Cardona (1–4, 9–11, 13), Geoffrey Martin (5–8), David Millard (12)

**Season Two**
**13 episodes** ('The Meeting'; 'The Globe'; 'The Heir'; 'The Letter'; 'The Diary'; 'The Locket'; 'The Valentine'; 'The Conspiracy'; 'The Messenger'; 'The Discovery'; 'The Attempt'; 'The Homecoming'; 'The Solution')
**Broadcast:** Sundays 20/9/70 – 13/12/70

**Main Cast:** Moultrie Kelsall (Andrew Flaxton), Hugh Cross (Archie Weekes), Lila Kaye (Sarah Weekes), Dai Bradley (Peter Weekes), Philip Maskery (David Stilgoe), Victor Winding (Barnaby Sweet), Gerry Cowan (Jacklin Flaxton/Narrator)

**Written by** Don Houghton (1, 2, 4, 10, 13), Michala Crees (3, 7), Patrick Scanlan (5), Jeremy Burnham (6, 11), Sid Waddell (8), Richard Lorne (9), Barry Cockcroft (12)
**Script Editor:** Don Houghton

**Designers:** James Weatherup (1–3, 6–8, 10, 12, 13), Richard Jarvis (4, 5, 9, 11)
**Producer:** Robert D. Cardona
**Directors:** Robert D. Cardona (1–3, 6–8, 10, 12, 13), David Goldsmith (4, 5, 9, 11)

**Season Three**
**13 episodes** ('All on a Summer's Day'; 'A Quiet Sunday'; 'A Fete Worse Than…'; 'Snake in the Grass'; 'In and Out of Hiding'; 'The Fastest Gun in the West Riding'; 'Trouble in the Air'; 'To See… A Fine Horse'; 'Things That Go Bump…'; 'The Ghost Catchers'; 'The Lady in White'; 'Down a Long Black Hole'; 'Goodbye, Summer – Goodbye')
**Broadcast:** Sundays 19/9/71 – 12/12/71

**Main Cast:** Alan Guy (Jonathan Flaxton), John Ash (William Pickford), Victor Winding (Benjamin Sweet), Veronica Hurst (Lady Jane Flaxton), Nicholas Pennell (Vicar), Gerry Cowan (Roger Grafton/Narrator)

**Written by** Gloria Tors (1, 8, 13), Gerry Andrews (2, 3, 6), John S. Weaver (4), John Ecke (5), Adrian Brown and Claudine Henry (7), Stuart Douglass (9–12)

**Designers:** Evan Hercules (1, 3, 4, 6–8, 13), Gordon Livesey (2, 5, 9–11), Bryan Hercules (12)
**Producer/Director:** Robert D. Cardona

### Season Four
**13 episodes** ('Is Your Journey Really Necessary?'; 'This Little Piggy'; 'What You Don't Know Might Hurt You'; 'No Place Like…'; 'The Bevin Boy'; '"Welcome Home" Tommy Atkins'; 'It Fell Off The Back of a Lorry'; 'Charity Begins At…'; 'Things Are Not What They Seem'; 'Cry Wolf'; 'A Funny Kind of Day'; 'Remember, Remember'; 'Keep the Home Fires Burning')
(colour)
**Broadcast:** Sundays 25/3/73 – 17/6/73 – networked except Scottish (delayed until Sunday 15/4/73) and LWT (Saturdays from 24/3/73 in 11.30a.m./noon slots)

**Main Cast:** Andrew Packett (Mathew Flaxton), Philip Baldwin (Terry Nichols), Joanna Jones (Elizabeth Flaxton), Victor Winding (Benjamin), Gerry Cowan (Narrator)

**Written by** Gloria Tors (1–3), Anthony Couch (4, 9), Gerry Andrews (6–8, 10, 12), John Gerard (11), (5 and 13 n/k)

**Designers:** Evan Hercules (1–5, 7, 8, 10), Jack Robinson (6, 9, 11, 12), (13 n/k)
**Producer/Director:** Robert D. Cardona

## A Handful of Thieves
The title of this drama refers to five children, Sid, Fred, Algy, Rosie and Clio, otherwise known as the Cemetery Committee. They have proven their bravery by risking their lives hurtling down Death Wall on pram wheels, an area of an old racetrack where many drivers were killed. When a robbery takes place, the beliefs of the children are brought into question. To regain the stolen money they too must behave like thieves.

Fred's gran has a new lodger, the sinister Mr Gribble. Sid, the leader of the Cemetery Committee and by far the most intelligent, is suspicious of the stranger from the moment he sets eyes on him. Sid's suspicions are confirmed when Gribble makes off with Gran's savings, leaving the poor old woman unable to pay her bills. The Cemetery Committee pool their resources to track the villain down but, to regain Gran's money, they must break into Gribble's home. Doesn't that make them just as bad as him?

Against Sid's wishes, the other members of the gang agree to steal the money back from Gribble. Sid strongly believes that it is wrong and refuses to be involved. Fred, Algy, Rosie and Clio leave Sid standing outside the local cinema as they begin their journey to Gribble's abode. *A Handful of Thieves* is just that little bit more than a mere adventure story.

**BBC**
**4 episodes** ('The Sinister Lodger'; 'The Fireworks Party'; 'Find Mr Gribble!'; 'Stop Thief!')
(b&w)
**Broadcast:** Mondays 22/9/69 – 13/10/69

**Main Cast:** Martin Ratcliffe (Fred), Martin Skinner (Sid), John Gugolka (Algy), Helen Worth (Rosie), Juliet Marshall (Clio), Barbara Leake (Gran), Frank Mills (Mr Gribble), Erik Chitty (Old Puffer)

Based on the novel by Nina Bawden (first UK publication 1967, Victor Gollancz)
**Dramatised by** Rosemary Anne Sisson
**Script Editor:** Victor Pemberton

**Designer:** Barrie Dobbins
**Producer:** John McRae
**Director:** Barry Letts

**Tie-in publications:** n/k

Also told as *Jackanory*, read by Keith Barron, broadcast 23/10/67 – 27/10/67

## The Battle of St George Without
Matt, Sidney and Henry, a gang of children living in Dove Square in contemporary London, have secrets and a secret hiding place but uncover plans that could jeopardise the upcoming St George's Day service at the local Church of St George Without. The gang do good and the Bishop arrives gratefully when the service goes ahead as planned.

Adapted from the novel by Irish writer Janet McNeill, the literary source, the three-part serial format and the adapting credit for John Tully again hint at yet another entry from the schools *Merry-Go-Round* serial repeated in an afternoon slot. The serial was later shown again in 1971.

**BBC**
**3 episodes** ('The Secret Place'; 'Guard Duties'; 'St George's Day')
(b&w)
**Broadcast:** Mondays 15/12/69 - 29/12/69

**Main Cast:** Stephen Shipp (Matt), Norman Sweeney (Sidney), Stephen Brassett (Henry), Drew Wood (Dan-Boy), David Littleton & Kenneth Littleton (The Flint Twins), John Woodnutt (The Bishop)

Based on the novel by Janet McNeill (first UK publication 1966, Faber & Faber)
**Adapted by** John Tully

**Music:** Jonathan Cohen
**Designer:** Oliver Bayldon
**Producer:** Dorothea Brooking

# 1970s

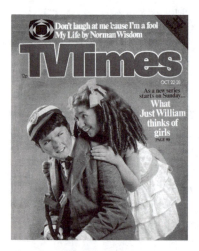

Don't laugh at me 'cause I'm a fool
My Life by Norman Wisdom

**TV Times**

12p

OCT 22-28

As a new series
starts on Sunday...
**What
Just William
thinks of
girls**
PAGE 90

**Above:** London Weekend's popular Sunday series *Just William* was one of the few children's dramas to make the front cover of *TV Times* magazine in the 1970s.

To usher in a new decade of increased profile and quality in children's drama required new initiatives by the BBC, not least in order to create a spirit of competition between the two rival channels. Spurred on by the success of the experiment that had been the live action film work on *The Witch's Daughter* for *Jackanory*, a new era was created through the dedication of Anna Home, her department head Monica Sims and the clever accounting of department manager George Ageros. With the BBC children's drama output shored up by European and American imports and even repeats of schools drama broadcasts, the time had come for home-grown produce to re-emerge. It began in a small way, with the three-part serial *Joe and the Gladiator* filmed in the North East of England. Home recalls that most of the tiny crew had to double up and cover all roles to get anything together, so low was the budget, but everyone who worked on the serials made in the early years seemed to do the very best they could.

*Joe and the Gladiator* may have marked a fresh start for the production of BBC children's drama but it was also important because it was tougher and more realistic than anything that had gone before. It admitted the working class and was far removed from the Corporation's period classics image. The 'search for truth' that had contentiously typified adult TV output of the early 60s (*Armchair Theatre*, *The Wednesday Play*, *Z Cars*) was now filtering through to children's drama. ITV broke new ground controversially with *The Owl Service*, a fantasy serial that drew its horror from its portrayal of violent adolescent jealousy. This had upped the age range of the 'children's' serial very quickly and dealt with difficult subjects expressed honestly albeit through a fantasy framework. Notably, *The Owl Service* was a modern 'classic' novel only two years old at the time.

The growing maturity of BBC children's drama in the early 70s can best be witnessed in the series of adaptations of books by Nina Bawden. From the muted runabout chase action of *A Handful of Thieves* there was an incremental progression to a story of jewel thieves encountering a sullen, uncommunicative outcast on a remote Scottish island in *The Witch's Daughter*. *The Runaway Summer* was next, a kids-on-the-run drama with an almost existential sense of doubt and impending responsibility. Finally, in 1974, *Carrie's War* was a serial that worked almost entirely at the level of internalised thoughts and feelings with little room for action and certainly without a coastal diamond smuggler in sight.

Among other advances was the first commissioned drama teleplay of the 70s, *Mandog*, written exclusively for the BBC by the noted children's author Peter Dickinson. Nineteenth-century dramas continued but these were usually held back for Sunday afternoons rather than weekdays. Many of the Sunday serials would be produced by the (adult) Drama Serials department and as such were not wholly intended as children's fare and unlikely to be based on any governing strategy as was material made by the Children's Unit.

At ITV the mid-70s witnessed a slight shift in the balance of power. Thames, the London weekday franchise created by an enforced merger of Rediffusion and ABC in 1968, was still the biggest producer of children's television and was headed by Lewis Rudd in 1970–72 and then Sue Turner from 1972 to 1978. The 70s saw smaller franchise-holders with a few years' profitability behind them try to move beyond regional news shows and into network production. Finding their path blocked by the clout of the 'Big Five' (Thames, ATV, Granada, LWT and Yorkshire) the backdoor way onto the network was through children's series and drama in particular.

The newcomers followed the path trodden by Southern in the mid-60s. Southern was still going strong by the mid-70s and remained the second biggest producer of children's television after Thames. HTV, the broadcaster for the West of England and Wales with production centres in Bristol (HTV West) and Cardiff (HTV Wales), made its name as a network producer of children's serials from 1972. Most of them were in the fantasy adventure arena, drawing on a rich vein of local Welsh and Arthurian tradition. *Arthur of the Britons* was at the time reportedly the biggest outlay on any series from a region outside of the Big Five and was followed by *Sky*, *The Georgian House*, *Children of the Stones*, *King of the Castle* and *The Clifton House Mystery*. North Eastern broadcaster Tyne Tees also got in on the act in 1977, with *Nobody's House* their first foray into the genre. *The Paper Lads* which followed the same year was far more markedly of its North East locale – a truly regionalised programme on the network which retained its Geordie accent.

Mention should be made of other regional flavours. Southern (for most of the 70s headed by Lewis Rudd after leaving Thames) made both period adaptations and new serials alike. Usually these had an open air, pastoral feel and an accent on location work, customarily in the nearby New Forest and out at sea. Thames' contemporary pieces tended to be that little more hip than the others – witness the metropolitan fashions of *Ace of Wands* and *The Tomorrow People*.

An overview of children's television in the 70s wouldn't be complete without a mention of *Look-In*. This comic, billed throughout its life as *The Junior TV Times*, was a powerful marketing tool which could promote forthcoming ITV productions. Its heyday was the 70s, the comic beginning in 1971 as a spin-off to Thames' new magazine show *Magpie* (indeed at the planning stages it was intended to be titled *Magpie*). Not only did the magazine give regional listings of programmes earmarked for children and help to aggressively trail them in a way that was totally unavailable to the BBC but what *Look-In* also did, even if unconsciously, was place the children's series of the time in among a mix of fashionable and sexy pop music. David Cassidy, ABBA and the Bay City Rollers rubbed shoulders with the likes of Susan Stranks and Mick Robertson of *Magpie*, who shared their pop pin-up status. As far as drama was concerned, many pages – and thus teenage wall space – were devoted to coverage of the pretty heroes of *Freewheelers*, *Follyfoot*, *Ace of Wands* and *The Tomorrow People*. Even *Black Beauty*'s strait-laced Judi Bowker and Stacy Dorning were included in this hormonal hegemony. In all possibility it was *Look-In* which

**Above:** Independent Television Publications launched the comic *Look-In* as *The Junior TV Times* in 1971 – it acted as a great publicity outlet for ITV children's programming and was highly successful throughout its first decade.

**Above:** *The Adventures of Black Beauty* and *Black Arrow* were two more series to be trailed on the front cover of *Look-In* during the early 70s.

throughout the decade helped to create the idea of a less staid and more sexy, more consciously adolescent culture around children's programmes on ITV rather than the programmes themselves. It was only on the cover of *Look-In* that Sian Phillips as the *Warrior Queen* could share space with punk band Eddie and the Hot Rods.

For all the froth of *Look-In*, children's drama in the 70s was a serious business. In breaking new ground and covering difficult and sometimes contentious topics, producing drama for children brought with it an onerous responsibility. The programme-makers were now seeking to carefully explore issues such as violence, race, parents, love and criminality and somehow arm their viewers for the realities of life.

When a mother wrote to *Radio Times* to complain about the BBC 1976 drama *Rocky O'Rourke*, Monica Sims gave a rare public statement that outlined the department's new attitudes. The letter-writer felt that child viewers looked up to television for their heroes, and that the criminal activities of Rocky and his brother were encouraging the audience to copy them. The complainant went on to suggest that while 'no doubt the programme intends to portray Rocky as an increasingly socially aware member of society as the series continues', the damage would be done among children who did not stay with the series and so catch on to its moral message: 'many may not understand the higher sentiments of social awareness as easily as they can associate with the leader figure of Rocky "the admired law breaker"'.

The assumption made that there would be a moral backbone to the serial was correct but it is interesting to note that the storyline was taken from a previously published novel, *A Pair of Jesus Boots*, which could be found in many a school library. The letter unintentionally reiterates two long-standing arguments: either television has an immediacy that increases its influence beyond that of the printed page, or only well-adjusted middle-class children read books while television is a medium open to all.

In reply, Sims duly confirmed the moral message of the serial. 'The intention is [not to promote juvenile crime but] the opposite and the point of the story is to show Rocky's realisation of the stupidity and thoughtlessness of his behaviour and his disillusion with his weak, criminal brother.' More tellingly she went on to reveal the central tenets of children's drama at the BBC in the 70s:

> We would be out of touch with the reality of children's lives if we only showed comfortable or sentimental stories. We hope it is helpful to give children an opportunity to think about some of the problems they have to face and also to realise the consequences of delinquent behaviour. Drama of many kinds can help children to understand themselves and other people and we believe that any child who identifies with Rocky is likely to share his struggle with his conscience. If we are to give a balanced view of the world in which children are growing up, we must occasionally include unpleasant aspects of life. Most of our drama in some way depicts a conflict between good and evil and unless we can show something of the bad it is difficult to see how we can emphasise the triumph of the good.

This was nothing compared to the storm of protest that was whipped up in 1978 with the advent of *Grange Hill*. Edward Barnes became Head of Children's Programmes at the BBC after Sims left to become Controller of Radio Four and he walked almost straight into the controversy. *Grange Hill* had been nurtured by Sims and Anna Home working alongside its writer Phil Redmond and was seen by many, then and now, as the coming of 'inner city'-styled realism to the BBC.

*Grange Hill* was so spot-on in its identification of school life that it made an impact bigger than any series that preceded it. It would be mildly ridiculous to suggest however, as the growing consensus seems to be, that nothing similar had come before either from the BBC or ITV. Phil Redmond, speaking to David Buckingham, has recently introduced the notion of 'Pre and post *Grange Hill* TV'. Two of its stars, Susan Tully (Suzanne Ross) and Terry Sue Patt (Benny Green), contributing to the 1998 TV documentary *From Grange Hill to Albert Square*, also approved the idea that before *Grange Hill* children's drama had featured 'middle class actors trying to play working class' and that 'there was nothing gritty' in the genre.

While the impact and thus influence of *Grange Hill* cannot be denied it is simply not true to say that *Grange Hill* was the first urban children's drama to admit the working class. *Rocky O'Rourke* (1976), as mentioned above, featured a criminal class in inner city Liverpool. *Sam and the River* (1975), while not remarkable at a story level, was nonetheless set in the grubbier parts of London's docklands, while the otherwise sentimental *Joe and the Gladiator* was an early attempt at realism filmed on Tyneside. Much under-documented has been ATV's *The Siege of Golden Hill*, filmed in inner city Birmingham and focusing on the lives of tower block kids. ATV followed up *Golden Hill* with a series set in a reasonably realistic comprehensive school, *A Bunch of Fives*. The title itself gives enough notice of its intent.

The 'grittier' children's drama had taken a long time to ferment but was an established style by the end of the 70s. Too many gritty, realistic contemporary pieces would, however, very quickly become as boring as a constant stream of Blyton adventures. The drama schedules of both channels were all about variety. Another myth should be questioned here – that somehow the BBC was about Edwardian period dramas and ITV dealt only in 'jeans and trainers' action series. In fact the output of both channels from the end of the decade, viewed side by side, suggested that the two sides couldn't have put together a more complementary menu if they had sat down and planned it between them.

ITV franchises produced the picturesque *Flockton Flyer*, trouble at Mill drama *Midnight is a Place*, the pseudo-Shakespeare of *Warrior Queen* and *The Feathered Serpent* as well as spy thrillers like *Quest of Eagles* and realistic pieces like *A Bunch of Fives*. In 1977, by way of contrasting example, the BBC produced both the thick-ear gangster drama *King Cinder* and period standard *Children of the New Forest*. 1978 brought the conspiracy thriller *Touch and Go* alongside period pieces like *The Hills of Heaven*. When viewed against the state of play a decade earlier, the 70s proved an embarrassment of riches for the genre.

**Above:** science fiction series *The Tomorrow People* and *Sky* on the cover of *Look-In*.

## The Owl Service

*The Owl Service* was possibly the most daring and dazzling example of children's drama up to that point, exemplifying the changes being wrought within the genre by both the BBC and ITV at the end of the 60s. Granada eschewed turn of the century literary standards, seeking inspiration from a more modern classic. Alan Garner's unsettling, fantasy-tinged book had been awarded the Carnegie Medal and Guardian Awards for children's fiction in 1967 so this was very much a cutting edge, contemporary source work.

The mantle of 'children's drama' sits rather uneasily with the serial – its themes are utterly adolescent and the story lacks the calming, reassuring passages that are to be found in a lot of children's fiction. *The Owl Service* links ancient Welsh legend to a present where a violent history seems to be repeating itself (this blurring of the boundaries between dream/reality and then/now is ever-present in Garner's work). At the centre of the storm is a triangle of love and hate, between the burgeoning sexuality of upper-class Alison and the affections of both her new stepbrother Roger and the Valley boy Gwyn.

Sexual jealousy had never been the topic of a children's drama before, and nor has it since, not to this degree. Alison is cast in the coquettish innocent girl/woman role. The camera, like Roger and Gwyn, lusts after her, with close-ups of bare thighs glimpsed beneath her nightshirt and a scene that sees her undress while Gwyn watches through the window. There is even implied teenage sex, when in episode three Gwyn and Alison spend the night alone in a small outhouse. Their expressions the next morning are the subject of much conjecture, more so than in the novel in fact. Shown in a Sunday teatime slot, controversy was inevitable.

Within the triangle a simmering class struggle is also being fought. Alison and Roger are resolutely upper middle class, almost unpleasantly so; Alison's life is run by 'Mummy' and Roger will be expected to follow his father into the family business. Roger considers Gwyn, with his jumper worn through at the elbows, to be 'a clever yobbo' at best, not 'one of us'. He and Alison are the landed gentry of this valley, the English owners of the holiday house, while the Welsh – like Gwyn, his 'Mam' Nancy and the gardener Huw – are employed as their domestics. Gwyn has bought elocution records in order to lose his Welsh accent and wants to go to university but complains that his mother's horizons are 'three inches high'. His attempt to escape the never-ending valley in episode six is an obviously metaphorical one.

The subject matter then is very much the stuff of contemporary drama, with the fantasy leanings quite hard to spot. There are the plates from which the design disappears when traced and made into paper owls by Alison but there are no ghosts or ghoulies, and fewer spooky lighting effects than we might expect. This is a story of the ever-present love, jealousy and anger that has been handed down through the ages, a tale of resentment and simmering tension always threatening to erupt into violence. One wonderfully understated 'cliffhanger' has a bottle thrown by Gwyn crashing against a wall, unnoticed by Roger as he calmly walks away.

The serial was shot between April and June 1969 in and around Dinas Mawddwy, North Wales (although the house was in reality Poulton Hall in Liverpool – the owners of Bryn Hall where Garner had written and set the novel had refused filming permission). The producer Peter Plummer was also directing, working closely with his chief cameraman David Wood. Alan Garner himself provided the scripts for the television adaptation. The serial was the first location drama production to be made in colour by Granada (only the briefest of scenes were filmed in studio and the earlier *The Flower of Gloster* had been only part scripted) which perhaps indicates the prestige that the company accorded it.

*The Owl Service* has a rough and ready, almost documentary-like quality that verges on the brutal, echoing the themes of the story. Its visual style is also partially informed by contemporary *nouvelle vague* and underground cinema with techniques such as flash jump-cuts used on occasion. In one scene, shots of an angry Alison are intercut with almost subliminal shots of Gillian Hills with her face painted with flowers, perhaps the clearest indication of counter-cultural influences at work.

In its story themes, visuals and production techniques *The Owl Service* is very much an experimental work in the children's drama canon. It broke new ground in all of these ways and most importantly it perhaps mapped the boundaries of what was and wasn't acceptable fare for children's television. Having extended the parameters so quickly, however, it may be that there was nowhere else left to go and subsequent children's productions appeared to be almost beating a retreat by comparison.

**Granada**
**8 episodes**
(colour)

**Episode One**
Title n/k (possibly 'The Owl Service')
Sunday 21/12/69 4.15–4.45p.m. (Granada, LWT and others); 4.25–4.55p.m. (Grampian); 5.30–6.00p.m. (Scottish, Border, Ulster and others)
Tuesday 6/10/70 4.50–5.15p.m. ATV Midlands and others
NB: All original transmissions in 1969–70 were in black and white, despite the serial being made in colour.
Gwyn and Alison find a dusty dinner service in the loft of the old house. The plates are covered in a flower pattern. Fascinated by them, Alison traces the pattern onto paper and from the tracings begins to make paper owls. Increasingly obsessed by the owls, Alison acts increasingly irrationally – until, appearing possessed, she scratches Roger's face so that she draws blood.

**Episode Two**
'The Mystery Deepens...'
Sunday 28/12/69 patterns as above and Tuesday 13/10/70 ATV
A violent force is briefly unleashed when Gwyn kicks the book of the Mabinogion from the hand of a surly Alison. The book tells the Welsh legend of Blodeuwedd, a tale of jealousy and violence. Then, the wood panelling in the billiard room breaks away to reveal a painting beneath – a painting of Blodeuwedd.

**Facing page:** Alison (Gillian Hills) becomes obsessed with tracing the flower pattern on an old dinner service to make paper owls – *The Owl Service*.

## Episode Three

'A Strange Picture…'

Sunday 4/1/70 patterns as above and Tuesday 20/10/70 ATV
Alison sneaks out of the house in the night, to a garden hut.
Frantically making her owls she is disturbed by Gwyn, who
comforts her. They spend the night there. Come the morning
Huw, talking gibberish, warns Gwyn of the evil to come.

## Episode Four

'The Plates Are Hidden…'

Sunday 11/1/70 patterns as above and Tuesday 27/10/70 ATV
Roger has developed photographs he has taken at the Stone
of Gronw – in the background of one can be made out a
figure waving a spear, in another a motorbike and rider.

## Episode Five

'The Missing Key…'

Sunday 18/1/70 patterns as above and Tuesday 3/11/70 ATV
Gwyn and Alison arrange to meet illicitly each day at four in
the afternoon, by the stables. Four days later Roger, Clive and
Alison are investigating a strange scratching sound coming
from a locked barn when Gwyn appears for his daily tryst.
Alison meekly allows herself to be led away by her stepfather.

## Episode Six

'Betrayal…'

Sunday 25/1/70 patterns as above and Tuesday 10/11/70 ATV
Alison tells Roger about the elocution records Gwyn has
bought to help rid himself of his accent and in the heat of an
argument Roger betrays the secret. Gwyn runs off and tries in
vain to climb the mountains and so escape the valley.

## Episode Seven

'Refuge in the Valley'

Sunday 1/2/70 patterns as above and Tuesday 17/11/70 ATV
In the hills Gwyn meets Huw. Huw confesses that many years
ago he killed Nancy's lover Bertram by accident when he
sabotaged the man's bike by way of a jealous prank. He then
reveals that he is Gwyn's father.

## Episode Eight

'The Legend Unravels'

Sunday 8/2/70 patterns as above and Tuesday 24/11/70 ATV
Roger discovers a stuffed owl and Bertram's old bike hidden
in the locked barn. A terrible rainstorm falls on the valley as
Alison finally becomes possessed by the ancient power and
the spirit of Blodeuwedd …

**Main Cast:** Michael Holden (Gwyn), Gillian Hills (Alison),
Francis Wallis (Roger), Edwin Richfield (Clive), Dorothy
Edwards (Nancy), Raymond Llewellyn (Huw)

Adapted from the novel by Alan Garner (first published 1967,
William Collins)

**Written by** Alan Garner
**Designer:** Peter Caldwell
**Producer:** Peter Plummer

First colour broadcast: 2/7/78 – 20/8/78; Sundays 5.45p.m. ITV

**Tie-in publications:** tie-in novel published by Peacock Books,
1969–70. *Filming The Owl Service – A Children's Diary* by
Ellen, Adam and Catherine Garner with Alan Garner and Peter
Plummer, published by Collins 1970 (hardback) and Armada
1971 (paperback).

# Redgauntlet

Scottish Television had enjoyed success with *Flight of the
Heron* in 1968 and another of their rare excursions into
serialised children's drama followed soon after. Like *Flight
of the Heron*, *Redgauntlet* centred upon the events of the 1745
Jacobite Rebellion, this time set in its aftermath.

Twenty years after the defeat of the Stuarts at Culloden,
Darsie Latimer leaves his Edinburgh college unconcerned
by such matters of history. He has an allowance from a
mother he never sees but still he wonders about his own
identity. He has always been told that he must never set
foot on English soil until he reaches twenty-five but has no
idea why. Finally Darsie's curiosity gets the better of him
and he sets out for the Solway Firth and Cumberland.
When Darsie arrives he is kidnapped by Cristal Nixon on
the instructions of the grizzled veteran of the '45,
Redgauntlet.

Darsie's friend Alan Fairford races off to rescue him
from Redgauntlet's clutches. Darsie's past is finally
revealed when he learns from the mysterious Greenmantle
that he is the son of the previous Laird of Redgauntlet and
the rightful heir to his title and estate. Redgauntlet,
brother to the laird who died at Culloden, has usurped
Darsie's birthright and has been using the Redgauntlet
fortune to fund his zealous desire for another Jacobite
uprising.

Scott's novel had been adapted for television by the
BBC in the late 50s, employing many Scottish actors in the
cast and with location filming in many of the novel's
genuine locations. For the 70s version Scottish writer Ian
Stuart Black provided the screenplay, while his daughter
Isobel played lady spy Greenmantle. This version
benefited from many filmed action sequences and a final
full-scale battle not likely to have been available to its
predecessor and these were no doubt its main draw.

*Redgauntlet* (1970)
**Scottish**
**8 episodes** ('The Man With the Sword'; 'Warning From a Lady';
'Race Against the Tide'; 'Held Prisoner'; 'The Trial'; 'The Storm';
'The Rebels'; 'Death of a Traitor')
(colour)
**Broadcast:** Wednesdays 7/1/70 – 25/2/70

**Main Cast:** Jack Watson (Redgauntlet), Roddy McMillan
(Cristal Nixon), James Grant (Darsie Latimer), Andrew
Robertson (Alan Fairford), Isobel Black (Greenmantle),
Malcolm Douglas (Tam), Isabel Begg (Lady Redgauntlet),
James Gibson (Wandering Willie), Taylor Smith (Maggie),
Walter Carr (James)

Based on the novel *Redgauntlet: A Tale of the Eighteenth
Century* by Sir Walter Scott (first UK publication 1824)

**Adapted by** Ian Stuart Black

**Designer:** Ron Franchetti
**Producer/Director:** Clarke Tait

*Redgauntlet* (1959)
**BBC**
**6 episodes**
(b&w)
**Broadcast:** Sundays 11/10/59 – 15/11/59

**Main Cast:** Tom Fleming (Redgauntlet), John Cairney (Alan Fairford), Donald Douglas (Darsie Latimer), Leonard Maguire (Mr Fairford), Terry Baker (Cristal Nixon), James Copeland (Joshua Geddes), Claire Isbister (Lilias Redgauntlet), Bryden Murdoch (Peter Peebles), Roddy McMillan (Captain Nanty Ewart)

**Adapted by** E. J. Bell

**Music:** Lawrence Leonard
**Designer:** Fanny Taylor
**Producer:** Kevin Sheldon

## A Stranger on the Hills

A short-run adaptation of the one of the more obscure winners of the Carnegie Medal fiction prize, obscured further by a substitution of title. Fifteen-year-old Nicholas Fetterlock is the son of a prosperous wool merchant in the Cotswolds of 1493, a typical middle-class fifteenth-century boy. The family's ordered life is turned upside down by the arrival of mysterious stranger Antonio de Bari, the Lombard, who places in jeopardy the Fetterlock family fortune.

Facing ruin, the only solution to their dissolution is for young Nicholas to marry Cecily Bradshaw, daughter of the moneyed Master Bradshaw, but Bradshaw senses the Fetterlock's imminent bankruptcy and is determined to refuse Nicholas his daughter's hand.

It's more than likely that this family saga was a 'children's hour' repeat broadcast of a *Merry-Go-Round* serial for schools.

**BBC South and West**
**3 episodes** ('The Lombard'; 'Cecily'; 'Thieves Discovered')
(b&w)
**Broadcast:** Mondays 2/2/70 – 16/2/70

**Main Cast:** Raymond Millross (Nicholas Fetterlock), Julian Sherrier (Antonio de Bari), Karen Newport (Cecily Bradshaw), Godfrey Quigley (Thomas Fetterlock), Michael Bird (Master Bradshaw), Thelma Barlow (Mistress Fetterlock), Angela Brooking (Mistress Bradshaw), Adrian Cairns (Master Richard), Artro Morris (Leach), Kenneth Watson (John Stern)

Based on the novel *The Wool-Pack* by Cynthia Harnett (first UK publication 1951, Methuen), aka *Nicholas and the Wool-Pack*
**Adapted by** John Elliot and Brian Miller

**Designers:** Desmond Chinn and Chris Robilliard
**Producer:** Brian Miller

## Catweazle

When Catweazle, an eleventh-century magician obsessed with flying but whose spells very rarely work, finds himself surrounded by Norman soldiers, the situation is desperate. He attempts to use his magic to fly away from his pursuers but instead travels through time, arriving in England 900 years in the future. Finding refuge in a nearby farmhouse he is befriended by a young boy called Carrot – the son of the farm owner.

Series creator and writer Richard Carpenter may well have taken inspiration from Barbara Euphan Todd's *Worzel Gummidge*, although at that point Worzel was still ten years

away from being adapted for television. The similarities between the two are not unnoticeable – a strange vagrant out of sorts with the human way of life becomes friends with local farm children and all become immersed in various comic escapades. Whereas *Worzel Gummidge* operated without any material end other than Worzel's infatuation with Aunt Sally, *Catweazle* had a definite premise driving the narrative – that of Catweazle's desire to escape the twentieth century and return home to his own time.

Regardless of the ongoing theme, the episode make-up is simple. Someone, usually Carrot, finds himself in a situation and relies on Catweazle to help, a sure passport to hilarious consequences and disastrous results. Carrot, deciding that Catweazle needs to be cleaned up, offers him use of the family bath with comedic results. Carrot's dad is ordered into the bank because he's 800 pounds in debt, which is a serious enough issue, except that Catweazle is on hand to unearth an ancient artefact with a street value of, yes you guessed it, 800 pounds. A failed spell and a missing pet leads Catweazle to believe that he's turned Carrot into a monkey.

At the end of the first season Catweazle at last discovers the way back home, leading to a touching farewell scene. The second season saw Catweazle once again returning to the twentieth century, this time in the grounds of King Farthing Manor where he meets Cedric, the son of Lord and Lady Collingford. In almost a carbon copy of the first season, Catweazle embarks on another thirteen comedy adventures, this time assisted by Cedric. The second season has a more pronounced structure – to return home Catweazle searches for the elusive thirteen signs of the Zodiac and each episode leads to the discovery of one of the signs. The last episode has a certain finality about it with Catweazle sailing off, in a similar manner to that of *The Wizard of Oz*, in a hot-air balloon.

A comparatively small cast of regulars was supplemented each week with various guest stars, including Peter Sallis, Bill Owen, Brian Wilde (anyone spotting a theme developing?), Hattie Jacques and Kenneth Cope. *Catweazle* became a highly respected children's series in its time and won the Writers Guild of Children's Broadcasting 1971 award for best children's TV drama script.

**Written by** Richard Carpenter

**London Weekend International**
**2 seasons**
(colour)

**Season One**
**13 episodes** ('The Sun in a Bottle'; 'Castle Saburac'; 'The Curse of Rapkyn'; 'The Witching Hour'; 'The Eye of Time'; 'The Magic Face'; 'The Telling Bone'; 'The Power of Adamcos'; 'The Demi Devil'; 'The House of the Sorcerer'; 'The Flying Broomsticks'; 'The Wisdom of Solomon'; 'The Trickery Lantern')
**Broadcast:** Sundays 15/2/70 – 10/5/70

**Main Cast:** Geoffrey Bayldon (Catweazle), Robin Davies (Carrot), Charles Tingwell (Mr Bennett), Neil McCarthy (Sam)

**Music Editor:** Ray Gravell
**Production Designer:** Evan Hercules
**Associate Producer:** Carl Mannin
**Executive Producer:** Joy Whitby
**Producer/ Director:** Quentin Lawrence

**Season Two**
**13 episodes** ('The Magic Riddle'; 'Duck Halt'; 'The Heavenly
Twins'; 'The Sign of the Crab'; 'The Black Wheels'; 'The Wogle
Stone'; 'The Enchanted King'; 'The Familiar Spirit'; 'The Ghost
Hunters'; 'The Walking Trees'; 'The Battle of the Giants';
'The Magic Circle'; 'The Thirteenth Sign')
**Broadcast:** Sundays 10/1/71 – 4/4/71

**Main Cast:** Geoffrey Bayldon (Catweazle), Gary Warren
(Cedric), Peter Butterworth (Groome), Moray Watson
(Lord Collingford), Elspet Gray (Lady Collingford)

**Story Editor:** Jeremy Godwin
**Supervising Editor:** Rod Nelson-Keys
**Production Designer:** Denys Pavitt
**Produced by** Carl Mannin
**Directors:** David Reid and David Lane

**Tie-in publications:** novelisations by Richard Carpenter.
*Catweazle* based on Season One episodes published in
paperback by Puffin, 1970. *Catweazle and the Magic Zodiac*
based on Season Two published in paperback by Puffin, 1971.

**Video:** both seasons released in their entirety across eight
cassettes by Network, 1998

## Smith

Typically entertaining Leon Garfield adventure where, by
circumstance and coincidence, a young urchin boy
becomes embroiled in hugely important wrongdoing.
Smith is a ruffianly yet rather sweetly innocent pickpocket
who one day purloins some seemingly rather worthless
papers from a gentleman's pocket only to see him
murdered a few minutes later. It transpires that the man
has been killed for the very document in Smith's
possession. Three mysterious men, Mr Black, Grey and
Brown, want that document and Smith now knows full
well what they will do to get it back. Smith can't read but
his sisters are sure that it promises a fortune to the bearer
of the deed. Smith finds a blind magistrate with a claim to
the papers and finds himself helping him, hoping to earn
his share of the spoils while trying to stay alive.

A fun production with its tongue firmly in its cheek, it
was also exciting, not just for its use of a bad boy hero but
also for hinted-at gore and the threat of imminent violence
and murder.

**Thames**
**8 episodes** ('Not Nubbed Yet'; 'Finders, Keepers'; 'Live and
Learn'; 'Blind Justice'; 'A Long Spoon'; 'The Newgate Star';
'The Black Angel'; 'God Save the King!')
(colour)
**Broadcast:** Wednesdays 4/3/70 – 22/4/70

**Main Cast:** Ian Ramsey (Smith), Jo Rowbottom (Bridget),
Cheryl Hall (Fanny), David Sumner (Mr Billing), Leon Collins
(Mr Brown), Michael Goldie (Mr Grey), George Innes
(Mr Black), Windsor Davies (Mr Welsh), Louise Dunn (Meg),

Lewis Fiander (Lord Tom), Michael Beint (Joseph), Moultrie
Kensall (Mr Mansfield), Meg Wynn Owen (Miss Mansfield)

**Based on the novel by Leon Garfield** (first UK publication
1967, Constable)
**Dramatised by** Stanley Miller

**Designer:** Roger Allen
**Producer:** Pamela Lonsdale
**Director:** Michael Currer-Briggs

## Ace of Wands

Tarot is an enigmatic stage magician and escapologist
with telepathic capabilities who, in his spare time, solves
mysteries of a strange or magical nature. Three close
friends assist Tarot in his adventures. The first of these is
twenty-year-old orphan girl Lillian Palmer, known as
Lulli, who shares a telepathic link with Tarot, allowing
them to perform amazing feats on stage and
communicate while several miles apart. Sam Maxstead, a
worldly cockney, has spent time in prison and held down
a variety of jobs. He now acts as Tarot's stage manager but
also has the handy knack of being able to open locks,
essential in many of Tarot's investigations. Mr Sweet, the
elderly owner of an antiquarian bookshop, completes the
team. He acts as Tarot's front man and has a vast number
of contacts in different areas, an excellent resource for
Tarot's enquiries.

In essence, writer Trevor Preston created a crime series
but, in writing the main character as a magician who dealt
increasingly in crimes of the supernatural, he broadened
the scope of potential script ideas, which in turn allowed
the development of some eye-catching, innovative stories.

Although there is the presence of magic and fantasy in
the first season, Tarot's initial investigations are a little
more conventional – here E-Type-Jaguar-driving Tarot
enjoys adventures more in a *Freewheelers* vein. Tarot tackles
Madame Midnight to recover an invention capable of
reversing paralysis but which could also cause great
damage in the wrong hands. He next has to recover two
missing government officials captured by Senor Zendor.
The magician then finds himself up against Falk, a villain
working in league with Nazis. Finally, Tarot battles against
Tun-Ju, an art thief who has successfully stolen *Venus* and
now plans to swipe the *Mona Lisa*.

For Season Two the emphasis on magic and fantasy
increased. Tarot still finds himself trying to recover a
stolen top-secret gas but the story has a science fiction
edge to it as the gas is capable of inducing deep sleep and
killing people through the power of nightmares.
Ceribraun, a crippled chess master, plans to steal a
priceless diamond. While attempting to stop him, Tarot
finds himself held prisoner by a talking computer and
harassed by giant chess pieces. 'Joker', P. J. Hammond's
first story, concerns the disturbing tale of ordinarily well-
behaved children suddenly going mad and destroying their
classrooms. 'Seven Serpents, Sulphur and Salt' is one of
Preston's favourite stories and also his last for the series. It
introduces the well-remembered villain, Mr Stabs, a
corrupt magician of the brotherhood. Many people who
fondly recall the series are often under the impression that
Stabs was a recurring villain and Tarot's nemesis. This is far
from the truth and he in fact only appeared in one story.
Preston would later revive the character in two anthology
series, *Shadows* and *Dramarama*.

It should be noted that Thames' master tapes for seasons one and two were completely destroyed, an act Preston described as 'typical vandalism by a television company'. Following completion of the second season, both Tony Selby and Judy Loe opted not to return for the third. Both actors had commitments but Loe seemed discontent with her contribution to the show, stating, 'My part was decorative even in a children's programme. I was allowed some intelligence, but was always having to be rescued by the man.' Two new characters, brother and sister Mikki and Chas, were brought in as replacements. Rather than change a winning formula, it was decided that Mikki too would have a telepathic link with Tarot. Both Petra Markham and Roy Holder played the characters as if younger than themselves but any fears that the series would become more juvenile were dispelled in a season of even more sophisticated and adult storylines.

Inventive narratives brought to the fore bizarre crimes of the mind. The season's zenith is perhaps Tarot's encounter with the haunting Mr Peacock, an old man with extraordinary powers of suggestion. Written by P. J. Hammond, the story contains ideas he would develop for his future project, *Sapphire and Steel*. 'Peacock Pie' made it clear to the audience that Tarot was not invulnerable. He is clearly unable to defeat Peacock and wins through only because the old man gives up through boredom at his own omnipotence. Tarot also deals with Mama Doc in a sinister story where people are turned into dolls. 'The Beautiful People' sees Tarot tackling extra-terrestrials with the power to exert control over inanimate objects.

The production was largely studio-bound with small sections of location filming. Restrictions were such when the programme started that the crew were limited to a maximum of three minutes of outside filming for every twenty-six-minute episode. The crew were also unable to film outside a thirty-mile radius of the Teddington Studios but this at least allowed them free rein of London and the Thames. Preston wanted Tarot's magic tricks to look as professional as possible and TV magician Ali Bongo was therefore hired to tutor MacKenzie in the required skills.

*Ace of Wands* was replaced by *The Tomorrow People* and although this would turn out to be just as popular, if not more so, than its predecessor it certainly lacked the innovative, intelligent writing and dashing hero that bestows upon *Ace of Wands* a real touch of class.

**Thames**
**3 seasons**
**46 episodes**
(colour)

**Main Cast:** Michael MacKenzie (Tarot), Tony Selby (Sam – Seasons 1 and 2), Judy Loe (Lulli – Seasons 1 and 2), Donald Layne-Smith (Mr Sweet), Roy Holder (Chas – Season 3), Petra Markham (Mikki – Season 3), Fred Owl (Ozymandias the owl)

**Created by** Trevor Preston
**Music:** Andrew Bown (stock incidental music also used)
**Producers:** Pamela Lonsdale (Seasons 1 and 2), John Russell (Season 3)

**Season One**
**4 stories** (13 episodes)
**Broadcast:** Wednesdays 29/7/70 – 21/10/70 5.20p.m.

**'One and One and One Makes Four'** by Trevor Preston
**3 episodes:** 29/7/70 – 12/8/70
**Designer:** Tony Borer
**Director:** John Russell

**'The Mind Robbers'** by William Emms
**4 episodes:** 19/8/70 – 9/9/70
**Designer:** Bernard Spencer
**Director:** Michael Currer-Briggs

**'Now You See It, Now You Don't'** by Don Houghton
**2 episodes:** 16/9/70 – 23/9/70
**Designer:** Colin Andrews
**Director:** John Russell

**'The Smile'** by Trevor Preston
**4 episodes:** 30/9/70 – 21/10/70
**Designer:** Frank Gillman
**Director:** Michael Currer-Briggs

**Season Two**
**4 stories** (13 episodes)
**Broadcast:** Wednesdays 21/7/71 – 13/10/71 5.20p.m.

**'Seven Serpents, Sulphur and Salt'** by Trevor Preston
**3 episodes:** 21/7/71 – 4/8/71
**Designer:** Tony Borer
**Director:** Pamela Lonsdale

**Above:** the first season team from Thames' *Ace of Wands*; (l to r) Sam (Tony Selby), master magician Tarot (Michael MacKenzie), Lulli (Judy Loe) and Mr Sweet (Donald Layne-Smith) say hello to feathered friend Ozymandias the owl.

**'Joker'** by P. J. Hammond
**3 episodes:** 11/8/71 – 25/8/71
**Designer:** Bernard Spencer
**Director:** John Russell

**'Nightmare Gas'** by Don Houghton
**3 episodes:** 1/9/71 – 15/9/71
**Designer:** Harry Clark
**Director:** Ronald Marriott

**'The Eye of Ra'** by Michael Winder
**4 episodes:** 22/9/71 – 13/10/71
**Designer:** Bernard Spencer
**Director:** John Russell

**Season Three**
**6 stories** (20 episodes)
**Broadcast:** Wednesdays 19/7/72 – 29/11/72 (times varied for different stories – 5.20, 4.50 and 4.25p.m.)

**'The Meddlers'** by P. J. Hammond
**3 episodes:** 19/7/72 – 2/8/72
**Designer:** Bill Palmer
**Director:** John Russell

**'The Power of Atep'** by Victor Pemberton
**4 episodes:** 9/8/72 – 30/8/72
**Designer:** Harry Clark
**Director:** Nicholas Ferguson

**'Peacock Pie'** by P. J. Hammond
**3 episodes:** 6/9/72 – 20/9/72
**Designer:** Gordon Toms
**Director:** John Russell

**'Mama Doc'** by Maggie Allen
**3 episodes:** 27/9/72 – 11/10/72
**Designer:** Philip Blowers
**Director:** Nicholas Ferguson

**'Sisters Deadly'** by Victor Pemberton
**3 episodes:** 18/10/72 – 1/11/72
**Designer:** Andrew Drummond
**Director:** Darrol Blake

**'The Beautiful People'** by P. J. Hammond
**4 episodes:** 8/11/72 – 29/11/72
**Designer:** Eric Shedden
**Director:** Vic Hughes

## Timeslip

As an ITV rival to *Doctor Who*, *Timeslip* upped the ante by making this a series *about* time travel, in preference to using it as a very sophisticated bus that could take the heroes from one separate adventure to another. Thus we saw threads from the same characters' lives at different points in time. These included the leads themselves – Simon Randall met himself as a technocratic scientist twenty years into the future while Liz Skinner, even more complicatedly, had two alternate time streams, one in which she was a cold-hearted scientist and another where she had turned out a friendly earth-mother.

In addition to this, *Timeslip* was set up as *serial* of serials, all of the episodes heading towards a satisfying resolution

**Above:** Simon Randall (Spencer Banks) and Liz Skinner (Cheryl Burfield) trespassing on Ministry of Defence property at the beginning of their adventure in time – *Timeslip*.

by either building upon previous adventures or apparently contradicting them. A logistical nightmare but one which the serial overcame with aplomb in its twenty-six-week run, a span making it perhaps the most ambitious serial of the 70s in storytelling terms at least.

The complex time travel ideas were also backed up by some time travel theory. In the dialogue these came courtesy of the series' scientific adviser Geoffrey Hoyle and there were also presentation links from ITN's science correspondent Peter Fairley to open the first two stories. These rather fanciful theories are the weakest science presented in the series, time apparently being a series of bubbles that you could step into. Elsewhere, the science behind the fiction was spot-on. Innovative notions of cloning were presented throughout the series and the serial earned its 'prophetic' tag after predicting the collapse of the ozone layer and the onset of global warming.

Now recognised as a cult science fiction show among fans of that genre, it's easy to forget that this was intended as children's fare. As such, the child leads act in very much the prescribed manner of the time. Their gender roles are very traditional, Simon explaining all the scientific wonders and Liz generally doing lots of screaming. Despite both being teenagers, Simon comes across at times as a rather pre-pubescent little boy more interested in science than silly girls, seemingly oblivious to Liz's running around in tight trousers. Usually the two share a 'babes in the wood' type relationship and, while he isn't quite pulling her pigtails, Simon is often dismissive of Liz ('You're always getting scared or bursting into tears'). To be fair, Liz has one wonderfully assertive moment where she shouts at one of her future selves, 'You're a rotten old cow and what's more you're not even pretty!' Through their adventures Liz and Simon do begin to depend on each other and there's a lovely moment right at the end of the final adventure which sees the two walk off arm in arm, finally having grown up that little bit.

The opening story, 'The Wrong End of Time', was in a very traditional vein. The gypsy-caravanning holiday that Liz and Simon are on when we first meet them is pure Enid Blyton. Similarly the storyline, of travelling back in time to encounter marauding Nazis, is one of escape and capture runaround. It's Liz meeting her father as he was thirty years ago that suggests the sophistication to come. Meanwhile, the sinister machinations of the ambivalent Commander Traynor (who also exists in the 1940 time period) hint at a far-reaching plot. One of this adventure's best moments comes when Liz is shot by a Nazi's revolver. She survives since she does not really exist in this time (another sign of the series' scientific pretensions) but nonetheless, for those familiar with the sort of villains who are regularly outwitted by small children and who couldn't fight their way out of a paper bag, it's a genuinely frightening moment.

Thereafter the stories step up a gear as the complex continuity of the time zones begins to knit together. 'The Year of the Burn-Up' is probably the series' finest instalment and not only because of its foresight. Here Traynor is now a deranged lunatic, appearing genuinely dangerous rather than merely scheming. Simon is left to wonder how he can avoid becoming the self-obsessed 2957 by 1990 while Liz is left with a similar quandary, pondering which path leads to the caring Beth of the Burn-Up and which to the hard-hearted Beth of the Ice Box. The conclusion to 'Burn-Up' is very downbeat, Simon returning to 1970 and musing on England's apparent destruction in 1990: 'By now it's probably over.' The final story sees them fight to avert either projected technological nightmare.

Many serials have sagged over even a thirteen-week period but, aside from its rather slow-moving opening instalment and a muddled handover between the third and fourth serials, *Timeslip* sustained itself marvellously over a half-year of adventure. A comic strip in *Look-In* which ran until the end of 1972 helped prolong its memory as did a complete repeat showing in 1973–74.

**ATV**
**26 episodes**
(colour; some episodes transmitted in black and white due to industrial action)

**Main Cast:** Spencer Banks (Simon Randall), Cheryl Burfield (Liz Skinner), Denis Quilley (Commander Traynor), Iris Russell (Jean Skinner), Derek Benfield (Frank Skinner)

**Created by** Ruth and James Boswell
**Written by** Bruce Stewart (episodes 1–19) and Victor Pemberton (episodes 20–26)

**Scientific Adviser:** Geoffrey Hoyle
**Script Editor:** Ruth Boswell
**Producer:** John Cooper

**Episodes 1–6**
**'The Wrong End of Time'**
**Broadcast:** Mondays 28/9/70 – 2/11/70 5.10 and 5.15p.m. ATV and rest of network
Fridays 2/10/70 – 6/11/70 5.15p.m. Thames and Southern
**Designer:** Gerry Roberts
**Director:** John Cooper

**Episodes 7–12**
**'The Time of the Ice Box'**
**Broadcast:** Mondays 9/11/70 – 14/12/70 5.10 and 5.15p.m. ATV and network
Fridays 13/11/70 – 18/12/70 5.15p.m. Thames/Southern
**Guest Cast:** Mary Preston (Beth), John Barron (Devereaux)
**Designer:** Michael Eve
**Director:** Peter Jefferies

**Episodes 13–20**
**'The Year of the Burn-Up'**
**Broadcast:** Mondays 21/12/70 – 8/2/71 5.10 and 5.15p.m. ATV and network
Fridays 25/12/71 – 12/2/71 5.15p.m. Thames/Southern
**Guest Cast:** Mary Preston (Beth), David Graham (2957)
**Designer:** Michael Eve (14–19), Gerry Roberts (13 and 20)
**Director:** Peter Jefferies (14–19), Ron Francis (13 and 20)

**Episodes 21–26**
**'The Day of the Clone'**
**Broadcast:** Mondays 15/2/71 – 22/3/71 5.10 and 5.15p.m. ATV and network
Fridays 19/2/71 – 26/3/71 5.15p.m. Thames/Southern
**Guest Cast:** John Barron (Devereaux)
**Designer:** Gerry Roberts
**Director:** Dave Foster (21–24), Ron Francis (25 and 26)

**Tie-in publications:** Paperback novelisation of 'The Wrong End of Time' and 'The Time of the Ice Box' (titled *Timeslip*) by 'Bruce Stewart on an original format by J. and R. Boswell' published by Pan Books, 1970 (black cover). Second edition by Piccolo, 1971 (red cover).

**Video release:** Four double-tape packs of all episodes released by ITC Home Video. All episodes as black and white only, advert breaks and ATV captions removed.
'The Wrong End of Time', released 8/2/93, deleted 1/8/96.
'The Time of the Ice Box', released 24/5/93, deleted 31/7/96.
'The Year of the Burn-Up', released 23/8/93, deleted 1/8/96.
'The Day of the Clone', released 24/1/94, deleted 10/4/97.

NB: Although it is something of an academic argument – since the original colour tapes of *Timeslip* have long been wiped or lost – all colour transmissions were in doubt from episode 16 onwards due to industrial action at ITV in spring 1971. Some records suggest that episodes 22, 23 and 26 were possibly recorded and transmitted in black and white only (even though original location filming material would have been in colour). For the 1973–74 repeat run the *TV Times* listed episodes 16, 25 and 26 as being b&w.

## Wreckers at Dead Eye

A ferocious night in 1770 and another storm-lashed ship crashes into the deadly rocks at Dead Eye after following a flickering light on the shore. The disasters are not accidents, however – they are organised by the Wreckers, inhabitants of a small coastal village called Thriabbas who use their lanterns to lure ships onto the rocks so that they can loot the cargo.

The villagers' luck takes a downward turn when a survivor from their latest act of piracy, an eastern girl called Soraya, manages to swim ashore. They must find her and silence her before she can reach the authorities and give evidence against them. The only villagers not involved in the criminal activities are the occupants of Moor House, home of retired sea captain Shadrach, his bosun Tobias, niece Caroline and stable lad Zac. They must find Soraya and get her to safety before the Wreckers catch her.

The series was filmed entirely on location at Westleton in Suffolk, Walton-on-the-Naze in Essex, but mainly on the East Anglia coast.

**Wreckers at Dead Eye**
**Thames**
**6 episodes** ('The Stranger'; 'Hand of Evil'; 'The Legend of Thriabbas'; 'Boomer Hole'; 'Ship in the Night';
'Shivering Sands')
(colour)
**Broadcast:** Wednesdays 28/10/70 – 2/12/70

**Main Cast:** Claire Benjamin (Soraya), Jack Allen (Shadrach), Catherine Organ (Caroline), Arthur Lovegrove (Tobias), Tom Owen (Zac), Arthur White (Eye Patch), Jack Smethurst (Jon-Jo)

**Written by** Paddy Manning O'Brine

**Designer:** Frank Gillman
**Producers:** Adrian Cooper and Paddy Manning O'Brine
**Director:** Adrian Cooper

## Joe and the Gladiator

Joe Darling is a teenage apprentice on the Newcastle shipyards who, to his surprise, befriends old Ted Prodhurst the rag-and-bone-man and his horse Gladiator. Joe does not have his problems to seek – Gran living in the family home is setting his Dad against his Mam and his parents threaten to separate; at work he has to put up with the bullying ways of his boss and the daft banter of fairweather friend Willie Styles. When Old Ted dies he leaves Gladiator to Joe and, though he cannot really afford to, he selflessly devotes his time to looking after the old nag. By doing so he earns the respect of many in the community.

This was one of the earliest modern dramas to be made by the BBC Children's Department and, as Anna Home recalls, the budget was so low that the crew had to double up as costume and design. Surprisingly, for what was really no more than a toe in the water, the crew did not stay in the environs of Shepherd's Bush but instead travelled to the book's real locations of South Shields, Tyneside and Wallsend to film the three episodes. The short run was all that could be afforded – in a reverse of the way Home had added drama inserts to late 60s' *Jackanory* tales, a narrator's commentary would be used to fill in those scenes that couldn't be included within the runtime.

The genuine locations added hugely to the working-class realism of it all although it's reported that Dennis Lingard, as Joe, was asked to moderate his Geordie accent for the sake of a wider audience. Lingard was certainly an authentic 'actor' and was back working on the docks and on the buses after his starring role. Working against the realism of the backdrop was the sentimental and unlikely ending to Catherine Cookson's tale in which it transpires that Old Ted had in fact set Joe a test. When Joe keeps the horse safe and well for two months, a solicitor advises him that the poor old rag-and-bone-man had left more than £2,000 to Joe in his will should this condition be met.

**BBC**
**3 episodes** ('Taggerine Ted'; 'Gladiator in Danger'; 'The Letter')
(colour)
**Broadcast:** Mondays 22/2/71 – 8/3/71

**Main Cast:** Dennis Lingard (Joe Darling), James Garbutt (Mr Prodhurst and as 'Storyteller'), Sheila Whitmill (Anna Billings), Ursula Smith (Mrs Darling), Richard Steele (Mr Darling), Ken Purvis (Willie Styles)

Based on the novel by Catherine Cookson (first UK publication 1968, Macdonald)
**Adapted by** Anna Home

**Producer/Director:** Anna Home

**Tie-in publications:** editions of novel published in paperback by Puffin, 1971–76

## Island of the Great Yellow Ox

When a terrifying storm washes Conor, his little brother Babo, and their two American friends up on to Ox Island, off the coast of Ireland, they become prisoners of the eccentric Lady Agnes and the Captain. This pair of scallywags are determined to uncover the Druid treasure they know is hidden somewhere on the island and these unwelcome children will not be allowed to get in the way.

This was another of the earliest three-part serials attempted by the BBC's embryonic Drama Unit and is remarkable for its being a co-production with the Irish broadcaster RTE – an enterprising way of finding more budget. The cast largely comprised Irish actors. As with *Joe and the Gladiator*, a storyteller was used to cram the story into the compressed timescale while saving money on the more difficult to achieve scenes.

**BBC/RTE Co-production**
**3 episodes**
(colour)
**Broadcast:** Mondays 15/3/71 – 29/3/71

**Main Cast:** Brian Sullivan (Conor), Jimmy O'Toole (Babo), Sandra Ross (Mary), Simon Tully (George), Harry Towb (Captain), Blanaid Irvine (Lady Agnes)
and with Oliver Maguire as 'The Storyteller'

Based on the novel by Walter Macken (first UK publication 1966, Macmillan)
**Adapted by** Marilyn Fox

**Director:** Marilyn Fox

## Jamie

*Timeslip* had been a huge success, so further time travel adventures for children seemed inevitable. *Jamie* was the story of a boy who bought a magic carpet which could not only fly through the air but also travel in time. This led to the sort of adventures which attempted to bring the history books to life, with Jamie and his friend Tink meeting Guy Fawkes, Robert the Bruce and William, Duke of Normandy, along the way and fighting alongside Nelson at Trafalgar.

Jamie was encouraged in his travels by the enigmatic Mr Zed, who seemed to know an inordinate amount about Jamie's carpet. The series was by and large intended as an exciting adventure serial, so Jamie and Tink would, for example, get caught up in events in nineteenth-century London and lose the carpet, leading to a desperate race to get it back and return to the present.

The series also took an interesting position regarding theories of time travel. In the episode 'Remember, Remember' Mr Zed suggests Jamie try to change history and warn the gunpowder conspirators of treachery afoot.

Jamie's warnings are unheeded, however, and he is suspected of being a spy. History runs its destined course and Jamie has been unable to affect what has gone before. Later journeying to 1666 and the time of the Great Fire of London, Jamie's attempts to prevent the fire appear to have failed when it begins as expected. However, Mr Zed tells Jamie that without his intervention the fire would have been much worse – on this occasion Jamie has become part of history.

Perhaps the sweetest tale comes in 'Summer Holiday'. When Jamie tries to tell his parents that he owns a magic carpet they refuse to believe him and so Jamie travels back in time to meet his father when he was Jamie's age. The two boys share an adventure but on Jamie's return to the present day he is dismayed to find that his father's grown-up attitudes remain the same – time has eroded his father's capacity for imagination.

**LWT**
**13 episodes** ('The Carpet'; 'Remember, Remember'; 'Sugar Islands'; 'England Expects'; 'Summer Holiday'; 'Prince of Fire'; 'The Climbing Boy'; 'The Devil's Rookery'; 'London Bridge is Falling Down'; 'New Lamps For Old'; 'Ettercap'; 'The Last Adventure'; 'Dragon's Wake')
(colour)
**Broadcast:** Sundays 6/6/71 – 5/9/71 (no broadcast 15/8/71 due to sports coverage. Series fully networked except in ATV region which broadcast from Sunday 25/7/71)

**Main Cast:** Garry Miller (Jamie Dodger), Nigel Chivers (Tink Bellow), Aubrey Morris (Mr Zed), Jo Kendall (Molly Dodger), Ben Aris (David Dodger)

**Written by** Denis Butler

**Theme Music:** Larry Adler
**Designers:** Roger Hall (1, 2, 5–7, 9, 10), David Catley (3, 4, 8, 11–13)
**Producer:** Anthony Kearey
**Executive Producer:** Francis Coleman
**Directors:** Anthony Kearey (1, 2, 5), Geoffrey Nethercott (3, 4), Bryan Izzard (6, 11), John Reardon (7, 8, 12, 13), David Coulter (9, 10)

## Follyfoot

The 70s might well have been a time of strictly defined gender roles when horses were 'a girl's thing' but if you remember *Follyfoot* as the twee, picturesque adventures of frolicking foals then you're very much mistaken. Aimed squarely at an adolescent rather than child audience, *Follyfoot* was a well-written series that never shied away from emotional complexities, cruelty and violence despite its sunny backdrop of the rolling Yorkshire Dales.

The central character was Dora, a teenage girl who doesn't fit in with the upper-crust set she has been born into. When her parents leave for a government commission in Brazil, Dora is left with her Uncle Geoffrey at his country mansion. Dora finds that the vast, lifeless house is dull compared with the 'retirement home' for old nags which Uncle runs as a hobby. Here she finds new purpose caring for the waifs and strays but also discovers that managing her new found independence isn't easy and brings all kinds of attendant problems.

A great ensemble cast are fondly remembered but,

**Above:** time-traveller *Jamie* (Garry Miller, right) and his friend Tink (Nigel Chivers) ponder the mystery of Mr Zed (Aubrey Morris). How is Jamie's destiny linked with that of this enigmatic stranger?

again, possibly inaccurately. They are not always the cheery bunch who jape around for the camera in the series' title sequence. Steve has a criminal record, but is an intelligent rough diamond with the same love for horses as Dora. Ron Stryker can sometimes be the joker but it's continually hinted that he keeps shady company and he retains an uneasy mystery throughout the series. Slugger is usually there for comic relief, a trusty ex-boxer who looks after Dora and offers kindly advice. Uncle Geoffrey is 'The Colonel' who can have run-ins with Dora when her sentimentality means Follyfoot takes on more strays than it can handle. All of the characters interact brilliantly, most realistically portrayed in 'Rain on Friday' – an episode which sees them cooped up in the house all day amid rising tensions and home truths.

The half-hour drama form can sometimes lead to rather too neat and contrived instalments but *Follyfoot* excelled with clever continuity and running storylines played out over several episodes. This was no doubt made possible by having one writer pen the bulk of the episodes. Thus the series was able to cover more ambiguous ideas with greater subtlety than a 'story of the week' affair while retaining consistency of character. Characters could develop over the series' run, with each season able to shift emphasis but still forming a coherent whole.

There were inevitably some format and character changes each season. Season One saw the regulars joined by a couple of younger 'staff', Callie and Gip, who were enthusiastic but sometimes irresponsible. In 'Moonstone' Callie steals a circus horse she thinks is being maltreated and in 'Know-All's Nag' Gip learns that sometimes you have to let more experienced heads help out.

Season Two closed with the Colonel very ill and Dora facing the choice of taking on the running of Follyfoot or returning to live with her parents, now returned from Brazil, and this set up the third-season format where Dora struggles with the responsibility of being Mistress of Follyfoot. This theme was most explicit in 'The Distant Voice' where Dora learns to make her own decisions instead of second-guessing what her Uncle would have done. 63

**Above:** Dora (Gillian Blake) and Steve (Steve Hodson) tend to the horses of Follyfoot Farm.

The consistently challenging third season also saw a new Nemesis for the folk of Follyfoot in the shape of bent horse-dealer Lockwood. Added complications came in the shape of his son Chip, whose amorous intentions towards Dora are initially reciprocated until she realises Chip's loyalty to his father and a tendency to turn a blind eye to Mr Lockwood's cruelty to animals. Season Three also includes the violent 'The Dream' where Dora (rather inexplicably) predicts a bloodied Steve standing up for what he believes, a scenario which to her disgust comes true.

Romance is a staple of the teenage series but there are no soft-focus tales of soppiness here. Dora's love life seems to consist of an unspoken attachment to Steve which leads to tensions and stand-up arguments. In 'The Prize' Dora is jealous of the time Steve devotes to the pretty Wendy and in 'The Awakening' Steve is furious when he believes the Colonel is trying to set up an aristocratic marriage for Dora and Lord Beck (Anthony Andrews). 'Uncle Joe' sees Dora develop a crush on an older man (played by David Hemmings, who was also a director on several episodes this season).

The chief strength of the scripts is that they are not just stories of mistreated horses. The horses are a means to an end, a device to illustrate the failings of their human owners. Cruelty and selfishness are universal weaknesses whose victims in this case happen to be horses. 'Miss Him When He's Gone' is the story of a family living in a street that is being torn down around them (proof that *Follyfoot* was not exclusively concerned with rural idyll). The itinerant father becomes very ill and his zealous son sees this as a chance to gain control of the old man's fruit cart. The horse that pulls this cart leads to Dora's involvement but that's not what the episode is about. When the old

man is killed setting fire to the cart and stables, so as to prevent his son taking over the business, it's Dora's feelings of complicity in his death and her horror at the total lack of grief shown by the family who hated him that are the focus.

A very thoughtful series of hard lessons, nonetheless *Follyfoot* was phenomenally popular with its target audience and beyond. Teenage fans treated the young leads as pop pin-ups while books, jigsaws and even a board game stand as testament to the series' success. Moving to a Sunday afternoon slot for Season Two, the series attracted a large contingent of adult viewers. The series became one of the few programmes for children to make the Top Twenty ratings when 'The Debt' was watched in 5.2 million homes. The series was sold to twenty countries and was a huge hit in Germany in particular where it was known as *Follyfoot Farm*, a name often mistakenly recalled as the original UK title.

Comparisons with the other equine phenomenon of the early 70s – *The Adventures of Black Beauty* – are inevitable. While never as lavishly staged as its period rival, *Follyfoot* was certainly first out of the trap, a full fifteen months ahead of *Beauty* and perhaps even spawning the LWT series. It also boasted scripts that were more than a match for its rival's more tidy adventures. Was it a coincidence that LWT was the only ITV region to move *Follyfoot* from its prime Sunday slot to Saturday mornings for the third season, or was it a case of knobbling the front runner?

**3 seasons**
(colour)

**Main Cast** (all three seasons): Gillian Blake (Dora), Steve Hodson (Steve), Arthur English (Slugger), Christian Rodska (Ron Stryker), Desmond Llewellyn (The Colonel)

**Season One**
**Yorkshire**
**13 episodes** ('Dora'; 'Steve'; 'Gypsy'; 'Shadow'; 'One White Foot Charley'; 'The Charity Horse'; 'Know-All's Nag'; 'Moonstone'; 'Stryker's Good Deed'; 'Mr She-Knows'; 'The Standstill Horse'; 'Birthday at Follyfoot'; 'A Day in the Sun')
**Broadcast:** Mondays 28/6/71 – 20/9/71 in most regions (shown Fridays 2/7/71 – 24/9/71 Thames, Southern, Grampian)

**Additional Cast:** Gillian Bailey (Callie), Bryan Sweeney (Gip), Paul Guess (Lewis)

**Written by** Francis Stevens (1–3, 5–8, 10, 11, 13), Audley Southcott (4, 12), Audley Southcott and Jennifer Stuart (9)
Based on *Cobbler's Dream* by Monica Dickens (first UK publication 1961, Michael Joseph)

**Theme song:** 'The Lightning Tree' by Steven Francis, sung by The Settlers
**Incidental scores** by Robert Sharples, Trevor Duncan, Dennis Farnon
**Art Director:** Geoffrey Martin
**Producer:** Audley Southcott
**Executive Producer:** Tony Essex
**Directors:** Stephen Frears (1, 6, 7), Frederic Goode (2, 4), Ian McFarlane (3, 5, 11), Michael Apted (8), Maurice Hatton (9), Vic Hughes (10), Michael Tuchner (12), Mike Purcell (13)

**Season Two**
**Yorkshire**
**13 episodes** ('Someone Somewhere'; 'The Debt'; 'Family of Strangers'; 'Present for Sandy'; 'The Innocents'; 'The Hundred Pound Horse'; 'Poor Bald Head'; 'The Prize'; 'Treasure Hunt'; 'Debt of Honour'; 'Out-of-the-Blue Horse'; 'The Awakening'; 'Fly Away Home')
**Broadcast:** Sundays 28/5/72 – 27/8/72 fully networked (only slight timing variations apply)

**Written by** Francis Stevens (1, 2, 4, 5, 7–9, 11–13), Francis Stevens from a story by Christine Bright (3), Rosemary Anne Sisson (6, 10)

**Executive Producer:** Tony Essex
**Directors:** Claude Whatham (1, 2), Desmond Davis (3–5, 12, 13), Jack Cardiff (6, 8), Michael Apted (7), Gerry Mill (9, 10), Peter Hammond (11)

**Season Three**
**A Yorkshire Television/Tele-Munich Co-production**
**13 episodes** ('The Distant Voice'; 'The Four Legged Hat'; 'Barney'; 'Miss Him When He's Gone'; 'The Dream'; 'The Challenge'; 'The Letter'; 'The Bridge Builder'; 'Uncle Joe'; 'The Helping Hand'; 'Rain on Friday'; 'Hazel'; 'Walk in the Wood')

**Broadcast:** Sundays 24/6/73 – 16/9/73 (Networked but some episodes missed by Scottish. LWT broadcasts Saturdays 23/6/73 – 15/9/73 initially evenings, later moved to morning)

**Additional Cast:** Frederick Treves (Sam Lockwood), Nigel Crewe (Chip Lockwood), Veronica Quilligan (Hazel)

**Written by** Francis Stevens (1–8, 10–13), Francis Stevens from a story by Rosemary Gee (9)

**Art Directors:** Howard Dawson, Geoffrey Martin, Ray Berger, Christine Kinder
**Executive Producer:** Tony Essex
**Directors:** Stephen Frears (1), Gareth Davies (2), R. Thomas (3), Peter Hammond (4, 9), Ken Hannam (5), Jack Cardiff (6, 7), David Hemmings (8, 13), Anthony Thomas (10), Michael Tuchner (11, 12)

**Tie-in publications:** four novels by Monica Dickens published by Piccolo (paperback) and William Heinemann (hardback). *Follyfoot*, 1971. *Dora at Follyfoot*, 1972. Both books reprinted as *Follyfoot Farm*, William Heinemann (hardback only), 1973. *The Horses of Follyfoot*, 1975. *Stranger at Follyfoot*, 1976. *Follyfoot Pony Quiz Book* by Christine Pullein-Thompson, published by Piccolo, 1974.
*Follyfoot, Dora at Follyfoot, Horses of Follyfoot, Stranger at Follyfoot* reprinted in paperback with new tie-in covers by William Heinemann, 1988.
Annuals published by World Distributors 1972–1976 (cover dated 1973–1977)
*Look-In Follyfoot Special*, 64-page magazine, summer 1973.

**Video:** first three episodes ('Dora', 'Steve', 'Gypsy') issued by Polygram Video. Released 8/5/95. Deleted 1/8/96.

## The Witch's Daughter

This Nina Bawden tale was to provide another step on the way to provide proper drama made for children at the end of the 60s. When adapted for *Jackanory* (transmitted 18/11/68 – 22/11/68, since destroyed) the narration was accompanied by a small amount of live action drama, directed by Anna Home. Though the results were not stunning these were the first inserts to include spoken dialogue.

The benefits of this policy could be seen three years later with a five-part live action adaptation of the same story. It's a very traditional adventure serial, with jewel thieves uncovered by a gang of children who find themselves in danger among Blyton-esque caves but it was enlivened by extensive location work on the beautiful but forbidding island of Mull off the West Coast of Scotland (production was completed with subsequent London studio work). The most fascinating aspect must be the character of Perdita, the strange and uncommunicative orphan girl known locally as the witch's daughter (Perdita means 'lost' and was the name of Bawden's own daughter). The character is an embryonic version of the outcast loner that would typify the lead of many dramas well into the 80s. Perdita was played by Fiona Kennedy, who had a small part in the film *The Wicker Man* around the same time and went on to become a Scottish folk singer and TV presenter. The two other child leads were both hot property at the time: Spencer Banks after the success of *Timeslip* and Gillian Bailey having just starred in *Here Come the Double Deckers!*.

65

A feature-length TV movie was made by American company Hallmark Entertainment in 1996 (transmitted in the UK ITV 20/2/99), filmed in Scotland and with some backing from Scottish Television. This version took a free hand in adapting the novel to its own ends. Old Annie shed thirty years and became Perdita's Aunt. Annie develops a romantic relationship with lodger Smith, unaware he is a jewel thief. Tim's blind sister, Janey, was written out and it transpired Tim's real father was a policeman killed in the line of duty. Perdita would seem to have second sight in at least one instance and is believed to have cursed the island, resulting in a dearth of the lobster fishing vital to Skua's economy. In a clear example of missing the point, Perdita is now English! The retelling ends, happily if preposterously, with Smith evading arrest and setting up a family unit with Annie and Perdita.

The BBC version had stayed faithful to the book, retaining its couple of layers of emotional depth; the Hallmark remake was over-complicated and over-egged, ending up as pure melodrama.

**BBC**
**5 episodes**
(colour)
**Broadcast:** Mondays 4/10/71 – 1/11/71

**Main Cast:** Fiona Kennedy (Perdita), Spencer Banks (Tim), Gillian Bailey (Janey), John Abineri (Smith), Barry Linehan (Jones), Helena Gloag (Annie MacLaren)

Based on the novel by Nina Bawden (first UK publication 1966, Victor Gollancz)
**Adapted by** Alistair Bell

**Designer:** Peter Brachacki
**Producer:** John McRae
**Director:** David Maloney

**Tie-in publications:** n/k

## The Runaway Summer

Central 'heroine' contrary Mary is spending the summer holidays at the seaside with her Grandfather and Aunt Alice but there any similarity to the Edwardian model ends. Mary is a badly behaved young girl at first, frustrated and angry at the imminent divorce of her parents – in the first episode she steals sweets from a seafront kiosk.

Mary meets local boy Simon and together they become embroiled in what is nominally an 'adventure thriller'. In fact this particular thriller is quite short on incident – there are no dogged detectives, car chases or bank robbers involved. Mary happens to spy a Kenyan boy landing on the beach by boat in order to beat the new British colonial immigration laws and she decides, along with Simon, to try and hide the boy from the police until they can find his uncle in London. Via this the story airs liberalist issues of the early 1970s.

*The Runaway Summer* is largely about secrets and lies: the children hiding Krishna from the authorities; Simon knowing more than he lets on about Mary, who tells him ridiculous stories about a cruel stepaunt; Simon's personal refuge, an island hideaway where they take Krishna for safety. More than anything it's about the secret world of children to which adults are rarely privy.

The surviving clip (almost certainly from part three and retained from an edition of *Blue Peter*) shows the three children enjoying a carefree game of chase in the hideaway but this is the counterpoint to the serial's main message. For all runaways there must come a time for decision and responsibility. Every summer turns inevitably to autumn.

**BBC**
**4 episodes**
(colour)
**Broadcast:** Mondays 8/11/71 – 29/11/71

**Main Cast:** Carol Davis (Mary), Stephen Bone (Simon), Jeffrey Sirr (Krishna), John Welsh (Grandfather), Beryl Cooke (Aunt Alice)

Based on the novel by Nina Bawden (first UK publication 1969, Victor Gollancz)
**Dramatised by** Rosemary Anne Sisson
**Script Editor:** Alistair Bell

**Designer:** Chris Pemsel
**Producer:** John McRae
**Director:** Mary Ridge

## Mandog

Wheelchair-bound Kate, brother Duncan and her friend Samantha discover seven strange men in a local car dump. It soon transpires that 'The Group' are revolutionaries who have travelled back in time from the year 2600 in an attempt to engineer the defeat of their enemies, the Galas. Levin, the group leader, takes hostage the mind of Samantha's dog, Radnor, and uses this to coerce the children into saying nothing about the presence of the group. In exchange Levin places the mind of one of his people, Justin, into Radnor's body. The Galas soon follow The Group through time and the children's home town becomes the setting for a power struggle from the future in which Radnor will play an essential role.

*Mandog* was filmed entirely on location in and around Southampton in the summer of 1971. The production was amateurish by Anna Home's own admission, roughly shot and edited all on film. Perhaps its most interesting aspect was the matter-of-fact use of a disabled lead character.

**BBC**
**6 episodes** ('The Man Who Could Walk Through Doors'; 'Mister Makes His Mark'; 'There Is No Duncan'; 'The Consignment'; 'On The Run'; 'You Have 30 Seconds…')
(colour)
**Broadcast:** Mondays 3/1/72 – 7/2/72

**Main Cast:** Carol Hazell (Kate), Jane Anthony (Sammy), Sebastian Graham-Jones (Justin), Adrian Shergold (Duncan), Christopher Owen (Levin), Ben (Radnor)

**Written by** Peter Dickinson

**Designer:** Ros Inglis
**Director:** Anna Home

**Tie-in publications:** novelisation written by Lois Lamplugh and Peter Dickinson published by BBC, 1972 (hardback only)

## Tightrope

Martin Clifford is studying for his A-levels during his final year at Redlow Comprehensive School, which is situated close to an American air force base involved in NATO exercises. A series of sudden events brings danger to Martin's otherwise ordinary life. While he is watching a schools television broadcast, the programme is interrupted by the mysterious 'Voice of Truth'. When a British intelligence officer by the name of Forrester tells Martin that he suspects there are spies in the nearby village who will attempt to sabotage the base, Martin finds himself drawn into a dangerous world of spies and espionage where he doesn't know who he can trust and his very life is at risk.

This was really a star vehicle from ATV, with Spencer Banks coming in fresh from *Timeslip* and automatically earning a *Look-In* front cover to promote the series.

**ATV**
**13 episodes**
(colour)
**Broadcast:** Wednesdays 19/1/72 – 12/4/72 (fully networked)

**Main Cast:** Spencer Banks (Martin Clifford), John Savident (Forrester), David Munro (Mr Harvey)

**Written by** Victor Pemberton
**Script Editor:** Ruth Boswell

**Designer:** Gerry Roberts
**Producer:** John Cooper
**Directors:** Ron Francis (1, 2, 5, 6, 9, 10, 13), David Foster (3, 4, 7, 8, 11, 12)

## The Intruder

Sixteen-year-old Arnold Haithwaite leads an uneventful life in the Cumbrian coastal town of Skirlston. He spends much of his time guiding tourists across the miles of treacherous sands while staying with Ernest Haithwaite, a man whom he calls father even though he is not. It is on the sands that Arnold first encounters 'the intruder', a stranger in a shabby mackintosh, black beret and eyepatch who claims to be the real Arnold Haithwaite.

Before long he has infiltrated Ernest's home, convincing the gullible old man that he is a relative. The intentions of the man, who goes under the name of Sonny, soon become obvious. He plans a series of developments that will turn Skirlston into a tourist magnet and to do so he needs a base from which to build his empire. Ernest's home is to be his headquarters and if young Arnold isn't even a real member of the Haithwaite family then the boy can have no claim to any of Ernest's belongings.

Dumped on a doorstep sixteen years previously, Arnold now begins a quest to discover his real identity but no-one, with the exception of his two new friends, Jane and Peter, seems willing to help.

Although not quite as prominent as Peter Plummer's earlier *Owl Service*, *The Intruder* finds similar sexual undercurrents in the shape of the enigmatic Jane. It is strongly hinted in the novel that Jane is indulging in extra-curricular activities with one of her tutors. On the whole this is a story of self-discovery set against the backdrop of a dying town with a limited future.

**Granada**
**8 episodes** ('The Stranger'; 'Jane'; 'Norma'; 'Miss Binns'; 'Peter'; 'Jane Again'; 'Mavis'; 'Me')
(colour)
**Broadcast:** Sundays 6/2/72 – 26/3/72 fully networked except Scottish (Sundays 2/1/72 – 20/2/72)

**Main Cast:** James Bate (Arnold Haithwaite), Sheila Ruskin (Jane Ellison), Simon Turner (Peter Ellison), Milton Johns (Sonny), Jack Woolgar (Ernest Haithwaite), Jean Alexander (Miss Binns), Maggie Don (Norma Benson)

Based on the novel by John Rowe Townsend (first UK publication 1969, Oxford University Press)
**Adapted by** Mervyn Haisman and Peter Plummer

**Designer:** Peter Caldwell
**Producer:** Peter Plummer

**Tie-in publications:** n/k

## Pretenders

Set in 1685, the majority of the background to this adventure story is based on historical fact. The Duke of Monmouth was the illegitimate son of Charles II. Following the death of Charles, his brother James was crowned king, much to the displeasure of Monmouth, who immediately set sail from Holland for England claiming that he was the rightful heir. Landing at Lyme Regis, Dorset, he started a rebellion to depose James II. Hopelessly outnumbered with a small band of mainly rebel Protestants from Europe at his side, the 'pretender' to the throne was ultimately defeated at the Battle of Sedgemoor, imprisoned in the Tower of London and executed.

The fictional element of the story concerns the voyage of Elam, a boy who believes Monmouth to be his father. Assisted on his travels by his sister Perfect and the German mercenary Joachim, Elam must risk his life on the Bristol Channel, dodge the King's dragoons and outsmart a devious merchant if he is to have any chance of reaching the Duke.

The climactic battle scenes required 150 actors and extras alongside cannons, muskets and thirty horses. Filming took place near the town of Bridgwater, three miles from Somerset, the location of the original battle.

**HTV**
**13 episodes** ('Rebellion'; 'Not a Live Thing Left'; 'Escape!'; 'In Safe Keeping'; 'The Players to the Rescue'; 'Shipwreck!'; 'The Paymaster'; 'Prince of Avalon'; 'Into Battle'; 'The Last Battle'; 'The Eye of the Drum'; 'Prizemen'; 'Fare Thee Well')
(colour)
**Broadcast:** Sundays 27/2/72 – 21/5/72

**Main Cast:** Frederick Jaeger (Joachim), Curtis Arden (Elam), Elizabeth Robilliard (Perfect), Jonathan Frewth (Monmouth), John Thaw (Fast Jack)

**Written by** Christopher Robinson (2, 4, 5), Paul Nicholson (3), Martin C. Rodgers (6), Ivan Benbrook (7), Carole Boyer (8), A. C. H. Smith (9, 10), Eric Pringle (11), Bob Baker and Dave Martin (12), Denis Constanduros (13), (episode 1 n/k)
**Story Editors:** Bob Baker and Dave Martin

**Designers:** Doug James (1, 2, 4, 5, 9–11, 13), Ken Jones (3, 7, 8), Leo Austin (6, 12)
**Producers:** Leonard White and Patrick Dromgoole
**Directors:** Patrick Dromgoole (1, 2, 6, 9), David Boisseau (3), Leonard White (4, 5, 13), Bill Bain (7, 12), Fred Burnley (8), Terry Harding and Patrick Dromgoole (10), Terry Delacey (11)

**Tie-in publications:** novelisation by Kenneth Bulmer published by New English Library, 1972

## Escape Into Night

Marianne is a young girl with a vivid imagination which becomes almost all too real, placing both herself and a boy called Mark in a strange kind of danger. One day Marianne draws a big old house ringed with standing stones in her sketch book and is able to dream herself into it. Next she dreams Mark into it, a boy who is ill and confined to bed, but in a fit of temper she scribbles all over the picture of the boy and places prison bars and high walls around the house, trapping him there. She draws a single green eye on each of the stones and they come to life in her dreamworld, further preventing Mark's escape. Mark is real, however – unable to walk he seems doomed to convalescence. Only by rescuing Mark from the house in Marianne's dream can she help him recover in the real world.

The creepy stones and their harsh, metallic voices made this a nightmarish serial in all senses of the word. It was complex too, challenging the audience to perceive which

sections were real and which were dreams. The subtext to the psychodrama concerned the capacity that all of us have for evil thoughts, Marianne earning redemption through her efforts to save Mark. Well rendered by the use of dimly lit sets of the old house, the lack of budget only became apparent when the children's final rescue from a lighthouse by helicopter wasn't seen on screen.

The original novel was later adapted for the cinema, undergoing another change of title as the movie *Paperhouse* (1988).

**ATV**
**6 episodes**
(colour)
**Broadcast:** Wednesdays 19/4/72 – 24/5/72 (fully networked)

**Main Cast:** Vikki Chambers (Marianne), Steven Jones (Mark), Patricia Maynard (Miss Chesterfield), Sonia Graham (Mrs Austen), Edmund Pegge (Dr Burton)

Based on the novel *Marianne Dreams* by Catherine Storr (first UK publication 1958, Faber & Faber)
**Adapted by** Ruth Boswell

**Designer:** Don Davidson
**Producer:** Alan Coleman
**Director:** Richard Bramall

## Fly Into Danger

When car mechanic Chris Lomax arrives at Chilford Green airfield to begin a new job as a flight engineer he is hoping for excitement and a chance to get airborne. He gets more than he bargained for when on his first test flight the plane's engine dies. Surviving this sabotage, Chris uncovers a smuggling ring centred on Chilford and wonders what the mysterious cargoes coming and going in crates marked Computapac could contain and their source.

There is the usual air of paranoia and distrust – can Chris really confide in Sarah, the pretty airport secretary he has befriended? Or is flight trainer Jeff Strong involved? And what of the suspicious airport manager Mr Ritchie? Meanwhile an Asian man is looking for his missing son, Chambra Lal ...

Typical thriller fare from a time when having hero pilots called Jeff Strong didn't appear unsophisticated. Exciting flying sequences were the series' main draw and these were shot at Halfpenny Green airfield, Staffordshire, which doubled as Chilford. One more interesting advance in this serial was the use of an ethnic family in the cast of lead characters.

**ATV**
**7 episodes** ('Take-Off'; 'In a Spin'; 'Grounded'; 'Mayday, Mayday'; 'Turbulence'; 'Forced Take-Off'; 'Final Approach') (colour)
**Broadcast:** Wednesdays 31/5/72 – 12/7/72 (fully networked)

**Above:** Marianne (Vikki Chambers) and once-imaginary boy Mark (Steven Jones) plan their *Escape Into Night*.

**Main Cast:** Louis Cabot (Chris Lomax), Susan Holderness (Sarah Davenport), Leigh Anthony (Lofty), Edward Peel (Jeff Strong), Bernard Kay (Gordon Ritchie), Marc Maharaj (Chambra Lal), Robert Keegan (Bill Hurst), Sam Dastor (Moji Patel), Mohan Singh (Bandara Lal)

**Written by** Roy Russell (episode 5 credited to David Stevens)

**Designer:** Martin Davey
**Producer:** David Foster
**Director:** Jonathan Wright Miller

## The Adventures of Black Beauty

The opening credits of *The Adventures of Black Beauty* state that the series is 'with acknowledgement to the classic by Anna Sewell'. To have said that it was based on the novel would be a far cry from the truth. The only link between the two is a horse called Black Beauty. While Sewell's novel depicted the difficult experiences of a horse, told from the animal's point of view, as it passed from owner to owner, the series shifted the emphasis away from the horse and concentrated instead on human characters.

Doctor Gordon has moved from London to the small country village of Five Oaks with his daughter Vicky, son Kevin and housekeeper Amy. Exploring nearby woodland, the children discover a wounded black stallion and return with him to their house in the hope that he may be cured. When the horse's master, a burly figure intent on breaking the beast's spirit, arrives to collect the animal, Vicky is distraught that they cannot afford to buy it. When Doctor Gordon saves the life of the master's uncle, they are given the horse as payment.

The village locals are suspicious of the Gordons' arrival, as Amy discovers when she asks one of them to tell the inhabitants of the area that Doctor Gordon's practice is now open. 'It won't do you no good, will it?' he replies. 'You're from London. You're foreigners.' This conflict of cultures is an engaging theme and, had it formed an ongoing subplot, detailing the way in which the Gordons adapt to village life and their struggle to gain acceptance, the series may have contained a bit more grit. Such notions are however forgotten by the second episode by which time the family seem to be living comfortably with their fellow villagers.

The series is made up of stand-alone episodes, many of which come with a moral or humane tale. 'The Hostage' tells of an escaped criminal who kidnaps Kevin and Beauty so that he can force Vicky into providing materials essential to his continued liberty. When Kevin is injured the criminal faces the choice of escape or helping the boy, which will ultimately lead to his capture. In nursing Kevin he demonstrates that, although he is labelled a dangerous man, he is still capable of great humanity.

*Black Beauty* is the mix of the good and the predictable that one might expect of a series of its length. In 'The Recruiting Sergeant', a unit of British Army soldiers arrives in the village and Vicky shelters a young AWOL Private. The scheming regiment sergeant commandeers Beauty, promising to release him only if Vicky turns in the runaway. Needless to say, one of Doctor Gordon's patients is an army general, who soon has the problem sorted.

Filming of the second season rapidly followed the broadcast of the first and there would be some notable changes. The character of Vicky had disappeared without explanation (actress Judi Bowker having decided to pursue

a more varied career) and in stepped a new character, Jenny, played by fifteen-year-old Stacy Dorning in her first television role. In the first story of the new season, 'A Member of the Family', Jenny narrates to us that she had been attending school in London and was now joining her father in the country. The audience is then left to assume that Jenny is Vicky's little sister while pondering what has happened to Beauty's former owner.

Two other new characters are also introduced. Squire Armstrong, the uppity new owner of the local manor and its surrounding estates, would have several disagreements with Doctor Gordon, usually regarding the actions of the children. Cockney street urchin Ned, Amy's nephew, arrives from London and immediately causes havoc, first of all accidentally setting light to the Gordons' barn and also unwittingly attracting the attentions of an unscrupulous thief he used to work for. This meant that there were now four children in the series: Jenny, Kevin, Ned and Albert, who had made occasional appearances in the first season. As a result of Dorning's age, there were strict guidelines governing the hours that she could work, but the greater number of child actors allowed the writers to 'rest' certain characters in particular episodes.

*The Adventures of Black Beauty* is a slick production. Shot on location, primarily in and around Stocker's Farm in Hertfordshire, the series benefits from the natural beauty of its scenic backdrops, and the many dynamic pursuits on horseback are directed with panache. Denis King's incidental music is excellent throughout and his majestic opening theme is infinitely memorable.

When a third season failed to materialise, it seemed that Black Beauty had enjoyed his final adventure. Twenty years later, however, a horse of the same name would appear in *The New Adventures of Black Beauty*. Twelve-year-old Vicky gains a new mother when her widower father plans to marry Jenny Gordon. The couple plan to emigrate to New Zealand. Vicky's father travels ahead of the family but the ship is soon reported missing. Jenny and Vicky go to New Zealand in the hope that they may find him, but instead discover a wild stallion – the new Black Beauty.

The series presents the same tales of humanity, morals and devious vagabonds, this time set against the more luxurious background of coastal New Zealand. William Lucas reprises his role as Doctor Gordon and Stacy Dorning returns as the now considerably older Jenny.

A further season of *The New Adventures of Black Beauty* was screened in a children's slot on BBC1 (transmitted 11/4/94 – 18/7/94). There was no British input to this venture and no apparent connection to its immediate predecessor.

An extremely memorable series which, while it lacks the gritty edge of its nearest rival, Yorkshire's *Follyfoot*, exudes a simplicity that makes the series a prime example of all-round children's entertainment.

Based on the novel *Black Beauty: the autobiography of a horse* by Anna Sewell (first UK publication *c.* 1885)

**The Adventures of Black Beauty** (1972–74)
**London Weekend International and Talbot** (Distributed by The Fremantle Corporation)
**2 seasons**
**52 episodes**

**Above:** the young cast of Season Two of *The Adventures of Black Beauty* with the famous horse; (l to r) Kevin Gordon (Roderick Shaw), Jenny Gordon (Stacy Dorning), Ned (Stephen Garlick) and Albert (Tony Maiden).

**Series developed by** Ted Willis
**Story Consultant** (Season One): Jeremy Godwin
**Story Consultant** (Season Two): Max Wilk

**Music** composed and arranged by Denis King and directed by Harry Rabinowitz (includes theme 'Galloping Home')
**Associate Producer:** Anthony S. Gruner
**Production Designer:** John Blezard
**Executive Producer:** Paul Knight
**Producer:** Sidney Cole

**Season One**
**26 episodes**
(colour)
**Broadcast:** Sundays 17/9/72 – 18/3/73 5.35p.m. (fully networked except LWT and Scottish). LWT screenings Saturdays from 30/9/72 5.10/5.15p.m.

**Main Cast:** William Lucas (Dr James Gordon), Charlotte Mitchell (Amy Winthrop), Judi Bowker (Vicky Gordon), Roderick Shaw (Kevin Gordon), Black Jet (Black Beauty)

'The Fugitive' by Ted Willis. Dir: John Reardon
'The Hostage' by Victor Pemberton. Dir: Charles Crichton
'The Pit Pony' by Ted Willis. Dir: Charles Crichton
'Horse Thieves' by Richard Carpenter. Dir: Alan Gibson
'Runaway' by Richard Carpenter. Dir: Charles Crichton
'Warhorse' by David Butler. Dir: John Reardon
'The Horsemen' by Lindsay Galloway. Dir: John Reardon
'The Duel' by Richard Carpenter. Dir: Charles Crichton
'The Viking Helmet (part 1)' by David Butler. Dir: Alan Gibson
'The Viking Helmet (part 2)' by David Butler. Dir: Alan Gibson
'Day of Reckoning' by Richard Carpenter. Dir: Charles Crichton
'Mantrap' by David Butler. Dir: Alan Gibson

'Clown on Horseback' by David Butler. Dir: Alan Gibson
'Three Locks to Fortune' by David Butler. Dir: Gerry Poulson
'The Recruiting Sergeant' by Lindsay Galloway. Dir: Charles Crichton
'The Debt' by Richard Carpenter. Dir: Charles Crichton
'The Horse Healer' by Lindsay Galloway. Dir: John Reardon
'The Witch' by John Kane. Dir: Alan Gibson
'The Ponies' by David Butler. Dir: David Askey
'The Ruffians' by Richard Carpenter. Dir: Ray Austin
'Two of a Kind' by David Hopkins. Dir: Charles Crichton
'Foul Play' by Richard Carpenter. Dir: David Askey
'Sailor on a Horse' by David Butler. Dir: Gerry Poulson
'Wild Justice' by Richard Carpenter. Dir: David Askey
'The Barge' by Victor Pemberton. Dir: John Reardon
'Father and Son' by David Hopkins. Dir: David Andrews

**Season Two**
**26 episodes**
(colour)
**Broadcast:** Sundays 23/9/73 – 10/3/74
4.50p.m. (LWT, Anglia, Granada, Yorkshire, Tyne Tees, Border, Grampian, HTV, Ulster)
5.35p.m. (ATV Midlands, Channel, Southern, Westward)

**Main Cast:** William Lucas (Dr James Gordon), Charlotte Mitchell (Amy Winthrop), Michael Culver (Squire Armstrong), Stacy Dorning (Jenny Gordon), Roderick Shaw (Kevin Gordon), Stephen Garlick (Ned Lewis), Tony Maiden (Albert), Black Jet (Black Beauty)

'A Member of the Family' (2 parts) by David Butler. Dir: Charles Crichton
'The Outcast' by Richard Carpenter. Dir: Gerry Poulson
'Good Neighbours' by Lindsay Galloway. Dir: Charles Crichton
'Mission of Mercy' by Richard Carpenter. Dir: Charles Crichton
'Battle of Wills' by John Kane. Dir: Peter Duffell
'The Medicine Man' by Richard Carpenter. Dir: Gerry Poulson
'Out of the Night' by David Butler. Dir: Peter Duffell
'Panic' by Victor Pemberton. Dir: Charles Crichton
'The Challenge' by David Butler. Dir: Freddie Francis

'Pocket Money' by Richard Carpenter. Dir: Gerry Poulson
'The Quarry' by David Butler. Dir: Peter Duffell
'Secret Fear' by Richard Carpenter. Dir: Ray Austin
'Lost (parts 1 & 2)' by James Karner. Dir: Charles Crichton
'Lost Goddess' by John Kane. Dir: Charles Crichton
'Where's Jonah?' by Richard Carpenter. Dir: Charles Crichton
'A Long Hard Run' by Richard Carpenter. Dir: Ray Austin
'The Horsebreaker' by David Butler. Dir: Ray Austin
'The Last Round-Up' by David Butler. Dir: Gerry Poulson
'Goodbye Beauty' by John Kane. Dir: Freddie Francis
'The Escape' by Richard Carpenter. Dir: Ray Austin
'A Ribbon for Beauty' by David Butler. Dir: Freddie Francis
'The Last Charge' by Peter Duffell. Dir: Freddie Francis
'Race Against Time' by David Butler. Dir: Freddie Francis
'Game of Chance' by Richard Carpenter. Dir: Ray Austin

**Tie-in publications:** large format hardback novelisation *The Adventures of Black Beauty: stories from the popular television series* by Tessa Bridger published by Hamlyn, 1972 (contains 'The Fugitive', 'The Horse Healer', 'The Pit Pony', 'Day of Reckoning', 'Warhorse').
Paperback novelisation *The Adventures of Black Beauty* by Mark Tyler published by Piccolo/Pan Books Ltd, 1972 (contains 'The Fugitive', 'Mantrap', 'Clown on Horseback', 'Horse Thieves' and 'The Horsemen').
Paperback novelisation *The Best of Black Beauty* by Richard Carpenter published by Everest Books Ltd, 1975 (contains 'The Outcast', 'The Quarry', 'Secret Fear', 'The Medicine Man', 'Mission of Mercy', 'A Long Hard Run', 'The Escape').
Annuals published by World Distributors 1974–6 (cover-dated 1975–1977). Annuals cover-dated 1978–80 were unlicensed and did not use the TV format.

**Video:** 'The Viking Helmet' (includes parts 1 and 2) released as a 46-minute compilation by The Video Collection, 13/8/90. Deleted 14/12/94.
*Father and Son* (containing 'Father and Son', 'Two of a Kind', 'Clown on Horseback', 'The Horse Healer') released as a 92-minute compilation by Video Gems, 27/3/95. Deleted 1/4/96.
*The Adventures of Black Beauty – The Best of Series One* (containing 'The Fugitive', 'The Hostage', 'The Recruiting Sergeant', 'Sailor on a Horse'*, 'Father and Son') released unedited at 125 minutes by Network Video, 2000.
*Although video box details episode as 'Sailor on a Horse', early copies actually include 'Warhorse'.
*The Adventures of Black Beauty – The Best of Series Two* (containing 'A Member of the Family' parts 1 and 2, 'The Medicine Man', 'Out of the Night', 'The Escape', 'Game of Chance') released unedited at 150 minutes by Network Video, 2000. Region 2 DVDs of both Network releases issued 17/9/01.
US video releases 1980s by Sony on VHS and Betamax: six volumes including 'The Fugitive'/'The Pit Pony'; 'A Member of the Family' parts 1 and 2; 'A Ribbon for Beauty'/'Mission of Mercy'; 'Lost' parts 1 and 2; 'Out of the Night'/'Good Neighbours'; 'The Quarry'/'The Challenge'.

**The New Adventures of Black Beauty** (1990)
**Isambard (Black Beauty) Limited in association with Fremantle Corporation, LWT and Beta/Taurus**
**16 episodes**\*\* ('That Old World Beauty'; 'Breaking In'; 'Ride A Black Horse'; 'Deceptive Appearances'; 'Fear of Water'; 'Treasure Hunt'; 'The Birdman'; 'Different Races'; 'A Question of Justice'; 'Horsepower'; 'Horse Sense'; 'Surprise'; 'A Present For Beauty'; 'Sea Horses'; 'Hope'; 'At Risk')
\*\* the first episode as transmitted in the UK was a 55-minute compilation of the two original half-hour episodes 'The Old World' and 'A Horse Like Beauty'. The series is more usually broadcast as 17 episodes.
(colour)
**Broadcast:** Saturdays 1/9/90 – 15/12/90 on ITV

**Main Cast:** Amber McWilliams (Vicky), Stacy Dorning (Jenny), Bill Lucas (Dr Gordon), Gedeon Burkhard (Manfred)

**Written by** Ken Catran (1–8), Graeme Farmer (9, 11, 12, 16), Peter Eyers-Hill and Marya Winstanley (10, 13, 15, 17), Cary Bay and James Griffin (14)
**Creative Consultant:** Anthony S. Gruner
**Original script devised by** Murray Newey
**Originating Writer:** Ken Catran (credited on 9, 10)
**Story Editor:** Christina Milligan

**Theme composed by** Denis King
**Music:** Chris Neal
**Production Designer:** Peta Button (1, 2), Kirsten Shouler (3–17)
**Producers:** John Crome (1–3), Murray Newey (4–17)
**Executive Producer for LWT:** Nick Elliott
**Executive Producer for Freemantle:** Richard Becker
**Executive Producer for 7 Network, Australia:** Des Monaghan
**Executive Producer:** Tom Parkinson
**Directors:** John Crome (1–5, 9, 12, 13, 15), Mike Smith (6–8), Catherine Millar (10, 11, 14, 16, 17)

**Tie-in publications:** *The New Adventures of Black Beauty 1: Beauty's Story* and *The New Adventures of Black Beauty 2: A Home at Last* by Jonathan Dowling (first UK publication 1991, Knight Books)

**Video:** US releases only – six volumes: 'The Old World'/'A Horse Like Beauty'; 'Breaking In'/'Ride A Black Horse'; 'Deceptive Appearances'/'Fear of Water'; 'Treasure Hunt'/'The Birdman'; 'Different Races'/'A Question of Justice'; 'Horsepower'/'Horse Sense' all released episodically at 60 minutes per volume by Questar Video, 1995. Deleted.

## The Long Chase

When John Corby's father disappears, he and friend Susan trek the length and breadth of Britain, becoming ever further embroiled in espionage. Amid jet boat action and shadowy hit men, the chase takes them to ports of call as far afield as Yorkshire, Cumberland and the Edinburgh Military Tattoo. The travelogue's epic length was highly ambitious for the BBC at this time even if the subject matter was not. The title said it all.

**BBC**
**13 episodes**
(colour)
**Broadcast:** Mondays 25/9/72 – 18/12/72

**Main Cast:** Simon Turner (John Corby), Jan Francis (Susan Fraser), Glyn Houston (Tom Corby), David Sinclair (Selby), Brian Peck (Bowers), Edward Brooks (Kessler), Walter Jackson (Bartas)

**Written by** N. J. Crisp (devised with Gerard Glaister)

**Producer:** Gerard Glaister
**Director:** Philip Dudley

## Jackanory Playhouse

This halfway-house approach between the talking head and rostrum stills storytelling of *Jackanory* and the expense and logistical undertaking of a full-scale drama production persisted in the 70s when drama budgets were at their tightest but surprisingly lasted into the early 80s.

Productions were made almost exclusively in the studio, apparently in as few takes as possible, against pared-down, theatre-style settings. A handful of actors, a plain diorama backing, a couple of castle walls, basic props and some stock costumes were usually all that was needed for a *Playhouse*.

The series rarely used original script ideas, with the first adventure of Helen Cresswell's *Lizzie Dripping* being among its few innovations. The majority of stories were instead quickly adapted from well-known fairy stories and folk tales. Among typical productions were 'The Long Nosed Princess' (31/12/73), 'Dick Whittington' (13/2/74), 'The Sleeping Princess' (5/1/76), 'The Emperor's Nightingale' (16/4/76), 'The Princess Who Couldn't Laugh' (7/3/78) and many more tales set in hastily realised royal courts.

There were nominally twelve seasons in all but episodes could be shown – and, one suspects, made – at short notice so that odd instalments would often crop up, employed almost in a filler capacity and often used in Christmas schedules.

**BBC**
**60 episodes**
(colour)
**Broadcast:** 17/11/72 to 5/11/85

## Black Arrow

Set in fifteenth-century England during the Wars of the Roses, this tale of betrayal, mystery and vengeance played out against the shrubbery of Hampshire's New Forest lies somewhere between *The Lone Ranger* and *Robin Hood*. This series took the basic premise and lead character of Robert Louis Stevenson's novel and moulded it for a 70s audience (a more faithful two-part pseudo-theatrical adaptation of Stevenson's story had been made by the fledgling BBC, aired 20/5/51 and 27/5/51 and the BBC again adapted it as a six-part serial shown 19/1/58 – 23/2/58).

Following his father's mysterious death, teenager Richard Shelton has been left in the care of Sir Daniel Brackley, an unpleasant and domineering nobleman. Rumours suggest Brackley was involved in Shelton senior's death and now plans to rob Richard of his inheritance.

Richard joins a band of dissidents determined to challenge Brackley's subjugation of the poor. The outlaws find themselves assisted by a hooded stranger on horseback whose face is permanently eclipsed by a black mask. The stranger carries a chilling message, which he leaves attached by a dagger to a church door. It reads, 'Four black arrows under my belt. Four for the sorrows we have felt. Four men who played the evil part. One black arrow in each black heart.' Four men are named on the parchment and, one by one, they are picked off by master archer Black Arrow until only Sir Daniel remains.

The second season is set four years later. Simon Cuff replaced Robin Langford in the role of the now older Shelton. This has the immediate effect of causing a great deal of confusion, as Cuff had played the part of the unnamed chief outlaw, a completely different character altogether, in the first season. This confusion may have been intentional, as the series seems obsessed with disguise and subterfuge.

It is discovered that Brackley has miraculously escaped the wrath of the Arrow and has been in hiding in France. Now that he has returned to England, the Black Arrow too reappears, determined to fulfil the prophecy.

Keeping the viewers guessing as to the identity of the Black Arrow, no actor was credited against the part until the third season, when it is revealed that Richard Shelton is the alter ego. This throws forth more confusion because the viewer knows that young Shelton certainly wasn't the Black Arrow of the first season. This leaves the audience to draw their own conclusions.

There are several strong theories. Was Brackley in error to believe he had killed Shelton's father? Could Shelton senior have returned disguised as the Black Arrow to gain vengeance over his would-be murderer? Or is there a close relative abroad seeking retribution in the family name? When Brackley returns alive from exile in France, it is Master Shelton who must take over the mantle to complete the Arrow's work.

With the blood feud over by the third season, it lacks the focus of its predecessors. Richard Shelton is now a Robin Hood figure meandering through the forest rescuing deserving minions from their misfortune. First he saves a young lad called Peterkin from the clutches of the wicked Lord William. With Peterkin's help he then aids a young couple who wish to marry against William's wishes, leading the cruel overlord to try and have the bride-to-be burned at the stake as the witch who has conjured up Black Arrow.

Based on Robert Louis Stevenson's famous character from the novel *The Black Arrow* (first UK publication 1888)

**Southern**
**3 seasons**
(colour)

**Season One**
**7 episodes** ('The Prophecy'; 'The Leper'; 'Richard Changes Sides'; 'The Cattle Drive'; 'The Chess Game'; 'The Crossroads'; 'The Last Arrow')
**Broadcast:** Mondays 4/12/72 – 22/1/73

**Main Cast:** Robin Langford (Richard Shelton), William Squire (Sir Daniel Brackley), Eric Flynn (Will Lawless), Helen Stronge (Joanna Sedley*), Simon Cuff (Chief Outlaw)
* Credited as 'John Matcham' for earlier episodes, since Joanna is disguised as a boy

**Written by** Ben Healey
**Designer:** Gregory Lawson
**Producer:** Peter Croft

**Season Two**
**6 episodes** ('The Stranger from France'; 'The Return of Black Arrow'; 'Sir Daniel at the Inn'; 'Plot and Counterplot'*; 'The Ambush'; 'The Lady Prioress')
**Broadcast:** Wednesdays 5/12/73 – 16/1/74
* Not broadcast in Scottish region

**Main Cast:** Simon Cuff (Richard Shelton), William Squire (Sir Daniel Brackley**), Glyn Owen (Will Lawless), Eddie Byrne (Brock), Dorothea Phillips (Mistress Hatch), Michael McStay (Knoles)
** Credited as The Stranger for earlier episodes to hide Brackley's surprise appearance

**Written by** Ben Healey
**Designer:** Gregory Lawson
**Producer:** Peter Croft

**Season Three**
**7 episodes** ('Peterkin'; 'The Wedding'; 'Trapped'; 'The Stake'; 'The Adventure of The Holy Finger'; 'Captured'; 'Winner Take All')
**Broadcast:** Sundays 24/11/74 – 12/1/75

**Main Cast:** Simon Cuff (Richard Shelton), John Sanderson (Peterkin), Brian Coburn (Lord William), Roberta Tovey (Anne), Nigel Havers (Roger)

**Written by** Anthony Read
**Designer:** Greg Lawson
**Director:** Bob Leng

## Arthur of the Britons

'No Guineveres, Lancelots, Galahads or Merlins. No armour, no romance. Just grime.' It might seem odd but that was how HTV trailed this ambitious twenty-four-part series. This take attempted to find a new angle by disposing of the fanciful fantasy and guessing at the grain of truth that spawned the legend. In place of magic and myth were a ragged band of long-haired warriors on horseback, fighting back against the Saxon overlords. Camelot was no longer an imposing castle but a collection of mud huts (in reality built on Forestry Commission land near Stroud for a six-month shoot). Of the Lady of the Lake there was no sign while Merlin the magician was also absent. Plans to include a revised, rationalised Merlin, a scientist and medicine man, were dropped at the early stages.

The three main characters were Arthur, the rugged Oliver Tobias in a very 1972 haircut, Kai, a near brother to his Lord, and Llud The Silver-Handed, the faithful retainer who had raised both Arthur and Kai. Kai had been born a Saxon and reared a Celt, a source of friction between him and Arthur from time to time. Arthur's sweetheart Rowena also featured, played by a German actress to accommodate the series' European backers.

Arthur's aim throughout the series was to unite the warring Celtic tribes and so overthrow Cerdig the Saxon warlord. In the first episode Arthur fakes his own death to draw the tribes together. The episodic series had Arthur and his men do battle each week with passing Saxon Thanes or belligerent Celtic chiefs.

The series' mainstay was of course the rough-edged action sequences. Shot all on film on location, there was none of the laboured choreography of similar efforts made in-studio. For its time the series was really quite violent – when Australia screened the series a large number of sequences were crudely trimmed to make it acceptable for a child audience. Sales were also made to America, helping to recoup HTV's massive investment.

**HTV West in association with Heritage Enterprises Inc and Taurus Film Gmbh & Co.**
**24 episodes** broadcast in the UK as two seasons (colour)

**Main Cast:** Oliver Tobias (Arthur), Jack Watson (Llud), Michael Gothard (Kai), Brian Blessed (Mark of Cornwall), Rupert Davies (Cerdig), Gila von Weiterhausen (Rowena)

**Theme Music:** Elmer Bernstein
**Incidental Music and Orchestration:** Paul Lewis
**Art Director:** Douglas James
**Producer:** Peter Miller
**Associate Producer:** John Peverall
**Executive Producer:** Patrick Dromgoole

**Season One**
**12 episodes** ('Arthur is Dead'; 'The Gift of Life'; 'The Challenge'; 'The Penitent Invader'; 'People of the Plough'; 'The Duel'; 'The Pupil'; 'Rolf the Preacher'; 'Enemies and Lovers'; 'The Slaves'; 'The Prize'; 'The Wood People')
**Broadcast:** Wednesdays 6/12/72 – 14/2/73. Transmission date for episode 'The Wood People' not known. May have been dropped from initial run in some regions.

**Written by** Terence Feely (1–4, 6–8), Bob Baker and Dave Martin (5), Scott Forbes (9), Robert Banks Stewart (10, 11), David Osborn (12)

**Directors:** Peter Sasdy (1), Pat Jackson (2, 6, 10, 11), Sidney Hayers (3, 5, 7–9, 12), Patrick Dromgoole (4)

**Season Two**
**12 episodes** ('The Swordsman'; 'Rowena'; 'The Prisoner'; 'Some Saxon Women'; 'Go Warily'; 'The Marriage Feast'; 'In Common Cause'; 'Six Measures of Silver'; 'Daughter of the King'; 'The Games'; 'The Treaty'; 'The Girl from Rome')
**Broadcast:** Wednesdays 12/9/73 – 28/11/73

**Written by:** Terence Feely (1, 6, 11, 12), Robert Banks Stewart (2, 3, 8), Jonathan Crown (5), Michael J. Bird (7), David Pursall and Jack Seddon (9), David Osborn (4, 10)

**Directors:** Sid Hayers (1, 5, 6, 10, 12), Patrick Dromgoole (2, 4, 7, 11), Pat Jackson (3, 8), Peter Sasdy (9)

**Tie-in publications:** novelised by Rex Edwards, published by Target, 1975.
Large format illustrated book by Terence Feely, published by HTV, 1974.

**Video:** feature compilation of episodes including 'The Marriage Feast' issued in the US only as *King Arthur, the Young Warlord*. Two releases, first by Video Gems.

## Thursday's Child

When the Rector finds an abandoned baby girl on the steps of his church, she carries a note stating, 'This is Margaret whom I entrust to your care. Each year fifty-two pounds will be sent for her keep and schooling.' Naming her Margaret Thursday, the day on which he discovered her, the Rector sends the child to stay with the well-off Cameron family. However, the family's fortune has dwindled over the years and the surviving Cameron sisters are now too old to look after Margaret. When the Rector receives advice from Margaret's mysterious benefactor that money for her upkeep is no longer available, the girl is sent to stay in an orphanage. Margaret makes herself an enemy of the cruel matron and is soon forced to run away. Taking with her two small boys, Horatio and Peter, they become unlikely leggers on a canal boat.

A tale of the strength of youth and innocence over the cruel and oppressive, very much in the style of Frances Hodgson Burnett or Dickens and typical of Sunday afternoon family fare, though actually shown Wednesdays.

**BBC**
**6 episodes** ('Three of Everything'; 'Sedgecombe'; 'I Hate Her'; 'The Crusader'; 'Rain in the Night'; 'Light in the Window') (colour)
**Broadcast:** Wednesdays 27/12/72 – 31/1/73

**Main Cast:** Claire Walker (Margaret Thursday), Gillian Bailey (Lavinia Beresford), Simon Gipps-Kent (Peter Beresford), David Tully (Horatio Beresford), Anne Ridler (Lady Corkberry*), Peter Williams (Lord Corkberry)
*Lady Corkberry credited as Sonia Graham episodes 4 and 5.

Based on the novel by Noel Streatfeild (first UK publication 1970, William Collins and Co)
**Adapted by** John Tully

**Music:** Tom McCall, arranged by Alfred Ralston
**Designer:** Antony Thorpe
**Producer:** Dorothea Brooking

**Tie-in publications:** edition published in paperback by Armada Lions, 1972

## Fish

Fish is the nickname of Jimmy Barnes, a lonely boy with an unsettled background finding it hard to fit in with the tight-knit community of a Welsh village. Things begin to change when he and Jimmy Price, the closest thing Fish has to a friend, come across a stray dog one night. Fish petulantly lies his way into keeping the dog, which becomes something of a local celebrity when it trots into the local shop each day to pick up the paper. Things only start to go wrong when local sheep are savaged at nights and Jimmy Price realises that the attacks began the night Floss, as Fish names his dog, appeared in the village.

This is a subtle tale of secrets kept between children and lies told to grown-ups. Sometimes lies can escalate until the truth becomes inescapable. When some older boys swap reflector posts on a dark country road, causing a serious accident, the two Jimmys succumb to peer pressure and sneak out in the night to change the reflectors back for the boys. The local bobby is out to catch the culprits but PC Morgan finds only Floss roaming around. Now Floss is

thought to be the sheep worrier and her innocence cannot be proved without implicating the boys in the road accident. When Fish's father threatens to have the dog put down, Fish runs away. Will keeping the boy's whereabouts secret place him in danger?

**BBC**
**4 episodes** ('I am going to keep her...'; 'The dog must go...'; 'I need somewhere to hide'; 'Fetch the paper, Floss') (colour)
**Broadcast:** Mondays 8/1/73 – 29/1/73

**Main Cast:** David Hogarth ('Fish'), Alan Jones (Jimmy Price), Robert Fellowes (Pete), Gareth Evans (Tom), Leslie Mitchell (Gary), Hubert Rees (PC Sam Morgan), Jimmy Gardner (Mr Barnes), Bernadette Milnes (Mrs Barnes), Janet Davies (Mrs Price), David Garfield (Mr Price), Queenie (Floss)

Based on the novel by Alison Morgan (first UK publication 1971, Chatto & Windus)
**Adapted by** Anna Home

**Director:** Anna Home

**Tie-in publications:** edition published in paperback by Puffin, 1973

## The Viaduct

Phil Benson lives in an old house by the railway viaduct with his grandfather George and their devoted friend Mrs Partridge. Almost all of the Bensons have throughout the years been servants of the railways and George harbours ambitions that Phil will become a great railway engineer like their ancestor Ebenezer. Ebenezer had been a rich man but miserly. What happened to his wealth after he died? Why is Phil's grandfather so secretive about the attic in the house and what is it that he doesn't want Phil to see?

Phil is trying to decide whether to go against George's wishes and look in the attic but the choice is taken out of his hands when George dies suddenly. Phil's Uncle Ern, a man whom George had little trust in, turns up and begins to search through George's belongings. Will he discover George's secret and Ebenezer's missing money? With the help of his new friend Andy, Phil attempts to solve the mystery of the viaduct.

Set in Deptford, South East London, this is an engaging story of an old man's pride at his family's past achievements and a young boy's desire to fulfil his grandfather's hopes.

**BBC**
**3 episodes** ('The Last of the Bensons'; 'Who are the Spies?'; 'Child of Brass and Iron') (colour)
**Broadcast:** Tuesdays 13/2/73 – 27/2/73
First broadcast for schools as *Merry-Go-Round* 6/3/72 – 20/3/72

**Main Cast:** David Arnold (Phil Benson), Julie May (Mrs Partridge), Michael Raghan (Grandad and Ebenezer), Adrian Hall (Andy Smith), Jeffrey Segal (Uncle Ern), Dempsy Cook (Lenny Eccles), Margaret Wedlake (Aunt Luce), John Vaughan (Jim), Bill Gavin (Mr Felix), Michelle Miller (Molly)

Based on the novel by Roy Brown (first UK publication 1967, Abelard-Schuman)
**Script:** John Tully

**Producer:** Dorothea Brooking
**Executive Producer:** Claire Chovil

**Tie-in publications:** n/k

## The Jensen Code

Terry Connor is a rough sixteen-year-old Birmingham kid sent with his friends to an outdoor activity centre in Derbyshire. When Terry goes pot-holing with Alex, he gets more excitement than he bargained for when he inadvertently becomes involved in espionage and intrigue at a nearby Ministry of Defence (MoD) establishment.

Jensen, an MoD worker and creator of the Jensen Code, is ambushed and kidnapped and Terry's life is also in danger. Terry is taken to a farmhouse where he is told he will be safe. A mysterious figure watches him from an upstairs window. Learning the truth about the Jensen Code, Terry is entrusted with its safety but after meeting the sinister Mr Richards he wakes in hospital with his memory all but erased. He starts to work out what has happened to him but, following a hospital visit from two 'friends', Terry is made to believe a different series of events. If Terry is unable to remember what has happened, he will be unable to prevent the planned space laboratory launch. His chances of succeeding are slim when he finds himself trapped in an old mine shaft with the water levels rising ...

The serial was written by Carey Harrison, son of entertainer Rex and brother of actor Noel. Among the cast was a young Karl Howman playing a character called Jacko – no relation to his comedy persona in the 80s' BBC sitcom *Brushstrokes*.

**ATV**
**13 episodes**
(colour)
**Broadcast:** Wednesdays 28/2/73 – 23/5/73

**Main Cast:** Dai Bradley (Terry Connor), Tony Wright (Alex), Brian Croucher (Gordon), Leon Eagles (Jensen), Milton Johns (Mr Richards), Paul Alexander (Ron), Karl Howman (Jacko), John Barrett (Mr Buckle), Dan Meaden (Kurtz), Daphne Heard (Granny Power), Barbara Angell (Miss Howard), John Scott Martin (Mr Connor), Angela Crow (Mrs Connor)

**Written by** Carey Harrison

**Designer:** Norman Smith
**Producer:** Alan Coleman
**Director:** Jonathan Wright Miller

## Lizzie Dripping

Penelope Arbuckle, otherwise known as Lizzie Dripping, has a vivid imagination. but is surprised to discover a witch in the church graveyard, propped up against a gravestone, knitting. Out of all the people in Little Hemlock, Lizzie is the only person who can see the witch, who has the habit of turning up at inopportune moments.

**Above:** the Witch (Sonia Dresdel) tries to lead *Lizzie Dripping* (Tina Heath) astray once again.

Helen Cresswell's *Lizzie Dripping* came about after a chance conversation between the author and a neighbour. During the course of discussions the neighbour addressed her daughter with the words: 'Wake up, Lizzie Dripping.' The name is a parochial term around the Nottingham area for a girl who, while certainly gutsy, has difficulty determining the difference between fact and fiction. Cresswell felt the name had an inherent magical quality she found inspirational.

It's little wonder that Lizzie is a dreamer. There's very little else for her to do in the quiet village of Little Hemlock. She is a solitary figure and it would appear that there are very few, if any, children her own age. Twelve-year-old Lizzie is frustrated also by the fact that her mother treats her like a child. When Jonathan comes to stay with his busybody Aunt Blodwen, and Lizzie's father asks why, her mother quietly says, 'More a family matter, Albert, mother going into hospital.' Lizzie isn't fooled, saying to herself, 'His mam's having a baby. Why don't she just say? They never still think I think babies get found under gooseberry bushes?' Lizzie may well seem like a dreamer but the girl is no fool. She is very observant, seeing and hearing almost everything that happens round about her.

It shouldn't be surprising that Lizzie is the only villager who can see the witch. The witch is a metaphor representing Lizzie's desire to ease the boredom of Little Hemlock. Wherever and whenever the witch appears Lizzie usually finds herself in situations that give her a buzz even if they may not please her mother. 'Wherever you be, there am I,' the witch tells her. 'Anywhere you can go, I can go.' 'The things I'll do if I turn out to be a witch,' Lizzie contemplates. The witch acts as a physical representation of Lizzie's inner conscience, the part that dares her to do things that will ultimately land her in trouble.

Lizzie Dripping first appeared on television as part of the *Jackanory Playhouse* series in 1972. Seventeen-year-old Tina Heath, later a presenter on *Blue Peter*, played Lizzie 'strapped down' and maintained the part when the BBC commissioned the character's own series (*Blue Peter*'s Biddy Baxter recalled an anecdote about how surprised the crew of the series were when they finally saw Heath as herself without her little girl's costume but her age was clearly stated in *Radio Times* when the Playhouse was transmitted). Location shooting took place in the Nottinghamshire village of Eakring, where Cresswell lived at the time.

The story is told completely from Lizzie's point of view. It was therefore necessary to incorporate frequent narration, the words spoken by Tina Heath, to convey the character's thoughts. The amount of narration is such that it's likely Heath delivered a higher percentage of her lines in the dubbing studio. For the pilot episode Hannah Gordon filled in the gaps with a third-person narration.

Cresswell would further explore the concept of young girls at odds with their surroundings in *Moondial* and *The Secret World of Polly Flint,* the latter of which is almost a reworking of *Lizzie Dripping*. *Lizzie Dripping* is certainly the simplest of the three but has an undeniable summery charm, a by-product of the lead character's innocence and mischievousness.

**BBC**

**2 seasons and one pilot**
(colour)

**Pilot**
*Jackanory Playhouse*: **'Lizzie Dripping and The Orphans'**
**Broadcast:** Friday 15/12/72
**Written by** Helen Cresswell
**Narrator:** Hannah Gordon
**Designer:** Paul Munting
**Executive Producer:** Anna Home
**Director:** Angela Beeching

**Season One: *Lizzie Dripping***
**4 episodes**
('Lizzie Dripping and the Witch'; 'Lizzie Dripping's Black Sunday'; 'Lizzie Dripping Runs Away'; 'Lizzie Dripping and the Leek Nobblers')
**Broadcast:** Tuesdays 13/3/73 – 3/4/73

**Season Two: *Lizzie Dripping Again***
**4 episodes**
('Lizzie Dripping and the Little Angel'; 'Lizzie Dripping Tries a Spell'; 'Lizzie Dripping By the Sea'; 'Lizzie Dripping Says Goodbye')
**Broadcast:** Thursdays 27/2/75 – 27/3/75

**Main Cast:** Tina Heath (Lizzie Dripping), Sonia Dresdel (Witch), Barbara Mitchell (Patty), Geoffrey Matthews (Albert), Sheila Raynor (Gramma), Ann Morrish (Miss Platt – Season 1), Keith Allingham (Jonathan – Season 2)

**Written by** Helen Cresswell

**Designer:** David Crozier
**Executive Producer:** Anna Home
**Producer:** Angela Beeching
**Director:** Paul Stone

**Tie-in publications:** *Lizzie Dripping* (hardback and paperback), *Lizzie Dripping By the Sea* (paperback), *Lizzie Dripping and the Little Angel* (paperback), *Lizzie Dripping Again* (hardback-only compilation of the two paperbacks *... By the Sea* and *... Little Angel*) all published by BBC, 1974.

**Video:** *Lizzie Dripping and the Little Angel* – three unedited episodes at 70 minutes by BBC, 1990 (contains '... Little Angel', '... Tries a Spell' and '... By the Sea'). Deleted. Reissued by Paradox, 1995. Deleted 2/6/2000.

## The Tomorrow People

*'Most of the children alive today are potential telepaths. All they have to do is find the key within themselves and unlock the special powers we telepaths possess ...'*

*The Tomorrow People* always seemed an almost attainable fantasy which was presumably why it struck a chord with its young audience. Its teenage leads were so similar to that target audience that it was easy to believe that one day you might develop their powers and be able to teleport or 'jaunt' to other planets, or at least to the other side of the school playground. The Tomorrow People were a very exclusive set – once the teenagers had gone through the painful process of 'breaking out' (unsettlingly presented in the series' first episode) and realised their special powers they would sever all ties with parents, teachers and all of that boring stuff and get on with saving the planet. The series' creator Price had latched onto the fact that all kids think themselves superior to their elders and yearn to be special.

The Tomorrow People were the next step in human evolution, termed 'Homo Superior', with powers of teleportation, telepathy and telekinesis. Roger Price had been influenced equally by a meeting with David Bowie on the set of a TV pop show (the 'homo superior' label came via a Bowie lyric) and a mind-expanding novel called *The Mind in Chains*, by psycho-scientist Dr Christopher Evans. Evans would stay on as the programme's scientific adviser although to be honest there was precious little scientific theory on show in this rather knockabout 'science fiction' series.

A variety of line-ups came and went throughout the series' sporadic six-year run, child actors not being the most dependable of stars. The slightly older Nicholas Young stayed the course, however, as sensible big brother figure John. *The Tomorrow People* was a very spunky and enthusiastic series and this was its chief strength. Part of its utopian freshness came from its egalitarian casting policy – the first line-up included Sammie Winmill as Carol, no doubt to keep the girls interested in the sci-fi shenanigans, and Kenny, a streetsmart black boy. When Stephen Salmon was replaced, Kenny gave way to the stronger character of Liz, with actress Elizabeth Adare becoming something of a role model for black youths. There was the gypsy boy Tyso (underused when actor Dean Lawrence broke his leg) and popular pretty boy and fashion leader Stephen.

Later castings revolved around Roger Price's TV empire. Much hyped were Price's pop group Flintlock, who were the house band on his kids' comedy shows *Pauline's Quirkes* and *You Must Be Joking*. Flintlock drummer Mike Holoway became a Tomorrow Person and roped into the marketing effort was the comic *Look-In*, always a Thames-biased journal and staunch supporter of *The Tomorrow People*, Holoway and Flintlock. This gave the series a real pop edge

– indeed Flintlock themselves were central to the story 'The Heart of Sogguth'. One of the last Tomorrow People was Scots boy Andrew, played by Nigel Rhodes from Price's most recent comedy vehicle *You Can't Be Serious*. Somehow Pauline Quirke failed to jaunt in to join the gang (though she had a walk on in 'The Blue and The Green').

*The Tomorrow People* is often dismissed by its detractors for being rather dumb by comparison with its more cerebral ITV predecessors *Timeslip* and *Ace of Wands* (indeed it *was* joyously dumb most of the time). Still, 'The Vanishing Earth' was spookily eerie, despite a hotpants-wearing villainess, carrying an ecological message and possessing a genuinely doom-laden atmosphere as the Earth faced destruction due to violent climatic change. Most thought-provoking of all was 'The Blue and the Green'. A schoolboy's drawing pinned to the wall of his classroom can change its colour and its mood. The picture exerts a strange influence on the schoolkids who begin fighting with each other and the violence escalates when Robert, the boy who painted the picture, hands out badges to his classmates, thus separating them into two factions, the blues and the greens. References to real world confrontations such as those of Northern Ireland are atypical of the series as a whole.

The series was mostly honest runaround – or jauntaround – adventure. Season Three sustained a little conspiracy-styled tension by introducing the notion of the Tomorrow People's importance to various superpowers as a potential secret weapon. By and large though the series was becoming increasingly jokey, reaching its nadir – or zenith if that's your taste – with the extremely camp 'A Man for Emily' which featured future *Doctor Who* Peter Davison dressed variously in a cowboy outfit, a traffic warden's uniform and a fetching combination of blue underpants and curly blonde wig.

Seasons five to seven seemed ever more slapdash if admittedly great fun. The series was by now made up of flimsy two-parters, bringing the on-screen variant ever closer to the *Look-In* comic strip (also written by Price). Indeed the television story 'A Much Needed Holiday' was actually adapted from a 1975 *Look-In* strip. The action and ropey special effects took centre stage and the plots a back seat.

Its kitsch style and 70s fashion sense have marked *The Tomorrow People* out as a camp cult item many years later. Early in their career *The League of Gentlemen* team performed a stage play by way of an affectionate tribute, entitled *The Teen People*. The (one presumes) entirely innocent preponderance of naked young male flesh in the series has created a post-modern gay following for the show while the innuendo of 'breaking/coming out' has also been co-opted. The series' keenest followers have recently reunited many of the 70s cast in audio CD adventures.

The original series had ended, fittingly, with the decade in 1979 when the ITV strike curtailed an intended run and Roger Price headed to Canada to pursue other projects. With *The Tomorrow People* as much a part of a 70s childhood as Chopper bikes, a revival seemed most unlikely, but it happened nonetheless.

Fashion has a tendency to operate in twenty-year cycles and while the 90s embraced the ABBA revival and the return of flared trousers, so it also witnessed the re-emergence of the Homo Superior. Original series creator Roger Price was heavily involved but it is immediately clear that the new series has no real connection with the original series and therefore shouldn't be described as a sequel. It's more a glossy reworking of the original concept, starting from scratch for a new generation.

The series has the same basic make-up as before. A small group of children discover that they have telepathic abilities and are capable of teleportation. They are drawn by a beacon on a spacecraft beneath the sand of a foreign island where they discover they have a higher purpose in life. Adam, played by *Neighbours* star Kristian Schmid, is the eldest of the group and acts as the leader. Lisa, later replaced by Ami, is a confident black girl and Kevin is the child of the group. They are assisted by Kevin's school friend Megabyte who, by remarkable coincidence, eventually becomes a Tomorrow Person himself. The new series of *The Tomorrow People* has a noticeable international flavour missing from the 70s series.

Roger Price had attempted to gravitate the 70s series towards out-and-out comedy but had backtracked on the idea following extreme negative reaction to 'A Man for Emily'. In the 90s he clearly still maintained this desire. Megabyte and Kevin form a comedy double act, parents faint in a hilarious manner when they witness their offspring teleporting, and the villains are more camp than they are, well, villainous. Price was determined that the central characters in the new season, particularly Adam, wouldn't have John's air of pomposity. 'I think today's audience would have found John too serious,' Price commented. It's therefore ironic that Kristian Schmid is practically the only member of the cast who doesn't seem to be playing it for laughs.

In a decade of here today, gone tomorrow fads, ABBA and flares once again came and went. So too did *The Tomorrow People* after three short seasons. There's a danger in trying to recreate past glories and, if this was Roger Price's intention, he must surely have been disappointed. In the 70s *The Tomorrow People* was an exciting and much talked about trend setter. In the 90s it was a passable, enjoyable trend follower.

### The Tomorrow People (1973–79)

**Thames**
**8 seasons**
**68 episodes**
(colour)

**Main Cast:** Nicholas Young (John – Seasons 1–8), Peter Vaughan-Clarke (Stephen Jameson – Seasons 1–4), Sammie Winmill (Carol – Season 1), Stephen Salmon (Kenny – Season 1), Elizabeth Adare (Elizabeth M'Bondo – Seasons 2–8), Dean Lawrence (Tyso – Seasons 3–4), Mike Holoway (Mike Bell – Seasons 4–8), Misako Koba (Hsui Tai – Seasons 6–8), Nigel Rhodes (Andrew Forbes – Seasons 7–8), Philip Gilbert (Voice of TIM)

**Created by** Roger Price
**Title Music:** Dudley Simpson
**Script Editor:** Ruth Boswell (Season 4)
**Producers:** Ruth Boswell (Seasons 1–3), Roger Price (Seasons 1 and 4), Vic Hughes (Seasons 5–8)

**Season One**
**Broadcast:** Mondays 30/4/73 – 30/7/73 4.50p.m.

**'The Slaves of Jedikiah'** by Brian Finch and Roger Price
**5 episodes:** 30/4/73 – 4/6/73
**Designer:** Harry Clark
**Director:** Paul Bernard

**'The Medusa Strain'** by Brian Finch and Roger Price
**4 episodes:** 11/6/73 – 2/7/73
**Designer:** Harry Clark
**Director:** Roger Price

**'The Vanishing Earth'** by Brian Finch and Roger Price
**4 episodes:** 9/7/73 – 30/7/73
**Designer:** Harry Clark
**Director:** Paul Bernard

**Season Two**
**Broadcast:** Mondays 4/2/74 – 6/5/74 4.50p.m.

**'The Blue and the Green'** by Roger Price
**5 episodes:** 4/2/74 – 4/3/74 ('An Apple for the Teacher'; 'The Changing Picture'; 'The Trojan Horse'; 'Cuckoo in the Nest'; 'The Swarming Season')
**Designer:** Michael Minas
**Director:** Roger Price

**'A Rift in Time'** by Roger Price
**4 episodes:** 11/3/74 – 1/4/74 ('Vase of Mystery'; 'Turn of the Thumb'; 'From Little Acorns'; 'Rise of the Roman Empire')
**Designer:** Michael Minas
**Director:** Darrol Blake

**'The Doomsday Men'** by Roger Price
**4 episodes:** 8/4/74 – 6/5/74 ('Dressed to Kill'; 'The Burning Sword'; 'Run Rabbit Run'; 'The Shuttlecock')
**Designer:** Michael Minas
**Director:** Roger Price

**Season Three**
**Broadcast:** Wednesdays 26/2/75 – 21/5/75 4.50p.m.

**'Secret Weapon'** by Roger Price
**4 episodes:** 26/2/75 – 19/3/75 ('Lost and Found'; 'Not Quite A Sleeping Beauty'; 'Whose Side Are You On Professor?'; 'A Present From Russia')
**Designer:** Philip Blowers
**Director:** Stan Woodward

**'Worlds Away'** by Roger Price
**3 episodes:** 26/3/75 – 9/4/75 ('Secret of the Pyramid'; 'Hound of the Night'; 'More for the Burning')
**Designer:** Philip Blowers
**Directors:** Dennis Kirkland (Studio) and Vic Hughes (Location)

**'A Man for Emily'** by Roger Price
**3 episodes:** 16/4/75 – 30/4/75 ('The Fastest Gun'; 'Here We Go Round The Doozlum'; 'A Man for Emily')
**Designer:** Philip Blowers
**Director:** Stan Woodward

**'The Revenge of Jedikiah'** by Roger Price
**3 episodes:** 7/5/75 – 21/5/75 ('The Curse of the Mummy's Tomb'; 'Last Chance'; 'Farewell Performance')
**Designer:** Philip Blowers
**Director:** Vic Hughes

**Season Four**
**Broadcast:** Wednesdays 28/1/76 – 10/3/76 4.50p.m.

**'One Law'** by Roger Price
**3 episodes:** 28/1/76 – 11/2/76 ('One Law for the Poor'; 'Another for the Rich'; 'Which Prohibits Them Equally From Stealing Bread')
**Designer:** Peter Elliot
**Director:** Leon Thau

**'Into the Unknown'** by Jon Watkins
**4 episodes:** 18/2/76 – 10/3/76 ('The Visitor'; 'The Father-Ship'; 'The Tunnel'; 'The Circle')
**Designer:** Peter Elliot
**Director:** Roger Price

**Season Five**
**Broadcast:** Mondays 28/2/77 – 4/4/77 4.45p.m.

**'The Dirtiest Business'** by Roger Price
**2 episodes:** 28/2/77 – 7/3/77 ('A Spy is Born'; 'A Spy Dies')
**Designer:** David Richens
**Director:** Vic Hughes

**'A Much Needed Holiday'** by Roger Price
**2 episodes:** 14/3/77 – 21/3/77 ('Spilled Porridge'; 'Just Deserts')
**Designer:** David Richens
**Director:** Richard Mervyn

**'The Heart of Sogguth'** by Roger Price
**2 episodes:** 28/3/77 – 4/4/77 ('Beat the Drum'; 'Devil in Disguise')
**Designer:** David Richens
**Director:** Vic Hughes

**Season Six**
**Broadcast:** Mondays 15/5/78 – 26/6/78* 4.45p.m.
*No broadcast on 29/5/78 due to Bank Holiday schedules

**'The Lost Gods'** by Roger Price
**2 episodes:** 15/5/78 – 22/5/78 ('Flight of Fantasy'; 'Life Before Death')
**Designer:** David Richens
**Director:** Vic Hughes

**'Hitler's Last Secret'** by Roger Price
**2 episodes:** 5/6/78 – 12/6/78 ('Men Like Rats'; 'Seeds of Destruction')
**Designer:** Allan Cameron
**Director:** Leon Thau

**Facing page:** *The Tomorrow People* and computer TIM in their underground lab for Season Three of the Thames series; (l to r) Stephen (Peter Vaughan-Clarke), Liz (Elizabeth Adare), Tyso (Dean Lawrence) and leader John (Nicholas Young).

**'The Thargon Menace'** by Roger Price
**2 episodes:** 19/6/78 – 26/6/78 ('Unexpected Guests';
'Playing With Fire')
**Designer:** Martyn Herbert
**Director:** Peter Yolland

**Season Seven**
**Broadcast:** Mondays 9/10/78 – 13/11/78 4.45p.m.

**'Castle of Fear'** by Roger Price
**2 episodes:** 9/10/78 – 16/10/78 ('Ghosts and Monsters';
'Fighting Spirit')
**Designer:** Gordon Toms
**Director:** Vic Hughes

**'Achilles Heel'** by Roger Price
**2 episodes:** 23/10/78 – 30/10/78 ('A Room at the Inn';
'Everything to Lose')
**Designer:** Gordon Toms
**Director:** Vic Hughes

**'Living Skins'** by Roger Price
**2 episodes:** 6/11/78 – 13/11/78 ('Harmless Fashion';
'Cold War')
**Designer:** Gordon Toms
**Director:** Stan Woodward

**Season Eight**
**Broadcast:** Mondays 29/1/79 – 19/2/79 4.45p.m.

**'War of Empires'** by Roger Price
**4 episodes** ('Close Encounter'; 'Contact!'; 'Standing Alone';
'All in the Mind')
**Designer:** John Plant
**Director:** Vic Hughes

**Tie-in publications:** novelisation by Roger Price and Julian R.
Gregory, *The Tomorrow People in The Visitor* published in
paperback by Piccolo/TV Times, 1973. Further novelisations by
Roger Price all published by Piccolo/TV Times: *The Tomorrow
People in Three in Three*, 1974; *The Tomorrow People in Four
into Three*, 1975; *The Tomorrow People in One Law*, 1976; *The
Tomorrow People in The Lost Gods with Hitler's Last Secret
and The Thargon Menace*.
*The Tomorrow People Annual 1979*, Stafford Pemberton, 1978.

**Video:** 'The Slaves of Jedikiah' (episodes 1–3) and 'The Slaves
of Jedikiah' (episodes 4–5) released episodically in UK as 78
minutes and 52 minutes on separate cassettes by
Thames/Video Gems 11/9/95. Deleted 1/4/96.
Simultaneous releases on VHS and Region 0 DVD from
Revelation Films: 'The Slaves of Jedikiah' 25/2/02;
'The Medusa Strain' 22/4/02; 'The Vanishing Earth' 24/6/02.
All episodic and unedited. Also available as three-disc DVD
box set.

**The Tomorrow People** (1992–95)

**Tetra Films in association with Reeves Entertainment for
Thames and Nickelodeon**
**3 seasons**
**25 episodes**
80    (colour)

**Main Cast:** Kristian Schmid (Adam), Kristen Ariza (Lisa –
Season 1), Adam Pearce (Kevin – Seasons 1 and 2), Christian
Tessier (Megabyte), Naomi Harris (Ami – Seasons 2 and 3)

**Created by** Roger Damon Price

**Music:** Andrew Phillips
**Producer:** Roger Price (Season 1), Alan Horrox
(Season 2 and 3)
**Executive Producer for Reeves Entertainment:** Michael Yudin
(Season 1)
**Executive Producer for Nickelodeon:** Jay Mulvaney
**Executive Producer:** Alan Horrox (Season 1), Roger Price
(Season 2 and 3)

**Season One**
**5 episodes**
**Broadcast:** Wednesdays 18/11/92 – 16/12/92

**Written by** Roger Price
**Music by** Tim Pitt and Bobby Boughton
**Designer:** Mark Tildesley
**Director:** Ron Oliver

**Season Two**
**Broadcast:** Tuesdays 4/1/94 – 8/3/94

**'The Culex Experiment'** by Lee Pressman and Grant Cathro
**5 episodes:** 4/1/94 – 1/2/94
**Designer:** Mark Tildesley
**Directors:** Alex Horrox and Vivianne Albertine

**'Monsoon Man'** by Grant Cathro and Lee Pressman
**5 episodes:** 8/2/94 – 8/3/94
**Designer:** Jon Henson
**Director:** Niall Leonard

**Season Three**
**Broadcast:** Wednesdays 4/1/95 – 8/3/95

**'The Rameses Connection'** by Grant Cathro
**5 episodes:** 4/1/95 – 1/2/95
**Director:** Roger Gartland

**'The Living Stones'** by Lee Pressman
**5 episodes:** 8/2/95 – 8/3/95
**Director:** Crispin Reece

**Tie-in publications:** novelisations *Monsoon Man*, *The Culex
Experiment*, *The Rameses Connection* and *The Living Stones*
published in paperback by Boxtree, Boxtree, Sapling and
Sapling respectively, 1995

**Video:** *The Tomorrow People* (78-minute compilation of first
story) released in UK by Thames 17/5/93. Deleted 14/12/94.

## Pollyanna

Polly Harington is middle-aged, rich and extremely bitter following a broken love affair. She has grown accustomed to her solitary existence and it is therefore only out of duty that she feels she should take responsibility for Pollyanna, her recently orphaned niece.

Regardless of her own personal grief, Pollyanna believes that there is nothing that cannot be overcome by a positive attitude, something she refers to as her 'just being glad game'. She has much work to do in a town where there are many unhappy people but within a very short space of time Pollyanna's happy disposition has warmed the hearts of those she meets. Mr Pendleton, the ill-tempered bachelor, soon yearns for a child of his own, and Mrs Snow, confined to her bed, grows to cherish every one of Pollyanna's visits. Even Aunt Polly finds herself charmed and slowly begins to unearth a happiness she had long forgotten.

Tragedy strikes when, returning from school, Pollyanna is run over. Although she survives, her legs are badly broken. Pollyanna's positive attitude is put to the test as she comes to terms with the fact that she cannot walk.

Worthy of note is the serial's American setting of Vermont. This meant the BBC had to recreate US locales, with varying degrees of success, in studio and in filmed environs closer to home (you might be surprised but English countryside looks nothing like American countryside). Elaine Stritch is the only genuine American in the cast and elsewhere there are various struggles with accents.

**Pollyanna**
**BBC**
**6 episodes**
(colour)
**Broadcast:** Sundays 7/10/73 – 11/11/73

**Main Cast:** Elaine Stritch (Aunt Polly), Elizabeth Archard (Pollyanna Whittier), Paddy Frost (Nancy), Ray McAnally (John Pendleton), Paul Maxwell (Dr Chilton), Stephen Galloway (Jimmy Bean), Donald Bisset (Old Tom), Robert Coleby (Timothy), Bessie Love (Mrs Snow), Valerie Colgan (Milly Snow)

Based on the novel by Eleanor H. Porter (first UK publication 1927, Harrap)
**Dramatised by** Joy Harington
**Script Editor:** Alistair Bell

**Music** composed by Wilfred Josephs, conducted by Marcus Dods
**Designer:** Allan Anson
**Producer:** John McRae
**Director:** June Wyndham-Davies

**Tie-in publications:** editions of novel published by Puffin, 1973

**Video:** released in UK as a 155-minute compilation on double cassette by BBC, 3/2/92

## The Terracotta Horse

The Jackson family are leaving Britain for Morocco, taking with them the small ornamental terracotta horse which young Linda Jackson believes could lead them to the greatest discovery in history, the location of the Holy Grail. It may not be plain sailing for the Jackson family, however, when they discover that they are being followed by a mysterious man in a Citroën. Another man, called Walters, also becomes aware that the horse could lead Linda to the Grail and he too starts to tail the family. David Jackson overhears a conversation that immediately places him in danger and Linda, travelling to Marrakesh, discovers a further inscription that brings her closer to the treasure. Will Linda find the Grail before those who pursue her? If she does, can she prevent them from taking it?

*The Terracotta Horse* is a basic adventure series, some of which was filmed in overseas European locations.

**BBC**
**6 episodes** ('The Seal of Solomon'; 'The Third Pentangle'; 'The Legend of the Grail'; 'The House of Columns'; 'The Stones of Ain Khalifa'; 'The Place of Solomon's Seal') (colour)
**Broadcast:** Mondays 12/11/73 – 17/12/73

**Main Cast:** Godfrey James (Bob Jackson), Kristine Howarth (Maggie Jackson), Lindy Howard (Linda Jackson), Patrick Murray (David Jackson), James Warwick (Dan Walters), Constantin De Goguel (Meissner), Nadim Sawalha (Hussein)

**Written by** Christopher Bond
**Script Editor:** Douglas Watkinson

**Producer:** Bill Sellars

**Tie-in publications:** n/k

## Carrie's War

It is odd to think that for many years Nina Bawden's novel was required reading on the school curriculum, set to give youngsters an insight into the lives of children during the Second World War – mainly because neither the book nor the resulting television adaptation actually has anything much to say about the war, bar some initial scene setting and info dumping. The title in fact describes an emotional war fought by twelve-year-old Carrie Willow, her attempts to reconcile the various parties in the story without taking sides and the battle to make her voice heard in a world run by adults.

*Carrie's War* is very much a character-driven novel, where interaction, emotion and internalised thoughts are more important than actions. Although the story is full of small incidents, there is very little plot and as such *Carrie's War* wouldn't seem a front-runner for television adaptation. To its credit the production is entirely faithful to the intent of the original work.

The novel is set up very much as a flashback piece, using the narration of a nostalgic, grown-up and widowed Caroline Willow, but the TV drama is seen through a child's eyes and sets itself very much in its period. It opens with a steam train puffing its way through peaceful countryside to stop at a remote station. A school of evacuees are reminded not to forget their gasmasks as they alight the train to start a new life in this Welsh valley town. The gaggle of uniforms are taken to a local hall where Carrie and her younger brother Nick are taken in by their new 'Auntie Lou'. A timid, fretful woman, she lives in the local general store with her brother, the overbearing 'fire 81

**Above:** Carrie Willow (Juliet Waley) finds the old skull residing in Mrs Gotobed's house.

and brimstone' figure Samuel Evans. The children are frightened by the mean-spirited ogre who oversees a cold, inhospitable household.

The children find comfort in the farmhouse at Druid's Bottom, where fellow evacuee Albert Sandwich is billeted. Evans' elderly sister Dilys Gotobed lives here with her housekeeper Hepzibah Green – whom some say is a 'white witch' – and distant cousin, the simple and near-mute Mr Johnny. Relations between Evans and his sister are strained to say the least – Dilys married the mine-owner's son while their father was 'still warm' after being killed in a mine disaster. A full life of socialising later Mrs Gotobed is now dying but still neither sibling will contact the other. Thus the sympathetic Carrie becomes something of a go-between, a message carrier for Mrs Gotobed and a spy for Mr Evans.

The story depends upon the complex relationships between some wonderful characters. As the story progresses Carrie discovers Evans is not wholly evil. His final scene is a wonderfully intimate tête-à-tête with Carrie, where Evans finds a note from Lou telling him that she has run off to marry her American forces sweetheart.

Hepzibah is the motherly figure, usually to be seen at the roaring hearth of her kitchen, with any suggestion of her witchcraft largely removed from the story. A potentially sinister scene from the novel where Hepzibah tells the story of the old skull was altered so that she instead told a nostalgic tale of visiting a travelling fair as a child. Despite the softening of this particular character, *Carrie's War* is far from toothless and cosy. One of the more interesting aspects explored is the death of Mrs Gotobed. The character is at once both eccentric and dignified.

In 1973 *Carrie's War*, at five episodes in length, was one of the most ambitious children's productions yet undertaken by the BBC. The serial was filmed all on location in among the steeply terraced houses and bleak hills of Blaengarw, a typical Welsh mining town. Although not mentioned by name in the novel this was in fact the intended setting of Bawden's tale. The author had been evacuated here, albeit for one week, in 1940.

What many remember of *Carrie's War* is the spooky air and a misplaced sense of menace. Some even hold the mistaken memory that it was in fact a telefantasy or supernatural serial. There is good reason for this – the road to Druid's Bottom is dark and stormy and there are strange noises in the grove; Mrs Gotobed's house meanwhile is all long shadows and candlelight. The 'cursed' skull is of course central to the story.

*Carrie's War* attracted praise from entranced child viewers as well as adults nostalgically recalling their own wartime experiences. The series' appeal widened yet further with a 1975 repeat in the Sunday afternoon 'family' slot. While there had been earlier breakthrough successes it was this watershed production that really set the standard for all BBC children's drama that followed.

**BBC**
**5 episodes**
(colour)

**Episode One**
Monday 28/1/74 5.15p.m.
Carrie and Nick Willow are evacuated to a village in South Wales during World War II and are taken in by the strict Mr Evans and his timid sister, Lou.

**Episode Two**
Monday 4/2/74 5.15p.m.
The children visit Mr Evans' sister, Mrs Gotobed, in her old house in Druid's Bottom.

**Episode Three**
Monday 11/2/74 5.15p.m.
Mr Evans' son Frederick visits on leave from the fighting but Mrs Gotobed is dying.

**Episode Four**
Monday 18/2/74 5.15p.m.
Mr Evans threatens to throw Hepzibah and Johnny out of the Gotobed house. When Carrie hears of the cursed skull that is believed to keep the house safe she throws it down the well.

**Episode Five**
Monday 25/2/74 5.15p.m.
Mr Evans is left alone when Carrie and Nick take the train back to stay with their mother but there is one last terrible shock to come.

**Main Cast:** Juliet Waley (Carrie), Andrew Tinney (Nick), Aubrey Richards (Mr Evans), Avril Elgar (Auntie Lou), Rosalie Crutchley (Hepzibah Green), Matthew Guinness (Mr Johnny), Tim Coward (Albert Sandwich), Patsy Smart (Mrs Gotobed)

Adapted from the novel by Nina Bawden (first published 1973, Victor Gollancz)
**Dramatised by** Marilyn Fox

**Designer:** David Crozier
**Executive Producer:** Anna Home
**Director:** Paul Stone

**Tie-in publications:** editions published in paperback by Puffin, 1974–88

**Video:** five-episode version issued by BBC Educational Publishing, for sale to schools only (opening recaps on episodes two to five removed)

## Boy Dominic

It's 1820 and young Dominic Bulman's world is torn apart the day he hears that his father's ship, *The Bright Star*, has been wrecked off the coast of North Africa. With no money coming in, he and his mother are forced to sell their comfortable home in Greenwich to face an uncertain future without the Captain. Unknown to them, Charles Bulman has survived the shipwreck but must avoid white slavers and prison before he can escape Africa.

Nick and his mother travel to Yorkshire and the ruined Bulman family pile but are turned away by Lady Bulman who considers Dominic's mother Emma to be a usurper only after the Captain's money. With nowhere else to turn, mother and son throw in their lot with an old seafaring friend of the Captain's, a rather wild and often drunken salt called William Woodcock. They open a guest house, welcoming all manner of patrons including the famous highwayman Harry Darkness.

Events take another turn when the Captain makes his way back to England and discovers that the sinking of the *Star* was sabotage and not an accident – Joshua Kemp and the scheming Jackson planned all along to take the Captain's money. The blaggards receive their comeuppance and the Bulmans are together again.

Not for long though. The next series ditched its slightly cosy family feel – and how – when Nick's parents were murdered in the opening episode of the sequel series. Now titled just *Dominic*, with the boy turning to man to avenge his parents' death, this was a tougher adventure mystery than before. The clue to the murder was a Hunter – a gold watch found at the scene of the crime. On the back is an engraving of the family crest of Lord Stainton, a scientist with an interest in rocketry, and this starts a trail that leads Nick into foul company among smugglers.

**Boy Dominic (1974)**
(NB: series developed and publicised as *The Log of the Boy Dominic*)
**Yorkshire**
**13 episodes** ('Lost at Sea'; 'Lodgings to Let'; 'The Man Who Loved Children'; 'Captain Darkness'; 'Fair Game'; 'Medicine Man'; 'The Man With The Painted Face'; 'A Frog He Would A-Wooing Go'; 'Sermons and Snuff'; 'Friends of the Family'; 'Ghost in Greenwich'; 'Lady Bulman Regrets'; 'Charles and Emma')
(colour)
**Broadcast:** Sundays 24/3/74 – 16/6/74 (networked with timing variations – 3.35p.m. Scottish, ATV and Westward 5.35p.m., 4.50p.m. in rest of ITV regions)

**Main Cast:** Murray Dale (Dominic Bulman), Richard Todd (Captain Charles Bulman), Hildegard Neil (Emma Bulman), Brian Blessed (William Woodcock), Ruth Kettlewell (Bessie

Dearlove), Julian Glover (Jackson), Ivor Dean (Joshua Kemp), Mary Morris (Lady Bulman)

**Written by** Keith Dewhurst (1, 4), Nick McCarty (2, 6, 8, 11), John Brason (3, 7), Penelope Lively (5, 9, 10), Denis Constanduros (12, 13)
**Story Editor:** Joy Whitby

**Designer:** Roger Andrews
**Producer:** Terence Williams
**Production Associates:** Peter Max-Wilson, Ian Frazer
**Executive Producer:** Jess Yates
**Directors:** Gareth Davies (1, 4, 5), John Davies (2, 3, 6, 7, 12, 13), Jeremy Summers (8, 9), Terence Williams (10, 11)

**Tie-in publications:** novelisation by Geoffrey Morgan published in paperback by Armada, 1974

**Dominic (1976)**
**Yorkshire**
**8 episodes** ('Hangman's Hollow'; 'The Hunter'; 'Miss Sarah'; 'The Crypt'; 'The Brotherhood'; 'Lucy and Harriet'; 'Twenty Years Ago'; 'Beyond Gravity')
(colour)
**Broadcast:** Sundays 15/2/76 – 4/4/76 (networked)

**Main Cast:** Murray Dale (Dominic Bulman), Stacey Tendeter (Lucy), John Hallam (Captain Beever), Louise Jameson (Lady Harriet), Gordon Gostelow (Bartholemew Finn), Thorley Walters (Lord Stainton), Edwin Richfield (Wardley)

**Written by** Keith Dewhurst (1–6), David Corbey (7, 8)
**Deviser:** Joy Whitby

**Designer:** Gordon Livesey
**Producer:** Hugh David
**Executive Producer:** Robert Corder
**Director:** Hugh David (1, 2, 7, 8), David Reynolds (3–6)

## Soldier and Me

A chase epic that saw two boys on the run from four sinister assassins. Jim Woolcott befriends Istvan Szolda after rescuing him from a beating by a gang of bullies and nicknames him 'Soldier' in a mispronunciation of his name. Istvan and his family escaped from Czechoslovakia in the aftermath of the 1968 revolt and so it is that he comes to overhear four Czech assassins plotting the execution of a dissident hiding out in Manchester. Of course, no-one will believe these kids when they try to report what they have heard to the police. Soldier and Jim witness the murder and when the two boys are spotted by the 'Boss' he and his three henchmen set off in pursuit of the pair, intending to silence them.

The serial was adapted by David Line from his own novel, the only revision updating the action to take place in the wake of the Czech revolt instead of the original Hungarian revolution around ten years before. The change was suggested by producer Brian Armstrong who, while working as a *World in Action* reporter, had risked certain death in Prague by smuggling out film of the uprising from under Russian noses.

The chase took in the less salubrious parts of Manchester and Stockport as well as the wilds of the Pennines and the Lake District, with the boys jumping off speeding trains and crossing stormy lakes to escape their pursuers. The shoot took a twenty-five-strong unit four months to film.

### Granada
**9 episodes** ('Conspiracy'; 'The House of Secrets'; 'Alibi'; 'Jump'; 'Cross Country'; 'Alone'; 'Hunted'; 'Trapped'; 'No Escape') (colour)
**Broadcast:** Sundays 15/9/74 – 10/11/74 (4.50p.m. in most regions, 5.35p.m. in others)

**Main Cast:** Richard Willis ('Soldier'), Gerald Sundquist (Jim Woolcott), Milos Kirek ('Boss'), Derrick O'Connor, Richard Ireson, Constantin de Goguel (henchmen)

Based on the novel *Run For Your Life* by David Line (first UK publication 1966, Jonathan Cape)
**Adapted by** David Line

**Designer:** Michael Grimes
**Producer:** Brian Armstrong
**Director:** Carol Wilks

**Tie-in publications:** editions published in paperback (as *Run For Your Life*) by Puffin, 1974–79

## Rogue's Rock

Rogue's Rock, a small island off the South Coast of Britain, is found to contain an abundance of uranium ore highly sought after by the world's superpowers. Having declared their independence, the islanders can only rely on themselves for help and protection as the island becomes the focal point for international leaders and mining experts.

Leading the charge against any invaders is Commander Rogue. Assisted by his faithful retainer, Hawkins, Rogue sets about ensuring that Maynard, a mining engineer who arrives on the island, leaves as soon as possible. Then, when ambassadors arrive on the Rock, the islanders start to feel as if they are being pushed and pulled between two superpowers.

*Rogue's Rock* was described by *TV Times* as a 'comedy adventure with rough and tumble chase'. Will Polberry, played by Royston Tickner, is the resident comedy character, bringing light relief in amongst treasure troves, spies and intrigue. The only person on the island with a television, Will makes money by selling tickets to watch his TV and ice cream to go with it.

Sadly, Clive Morton had passed away following completion of the first season and Donald Hewlett took over the lead role for Season Two, playing Wing Commander Julius Rogue. It was explained that his brother had left to represent the island at the United Nations. Rogue was helped by two intrepid young assistants, Tom and *Avengers*-girl type Jane.

Intrigue is high on the agenda as Asian agents arrive with a plot to make off with the Mask of Bakonga. The island also makes a trade pact with the Soviet Union, which brings attention from the Americans. Will and Hawkins soon uncover a plot by the American government to invade Rogue's Rock. The third and final season presented further adventures of this ilk. Two strangers to the island find a chest full of silver ingots, while Will and Hawkins concoct a plan to attract tourists

to the island. When the island strikes oil it has consequences for the wildlife when the rig frightens the fish away. A young American thinks that he has the answer.

### Southern
**3 seasons**
(colour)

**Main Cast:** Clive Morton (Commander Rogue – Season 1), Donald Hewlett (Wing Commander Rogue – Seasons 2 and 3), Kristin Hatfield (Katy – Season 1), Royston Tickner (Will), Graham Simpson (Tom – Seasons 2 and 3), Harold Goodwin (Hawkins), Susan Dury (Jane Steele – Season 2)

**Producer:** Chris McMaster

**Season One**
**6 episodes** ('On the Rock'; 'Runes'; 'Treasure'; 'Blockade'; 'Raising the Wind'; 'Raising the Flag')
**Broadcast:** Wednesdays 6/11/74 – 11/12/74

**Written by** Peter Miles (1), Keith Miles (2, 3, 5), Paul Erikson (6), (4 n/k)
**Designer:** John Dilly
**Executive Producer:** Lewis Rudd

**Season Two**
**13 episodes** - nominally as 3 stories (4-5-4) ('Refugee'; 'Network'; 'Kidnap!'; 'Double Trouble'; 'Taped!'; 'Crisis!'; 'Minisub'; 'Intrepid'; 'Invasion'; 'Wrecked!'; 'Aged!'; 'Slaves'; 'Mayday!')
**Broadcast:** Mondays 8/12/75 – 1/3/76

**Written by** Royston Caws (1–4), Ralph Wright (5–9), David Stevens (10–13)

**Film Editor:** Mike Womersley
**Designer:** John Dilly

**Season Three**
**8 episodes** ('Galleon'; 'Waterloo'; 'Black Gold'; 'Phoenix'; 'El Akhram'; 'Penny'; 'Up the Spout'; 'El Aziz')
**Broadcast:** Wednesdays 8/9/76 – 27/10/76 (no Scottish/Grampian broadcast 13/10/76 due to Scotland football match; broadcast 14/10/76 in those regions)

**Written by** Ian Cullen (1–4), Royston Caws (5–8)

**Designer:** John Dilly
**Director:** Chris McMaster

## The Secret Garden

Mary Lennox is a spoilt, ill-tempered young girl recently orphaned. Returning to Britain from India, she is to stay at her uncle's remote Yorkshire mansion, Misselthwaite Manor. There she discovers an oppressive atmosphere of sadness, a hidden garden and a hypochondriac boy called Colin. With the help of Dickon, a local village lad, Mary resurrects the secret garden where Colin's mother died, a garden that lies at the heart of discontent at her uncle's home.

On its initial publication Frances Hodgson Burnett's *The Secret Garden* received unfavourable press, described by the American Library Association as 'over sentimental and dealing almost wholly with abnormal people'. These comments are indicative of a time when the function of the child was to be seen and not heard. *The Secret Garden* takes this strict Victorian stance still prevalent in Edwardian times and throws it right out of the window. Now, nearly ninety years later, the book is regarded as Burnett's best work. It is therefore little wonder that it has been adapted twice for the cinema and on no less than three occasions for children's television.

The first two were shot in black and white in the 50s and 60s. The adaptation in 1952 utilised both studio VT and a small amount of film shot on location in the South of England. The 1960 production used a greater amount of filmed location work. On this occasion the production team had to overcome two main areas of concern. Burnett's book incorporated various animals and this problem was resolved thanks to Chessington Zoo. Also, with the story starting in mid-winter and ending in late spring but with filming taking place in winter at Penhurst Place, Kent, the production team had to recreate spring by planting daffodils and crocuses in the flower-beds.

In 1975 the BBC pushed the boat out a little further for the third incarnation. It is, however, a victory of period style over actual content. Burnett's novel is as far removed from frenetic action and incident as you could possibly get, laden instead with long scenes containing either large chunks of dialogue or much meandering through the grounds of Misselthwaite Manor. On screen it's too long at seven episodes and on some occasions the viewer could be forgiven for thinking that nothing had happened by the end of an episode.

As a child Dorothea Brooking had been greatly impressed with the novel. This was the third time she had produced the story as a serial, something she considered to be a personal achievement. Brooking had been involved in the BBC's adaptation of *Tom's Midnight Garden* the year previously and unfortunately *The Secret Garden* suffers from the same distracting production errors. The frequency of editing between VT in studio, location filming and stock footage is really quite off-putting. Although such switching was a much used technique of the time its often illogical use here rests uneasy on the eye of the viewer, particularly when the key setting of the Secret Garden itself is rendered in a studio that seemingly exists at the centre of filmed locations.

Regardless of the production's technical issues *The Secret Garden* is still a good demonstration of character development and gently worked themes. The garden is a clear metaphor of Mary and Colin's situation. Like the garden, both of them have been neglected to an extent and have become spoilt as a result. In healing the garden they heal themselves, an indication of Burnett's belief in the importance of nature and its therapeutic effects.

*The Secret Garden*, content to canter along at a slow pace, requires quite a degree of patience and concentration. It looks and feels like your archetypal Sunday teatime family drama and it's therefore strange to note that it was originally broadcast on Wednesday afternoons.

Based on the novel by Frances Hodgson Burnett (first UK publication 1910, Heinemann)

## *The Secret Garden* (1952)
### BBC
**8 episodes** ('There Is No-one Left'; 'Across the Moor'; 'Cry in the Corridor'; 'Door in the Wall'; 'Colin'; 'Tantrum in the Night'; 'It Has Come'; 'When the Sun Went Down')
(b&w)
**Broadcast:** Tuesdays 29/4/52 – 17/6/52

**Main Cast:** Elizabeth Saunders (Mary Lennox), Brian Roper (Dickon), Dawson France (Colin), Herbert Smith (Ben Weatherstaff), Billie Whitelaw (Martha), Richard Wade (Thomas)

**Written by** Alice De Gray
**Settings by** Lawrence Broadhouse
**Producer/Director:** Dorothea Brooking

## *The Secret Garden* (1960)
### BBC
**8 episodes** ('There Is No-one Left'; 'Misselthwaite Manor'; 'Cry in the Corridor'; 'Door in the Wall'; 'I am Colin'; 'Tantrum'; 'Magic'; 'I Shall Live Forever')
(b&w)
**Broadcast:** Sundays 3/1/60 – 21/2/60

**Main Cast:** Gillian Ferguson (Mary Lennox), Colin Spaull (Dickon), Peter Hempson (Colin), Fred Fairclough (Ben Weatherstaff), Prunella Scales (Martha), Stuart Hutchison (Thomas)

**Written by** Dorothea Brooking
**Settings by** Richard Henry
**Produced by** Dorothea Brooking

## *The Secret Garden* (1975)
### BBC
**7 episodes**
(colour)

### Episode One
'There is no one left'
Wednesday 1/1/75 5.00p.m.
Following the death of her parents, Mary Lennox is sent to stay at her Uncle Craven's mansion. Her maid tells her that there is a garden in the grounds that has remained locked for ten years. Mary is determined to find the garden.

### Episode Two
'The cry in the corridor'
Wednesday 8/1/75 5.15p.m.
Mary finds an old key buried in the earth, revealed to her by the robin that sings in the garden. At the house she thinks she hears the sound of crying and concludes that there is someone hidden there.

### Episode Three
'The door in the wall'
Wednesday 15/1/75 5.15p.m.
Mary discovers a hidden door out in the grounds. Using the old key she has found she opens it and finds herself in a walled garden. Mary then meets young Dickon and makes him promise to keep the garden their secret.

**Facing page:** orphan Mary Lennox (Sarah Hollis Andrews) arrives at Misselthwaite Manor and stumbles across *The Secret Garden* (BBC 1975).

### Episode Four
'I am Colin'
Wednesday 22/1/75 5.15p.m.
Mary meets her uncle for the first time and asks him if she may have some earth for a garden. During the night Mary hears crying again. Investigating, she discovers a hidden room and a boy called Colin.

### Episode Five
'A tantrum'
Wednesday 29/1/75 5.15p.m.
Dickon and Mary believe that the garden could make Colin well again and cure his tantrums. She tells Colin that he isn't ill at all and only does it for attention.

### Episode Six
'When the sun went down'
Wednesday 5/2/75 5.15p.m.
Colin is taken to the garden and gradually discovers that he is able to walk again.

### Episode Seven
'Magic'
Wednesday 12/2/75 5.15p.m.
Colin's health continues to improve. When his father returns to the manor he discovers there has been much change for the better.

**Main Cast:** Sarah Hollis Andrews (Mary Lennox), Andrew Harrison (Dickon), David Patterson (Colin), Tom Harrison (Ben Weatherstaff), Jacqueline Hoyle (Martha), William Marsh (John), Hope Johnstone (Mrs Medlock), John Woodnutt (Mr Archibald Craven)

**Dramatised by** Dorothea Brooking

**Oboe Soloist:** Malcolm Messiter
**Designer:** Guthrie Hutton
**Producer:** Dorothea Brooking

**Tie-in publications:** paperback editions of novel published by Puffin, 1975

**Video:** Released in UK as a 107-minute compilation by BBC Video, 1984. Deleted. Reissued in *Family Classics* series by BBC Video, 3/4/95.
Released in US as 107-minute compilation by Playhouse Video. Deleted.

## The Changes

In terms of both scale and epic length *The Changes* was certainly the most ambitious production thus far tackled by the BBC Children's Department. It was Children's Drama Producer Anna Home who adapted Peter Dickinson's trilogy of novels in close consultation with the author. *The Changes* trilogy had consisted of unconnected episodes set at various points in Britain's future and Home sweepingly rearranged these events into a linear storyline. She condensed what was as much as a decade of events into a tight and manageable story covering just a few months with one central heroine constant throughout. Nicky Gore, from Dickinson's third novel *The Devil's Children*, was aged upwards to fifteen and appeared in all ten episodes. The choice of a consistent heroine is a wise one leading to greater audience identification. Choosing a female character no doubt helped give more across-the-board appeal, seeing as the story itself – science fiction-tinged adventure – is traditionally viewed as boys' fare.

Though the joins are fairly seamless, close examination reveals the adventure's episodic origins. Episode one tells of the coming of *The Changes* in brutal style. It's violent and unsettling; by the end the towns and cities are laid waste and deserted as people rage against the machine and destroy all modern technology. Much quoted similarities between *The Changes* and other post-apocalypse fiction such as *Day of the Triffids* are really only noticeable here.

In the search for her parents Nicky comes across a caravan of Sikh people and this leads into a retelling of Dickinson's *Devil's Children*, a metaphor for racism at a time when many English cities were becoming homes to growing ethnic populations with an accordant upswing in the activities of the National Front. As the Sikhs, unaffected by The Changes, pass through a village, they are stoned by a gang of locals. The Sikh leader, Chacha, explains to Nicky: 'It is all part of the madness ... They are frightened because they do not know what has happened and we are strangers and therefore we might be dangerous.' That the Sikhs are proud of their traditions (their folklore, storytelling and community history is heavily foregrounded) somehow spares them The Changes. It's also interesting to see how Nicky, allowed to join their closed group, becomes a 'white stranger' with the roles reversed.

Telefantasy enthusiasts often compare *The Changes* with the (later) 1975 BBC series *Survivors*, and episodes five to eight, as a look at a superstitious Britain run by self-appointed guardians, are as close at it comes. Episodes nine and ten are broadly speaking the story conclusion, with Nicky and new-found friend Jonathon setting out to find and reverse the cause of The Changes. Home opted to rework the ending seen in Dickinson's *The Weathermonger*, claiming that it did not work in dramatic terms, but it is just as likely that she objected to the idea of a revived Merlin addicted to morphine.

It's in the latter episodes that the work's main themes are explicitly aired. Nicky meets Mary and Michael, two recognisable opt-out middle-class liberals of the 1970s. The serial's message is not a militantly ecologist one and prefers typically BBC balance and neutrality. For instance, as Michael says, 'I don't think you can just stop progress because there are things about it you don't like.' Mary is worried that one day her baby might get ill and there will be no treatment; she'd like to contact old friends on the phone; she'd like to go the hairdressers once in a while and read glossy magazines. She feels that people don't have a choice in this anymore. And it's the responsibility that comes with that freedom of choice that the serial is keen to promote.

The very end of the serial is inconclusive, however. The final shots are of heavy traffic running again in the towns and cities of Britain – is this a happy ending in which man has regained his destiny, or a bleak one which suggests he is a doomed polluter who has learned nothing from his experience?

As well as being thought-provoking *The Changes* also contains a lot of quite hard-hitting scenes: there are extended fight sequences between the Sikhs and the bandits; Davey Gordon's skewed religious fanaticism is unsettling at times and his death by drowning is unforgiving and final. On its original airings, warnings that the serial might not be suitable for younger children were broadcast before each episode.

*The Changes* was made all on location (in Bristol, Gloucestershire and the Forest of Dean) on film and was, up to that point, the most lavish production to be made outside of the 'Sunday Classics'. The serial benefited from having an experienced director and photographer at the helm and is perhaps the first example of the BBC using a proper crew on a children's drama as opposed to the 'all hands on deck' approach necessitated in earlier efforts.

**The Changes**
**BBC**
**10 episodes**
(colour)

### Episode One
'The Noise'
Monday 6/1/75 5.20p.m.
The peace of the Gore household is shattered by a tremendous noise – suddenly Mr Gore starts smashing the TV set as if possessed. The family wreck all of the electrical items in the house. All over Britain the scene is repeated while earthquakes and tidal waves strike the country. The Gores pack up and head for France, where it is believed the Noise has had no effect, but young Nicky becomes separated from her parents. Soon she is forced to leave the house – there is sickness in the towns, as the water becomes infected.

### Episode Two
'The Bad Wires'
Monday 13/1/75 5.20p.m.
Nicky joins up with a band of travelling Sikhs who are oddly unaffected by the Noise. Passing through a village they are attacked by stone-throwing locals. Heading further up the road the group pass under overhead power lines and Nicky hears the Noise starting up again …

### Episode Three
'The Devil's Children'
Monday 20/1/75 5.20p.m.
… but the 'bad wires' are dead and so the band carry on until they settle at an abandoned farm. They set up a rudimentary blacksmiths and offer to trade tools with the suspicious nearby village in exchange for other supplies, with Nicky acting as an intermediary.

### Episode Four
'Hostages!'
Monday 27/1/75 5.20p.m.
A group of bandits attack the village, killing the leader Barnard and taking the local children hostage as insurance for their safety. The Sikhs rescue the children in a pitched battle and thus earn the villagers' respect.

### Episode Five
'Witchcraft!'
Monday 3/2/75 5.20p.m.
Nicky heads to find her aunt in the Cotswolds but en route her cartwheel breaks and she is knocked unconscious. Waking, she stumbles on to the nearest village and falls asleep in a barn. She is locked in and tries to break out using a tractor stored in the barn – for this she is tried by the head man Davey Gordon as a witch. The villagers find her guilty.

### Episode Six
'A Pile of Stones'
Monday 10/2/75 5.20p.m.
Gordon decrees that Nicky be stoned to death the next day and she is shut up in an attic overnight. John rescues her before setting fire to the building to cover their tracks. He and Nicky flee to John's tug barge Heartsease as soon as it is light the next day but Gordon and his men are after them.

### Episode Seven
'Heartsease'
Monday 17/2/75 5.20p.m.
Nicky and John set sail up the canal, aiming for the sea and France, but before long they approach a bridge and discover that Gordon is on it waiting for them.

### Episode Eight
'Lightning!'
Monday 25/2/75 5.20p.m.
Peter, now convinced Gordon is mad, struggles with the self-proclaimed leader who falls into the canal and drowns. The Heartsease continues its journey but the engine mysteriously fails and then the boat is struck by lightning and destroyed. Struggling ashore, Nicky and John are taken in by a kindly couple – but Nicky still wonders what has caused The Changes.

### Episode Nine
'The Quarry'
Monday 3/3/75 5.20p.m.
Nicky and John travel to find the source of The Changes. Stumbling across a quarry they find a madman called Furbelow, rambling that he cannot control the power he has awoken. His journal transcribes a message he has heard in the cavern – Nicky translates it to mean 'I am Merlin … whoever touches me unbalances the world.'

### Episode Ten
'The Cavern'
Monday 10/3/75 5.20p.m.
In the cavern is a monolithic rock – Nicky is able to converse with the power held within the rock and she pleads for the balance between nature and man's machines to be restored. The force agrees and allows man to retake control of his destiny. Before long, traffic has returned to the streets of Britain.

**Main Cast:** Vicky Williams (Nicola Gore), Keith Ashton (Jonathon), Bernard Horsfall (Mr Gore), Sonia Graham (Mrs Gore), David Garfield (Davey Gordon), Rafiq Anwar (Chacha), Marc Zuber (Kewal), Sahab Qizilbash (Grandmother), Rugby Brar (Gopal), Rebecca Mascarenhas (Ajeet), Arthur Hewlett (Mr Tom), Edward Brayshaw (Chief Robber), James Ottoway (Maxie), David King (Mr Barnard), Jack Watson (Peter), Zuleika Robson (Margaret), Stella Tanner (Anne), Tony Hughes (Jack), Tom Chadbon (Michael), Merelina Kendall (Mary), Oscar Quitak (Mr Furbelow)

Based on *The Changes* trilogy of novels by Peter Dickinson (*The Weathermonger*, first published 1969; *Heartsease*, first published 1969; *The Devil's Children*, first published 1970; all by Victor Gollancz)

**Adapted by** Anna Home

**Music:** Paddy Kingsland
**Designer:** Paul Munting
**Producer:** Anna Home
**Director:** John Prowse

**Tie-in publications:** possible hardback unconfirmed; three
Dickinson books issued as *The Changes Trilogy* 1975, Victor
Gollancz.
Box set of three paperback novels with tie-in slip case
(illustrated with BBC photos) issued c. 1975, Puffin (all three
book covers are still those of the regular paperbacks of the
time).

## Sky

Aliens in TV science fiction inevitably tend to be depicted
as malevolent monsters hell-bent on destroying the planet,
or occasionally as ambassadors on missions to rescue
mankind from its own folly. Bob Baker and Dave Martin
broke the science fiction mould with *Sky*, eschewing the
cliché of flying saucers and removing such simple notions
as good and evil.

A creature materialises on Earth with a specific purpose
in mind but finds himself in the wrong time. He tells the
farmboy Arby that he expected to arrive 'after the chaos',
a period in which he clearly expects to be recognised.
Instead he has taken shape during 'the decline'. Now he
seeks the 'Juganet', a circle and machine that can transport
him to the desired location. These words suggest that
mankind is heading towards a catastrophe. More
importantly, whatever event is going to take place, Sky has
no intention of preventing it. 'In your terms I am to be a
god,' he tells Arby's sister. The icy indifference he displays

**Above:** the mysterious alien known as *Sky*
(Marc Harrison) appears on Earth.

to events on contemporary Earth and the wellbeing of
those trying to help him is unsettling. 'Your problems do
not concern me,' he dispassionately informs Arby. As a
result, Sky's hidden agenda and motives are never above
suspicion, making him more anti-hero than hero.

If Sky is strange, Goodchild is positively bizarre. As
soon as Sky arrives on Earth he is attacked by nature. 'The
animus of the organism ... all natural organisms reject that
which is foreign to them,' he informs Arby. These attacks
increase in strength until a physical manifestation takes
place and Goodchild is created from the wind and leaves.
Goodchild is basically an Earth spirit in the tradition of
the Green Man, working not for the benefit of man but the
good of life. The presence of a second ambivalent figure
furthers the tension in the drama although some viewers
might wonder why, if Goodchild's purpose is to rid the
Earth of an unnatural invader, his manifestation had not
already taken place in response to environmental
pollutants? Then again, is Sky himself the pollution?

Although the ecological message is apparent from an
early stage in the story, the full impact is kept from the
viewer until the final episode. Arby finds himself
transported with Sky to the time following the chaos,
where he discovers a tribe of telepaths who have learned to
live at one with nature. Arby cannot understand where his
people went wrong. Sky philosophically tells him, 'You do
not reach the stars with rockets anymore than you invent
radio by shouting at the sky. You believe in machines and
that is not the way.' The intent is clear; following the
chaos, man has learned to exist without the machines that
destroy the equanimity man should have with the Earth. 89

Sky's purpose is also clear. 'It is the destiny of all intelligent beings to stand outside space and time,' he explains to Arby. Now that mankind has learned to respect nature, Sky has arrived to guide the race towards the next stage in its evolution, thus ultimately confirming that he is a force for good. Elements of *2001: A Space Odyssey* and *Beneath the Planet of the Apes* are evident in *Sky*. One could even say that there are hints of the Bible's prophesied second coming of Christ.

The production's special effects are a triumph of imagination over budget constraints. The natural colour of Sky's eyes, a striking blue, is an obvious premeditated design which enabled the crew to alter the colour and pattern of the eyes using chromakey. Wearing cumbersome contact lenses for sustained periods of time must have been difficult for actor Marc Harrison but the end result, although not outstanding, looks more than competent for its time. The independent movement of the leaves in the first few episodes is also simple but effective. They are filmed being removed from a particular object with the help of a wind generator and the film is then played backwards at reduced speed, creating an unnatural but entirely fitting effect. The crew visited some of the most recognisable ancient sites in Britain. Glastonbury Tor and Avebury are both Juganet candidates, before the machine is finally located at Stonehenge.

**HTV West**
**7 episodes**
(colour)

**Episode One**
'Burning Bright'
Monday 7/4/75 4.50p.m.
While out shooting pheasants, Arby Vennor discovers a mysterious alien entity called Sky. Sky seems disturbed that Earth is not in a period of chaos and surmises that he has arrived at the wrong time. Sheltered by Arby in a nearby cave, the being would appear to be under attack from nature itself.

**Episode Two**
'Juganet'
Monday 14/4/75 4.50p.m.
Arby's sister, Jane, now knows of Sky's arrival and Sky tells the Vennor children that he must find the Juganet – a machine required to return him to his proper place. Arby and Jane take Sky to the school to try and find information on the Juganet but they are followed by Roy Briggs and his father. Sky and friends are then captured by the police as a mysterious figure manifests itself.

**Episode Three**
'Goodchild'
Monday 21/4/75 4.50p.m.
Sky is interrogated at the police station but uses his powers to influence the police into letting him go. On the way home, a strange figure appears on the road causing the Land-Rover to swerve. Mrs Vennor is flung from the vehicle and injured. Sky once again exerts his powers, this time healing Mrs Vennor, leaving himself very weak. Ambrose Goodchild, the manifested being, searches for Sky and attacks him at the Vennor's house. Rescued by the children, the injured alien is taken to hospital.

**Episode Four**
'What Dread Hand'
Monday 28/4/75 4.50p.m.
Sky begs help of a patient in the hospital, receptive to his telepathic abilities. Goodchild arrives at the hospital claiming he is a surgeon and suggesting that Sky be operated on immediately. The children consider the possibility that the Juganet could be located at the stone circle in Glastonbury.

**Episode Five**
'Evalake'
Monday 5/5/75 4.50p.m.
Escaping Goodchild, the children travel to Glastonbury where Sky finds himself confronted by a hippy believing him to be the long-awaited 'Keeper of the Grail'.

**Episode Six**
'Life Force'
Monday 12/5/75 4.50p.m.
After another Goodchild attack, the children take Sky to a deserted country house but discover Goodchild is ahead of them. The house is a trap, a non-existent creation of Goodchild's. Cornered, Sky attempts to make a bargain with Goodchild.

**Episode Seven**
'Chariot of Fire'
Monday 19/5/75 4.50p.m.
The Juganet is located at Stonehenge and Sky is taken there by Arby and Jane. Sky refuses to show the children the future and Arby tries to follow him, inadvertently triggering the Juganet. Goodchild appears at the circle but Jane doesn't recognise him. Sky has made her forget the whole adventure. Goodchild concludes that Sky has gone from the Earth and disappears, his job complete. Propelled through time, Arby arrives in a settlement populated by a telepathic tribe. The tribe attempt to sacrifice Arby but Sky intervenes and allows him to return home.

**Main Cast:** Marc Harrison (Sky), Stuart Lock (Arby Vennor), Cherrald Butterfield (Jane Vennor), Richard Speight (Roy Briggs), Jack Watson (Major Briggs), Robert Eddison (Goodchild), Frances Cuka (Mrs Vennor), Thomas Heathcote (Mr Vennor)

**Written by** Bob Baker and Dave Martin

**Music:** Eric Wetherell
**Design:** John Briggs (all) with Chris Cook (4 and 6)
**Executive Producer:** Patrick Dromgoole
**Producer:** Leonard White
**Director:** Patrick Dromgoole (1, 2), Terry Harding (3, 5), Derek Clark (4, 7), Leonard White (6)

## Sam and the River

A welcome diversion from more typical BBC home counties fare, this adventure thriller was set in the heart of London's docklands long before its 80s redevelopment. Sam Leigh was the story's hero, a boy who lived above a pub, bringing a working-class touch to an otherwise predictable tale of crooks undone by a young boy's ingenuity and the help of a trusty coastguard.

Written and produced by Peggy Miller, more usually responsible for buying in and adapting European imports for the department, the story seems to have been built around whatever interesting locations were convenient for filming. The plot takes in an old sea fort overlooking the Thames estuary, Greenhithe, Greenwich and a trip by hydrofoil.

Interesting as an at least visually gritty 16mm glimpse into a world many viewers probably didn't know existed.

**De Lane Lea for BBC**
**6 episodes**
(colour)
**Broadcast:** Thursdays 24/4/75 – 29/5/75

**Main Cast:** Simon West (Sam Leigh), Jo Rowbottom (Katie Leigh), Harry Markham (Patrick Flint), Bryan Marshall (Alan Flint), Peter Woodthorpe (Smithy), Ben Aris (Lt Hodges), George Mikell (Andre), Mark Dightam (Paul Redmond)

**Writer:** Peggy Miller

**Producer:** Peggy Miller
**Director:** Joe McGrath

## The Siege of Golden Hill

'If children are more aggressive, more angry, more intractable, perhaps it is because they have seen the writing on the wall and realise what is in store if they don't kick against it ...' So said writer Nick McCarty of the problems of the inner cities as portrayed in his Sunday afternoon serial. The Sunday serial conjures up images of cosy Edwardiana from the BBC, rightly or wrongly, but *The Siege of Golden Hill* was light years removed from those expectations, purely by being set 'next door'.

The setting, painted in publicity material as 'a world of eviction and extortion, demolition and tower blocks, violence and vandalism', is the graffiti-sprayed concrete jungle of 'a large Midlands city' (recognisably Birmingham). Here bored youths turn to gangs for a sense of purpose and belonging. One such gang is Anvil and they are involved in efforts to frighten Old Tom out of his lifelong home. This is not mindless thuggery, however – the youths are pawns in the game of the real villains, in the pay of unscrupulous property developers who want Tom and his kind moved on so they can build their tower blocks and profits.

Tom's grandson Billy, a fifteen-year-old member of the Anvil gang, must fight to help his grandfather while falling in love with Sarah, a girl who wants to help. Sarah's father is on the council but her pleas fall on deaf ears since the councillors are in the sway of the developers. How deep does the corruption run? There are protection rackets, with an Asian shopkeeper called Suliman Khan among those threatened and hospitalised in attacks.

Now largely forgotten in the rush to praise *Grange Hill* as ushering in a new dawn of urban realism (was the similarity in location name just coincidence?), *Golden Hill* was a gritty and cynical portrayal of modern social problems in the multiracial Britain of the mid-70s. McCarty, who won a Pye Broadcasting Award for the series, summed it up as being about 'age and youth; poverty and the new affluence; education and dead-end jobs; love, housing and an era of change'. That it was.

The life of Anvil leader Jacky after the days of the gang has passed was the focus of a sequel, which saw him as easy prey for another businessman on the make. This time Jacky was implicated in the disposal of toxic waste.

***The Siege of Golden Hill*** (1975)
**ATV**
**12 episodes** ('Ultimatum'; 'Threats'; 'The Vandals are Coming'; 'Bribery'; 'The Frighteners'; 'Besieged'; 'New Victims'; 'Extortion'; 'Undercover'; 'Intimidation'; 'Last Straw'; 'Nailed') (colour)
**Broadcast:** Sundays 8/6/75 – 24/8/75

**Main Cast:** Gerry Sundquist (Billy), Sara Clee (Sarah), Billy Hamon (Jacky), Peter Dudley (Des), Walter Dalby (Old Tom), Arnold Peters (Mr Small), John Malcolm (Allen), Chris Sanders (Herbert Franks), Karen Berlinski (Mary), Gregory Munroe (Kenny), Frederick Schrecker (Sam), Dev Sagoo (Suliman), Rafiq Anwar (Shastri)

**Created by** Nick McCarty and John Sichel
**Written by** Nick McCarty

**Designers:** Bryan Holgate (1–6), Stanley Mills and Bryan Holgate (7–12)
**Producer/Director:** John Sichel

***Golden Hill*** (1976)
**ATV**
**6 episodes** ('The Spoilers'; 'Dead on Arrival'; 'Escape'; 'Down to The Golden City'; 'All That Glisters'; 'Trap') (colour)
**Broadcast:** Sundays 26/9/76 – 31/10/76

**Main Cast:** Billy Hamon (Jacky), Karen Berlinski (Mary), Gregory Munroe (Kenny), Robin Meredith (William Evans)

**Written by** Nick McCarty and John Sichel (1), Nick McCarty (2–6)

**Designer:** Bryan Holgate
**Producer/Director:** John Sichel

## Shadows

To be given licence to frighten children but not scare them witless is a huge responsibility. While *Shadows* was undoubtedly a very frightening anthology series it dealt in psychological tales rather than out-and-out schlock or gore – the 'shadows' of the programme's title could not only refer to a creepy night with spirits abroad but also to alternate realities very close but also far removed from the rational world.

As with many ghost stories for children, several episodes functioned as exciting ways of teaching history. Producer Pamela Lonsdale was no doubt aware of the flak a horror series might bring from concerned parents if it were seen purely as gruesome entertainment. The ghosts who haunted the present gave us vivid glimpses of the past, be it wartime France ('Eleven o'Clock'), the life of a Victorian servant girl ('Time Out of Mind') or the miserable existence of a boy working in the Welsh coalmines 150 years earlier ('After School'). This desire to bring to life the pages of history was made explicit in 'Peronik', where a beautifully illustrated legend was revisited upon a teenage boy, while 'The Dark Streets of Kimballs Green' saw a girl imagine her everyday enemies personified as characters from her history book.

The flipside to this was that the present day was realistic and recognisable, with glam-rock sounds of 1976 playing at  91 the school dance in 'Peronik' and a pop star's mansion providing the setting for 'Honeyann'. The stories were populated by a wide variety of ordinary children. Several pitted more traditional middle-class brother and sister pairings against the terrors of the mind – in 'The Waiting Room' Jenny Agutter was positively posh in her last British TV role before leaving for Hollywood. Other tales admitted the working classes; there were dingy flats in 'Peronik' and a gang of rather badly behaved kids were up for 'larking about' in a museum in 'Optical Illusion', among them a young and unashamedly Cockney Pauline Quirke. The horrors encountered were often an amplification of the very real fears of the teenage audience. The startling 'Peronik' sees a teenage boy who is constantly being put down by his parents finally come of age and win the affections of the girl he longs for in an allegorical rites of passage drama filled with bizarre imagery. In 'The Inheritance' a school leaver has a vivid dream that sees him struggle to deny the office job existence his parents have mapped out for him.

Often the stories seemed written to be made as cheaply as possible but this seemed positively advantageous at times, rather than unfortunate. 'After School' cleverly deploys a minimum of establishing shots of a run-down Welsh mining village before using only two sets and two schoolboy actors for the remainder of the piece. 'The Waiting Room', despite the prominent casting of Agutter, was a textbook example of cheap but effective television, using only one set (the titular waiting room of a run-down, remote railway station at midnight) and accommodating four speaking parts.

The lack of music, for example, led to many eerie silences which only added to the icy tension of many episodes. Among these was the very weird 'The Eye' and also 'The Witch's Bottle', which saw young Jill visited by the spirit of a long-dead witch girl in a spooky cottage. The gothic overtones to the story, with storm-lashed nights and bodily possession, made it the most obvious horror tale of the run and even featured a black mass in miniature which flew dangerously close to occultism. It's unlikely such a story would be aired today.

While the production techniques demonstrated a canny awareness of the available funds, the series was really driven by a top-notch line-up of writers. J. B. Priestley wrote his first children's story here together with his archaeologist wife; noted author Penelope Lively submitted an early teleplay with 'Time Out of Mind'; while Joan Aiken and Fay Weldon also contributed.

The series also provided a platform for a couple of pilot episodes. 'Dutch Schlitz's Shoes' was an obvious attempt at setting up a new format utilising the Mr Stabs character from Thames' own *Ace of Wands*. Russell Hunter reprised his role as the loquacious, diseased magician, forming a double act with his obsequious stooge companion Luko (recast for this episode). A wilfully odd story of Stabs being taken over by the spirit of a cigar-smoking Chicago gangster from the 1920s, this was a rare comedic excursion for *Shadows*, slightly out of step with the rest of the series. A run of adventures for Stabs failed to materialise although their creator Trevor Preston made one more attempt in a 1984 *Dramarama*. *Shadows* did spawn one spin-off series, however, when *The Boy Merlin* made a full series of six episodes in 1979.

The *Shadows* horror anthology format was revived in all but name by Thames in 1983, as *Dramarama: Spooky*, with *Dramarama* itself doing much to carry on the tradition of scary but intelligent fiction into the next decade. For consistent quality, however, the frighteningly good *Shadows* was a hard act to follow.

**Thames**
**3 seasons**
(colour)

**Season One**
**7 episodes**
Broadcast: Wednesdays 3/9/75 – 15/10/75

'The Future Ghost' by Roger Marshall. **Dir:** Leon Thau
'After School' by Ewart Alexander. **Dir:** Audrey Starrett
'The Witch's Bottle' by Stewart Farrar. **Dir:** Vic Hughes
'The Waiting Room' by Jon Watkins. **Dir:** Stan Woodward
'Optical Illusion' by Tom Clarke. **Dir:** Peter Webb
'Dutch Schlitz's Shoes' by Trevor Preston. **Dir:** Stan Woodward
'The Other Window' by J. B. Priestley and Jacquetta Hawkes. **Dir:** Darrol Blake

**Script Editor:** Ruth Boswell
**Producer:** Pamela Lonsdale

**Season Two**
**6 episodes**
Broadcast: Wednesdays 28/7/76 – 1/9/76

'The Dark Streets of Kimballs Green' by Joan Aiken. **Dir:** Stan Woodward
'Time Out of Mind' by Penelope Lively. **Dir:** Audrey Starrett
'The Inheritance' by Josephine Poole. **Dir:** Peter Webb
'Dark Encounter' by Susan Cooper. **Dir:** Leon Thau
'Peronik' by Rosemary Harris. **Dir:** Vic Hughes
'The Eye' by Ewart Alexander. **Dir:** Neville Green

**Producer:** Ruth Boswell

**Season Three**
**7 episodes**
Broadcast: Wednesdays 20/9/78 – 1/11/78

'Eleven o'Clock' by Ewart Alexander. **Dir:** Joe Boyer
'The Rose of Puddle Fratrum' by Joan Aiken. **Dir:** Neville Green
'And For My Next Trick…' by P. J. Hammond. **Dir:** Michael Custance
'The Boy Merlin' by Stewart Farrar from a story by Anne Carlton. **Dir:** Vic Hughes
'The Man Who Hated Children' by Brian Patten. **Dir:** Neville Green
'The Silver Apple' by Philip Glassborow. **Dir:** Gabrielle Beaumont
'Honeyann' by Fay Weldon. **Dir:** Pamela Lonsdale

**Producer:** Pamela Lonsdale

**Tie-in publications:** *The Best of Shadows* published by Carousel, 1979. Written by Joan Aiken, Josephine Poole, Brian Patten, P. J. Hammond, Ewart Alexander (novelisations of 'The Dark Streets of Kimballs Green', 'The Inheritance', 'The Eye', 'Eleven o'Clock', 'The Rose of Puddle Fratrum', 'And For My Next Trick...', 'The Man Who Hated Children').

## The Hill of the Red Fox

Young Scotsman Alasdair Cameron has lived in London with his mother for many years following the death of his father. During the school holidays he returns to Skye to claim his inheritance – a small croft and cottage owned by his father. During the journey north, Alasdair is handed a desperate message from a man later found dead. It says 'Hunt at the Hill of the Red Fox D15'. Mysterious happenings on the island, most of which involve the sinister Murdo Beaton, make little sense either. Alasdair soon discovers that atomic scientists are disappearing and conspiracy and espionage has followed him to Skye.

At first glance *The Hill of the Red Fox* could be mistaken for a mere thriller, yet it has a breadth of narrative missing from those typical of the time. The thriller aspect is foremost in the plot, driving the pace and maintaining the suspense, but it is the subtext, that of the meeting of two differing cultures and a young boy's coming of age, that provides the more intriguing angle.

Alasdair's assumptions of island life are nothing compared to the opinions some of the islanders have of city dwellers. When Alasdair meets Mairi, Murdo Beaton's daughter, he asks her if she would like to visit London. 'The cailleach says that everyone in the cities is bad,' Mairi replies, reinforcing the chasm between her people and mainstream life.

Not all of the islanders are as deceitful as Murdo Beaton. The other men of the village extend a warm welcome to Alasdair, treating him as an adult rather than a child. It's entirely fitting considering the situations that the boy encounters on Skye. In a relatively short period of time he adapts to a radically different way of life while his exposure to danger opens his eyes to life's complexities.

The adaptation differs in a number of ways from Allan Campbell McLean's novel. Most noticeable is the surface updating that brings the setting forward in time from the 50s to the 70s. In doing so the production was able to incorporate current hardware, such as a submarine, as extra visual stimulus in what could otherwise have been a relatively static script. The book had also depicted Alasdair as being very unhappy with the uncomfortable way of island life, whereas the character on screen approaches every situation with little in the way of apprehension and seems to enjoy each challenge thoroughly.

The production, as can often be the case with regional drama, borders precariously close to stereotyping on a couple of occasions but generally looks good. It is particularly refreshing to see that the scenes taking place on the train journey north are actually filmed on a moving train, as opposed to the expected studio insert with superimposed backdrop. Much of the story is filmed among rugged locations but the cottage interiors with their implausibly bright lights were certainly shot in-studio.

*The Hill of the Red Fox* doesn't exude the dynamics of contemporaries like *Freewheelers* but it competently delivers engaging characters and a more original approach to the espionage thriller.

**BBC Scotland**
**6 episodes**
(colour)
**Broadcast:** Wednesdays 24/9/75 – 29/10/75

**Main Cast:** Mark Rogers (Alasdair Cameron), Donald Douglas (Murdo Beaton), Bernard Horsfall (Duncan Mor – 'Big Duncan'), Gillian Barclay (Mairi), Roy Boutcher (Hunt), George Howell (Man With Blue Eyes), Victor Carin (Hector Macleod), Peter Miles (Dr Reuter)

Based on the novel by Allan Campbell McLean (first UK publication 1955, William Collins & Co. Ltd)
**Adapted by** Scot Finch

**Title Music:** Andy Park
**Designer:** Walter Miller
**Producer:** Pharic MacLaren
**Director:** Bob McIntosh

**Tie-in publications:** paperback edition published by Lions/Collins, 1975

## Ballet Shoes

Adopted as babies by the eccentric fossil collector Matthew Brown, Pauline, Petrova and Posy have been left in the care of his niece Sylvia while he ventures abroad on another long expedition. Nobody knows when he will return and, as time passes without contact, the money to maintain the house and the girls' education runs out. Sylvia therefore has no option but to educate the children herself as best she can and advertise for tenants to bring in enough to live on.

The arrival of one lodger in particular, a music and drama teacher called Theo Dane, brings about a remarkable change in fortune for the girls when she gets all three accepted at the music academy of the famous dancer Madame Fidolia. Fame beckons for all three girls but will they be able to cope with the rigorous training regime demanded by Fidolia? More importantly, is it really what each of them wants?

*Ballet Shoes* is, beyond shadow of a doubt, gender specific and it's difficult to see what interest it would hold for anyone other than those in the young female bracket. The narrative can be very slow in places, taking the viewer step by step through the pain that must be endured before one can become a professional dancer. The plot also has the capacity to be hopelessly romantic and demands a thorough stretch of the imagination to accept the girls' outrageous good fortune. Sylvia cannot afford the girls' education but it just so happens that their three new tenants are between them able to teach literature, history, French, maths, physics and dance.

The enrolment of the girls without cost at Fidolia's academy is also remarkably fortunate but pivotal in the plot, incorporating themes of self-discovery and differing ambitions. Posy is a natural dancer while Pauline shows an aptitude for drama and both of them enjoy their classes. Petrova, on the other hand, isn't comfortable at the academy. Although she meets Fidolia's requirements and is capable of winning auditions, the tomboy would far rather spend her time helping to mend cars at John Simpson's garage.

The pressures of looming debt bring out the best in the girl's characters, particularly Pauline who sets about  93 encouraging Posy and Petrova to seek auditions that will lead to a wage, thus enabling them to help Sylvia pay the bills. After a very short time, it also highlights a darker side to Pauline's personality when it is insinuated that she has arranged for the adversaries of one audition to turn up at the wrong theatre. Her thirst for success is such that, for a time, she becomes a thoroughly petulant girl with ideas above her station.

*Ballet Shoes* may well be television strictly for girls but this doesn't prevent it from tackling the issues of personal identity universal in children's drama.

**BBC**
**6 episodes**
(colour)
**Broadcast:** Wednesdays 5/10/75 – 9/11/75

**Main Cast:** Angela Thorne (Sylvia), Barbara Lott (Nana), Elizabeth Morgan (Pauline Fossil), Jane Slaughter (Petrova Fossil), Sarah Prince (Posy Fossil), Joanna David (Theo Dane), Sheila Keith (Dr Jakes), Terence Skelton (Mr Simpson), Mary Morris (Madame Fidolia)

Based on the novel by Noel Streatfeild (first UK publication 1936, Dent)
**Dramatised by** John Wiles
**Script Editor:** Alistair Bell

**Designer:** Anthony Thorpe
**Producer:** John McRae
**Director:** Timothy Coombe

**Tie-in publications:** paperback edition published by Puffin, 1975

**Video:** Released in UK as a 120-minute compilation by BBC Worldwide, 1990. Deleted 11/1/94. Released in US as a 120-minute compilation by BFS Video/BBC Gold. Issued on Region 1 DVD in the US, 2000.

## Striker

When Ben Dyker and his father move into the village of Brenton they are viewed with suspicion. A poor kid living in a caravan, Ben is taunted by the local boys but eventually earns their respect with his skills on the football field. Ben's father is not keen on his boy mixing, however, and is regretful over an injury which ended his own football career. Ben has to go behind his father's back to turn out for the Brenton Boys side. His father is furious when he finds out the truth but relents when he realises that by doing so Ben has gained acceptance among the villagers.

This initially three-part drama begat a sequel, though for the second run Ben 'Striker' Dyker was no longer the focus. Traditional tales of junior football endeavour and *Roy of the Rovers*-style last-gasp winners prevailed for the Brenton side. If the second run had a central character it was the team's biggest fan, a girl called Jacky. Jacky was always on the sidelines but harboured a desire to play for the Brenton Boys. Upset at not being included she runs away but her chance comes on cup final day when Brenton lose a player in an accident. With no option but to play Jacky, the girl gets a boy's haircut and wins the cup for the team. Thus the season mirrors the first, being a tale of prejudice overcome by talent.

The series was written by actor Kenneth Cope, best remembered as the white-suited ghost Marty in the 1969 detective drama *Randall and Hopkirk (Deceased)*. *Striker* was largely based on fact – Cope had moved to the quiet village of Islip in the early 70s and before long had begun coaching the local boys' football team. His side included boys nicknamed Bomber and Soggy as in the series, Mark and Nicky were based on his own sons, while Jacky was a girl who worked in the local post office.

**BBC**
**2 seasons**
(colour)

**Main Cast:** Kevin Moreton (Ben Dyker), Geoffrey Hinsliff (Mr Dyker), Keith Allingham (Bomber), Simon Manley (Soggy), Stephen Howe (Mark), Sylvia O'Donnell (Jacky), Ian Sinclair (Wayne), Sam Williams (Nicky), Joe Gladwin (Harry), Patrick Murphy (Paddy – Season 2 only)

**Written by** Kenneth Cope

**Producer:** Anna Home
**Director:** Colin Cant

**Season One**
**3 episodes**
**Broadcast:** Wednesdays 31/12/75 – 14/1/76

**Season Two**
**5 episodes**
**Broadcast:** Wednesdays 6/10/76 – 3/11/76 (episode 2 shown on BBC2 in Scotland due, ironically, to live football coverage)

**Tie-in publications:** novelisation of first season by Kenneth Cope published in paperback by BBC, 1976

## The Georgian House

Dan and Abbie, two students from very different backgrounds, have obtained placements in a beautiful Georgian house in Bristol. The house, owned 200 years ago by the rich Leadbetter family, has been restored to its former glory and is to be opened to the public. Dan and Abbie hope to carry out additional research for their studies while acting as tour guides to the public.

While unpacking valuable ornaments for display, the pair are attracted to an African wood carving which emits a mysterious noise. They find themselves transported in time to become involved in the affairs of the Leadbetter family. Abbie is transformed into a member of the family, while Dan finds himself dressed in the clothes of a kitchen boy. It transpires that they have been summoned to save a black servant about to be returned to the plantations. Assisting the boy won't be easy, especially as Abbie seems to have forgotten her twentieth-century origins.

*The Georgian House* is interested in themes of class and social status. This is apparent right at the off when Dan arrives at the house. Clearly educated at a private school, he tells janitor Ellis that he is sure the time spent at the house will be educational. The working-class Ellis makes his feelings quite clear, saying, 'Education comes from life ... getting on with other people.' Abbie too seems unimpressed with the privileges she believes Dan's wealthy status will bring him. She attends an ordinary comprehensive school and has ambitions to be an archaeologist. When Dan tells her that he wants to qualify in economics and will then go straight into his father's firm, she mockingly replies, 'a nice steady little job'. Abbie herself feels the brunt of Ellis' scepticism when she tells him that she would like to put together a demonstration for tourists that will highlight the problems of life 200 years ago. Ellis is quick to tell her, 'You just tell them that the Leadbetters were rich and that the rich don't have any problems.'

When Dan and Abbie travel back in time it is Abbie who is transformed from a comprehensive school girl to a rich aristocrat. Dan meanwhile must suffer life as a kitchen boy, experiencing first-hand the healthy disdain offered by those in the upper class and learning something about himself in the process.

*The Georgian House* isn't going to hold much interest for those children motivated by dynamic action sequences and fast-moving plots. The narrative has a propensity towards the educational but effectively uses the fantasy element of the story – two teenagers travelling through time – to disguise this.

**HTV West**
**7 episodes** ('New Recruits'; 'We'll Never Get Back'; 'Treachery'; 'A Dose of Sulphur Water'; 'Duwamba'; 'Trapped'; 'Look To Your Future')
(colour)
**Broadcast:** Fridays 2/1/76 – 13/2/76 (except HTV; shown Sundays 28/12/75 – 8/2/76)

**Main Cast:** Jack Watson (Ellis), Adrienne Byrne (Abbie), Spencer Banks (Dan), Brinsley Forde (Ngo), Constance Chapman (Mistress Anne Leadbetter), Peter Schofield (Thomas Leadbetter), Janine Duvitski (Ariadne)

**Written by** Jill Laurimore and Harry Moore

**Designer:** Ken Jones
**Producer:** Leonard White
**Executive Producer:** Patrick Dromgoole
**Directors:** Derek Clark (1, 2), Sebastian Robinson (3), Terry Harding (4, 6), Leonard White (5, 7)

## A Place to Hide
This was truly a family adventure serial since it pitted a family against a gang of crooks rather than taking the more usual 'kids on their own' tack. Head of the Valenta household is Bruno, an ex-magician, and it doesn't take a genius to work out that his magic tricks will no doubt save the day for the Valenta family.

One day a strange family arrive at the Valenta's remote guest house. Bill Smith and his grown-up son and daughter, Ann and Derry, immediately raise the suspicions of the Valenta children and before long the trio are uncovered as a gang of bank robbers on the run, looking for somewhere to stash their £100,000 loot. With the Smith family's cover blown, a routine kidnap/siege plot unfolds, dragging in the local bobby. Though Bill Smith did carry a gun, *A Place to Hide* is unlikely to go down as a tough and uncompromising thriller.

**ATV**
**6 episodes** ('The Hideout'; 'The Secret Place'; 'The Giveaway'; 'The Contact'; 'The Trick'; 'The Illusion')
(colour)
**Broadcast:** Sundays 4/1/76 – 8/2/76

**Main Cast:** Terry Duggan (Bruno Valenta), Hilary Crane (Laura Valenta), June Page (Madeleine Valenta), David Nunn (Mark Valenta), Arthur White (Mr Smith), Frances Tomelty (Ann Smith), Brian Capron (Derry Smith), Lloyd McGuire (PC Brockhurst)

**Written by** Roy Russell

**Designer:** Stanley Mills
**Producer/Director:** Shaun O'Riordan

## Kizzy
Kizzy Lovell is a traveller girl living with her great-great-grandmother in a covered wagon – a gypsy as the old term would have it. Kizzy is only a Diddakoi, a half gypsy, but all it means is that the cruel girls at school have another name with which to taunt her.

One interesting aspect of the character is that little Kizzy is no shrinking violet – she's quite prepared to bite, scratch, spit and hit back at her tormentors. Astoundingly this drew some complaints from adult viewers, who felt her behaviour was a bad example to children watching.

Kizzy's is a heartbreaking tale although it's unevenly both tough and sentimental. When Kizzy's Gran dies and her wagon home burnt according to gypsy tradition, the now homeless Kizzy's case is heard in juvenile court. She is lucky to avoid being sent into care, particularly when the spiteful busybody Mrs Cuthbert calls for it. The kindly Miss Brooke offers to look after her but still Kizzy is ungrateful and wants to stay with her friend, the Admiral. When Kizzy is sent back to school she is subjected to a shocking mob attack by a gang of girls (another cause for viewer concern) and then her old horse Joe dies. After all the girl has had to put up with, sentimentality finally wins out in the shape of a rather contrived romantic ending, but on the whole *Kizzy* stands as a well-observed piece on children's capacity for cruelty and intolerance.

**BBC Birmingham**
**6 episodes** ('The Wagon'; 'What Shall We Do With Kizzy?'; 'She Can't Stay There!'; 'Into Care'; 'No Escape'; 'The Bonfire')
(colour)
**Broadcast:** Wednesdays 21/1/76 – 25/2/76

**Main Cast:** Vanessa Furst (Kizzy), Betty Hardy (Gran), John Welsh (Admiral Twiss), Anne Ridler (Olivia Brooke), Melissa Docker (Prue Cuthbert), Miriam Margolyes (Mrs Doe)

Based on the novel *The Diddakoi* by Rumer Godden (first UK publication 1972, Macmillan)
**Adapted by** John Tully

**Music:** Peter Gosling
**Designer:** Myles Lang
**Producer:** Dorothea Brooking
**Director:** David Tilley

**Tie-in publications:** paperback editions of novel as *The Diddakoi* published by Puffin, 1975–84 (two different covers)  95

## Jumbo Spencer

Jumbo Spencer's mother wonders why her son can't be like any normal boy. Jumbo, however, revels in the fact that he isn't like anyone else. He's the leader of the gang and determined to make sure that his people, Mike, Freckles and Maggots, have the best school holiday ever. Proclaiming himself a leader of men, he tells his friends that they will spend the summer reforming their home town of Shoredale, ridding it of vice and poverty.

The series comprises a sequence of set-piece adventures. Jumbo manages to trick the rival gang into trimming the shrubbery and generally tidying up the local high street, one of the areas the local folk thought could be improved. He then sets about ensuring that Miss Mog has a zebra crossing painted on the road outside her house so that the old lady can safely cross the road. Bill Stiggins, leader of the rival gang, informs the police of Jumbo's illegal road work but ends up removing the paint himself when the police decide there really should be a crossing.

Jumbo next influences rich villager Mr Bennet into agreeing to fund a youth club, pavilion and playing fields if Jumbo himself can raise £100 in a month. To this end Jumbo forms an employment agency to enable children to do odd jobs for payment and then turns Shoredale into a village of historic interest.

**BBC**

**5 episodes** ('The Jumbo Spencer Reform Club'; 'Jumbo and the Police'; 'Kidnapped!'; 'On the Map'; 'In the Bag')
(colour)
**Broadcast:** Mondays 9/2/76 – 8/3/76

**Main Cast:** Mark Weavers (Jumbo), Natalie Boyce (Maggots), John Weavers (Freckles), Huw Higginson (Mike), Christopher Watts (Bill), John O'Farrell (Dick), Jeffrey Chapman (Steve), Jim Smilie (Mr Spencer), Helen Fraser (Mrs Spencer)

Based on the novel by Helen Cresswell (first UK publication 1963, Brockhampton Press)
**Adapted for televison by** Helen Cresswell

**Producer:** Daphne Jones
**Executive Producer:** Anna Home
**Director:** Jeremy Swan

**Tie-in publications:** paperback published by Knight, 1975

## Rocky O'Rourke

Thirteen-year-old Rocky O'Rourke lives in the least affluent area of Liverpool and has two very different ambitions: to be a professional footballer or a successful crook. As leader of a street gang called The Cats, he is well on his way to being notable in the latter, stowing away in lorries and breaking into abandoned buildings. It's not enough for Rocky. He idolises his big brother Joey, currently spending time at Her Majesty's pleasure, and looks forward to pulling off a really big job to earn his brother's respect. Rocky soon comes to appreciate the frailties of his ambitions when he becomes entangled in the activities of a very real and dangerous villain.

*Rocky O'Rourke* generated criticism from a minority of parents. 'Is *Rocky O'Rourke* part of a BBC "promote juvenile crime campaign"?' commented one. Monica Sims, Head of Children's Programmes replied, 'The intention is the opposite and the point of the story is to show Rocky's realisation of the stupidity and thoughtlessness of his behaviour and his disillusion with his weak, criminal brother.'

**BBC**
**4 episodes**
(colour)
**Broadcast:** Wednesdays 3/3/76 – 24/3/76

**Main Cast:** The Cats – Michael Mills (Rocky), James Hoey (Nabber), Eamonn Deery (Billy), Peter Chan (Chan); Alan Pope (Joey), Kenny Walker (Chick), John Dalziel (Spadge)

Based on the novel *A Pair of Jesus-Boots* by Sylvia Sherry (first UK publication 1969, Jonathan Cape). US title *The Liverpool Cats*
**Dramatised by** Alan England

**Producer:** Anna Home
**Director:** John Prowse

**Tie-in publications:** paperback published by Puffin, 1975

## The Molly Wopsies

*Funny Ha Ha* had been a showcase of six comedies made by Thames in 1974. Viewers were asked to write in and say which of the six they liked the best and it was 'The Molly Wopsy', fifth in the series, which proved the most popular and returned as a full series a year and a half later.

The series presented the light-hearted adventures of a gang of four children, enjoying themselves despite the shadow of World War II and getting up to all sorts of mischief in a sleepy Oxfordshire village. Their arch-enemy was the local bobby PC Berry but he couldn't stop them getting into all sorts of gently rustic scrapes. The gang got up to little more than causing mild havoc at the harvest festival, or stealing the odd chicken in a sitcom manner. Perhaps the most interesting episode saw the kids discover a German pilot who had bailed out over the village.

This was something of a nostalgic view of the war, written by someone who was there. Ron 'Mr' Smith, who was working on a car production line when he wrote the series, was a boy in 1941 and the Molly Wopsy was the local ghost in the village where he grew up and also became the name of his gang of friends. The ghost storyline surfaced in the series' opening episode, a clear example of how much the series was based on fact. The series was notable for providing the first TV role for Phil Daniels (later the lead in *Raven* and the classic Who film *Quadrophenia*), a local lad from the village of Turville where the series was made.

**Thames**
**1 pilot** and **6 episodes** ('The Initiation'; 'All Was Safely Gathered In'; 'The German Hunters'; 'Arrowing Times'; 'The New Uniform'; 'Sunday Morning')
(colour)

Pilot as part of *Funny Ha Ha* showcase series 21/6/74: 'The Molly Wopsy'

Full series of six episodes broadcast: Wednesdays 17/3/76 –
21/4/76

**Main Cast:** Ben Forster (Dinkey Dunkley), Phil Daniels
(Alan Musgrove), Matthew Whiteman (Norman Yates),
Julie Taylor (Dotty Minton), Aubrey Morris (PC Berry),
Patrick Barr (Farmer Brown)

**Written by** Mr Smith (Ron Smith)

**Theme Music:** 'Run Rabbit Run' sung by Arthur Askey
**Designer:** Bill Palmer
**Producer:** Ruth Boswell
**Director:** Stan Woodward

## Four Idle Hands

The devil will find work for idle hands to do ... and in this
case the four idle hands belong to two rather workshy
sixteen-year-olds, Mike and Pete. This serial took a light-
hearted though still realistic look at what was a serious
subject in the mid-70s as unemployment and inflation
began to rise.

The lads come across the problems facing all school
leavers: unhelpful careers teachers, a lack of direction and
a lack of cash. What work they get is unfulfilling and after
all they would rather be spending their time shooting the
breeze in Emilio's cafe. If they can't make an honest living
the two wonder if they might somehow be able to make a
*dishonest* living. The boys drift through various work
schemes until they meet the attractive Frances, a social
worker who tries to help them on their way.

*Four Idle Hands* was a groundbreaking series which has
gained less attention than it deserved, no doubt due largely
to its awkward slot of 4.20p.m. Younger children would
have found it confusing and boring, while it probably
passed unnoticed by the older teenagers it was aimed at.
Only with the 80s and the development of new timeslots
for teenagers could series such as the thematically similar
*Tucker's Luck* succeed.

**ATV**
**6 episodes** ('Out of the Frying Pan'; 'Taking the Plunge';
'Do Unto Others'; 'A Clean Sweep'; 'Reds Under the Bed';
'Win a Few, Lose a Few')
(colour)
**Broadcast:** Fridays 26/3/76 – 30/4/76

**Main Cast:** Phil Daniels (Mike Dudds), Ray Burdis (Pete
Sutton), George Innes (Emilio), Royston Tickner (Mr Dudds),
Howard Goorney (Mr Sutton), Sally Tinker (Frances)

**Written by** John Kane

**Designers:** Ken Wheatley (1, 3, 5), Tony Waller (2),
Lewis Logan (4, 6)
**Producer:** David Foster
**Director:** Jonathan Wright Miller

## Westway

The self-sufficiency lifestyle that filled the Sunday
supplements of the early 70s was reflected on the BBC in
series as different as *The Good Life* and *Survivors*. An ITV
take came in the unlikely guise of a children's drama serial.

The new arrivals to the Bristol commune in the old
Westway house were the Saxby family, providing an
outsider's viewpoint to this strange new way of life. Dad
Len had answered a newspaper advert to join Westway,
bringing his two young sons and teenage daughter.

The togetherness and idealism expected fall apart on
occasion and tensions rise among the tenants of Westway.
The children of the Saxby, Ryder and Harvey families take
an active role in the community only to find that when
their enthusiasm for the market garden begins to pay off it
leads to adults squabbling over the profits.

The dramas of community life were complemented by a
more traditional plotline, when Mark Saxby discovers from
the cantankerous old Miss Marlbury that there is some
kind of treasure hidden in the big old house. The lost diary
of Marlbury's ancestor, 'the Yellow Lord', has great
significance when the future of Westway becomes
untenable and a price is offered for the mansion.

Note should be made of an excellent young cast of
established and soon-to-be child stars, among them the
prolific Simon Gipps-Kent (probably the foremost juvenile
actor of the 70s who later died in tragic circumstances at a
young age), Sarah Sutton (later of *The Moon Stallion* and
*Doctor Who*) and no less than two Tomorrow People (Dean
Lawrence and Nigel Rhodes). Proving meanwhile that the
self-sufficiency lifestyle was more than mere media
invention, Ann Lynn – Jan Ryder in the series – really did
live on a commune at the time.

**HTV**
**7 episodes** ('The Saxby Invaders'; 'A Do-It-Yourself School';
'A Growing Concern'; 'Happy Families'; 'Noughts and Crosses';
'A Highly Desirable Property'; 'The Tenants' Feast')
(colour)
**Broadcast:** Wednesdays 28/4/76 – 9/6/76

**Main Cast:** Donald Morley (Pete Ryder), Ann Lynn (Jan Ryder),
Simon Gipps-Kent (Crispin Ryder), Sylvestra le Touzel
(Samantha Ryder), Ivor Salter (Len Saxby), Chris Range (Anna
Saxby), Ashley Knight (Phil Saxby), Nigel Rhodes (Mark Saxby),
Jane Lowe (Paula Harvey), Dean Lawrence (Ron Harvey),
Sarah Sutton (Sue Harvey), Daphne Heard (Miss Marlbury),
Tim Preece (Graham Lawrence)

**Written by** Guy Slater

**Designer:** John Biggs
**Producer:** Leonard White
**Executive Producer:** Patrick Dromgoole
**Directors:** Mike Vardy (1, 2), Don Leaver (3, 4), Leonard White
(5, 7), Derek Clark (6)

## Operation Patch

It's 1805 and the British fleet, under Lord Horatio Nelson,
prepares for a decisive battle with the French that history
will know as Trafalgar. On the English South Coast, where
Napoleon's forces threaten invasion, two youngsters, Tom
and Betsy, discover a young deserter boy on the run from
the feared Navy press gangs. Slowly but surely this leads
them into a plot to assassinate Admiral Nelson before the
HMS *Victory* can set sail ('Operation Patch' referring to the
famous eyepatch of the intended victim). The children
must learn who are the spies and who are the counter-spies
in time to stop the killing.

What could easily have been another swashbuckling runaround operating at one level is enriched by John Lucarotti's attention to social and political history. The story is played out against a background of call for social change – the murder plot is tied up in the workers' Jacobin Movement of the late eighteenth century and their wish to overthrow the privileged few who run England. The movement has been forced underground by the outlawing of Jacobin Society meetings and some supporters have become fanatical in their desire for violent change. Lucarotti also ups the stakes by directly involving the families of Tom and Betsy in the affair, with Betsy's father a Master-at-Arms on the *Victory* and Tom's a liberal Jacobin who is framed for possessing seditious pamphlets.

**Southern**
**7 episodes** ('The Deserter'; 'The Informers'; 'The Prisoner'; 'The Rebel'; 'The Spies'; 'The Assassin'; 'The Admiral')
(colour)
**Broadcast:** Sundays 13/6/76 – 25/7/76

**Main Cast:** Nigel Greaves (Tom Moyes), Lynsey Baxter (Betsy Cosserat), Barry Lowe (Dick Moyes), Michael Robbins (George Cosserat), Virginia Balfour (Beulah Cosserat), Anthony Pedley (Ralph Page), Diane Mercer (Merry), Aubrey Morris (Matthew Snell), Donald Pickering (Mr Scott), Tony Calvin (Nelson)

**Written by** John Lucarotti

**Music:** Leon Cohen
**Designer:** John Dilly
**Producer/Director:** Don Leaver
**Executive Producer:** Lewis Rudd

**Tie-in publications:** novelisation by John Lucarotti published by Target, 1976

## The Feathered Serpent

All-in-studio skullduggery and sacrifice in this Aztec period drama; certainly such implied savagery would not be allowed in a modern context lacking *Feathered Serpent*'s educational aspect. With Emperor Kukulkhan wishing to see an end to sacrifice and other barbaric practices, his conniving High Priest Nasca disingenuously sets about maintaining his power base. Kukulkhan's beautiful daughter Chimalma, the boy prince Heumac and his servant lad Tozo are all drawn into Nasca's web of ruthless deceit. At the conclusion to the first series Nasca looks set to realise his goal and have Heumac sacrificed on the summit of the Pyramid of the Sun.

Heumac survived this treachery and returned in a second series. This time round his main rival was Xipec, Governor of the Gold Region. Xipec challenges Heumac's intended marriage to Chimalma and sets him an ordeal which he must complete. Nasca is still a threat and now there is the suggestion of magic and sorcery as the Priest consorts with mad old witch Keelag.

While the studio-based exteriors were impressive if never really convincing, the colourful costumes were superb. Most were historically accurate although Chimalma's outrageous wedding dress was designed by a *Look-In* reader via a competition.

**Thames**
**2 seasons**
(colour)

**Main Cast:** Patrick Troughton (Nasca), Diane Keen (Empress Chimalma), Brian Deacon (Prince Heumac), Richard Willis (Tozo), Robert Gary (Mahoutec), George Lane Cooper (Chadac), George Cormack (Otolmi)

**Written by** John Kane

**Music:** David Fanshawe
**Producer:** Vic Hughes

**Season One**
**6 episodes**
**Broadcast:** Mondays 21/6/76 – 26/7/76

**Additional Cast:** Tony Steedman (Kukulkhan)

**Designer:** Patrick Downing
**Directors:** Vic Hughes (1, 4), Michael Custance (2, 3, 5, 6)

**Season Two**
**6 episodes**
**Broadcast:** Mondays 3/4/78 – 8/5/78 (4.45p.m. except episode 5 1/5/78 at 4.15p.m.)

**Additional Cast:** Granville Saxton (Xipec), Sheila Burrell (Keelag)

**Designer:** Jan Chaney
**Directors:** Vic Hughes (2–6), Stan Woodward (1)

**Tie-in publications:** *TV Times* cover for week 19/6/76 – 25/6/76

## Nobody's House

To make a children's series about having fun with ghosts only to find yourself beaten to the punch by the BBC's *Rentaghost* must have been galling for the team behind *Nobody's House*. Still, although it was a light-hearted and good-natured comedy drama, *Nobody's House* was just that little bit more sophisticated than the more outright slapstick of the BBC comedy series.

*Nobody's House* concerned the adventures of a fourteen-year-old ghost boy who finds two children his own age moving into his house after more than a century of boredom and loneliness. It was about fairly robust japes on the surface but always shot through with a dose of pathos. Dubbed 'Nobody' by Tom and Gilly, the Sinclair children, on account of his being an orphan, the ghost boy will often let slip the misery of his brief life on earth. On meeting them he brazenly explains, 'I used to live here in the old workhouse – 'til I caught plague and snuffed it.' In other stories we sense his alienation when the children are too busy with their everyday lives and homework to bother with him. In 'Nobody's Family' he is discovered weeping because although he 'lives' in the house he is not considered a part of the Sinclair family, a family whom to him are ever-present but merely remind him of something he has never had. The novelisation is more direct about this tragic side to the ghost boy, detailing the whippings he

**Above:** Armada published this paperback novelisation to tie-in with Tyne Tees' *Nobody's House*.

endured in his time as no more than a slave. The book describes his situation beautifully: 'He had yearned for some children of his own age to come and live in the house so that they could all become friends together, play games and share each other's secrets.'

In 'Nobody Loves Me' we meet another similarly forlorn ghost child, Beatrice-Ellen. A spoilt rich girl from Nobody's time, she is sulky and mean-spirited and gets up to all sort of tricks. Gilly eventually realises that she is only doing this to get attention and, by sitting down with her and offering to be the girl's friend, lonely Beatrice is at last shown the kindness her Victorian socialite family could not afford.

To see *Nobody's House* purely as a metaphor for the alienated child would be to read too much into it. There are as many children who will recall it as the funny series with the boy who tugged on his scarf when it was time to disappear. Usually the darkness is outshone by the series' brighter side, with Nobody scaring away burglars and foiling a forger of old paintings who tries to con antique dealer Mr Sinclair. When he's not so self-absorbed, Nobody is a naturally mischievous ghost, given to moving household objects about to amuse himself. In the opening episode, with the Sinclairs moving in, he has lots of low comedy fun with paint pots, almost to *Rentaghost* extremes. There's some punning wordplay too, Nobody complaining to Tom at one point 'you nearly frightened me to death!'.

Perhaps surprisingly, the series isn't that frightening either. Only Silver Ned, a glam-rock-influenced nasty ghost exorcised by a scientific ghost hunter in 'Nobody's Ghost' is a little disturbing. On the whole the series was an amiable comedy based around an engaging and well-rounded central character.

**Tyne Tees**
**7 episodes** ('There's Nobody There…'; 'Nobody's Perfect'; 'Nobody's Fool'; 'Nobody's in Charge'; 'Nobody Loves Me'; 'Nobody's Family'; 'Nobody's Ghost')
(colour)
**Broadcast:** Mondays 27/9/76 – 8/11/76
**Main Cast:** Kevin Moreton (Nobody), Stuart Wilde (Tom Sinclair), Mandy Woodward (Gilly Sinclair), William Gaunt (Peter Sinclair), Wendy Gifford (Jane Sinclair)

**Written by** Martin Hall and Derrick Sherwin

**Music:** Anthony Isaac
**Designer:** Roger Andrews
**Producer:** Margaret Bottomley
**Directors:** Michael Ferguson, David Green

**Tie-in publications:** novelisation published in paperback by Armada, 1976

## The Canal Children

The year is 1845, and the coming of the railways bites hard for those in the canal haulage business. To make matters worse for Colonel Russell, head of the Warwick and Birmingham Canal Company, cargoes are being stolen somewhere along the route north from Hatton to Knowle Locks.

Russell is too concerned with this business to notice too much when his granddaughter Betsy comes to Cuttle Hall for the holidays. The Colonel had disowned Betsy's father before his death and shows little affection to the girl. Betsy is made of stern stuff, however, and when her new friend from 'below-stairs', lock-keeper's boy Tom Brill, is dismissed on suspicion of aiding and abetting the barge thieves she resolves to help him clear his name. At first this Midlands urchin and his friend Dan Trugg are distrustful of such an upper-class 'gongoozler' (a bargee's word for a 'useless person who lazes around while other folks work') but Betsy's spirit wins them over.

There's a touch of the Hodgson Burnetts, given the subplot of Betsy warming the heart of her cold grandfather, but it's all rather low on real adventure until the three children finally set off to catch the thieves. 'Buggets' are thought to be responsible, the ghosts who are said to haunt the long, dark tunnel at Shrewley – but is that likely, or might there be a more rational explanation?

Made with the usual BBC attention to period detail, this rather obscure serial might have been better remembered had it aired in the Sunday slot one might have expected.

**BBC**
**6 episodes** ('A Gongoozler'; 'Buggets and Tonnage'; 'Poor Man's Morris'; 'Gunpowder'; 'The Secret Agent'; 'The Wager')
(colour)
**Broadcast:** Wednesdays 10/11/76 – 15/12/76

**Main Cast:** Maxine Gordon (Betsy Russell), Andrew O'Connor (Tom Brill), Peter Berry (Dan Trugg), Eric Porter (Colonel Russell), Gwen Cherrell (Aunt Sarah Russell), Barbara Hickmott (Mary Brill), William Wilde (Charlie-the-Mule), Brian Hayes (Joe Collingtree), Don McKillop (Walter Crumlow)

**Written by** Brian Wright

**Music:** Jack Emblow
**Designer:** Geoff Powell
**Producer:** Anna Home
**Director:** John Prowse

**Tie-in publications:** novelisation by Brian Wright published by William Heinemann (hardback) and Piccolo (paperback), 1976

## James and the Giant Peach

James is a desperately unhappy orphan child left in the care of his two cruel aunts, Spiker and Sponge, who treat him like a slave. One day he encounters a mysterious old man at the bottom of the garden who hands James a bag containing hundreds of magical organisms. James is told to be wary and never let the bag drop from his hand or someone else will benefit from their powers. In his excitement, James drops the bag at the base of an old peach tree and, very shortly, the tree is sporting a plump peach on its top branch.

The peach grows in size until it's far bigger than a person and, when James finds a hole in the side of the huge fruit, he crawls inside. There he finds a variety of oversized insects and worms, all recipients of the magic power. Severing the peach from the tree, they set out on an amazing adventure.

This fascinating play doesn't take itself particularly seriously and seems something of an offering for the panto season. It doubles up as a musical, containing a number of comical songs that allow the actors to further ham it up. Produced on a minimal budget it was taped entirely in the studio and utilised simple, two-dimensional storybook backdrops akin to those one would expect to find on *Rainbow* or *Play School*. The costumes achieved an almost gruesome effect, comprising the actors, with their faces painted, standing inside exaggerated if accurate insect suits. The special effects weren't complex – CSO was apparent in many areas of the production and the effect of the growing peach was achieved simply by using a balloon, slowly inflated as required.

The late Roald Dahl is the most popular children's author in Britain but thus far *James and the Giant Peach* is the only one of his works to have been adapted for children's television using live action – most have leapfrogged direct to the big screen.

BBC
1 episode
(colour)
**Broadcast:** Tuesday 28/12/76

**Main Cast:** Simon Bell (James), Anna Quayle (Aunt Spiker), Ann Beach (Aunt Sponge), Arthur Hewlett (Old Man), Thorley Walters (Grasshopper), Pat Coombs (Spider), Kate Lock (Ladybird), Bernard Cribbins (Centipede), Hugh Lloyd (Earthworm), Christopher Owen (Silkworm/2nd naval officer), Jo Kendall (Glow-Worm/American Woman)

Based on the novel by Roald Dahl (first UK publication 1961, HarperCollins)
**Adapted by** Trevor Preston

**Music:** Peter Howell
**Designer:** Anna Ridley
**Producer:** Anna Home
**Director:** Paul Stone

## The Phoenix and the Carpet

Nostalgia can be hopelessly inaccurate; one of the best remembered of all the BBC's Sunday serials for children was in fact shown on Wednesday afternoons. A mix of innocent fantasy and Edwardian period settings, E. Nesbit's tale was first translated to the screen in the 70s as a story of low budget magic amid sailor suits and straw boaters.

Nesbit's original tale was essentially a sequel to the successful *Five Children and It*. For the follow-up, the wish-granting Psammead is directly replaced by the Phoenix and his wish-granting magic carpet. The Psammead had been tetchy but the Phoenix was almost downright rude. The bird's vanity and sulks were faithfully translated in this adaptation. When the Phoenix off-handedly suggests that he 'cannot say I am fond of anyone', young Cyril mutters, 'Except yourself.' He may be a wise old bird but he has the personality of a spoilt child and this of course makes him a favourite with the audience.

The wishes granted by the Psammead had been cautionary lessons for the children, but here the journeys of the carpet lead them into good-spirited adventure and mild danger. *The Phoenix and the Carpet* seems to have been written as instalments for bedtime reading, also betraying its original serialised publication in *The Strand* magazine. Likewise this largely unabridged adaptation (though it does manage to join two previously unrelated French adventures into one) flits between various vignettes with little in the way of an unfolding narrative. Only a few nominal overlaps suggest any sort of interlinked plot development.

Mention should be made of the completely revised and genuinely teary ending, which has the carpet and the Phoenix's egg floating off into space with Bobs gazing after it. The Phoenix never got to say his farewells before returning to his egg but, just as Bobs is about to turn away, a golden feather falls to the floor in slow motion. 'It's alright, he did say goodbye after all.'

The biggest technical headache was the demonstration of the magic of the bird and its carpet. *Radio Times* brought up an old chestnut, commenting: '... that the Phoenix and the Carpet have never before displayed their magical talents on screen is entirely due, it seems, to technical barriers. How could a wishing carpet have taken to the air under its own steam in the days before CSO?' Indeed, CSO (colour separation overlay) is used to the full here but, one suspects, without enough time to devote to finer details. The carpet flies completely flat and never flaps in the wind, the children are often caught in the overlay and partially disappear, while some aerial footage of London beneath the carpet clearly shows modern parked cars in Edwardian London. Still, the art nouveau kaleidoscope animation that fills the screen when the carpet takes off is a wonderful touch.

The Phoenix meanwhile is ingeniously realised as a simple puppet. The stroke of genius here was not to attempt to make the bird look real in any way, instead making him look like a carving or statue come to life. The ornate antique look (something akin to the bookend Yaffle in *Bagpuss*) is impressive even if its CSO flying is sometimes less so. A valiant try, technically speaking. It is better to have tried and sometimes lost than to have complained about the technology not being good enough and shelved the project for another twenty years.

Twenty years later the story *was* revived. With terrific special effects, subtle lighting the original had lacked and, of course, a lot more money thrown at the production, it had a big screen quality the first couldn't hope to match. Now the carpet didn't just fold and swish through the skies at high speed, it even had an animated shadow when it landed. Made as a sequel to the two Psammead television adventures (the Psammead's cameo from Nesbit's novel was now reinstated to tie in with the TV prequels), *Phoenix* was remade to capitalise on those serials' success in America, with a much greater budget committed on this occasion.

The only disappointing visual aspect in the more recent version was the Phoenix itself. While it benefited from animatronic control it looked like a cross between Rod Hull's Emu and Orville the Duck and wasn't a patch on the inventive if cheapskate bird of the original.

It wasn't just technically improved – the 90s version was more tightly written at six episodes and the South Sea islanders were now thankfully played with far more dignity by black actors. The 70s version had been naively racist in using white actors painted with gravy browning and sporting afro wigs. All roads up, the 90s adaptation was better and only an inaccurate nostalgist would disagree. For all that, it's difficult to ignore the sneaking suspicion that in the 70s *The Phoenix and the Carpet* was a serial that children genuinely wanted to watch. The 90s remake, made with more calculated and less altruistic intentions, comes across as being something they were *expected* to watch.

Based on the novel by E. Nesbit (first UK publication 1904, T. Fisher Unwin)

### *The Phoenix and the Carpet* (1976–77)
**BBC Birmingham**
**8 episodes**
(colour)

### Part 1
'The Magic Fire'
Wednesday 29/12/76 5.10p.m.
Four children find a strange egg inside their new Persian carpet. As they drop the egg accidentally onto the fire, a Phoenix is hatched. The fabulous bird of antiquity can grant wishes and tells them that the rug is a magic carpet. Flying to France on the carpet they land inside an old tower. They find a casket of treasure there but are chased by two ghostly forms.

### Part 2
'Queen of the Island'
Wednesday 5/1/77 5.10p.m.
The ghosts turn out to be a widow and her son. They are trying to protect the tower's lost treasure from thieves – the children give her back the casket they have found. Next day they travel to a sunny South Sea island. Cook, transported by accident, is taken to be a prophetic figure by the natives and they crown her their queen.

**Above:** that fabulous bird of antiquity, the Phoenix, spirits the magic carpet and passengers (l to r) Anthea (Tamzin Neville), Bobs (Max Harris), Jane (Jane Forster) and Cyril (Gary Russell) away to a desert island in the 1977 adaptation of *The Phoenix and the Carpet*.

### Part 3
'Some Indian Things'
Wednesday 12/1/77 5.10p.m.
The children travel to India to find some items for the church bazaar. They cheer up a melancholy Ranee and she rewards them with gifts. Miss Peasmarsh's stall does very well out of the items but at the end of the day it transpires that the carpet has mistakenly been sold to nasty old Mrs Biddle.

### Part 4
'The Temple of the Phoenix'
Wednesday 19/1/77 5.10p.m.
With the children wishing for Mrs Biddle to become nice, she offers to give them back the carpet. The carpet restored to them, they take the Phoenix out to see London. They visit the offices of Phoenix Insurance, which the vain old bird believes to be a temple to his honour.

### Part 5
'Gifts from Persia'
Wednesday 26/1/77 5.10p.m.
The carpet is sent to Persia to bring back gifts for the children but it ends up bringing back a hundred Persian cats. It is then sent to fetch milk to feed the cats but brings back a whole cow. Bobs, Cyril and Anthea go out to put the cats on local doorsteps, leaving Jane asleep alone in the house. She is awakened by a burglar breaking in …

**Part 6**
'What To Do with a Burglar'
Wednesday 2/2/77 5.10p.m.
The burglar turns out to be a rather cowardly sort – and helps to milk their cow. The cats fed, the children offer him them to sell and he gladly does so until he is caught by the police, suspicious he has stolen the moggies. The carpet frees him from prison and takes him to the island where he and Cook are married by a 'kidnapped' Reverend Blenkinsop.

**Part 7**
'The Hole in The Carpet'
Wednesday 9/2/77 5.10p.m.
One day, out flying, Bobs and Jane fall through a large hole in the now rather battered carpet. Luckily they land on the roof of Reverend Blenkinsop's house and he is thus able to convince his fearsome aunts that his 'vision' of the magic carpet was true.

**Part 8**
'A Night at The Theatre'
Wednesday 16/2/77 5.10p.m.
Though the Phoenix feels old and tired he joins the children for a night at the theatre. He gets very excited at it all and causes their viewing box to burst into flames. The fire brigade arrive but with one last great effort the Phoenix puts out the fire. His energies spent, the bird returns to his egg. The children watch as the carpet, with the egg inside, floats off for another 1,000 years.

**Main Cast:** Richard Warner (The Phoenix), Gary Russell (Cyril), Tamzin Neville (Anthea), Max Harris (Robert), Jane Forster (Jane), Daphne Neville (Mother), Edward Brooks (Father), Trisha Mortimore (Eliza), Susan Field (Cook), Bernice Stegers (Madame), Adam Stafford (Henri), Hilary Mason (Mrs Biddle), Surya Kumari (Ranee), Bernard Holley (Burglar), Nigel Lambert (Rev Septimus Blenkinsop), Seymour Green (Theatre Manager) Phoenix made and operated by Joe Barton

**Dramatised by** John Tully

**Insurance song (episode 4):** Jonathan Cohen
**Operetta song (episode 8):** Paul Horner
**Designer:** Myles Lang
**Director:** Clive Doig (credited as film sequences only for episode 4)
**Producer:** Dorothea Brooking

**Tie-in publications:** paperback editions of novel published by Puffin, 1976–8

**E. Nesbit's The Phoenix and the Carpet (1997)**
**A BBC/HIT Entertainment Co-production**
**6 episodes**
(colour)
**Broadcast:** Sundays 16/11/97 – 21/12/97 (episode 3 shown on BBC2 in Scotland due to live football coverage)

**Main Cast:** David Suchet (Voice of the Phoenix), Ben Simpson (Cyril), Jessica Fox (Anthea), Ivan Berry (Robert), Charlotte Chinn (Jane), Mary Waterhouse (Mother), Ian Keith (Father), Lesley Dunlop (Eliza), Miriam Margolyes (Cook), Francis Wright (Voice of the Psammead)

**Screenplay by** Helen Cresswell

**Music:** Paul Hart
**Art Director:** Clara Morland
**Production Designer:** George Kyriakides
**Executive Producer for HIT:** John Bullivant
**Executive Producer for BBC:** Anna Home
**Director:** Michael Kerrigan

**Tie-in publications:** paperback edition of novel published by Puffin, 1997. Abridged and adapted short-form of Nesbit's novel by Helen Cresswell published by Puffin, 1997 (includes colour photos from the serial).

## Children of the Stones

In some cases, calling a children's drama 'adult' can be seen as a pejorative term. Some can come across as mainstream dramas rejected and then partly reworked for the children's market in hope of a sale. To call *Children of the Stones* 'adult' is a compliment.

An unwritten rule of children's drama is that you must get rid of any parental or authority figures as soon as possible to let the child leads come into their own, but *Children of the Stones* gives as much prominence to its adult cast as to the younger actors. Unexpectedly this gives it an air of gravitas and threat and is due at least partly to excellent performances by Gareth Thomas and Veronica Strong (Strong's husband was in fact the serial's writer Jeremy Burnham). Iain Cuthbertson, one of the small screen's most ebullient character actors, gives perhaps the most carefully subdued performance of his career in the serial.

The script is a fairly complex blend of supernatural horror and science fiction which never talks down to the audience. Admittedly several plot strands are derivative but undoubtedly gripped the child audience to whom these ideas appeared exciting and new. Certainly it's not difficult to imagine this serial made as a lowish budget British horror picture a few years earlier. *Children of the Stones* is a dash of *Village of the Damned* (trapped in a picturesque but spooky village with no outside phone lines) and a pinch of an Anglified *Wicker Man* (legends and folk tradition with a sinister edge). *Quatermass* is in there and so too is *The Owl Service*.

Most clearly it's very much a late entry to the early 70s canon that tried to update the horror movie for a more sophisticated audience. Here Professor Brake seeks to rationalise paranormal phenomena with his electronic devices and scientific measurement just as happened in the horror curio *The Legend of Hell House* or Nigel Kneale's *The Stone Tape*. No matter the weirdness – psychic abilities, ley lines, the power that lies in the stones – Brake is always on hand to give a possible scientific explanation. These seem, as is so often the case, mindful of an educational remit – nothing in children's television can ever be purely damn good fun. Scientific advisor Dr Peter Williams gives plausible and up to date explanations for black holes, supernovas, psychokinesis and ammonia-powered atomic clocks among other topics.

*Children of the Stones* prefers a quiet menace to the more frenetic action adventure pace these things can fall into. It is certainly adult in tone, but it doesn't forget its target audience. Much of the tension is created in the recognisable but oddly different classroom of the village school. Certain pupils sit at desks on their own while the rest sit together in groups. The group members are brilliant mathematicians despite being barely into their teens and are curiously happy and calm, with little of the boisterous behaviour one would expect (a clear nod to John Wyndham again). By twisting settings familiar to the child audience, so it keeps them intrigued. The story is also careful to involve Matthew as much as his father to keep the younger viewer interested. It's Matthew who makes the most telling deductions and his latent psychic abilities allow him to advance the story far more than his father can despite his wealth of academic knowledge.

However, it is, for all its accurate science, a superbly scary piece of hokum at heart. What's most frightening and unsettling of all is the way the few 'unconverted' villagers who remain are taken over by Hendrick's idea of 'happiness' episode by episode. 'Village idiot' Dai is killed – violent death is less common than you might imagine in children's drama – and by the outset of episode six the unthinkable happens when even Margaret and Sandra are taken over, leaving the Brakes the last free wills remaining.

Even more bravely, at the story's climax Sandra and Margaret fail to reach the Sanctuary with Matthew and Adam and are turned into twisted stone parodies of human beings. The conclusion is wonderfully overwrought although deciphering what was going on must have been challenging, to say the least, for a young audience; Hendrick is blasted by the psychic beam and is momentarily glimpsed as a bearded figure of ancient times while the villagers are turned to stone *en masse*. Even more thought-provoking is the coda to the story, in which Brake theorises that it is not just the stones that encircled the village but also a ring of time. As the serial concludes, the events of the story appear not to have happened at all but, just when you think that's a bit of a cheat, you realise that in fact time has turned the circle and the whole nightmare is about to begin again. It's a resolution that clearly illustrates the unpatronising stance of this serial.

**HTV West**
**7 episodes**
(colour)

**Episode One**
'Into the Circle'
Monday 10/1/77 4.45p.m.
Scientist Adam Brake and his son Matthew arrive in the quiet village of Milbury to study the ancient stone circle that stands there. At school Matthew befriends Sandra, while his father meets Sandra's mother Margaret, curator of Milbury's museum. Margaret invites Adam to touch one of the mysterious stones – he receives some kind of psychic shock and is thrown to the ground.

**Episode Two**
'Circle of Fear'
Monday 17/1/77 4.45p.m.
Matthew meets a strange man called Dai, who appears to be some kind of 'village idiot' but warns Matthew of the danger here. That night the villagers gather outside and sing a weird incantation …

**Episode Three**
'Serpent in the Circle'
Monday 24/1/77 4.45p.m.
Dai finds a stone amulet, decorated with a serpent, which he

mutters is his protection and a key. Meanwhile one of the more normal children at the strange village school, Jimmo, heartily joins in a morris dance on the green despite he and his father having said they hated them only days before. The pair now seem curiously happy.

**Episode Four**
'The Narrowing Circle'
Monday 31/1/77 4.45p.m.
Dai's amulet is broken – he runs off and is found soon after lying dead on the grass where only a few minutes earlier had lain a stone carved with a serpent.

**Episode Five**
'Charmed Circle'
Monday 7/2/77 4.45p.m.
Matthew reassembles Dai's amulet and receives a psychic message; 'Visitor … bright … stones … power … beam … always!' Brake wonders if it refers to a 'guest star' – a supernova. The Smythes are invited to dinner by Hendrick; at a set time the dining room roof slides open and an intense beam of light shoots to the heavens. Margaret and Sandra are transfixed …

**Episode Six**
'Squaring the Circle'
Monday 14/2/77 4.45p.m.
The Smythes are now under Hendrick's power. Matthew and Adam try to leave the village but as they drive away something looms up in front of their car and Adam loses control. They wake up prisoners of Hendrick. 'Dinner' is in less than an hour …

**Episode Seven**
'Full Circle'
Monday 21/2/77 4.45p.m.
By tampering with Hendrick's digital clocks, Adam tricks him into trying to 'process' Matthew and himself a few minutes too early. Hendrick's protection is lost and he is blasted by the light beam. The villagers are turned to stone as the Brakes run to Dai's Sanctuary. When they wake, Dai is there while the village has apparently returned to normal. Leaving the village, Adam and Matthew pass a man bearing an uncanny likeness to a younger Hendrick driving in the opposite direction …

**Main Cast:** Iain Cuthbertson (Raphael Hendrick), Gareth Thomas (Professor Adam Brake), Peter Demin (Matthew Brake), Veronica Strong (Margaret Smythe), Katharine Levy (Sandra Smythe), Freddie Jones (Dai)

**Written and created by** Jeremy Burnham and Trevor Ray

**Music:** Sidney Sager
**Designer:** Ken Jones
**Producer/Director:** Peter Graham Scott
**Executive Producer:** Patrick Dromgoole

**Tie-in publications:** novelisation by Trevor Ray and Jeremy Burnham published in paperback by Carousel, 1977

**Video:** 98-minute compilation as a single tape on Betamax and VHS formats by Guild Home Video c. 1981. 98-minute compilation reissued late 1980s, label not known. Re-released as two-part 180-minute compilation on double tape format by Video Gems, 5/4/93. Deleted 1/4/96. Region 2 DVD of uncut episodic serial released by Network Video 21/10/02.

103

## Just William

'They were funny adventure stories for kids ... but they were funny for adults in a sort of social, satirical fashion ...'. John Davies, producer/director of the 70s TV revival of *William*, identified just what has made Richmal Crompton's novels so popular since the late 20s. The comic adventures of naughty schoolboy William Brown and his gang, the Outlaws, set William up as the rebel to all of the mores and conventions of Britain between the wars.

Successful in other media, the first TV version starred Robert Sandford, was produced by Joy Harington and shown by the BBC 24/1/51. A 1956 series by an ITV company is similarly lost in the mists of time. The BBC later followed with a series which for its first season starred a fourteen-year-old Dennis Waterman in the lead role.

Despite the first books being nearly fifty years old by the mid-70s, it was the LWT series that perhaps became the most popular of all, scheduled in a Sunday afternoon slot ideal for capturing both the children and adults to whom William supposedly appealed equally. John Davies realised that the adults in the books were grotesque, over-life-size and fairly unsympathetic and so encouraged his cast to play the parts likewise. Mr Brown 'would prefer to be working in his office twenty-four hours a day'. Mum was well-meaning but naive and rather dizzy. Brother Robert was 'a pompous bore, always chasing girls usually of a social standing above his own'. Sister Ethel was of the same ilk as her elder brother and, when William's latest antics had scared off another of the girl's hapless suitors, Mr Brown would often slip his young son some extra pocket money in gratitude. Into this stultifying middle-class boredom William couldn't help but come across as the anti-hero.

If the Browns were exaggerated in their dullness, the Botts who lived at the Manor Hall were a truly appalling bunch of *nouveau riche* snobs (they had made their money out of bottled sauce). The two best-remembered co-stars were Diana Dors as the gaudy, aitch-dropping ogre Mrs Bott and, in particular, Bonnie Langford as her daughter Violet Elizabeth. Langford quickly became the star of the show as the villain with the ginger ringlets, introducing a bona fide catchphrase – 'I'll thcweam and thcweam until I'm sick!' – to the national consciousness and the country's impressionists. It's tribute to Langford's performance that many thought the precocious actress was playing herself. The actress feels she is still fighting preconceptions created by this one role twenty-five years ago.

Producer Davies, feeling that the way Crompton's books had kept up with the times had damaged their appeal, kept the series firmly in period and plumped for a 1928 setting. Thus William was pitted against what Davies described as 'irate colonels, dry-stick spinsters and angry men who get their cucumber frames smashed by cricket balls'. Allied to this nostalgic view of England was an occasionally playful visual sense, which even admitted a dream sequence of Violet as Queen Elizabeth I and the Outlaws as her courtiers in one episode.

The series' most recent revival, by an independent producer for the BBC, failed to become a mini-phenomenon as the 70s series had done. Certainly it traded on a similar antique setting, this time no doubt with an eye on American PBS sales (to the Public Broadcasting Service stations). The second season was moved into a peak-time Sunday evening slot at 7p.m., suggesting that the schedulers saw its appeal as lying more with nostalgic parents than their offspring.

**Just William (1977)**
**LWT**
**27 episodes**
(colour)

**Main Cast:** Adrian Dannatt (William Brown), Diana Fairfax (Mrs Brown), Hugh Cross (Mr Brown), Stacy Dorning (Ethel Brown), Simon Chandler (Robert Brown), Michael McVey (Ginger), Craig McFarlane (Henry), Tim Rose (Douglas), Bonnie Langford (Violet Elizabeth Bott), Diana Dors (Mrs Bott), John Stratton (Mr Bott)

Based on the novels by Richmal Crompton
**Adapted by** Keith Dewhurst

**Theme:** Denis King
**Producer/Director:** John Davies
**Executive Producer:** Stella Richman

**Season One**
**13 episodes** ('William and the Begging Letter'; 'William – the Great Actor'; 'The Outlaws and the Tramp'; 'The Sweet Little Girl in White'; 'William and the Badminton Racket'; 'A Little Interlude'; 'William and the Prize Pig'; 'William and the Wonderful Present'; 'William the Matchmaker'; 'Waste Paper Please'; 'Only Just in Time'; 'William and the Sleeping Major'; 'William Clears the Slums')
**Broadcast:** Sundays 6/2/77 – 1/5/77 (fully networked at 4.35p.m. but moving to new time of 5.45p.m. for last few episodes in most regions)

**Designer:** Bryan Bagge

**Season Two**
**13 episodes** plus **1 hour Christmas Special** ('William's Lucky Day'; 'The Great Detective'; 'Violet Elizabeth Wins'; 'William Holds the Stage'; 'William the Philanthropist'; 'It All Began with the Typewriter'; 'A Rescue Party'; 'William Finds a Job'; 'Parrots for Ethel'; 'William's Worst Christmas'*; 'William at the Garden Party'; 'Two Good Turns'; 'Finding a School for William'; 'William and the Tramp')
**Broadcast:** Sundays 23/10/77 – 22/1/78 (fully networked)
*Christmas Special Sunday 25/12/77 (12.30p.m.)

**Designers:** Rae George, Bryan Bagge, Colin Monk

**Tie-in publications:** editions of the Crompton novels published in paperback by Armada, 1977.
*TV Times* covers for weeks 5/2/77 – 11/2/77 and 22/10/77 – 28/10/77 (Violet also makes a guest appearance on cover of the Christmas 1977 issue). *The Just William Annual*, published by World Distributors 1977 and 1978 (dated 1978 and 1979)

*Over to William* (1956)
**unknown independent company for ITV broadcast (b&w)**
**13 episodes** ('Violet Elizabeth Wins'; 'Claude Finds a Companion'; 'William and the Ebony Hairbrush'; 'The Brown Check Sports Coat'; 'Aunt Louie's Birthday Present'; 'William and the Three-Forty'; 'William the Bold'; 'William's Lucky Day'; 'William and the Tramp'; 'Cats and White Elephants'; 'Esmeralda Takes a Hand'; 'The Begging Letter'; 'William Meets a Professor')
**Broadcast:** 20/9/56 – 13/12/56
**Starring** Keith Crane as William

*William* (1962–63)
**BBC**
(b&w)

**Main Cast:** Dennis Waterman (William – Season 1), Denis Gilmore (William – Season 2), Carlo Cura (Douglas), Kaplan Kaye (Henry), Christopher Witty (Ginger), Gillian Gostling (Violet)

**Season One**
**6 episodes** ('William and the Wonderful Present'; 'William and the Leopard Hunter'; 'William Finds a Job'; 'William The Counterspy'; 'William and the Parrots'; 'William and the American Tie')
**Broadcast:** Saturdays 26/5/62 – 30/6/62

**Season Two**
**6 episodes** ('William The Peacemaker'; 'William and the Little Girl'; 'William and the Three Bears'; 'William and the Sleeping Major'; 'William and the Real Laurence'; 'William Goes Shopping')
**Broadcast:** Saturdays 30/3/63 – 4/5/63

**Adapted by** C. E. Webber
**Producer:** Leonard Chase

*Just William* (1994–95)
**Talisman Films for BBC**
(colour)

**Main Cast:** Oliver Rokison (William Brown), Jonathan Hirst (Ginger), Stephen Wilmot (Henry), Alastair Weller (Douglas), Tiffany Griffiths (Violet), David Horowitch (Mr Brown), Polly Adams (Mrs Brown), Rebecca Johnson (Ethel), Benjamin Pullen (Robert Brown), Robert Austin (Mr Bott), Lil Roughley (Mrs Bott)

**Producer:** Alan Wright
**Director:** David Giles

**Season One**
**6 episodes** ('William and the White Elephants'; 'Finding a School for William'; 'William the Great Actor'; 'William's Birthday'; 'William and the Russian Prince'; 'William's Busy Day')
**Broadcast:** Sundays 13/11/94 – 18/12/94

**Written by** Simon Booker (1–3), Allan Baker (4–6)

**Season Two**
**6 episodes** ('William Clears the Slums'; 'Boys Will Be Boys'; 'William and the Ebony Hairbrush'; 'William and the Old Man in the Fog'; 'Parrots for Ethel'; 'William Turns Over a New Leaf')
**Broadcast:** Sundays 12/11/95 – 17/12/95

**Written by** Simon Booker

**Tie-in publications:** *Radio Times* cover for 18/11/95 – 24/11/95 edition

**Video:** two volumes released by BBC Video, 3/4/95. Two episodes each: 'William and the White Elephants'/'Finding a School for William'; 'William the Great Actor'/'William's Birthday'. Deleted 16/7/97.

## Horse in the House

After the phenomenal success of *Follyfoot* and *The Adventures of Black Beauty* it was inevitable that somebody would try to find a successor to air alongside the popular repeats of the early 70s hits. Indeed both Rosemary Anne Sisson and Audrey Starrett had worked on *Follyfoot* and joined the crew of this new pretender. The series was the realisation of a five-year ambition by executive producer Sue Turner, herself a keen horsewoman, to adapt a novel by American writer William Corbin. Its US setting was transposed for television to an utterly middle-class English locale.

Melanie Webb was some sort of aspirational figure for little girls all over Britain, a pony-loving teenager living in the country. Among her family are two precocious sisters (a novel-writing thirteen-year-old and a would-be astronaut) and a horse called Orbit. When her parents are away, Melanie brings the horse into the family home – hence the series' title.

The first season was a six-part thriller, with Melanie and family trying to save a kidnapped Orbit. The second season was a more obvious clone of *Follyfoot*, adapting a two-part episodic format which saw Melanie coping with two rival jockeys, an outbreak of strangles (a second-hand *Follyfoot* topic) and an old woman threatened with eviction from her cottage. Melanie now lived with her aunt and uncle, the set-up inherently lacking any of the inter-character friction that typified *Follyfoot*.

**Thames**
**2 seasons**
(colour)

**Season One**
**6 episodes**
**Broadcast:** Wednesdays 9/2/77 – 16/3/77 4.45p.m.

**Main Cast:** Kim McDonald (Melanie Webb), Alison Glennie (Katie), Katrina Rose (Diana), Charles Bolton (Richie Webb), Bridget Armstrong (Mrs Webb), Michael Coles (Mr Webb), Mandao (Orbit)

Based on the book by William Corbin (first UK publication 1966, Methuen; first US publication 1964, Coward-McCann)
**Adapted by** Rosemary Anne Sisson

**Music:** Carl Davis
**Designer:** Jack Robinson
**Producer:** Ruth Boswell
**Executive Producer:** Sue Turner
**Director:** Stan Woodward (1, 2, 5), Audrey Starrett (3, 4, 6)

**Season Two**
**3 x 2-part stories** ('Strangles'; 'Stable Girl'; 'Right of Way')
**Broadcast:** Mondays 26/2/79 – 2/4/79

**Main Cast:** Kim McDonald (Melanie Webb), Pete Postlethwaite (Uncle Doug), Venetia Maxwell (Aunt Jen)

**Written by** Ian Cullen (1, 2), Julie Welch (3, 4), Phil Redmond (5, 6)

**Designer:** Jack Robinson
**Producer:** Ruth Boswell
**Director:** Stan Woodward

**Tie-in publications:** n/k

## Out of Bounds

Helen and Terry, two promising young gymnasts, have their training for the county trials abruptly interrupted the day Terry receives an unexpected birthday gift of a watch. It soon transpires that the present is stolen property – Terry's brother Pete is involved in shady goings-on up to his neck. When Terry and Helen try to investigate why Pete is being blackmailed by a gang of local thugs and attempt to find the whereabouts of a stolen gun, Len Morgan's gym is vandalised as a warning to the young detectives.

This fairly obscure BBC filmed drama entry benefited from stunts and action and the expertise of Nik Stuart MBE as gymnastics adviser.

**BBC**
**6 episodes**
(colour)
**Broadcast:** Wednesdays 16/3/77 – 20/4/77

**Main Cast:** Melvin McClymont (Terry Ashmoore), Barbara Slater (Helen Parkin), Kim Smith (Pete Ashmoore), Gaynor Ward (Linda), John Price (Len Morgan)

**Written by** Brian Clark and Jim Hawkins from an idea by Dorian Cowland

**Music:** Carl Davis
**Designer:** Peter Kindred
**Producer:** Anna Home
**Director:** Colin Cant

**Tie-in publications:** novelisation by Brian Clark and Jim Hawkins published in paperback by BBC, c. 1979

## The Flockton Flyer

It would be too easy to describe this series glibly as a present-day *Railway Children* but in truth the famous Edwardian trio were far more independently minded than the three Carter children who live on a preservation society steam railway. Detracting from the excitement of what was billed as an adventure serial is the portrayal of a firm family unit. The cosy domestic chats round the dinner table, not to mention the fact that it's usually Dad's resourcefulness that saves the day, mean the Carter kids become bit players in a bigger ensemble.

When their landlord turfs the Carters out of their garage business, the family become caretakers of Somerset's Flockton and Lane End branch line on behalf of Commander Jack Frost and his steam preservation society. Their aim is to reopen the line to the public and have the *Flockton Flyer*, GWR engine 6412, take to the tracks once more.

The teenagers of the cast were Peter Duncan, pre-*Blue Peter*, and Gwyneth Strong (much later Cassandra in *Only Fools and Horses*). Curiously the pin-up potential of boy-next-door hunk Duncan and rake-skinny Strong are under-

utilised, with a dearth of adolescent plotlines. Jan doesn't locate a boyfriend until Season Two. Jessica Carter meanwhile is a little girl who takes in all the waifs and strays, unruly animals usually put to comic purposes. Gwyneth Strong's younger sister Catrin took over the role of Jessica for the second run, a slightly older and rather less sickly sweet girl.

Dad Bob is a conventionally stoic type although there's a very interesting scene in ''Op It' where we see his guilt at having been too busy to pay attention to Jess, who has run away. 'You hear about such awful things happening to kids these days,' he says in a wavering voice. Mum Kathy receives rather sexist comments about her lack of cooking expertise but more interestingly also studies history part time. In fact she is absent from Season Two altogether and we are told she has gone to Ontario University to take a degree. The family was complemented by the yarn-spinning, workshy but kindly old tramp Bill Jelly – occasional glimpses of his unsettled wanderlust and references to a dubious criminal past were never really developed. Jelly formed a comic partnership with Jack Frost, a retired Naval Commander who refers to everything in seafaring terms (his catchphrase 'Hell's Bells and Buckets of Blood!').

The series' real failing was that it was never life-or-death stuff. An accident in 'Under the Circumstances...' turns out to be a lorry shedding hay over a level crossing, which the *Flyer* crew sort out by turning up with a first aid kit. Jan meanwhile 'rescues' a lady writer who has fallen over in some mud. Heady stuff. An episode which sees two mail-train robbers diverted onto the Flockton branch is more promising but the armed raiders revert to bungling type (it turns out they stole the wrong mail bag and would only have got away with some postal orders). In ''Op It' Jess runs away to a mysterious island where *absolutely nothing happens* and she is found safe and well the next day. Many episodes were comic affairs, particularly 'Ready When You Are, Mr Cutley' which saw the family dress up as Indian mutineers for a film shoot.

Perhaps the most interesting episode is 'Pull the Other One' which shows that there is some sort of real world impinging upon the idyll of Flockton. When a yob vandalises the trains one night the tearaway is taken in and rehabilitated by becoming a useful part of the restoration team. Another early performance by Phil Daniels, it's a shame this more abrasive character couldn't have become a regular part of the cast.

Primary location work for the series was on the West Somerset Railway, the longest private railway in England, which runs from Minehead to Taunton. The second season saw the *Flyer* travel further afield as Flockton gained a coastline and the Carters moved downline to Crowcombe Station. Despite the potential for more wide-ranging adventures the *Flyer* continued to chuff along contentedly in six more gentle episodes.

**Southern**
**2 seasons**
(colour)

**Main Cast:** David Neal (Bob Carter), Sheila Fearn (Kathy Carter – Season 1 only), Peter Duncan (Jimmy Carter), Gwyneth Strong (Jan Carter), Annabelle Lanyon (Jessica Carter – Season 1), Catrin Strong (Jessica Carter – Season 2), Geoffrey Russell (Bill Jelly), Anthony Sharp (Cmdr Jack Frost)

**Season One**
**6 episodes** ('Be It Ever So Humble'; 'Game, Set and Match'; 'Pull the Other One'; 'Under the Circumstances...'; 'Oo Do You Suppose Will Get the Medal?'; 'I Name This Ship')
**Broadcast:** Mondays 18/4/77 – 23/5/77

**Written by** Peter Whitbread

**Music:** Jugg Music
**Designer:** John Dilly
**Producer:** Colin Nutley

The Flockton Flyer driven by Harry Lee, fired by Keith Hawkins

**Season Two**
**6 episodes** ('Race You For It'; 'Ready When You Are, Mr Cutley'; 'What A Little Beauty'; 'A Question of Honour'; "Op It'; 'A Little Bit of Somewhere')
**Broadcast:** Mondays 9/1/78 – 13/2/78

**Written by** Peter Whitbread

**Music:** Jugg Music
**Designer:** Gregory Lawson
**Producer/Director:** Colin Nutley

**Tie-in publications:** *The Flockton Flyer* by Peter Whitbread published by Arrow/Look-In Books, 1977; novelisation of first-season episodes with additional original plotlines

## King of the Castle

Teenager Roland Wright is a shy, sensitive boy who has recently moved into a block of council flats with his father and stepmother, taking up a music scholarship in a nearby college. Roland often incurs the wrath of the headmaster when he fails to sing to the highest standard. His father has little time for him, being more interested in his own music, and Roland hasn't yet formed a trusting relationship with his stepmother June. Worst of all, he finds himself being harassed by the thugs who inhabit the stairwell in his tower.

It's all too much for Roland and matters come to a head after a particularly vicious confrontation with Ripper, the gang leader, when Roland escapes into a malfunctioning lift which then hurtles to the basement. The doors of the lift open to reveal a disturbing underground labyrinth where people look strangely familiar.

Roland is knocked out during his descent in the elevator and, while unconscious, is subjected to a terrible nightmare where all his subconscious insecurities are magnified and distorted in front of him. It's a terrifying odyssey for Roland as the people who impact on his day-to-day life appear in his nightmare as twisted caricatures.

The first person Roland meets is a reflection of Vine, the concierge of his tower block. In the fantasy landscape he is known as Vein, the keeper of the keys, an ambivalent but ghoulish character who guides Roland through the various levels of the labyrinth and continually leaves the audience guessing as to whether he is working for or against Roland. As the boy's journey continues he meets more characters whose meaning, to the audience at least, is far more obvious.

Roland's domineering headmaster, Spurgeon, becomes Hawkspur, a demented scientist reminiscent of

Frankenstein, obsessed with creating the perfect organism. He brings his creature to life using music and then tries to transplant Roland's voice into the being. This is certainly a metaphor for Roland's real-life dissatisfaction with his school and his perception of Spurgeon as being completely single-minded in trying to make him someone he doesn't want to be. Even more meaningful is Roland's encounter with the Lord of the Castle, a reflection of his father. When the Lord tells Roland that he can't see him and that he has too many things piling up, Roland replies, 'What about me?' The Lord is dismissive, saying, 'I can't solve your problems.' Roland comes straight to the point, telling him, 'You're responsible for them.'

Roland is confronted by other aspects of his troubled life. The bully Ripper becomes a Samurai warrior and the pair fight on a number of occasions. His stepmother appears as a witch and even insignificant players, like the two police officers called out to a disturbance at the flats, appear as castle guards.

The nightmare doesn't just stop at people but also encompasses situations that frustrate Roland in his waking hours. His tirade about the pointlessness of his work as a kitchen skivvy reflects his fears of a future where work is nothing but an endless treadmill of the same old tasks with no material end in sight. Roland's apprehensions of bureaucracy are also explored when, trying to gain an interview with the Lord, he finds himself shunted around endless identical departments where he is always met by a variation of the same individual.

Roland also has his lessons to learn, none more important than when he finally becomes the King of the Castle. It is his hope that in making it to the figurative top he will be able to free himself but he only finds himself bogged down by the effort required to run his kingdom. He wants all his subjects to be happy and enforces upon them what he believes will make them happy. In doing so he becomes that which he loathes. His subjects revolt, putting him on trial for treason and finally banishing him. This allows him to return to 'reality' but as a changed person. He is now someone brave enough to tell Spurgeon that he will no longer be attending choir and clever enough to beat Ripper without the need for violence. Most importantly he has the courage to begin to build an understanding with his father.

At the time, *King of the Castle* was one of ITV's most ambitious projects for children's television. Although it's primarily studio-bound, HTV spent £300,000 on the production and nine months auditioning 200 children in an attempt to ensure that they cast the right boy in the part of Roland. The directors on the production, Peter Hammond in particular, demonstrated clever use of the camera, shooting at unusual angles while optical effects, like lights or shapes, were matted over the top of the primary image, adding to the nightmarish vision of Roland's dream. As one might expect, film and video are used throughout but with a specific design in purpose, film being used to represent the 'real world', while tape is used in Roland's fantasy world.

*King of the Castle* isn't a drama for faint-hearted children. It was considered so strong at the time that ITV's Network Planning Committee delayed transmission by four months, removing it from its proposed weekday children's slot and placing it instead in a more family-friendly Sunday teatime slot. Although it is sometimes too proud of its subtext to remember to add a narrative layer on top, it is clearly a highly intelligent and particularly

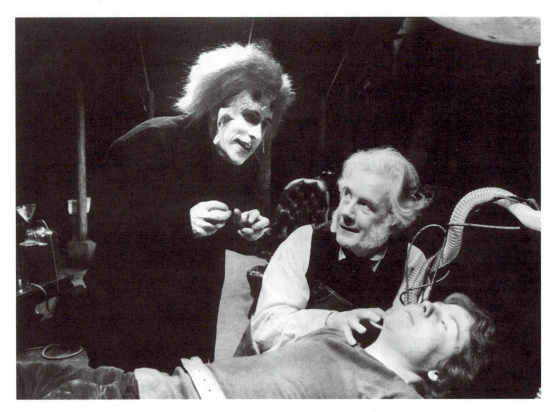

**Above:** a scene from HTV's bizarre allegory *King of the Castle*. Mad scientist Hawkspur (Fulton MacKay) hopes to make young Roland (Philip Da Costa) in his own image, as an earlier attempt – the Ergon (Milton Johns, left) – looks on.

sinister story, containing elements of *The Prisoner* and Kafka's *The Castle* (and possibly even the Genesis concept album *The Lamb Lies Down On Broadway*!). Created at a time when television could still be something of an experimental medium, *King of the Castle* is one of a kind and children's television hasn't seen the like of it since.

**HTV West**
**7 episodes**
(colour)

**Episode One**
Sunday 8/5/77 4.45p.m.
Roland stumbles into an unsafe lift when he tries to flee from the bullies that terrorise the residents of the block of flats where he lives. The lift plummets to the basement and, when the doors open, Roland finds himself in a strange underground cavern.

**Episode Two**
Sunday 15/5/77 5.45p.m.
Roland is now in a nightmare fantasy world where the inhabitants closely resemble those that he knows in real life. He meets Vein, the keeper of the keys, and is told that he must earn certain keys to escape.

**Episode Three**
Sunday 22/5/77 4.45p.m.
Roland is confronted by a warrior but manages to escape. He then meets a glamorous self-styled clairvoyant known as 'The Lady'.

**Episode Four**
Sunday 29/5/77 5.45p.m.
Roland must flee from the warrior once again but is seized by the castle guard. From there he is sent to the kitchens to work as a skivvy but is quickly planning his own escape.

**Episode Five**
Sunday 5/6/77 5.00p.m.
Roland escapes a bureaucratic vicious circle and attempts to argue his case for freedom with the Lord. He fails in his bid and is advised by Vein that the Lord stands between Roland and the last key, which the boy needs if he is to escape.

**Episode Six**
Sunday 12/6/77 5.45p.m.
The Lord hands over the final key, making Roland King. The boy intends to escape but finds that he is unable because he is so busy being King. Unhappy with his rule, Vein leads Roland's subjects to revolt against him.

**Episode Seven**
Sunday 19/6/77 5.45p.m.
Roland must defend himself when he stands trial on a number of charges, including treason.

**Main Cast:** Philip Da Costa (Roland), Talfryn Thomas (Vine/Vein), Angela Richards (June/Lady), Derek Smith (Voss/Voysey), Fulton MacKay (Spurgeon/Hawkspur), Milton Johns (Hawker/Ergon), Jamie Foreman (Ripper/Warrior)
NB: The name pairs here refer to the real world/dreamworld characters, given in that order

**Written by** Bob Baker and Dave Martin

**Musical Director:** Sidney Sager
**Designer:** John Biggs
**Producer:** Leonard White
**Executive Producer:** Patrick Dromgoole
**Director:** Peter Hammond (1, 2), Terry Harding (3, 5, 7), Leonard White (4, 6)

## A Bunch of Fives

Chris Taylor, a fifth former at Oxford Lane School, is accused of something he didn't do. He decides to set the record straight in the school magazine but one of the teachers refuses to print it. Unhappy at the treatment he has received, Chris musters a group of fellow fifth formers (hence the title of the programme) to start their own school magazine with free speech firmly in mind. All they need do is find the stories to fill it.

Series director John Sichel derived the idea for *A Bunch of Fives* while following the American presidential elections on television. His attention was caught by an interview with two teenagers who had written about Jimmy Carter for their school newspaper. He immediately got in contact with Colin Rogers, with whom he had worked on the *Siege of Golden Hill* series, and told him he had an idea for a follow-up.

Following on from *Golden Hill*, Rogers had for some time been considering the idea of a series set not in a school but around it. The two ideas merged together, resulting in a drama based on an independent magazine driven by pupils and their interests in and out of school, rather than a school magazine dictated by the institutional authorities.

Sichel and Rogers travelled to various comprehensive schools and sampled the opinions of a great many teachers and pupils. When the series had been commissioned, casting took place before any scripts had been developed. They specifically wanted actors with presence and an ability to contribute to the series. This in turn permitted the writers to construct scripts with particular personalities in mind.

The series is recorded entirely on video and, for the scenes that take place around the school grounds, the cast and crew travelled to Ravenscroft Comprehensive in Barnet, which, ironically, had its own student newspaper, *The Raver*.

*A Bunch of Fives* was certainly in touch with the youth of the day, incorporating trendy street lingo into the dialogue at various points. It perhaps wasn't quite as hard-hitting as *The Siege of Golden Hill* but still stands out as a contemporary school drama which beat *Grange Hill* to the punch.

**Above:** *A Bunch of Fives*; Philippa Stokes (Lindsay-Jane Bartlett) meets aspiring rock star Danny Reid (Dougal Rose) and finds out what it means to be music correspondent on the Oxford Lane school newspaper in the episode 'The Critic'.

**ATV**
**2 seasons**
(colour)

**Main Cast:** Jamie Foreman (Chris Taylor), Lesley Manville (Helen Wyatt), Richard Willis (Dave Jenner), Julia Gale (Sally Morris), Andrew Rindus (Ken McCall), Lindsay-Jane Bartlett (Philippa Stokes), Julia Carey (Mrs Carol Walsh), Chris Sanders (Mr Buck), Jennifer Hill (Miss Begg), Richard Mayes (Mr Oakley)

**Series created by** Colin Rogers and John Sichel

**Theme Music:** Miki Antony and Dave Jordan
**Designer:** Stanley Mills
**Producer:** Colin Rogers
**Directors:** John Sichel (Season 1), Richard Bramall (Season 2)

**Season One**
**7 episodes** ('Do-It-Yourself'; 'The Critic'; 'The Gig'; 'A Cry for Help'; 'The Chip Shop Mafia'; 'Proof'; 'The Sell Out')
**Broadcast:** Wednesdays 18/5/77 – 29/6/77
**Written by:** Paula Milne (1–3, 7), William Humble (4–6)

**Season Two**
**7 episodes** ('Influences'; 'A Star is Born'; 'Playback'; 'The Mock'; 'The Letter'; 'Making Deals'; 'Celebration')
**Broadcast:** Wednesdays 12/4/78 – 24/5/78
**Written by:** Paula Milne (1–5), Jim Haddon (6, 7)

**Tie-in publications:** novelisation of first season by Colin Rogers published in paperback by *Look-In* Books (ITV/Arrow), 1977

## Follow Me

With *Follow Me* HTV had come up with another Sunday afternoon adventure serial which once more suggested Bristol was the world centre of seaborne crime.

Young Tom Dawes and his father Sid investigate the mystery of a missing girl, Lynn, when they find an unfinished tape message. They recover the runaway but stumble across a plot by seafaring bad guys led by Colonel

Gaines. Thus ensues kidnap, rescue and runaround on the Bristol Channel and its environs. Inoffensive, escapist fare but not one of HTV's most memorable offerings.

**HTV**
**7 episodes**
(colour)
**Broadcast:** Sundays 26/6/77 – 7/8/77

**Main Cast:** Ronald Fraser (Sid Dawes), Ian Donnelly (Tom Dawes), Murray Hayne (Colonel Gaines), Tony Wright (Baxter), Katharine Levy (Lynn), Ewen Solon (Bert), Godfrey James (Southways), June Barrie (Brenda), Richard Bartlett (Nigel), Steve Emerson (Green), Hubert Tucker (Jones)

**Written by** Bob Baker and Dave Martin

**Designer:** Ken Jones
**Producer/Director:** Peter Graham Scott
**Executive Producer:** Patrick Dromgoole

## The Paper Lads

Five children delivering newspapers from a corner shop in deepest darkest Tyneside isn't the most obvious choice in subject matter for a children's drama. Thankfully there's more to *The Paper Lads* than the pros and cons of foot-powered tabloid distribution.

Harsh images paint a more than adequate picture of life in the brick and concrete sprawl of working-class Tyneside. Many of the houses in the endless terraces are in poor condition, their garden spaces littered with mud and stone debris. Grimy youngsters occupy the street, content to draw chalk pictures on the pavements. Lack of local entertainment is the main reason the paper lads spend so much of their time at the newspaper shop, set up by retired police officer Jack Crawford and his wife Anne. The couple try to teach the kids the virtue of honest hard work, fulfilling the role of mentors while inadvertently becoming involved in many of the children's escapades.

The first episode presents the audience with a graphic level of violence for a children's drama. Snaith, the local teenage nutcase, robs Baz of his papers and proceeds to sell them to the crowd at a football match. Anne's son Davey tracks Snaith down to a sports club, punches him in the stomach and watches while a baying crowd turn the thief upside down and shake him until the money falls out of his pockets. Later, Snaith gets his own back by ambushing Davey and chief paper lad J. G. on their way home. Davey gets a brick in the head and J. G. gets a thorough kicking. Strong stuff then, but not a reflection of the series in its entirety. The hard-hitting approach adopted by the first episode is replaced in the following instalments by a number of more predictable adventures. Gog's father, a security officer at the docks, happens to mention that there's only one person to guard a safe containing £20,000. The dock is of course robbed and it's up to the paper lads to lead the police to the criminals. The paper lads also involve themselves in the shady world of vegetable sabotage when they attempt to discover who has destroyed some prize-winning leeks.

*The Paper Lads* is to an extent *The Famous Five* without the middle-class trappings but with a little more depth. 'Enter Picasso' sees Ian abscond with a five pound note to buy new paints and drawing material. Unhappy at his father always being away at sea, still unable to cope with his mother's death two years previously and discontent staying with his father's girlfriend, Ian considers art to be his only hope of escaping life in Tyneside. This thread is picked up again in the second season in 'The Sailor's Return'. Ian's father returns home and announces that he intends to marry again. Ian finally has to accept his mother's death and establishes a common ground with his father's girlfriend. In doing so, he grows up a little.

The character of girl paper lad Sam is also excellent. She demands that Jack give her a job and claims sexual discrimination when he at first refuses. A tomboy by nature, she is however capable of demonstrating great femininity, assisting Baz in a ballroom dancing competition. Her transition from scruffy tomboy to attractive young woman takes many of her friends by surprise.

The majority of the series was filmed on location in and around Tyneside. The striking theme tune, 'Back Home Once Again', was penned by folk-rock group Renaissance.

**Tyne Tees**
**2 seasons**
(colour)

**Main Cast:** Tony Neilson ('J. G.' – John George Bell – Season 1 only), Andrew Edwards (Ian Armstrong), Peter Younger ('Gog' – Paul Golightly), Gavin Kitchen ('Baz' – Barry Moorhead), Judith Pyle (Sam Moorhead), Glynn Edwards (Jack Crawford), Anne Jameson (Jinny Crawford), Barry Braund (Neville – Season 2)

**Series created by** J. G. Holland

**Season One**
**7 episodes** ('Round One'; 'Cash and Carry'; 'The Sweetie Shop Kid'; 'Fifty Years A Showman'; 'Enter Picasso'; 'Best Foot Forward'; 'Eyewitness')
**Broadcast:** Wednesdays 24/8/77 – 5/10/77

**Written by** Ian Cullen (1, 4, 7), Sid Chaplin (2), William Corlett (3, 5), Larry Wyce (6)

**Music:** Renaissance
**Designers:** Roger Andrews (1, 2, 4, 5), Ashley Wilkinson (3, 6, 7)
**Producer:** John K. Cooper
**Directors:** Derek Martinus (1, 2, 6), John Frankau (3, 5, 7), John K. Cooper (4)

**Season Two**
**7 episodes** ('New Boy'; 'Paddy for Champ'; 'Intruders'; 'A Day to Remember'; 'The Sailor's Return'; 'Presents from Paris'; 'It Takes Two to Tango')
**Broadcast:** Mondays 20/11/78 – 22/1/79

**Written by:** William Humble (1, 4, 6), Ian Cullen (2, 3), William Corlett (5, 7)

**Music:** Renaissance
**Additional incidental music:** Anthony Isaac
**Designers:** Chris George (1, 2, 7), Ashley Wilkinson (3–6)
**Producer:** Keith Richardson
**Executive Producer:** Margaret Bottomley
**Directors:** Gerry Mill (1–3, 5, 6), Roger Cheveley (4, 7)

**Tie-in publications:** *The Paper Lads* – novelisation of the first season by Pat Sandys published in paperback by Target, 1977. *News of the Paper Lads* – novelisation of second season by William Humble published in paperback by Target, 1978

## Raven

ATV's *Raven* incorporates many of the elements more readily associated with HTV's fantasy output for children from Wales and the West. Arthurian legend, caves and standing stones are all present and correct.

Teenage tearaway Raven has been released from borstal to participate in a rehabilitation programme, helping Professor Young on an archaeological exploration of a cave system which contains ancient symbols. The government has decided that a nuclear waste processing plant should be built on the site and the caves used to house the toxic residue. The cave system must be saved. But how? Strange powers are gathering at the cave and Raven, a part of everything that is happening, realises that the preservation of the caves lies in his hands.

Jeremy Burnham and Trevor Ray present a surprising piece of social realism through the character of Raven. The 'hero' of the piece is a tough juvenile delinquent, a convicted criminal who has served time in borstal. Burnham and Ray thankfully avoided writing the character steeped in stereotype. Rather than being the disruptive and disrespectful youth one might expect, Raven clearly wants to make a go of his one chance of proving he can manage himself without close guidance from authority. It does, however, take him time to adjust to this new way of life. In one particularly good scene, Professor Young's wife enters Raven's room while he is asleep. Momentarily confused, he jumps out of bed, startled, and shouts, 'Sir!' Later, when Mrs Young tells Raven that they are missing kitchen cutlery, Raven produces a knife and fork from his pocket, explaining that in borstal they had to wash their own cutlery and keep it until their next meal.

The fantasy trappings meanwhile act as a clear metaphor for Raven's voyage of self-discovery. However, it is the realist expression of the drama that continues to surprise. Raven may have saved his kingdom, preventing the development of the nuclear processing plant and ultimately ensuring the safety of the caves, but a happy ending is not entirely forthcoming. There is no blossoming relationship between himself and the pretty reporter Naomi, and Professor Jones dies, making way for an ending of mixed emotions where Raven's triumph is tempered by the loss of his friend.

The serial is recorded entirely on videotape both in studio and on location, unusual at the time. Noticeably, the production doesn't rely on incidental music to enhance the appropriate scenes, favouring instead what could be described as an opressive 'wall of noise'. Special sounds were also used to simulate the disturbing sound of angry bird-squawking and the furious beating of wings. Imaginative use of light, shadow and movement was deployed in tandem with this. A simple but effective combination of the three in the first episode suggests a link between Professor Young and the merlin. The camera rapidly cuts between two close-up stills – one of Jones and one of the merlin bird, both on a plain black background – to the accompaniment of the almost unnatural sound of the bird.

It is surprising that *Raven* – which breaks the mould through its central character as well as operating on a par with many psychedelic eco-fantasies of the 70s such as *Sky*, *The Changes* and *King of the Castle* – is now a forgotten entry.

**ATV**
**6 episodes**
(colour)
**Broadcast:** Mondays 19/9/77 – 24/10/77

**Main Cast:** Phil Daniels (Raven), Michael Aldridge (Professor James Young), Patsy Rowlands (Mrs Young), Shirley Cheriton (Naomi Grant), James Kerry (Bill Telford), Hugh Thomas (Clive Castle), Elis Jones (Vicar Wakefield), Tenniel Evans (Editor)

**Created and written by** Jeremy Burnham and Trevor Ray

**Designer:** John Hickson
**Producer:** Colin Shindler
**Director:** Michael Hart

**Tie-in publications:** novelisation by Jeremy Burnham and Trevor Ray published in paperback by Corgi Carousel, 1977

## The Peppermint Pig

Another in a long line of Nina Bawden adaptations by the BBC, at the time in print just two years. There's undeniably a touch of *The Railway Children* about this story – two children and their mother move from suburban London to their aunts' farm in Norfolk after their father heads for America to avoid questions about a robbery he didn't commit.

Little Poll Greengrass and her brother Theo find out what it means to be hand-me-down poor, discover a wandering grandfather they thought was dead and encounter mean old Mrs Bugg and her son Noah's bullying ways. Poll also comes down with the fever but is lucky enough to recover – the little brother of her friend Annie is not so fortunate and dies from his illness. Most importantly Poll is given a little piglet to keep as a pet. The pig becomes something of a celebrity in the village but its real purpose is to stand as a metaphor for Poll's growing up. There can be only one fate for a pig raised in a farming community and when at the end of the tale it ends up at the butcher's it is time for Poll to move on.

The serial, made all on film, is very similar in tone to Bawden's more famous *Carrie's War* – low on incident, rich in subtle character interactions.

**BBC**
**5 episodes**
(colour)
**Broadcast:** Wednesdays 21/9/77 – 19/10/77

**Main Cast:** Lucy Durham-Matthews (Poll Greengrass), Ben Bethell (Theo Greengrass), Anne Stallybrass (Emily Greengrass), Tom Georgeson (James Greengrass), Sarah Hollis Andrews (Annie Dowsett), Rosalie Crutchley (Aunt Sarah), Pat Keen (Aunt Harriet), Sarah Prince (Lily), David Parfitt (George), Aimee Delamain (Miss Mantripp), Maryann Turner (Mrs Bugg), Paul Wilson (Noah Bugg), Russell Waters (Old Rowland), Lally Bowers (Lady March)

Based on the novel by Nina Bawden (first UK publication 1975, Victor Gollancz)
**Adapted by** Julia Jones

**Designer:** Bob Berk
**Producer:** Anna Home
**Director:** Paul Stone

**Tie-in publications:** n/k

## Midnight is a Place

Orphan boy Lucas Bell lives at run-down Midnight Court with his erratic, drunken guardian Sir Randolph. Oakapple, the boy's tutor, takes him to Midnight Mill, which Sir Randolph owns. There Lucas gains an insight into the appalling conditions suffered by the working class.

Lucas is bored and longs for a friend but doesn't get quite what he hoped for when French girl Anna-Marie comes to stay at the Court. When Randolph sets fire to the mansion, killing himself and seriously injuring Oakapple, the two children need to pool their resources to find work and shelter. Lucas ends up labouring in the sewers and Anna-Marie collects cigar butts from the street.

When the two children decide to move into the Ice House that stands next to the ruins of Midnight Court, they meet Lady Murgatroyd whose past is intertwined with that of Oakapple. Anna-Marie starts working at Midnight Mill, where she encounters the menacing Bludward. Can the two children survive in such dangerous environments? How will they find out Randolph's secret? If they do find out, will it bring about a change in fortune?

Although there is no music credit for *Midnight is a Place*, fans of David Collings will be delighted to know that the the folk(ish) theme song is sung by none other than the man himself in which he posits the rather romantic theory that midnight is not a time, but a place.

**Southern**
**13 episodes**
(colour)
**Broadcast:** Wednesdays 12/10/77 – 4/1/78

**Main Cast:** Simon Gipps-Kent (Lucas), Maxine Gordon (Anna-Marie), David Collings (Julian Oakapple)

Based on the novel by Joan Aiken (first UK publication 1974, Jonathan Cape)
**Adapted by** Roy Russell

**Designer:** Greg Lawson
**Executive Producer:** Lewis Rudd
**Producer/Director:** Chris McMaster

**Tie-in publications:** paperback edition of novel published by Puffin, 1977

## King Cinder

An incongruously *Sweeney*-like tale of extortion rackets, kidnap and revenge among the speedway set. King Cinder was what they used to call Richard Hutson when he was a top speedway rider for The Barons; now, more than ten years retired, King Cinder is merely the name of the restaurant he runs in the seaside town of Barton.

A gang of black-leather-clad ton-up boys start to cause trouble for the traders of Barton, including Hutson, and before long the shady Todd Edwards arrives back in his home town after years of exile, offering the traders 'protection' from the thugs he himself has hired.

However, the racket is only part of the picture – Edwards wants revenge after being run out of town by Hutson back when Edwards was just a minor league crook. Edwards takes Hutson's speedway-keen son Trevor under his wing, offering him big but crooked money to race, thus turning Trevor against his father. It's up to Hutson's younger son Kerry, another promising speedway rider, to be the hero in all of this.

Hired muscle carried shooters in intoxicating locations like Saturday night funfairs and smoky pubs amid shouts of 'Leave it!'. Peter Duncan was less than clean-cut but always honourable as Kerry, and he and co-star Lesley Manville, as girlfriend Nikki, were a match of jeans and sneakers cool.

*King Cinder* came across like a bowdlerised adaptation of a dog-eared New English Library paperback. There was much scrapping and plenty of squealing-tyre bike chases while at the denouement the villain perished in a cliff-edge car plunge. One can question the validity of all this to a child audience but most were left enthralled nonetheless.

**BBC**
**6 episodes** ('The Barons'; 'Todd'; 'Spider's Web'; 'Speedway'; 'Home Truths'; 'On the Track')
(colour)
**Broadcast:** Wednesdays 2/11/77 – 7/12/77

**Main Cast:** Peter Duncan (Kerry Hutson), Tony Caunter (Richard Hutson), Lesley Manville (Nikki), Jeremy Arnold (Trevor Hutson), Daniel Abineri (Lacey), Michael Hawkins (Todd Edwards), Derek Ware (Clayton), Howard Goorney (Nulty)

**Written by** John Foster

**Title Music:** Nic Rowley
**Designer:** Barrie Dobbins
**Executive Producer:** Anna Home
**Director:** John Prowse
Speedway sequences courtesy of Rye House Speedway

**Tie-in publications:** novelisation by John Foster published in hardback and paperback by BBC, 1977

## A Traveller in Time

Two period dramas for the price of one as an Edwardian girl sensitive to the layers of time is able to pass through into the late 16th century. There she helps to try and save the life of Mary, Queen of Scots, despite knowing that the deposed Queen's beheading will surely come to pass. Penelope becomes involved in the Babington Plot to free Mary from prison when she visits her Aunt Tissie and Uncle Barnabas on their farm in Derbyshire and is transported through the ages. Penelope has little control over her visits into the past and is always fearful that she will not be able to get back to her own time.

The source novel had been a very gentle, pastoral piece full of descriptions of lazy summer days, so efforts were made to render the TV adaptation in a rather more exciting style. An offhand casual comment from the book, suggesting the evil Arabella may be burning effigies of Penelope at night, becomes a concrete reality and the scene of her burning a wax 'voodoo' doll by candle flame, backed by the serial's theme of 'Greensleeves', provides the cliffhanger to episode four.

Most location shooting was at the Groom farm in Dethick, Derbyshire. This led to farmer's son Simon Groom becoming a long-running *Blue Peter* presenter when he chanced a radio interview with Brooking, leading to him auditioning for Biddy Baxter.

**BBC Scotland**
**5 episodes** ('The Door'; 'The Kitchen'; 'The Locket';
'The Tunnel'; 'The Ribbon')
(colour)
**Broadcast:** Wednesdays 4/1/78 – 1/2/78

**Main Cast:** Sophie Thompson (Penelope Taberner), Gerald James (Uncle Barnabas), Elizabeth Bradley (Aunt Tissie/Dame Cicely), Louis Hammond (Jude), Mary Maude (Mistress Babington), Sarah Benfield (Tabitha), Simon Gipps-Kent (Francis Babington), Charles Rogers (Anthony Babington), Heather Chasen (Mary, Queen of Scots), Michelle Copsey (Arabella)

Based on the novel by Alison Uttley (first UK publication 1939, Faber and Faber)
**Dramatised by** Diana de vere Cole

**Designer:** Walter Miller
**Executive Producer:** Anna Home
**Producer/Director:** Dorothea Brooking

## Grange Hill

There is probably no better-known children's television drama than *Grange Hill*. Twenty-four seasons and counting make it the longest running and in that time it's been the most watched and the most consistently controversial within the genre bar none. While this book will hopefully show the breadth and variety demonstrated within this genre and show that it did not begin and end with *Grange Hill*, the innovation and influence of the series cannot be denied or underestimated.

The *Grange Hill* story began in 1975 when ATV comedy writer Phil Redmond first developed the idea of a series set in a modern mixed-background, mixed-ability comprehensive school. The idea was initially turned down by many ITV companies, although it's interesting to note the appearance of the school drama *A Bunch of Fives* from ATV themselves in 1977. Redmond's idea finally found a receptive welcome at the BBC in 1976. In a case of right place, right time, children's drama executive Anna Home already had a folder of aborted outlines marked 'SCHOOL?' among her files.

Director on the first trial run of nine episodes was Colin Cant, who didn't think the scripts were that strong – indeed the first season lacks much of a thread and perhaps seemed rather rambling to Cant who was more used to the one-off serial format. Cant also voiced doubts that children would want to come home from a day of school to watch more of the same on television. How wrong he was.

The first season has much to say about class – Redmond constructed almost the first full ten minutes of episode one to sketch in the backgrounds of the pupils making

their way to Grange Hill for the first time. Tucker Jenkins raced out the door of a flat in a working-class estate; Justin Bennett got a lift from his father in a Rover saloon. Benny Green turned up, in jeans rather than uniform, before the gates had even opened, leaving us to wonder just what his home life might be like. The first formers, with whom this season is almost exclusively concerned, learn to come together whatever their background to turn over the bullies of the school. Tucker, Benny, Alan Hargreaves and Trisha Yates were very East London while Justin, Judy Preston and Ann Wilson could only have failed the entrance exam to a public school. Benny Green is the focus of the series' class essay. Coming from a poor West Indian immigrant family, he is picked on because he cannot afford a uniform and is almost excluded from the school football team, despite his sporting talent, because he cannot afford proper boots.

Benny is also picked on because of his race, Doyle calling him a 'golly', thus signalling *Grange Hill*'s first 'issue'. Trisha befriends Benny when the two bunk off lessons and he explains to her about Doyle's name-calling. Trisha thinks this is terrible; after all, she tells Benny, 'you can't help it if you're a nig-nog'. Benny replies very amiably that she in turn can't help being 'a honky'. Trisha was a rounded and thus flawed character as this exchange shows – she was fiercely working class and not one to be pushed around although her headstrong nature sometimes meant she all too willingly got herself into trouble as a rebel without a cause. Trisha was easily as good a character as Tucker; indeed the fact she was a girl can only have made her more revolutionary. The casting of Michelle Herbert, a genuine North London tower block kid who went to acting classes after school because there was nothing else to do, is a shining example of *Grange Hill*'s innovative casting policy which took in amateur groups as well as the more practised budding thesps from the stage school arena.

The intelligence and worthiness of Redmond's writing was all very well, but what really set *Grange Hill* apart early on, and has continued to sustain it, was that its apparent 'gritty' reality was in fact a heightened one. Sean Maguire, who later played Tegs in the series, nicely summed up the appeal to young viewers. 'It was always a bit naughty and rebellious ... we all thought, "Oh we'd never do that," but you loved to watch the ones that had the guts to do it.' The realism and ordinariness of the setting made it seem familiar on the surface but it was populated by the likes of the cheeky Tucker or the rebellious Trisha and events were always slightly larger than life. When the perpetrators went too far they were justly punished and an inordinate amount of time is taken to show exactly the consequences of bad behaviour, be it suspension, expulsion, the police or, on a few occasions, the cane. (Tucker and Benny are the first to receive it in the era of Grange Hill as a comprehensive. Perhaps even more disturbingly, the pretty but easily led Cathy Hargreaves receives the same punishment in Season Four as a demonstration of new head Mrs McClusky's disciplinary stance.) The beauty of the deal was that the viewers got vicarious pleasure from watching the on-screen antics but didn't have to take the rap at the end of it. The official line from BBC chiefs was always to point out that the stories constituted moral lessons. As Anna Home later recalled, 'we always made a policy of showing the consequences of actions'.

It's worth highlighting that there were nonetheless more than a few low-powered, incidental and traditional plots among the heightened high-jinks, particularly among those 113

**Above:** central characters in the very first season of *Grange Hill* were first year boys (l to r) Tucker (Todd Carty), Alan (George Armstrong) and Benny (Terry Sue Patt).

early episodes: a cricket match, a general knowledge quiz, a puma on the loose at an outdoor trip, a runaway hamster that took up a whole first season episode in sitcom fashion. Despite this, after the first nine episodes (sedate by later standards) *Grange Hill* had already caused more concern than any other drama for children. The episode which saw Tucker and the gang clowning around in the swimming lesson when left unattended was dropped from a repeat run after many teachers and parents complained that this would never happen, even though in this case a boy had cut his foot and been taken to the nurse by the teacher. One irate mother wrote to *Radio Times* to complain in no uncertain terms: 'Until now I have greatly admired BBC's children's drama presentations but I am disgusted with *Grange Hill*... this is no entertainment but a glamorisation of hooliganism and the abominable attitude of children to their teachers.' Anna Home pointed out that children were aware this was fiction and just a little larger than life.

It was undoubtedly the realism of the setting that created such concern in parents; there had surely been violence and action in period dramas before, for example. What made the difference here was that these irresponsible kids went to a school just like those attended by their own offspring. Parents were horrified to think that their kids were behaving like this at school and, if they weren't, then wouldn't such actions be all too easy to copy? If Tucker was really a modern-day William Brown or Jennings – and he no doubt was – it was this modernity

which caused all the problems. It was difficult for parents to see *Grange Hill* as escapism but that is presumably how their children primarily viewed it.

The second season, now in the extended twice-weekly format that would become the norm, was more outrageous still and very few hamsters went missing. Cathy fell out with Trisha and they scrapped on the floor of the art class – when Miss Summers tried to intervene she accidentally hit Cathy and was suspended from work until the matter was cleared up. Cathy went off the rails when she found out her 'dead' dad was alive and well (having been chased down the street by him, mistaking him for a prowler – or 'rapist' as she herself put it). She fell in with the bad girl Madelin Tanner, was nearly caught smoking round the back of the school and very definitely caught for shoplifting. Madelin thought Trisha 'a stuck up bitch' while Miss Summers was referred to as 'an old cow' by some third formers' graffiti. Yes, there had been realist, contemporary children's drama before but never anything as heady and intoxicating as this.

The second season's main narrative drive revolved around the actions of the Students' Action Group (SAG), a group of extremist older pupils who tried to bypass the elected school council to get things done their way, boycotting games and forming picket lines in an effort to draw attention to their call for the abolition of uniforms. The interesting dynamic placed these extremists against the new, liberal and progressive headmaster Mr Llewellyn. His first test came when a spontaneous demonstration in the canteen saw pupils climb onto the tables to protest against the segregated dining area for free meals pupils (this was in fact Tucker's sensible idea after he was stopped from sitting with Benny). Despite the near-riot of the rabble, Llewellyn finds their suggestion a sensible one and accedes to their demands. Parents protested against the 'weak' stance taken, seeing it as undermining the teacher's authority. Only later do we see him adopt strong-arm tactics when a sit-in by the SAG turns into wanton vandalism.

The politics of playground democracy and the empowerment of the pupils would be re-examined time and again in subsequent seasons and continues to this day. Often censorship of the school magazine was a flashpoint – in Season Six, Mr McGuffy advises Claire and Suzanne to publish and be damned and finds himself suspended over approving and encouraging contentious material. A rally in support of 'Scruffy' is undermined by Mrs McClusky's clever manipulation and she reinstates him before the protest has really begun. Calley Donnington, Ronnie Birtles, Danny Kendall and many more successors would inherit these concerns over free speech in later years. Nowadays the same arguments rage over the pupils' school website.

What little praise parents and teachers had for the second season applauded the more worthy and less abrasive topics, such as Andrew Stanton's family break-up or Simon Shaw's dyslexia (even if they complained that Shaw's condition would have been spotted much earlier). Season Two was the template for the entire series' resultant run: controversy, politics, over-the-top action, sensitive issues, comic scrapes (although there was virtually nil in the way of s-e-x). If viewed today by those who grew up with it they will probably be surprised by how far it goes in places. Phil Redmond was invited to lunch by BBC executives and 'agreed' that if the series wasn't toned down there would probably not be a series at all.

The main development of the third series was the expansion of the school as we viewed it. The first formers were moved up the school and a new intake brought in to replace them. Now we followed the adventures and concerns of two age ranges. Subsequent seasons would see a new first year introduced each time until the cast encompassed from first to sixth form, broadening the topics available to cover and the demographic appeal of the series as a whole.

Subjects covered in the next few years included an extended examination of racism in Season Six. Gripper Stebson's shadow of bullying and extortion loomed large for the whole year, leading to a final multiracial scrap in the toilets and a dressing down from an explosive Bullet Baxter.

*Grange Hill*'s most famous 'campaign' dominated Season Nine and saw Zammo Maguire become addicted to heroin. The choice of Zammo as the victim was deliberate – the favourite cheeky chappie of the school had to be shown to be almost destroyed by the drug. Had a character like Gripper become the addict, who would care? Moreover, the young audience would probably associate drugs as being something only recognisably 'bad' people could succumb to. Again, the plain adoption of the issue is not enough. Put across in the wrong way, the series could end up looking patronising, didactic and, worst of all, not make for very good drama. There is the need for thrills and excitement as well as accurate portrayal of the issue and in this case the series didn't disappoint. The storyline was resolved in one of the series' most electrifying scenes, with Zammo smashing his friend Kev in the face, knocking his girlfriend Jackie around the locker room with real force and finally left scrabbling around pathetically on the floor for his smack as the police burst in.

While the drugs theme was among the most controversial tackled by the series, the strong warning it represented meant it was universally praised. A word of commendation was even spoken in the House of Commons (the very same place Season Two's SAG action had earned condemnation). The Zammo plot marked *Grange Hill*'s transformation from *enfant terrible* to mature and responsible force for social change and education. The cast made the hit record 'Just Say No', their own take on an American anti-drugs song, and many of them were invited to the White House to meet the Reagans in recognition of their good work. *Grange Hill* was now a campaigner and with this status came a responsibility. Some perceive that the series became more politically correct after this.

Certainly the bullies seemed weaker somehow – the utterly irresponsible headcase Imelda Davies was putting asbestos down Ziggy Greaves' back in Season Nine, but the following year was spraying coloured dye in people's hair. Season Eleven's baddies were the Grid Iron Crew led by Mauler McCaul, unthreatening comedy villains in American football uniforms. McCaul had neither an axe to grind nor any real malice. An ongoing plot strand in Season Ten meanwhile concerned the escapades of Harriet the donkey – surely the most twee caper since Trisha lost that hamster.

The final taming of the loose cannon possibly came with the adoption of the purple and yellow school shield badge (fictionally designed in Season Nine by a pseudonymous Danny Kendall) as a logo for the *Grange Hill* brand, now a respected byword for BBC quality.

Around the same time there was a shift away from the Grange Hill school as the centre of the action. Previously the series had looked at aspects of school life, with the occasional glimpse into the secret home lives of its more troubled pupils. Now more action seemed to take place at parties or in burger bars. Some of the night life was worthwhile. Ziggy and Robbie's underage trip to the pub ended in a bar brawl and had Robbie throwing up outside with pure fear at having witnessed real adult violence. Some merely showed how much more teenage and fashion conscious the show had become – it was no longer enough to namedrop UB40 from time to time. One rather silly scene had two Grange Hill girls dolled up for a night out only to be stopped by kerb-crawlers looking for trade.

The issues continued of course: teenage pregnancy was finally tackled to some outcry in Season Fourteen. The initially realistic handling gave way to a melodramatic climax of sorts, when Chrissy pushes her pram across a desolate urban wasteland to break up an epic, gladiatorial gangfight – this over-the-top scene probably marked *Grange Hill*'s nadir. An AIDS storyline formed the backbone to Season Eighteen, though when you have a disabled actress taking part in an AIDS tutorial class you wondered how much more of a PC pamphlet the series could become. The hard lessons such as those taught by Gripper or Zammo had given way to a softer soap(box). One of the better 90s storylines involved the harassment of a gay teacher, Mr Brisley.

After almost a quarter of a century it is inevitable that *Grange Hill*'s trail-blazing days are behind it even if, at the time of writing, letters in *Radio Times* are complaining about a lesbianism storyline. It has now entertained and given food for thought to five 'generations' of children, each watching for a five year span that reflects their own progression through school. This has led to the repetition and retreading of plotlines, each probably appearing fresh and interesting to the incumbent audience. For example, there have been sudden deaths (due to a dare gone wrong, a swimming pool accident, terminal illness, a random stabbing, a fall while escaping a fire) at regular intervals since 1980 and subsequent grieving. Justine's tutoring of Tegs in 1989 echoes Trisha's similar efforts with Simon in 1979, and so on.

While the programme's nature is now cyclical, like all soaps, it is interesting to observe how *Grange Hill* also acts as a yardstick – a constant control in the changing world of children's television. Once a nine-week low-key drama serial it is now almost a fully fledged soap preparing a move from its backlot at Elstree to Liverpool and back into the hands of its creator Phil Redmond at Mersey TV. It represents an immovable given in the BBC children's drama schedules. Unlikely as it would have seemed in 1978, *Grange Hill* is now an institution in both senses of the word. Flippin' 'eck!

**BBC**
**25 seasons** (by 2002 – ongoing)
(colour)
NB Mersey TV will produce Season 26 for the BBC

**Season One**
**9 episodes**
**Broadcast:** Wednesdays 8/2/78 – 5/4/78

**Main Cast:** Todd Carty (Peter 'Tucker' Jenkins), Terry Sue Patt (Benny Green), Robert Morgan (Justin Bennett), Michelle Herbert (Trisha Yates), Abigail Brown (Judy Preston), Lucinda Duckett (Ann Wilson), George Armstrong (Alan Hargreaves), Vincent Hall (Michael Doyle), Michael Percival (Mr Mitchell), Dorothea Phillips (Mrs Monroe), Roger Sloman (Mr Foster), Denys Hawthorne (Mr Starling)

**Writer:** Phil Redmond
**Director:** Colin Cant
**Executive Producer:** Anna Home

## Season Two
**18 episodes**
**Broadcast:** Tuesdays and Fridays 2/1/79 – 2/3/79

**Main Cast:** Todd Carty (Tucker), Terry Sue Patt (Benny), Robert Morgan (Justin), Michelle Herbert (Trisha), Lyndy Brill (Cathy), Mark Farmer (Gary Hargreaves), Linda Slater (Susi McMahon), Ruth Davies (Penny Lewis), George Armstrong (Alan Humphries*), Vincent Hall (Doyle), Paul Miller (Simon Shaw), Mark Chapman (Andrew Stanton), Donald Waugh (Joseph Hughes), Sara Sugarman (Jessica Samuels), Abigail Arundel+ (Judy Preston), Vivian Mann (Antoni Karamanopolis), Lesley Woods (Madelin Tanner), Michael Percival (Mr Mitchell), Michael Cronin (Mr Baxter), James Wynn (Mr Sutcliffe), Sean Arnold (Mr Llewellyn), Philomena McDonagh (Miss Summers)
\* For some reason Alan Hargreaves became Alan Humphries this year – presumably with the introduction of the unrelated Cathy Hargreaves in Season Two
\+ Several actors' stage names changed during the series as a result of them joining Equity at sixteen

**Writers:** Phil Redmond, Margaret Simpson, Alan Janes
**Directors:** Colin Cant, Roger Singleton-Turner
**Executive Producer:** Anna Home

## Season Three
**16 episodes**
**Broadcast:** Tuesdays and Fridays 8/1/80 – 29/2/80

**Main Cast:** Todd Carty (Tucker), Terry Sue Patt (Benny), Robert Craig-Morgan+ (Justin), George Armstrong (Alan), Paul McCarthy (Tommy Watson), Michelle Herbert (Trisha), Lyndy Brill (Cathy), Linda Slater (Susi), Ruth Davies (Penny), Vincent Hall (Doyle), Mark Eadie+ (Andrew Stanton), Donald Waugh (Hughes), Peter Moran (Pogo Patterson), Mark Baxter (Duane Orpington), Lesley Woods (Madelin), Vivian Mann (Antoni), Michael Cronin (Mr Baxter), James Wynn (Mr Sutcliffe), Brian Capron (Mr Hopwood), Lucinda Gane (Miss Mooney), Sean Arnold (Mr Llewellyn)

**Writers:** Phil Redmond, Margaret Simpson, Alan Janes
**Directors:** Brian Lennane, Jackie Willows, Roger Singleton-Turner
**Producer:** Colin Cant
**Executive Producer:** Anna Home

*The Great Grange Hill Debate* was a special discussion programme coming from the *Grange Hill* set, shown on BBC1 Tuesday 4/3/80.
**Presenters:** Toni Arthur, Paul Burden
**Producer:** Molly Cox

## Season Four
**18 episodes**
**Broadcast:** Tuesdays and Fridays 30/12/80 – 27/2/81

**Main Cast:** Todd Carty (Tucker), Terry Sue Patt (Benny), Robert Craig-Morgan+ (Justin), George Armstrong (Alan), Paul McCarthy (Tommy), Michelle Herbert (Trisha), Lyndy Brill (Cathy), Linda Slater (Susi), Rene Alperstein (Pamela Cartwright), Vincent Hall (Michael Doyle), Donald Waugh (Joseph Hughes), Peter Moran (Pogo), Mark Baxter (Duane), Paula Ann Bland (Claire Scott), Susan Tully (Suzanne Ross), Mark Burdis (Christopher 'Stewpot' Stewart), David Lynch (Booga Benson), Gwyneth Powell (Mrs Bridget McClusky), Michael Cronin (Mr Baxter), James Wynn (Mr Sutcliffe), Brian Capron (Mr Hopwood), Lucinda Gane (Miss Mooney), Allyson Rees (Miss Lexington)

**Writers:** Phil Redmond, Margaret Simpson, Alan Janes, Sandy Welch
**Directors:** Colin Cant, Christine Secombe, Graham Theakston
**Producer:** Colin Cant
**Executive Producer:** Anna Home

## Season Five
**18 episodes**
**Broadcast:** Tuesdays and Fridays 5/1/82 – 5/3/82
Preceded by **Christmas Special** 28/12/81

**Main Cast:** Peter Moran (Pogo), Mark Baxter (Duane), Paula Ann Bland (Claire), Susan Tully (Suzanne), Mark Burdis (Stewpot), Rene Alperstein (Pamela), Alison Bettles (Fay Lucas), Nadia Chambers (Annette Firman), Lee MacDonald (Samuel 'Zammo' McGuire), Lee Sparke (Gordon 'Jonah' Jones), Erkan Mustafa (Roland Browning), Mark Savage (Gripper Stebson), Dulice Liecier (Precious Matthews), Paula Taras (Belinda Zowkowski), Todd Carty (Tucker), George Armstrong (Alan), Robert Craig-Morgan (Justin), Gwyneth Powell (Mrs McClusky), Michael Cronin (Mr Baxter), James Wynn (Mr Sutcliffe), Brian Capron (Mr Hopwood), Lucinda Gane (Miss Mooney), Fraser Cairns ('Scruffy' McGuffy), Allyson Rees (Miss Lexington)

**Writers:** Alan Janes, Jane Hollowood, Margaret Simpson, Barry Purchese
**Directors:** Diarmuid Lawrence, Anthea Browne-Wilkinson, Christine Secombe, John Prowse
**Producer:** Susi Hush

## Season Six
**18 episodes**
**Broadcast:** Tuesdays and Fridays 4/1/83 – 4/3/83

**Main Cast:** Peter Moran (Pogo), Mark Baxter (Duane), Paula Ann Bland (Claire), Susan Tully (Suzanne), Mark Burdis (Stewpot), Alison Bettles (Fay), Nadia Chambers (Annette), Lee MacDonald (Zammo), Lee Sparke (Jonah), Erkan Mustafa (Roland), Mark Savage (Gripper), Dulice Liecier (Precious), Vincent Matthews (Jeremy Irvine), Simone Nylander (Janet St Clair), Kaka Singh (Randir Singh), Julie-Ann Steel (Diane Cooney), Gwyneth Powell (Mrs McClusky), Michael Cronin (Mr Baxter), Fraser Cairns ('Scruffy' McGuffy), James Wynn (Mr Sutcliffe), Lucinda Gane (Miss Mooney), Allyson Rees (Miss Lexington)

**Writers:** Barry Purchese, Jane Hollowood, Margaret Simpson, David Angus, Paula Milne
**Script Editor:** Anthony Minghella
**Directors:** Carol Wilks, Edward Pugh, Alistair Clark
**Producer:** Kenny McBain

*Speak Out on Grange Hill* was a special discussion programme transmitted directly after episode 18 and shown on BBC2 (4/3/83). Issues covered included the racist storyline of the season.
**Presenter:** John Craven
**Producer:** Eric Rowan

**Season Seven**
**18 episodes**
**Broadcast:** Tuesdays and Fridays 3/1/84 – 2/3/84

**Main Cast:** Peter Moran (Pogo), Mark Baxter (Duane), Paula Ann Bland (Claire), Susan Tully (Suzanne), Mark Burdis (Stewpot), Alison Bettles (Fay), Nadia Chambers (Annette), Lee MacDonald (Zammo), Melissa Wilks (Jackie Wright), Erkan Mustafa (Roland), Mmoloki Chrystie (Kevin Baylon), Dulice Liecier (Precious), Vincent Matthews (Jeremy), Simone Nylander (Janet), Kaka Singh (Randir), Julie-Ann Steel (Diane), David Rippey (Gluxo Remington), Gwyneth Powell (Mrs McClusky), Michael Cronin (Mr Baxter), Fraser Cairns ('Scruffy' McGuffy), Allyson Rees (Miss Lexington), Kara Wilson (Miss Gordon)

**Writers:** Barry Purchese, Jane Hollowood, Margaret Simpson, David Angus, Frances Galleymore, John Godber
**Script Editor:** Anthony Minghella
**Directors:** Carol Wilks, Edward Pugh, Nic Phillips, David Bell
**Assistant Producer:** Peter Sofroniou
**Producer:** Kenny McBain

**Season Eight**
**18 episodes**
**Broadcast:** Mondays and Wednesdays 18/2/85 – 22/4/85 (this season was transmitted in the unusual slot of 5.35p.m., after *Blue Peter*, rather than the usual 5p.m./5.10p.m. start time).
No episode Easter Monday 8/4/85.

**Main Cast:** Paula Ann Bland (Claire), Mark Burdis (Stewpot), Alison Bettles (Fay), Nadia Chambers (Annette), Lee MacDonald (Zammo), Melissa Wilks (Jackie), Tim Polley (Steven Banks), Erkan Mustafa (Roland), Mmoloki Chrystie (Kevin), Julie-Ann Steel (Diane), Simone Hyams (Caroline 'Calley' Donnington), Tina Mahon (Veronica 'Ronnie' Birtles), John McMahon (Luke 'Gonch' Gardner), Bradley Sheppard (Paul 'Hollo' Holloway), John Alford (Robbie Wright), John Drummond (Trevor Cleaver), Steven West (Vince Savage), Gwyneth Powell (Mrs McClusky), Michael Cronin (Mr Baxter), Michael Sheard (Mr Bronson), Karen Ford (Miss Booth), Mark Savage (Gripper Stebson)

**Writers:** Barry Purchese, Margaret Simpson, David Angus, Frances Galleymore, John Godber, Rosemary Mason
**Script Editor:** Anthony Minghella
**Directors:** Edward Pugh, David Bell, Roger Singleton-Turner, Margie Barbour, John Smith
**Producer:** Ben Rea

**Season Nine**
**24 episodes**
**Broadcast:** Tuesdays and Fridays 7/1/86 – 1/4/86 (now back in the more usual post-*Newsround* slot)
Preceded by **Christmas Special** 27/12/85

**Main Cast:** Lee MacDonald (Zammo), Melissa Wilks (Jackie), Tim Polley (Banksie), Erkan Mustafa (Roland), Mmoloki Chrystie (Kevin), Alison Bettles (Fay), Simone Nylander (Janet), Simone Hyams (Calley), Tina Mahon (Ronnie), John McMahon (Gonch), Bradley Sheppard (Hollo), John Alford (Robbie), John Drummond (Trevor), Steven West (Vince), George Wilson (Eric 'Ziggy' Greaves), Jonathan Lambeth (Danny Kendall), Ricky Simmonds (Ant Jones), Fleur Taylor (Imelda Davies), Ruth Carraway (Helen Kelly), Samantha Lewis (Georgina Hayes), Fiona Mogridge (Laura Reagan), Sara McGlasson (Julia Glover), Gwyneth Powell (Mrs McClusky), Michael Cronin (Mr Baxter), Michael Sheard (Mr Bronson), Karen Ford (Miss Booth), George A. Cooper (Mr Griffiths), Lucinda Curtis (Mrs Reagan), Jeffrey Kissoon (Mr Kennedy)

**Writers:** Barry Purchese, Margaret Simpson, David Angus, Frances Galleymore, John Godber, Rosemary Mason, Sarah Daniels
**Script Editors:** Anthony Minghella, Norma Flint
**Directors:** Edward Pugh, David Bell, Roger Singleton-Turner, Margie Barbour, John Smith
**Assistant Producer:** David Leonard
**Producer:** Ronald Smedley

**Season Ten**
**24 episodes**
**Broadcast:** Tuesdays and Fridays 6/1/87 – 27/3/87

**Main Cast:** Lee MacDonald (Zammo), Melissa Wilks (Jackie), Tim Polley (Banksie), Erkan Mustafa (Roland), Mmoloki Chrystie (Kevin), Alison Bettles (Fay), Simone Nylander (Janet), Simone Hyams (Calley), Tina Mahon (Ronnie), Bradley Sheppard (Hollo), John Alford (Robbie), John Drummond (Trevor), Steven West (Vince), George Christopher+ (Ziggy), Jonathan Lambeth (Danny), Ricky Simmonds (Ant), Fleur Taylor (Imelda), Ruth Carraway (Helen), Samantha Lewis (Georgina), Fiona Mogridge (Laura), Sara McGlasson (Julia), Jimmy Carr (Perry), Leah Finch (Lucy), Gwyneth Powell (Mrs McClusky), Michael Sheard (Mr Bronson), Karen Ford (Miss Booth), George A. Cooper (Mr Griffiths), Lucinda Curtis (Mrs Reagan), Jeffrey Kissoon (Mr Kennedy)

**Writers:** Barry Purchese, Margaret Simpson, David Angus, John Godber, Rosemary Wilson, Sarah Daniels, Chris Ellis
**Script Editors:** Anthony Minghella, Leigh Jackson
**Directors:** Edward Pugh, David Bell, Margie Barbour, John Smith, Albert Barber
**Producer:** Ronald Smedley

**Season Eleven**
**20 episodes**
**Broadcast:** Tuesdays and Fridays 5/1/88 – 11/3/88

**Main Cast:** Simone Hyams (Calley), Tina Mahon (Ronnie), John McMahon (Gonch), John Alford (Robbie), John Drummond (Trevor), Steven West (Vince), George Christopher+ (Ziggy), Jonathan Lambeth (Danny), Ruth Carraway (Helen), Samantha Lewis (Georgina),

117

Fiona Lee-Fraser+ (Laura), Sara Peters+ (Julia), Simon Vaughan (Freddie Mainwaring), Rachel Roberts (Justine Dean), Sonya Kearns (Chrissy Mainwaring), Paul Adams (Matthew Pearson), Sean Maguire (Terrance 'Tegs' Ratcliffe), Darren Cudjoe (Clarke Trent), Joshua Fenton (Francis 'Mauler' McCaul), Michelle Gayle (Fiona Wilson), Lynne Radford (Susi Young), Gwyneth Powell (Mrs McClusky), Michael Sheard (Mr Bronson), Karen Ford (Miss Booth), George A. Cooper (Mr Griffiths), Lucinda Curtis (Mrs Reagan), Stuart Organ (Mr Robson), Nicholas Donnelly (Mr Mackenzie), Julia Goodman (Mrs Pearson), Madeline Church (Miss Stone)

**Writers:** Barry Purchese, Margaret Simpson, David Angus, Sarah Daniels, Chris Ellis, John Smith, Kay Trainor
**Script Editors:** Anthony Minghella, Leigh Jackson
**Directors:** Albert Barber, Robert Gabriel
**Producer:** Ronald Smedley
**Associate Producer:** David Leonard

***Behind the Scenes at Grange Hill*** was a special programme aired 1/1/88 as a season opener to the eleventh year.
**Introduced by** Lee MacDonald
**Producer/Director:** Ronald Smedley

## Season Twelve
**20 episodes**
**Broadcast:** Tuesdays and Fridays 3/1/89 – 10/3/89

**Main Cast:** Simone Hyams (Calley), Tina Mahon (Ronnie), John McMahon (Gonch), John Alford (Robbie), John Drummond (Trevor), Steven West (Vince), George Christopher (Ziggy), Jonathan Lambeth (Danny), Ruth Carraway (Helen), Samantha Lewis (Georgina), Rachel Roberts (Justine), Sonya Kearns (Chrissy), Paul Adams (Matthew), Sean Maguire (Tegs), Darren Cudjoe (Clarke), Joshua Fenton (Mauler), Michelle Gayle (Fiona), Lynne Radford (Susi), Ian Congdon-Lee (Ted Fisk), Melanie Hiscock (Mandy Freemont), Gwyneth Powell (Mrs McClusky), Michael Sheard (Mr Bronson), Karen Ford (Miss Booth), George A. Cooper (Mr Griffiths), Stuart Organ (Mr Robson), Nicholas Donnelly (Mr Mackenzie), Madeline Church (Miss Stone)

**Writers:** Barry Purchese, Margaret Simpson, David Angus, Sarah Daniels, Chris Ellis, Kay Trainor
**Script Editor:** Leigh Jackson
**Directors:** Albert Barber, Robert Gabriel, John Smith, Ronald Smedley
**Producer:** Ronald Smedley
**Associate Producer:** Albert Barber

## Season Thirteen
**20 episodes**
**Broadcast:** Tuesdays and Fridays 2/1/90 – 9/3/90

**Main Cast:** Simone Hyams (Calley), Tina Mahon (Ronnie), John Alford (Robbie), John Drummond (Trevor), Samantha Lewis (Georgina), Rachel Roberts (Justine), Sonya Kearns (Chrissy), Paul Adams (Matthew), Sean Maguire (Tegs), Joshua Fenton (Mauler), Ian Congdon-Lee (Ted), Julie Buckfield (Natalie Stevens), Otis Munyangiri ('Locko' Lockery), Jamie Lehane ('Jacko' Morgan), Natalie Poyser (Becky Stevens), Ian Rushmere (Brian Shaw), Sundeep Suri (Akik Rashim), Jonathan Riesel (Dominic), Alice Dawnay (Alice Rowe), Margo Selby (Julie Corrigan), John Pickard (Neil Timpson),

Veena Tulsiani (Aichaa Rashim), Carl Pizzie (Raju), Wayne Norman (Rod), Rene Zagger (Mike Bentley), Gwyneth Powell (Mrs McClusky), Karen Ford (Miss Booth), George A. Cooper (Mr Griffiths), Stuart Organ (Mr Robson), Nicholas Donnelly (Mr Mackenzie), Lee Cornes (Mr Hankin), Anna Quayle (Mrs Monroe), Kevin O'Shea (Mr Hargreaves)

**Writers:** Barry Purchese, Margaret Simpson, David Angus, Sarah Daniels, Chris Ellis, Kay Trainor, Kevin Hood
**Script Editor:** Leigh Jackson
**Directors:** John Smith, Andrew Whitman, Richard Kelly, Riitta-Leena Lynn
**Producer:** Albert Barber

## Season Fourteen
**20 episodes**
**Broadcast:** Tuesdays and Fridays 8/1/91 – 15/3/91

**Main Cast:** Simone Hyams (Calley), Tina Mahon (Ronnie), John Alford (Robbie), John Drummond (Trevor), Samantha Lewis (Georgina), Rachel Roberts (Justine), Sonya Kearns (Chrissy), Paul Adams (Matthew), Sean Maguire (Tegs), Ian Congdon-Lee (Ted), Julie Buckfield (Natalie), Otis Munyangiri (Locko), Jamie Lehane (Jacko), Natalie Poyser (Becky), Ian Rushmere (Brian), Sundeep Suri (Akik), Alice Dawnay (Alice), Margo Selby (Julie), John Pickard (Neil), Rene Zagger (Mike), Nina Fry (Robyn Stone), Rebekah Gilgan (Fran), Luisa Bradshaw-White (Maria Watts), Kelly George (Ray Haynes), Desmond Askew (Richard), Gwyneth Powell (Mrs McClusky), Karen Ford (Miss Booth), George A. Cooper (Mr Griffiths), Stuart Organ (Mr Robson), Nicholas Donnelly (Mr Mackenzie), Lee Cornes (Mr Hankin), Anna Quayle (Mrs Monroe), Kevin O'Shea (Mr Hargreaves), William Brand (Mr van de Groot)

**Writers:** Barry Purchese, Margaret Simpson, Sarah Daniels, Chris Ellis, Kay Trainor, Kevin Hood
**Directors:** Albert Barber, Richard Kelly, Riitta-Leena Lynn
**Producer:** Albert Barber

## Season Fifteen
**20 episodes**
**Broadcast:** Tuesdays and Fridays 7/1/92 – 13/3/92

**Main Cast:** Rachel Roberts (Justine), Sonya Kearns (Chrissy), Ian Congdon-Lee (Ted), Julie Buckfield (Natalie), Clare Buckfield (Natasha Stevens), Jamie Lehane (Jacko), Natalie Poyser (Becky), Ian Rushmere (Brian), Alice Dawnay (Alice), Margo Selby (Julie), Nina Fry (Robyn Stone), Rebekah Gilgan (Fran), Luisa Bradshaw-White (Maria), Kelly George (Ray), Desmond Askew (Richard), Danny Cunningham (Liam Brady), Ricky Ward (Jake), Nick Fletcher (Luke), Stuart Organ (Mr Robson), George A. Cooper (Mr Griffiths), Nicholas Donnelly (Mr Mackenzie), Lee Cornes (Mr Hankin), Anna Quayle (Mrs Monroe), Kevin O'Shea (Mr Hargreaves), Marita Black (Ms Patty Janowitz), Flip Webster (Mrs Mason)

**Writers:** Barry Purchese, Margaret Simpson, Sarah Daniels, Chris Ellis, Kevin Hood, Alison Fisher

**Season Sixteen**
**20 episodes**
**Broadcast:** Tuesdays and Fridays 5/1/93 – 12/3/93

**Main Cast:** Rachel Victoria Roberts+ (Justine), Sonya Kearns (Chrissy), Ian Congdon-Lee (Ted), Julie Buckfield (Natalie), Clare Buckfield (Natasha), Jamie Lehane (Jacko), Natalie Poyser (Becky), Ian Rushmere (Brian), Alice Dawnay (Alice), Margo Selby (Julie), Nina Fry (Robyn), Luisa Bradshaw-White (Maria Watts), Kelly George (Ray), Desmond Askew (Richard), Danny Cunningham (Liam Brady), Ricky Ward (Jake), Nick Fletcher (Luke), Denzil Kilvington (Kenny), Joanna Stride (Ruth), Gareth Phillips (Nick), Paul Bigley (Dave Greenman), Alan Cave (Dennis Morris), Zander Ward (Andy 'Spanner' Walker), Helen McDonagh (Mary MaCarthy), Stuart Organ (Mr Robson), George A. Cooper (Mr Griffiths), Nicholas Donnelly (Mr Mackenzie), Lee Cornes (Mr Hankin), Anna Quayle (Mrs Monroe), Kevin O'Shea (Mr Hargreaves), Flip Webster (Mrs Mason), Adam Ray (Mr Brisley), Jenny Howe (Mrs Keele)

**Writers:** Sarah Daniels, Chris Ellis, Kevin Hood, Alison Fisher, Diane Whitley, David Angus

**Season Seventeen**
**20 episodes**
**Broadcast:** Tuesdays and Fridays 4/1/94 – 11/3/94

**Main Cast:** Rachel Victoria Roberts (Justine), Jamie Lehane (Jacko), Natalie Poyser (Becky), Ian Rushmere (Brian), Margo Selby (Julie), Nina Fry (Robyn), Luisa Bradshaw-White (Maria), Desmond Askew (Richard), Paul Bigley (Dave), Alan Cave (Dennis Morris), Kevin Bishop (Sam Spalding), Aidan David (James 'Arnie' Arnold), Amy Simcock (Jessica), Francesca Martinez (Rachel Burns), Jamie Groves (Josh), Belinda Crane (Lucy Mitchell), Colin Ridgewell (Colin Brown), Elisabeth Stainer (Rosa), Stuart Organ (Mr Robson), Lee Cornes (Mr Hankin), Adam Ray (Mr Brisley), Jenny Howe (Mrs Keele), Peter Leeper (Mr Parrott), Hakeem-Kae-Kalim (Mr Manyeke), David Quilter (Mr Arnold), Jenny Long (Anna Wright)

**Writers:** Sarah Daniels, Chris Ellis, Kevin Hood, Alison Fisher, Diane Whitley, Ol Parker

**Season Eighteen**
**20 episodes**
**Broadcast:** Tuesdays and Fridays 3/1/95 – 10/3/95

**Main Cast:** Jamie Lehane (Jacko), Natalie Poyser (Becky), Ian Rushmere (Brian), Margo Selby (Julie), Nina Fry (Robyn), Paul Bigley (Dave), Alan Cave (Dennis), Kevin Bishop (Sam Spalding), Aidan David (Arnie), Amy Simcock (Jessica), Jamie Groves (Josh), Belinda Crane (Lucy), Colin Ridgewell (Colin Brown), Jenny Long (Anna Wright), Francesca Martinez (Rachel), Steve Hammett (Dudley Webster), Laura Hammett (Sarah-Jane Webster), Darren Kempson (Gabriel), Andrew Henry (Gordon Wright), Amelda Brown (Wendy Wright), Daniell O'Grady (Con), Nicholas Pinnock (Jerome), Abigail Hart (Paula Webster), George Stark (Kevin Jenkins), Rochelle Gadd (Delia 'Dill' Lodge), Martino Lazzeri (Joe Williams), Stuart Organ (Mr Robson), Lee Cornes (Mr Hankin), Adam Ray (Mr Brisley), Peter Leeper (Mr Parrott), David Quilter (Mr Arnold), Sally Geoghegan (Miss Carver)

**Writers:** Sarah Daniels, Chris Ellis, Kevin Hood, Alison Fisher, Diane Whitley, Ol Parker, Judith Johnson

**Season Nineteen**
**20 episodes**
**Broadcast:** Tuesdays and Thursdays 23/1/96 – 28/3/96

**Main Cast:** Nina Fry (Robyn), Margo Selby (Julie), Jamie Lehane (Jacko), Natalie Poyser (Becky), Alan Cave (Dennis), Aidan David (Arnie), Amy Simcock (Jessica), Belinda Crane (Lucy), Colin Ridgewell (Colin), Jenny Long (Anna), Francesca Martinez (Rachel), Steve Hammett (Dudley), Laura Hammett (Sarah-Jane), Darren Kempson (Gabriel), Abigail Hart (Paula), George Stark (Kevin), Rochelle Gadd (Dill), Martino Lazzeri (Joe), Peter Morton (Wayne Sutcliffe), Ben Freeman (Chris Longworth), Ayesha Antoine (Poppy Silver), Sian Welsh (Laurie Watson), Fiona Wade (Joanna Day), Sabrina de Bellis (Edith), Alice Matcham (Chantal), Melanie Joseph (Lauren), Natalie Tapper (Jodie), Jenni Keenan-Green (Eilidh), Lisa Hammond (Denny), Stuart Organ (Mr Robson), Lee Cornes (Mr Hankin), Adam Ray (Mr Brisley), Peter Leeper (Mr Parrott), David Quilter (Mr Arnold), Sally Geoghegan (Miss Carver), Madelaine Newton (Mrs Jenkins), Karen O'Brien (Mrs Maguire), Catherine Chevalier (Mme Lefevre), Dominick Carrara (Christophe Urdy)

**Writers:** Sarah Daniels, Chris Ellis, Kevin Hood, Alison Fisher, Diane Whitley, Ol Parker, Judith Johnson

**Season Twenty**
**20 episodes**
**Broadcast:** Tuesdays and Thursdays 21/1/97 – 27/3/97

**Main Cast:** Alan Cave (Dennis), Aidan David (Arnie), Amy Simcock (Jessica), Belinda Crane (Lucy), Colin Ridgewell (Colin), Francesca Martinez (Rachel), Steve Hammett (Dudley), Laura Hammett (Sarah-Jane), George Stark (Kevin), Rochelle Gadd (Dill), Peter Morton (Wayne), Ben Freeman (Chris), Ayesha Antoine (Poppy Silver), Sian Welsh (Laurie), Fiona Wade (Joanna), Melanie Joseph (Lauren), Laura Sadler (Judi Jeffreys), Jamie Groves (Josh), Diana Magness (Evelyn), Ashley Walters (Andy Phillips), Oliver Elmidoro (Tom), Robert Stuart (Matt), Jonathan Marchant-Heatley (Sam 'Cracker' Bacon), Charlotte McDonagh (Lisa), Thomas Carey (Alec), Lorraine Woodley (Carlene), David Kendall (Harry), Duncan Robertson (Jonathan), Victoria Alcock (Ruth), Kelly George (Ray Haynes), Stuart Organ (Mr Robson), Lee Cornes (Mr Hankin), Adam Ray (Mr Brisley), David Quilter (Mr Arnold), Sally Geoghegan (Miss Carver), Madelaine Newton (Mrs Jenkins), Karen O'Brien (Mrs Maguire), Rachel Bell (Mrs Holmes), Clive Hill (Mr Dai 'Hard' Jones)

**Writers:** Sarah Daniels, Chris Ellis, Alison Fisher, Diane Whitley, Leigh Jackson, Tanika Gupta

**Season Twenty-One**
**20 episodes**
**Broadcast:** Tuesdays and Thursdays 27/1/98 – 2/4/98

**Main Cast:** Alan Cave (Dennis), Aidan David (Arnie), Amy Simcock (Jessica), Belinda Crane (Lucy), Colin Ridgewell (Colin), Francesca Martinez (Rachel), Steve Hammett (Dudley), Laura Hammett (Sarah-Jane), George Stark (Kevin), Rochelle Gadd (Dill), Peter Morton (Wayne), Ben Freeman (Chris),

Ayesha Antoine (Poppy), Sian Welsh (Laurie), Fiona Wade (Joanna), Laura Sadler (Judi), Diana Magness (Evelyn), Oliver Elmidoro (Tom), Robert Stuart (Matt), Jonathan Marchant-Heatley (Cracker), Charlotte McDonagh (Lisa West), Thomas Carey (Alec), Lorraine Woodley (Carlene), Kelly George (Ray), Maggie Mason (Gemma), Sam Bardens (Adam), Michael Obiora (Max), Jade Williams (Zoe Stringer), Tilly Gerrard (Sian), John Hudson (Ian), Francesco Bruno (Franco), Iain Robertson (Sean Pearce), Marcel McCalla (Nathan Charles), Stuart Organ (Mr Robson), Lee Cornes (Mr Hankin), Adam Ray (Mr Brisley), David Quilter (Mr Arnold), Sally Geoghegan (Miss Carver), Madelaine Newton (Mrs Jenkins), Karen O'Brien (Mrs Maguire), Rachel Bell (Mrs Holmes), Clive Hill (Mr Jones)

**Writers:** Sarah Daniels, Chris Ellis, Diane Whitley, Leigh Jackson, Tanika Gupta

## Season Twenty-Two
**20 episodes**
**Broadcast:** Tuesdays and Thursdays 26/1/99 – 1/4/99

**Main Cast:** Aidan David (Arnie), Colin Ridgewell (Colin), Laura Hammett (Sarah-Jane), George Stark (Kevin), Rochelle Gadd (Dill), Peter Morton (Wayne), Laura Sadler (Judi), Diana Magness (Evelyn), Oliver Elmidoro (Tom), Robert Stuart (Matt), Jonathan Marchant-Heatley (Cracker), Charlotte McDonagh (Lisa), Thomas Carey (Alec), Kelly George (Ray), Maggie Mason (Gemma), Sam Bardens (Adam), Michael Obiora (Max), Jade Williams (Zoe), John Hudson (Ian), Francesco Bruno (Franco), Marcel McCalla (Nathan), Lindsay Ray (Amy Davenport), Arnold Oceng (Calvin Braithwaite), Jalpa Patel (Anika Modi), Colin White (Spencer Hargreaves), Adam Sopp (Darren Clarke), Taylor Scipio (Kamal Hussain), Joanne Hildon (Cathy), William Christopher French (Mike), Kate Bell (Kelly Bradshaw), Christian Burgess (David Lyons), Emma Pierson (Becky Radcliffe), Daniel Lee (Ben Miler), Sally Morton (Tracy Long), Stuart Organ (Mr Robson), Lee Cornes (Mr Hankin), Adam Ray (Mr Brisley), David Quilter (Mr Arnold), Sally Geoghegan (Miss Carver), Rachel Bell (Mrs Holmes), Clive Hill (Mr Jones), Tam Hoskyns (Mrs Betterton), Michael Larkin (Bob), Jenny Galloway (Mrs Davenport), Doreen Ingleton (Mrs Braithwaite), Ann Davies (Mrs Singleton), Sheila Steafel (Mrs Walton), Colin Higgins (Mr Norris), Karen Gledhill (Miss Lacey)

**Writers:** Sarah Daniels, Diane Whitley, Tanika Gupta, Tim O'Mara, Jeff Povey, Annie Wood

## Season Twenty-Three
**20 episodes**
**Broadcast:** Tuesdays and Thursdays 25/1/00 – 30/3/00

**Main Cast:** Aidan J. David (Arnie), Colin Ridgewell (Colin), Laura Hammett (Sarah-Jane), Rochelle Gadd (Dill), Peter Morton (Wayne), Diana Magness (Evelyn), Oliver Elmidoro (Tom), Robert Stuart (Matt), Jonathan Marchant-Heatley (Cracker), Charlotte McDonagh (Lisa), Thomas Carey (Alec), Sam Bardens (Adam), Michael Obiora (Max Abassi), John Hudson (Ian), Francesco Bruno (Franco), Marcel McCalla (Nathan), Lindsay Ray (Amy), Arnold Oceng (Calvin), Jalpa Patel (Anika), Colin White (Spencer), Adam Sopp (Darren), Kate Bell (Kelly), Daniel Lee (Ben), Sally Morton (Tracy), Dominic Power (Simon), Emma Waters (Katy Fraser), Stuart Organ (Mr Robson), Lee Cornes (Mr Hankin), David Quilter (Mr Arnold), Sally Geoghegan (Miss Carver),

Rachel Bell (Mrs Holmes), Clive Hill (Mr Jones), Judith Wright (Miss Fraser), Don McCorkindale (Mr Forbes)

**Writers:** Sarah Daniels, Tanika Gupta, Tim O'Mara, Jeff Povey, Philip Gerard, Philip Gladwin, Michael Butt, Eanna O'Lochlainn, Judy Forshaw, Lin Coghlan, Paul Smith, Suzie Smith

## Season Twenty-Four
**20 episodes**
**Broadcast:** Tuesdays and Thursdays 23/1/01 – 29/3/01

**Main Cast:** Aidan J. David (Arnie), Colin Ridgewell (Colin), Peter Morton (Wayne), Diana Magness (Evelyn), Oliver Elmidoro (Tom), Robert Stuart (Matt), Jonathan Marchant-Heatley (Cracker), Charlotte McDonagh (Lisa), Michael Obiora (Max), Marcel McCalla (Nathan), Lindsay Ray (Amy), Arnold Oceng (Calvin), Jalpa Patel (Anika), Colin White (Spencer), Adam Sopp (Darren), Kate Bell (Kelly), Daniel Lee (Ben), Sally Morton (Tracy), Stephen Omer (Phil Parker), Jon Newman (Kieran 'Ozzie' Osborne), Max Brown (Danny Hartson), Mark Lewis (Frankie Abbott), Matthew Buckley (Martin Miller), Amanda Fahy (Shannon Parkes), Jessica Staveley-Taylor (Leah Stewart), Suzy Aitchinson (Sally West), Simon Pearsall (Don West), Sophie Shad (Shona West), Emma Willis (Vikki Meedes), Naomi Osei-Mensah (Clare Chaplin), Shane Leonidas (Josh Irving), Tom Savage (Billy), Kacey Barnfield (Maddie Gilks), Renee Montemayor (Briony Jones), Daniel Harcourt (Kev), Daniel Wilson (Jez), Sammy O'Grady (Kathy McIlroy), Le Charne Jolly (Amelia), Stuart Organ (Mr Robson), Lee Cornes (Mr Hankin), Sally Geoghegan (Miss Carver), Rachel Bell (Mrs Holmes), Clive Hill (Mr Jones), Judith Wright (Miss Fraser), Don McCorkindale (Mr Forbes), David Schaal (Mr Hargreaves), Joanne Howarth (Mrs Hargreaves)

**Writers:** Philip Gerard, Paul Smith, Philip Gladwin, Suzie Smith, Mark Hiser, Bridget Colgan, Sarah Daniels, Tara Byrne, Carolyn Sally Jones

## Season Twenty-Five
**18 episodes**
**Broadcast:** Tuesdays and Thursdays 29/1/02 – 28/3/02

**Main Cast:** Oliver Elmidoro (Tom), Robert Stuart (Matt), Jonathan Marchant-Heatley (Cracker), Charlotte McDonagh (Lisa), Michael Obiora (Max), Lindsay Ray (Amy), Arnold Oceng (Calvin), Jalpa Patel (Anika), Adam Sopp (Darren), Daniel Lee (Ben), Jon Newman (Ozzie), Max Brown (Danny), Matthew Buckley (Martin), Amanda Fahy (Shannon), Jessica Staveley-Taylor (Leah), Sophie Shad (Shona), Emma Willis (Vikki), Naomi Osei-Mensah (Clare), Shane Leonidas (Josh), Kacey Barnfield (Maddie), Renee Montemayor (Briony), Sammy O'Grady (Kathy McIlroy), Reggie Yates (Carl Fenton), Sara Stockbridge (Suzie Gilks), Nicholas Caunter (Michael Barton), Peter Shea (Chris), John Hudson (Ian Hudson), Max Brown (Danny Hartson), Victoria Goddard (Tina), Steven Di Meo (Rob), Stuart Organ (Mr Robson), Lee Cornes (Mr Hankin), Nicolas Tizzard (Mr Deverill), Sally Geoghegan (Miss Carver), Rachel Bell (Mrs Holmes), Clive Hill (Mr Jones), Judith Wright (Miss Fraser)

**Writers:** Si Spencer, Sarah Daniels, Philip Gerard, Lisselle Kayla, Rachel Dawson, Philip Gladwin, Lin Goghlan, Helen Eatock

**Tie-in publications:** all below issued in paperback, some as hardbacks also. *Grange Hill Stories* by Phil Redmond published by BBC, 1979. Six books published by Fontana Lions (hardbacks usually published by BBC, some by Andre Deutsch): *Grange Hill Rules – OK?* by Robert Leeson, 1980. *Grange Hill Goes Wild* by Robert Leeson, 1980. *Grange Hill For Sale* by Robert Leeson, 1981. (these three novels also issued as a gift set *Grange Hill x 3* by Fontana – reissued as *Grange Hill x 4* with addition of *Tucker and Co.*). *Tucker and Co. Stories of life in and out of Grange Hill* by Phil Redmond, 1982. *Grange Hill Home and Away* by Robert Leeson, 1982. *Great Days at Grange Hill* by Jan Needle, 1984. Seven books published by Magnet/Methuen (paperbacK) and Hamish Hamilton (hardback): *Grange Hill After Hours* by Phil Redmond, 1986. *Grange Hill On the Run* by Phil Redmond, 1986. *Grange Hill Graffiti* by Phil Redmond, 1986. *Grange Hill Heroes* by Phil Redmond, 1987. *Grange Hill Rebels* by Phil Redmond, 1987. *Grange Hill Partners* by Phil Redmond, 1988. *Ziggy's Working Holiday* by Phil Redmond and Margaret Simpson, 1988.
*Grange Hill Annual* published by Grandreams, 1980. *The Grange Hill Annual* published by Fleetway/IPC 1981–85 (on covers as Annual 1982–1986). *Grange Hill Storybook* (Grange Hill Annual 1988) published by World International (hardback) and World/Cliveden Press/Scholastic (paperback), 1987.

**Video:** *Grange Hill* (106-minute compilation of Season One episodes) released by BBC Video, 1983 on VHS, Betamax and laserdisk. *Grange Hill 2 – More Exploits of the 1st Years* (98-minute compilation of Season Two episodes) released by BBC Video, 1985 on VHS and Betamax. Both tapes deleted.

## Warrior Queen

This drama takes the audience back to AD61 when Boudicca, queen of the Iceni, battled to defend Britain from misrule by the invading Roman soldiers.

Seventeen years earlier Boudicca's husband, Prasutagus, had formed a treaty with Rome, giving him peace and independence under their rule. Now the dying Prasutagus bequeaths half of his kingdom to his two daughters, Tasca and Camora, and the other to emperor Nero. Boudicca believes that the prosperity of their land depends on the maintenance of peace with Rome. She therefore attempts to please the empire by giving her husband a Roman burial, rather than the traditional Celtic one. Boudicca invites the Roman tax collector, Catus Decianus, to the burial. Things start to go wrong, however, when Decianus announces that the treaty with Rome is finished and that her people will be required to pay him tax. War is inevitable.

*Warrior Queen* was recorded entirely on tape and on location in order to speed up production but ends up actually slowing down what is seen on screen. Like the earlier *The Feathered Serpent* the piece is weighty in dialogue, coming across like some kind of *I, Claudius* for kiddies. With regards to action the camera would usually cut away at the most brutal moments, while battle scenes seemed rather flat due to the static positioning of the camera. A strange choice for children's television all told, due largely to the fact that there are no child protagonists within it.

**Thames**
**6 episodes**
(colour)
**Broadcast:** Mondays 20/2/78 – 27/3/78

**Main Cast:** Sian Phillips (Boudicca), Patti Love (Tasca), Veronica Roberts (Camora), Michael Gothard (Volthan), Darien Angadi (Kuno), Nigel Hawthorne (Catus Decianus)

**Written by** Martin Mellett

**Music:** Dominic Muldowney and Stuart Orme
**Design:** Bill Laslett
**Producer:** Ruth Boswell
**Executive Producer:** Sue Turner
**Directors:** Michael Custance and Neville Green

**Tie-in publications:** novelisation by Martin Mellett published by Piccolo, 1978

## The Doombolt Chase

Having witnessed a mad scientist testing his sonic cannon, three adventurous teenagers have to escape from the villains' lair. But the gates are firmly shut. 'We'll smash our way through with that Land Rover,' grins Peter. 'What, James Bond style?' asks Lucy.

Yes, just about, although it's a Bond-like tale of advanced weapons technology and stolen nuclear missiles set purely in and around the exotic climes of the Bristol Channel and the Brecon Beacons.

This Sunday adventure serial concerned a convoluted scheme to sell a new secret weapon to the highest bidder. The Navy's top secret research into the Doombolt project has been hijacked and improved by Professor Bayard – this device uses ultrasonic triggers to redirect other people's missiles. With the UK coastline apparently ringed by hundreds of Navy 'missile canisters' this could prove catastrophic. It's something like that anyway – Peter Vaughan stumbles over the slide show that tries to explain the whole thing and no wonder.

*The Doombolt Chase* is an adventure runaround that falls into the trap of concentrating on action at the expense of consistent plotting. Traitors, a countdown to the weapon's operation, heroes who somehow manage to cut the ropes that bind them, secret bases where the walls are lined with reel-to-reel computer cabinets; all the clichés are present and correct.

The serial appears to be based on the same logic that underpins the Children's Film Foundation (CFF) output of the time – that teenage kids can run faster than either trained thugs or the Royal Navy's finest. Similarly it deals in the false drama of adventure and excitement that never seems to place the young heroes in any real danger. After running away from yet another scrape, Lucy gasps, 'I was scared stiff,' to which Richard replies, 'I quite enjoyed it,' and that probably best explains its outlook. The outrageous and omnipresent funk soundtrack is also in keeping with the CFF productions of the 70s.

The script falls uneasily between this sort of innocent action and an earnest, more adult, thriller style. The main failing of *Doombolt Chase* is that, for all their running around, the three kids do little to advance events. There's too much in the way of regular conferences between the members of the Admiralty, and the day is won by the Navy and Marines when they finally launch an all-out attack on the villains' base. Episode one in particular, concentrating on an accurately researched but slow-moving Naval court martial, has little to offer younger viewers.

An all-important end credit reads 'The producers wish to thank the Royal Navy and the Royal Marines for their   121 co-operation' but that's rather understating it. Without their assistance the script would doubtless have been thrown in the bin and it's more than likely that their help was sought while the script was at the draft stages. The forces' help is most obvious in the final storming of Bayard's hideout, utilising what looks like Marines on training manoeuvres and featuring no less than three helicopters on screen at one time. The *Freewheelers* would have been green with envy.

**HTV West in association with Wagner-Hallig Film and RPTP**
**6 episodes** ('Court of Shame'; 'Escape to Danger';
'Death Beacon'; 'Alarm at Gareth's Peak'; 'The Devil's Jaws';
'Assault on Cragfest')
(colour)
**Broadcast:** Sundays 12/3/78 – 16/4/78

**Main Cast:** Andrew Ashby (Richard Wheeler), Shelley Crowhurst (Lucy), Richard Willis (Peter Larapy), Donald Burton (Commander David Wheeler), Frederick Jaeger (Cmdr Vallance), George Colouris (Bayard), John Woodnutt (Spencer), Ewen Solon (Admiral Lupin), Peter Vaughan (Captain Hatfield), Simon MacCorkindale (Lt Cmdr Madock)

**Written by** Don Houghton

**Title Music:** Eve King
**Design:** Ken Jones
**Executive Producer:** Patrick Dromgoole
**Producer/Director:** Peter Graham Scott

## Come Back, Lucy

Timeslip fantasies where children – more often than not a sensitive young girl – would meet a new friend from the past have been a persisting trope in children's fiction. One of the earliest examples was Alison Uttley's *A Traveller in Time* in 1939 and notable modern variants have included Penelope Farmer's *Charlotte Sometimes* in 1969. While *Come Back, Lucy* was not startlingly original as a source novel it came to life very effectively on TV.

At a subtextual level the piece is about a journey of self-discovery for young Lucy. A timid and old-fashioned girl brought up by her Aunt Olive, she prefers the cosy nostalgia of years gone by to modern life. When her Aunt Olive dies, Lucy is taken in by her kindly aunt and uncle but cannot stand the modern reality of her high-spirited cousins, finding them brash and uncouth. Retreating into her own company she is only too happy when she realises she can travel back in time to play with Alice, a Victorian girl living in a time of governesses and rocking horses in the playroom. Alice becomes demanding of Lucy, however, and eventually turns out-and-out malevolent when she conspires to trap Lucy with her in the Victorian era. Lucy must truly believe that the 1970s is her rightful time and she must fight with all her will to get back to her cousins...

There was the engaging gimmick of Alice appearing unbidden in mirrors and other reflective objects but the real horror of *Come Back, Lucy* was the eventually unbridled malice and spite of Alice. The central performance was a good one, albeit achieved by sleight of hand – Bernadette Windsor was in fact nineteen years old playing twelve. Due to a medical condition the actress was a convincing four foot six when she played Alice.

The visual style of *Come Back, Lucy* was almost certainly a major influence on adult fantasy series *Sapphire and Steel* – itself originally conceived as a children's programme – which *Lucy*'s producer Shaun O'Riordan would work on the following year.

**ATV**
**6 episodes**
(colour)
**Broadcast:** Sundays 23/4/78 – 28/5/78 (fully networked)

**Main Cast:** Emma Bakhle (Lucy), Bernadette Windsor (Alice), Royce Mills (Uncle Peter), Phyllida Law (Aunt Gwen), Russell Lewis (Patrick), Oona Kirsch (Rachel), Francois Evans (Bill), Eve Karpf (Mademoiselle), Aimee Delamain (Aunt Olive)

Based on the novel by Pamela Sykes (first UK publication 1973, Hamish Hamilton)
**Adapted by** Colin Shindler and Gail Renard

**Music:** Ken Jones
**Designer:** Su Nash
**Producer:** Shaun O'Riordan
**Director:** Paul Harrison

**Tie-in publications:** editions of novel published in paperback by Puffin, 1978–80

## The Famous Five

It took the best part of a quarter of a century for television to bring Enid Blyton's most famous creations bang up to date in a 70s-set adventure serial. At least it *looked* bang up to date, with the Five no longer in short trousers and scratchy woollens but sporting anoraks, bad mop haircuts and flared jeans. And that was just the girls.

The TV series was a huge hit with British kids – another generation was ready and willing to suspend disbelief as four kids and a dog took on the criminal fraternity while on holiday from school. How many school holidays they got, the staggering crime rate of the sleepy coastal town of Kirrin and whether the gang met any adults who *weren't* crooks were irrelevant questions that went unasked. Week after week 'Julian, Dick and Anne, George and Timmy the dog' stumbled across jewel smugglers, secret passages, treasure maps and a plan to steal Uncle Quentin's top secret research papers as if it was the first time they had encountered such a thing. Blyton's genius, if it can be called genius, was to tap in to the unsophisticated adventures of any gang of children imagining themselves to have uncovered a mystery per day on an otherwise long and uneventful summer break.

The production itself was rather rushed-looking, despite being a textbook example in low budget factory television. James Gatward's independent company Portman took over the Exbury mansion in the New Forest locale for the summer of 1977 and kitted it out as a studio complex. Editing facilities and production offices were installed on the first floor, interiors were filmed in the ground floor rooms, while standing sets of secret passages and underground caverns were erected in the mansion cellars. German finance was involved, leading to the casting of German actor Michael Hinz as Quentin – whose strange accent was no doubt a mystery to many of the children watching. The backers even wanted one of the four leads to be played by a German youth but eventually Portman managed to convince them of Michelle Gallagher's German great-grandparentage.

If the written pages of Blyton's novels sometimes seemed ludicrous, the same material's lack of realism would only be amplified by the harsh truth of the camera eye. This is of particular concern when the children (and in the first series the leads do look very young) come face to face with some strapping baddie, with violent action the inevitable outcome. Blyton's world was a place where no-one ever got hurt and deserving baddies ended up in prison where they belonged, which seems a rather irreconcilable equation. No doubt as a result of the Enid Blyton Foundation's close control, this ethos was maintained by the TV adaptation. In some episodes in this first thirteen, upper-class and rather camp villains (the ones who wanted Quentin's research secrets) might carry a gun but you never thought they'd use it. Rather more working-class villains with Cockney accents (the ones who smuggled illicit goods) wouldn't carry guns, presumably as you might expect them to use them if they did. Timmy was very useful in this regard and he became the blunt instrument of the Five, the one permitted to acts of violence. The most credible approach to the villains' threat was, oddly, to play it for laughs and have the bad guys falling into rivers and the like while the gang looked on, laughing. 'You wait til I get my 'ands on you,' they'd shout, but they rarely did.

Children grow up fast and for the episodes filmed in summer 1978 the four now looked like the young teenagers they were. With their tousled hair, matching bomber jackets and tight jeans they looked if not sexy then definitely almost cool. With new producer Sid Hayers at the helm, the episodes were tighter, slicker and that little bit tougher this time round. 'Five Fall Into Adventure' is a great tale with real threats from the villains (one even utters, 'Stop or I'll shoot!'), tension as the kids are trapped in the house at night, and a poor kid whose wicked father is shown to leave bruises when he threatens her. The music meanwhile sounds as if it could have come from an episode of *The Professionals*.

The 70s series adapted all but two of Blyton's books: the rights to *Five On a Treasure Island* were with the Children's Film Foundation at the time, while *Five Have Plenty of Fun* was, incredulously, thought to be too similar to other stories! A possible third series was shelved when the Blyton Foundation forbade the team to write their own adventures. Infuriatingly for Portman, a French publisher was granted permission to create new novels based on the Five just a couple of years later.

It's worth mentioning *The Comic Strip*'s groundbreaking 'Five Go Mad in Dorset' (C4 2/11/82) and 'Five Go Mad on Mescalin' (2/11/83) which, in their time, were viewed as outrageous mockeries of the hitherto unassailable institution that was Blyton. This comedy was a right-on satire addressing the dubious middle-class seclusion and alleged racism of the Blyton canon. Despite the impact of the two films, they don't prove that the Five concept was dead – the Strip team's comic cynicism was only a perfectly natural adult rejection of the 'lie' of the idyllic world of Blyton, as childhood retreated from its makers.

The team behind the 90s TV revival didn't seem too convinced of this and their faithful period recreation seemed rooted in the belief that the Famous Five couldn't exist in a contemporary and more cynical setting without being smashed to a pulp by Moss Side crack dealers. Thus

**Above:** Southern's *Famous Five* (clockwise from top left); Julian (Marcus Harris), Dick (Gary Russell), Anne (Jennifer Thanisch), George (Michelle Gallagher) and (centre) Timmy the Dog (Toddy Woodgate).

the series was set in the same safe and far-off time of the novels – books which have increasingly in the past decade been sold as nostalgia pieces with faux-1940s jackets.

Despite a dream team of writers adapting Blyton's books and lavish production values, the core decision to relocate the tales in their period setting seemed the deciding factor in its failure. '... and if that all sounds a bit old-fashioned, don't worry, *The Famous Five* is perfect escapist fun!' enthused Tim Vincent on the *Radio Times* Children's Page at the launch of the series. The children seemed far from worried but nor were they apparently that interested in these alien attitudes, resulting in increasingly scattered showings across the ITV schedules. It took ITV almost four years to show all twenty-six episodes. The series may just have stood a chance if aired in slots more amenable to family viewing and thus more likely to hook some nostalgic parents. In Europe, meanwhile, the co-production has been shown many times over, while in Germany it was possible at one point to watch two different episodes on different satellite channels at the same time.

Based on the 21 books by Enid Blyton (first UK publication from 1942)

### Enid Blyton's Famous Five (1978–79)
**Portman Productions for Southern**

**Main Cast:** Michelle Gallagher (George), Jennifer Thanisch (Anne), Marcus Harris (Julian), Gary Russell (Dick), Michael Hinz (Uncle Quentin), Sue Best (Aunt Fanny), Toddy Woodgate (Timmy the Dog)

## Season One

**13 episodes** ('Five on Kirrin Island'* (2 episodes); 'Five Go Adventuring Again'; 'Five Go To Smuggler's Top' (2 episodes); 'Five Go Off in a Caravan'; 'Five Go Off To Camp' (2 episodes); 'Five on A Hike Together'; 'Five Go To Mystery Moor'; 'Five On A Secret Trail'; 'Five Go to Billycock Hill'; 'Five on Finniston Farm'+)
* Title incorrectly given on screen as 'Five on Kirren Island'
+ Title incorrectly given on screen as 'Five on Finiston Farm'
(colour)
**Broadcast:** Mondays 3/7/78 – 2/10/78 (no broadcast Bank Holiday 28/8/78)

## Season Two

**13 episodes** (transmitted in two blocks)
(colour)

**First block broadcast:** Sundays 19/11/78 – 31/12/78 (no broadcast 25/12/78)
('Five Get Into Trouble' (1: 'Prisoners', 2: 'Conspiracies'); 'Five Get Into a Fix'; 'Five Are Together Again' (2 episodes); 'Five Have a Wonderful Time')
Note: these six episodes were broadcast closer to Season 1 but were filmed in the second shooting block

**Second block broadcast:** Wednesdays 27/6/79 – 8/8/79
('Five Fall Into Adventure' (2 episodes); 'Five Run Away Together'; 'Five Go To Demon's Rocks' (2 episodes); 'Five Go Down to the Sea' (2 episodes))
(Repeats tacked on at end of this block from 15/8/79)

**Adapted by** Richard Carpenter, Gail Renard, Richard Sparks, Gloria Tors

**Music:** Rob Andrews
**Production Designer:** Bob Cartwright
**Art Director:** Fred Hole
**Producer:** Don Leaver (Season 1), Sidney Hayers (Season 2)
**Executive Producer:** James Gatward
**Directors:** Mike Connor, Peter Duffell, James Gatward, Sidney Hayers, Don Leaver

**Tie-in publications:** paperbacks of all 21 novels published by Knight Books, 1978. Annuals published 1978 to 1982 by Purnell. *Enid Blyton's Famous Five TV Special* (hardback – photo illustrated reprints of 'Camp', 'Mystery Moor', 'Caravan'), Hodder and Stoughton, 1978.

**Video:** Longman Video/Pickwick 1983. 'Mystery Moor'/'Camp'; 'Run Away Together'/'Have A Wonderful Time'/'Get Into a Fix'; and other volumes. Deleted.
Six volumes issued by Pickwick, 1992. 'Get Into Trouble'/'Demon's Rocks'; 'Go Down to the Sea'/'Together Again'; 'Mystery Moor'/'Fall Into Adventure'; 'Smuggler's Top'/'Caravan'; 'Run Away Together'/'Wonderful Time'/'Get Into a Fix'; 'Secret Trail'/'Billycock Hill'/'Finniston Farm'/'Hike Together'. Deleted.
Four volumes issued by ILC, 1999. 'Hike'/'Adventuring Again'/'Caravan'; 'Secret Trail'/'Camp'; 'Kirrin Island'/'Billycock Hill'; 'Mystery Moor'/'Smuggler's Top'. Note that in all of these releases, most two-part stories are edited into 42-minute compilation format.

## Enid Blyton's The Famous Five (1996–2000)

**A Zenith North/Portman Production in association with Frankfurter Films for ZDF/Tyne Tees Television/HTV and The Family Channel**
**26 episodes**
(colour)

**First block broadcast:** Mondays 1/7/96 – 2/9/96
('Five on a Treasure Island' (2 episodes); 'Five Get Into Trouble'; 'Five Fall Into Adventure'; 'Five Go Off to Camp'; 'Five on Finniston Farm'; 'Five Go To Smuggler's Top' (2 episodes); 'Five are Together Again', 'Five Go To Demon's Rocks')

**Second block broadcast:** Mondays 14/4/97 – 19/5/97
(no tx 5/5/97) ('Five Go Down to the Sea' (2 episodes); 'Five Run Away Together'; 'Five Go To Mystery Moor'; 'Five Get Into a Fix')

**Third block broadcast:** Sunday mornings 20/7/97 – 10/8/97
('Five Go Adventuring Again'; 'Five on Kirrin Island Again'; 'Five on a Secret Trail'; 'Five Have Plenty of Fun')

**Fourth block broadcast:** Mondays 26/7/99 – 23/8/99
('Five Have a Mystery to Solve'; 'Five on a Hike Together' 'Five Have a Wonderful Time' (2 episodes), 'Five Go Off in a Caravan')

**Fifth block broadcast:** Sunday mornings 11/6/00 – 25/6/00
(Unknown episode, possibly a repeat; 'Five Go To Billycock Hill' (2 episodes))

Above compiled using incomplete *Radio Times* listings and additional BFI data – all 26 episodes thought to have been shown once

**Main Cast:** Jemima Rooper (George), Laura Petela (Anne), Marco Williamson (George), Paul Child (Dick), Christopher Good (Uncle Quentin), Mary Waterhouse (Aunt Frances), Connal (Timmy)

**Dramatised by** Julia Jones, Helen Cresswell, Alan Seymour

**Music:** Joe Campbell and Paul Hart
**Art Director:** Iain Andrews
**Designer:** Ash Wilkinson
**Executive Producers:** for Portman – Ian Warren; for Tyne Tees – Peter Moth; for HTV – Dan Maddicott
**Executive Producer:** Peter Murphy
**Producer:** John Price
**Directors:** Michael Kerrigan, Tony Kysh, Andrew Morgan

**Tie-in publications:** most Blyton books reprinted in paperback with tie-in covers, 1996

**Video:** 12 tapes released by First Independent, June – August 1997. 'Treasure Island' 1 and 2; 'Fall Into Adventure'/'Demon's Rocks'; 'Off to Camp'/'Have Plenty of Fun'; 'Get Into Trouble'/'Adventuring Again'; 'Kirrin Island Again'/'Finniston Farm'; 'Smuggler's Top' 1 and 2; 'A Mystery to Solve'/'On a Hike Together'; 'Billycock Hill' 1 and 2; 'Get Into a Fix'/'Off in a Caravan'; 'Go Down to the Sea' 1 and 2; 'Wonderful Time' 1 and 2; 'Run Away Together'/'Mystery Moor'

## Touch and Go

When teenager Emily finds herself spending a night in hospital after a minor car accident she is sure she sees something she shouldn't have. Accidentally stumbling behind the door of Room 9 she sees a dead woman with a strange man leaning over the body ... Emily's peaceful country holiday soon becomes a nightmare and the foggy coastline of craggy Drumincombe is suddenly fraught with danger. She and Charles, a boy she meets at her hotel, find themselves being watched from all sides.

*Touch and Go* is a surface updating of the traditional children's adventure serial, now rendered as some kind of conspiracy thriller. The coastal setting is pure Kirrin Island but the smuggling that goes on here is but a small part of a bigger plan by a right-wing pressure group called The Dedicated Few to blow up a visiting African delegation. One modern touch is the use of a woman villain among the gang – the well-dressed superbitch Charmaine. Otherwise, things are plotted along traditional lines – the kids can't convince the authorities of the danger and so have to go it alone to solve the mystery. Along the way they find what seems like welcome help only to realise they've walked into the villains' lair. Trussed up, they manage to escape their captors and set off in a race against time to stop the bomb attack on the Naval College. The template of the 60s adventure serial may have mutated ever so slightly over time but at heart remained reassuringly familiar.

**BBC**
**5 episodes**
(colour)
**Broadcast:** Wednesdays 20/9/78 – 18/10/78

**Main Cast:** Maxine Gordon (Emily), David Parfitt (Charles), Aubrey Morris (Willy), Sandy Ratcliff (Charmaine), Shane Briant (Adam), Nigel Lambert (Mr Denman), Anne Cunningham (Emily's mother), Jane Freeman (Mrs Meighan)

Based on the novel by Josephine Poole (first UK publication 1976, Hutchinson & Co.)
**Screenplay by** Josephine Poole

**Designer:** Gerry Scott
**Executive Producer:** Anna Home
**Director:** Jonathan Ingrams

**Tie-in publications:** edition published in paperback by Knight Books, 1978

## The Clifton House Mystery

When old Mrs Betterton sells her family home it is bought by concert pianist and conductor Timothy Clare. Mrs Betterton also sells off many of her heirlooms in an auction and Clare's elder son Steven buys a dusty old military helmet. Daughter Jenny meanwhile is gifted an old musical box by Mrs Betterton's granddaughter. The two items are linked to the ghosts of an old lady and a soldier which have haunted the Clifton House for more than a century.

*The Clifton House Mystery* is to all intents and purposes a horror movie for those who would never be allowed to stay up late to see them on TV. All of the clichés of the Hammer genre are gleefully served up to this audience as 'new to you' (writer Farson was a published horror movie buff as well as a former TV presenter). Apparitions of a steely faced soldier and a sweet old lady haunt the place, a skeleton is found lying in a four-poster bed in a bricked-up room and poltergeists make plates fly out of hands. Some sections are very frightening for younger children, including a scene where spots of blood drip from the ceiling and onto the face of a dinner guest. Surprisingly though, producer Leonard White recalls there having been no viewer complaints.

Made on a budget far lower than that of even the most low-budget horror flick, *The Clifton House Mystery* was made almost entirely in HTV West's Bristol studios on videotape (a single establishing shot was taped on location). Much like ATV's later *Sapphire and Steel* the production uses a few darkly lit sets to create its atmosphere. The limited amount of music that could be afforded is turned to positive advantage, the long silences being used to create tension. Clever use of music is key to the serial, with the ghosts' appearances usually signalled by the music box rendition of the soldier's regimental march.

The lack of melodramatic incidentals also helps to create one of the serial's most frightening scenes. Guest's 'exorcism' of the soldier is achieved by a close-up on Peter Sallis' terrified face, a few video overlays and thunderous use of horse and battle noise sound effects. This makes one of several very effective cliffhanging episode endings to the serial. It's worth noting that the religious aspect of a bona fide exorcism is avoided here. The use of occult imagery has been a moot point several times in the history of children's drama and in 1978 memories of the attendant fuss that had surrounded *The Exorcist* would still be fresh in the programme-makers' minds.

A local history lesson is added almost guiltily to the shlock-fest, meeting some sort of educational remit and mindful of the need to meet the part of the franchise guidelines that stipulates programmes should reflect the concerns and colour of their region. To this end a mini-lecture is delivered, by a librarian no less, on the Bristol riots of 1831. The soldier ghost had been the commanding officer of the 3rd Dragoon guards on the night crowds of thousands had filled the streets of Bristol to protest against restricted voting rights. Captain Bretherton made a deal to withdraw his troops but the rioters reneged upon it and in the resulting destruction Bretherton fled to the safety of his mother's home. Untried for charges of cowardice he had been hidden by his mother until his death, upon which she walled up his body in the bedroom.

An oddly paced final episode (which includes a bizarre TV appearance by the Clares on HTV's *Report West* news programme) ties up loose ends very tightly only to then pull them apart just for sensationalist and illogical effect – but then sensationalist shock tactics was what *The Clifton House Mystery* was all about.

**HTV West**
**6 episodes**
(colour)
**Broadcast:** Sundays 8/10/78 – 12/11/78

**Main Cast:** Amanda Kirby (Jenny), Joshua Le Touzel (Steven), Robert Morgan (Ben), Sebastian Breaks (Timothy Clare), Ingrid Hafner (Sheila Clare), Michelle Martin (Emily), Margery Withers (Mrs Betterton), Peter Sallis (Milton Guest), Elizabeth Havelock (The Lady), Derek Graham (Officer)

**Written by** Harry Moore and Daniel Farson                    125

**Music:** Sidney Sager and Kenneth Mobbs
**Designer:** Ken Jones
**Producer:** Leonard White
**Executive Producer:** Patrick Dromgoole
**Directors:** Hugh David (1, 2), Jeffrey Milland (3, 5), Terry Miller (4, 6)

**Tie-in publications:** novelisation by Daniel Farson published in paperback by Look-In/ITV Books and Arrow Books, 1978

**Video:** 150-minute compilation by Guild Home Video, c. 1980. Deleted.

## The Hills of Heaven

John Farrimond's story was set in a mining town in 1930s' industrial Lancashire and based on the author's own childhood experiences of playing on slag heaps, stealing coal and running from the pit bobby. The television adaptation brought the scenario to life, played out in streets of terraced houses and replete with flat caps, bicycle clips, sparking clogs and a layer of sooty grime.

Three working-class kids, Billy Walsh, Mick Mack and the tomboyish Nancy 'Spindle Legs' Brindle, spend their days happily indulging in dares. The three don't realise the danger of such things until one day Mick sets off a line of parked coal trucks so that they are wrecked and derailed. Worse still is to come, when a tramp who has been sleeping in one of the trucks stumbles from the wreckage. The canny tramp demands shelter, clothes and food or else he will tell the pit bobby who is responsible for the damaged trucks. With no choice but to meet his blackmail request, the children hide the tramp in an abandoned house in the middle of the old mine workings but events take another turn when the house collapses due to subsidence. The kids now face a dilemma – whether to alert the authorities to the tramp trapped down the mine in need of rescue or keep their mouths shut to avoid blame over the derailment.

The slight story – a novella rather than a full-blown novel – fits the three episode format well and this, as well as the coincident publication and TV air-dates, suggests that the book and teleplay were written in tandem. The title referred to the low clouds the kids sometimes see over Southport and which to the children seem a world away.

**BBC**
**3 episodes**
(colour)
**Broadcast:** Wednesdays 25/10/78 – 8/11/78

**Main Cast:** David Haddow (Billy Walsh), Katie Armstrong (Nancy Brindle), Malcolm Sproston (Mick Mack), Ray Smith (Tramp), Frank Vincent (Tom Barraclough), Rowena Parr (Annie Walsh)

Based on the novel by John Farrimond (first UK publication 1978, BBC)
**Adapted by** Barry Collins

**Designer:** Chris Edwards
**Producer:** Angela Beeching
**Director:** Eric Davidson

**Tie-in publications:** edition published in hardback and paperback by BBC, 1978 (this was the book's first edition)

## The Moon Stallion

Horses, magic, mansions, period frocks and side whiskers; it's all here in the archetypal BBC children's drama of the 70s. While all of these icons and totems are present and correct it has to be said that this drama is largely about style and image and rather less about story and subtext.

*The Moon Stallion* is a pastiche of classic Victorian and Edwardian fantasy fiction. It's about night filming, a sense of mystery and vulnerable girls in nighties staring into the middle distance but in the final examination is no more than a entertaining hotchpotch of enticing legends and myths. Working within a real location gives Hayles' script a focus, the work springing naturally from the fascinating historic sites located within little more than a square mile of Uffington, Wiltshire. The principal icon was the chalk White Horse carved into the hillside just east of Uffington Castle and this would have led into the idea of the titular Moon Stallion, an occasional manifestation of the spirit depicted by the ancient artwork. Also involved were an ancient burial mound at Dragon Hill and Wayland Smithy, where legend tells the White Horse was shod.

Hayles may well have researched deeply into Arthurian myth but such legendary tales have a way of evolving over centuries until one is left with a vast amount of contradictory, embellished fiction. Hayles takes a fairly free hand, quite rightly, in adapting these tales for his purpose although Professor Purwell, a scholar of Arthurian myth, helps to suggest on screen where inventions occur. Just as important as the basis in legend, seemingly, is the influence of LWI's *The Adventures of Black Beauty*. *The Moon Stallion* does indeed come across as a long-form version of one of the spookier, fantasy-tinged episodes of the famous series, being a tale of rustic magic possessing both a well-spoken girl heroine and gratuitous shots of horses galloping over the hills.

While drawing together elements familiar from turn of the century fantasy fiction, Hayles is either unsure of how to deploy them or has been instructed to rein things in. For example, the discovery of strange magic by a vulnerable and pretty young virgin heroine is usually a metaphor for sexual awakening in the gothic novel but Hayles deploys Diana on a purely surface level. Sex and black magic are big enough no-nos on their own in children's drama but still there's not the smallest subtextual hint of their traditional co-existence here.

What *The Moon Stallion* is actually about, other than entertaining the kiddoes on a weekly basis, is hard to fathom. Resolution of events is far from tidy. Initially the Moon Stallion is being sought by Sir George Mortenhurze, a man who has become obsessed with the creature in his bereavement for his dead wife. In his grief he has believed the superstition that those who see the Stallion will be dead by Harvest and he vows to capture the horse for causing her death nine years previously. Mortenhurze ends up hunted and killed by the Stallion but has he really deserved this? His only crime was to have lived in a superstitious age – should he not be a more sympathetic figure?

Mortenhurze is used by Todman, who knows the true significance of the Stallion as messenger of Epona the Moon goddess (known to the Greeks as Diana) and wants the power she holds. The final climax turns out to be a rather Pythonesque wrestling match between Todman and the Green King for the secrets of Tir na Nog, which might as well have been an arm-wrestle or conker match, it seems so ludicrously low-powered.

Oddest of all is a cautionary warning to modern man, given by the Green King, embodiment of the natural forces of the Earth. He shows Diana man's past, present and future in the Shield of Knowledge (or more prosaically in the shape of stock footage and photographs of the Pyramids, Victorian London, Concorde and Skylab). The Green King foretells of the future's nuclear destruction and man's eternal instinct for survival. 'Wheel turns,' is his message but what purpose any of this serves is uncertain. It's also remarkably similar to 1975's *The Changes*, another drama based on aspects of the Merlin legend. The rare movie-length edit of *The Moon Stallion* released on video excised this supposedly key scene completely, so maybe the editors wondered what on earth it was all about too. What journey has Diana made after six episodes? How many members of the audience thought that Diana's sight would be restored, in expectation of some kind of epiphanic ending that doesn't come?

To give it its due *The Moon Stallion* is a wonderful piece of light melodrama fit for any Sunday afternoon (as it was deployed when repeated in three parts in 1980). *The Moon Stallion* is a looker, then, but rather directionless as a story.

**Above:** Sarah Sutton featured as Diana on the cover of Mirror Books' novelisation of *The Moon Stallion*.

**A BBC TV Production in association with Sudfunk Stuttgart**
**6 episodes**
(colour)

**Episode One**
Wednesday 15/11/78 5.10p.m.
Professor Purwell arrives at the mansion of George Mortenhurze, sponsor of his researches into Arthurian legend in the Uffington area. On the way to the house Purwell's blind daughter Diana is first to sense the presence of the white Moon Stallion, a mythical horse said to appear every nine years.

**Episode Two**
Wednesday 22/11/78 5.10p.m.
The Stallion comes to Diana and presents her with a vision of a rider in dark armour and a crown. Could this be King Arthur? She faints away.

**Episode Three**
Wednesday 29/11/78 5.10p.m.
Paul and Estelle spy Todman, a horse whisperer and Mortenhurze's stablemaster, making a magic talisman from toad bones which he hopes will help him catch the Moon Stallion. That night Diana is summoned from her bed by the Stallion, which carries her off into the night.

**Episode Four**
Wednesday 6/12/78 5.10p.m.
The Stallion takes Diana to the Smithy where Wayland the Green King grants her a vision of man's future. Mortenhurze approaches the barrow – trying to steal the Moon Stallion; the magic of the wild hunt is invoked and Sir George is hounded to his death by the Stallion.

**Episode Five**
Wednesday 13/12/78 5.10p.m.
Todman wants the Stallion in order to harness the power and secrets of Diana, the Moon Goddess. He kidnaps her present day namesake in order to gain an audience with the goddess' guardian, the Green King.

**Episode Six**
Wednesday 20/12/78 5.10p.m.
Diana and Todman are taken by the Moon Stallion to the Smithy, gateway to the mythical land of Tir na Nog. Todman must do battle with the Green King; whoever is the victor will hold the Hammer of Truth and the knowledge of the gods.

**Main Cast:** Sarah Sutton (Diana Purwell), James Greene (Professor Purwell), David Haig (Todman), John Abineri (Sir George Mortenhurze), Caroline Goodall (Estelle), David Pullan (Paul Purwell), Michael Kilgarriff (The Green King), Joy Harington (Mrs Brookes), Richard Viner (The Dark Rider) and Tabu (The Moon Stallion)

**Written by** Brian Hayles

**Music:** Howard Blake
**Designer:** Roger Cann
**Executive Producer:** Anna Home
**Director:** Dorothea Brooking

**Tie-in publications:** paperback novelisation by Brian Hayles published by Mirror Books, 1978

**Video:** 95-minute compilation released January 1985 by BBC Video. Deleted. Same compilation released in the US and Canada by BFS Video, 1990.

127

## Pinocchio

The BBC Sunday Classics may have a long tradition of conservatism but this fresh if faithful adaptation of Carlo Collodi's novel braved inevitable comparisons with the 1940 Walt Disney movie to examine the darker side of the written source work.

Although rendered partly with light entertainment trimmings and even a few songs (no 'When You Wish Upon a Star' here even if the rest of the score is a superb classical/electronic mixture), this is very much a minor part of the telling. The central tenets of Collodi's book remain true – the lonely Geppetto grieves so much for his dead son that his wishes for another are answered by the Blue Fairy. Her magic powers only extend to the woods and forests, however, and so all she can do is make Geppetto's carved puppet come to crudely animated life. Geppetto wants to love the boy but Pinocchio often rewards his father with loud tantrums which the woodcarver patiently bears. By turns innocent and gullible or thoughtless and selfish, the puppet tries to become a real boy but is all too easily led astray by the conmen Mr Fox and Mr Cat and the temptations of the idle life.

An at-times grotesque story – in keeping with the book's rather twisted premise – central to an unsettlingly strange air is that here Pinocchio is a real puppet playing against actors. Disney's film had a cartoon puppet interacting with cartoon people, but here, the truly unnatural concept of a living puppet can never be forgotten and thus Pinocchio's wish seems all the more urgent. The brilliantly played Mr Fox and Mr Cat appear whimsical enough, if cruel, but there are further, almost disturbing predicaments for the wooden boy. There is the antiquated psychedelia of the Land of Toys where Pinocchio and the lazy boys waste their days until they are turned into donkeys, and a cruel circus act where the Ringmaster whips the wooden puppet donkey into ever more dangerous stunts.

The production is imaginatively realised all in studio, usually through illustrated backdrops and models. Pinocchio himself is a simple, almost purposefully crude rod puppet, sometimes operated by a puppeteer out of shot, sometimes superimposed using CSO.

Almost certainly this is the most creatively off-kilter production to have been made by the Sunday Classics team. Whether children would prefer this over the bright and cheerful Disney animation is unlikely – if anything they would probably be too frightened to stick with it for long.

**BBC/Time Life Films**
**4 episodes**
(colour)
**Broadcast:** Sundays 3/12/78 – 24/12/78

**Main Cast:** Derek Smith (Geppetto), Rosemary Miller (Voice of Pinocchio), Roy MacReady (Mr Federico Fox), Neil Fitzwilliam (Mr Cat), Rhoda Lewis (The Blue Fairy), David Lynch (Lampwick), Timothy Bateson (Schoolmaster), James Berwick (Voice of the Cricket/Zaporelli)
Pinocchio by Theatre of Puppets. Puppetmaster: Barry Smith Operators: Gillian Robic, Trevor Trenton

Based on the book by Carlo Collodi (first English translation c. 1892 by MA Murray)
**Dramatised by** Alec Drysdale
**Script Editor:** Alistair Bell

**Incidental Music:** Stephen Deutsch
**Designer:** Ken Sharp
**Illustrator:** Julek Heller
**Producer/Director:** Barry Letts

**Tie-in publications:** n/k

**Video:** 108-minute compilation released by BBC Video on VHS and Betamax, 1985. Deleted.

## The Strange Affair of Adelaide Harris

For this work, writer Leon Garfield put aside his usual cast of urchins running from murder and danger through the back streets of a fantasised Dickensian London in favour of a period farce more akin to the likes of *Tom Jones*. The cast of this adaptation respond to the comedy tone of the script with some richly hammy performances. Freddie Jones in particular seems to enjoy his job as the villain of the piece, Mr Raven, always skulking in doorways hidden from view by the black cloak swept theatrically over his face.

The two child leads are hard to find in a story that concentrates far more on the to-ings and fro-ings between their families – indeed this would have made it an ideal candidate for a Sunday teatime slot. Nonetheless Bostock and Harris are two engaging wheeler-dealers, the plot concerning their attempts to find Harris' baby sister Adelaide after they rather carelessly lose her. A gypsy baby is substituted at one point before they finally locate the little soul in the local orphanage, The Asylum for Foundling Children.

The production had a quirky and larger than life visual style, coming across as period comic strip. The title sequence went even further by using 'penny dreadful' style caricatures of the roll of players, a sure sign of its comedic tone.

**BBC in association with Messischer Rundfunk**
**6 episodes**
(colour)
**Broadcast:** Wednesdays 3/1/79 – 7/2/79

**Main Cast:** Jim Harris (Harris), Matthew Beamish (Bostock), Freddie Jones (Mr Selwyn Raven), Timothy Davies (Mr Brett), Derek Francis (Dr Bunnion), Jean Harvey (Mrs Bunnion), Amanda Kirby (Tizzy Alexander), Patrick Newell (Major Alexander), John Ringham (Dr Harris), Jane Lowe (Mrs Harris), Tracey Childs (Mary Harris), Fiona Hendry (Catherine Harris)

Based on the novel by Leon Garfield (first UK publication 1971, Longman Young Books)
**Adapted by** Robin Miller

**Music:** Alan Roper
**Designer:** David Spode
**Executive Producer:** Anna Home
**Director:** Paul Stone

**Tie-in publications:** edition of novel published in paperback by Puffin, 1978

## Park Ranger

Former *Freewheelers* creator Chris McMaster developed this series about the Park Ranger of Bearsdale, a fictional Borders National Park. David Martin was the Ranger, accompanied by his new young assistant Paul and aided and abetted by local vet Margaret and her teenage daughter Katie. Without the globetrotting capabilities of the *Freewheelers* the team had to wait for the action to come to them. However improbably, it did.

In the most exciting National Park in the country there was a rabid dog from France on the loose to contend with, an escaped convict, two crooks seeking a mineral deposit in a mountain quarry, a bomber threatening a local nuclear power plant and a raging forest fire to end the series.

As ever McMaster drafted in as much hardware as possible – two American brats caused havoc with a hang-glider in one episode, while as many helicopters as could be fitted into the storylines also featured.

**Southern**
**6 episodes** ('New Boy'; 'Fugitive'; 'Contest'; 'Treasure!'; 'Waste'; 'Fire!')
(colour)
**Broadcast:** Wednesdays 21/2/79 – 28/3/79

**Main Cast:** Richard Gibson (Paul Graham), Norman Bowler (David Martin), Jane West (Katie Jackson), Jenny Logan (Margaret Jackson)

**Created by** Chris McMaster
**Written by** Brian Finch (1, 2), Roy Russell (4), 3, 5, 6 not known due to *TV Times* strike but possibly Chris McMaster

**Designer:** Greg Lawson
**Producer:** Chris McMaster

**Tie-in publications:** novelisation published by Carousel, 1979

## Worzel Gummidge

Children's novelist Barbara Euphan Todd could never have guessed that many years after retiring famous scarecrow Worzel Gummidge – a star of radio in the 40s and a one-off TV adventure in the 50s – he would become more popular than ever with the television generation.

After her death in 1976, the rights to the novels were bought by noted 60s cinema writers Keith Waterhouse and Willis Hall, seeing the potential for a children's feature film. Armed with a script about a scarecrow uprising, they managed to involve a very enthusiastic Jon Pertwee but it was the leanest of times for the British film industry and the three failed to raise the necessary finance. Turning next to television, the BBC and several of the larger ITV franchises turned the project down before Southern accepted it.

The Worzel known today was to a large extent an invention of the TV production. Worzelese, the West Country Yokel scarecrow language, and the gimmick of Worzel's interchangeable heads were both devised by Pertwee. Notable among Waterhouse and Hall's format changes was the replacing of Worzel's love interest Earthy Mangold by a revised version of Euphan Todd's Aunt Sally – in the original books she really had been Worzel's aunt! Most importantly, Euphan Todd's kindly village idiot type

became a sharper, more selfish and badly behaved scarecrow, much to the delight of the audience, it seemed.

The series was broadly a comedy of cake fights and falls into rivers on an almost weekly basis, with the guest players a Who's Who of 60s' British film comedy, but there is enough going on in dramatic terms to merit the series' inclusion here. Worzel had a pronounced anti-authoritarian streak – whether it was cocking a snook at the local bobby or the upper crust Mrs Bloomsbury-Barton, this no doubt appealed to the sizable adult audience as much, if not more, than it did to their children. While not wanting to read too much into it, there's much satisfaction to be had when the servant class of butler Worzel and maid Aunt Sally run off with Bloomsbury-Barton's cake trolley at the end of 'Very Good Worzel'.

Throughout, this was an engaging – and often surprisingly affecting – story of unrequited love. Aunt Sally, coconut shy with pretensions and the object of Worzel's devotion, was one of TV's most enduring villainesses, only ever wanting to be with Worzel when there were free cream cakes involved. Most heartbreaking of all are the last minute jilting of Worzel at the altar in 'The Scarecrow Wedding' and her jealous machinations in 'Will the Real Aunt Sally...?' which sees Worzel lose an identical-looking, but far more kind-hearted, Aunt Sally.

The series also possessed a darker side and, at times, a grotesque visual sensibility. In the first episode Worzel is 'born' in a lightning storm *à la* Frankenstein, while 'The Trial of Worzel Gummidge' has a ghoulish bunch of scarecrows coming from far and wide to attend Worzel's trial for dereliction of duty, with the on-screen results resembling a scene from *Night of the Living Dead*. Many episodes placed Worzel in very real mortal danger, as opposed to comic circumstances – his greatest fears being the compost heap and the bonfire.

Despite the series' success all was not plain sailing after the difficult enough origins. Filming on the second season in the summer of 1979 was halted by the ITV strike and the series was curtailed from thirteen to just eight episodes. The series finally ended when Southern lost their franchise at the end of 1981 and their successors TVS decided to pursue their own projects. A series to be filmed in Ireland and financed with American support was cancelled at the eleventh hour when one of the American producers publicly insulted HTV's Lord Harlech, another of the project's backers. Worzel finally returned to TV thanks to a New Zealand producer but *Worzel Gummidge Down Under*, aired by Channel Four on Sunday mornings, failed to catch the imagination as before. This was no doubt due at least in part to the timeslot, inaccessible to the family audience.

Until his death in 1996 Jon Pertwee continued to campaign for further adventures of Worzel, latterly as an animated series, eternally grateful to a character who had produced from him the most rounded acting performance of his career. Of Worzel, he said, 'He says and does all the things that all of us would like to do, but are too shy, self-conscious and respectful to. Being rude to those in authority, being selfish ... there is something of Worzel in all of us.'

**Above:** Sue and John (Charlotte Coleman and Jeremy Austin) watch *Worzel Gummidge* (Jon Pertwee) go into another of his infamous sulks.

***Worzel Gummidge Turns Detective* (1953)**
**BBC**
**4 episodes** ('Enter Two Scarecrows'; 'Aunt Sally';
'Gummidge, the Sweep'; 'Gummidge Disappears')
(b&w)
**Broadcast:** Tuesdays 10/2/53 – 3/3/53

**Cast:** Frank Atkinson (Worzel Gummidge), Mabel Constanduros (Earthy Mangold), Carole Oliver (Penny), David Coote (Andrew), Philip Ray (Mr Braithwaite), Margaret Boyd (Mrs Braithwaite), Janet Joye (Mrs Bloomsbury-Barton), Totti Truman-Taylor (Aunt Sally)

**Designer:** Stephen Taylor
**Producer:** Pamela Brown

***Jackanory: Worzel Gummidge Again* (1974)**
**BBC**
**Broadcast:** 4/11/74 – 8/11/74
**Read by** Geoffrey Bayldon

***Worzel Gummidge* (1979–81)**
**Southern**
(colour)
**4 seasons** and **1 Special**

**Regular Cast** (in all 4 seasons): Jon Pertwee (Worzel Gummidge), Charlotte Coleman (Sue Peters), Jeremy Austin (John Peters), Una Stubbs (Aunt Sally), Geoffrey Bayldon (Crowman), Mike Berry (Mr Peters), Megs Jenkins (Mrs Braithwaite), Norman Bird (Mr Braithwaite), Michael Ripper (Mr Shepherd), Norman Mitchell (PC Parsons)

**Written by** Keith Waterhouse and Willis Hall, based on characters created by Barbara Euphan Todd

**Season One**
**7 episodes** ('Worzel's Washing Day'; 'A Home Fit for Scarecrows'; 'Aunt Sally'; 'The Crowman'; 'A Little Learning'; 'Worzel Pays a Visit'; 'The Scarecrow Hop')
**Broadcast:** Sundays 25/2/79 – 8/4/79 networked 5.30p.m.

**Guest Cast:** Joan Sims (Mrs Bloomsbury-Barton)

**Music:** Neil Cameron and George Evans
**Production Designer:** Hazel Peiser
**Associate Producer:** David Pick
**Executive Producer:** Lewis Rudd
**Producer and Director:** James Hill

**Season Two**
**8 episodes** ('Worzel and the Saucy Nancy'; 'Worzel's Nephew'; 'A Fishy Tale'; 'The Trial of Worzel Gummidge'; 'Very Good Worzel'; 'Worzel in the Limelight'; 'Fire Drill'; 'The Scarecrow Wedding')
**Broadcast:** Sundays 6/1/80 – 24/2/80 networked 5.30p.m.

**Guest Cast:** Joan Sims (Mrs Bloomsbury-Barton), Barbara Windsor (Saucy Nancy), Bill Maynard (Sergeant Beetroot), Wayne Norman (Pickles), Sarah Thomas (Enid)

**Music:** Neil Cameron and George Evans
**Associate Producer:** David Pick
**Production Designer:** Hazel Peiser
**Art Director:** Keith Liddiard
**Executive Producer:** Lewis Rudd
**Producer:** James Hill
**Directors:** James Hill (all except 'Very Good Worzel' by David Pick)

### Season Three
**8 episodes** ('Moving On'; 'Dolly Clothes-Peg'; 'A Fair Old Pullover'; 'Worzel the Brave'; 'Worzel's Wager'; 'The Return of Dafthead'; 'Captain Worzel'; 'Choir Practice')
**Broadcast:** Saturdays 1/11/80 – 20/12/80 networked 5.15p.m. (later moving to 5.30p.m.)
**1-hour Christmas Special:** 'A Cup o' Tea an' a Slice o' Cake.' Saturday 27/12/80 (networked 5.20p.m.)

**Guest Cast:** Barbara Windsor (Saucy Nancy), Bill Maynard (Sergeant Beetroot), Lorraine Chase (Dolly Clothes-Peg), Thorley Walters (Colonel Bloodstock), Denis Gilmore (Harry)

**Music:** Neil Cameron
**Production Designer:** Hazel Peiser
**Art Director:** Keith Liddiard
**Executive Producer:** Lewis Rudd
**Producer/Director:** James Hill

**Christmas Special** – Additional Credits
**Music:** Denis King
**Music Editor:** Chris Wentzell
**Choreographer:** Geraldine Stephenson

### Season Four
**7 episodes** ('Muvver's Day'; 'The Return of Dolly Clothes-Peg'; 'The Jumbly Sale'; 'Worzel in Revolt'; 'Will the Real Aunt Sally...?'; 'The Golden Hind'; 'Worzel's Birthday')
**Broadcast:** Saturdays 31/10/81 – 12/12/81 networked 5.05p.m.

**Guest Cast:** Lorraine Chase (Dolly Clothes-Peg), Bernard Cribbins (Jolly Jack), Connie Booth (Other Aunt Sally)

**Music:** Neil Cameron
**Series Designer:** Hazel Peiser
**Production Designer:** Christine Ruscoe
**Art Director:** Mark A. Ward
**Executive Producer:** Al Burgess
**Producer/Director:** James Hill

**Tie-in publications:** *The Television Adventures of Worzel Gummidge* by Keith Waterhouse and Willis Hall, published by Puffin, 1979. *More Television Adventures of Worzel Gummidge* by Keith Waterhouse and Willis Hall, published by Puffin, 1979. *Worzel Gummidge at the Fair* by Keith Waterhouse and Willis Hall, Young Puffin, 1980. *The Irish Adventures of Worzel Gummidge* by Keith Waterhouse and Willis Hall, published by Severn House, 1984 (hardback) and Sparrow, 1984 (paperback). *Worzel Gummidge Down Under* by Keith Waterhouse and Willis Hall, A Channel Four book by Dragon,

1987. Also *Television Adventures* and *More Television Adventures* reprinted as *Worzel Gummidge's Television Adventures*, Kestrel, 1981 (hardback).
Reprints of Euphan Todd books by Target, published 1980 with artwork covers depicting Pertwee's likeness, were unlicensed. Annuals published by Purnell and Grandreams 1978–1982.

**Video:** Series of seven tapes, two episodes on each (except 52-minute Christmas Special) by Carlton Home Entertainment: 'Washing Day'/'A Home Fit for Scarecrows'; 'Aunt Sally'/'The Crowman'; 'A Little Learning'/'Worzel Pays A Visit'; 'Saucy Nancy'/'Worzel's Nephew'; 'Fishy Tale'/'Trial of Worzel'– deleted 20/10/92. 'The Scarecrow Wedding'/'Fire Drill'; 'Cup o' Tea ...' deleted 17/2/93.
Series of two tapes, three episodes on each by NTV Entertainment: 'Scarecrow Wedding'/'Will the Real Aunt Sally...?'/'Jumbly Sale'; volume 2 details n/k. Released 1994. Deleted.
Series of four tapes, three episodes on each by ILC/Primetime: 'Washing Day'/'Home Fit for Scarecrows'/'Aunt Sally'; 'Scarecrow Wedding'/'Will the Real ...'/ 1 other n/k; 'Scarecrow Hop'/'Saucy Nancy'/'Worzel's Nephew'; 'Fishy Tale'/'Trial of Worzel'/'Very Good Worzel'. Released 8/2/99.
Series of releases issued 8/10/01, simultaneously on VHS and Region 2 DVD by Laserlight: 'Captain Worzel'/'Choir Practice'/'Muvver's Day'; 'Moving On'/'Dolly Clothes-Peg'/'A Fair Old Pullover'; 'The Golden Hind'/'Will the Real ...'/'Jumbly Sale'; 'The Return of Dolly Clothes-Peg'/'Worzel's Revolt'/'Worzel's Birthday'; 'Worzel the Brave'/'Worzel's Wager'/'Return of Dafthead'; 'Cup o' Tea ...'.

## *Worzel Gummidge Down Under* (1987–89)
(colour)
**2 seasons**

**Main Cast:** Jon Pertwee (Worzel), Una Stubbs (Aunt Sally), Jonathan Marks (Mickey), Bruce Philips (Crowman), Joy Watson (Mrs Peacock)

### Season One
**Toti Productions for Channel 4** (UK/New Zealand co-production)
**10 episodes** ('As the Scarecrow Flies'; 'The Sleeping Beauty'; 'Full Employment'; 'Worzel's Handicap'; 'King of the Scarecrows'; 'Ten Heads are Better Than One'; 'Worzel to the Rescue'; 'Slave Scarecrow' (part 1 of 2-part story); 'The Traveller Unmasked' (part 2 of 2); 'A Friend in Need')
**Broadcast:** Sundays 4/10/87 – 6/12/87 Channel 4 11.30a.m.

**Written by** Keith Waterhouse and Willis Hall
**Producer:** Grahame McLean
**Director:** James Hill

### Season Two
**Creative Arts Production for Channel 4** (UK/New Zealand co-production)
**12 episodes** ('Stage Struck'; 'Red Sky In't Mornin'' (part 1 of 2-part story); 'Them Thar Hills' (part 2 of 2); 'The Beauty Contest'; 'Bulbous Cauliflower'; 'Weevily Swede'; 'Elementary, My Dear Worty'; 'Dreams of Avarish'; 'Runaway Train'; 'Aunt Sally RA'; 'Wattle Hearthbrush'; 'The Bestest Scarecrow')
**Broadcast:** Sundays 29/1/89 – 16/4/89 Channel 4 11.30a.m.

**Additional Cast:** Olivia Ihimaera-Smiler (Manu), Danny Mulheron (Blighty Tater), Ellie Smith (Wattle Hearthbrush), Ross Jolly (PC Peacock)

**Written by** Frances Walsh (5–9), James Hill (10), Anthony McCarten (11, 12), 1–4 n/k
**Producer:** Grahame McLean
**Directors:** James Hill (1–6, 8), Grahame McLean (7, 9–12)

**Video:** 94-minute compilation of episodes c. 1989. Deleted.

## The Boy Merlin

A rather studious adventure series based upon obviously extensive research into Arthurian myth and legend, *The Boy Merlin* spun off from the Thames anthology series *Shadows*.

Young Merlin is the fatherless son of the princess, Lady Iamena, fostered by Welsh blacksmith Dafydd and his wife Blodwen and brought up as their own. It is grandmother Myfanwy who knows of Merlin's true destiny and foresees the time of King Arthur and it is she who teaches the boy the art of magic, despite Dafydd's initial protests. Merlin makes an enemy the day King Vortigern's envoy, the Saxon Thane Octa, is sent to take back the son of Iamena. Vortigern wishes to build a tower in this Welsh wilderness and the mortar will be mixed with the blood of Iamena's long lost son Ambrosius – Octa suspects that Merlin is the lost prince. Merlin, under the tutelage of Myfanwy and her magic, sends him on his way by casting a spell on Octa's horse.

The series pitted Octa (recast with a different actor from the pilot) against the young magician as he tries to obtain Merlin's blood. Familiar aspects of the legend were woven into the episodes, with the arrival of the Round Table and the appearance of The Lady Vivien of the Lake both featuring.

A novel take on the Arthurian myth before the birth of Arthur, the production was largely studio-bound. Interesting to note is the predominantly Welsh tongue of the cast used in preference to the dramatic licence of stage English, particularly given that the series was made by Thames and not HTV. The series was hampered by the onset of industrial action at ITV, a *TV Times* dispute blacking out most promotion for the series.

**Thames**
**1 pilot** and **6 episodes**
(colour)

**Pilot episode**
*Shadows*: 'The Boy Merlin'
**Broadcast:** Wednesday 11/10/78

**Cast:** Ian Rowlands (Merlin), Donald Houston (Dafydd), Rachel Thomas (Myfanwy), Margaret John (Blodwen), Cassandra Harris (Iamena), Archie Tew (Octa)

**Written by** Stewart Farrar from a story by Anne Carlton
**Designer:** Bill Palmer
**Director:** Vic Hughes
**Series Producer:** Pamela Lonsdale

**Series**
**6 episodes** ('Red Dragon, White Dragon'; 'Book of Magic'; 'The Round Table of Destiny'; 'The Tide of Vengeance'; 'A Gathering of Armies'; 'The Lady and The Sword')
**Broadcast:** Mondays 23/4/79 – 11/6/79 (no scheduled episode Bank Holiday 28/5/79)

**Main Cast:** Ian Rowlands (Merlin), Donald Houston (Dafydd), Rachel Thomas (Myfanwy), Margaret John (Blodwen), Bryan Marshall (Iefan), Derek Smith (Grimbald), James Smith (Octa)

**Written by** Stewart Farrar

**Designer:** David Richens
**Producer:** Pamela Lonsdale
**Directors:** Joe Boyer (1, 5), Darrol Blake (2), Vic Hughes (6), 3 and 4 n/k due to *TV Times* strike

## The Danedyke Mystery

A thriller serial with a Reverend detective seems fitting for the Sunday afternoon slot. Septimus Treloar had been the hero of a couple of children's novels by Stephen Chance although this was the only one to be adapted for television.

Reverend Treloar has put his police days behind him until one night his organist Mrs Crowle is attacked by the church ghost – but, as Septimus deduces, what sort of ghost goes round knocking people out? It's thought that the perpetrator may well be after Our Lady's Cup, a religious relic that has been in the church for several centuries. Septimus is confused, however – surely no professional thief would come looking for such an unremarkable piece of silverware unaware that it currently resides in a bank vault? In fact the weasely Major and his burly henchman Armchair are after the long lost golden cup, the original work of art that is much, much older and may well still be hidden somewhere in the church of St Mary's …

A rather sedate piece somewhere between G. K. Chesterton's *Father Brown* and the later ruminations of *Inspector Morse*, this wasn't an obvious choice for a children's/family serial. One major format change from book to screen was the replacing of Tom and Rosemary Horton, a young married couple who help Septimus, with two new young(ish) assistants Angela Horton and Tom Richards. The freer agents were more likely to find identification with younger audience members who would have little interest in such adult ties.

**Granada**
**6 episodes**
(colour)
**Broadcast:** Sundays 3/6/79 – 15/7/79 (no broadcast 1/7/79 due to sports coverage)

**Main Cast:** Michael Craig (Reverend Septimus Treloar), Derek Thompson (Tom Richards), Tessa Peake-Jones (Angela Horton), Kenneth Colley (The Major), John Rhys-Davies (Armchair), Peter Vaughan (Det Insp Burroughs), Fanny Rowe (Mary Crowle)

Based on the novel *Septimus and the Danedyke Mystery* by Stephen Chance (first UK publication 1971, The Bodley Head)
**Adapted by** Willis Hall

**Music:** Alan Parker
**Production Designer:** Chris Wilkinson
**Producer:** Pauline Shaw
**Executive Producer:** Michael Cox
**Director:** Jonathan Wright Miller

**Tie-in publications:** edition of novel published in paperback by Puffin, 1979

## The Enchanted Castle

After the success of the adaptation of E. Nesbit's *The Phoenix and the Carpet* in 1977, a sequel was called for and luckily for the BBC one was to hand in the shape of the author's *The Enchanted Castle*. It certainly bears all the hallmarks of a sequel, however, and is very derivative of its predecessors, the popular Psammead and Phoenix tales.

As before there are four Edwardian children in sailor suits, plus-fours and petticoats who discover wish-granting magic which goes unexpectedly wrong and there's even a scatty maid who gets caught up in the secret, but what *Enchanted Castle* lacks is a charismatic confidant like the Psammead or Phoenix. In this tale the wishes come true rather more mechanically, courtesy of a magic ring. The guest star this time is the splendid castle the children discover in the middle of a lake, shown off in some good location work as well as in an animated title sequence.

There are some value for money set pieces, treading a fine line between imaginative fantasy and outright scares. The visual effects department was stretched by the need to create a host of statues which come to life including all manner of sprites and even a stone brontosaur. Possibly best remembered by those who watched as children were the Ugly-Wuglies – these scarecrow-like creatures, made by the children from broomsticks and old clothes, come to life by the power of the ring, their painted paper faces being one particularly visually arresting image.

**BBC**
**6 episodes** ('A Magic Day'; 'Moon Magic'; 'Magic Life'; 'Magic Journey'; 'Feast of Magic'; 'Magic End')
(colour)
**Broadcast:** Wednesdays 7/11/79 – 12/12/79

Based on the novel by E. Nesbit (first UK publication 1907, Ernest Benn)
**Dramatised by** Julia Jones

**Main Cast:** Candida Beveridge (Cathy), Simon Sheard (Gerald), Marcus Scott-Barrett (Jimmy), Georgia Slowe (Mabel), Diane Mercer (Mademoiselle), Sheila Beckett (Aunt), Gill Abineri (Eliza), Cavan Kendall (Bailiff/Lord Yalding)

**Designers:** John Stout, Chris Pemsel
**Executive Producer:** Anna Home
**Director:** Dorothea Brooking

**Tie-in publications:** editions of novel published in paperback by Puffin, 1979–83

**Above:** four Edwardian children, (l to r) Mabel (Georgia Slowe), Gerald (Simon Sheard), Cathy (Candida Beveridge) and Jimmy (Marcus Scott-Barrett), on another visit to *The Enchanted Castle*.

## Quest of Eagles

When Stefan Kolawski's father dies suddenly, the teenager finds himself thrown into a web of mayhem and intrigue. Fleeing from Poland during the war, Stefan's father took with him an important and immensely valuable treasure of the Polish people. To establish the destiny of the artefact, Stefan must find out what it is and where it's hidden. With the help of his two friends, Jane and Sinckla, Stefan begins a dangerous journey of discovery that sets him at odds with the British and Polish intelligence services and the enigmatic and ever-present Vladek Gora.

A father who wasn't what he seemed. A teenager who is more than just a Geordie schoolboy. A head teacher who used to be a spy for the Polish intelligence agency. A Polish naval officer who is actually a foreign government official, and an apparently distinguished gentleman secretly responsible for the death of many of his own people during the war. It's clear to see that *Quest of Eagles* harbours a  133 multitude of twists and turns. While certainly engaging, one cannot help but feel that the narrative is far too complicated for its target audience. Only the presence of Michael Yeaman and Gina McKee, in the respective roles of teenagers Stefan and Jane, define this as being drama for children.

It's difficult to sympathise with character predicament, especially that of Stefan, due to the emotional detachment demonstrated throughout. When Stefan's father passes away, the boy seems coldly removed and doesn't bat an eyelid later in the story when he is led to believe that the family priest has been murdered while trying to protect him. This ultimately has a detrimental effect on the character's development. Stefan's journey in the story isn't merely that of the search for missing treasure but one of self-discovery, establishing the true identity of his father and thus himself. The decision that will determine the destiny of Poland's lost treasure eventually rests on Stefan's shoulders. On this occasion, though, the effect is lost as the emotionally stunted Stefan makes his decision with comparative ease.

**Tyne Tees**
**7 episodes**
(colour)
**Broadcast:** Mondays 11/11/79 – 23/12/79

**Main Cast:** Michael Yeaman (Stefan), Gina McKee (Jane), Tom Harris (Sinckla), Vladek Sheybal (Priest), Ferdy Mayne (Vladek Gora), Robert Urquhart (Wilson), Michael Williams (Etherington), Milos Kirek (Andrei Beck), Bruce White (Harry)

**Written by** Richard Cooper

**Music** composed by Wilfred Josephs, conducted by Marcus Dods
**Designer:** Ashley Wilkinson
**Producer:** Margaret Bottomley
**Director:** Bob Hird

**Tie-in publications:** novelisation by Richard Cooper published in paperback by Target, 1979

## The Ravelled Thread

There were certain storyline similarities between this and Lucarotti's earlier historical drama *Operation Patch*. A child's father is framed and wrongly imprisoned to disguise a conspiracy that could affect the outcome of a war, while spies and double-crossers can be found at every turn.

This time round the backdrop was Portsmouth, launching point for the colonial forces fighting in the American Civil War. Silas Trumble is the innocent caught up in the plot, a warehouse clerk accused of stealing and thrown in jail. It is up to his daughter Abigail to prove his innocence. She at first appoints a duplicitous solicitor and then turns to a young journalist called Sedgwick, while her most trusted aides are a gang of street urchins led by a boy called Gegor.

Sedgwick begins to uncover the shadowy links between Silas Trumble's boss Higby and landowner Sir Daniel Maundy. Yet Sedgwick is almost too interested in Abigail's case; is he all he seems? Higby and henchman Dobbs soon get nasty and plan to get rid of Abigail and her father. Kidnap and rescue ensue as Abigail gets closer to uncovering a secret army. The climax featured a battle fought with long muskets in the New Forest, that perennial stand-by location for Southern dramas.

There was an interesting piece of casting for this serial. At the age of twenty-seven, fading child star Jack Wild, the Artful Dodger of the 1970 film musical *Oliver!*, once again played the young leader of a group of urchin kids.

Several out-takes from the serial exist courtesy of a videotape engineers' Christmas tape, which also featured a guest appearance from producer/director Chris McMaster atop a horse and dressed as Napoleon!

**Southern**
**6 episodes** ('Accused'; 'The Felon'; 'The Ledger'; 'Kidnapped'; 'The Ship'; 'The Spy')
(colour)
**Broadcast:** Sundays 31/12/79 – 4/2/80

**Main Cast:** Julia Lewis (Abigail Trumble), Robert James (Silas Trumble), Steven Grives (Sedgwick), Jack Wild (Gegor), Mark Wingett (Billyboy), Debby Cumming (Jennie), John Byron (Sir Daniel Maundy), Reginald Marsh (Higby), John Junkin (Dobbs)

**Written by** John Lucarotti

**Designer:** John Newton-Clarke
**Producer/Director:** Chris McMaster

**Tie-in publications:** novelisation by John Lucarotti published in paperback by Puffin, 1979

# 1980s

By the late 70s there was no doubting the excellence of much of the children's drama output from the ITV regions. The BBC is often recalled as the definitive children's service from around this time but ITV productions at least matched those of the BBC on a one-to-one basis. Given the expense of drama it was still a semi-precious commodity and was usually networked among the ITV regions but the patchwork nature of the rest of children's weekday afternoon schedules did its children's service no favours. What the BBC enjoyed was network scheduling and aggregate on-screen publicity which ITV could only counter via the pages of *Look-In*. New BBC series could be trailed on *Blue Peter* or *Multi-Coloured Swap Shop* and then viewed by all of the audience at one time thus helping to build up some kind of momentum.

ITV's programming seemed slipshod – there was too much haphazardly regional gap-filling using back catalogue Gerry Anderson puppet series, for example. The choice of material for children could seem arbitrary, possibly even lazy. Children's hour in some regions could consist of an episode of Irwin Allen's 60s' action series *Land of the Giants*, now 'downgraded' from prime-time to off-peak hours, or reruns of American soap *Little House on the Prairie*. With the addition of one undistinguished cartoon, that constituted the day's viewing. Other evidence of this lackadaisical approach could be seen on Saturday mornings where repeats such as *Batman* would be linked by low budget continuity material in various areas even though the revolutionary *TISWAS* was a phenomenon in the regions lucky enough to see it. A network slot was finally achieved by *TISWAS* in 1979 after five years on air, by which time the BBC's *Multi-Coloured Swap Shop* was already a TV institution.

What was required was a network initiative that would help sell the product of the regions better, without losing any regional distinctiveness or alienating any of the smaller but no less productive suppliers. To this end the Watch It! strand was set up at the end of 1980. In what would today be called a re-branding exercise, network slots were created and an overall umbrella of logo and continuity applied. Better targeted publicity for new shows in *Look-In* was an immediate by-product. The Watch It! brand established, a more concerted and cohesive approach to provision of programming was established between the regions after a conference in July 1981. The service now appeared ready to take on the BBC. Not only was drama well served by the more careful consideration of series across any given year (early output including *Stig of the Dump*, *Brendon Chase* and *Into the Labyrinth*) but new series such as *Dangermouse* and *CBTV Channel 14* also made an immediate impact with children across the country.

One region which would not take much part in the new Watch It! regime was Southern. While the region had done sterling service to build children's drama for ITV since the mid-60s, its other output was deemed lacking and the station closed at the end of

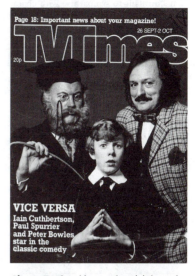

**Above:** *TV Times*' interest in celebrity and lifestyle meant few children's dramas ever made its cover, but Peter Bowles' star status put *Vice Versa* there in 1981.

**Above:** *Look-In* magazine continued to promote children's series into the 1980s, including *Brendon Chase* (top) and *Murphy's Mob* (above) although the publication faced difficult times by the end of the decade.

**Facing page:** teen drama *Maggie* made the front cover of *Radio Times* (top) but big budget fantasies *The Box of Delights* (middle) and *The Lion, the Witch and the Wardrobe* (bottom) really summed up BBC ambition in this decade.

1981. Southern's death was less keenly felt in the arena of children's television than might be expected, with the poaching of the highly experienced Anna Home from the BBC to head up children's output at TVS, the franchise's successor. Outgoing head of Children's at Southern, Lewis Rudd, left for Central and continued his good work there.

The clearest demonstration of improved co-ordination of activity by the ITV regions was the play strand *Dramarama*. Initially seen as a continuation of the semi-educational *Theatre Box*, the *Dramarama* title was first applied to seven episodes of the Thames series *Spooky*, a collection of ghost stories. For the second 1983 run the *Dramarama* strand became a sort of Eurovision Drama Contest for the ITV regions (with ITV the only winner). With Anna Home in nominal charge of the project, regions were invited to submit scripts. Regional producers who could barely afford full-run drama series took advantage of the set-up, with the likes of Scottish and Border contributing over the years. Not only did *Dramarama* allow small regions to develop their drama capability, no doubt acting as a training run for general drama, but it nurtured experimentation and new writing talent. Some episodes were better than others, some were conventional, some brave, but over a near century of episodes and an incredible variety of topics and styles *Dramarama* represented perhaps the ultimate high point of ITV children's drama, maybe even the zenith of any children's drama seen on either channel.

With timing that was surely more than coincidental the BBC launched a similar set of plays in 1982 including one-offs such as *Secrets*, *Billy Boy* and *Thief*. The plays were never scheduled consecutively, however, and lacked an attention-grabbing umbrella title – both factors would no doubt make the plays hard to promote. Single plays continued to be made by the BBC extremely sporadically up until *Billy's Christmas Angels* in 1988.

ITV's successful Watch It! strand gave way to a new identity in 1983 – Children's ITV now linked programmes with chatty asides and plugs for new series by guest presenters. Each host broadcast from a small studio or the deck of a spaceship set for a one-month run. Hosts included Charlotte Coleman in character as Marmalade Atkins, Mike Reid, The Krankies, Roland Rat, *Fraggle Rock*'s Uncle Travelling Matt, Matthew Kelly and Cheryl Baker. The glue of the new branding seemed to hold the viewers – ITV was winning the ratings battle before long. In 1985 the BBC borrowed the idea to great effect and had regular continuity presenters and a procession of puppet co-stars broadcast from a tiny studio known as The Broom Cupboard, beginning with the then unknown Phillip Schofield. Another – less successful – initiative for the Children's Department of the BBC the same year was the launch of *Beeb* magazine in January, intended to rival *Look-In*. Featuring a *Grange Hill* comic strip and new battles with *The Tripods*, among other supposed delights, the magazine ran to only a dozen or so issues.

Another interesting new development for the 80s were the attempts to provide fare for the older teenage audience. One of the hardest audiences to catch has always been the 15–21 age group, usually too busy going out to stay at home and watch television. A lack of scheduling time for a perceived minority audience sector was a particular problem in the days of three channel TV where the more contentious material demanded could become very visible. Channel 4 tried out many new 'Youth' programmes, such as rock show *The Tube*, when it began broadcasting in 1982. Not long after, both BBC and ITV were making inroads into the youth market with new drama series. ITV screened *Murphy's Mob* in the 4.45p.m. slot of Children's ITV, but more difficult to schedule was the Hazel O'Connor pop drama *Jangles*. With its plots concerning teenage violence and delinquency, some regions adjusted their schedules to make way for the series in the 5.15p.m. post-children's slot while others stuck with it in the rather out of place 4.45p.m. slot and one or two even placed it ill-advisedly in the 4p.m. slot usually reserved for the youngest part of the audience.

The BBC meanwhile, with a minority channel readily to hand, opened up a new slot at around 6 o'clock on BBC2. Drama dealing with more awkward teenage issues such as sex, relationships and the difficulties of modern family life came in the shape of *Tucker's Luck* and *Maggie*. Slightly more robust than series in the children's slot would ever be allowed to be, the close proximity to the 'children's hour' nonetheless provoked complaints from parents who felt it appeared a natural extension for that younger audience and this shows how difficult it was to schedule such drama in the early 80s.

Channel 4's prime slots were more minority-focused than other channels and so these were used to air the teenage *Brookside* spin-off *Damon and Debbie* (4/11/87 – 18/11/87). This three-part serial concerned the hardships of Damon Grant (Simon O'Brien) and his girlfriend Debbie McGrath (Gillian Kearney) on the run from the girl's disapproving and overprotective father. The serial ended with Damon fatally stabbed – even *Dramarama* would have found this kind of material hard to screen. Another *Brookside* spin-off, *South*, followed the trials of Tracy Corkhill and boyfriend Jamie seeking their fortune in London (and meeting Morrissey among other events). Again, this was scheduled at an odd hour, eventually going out as some form of social development parable in an *English Programme* schools broadcast (14/3/88 and 21/3/88). Several excellent and hard-hitting 'problem' dramas made for schools and colleges by the BBC had been airing since the 1960s under the *Scene* banner and many could easily have been transferred to more mainstream slots given this new environment but the option has rarely been taken up.

*Maggie*, *Tucker's Luck*, *South* and *Damon and Debbie* are among the series thought to echo most clearly the times of Thatcher's Britain. Topics such as joblessness and a growing class and North/South divide were everyday issues for school-leavers in the early 80s but did such issues really affect children of school age? Certainly dramas like *The Cuckoo Sister*, *Dodgem* and *Stookie* were recognisably set in Thatcher's time but they tended to concentrate on the personal rather than the political. Among the rare examples directly tackling Thatcher's policies head on were a small number of *Dramarama* episodes such as 'The Coal Princess', which viewed the miner's strike from a young girl's perspective, and 'The Macrame Man', which dealt with unemployment in the family.

**Above:** *Grange Hill* was the most popular children's drama in the 1980s. Spin-offs included a short-lived magazine from IPC in 1981 (top). A comic strip also appeared in the BBC's *Beeb* magazine, launched in 1985 (issue 2 pictured above) but the comic lasted only a couple of dozen issues.

Another major aspect that defined the 80s was the coming of the digital age. Technically, the biggest change seen in television drama in the 80s was the almost wholesale changeover to OB videotape from location filming and children's drama was not excluded from this. Early experiments in the genre in the mid to late 70s had included *A Bunch of Fives*, *Warrior Queen* and *Horse in the House*. While video had an economic function, generally allowing crews to get fifteen minutes of footage shot in a day as opposed to five with film, it also allowed for a faster pace. Tape editing and hand-held cameras worked to produce this effect, most clearly seen in the chase drama *Running Scared*. While the choice of location VT for an action piece requiring rapid movement may have seemed an obvious one, tape was also used on lavish fantasy period pieces like *The Children of Green Knowe* and *The Box of Delights*. The use of video for these kinds of production allowed for more seamless integration between raw footage and complicated post-production video effects such as CSO, Quantel and, towards the end of the decade, digital systems like Paintbox and Harry.

It was the expensive *The Box of Delights* that redefined the way children's drama could be made in this decade. Edward Barnes' comment to the press that *Box* would be a feast among the balanced diet of children's television demands scrutiny of the 1984 schedules leading up to *Box*'s screening at the end of the year. This reveals a meagre ration of drama in particular, a famine before the feast as funds were sequestrated and funnelled into production of *Box*. Repeats of *The Monkees* featured heavily, for example, and the number of European imports seemed at its highest since the late 60s.

The funding of *Box* went beyond penny-pinching in other areas, however. The bulk of the backing came via 215 PBS (Public Broadcasting Service) stations in the United States who were canvassed extensively by BBC Enterprises, the commercial sales arm of the corporation, before the serial had been made. This pre-selling of series abroad depends on a sellable and easily communicated big idea and leads inevitably to a dependence on the familiar. In this case what was no doubt being sold was a quaint notion of between-the-wars Englishness, easily imagined from a long line of preceding heritage productions from the UK. Buttered muffins and hot chestnuts are far easier to export than a regional or contemporary series which can also date very quickly, so most British co-productions are in the period vein and were populated by stock upper-class types. It was the sheer scale of the investment required for *Box* – £1 million – that meant there was no comparison with previous modest efforts in internationally co-funded children's drama, which trailed back as far as the early 70s.

Enterprises' real target was *The Chronicles of Narnia* and after several years resolving rights issues the production finally arrived on British screens – and the screens of many other countries besides – bankrolled by the same Enterprises route as *Box of Delights*. After thirty years, Owen Reed's vision of globally aired and funded drama serials from the BBC had come true. By the end of the 80s there was still some room for more regional dramas with more modest aims (*Billy's Christmas Angels* by BBC Bristol or *The Watch House* from BBC Newcastle) but the die was cast at this time and more postcards from the Old Empire would follow in years to come.

It was likely that it was only the American market that kept traditional period drama airing on British screens. The biggest question remains: which was the primary market for these dramas and which was a secondary benefit? *The Chronicles of Narnia* marked a brief return to prominence for the Sunday afternoon literary classic. For the BBC Sunday serials, the 80s was the decade they fell from favour. *The Swish of the Curtain* seemed very dated for 1980 and it was only by a sideways move into classic fantasies that the strand continued at all in efforts like *Pinocchio* (1978), *Gulliver in Lilliput* (1981) and *Alice in Wonderland* (1986). There was a move away from obvious child-friendly material such as *Children of the New Forest* towards more adult material in adaptations of *The Hound of the Baskervilles* (1982) and *H. G. Wells' Invisible Man* (1984). BBC chiefs deemed the latter too frightening for younger audiences and so it was moved into a peak-time weekday slot. ITV fared much better with Saturday evening and Sunday afternoon family fare, carrying on the tradition of period swashbuckling in action series like *Smuggler* (1981), *Dick Turpin* (1979–81) and the glossily mystic *Robin of Sherwood* (1984–86). More adolescent new angles for the ITV Sunday slot came in the shape of *Knights of God* and *Shadow of the Stone* in 1987. In the same year *Vanity Fair* became the last of the teatime Sunday Classics from the BBC Drama Serials department. Thereafter much bigger-budgeted film melodramas, preferably of a romantic nature, designed to air in peak-time slots and sell abroad, became the preferred format. The child audience had been abandoned by Sunday afternoons but in all possibility they had deserted the Sunday serials long before.

The 80s had been a decade of consolidation rather than the rapid change seen in the previous ten years. Ambition had grown but budgetary requirements were rising commensurately. By the close of the decade the power of market forces was changing the old regulated duopoly of television. Satellite loomed; global media powers amassed. The old model of regional production for ITV was slowly being dismantled too. Since the children's market had been served so well by the smaller regions, the coming era of producer choice and independent production houses meant the effects of this break-up were keenly felt.

*Dramarama* seems to have been the first casualty of the changes being wrought in ITV. Several of its later episodes came from independent producers such as KPO and Husson and this can be seen as positive progress of sorts. The downside was that by consisting of extremely disparate stand-alone instalments, *Dramarama* was difficult to schedule and promote. Consistently topical and reflecting its parent regions, it was also difficult to sell in America – packages did air in the US from time to time but were usually sold as 'some off-the-wall stuff from those crazy Brits' and never broadcast in very high profile positions. The increasing power of the larger regions and consolidation of 'network' products, allied to the growing lure of global television, ultimately meant the end for *Dramarama*. Its final episode aired in August 1989 and the strand failed to see out the decade. In the ten years plus since its demise, no similar one-off play strand has come to take its place on either channel.

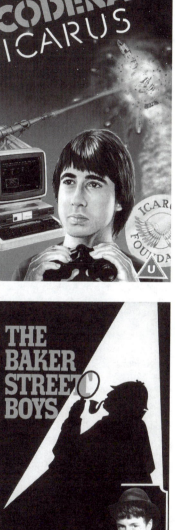

**Above:** the home video market was born in the 1980s. Among the children's dramas released by the BBC were *Codename Icarus* and *The Baker Street Boys*.

## Our John Willie

Times are bad for David Halliday and his deaf and dumb brother John Willie. They have been lucky enough to escape the flood in the pits but their father has been killed. Without a mother and deprived of their pit worker's cottage, the two boys find themselves orphaned and homeless.

They set up temporary shelter in one of the mines and David hopes to earn food at the local workhouse. John Willie, however, is too frail for the hard labour and David only earns one small loaf of bread for a full day's work. The boys are then threatened by the Coxons, a local family who delight in tormenting them because of John Willie's condition, and are forced to flee the mine.

They take refuge in the dilapidated summerhouse of Miss Peamarsh, a strange woman who hides herself away in her manor. David has had unfavourable meetings with the woman on a couple of occasions and therefore expects the worst when she discovers they have been squatting in her grounds. To his amazement Miss Peamarsh allows them to stay in her house so that John Willie can be nursed back to health. Furthermore, David cannot believe his luck when she offers him a wage to run errands and maintain the house. Then, to his horror, he discovers that Miss Peamarsh is being blackmailed by her former gardener, Dan Potter. When David's dog Snuffy unearths human bones in the garden, it seems likely that Miss Peamarsh may well have murdered her brother.

Set in nineteenth-century North England, Catherine Cookson's period story is primarily one of human endurance across the social classes but works equally well as a mystery.

**BBC Birmingham**
**5 episodes**
(colour)
**Broadcast:** Wednesdays 2/1/80 – 30/1/80

**Main Cast:** Antony Manuel (Davy), David Burke (John Willie), Madeleine Cannon (Miss Peamarsh), James Garbutt (Mr Cartwright), Anne Jameson (Mrs Cartwright), Malcolm Terris (Matt Coxon), Ian Mullaney (Jim Coxon), Paul Hanson (Fred Coxon), John Malcolm (Dan Potter), Ian Cullen (Peter Talbot)

Based on the novel by Catherine Cookson (first UK publication 1974, Macdonald & Co.)
**Dramatised by** Valerie Georgeson

**Music:** Howard Blake
**Designer:** Myles Lang
**Executive Producer:** Anna Home
**Director:** Marilyn Fox

**Tie-in publications:** edition published in paperback by Piccolo, 1979

## God's Wonderful Railway

Told as three separate stories, *God's Wonderful Railway* concerns the Grant family who, over several generations, devote their lives to the construction and maintenance of the Great Western Railway line, one of Britain's most famous train lines and now a major tourist attraction.

'The Permanent Way' details the genesis of the Great Western Railway. It is the 1860s and the navvies take over the countryside to begin construction of a new railway line. It is a project that will provide jobs for many people and will ultimately revolutionise the transport of goods and people. Will such change be welcomed with open arms by everyone? Perhaps not, but Robbie Grant is intent on proving that his injured leg will not prevent him from working.

'Clear Ahead' revisits the family in 1906. George Grant is determined that he will work on the railway, following in the footsteps of his grandfather. This involves working for Mr Jellicoe, the intimidating station manager.

'Fire on the Line' concludes the story. In 1939 George Grant has realised his dream and become a station master. It is now the turn of his son Andy to maintain the family tradition and take a job on the railway. As the company prepares for war, Andy soon finds out that there's more to life than trains.

Filmed mostly on location, this drama must have been really exciting for young train enthusiasts. The idea of having the action take place over different eras was an interesting one but the piece was rather slow moving.

**BBC**
**8 episodes** ('The Permanent Way' (2 episodes); 'Clear Ahead' (3 episodes); 'Fire on the Line' (3 episodes))
(colour)
**Broadcast:** Wednesdays 6/2/80 – 26/3/80
(episode 8 on BBC2)

**Main Cast:** 'The Permanent Way': Brian Coburn (Giant), Gerard Kelly (Robbie Grant), Anne Kristen (Martha), Anne Burns (Deborah), Brian Grellis (Spider), Ralph Arliss (Green Eye), Craig Stokes (Rusty), Gorden Kaye (Jem), Max Faulkner (Scarecrow), Eugene Geasley (Shorty), Hugh Dickson (John Fowler), Albert Shepherd (Henry Bridgman)
'Clear Ahead': Ian Sandy (George Grant), Shirley Cain (Jane Grant), John Barrett (Robbie Grant), Roger Hume (Vicar), Dale Bayford (Ted Jarvis), Richard Pearson (Mr Jellicoe), Frank Veasey (Davies), Ralph Lawton (Holmes), Terry Molloy (Fry), Terry Pearson (Harvey)
'Fire on the Line': Andrew Hughes (Andy Grant), Colin Douglas (George Grant), June Brown (Elsie Grant), Annette Ekblom (Marjorie Grant), Phillip Joseph (Geoffrey Green), Bill Dean (Ted Jarvis), Katherine Roberts (Alice Stone)

**Written by** Avril Rowlands

**Designers:** Spencer Chapman ('The Permanent Way'), David Spode ('Clear Ahead' and 'Fire on the Line')
**Executive Producer:** Anna Home
**Producer:** Paul Stone
**Directors:** Fiona Cumming ('The Permanent Way'), John Prowse ('Clear Ahead'), 'Fire on the Line' n/k

**Tie-in publications:** paperback novelisations by Avril Rowlands *The Permanent Way*, *Clear Ahead* and *Fire on the Line* published by BBC, 1980, 1981

## Jukes of Piccadilly

Brinsley Jukes is an old-fashioned English gentleman, rather out of step with the modern world. He is the owner of a fine and exclusive tea emporium in London while indulging his hobby as a private investigator. He is reluctantly assisted on his endeavours by colleague Cromarty.

When Brinsley witnesses a young metal-detecting enthusiast being kidnapped, his investigations involve him with a ruthless gangster, some unpleasant henchmen and buried treasure. Following that, Brinsley is hired by Sheikh Achmed to investigate the disappearance of his niece, Princess Ayallah. Finally, Brinsley is on hand when a convict makes a daring bid for freedom from prison.

This light-hearted piece borrows much of its style from the likes of Sherlock Holmes, simplifying that which is successful as adult drama for a younger audience.

**Thames**
**6 episodes** (3 x 2-part stories) ('The Corcelli Medallion'; 'The Case of the Arabian Kidnap'; 'The Dulverton Green') (colour)
**Broadcast:** Mondays 11/2/80 – 17/3/80

**Main Cast:** Nigel Hawthorne (Brinsley Jukes), Manning Wilson (Cromarty)

**Devised by** Robert Banks Stewart

**Written by** Robert Banks Stewart ('The Corcelli Medallion') and Robert Holmes ('The Case of the Arabian Kidnap'/ 'The Dulverton Green')

**Designer:** Frank Gillman
**Producer:** Ruth Boswell
**Director:** Terry Steel

## The Further Adventures of Oliver Twist

Born in a workhouse and made to work all hours of the day, orphan boy Oliver Twist suddenly finds himself thrown onto the streets after he has the cheek to ask for more food. In desperation he runs away to London only to fall in with a group of thieves led by the villainous Fagin. Dickens's classic novel then details Oliver's escape from the criminal and how he helps bring him to justice.

Although *Oliver Twist* concerns the story of an orphan boy's turbulent adventures in Victorian London, it isn't a children's book *per se*. It has never really been adapted for children's television and has thus far appeared only as a 'Sunday Classic' serial or in feature film format.

This was remedied in 1980 when David Butler brought to fruition an idea first voiced by Hugh Leonard. A few years previously, a gathering of well-known writers had been involved in a Granada Television parlour game and had been asked to create their own sequels to popular classic novels. Butler had been a lifelong fanatic of the works of Charles Dickens and set about creating a sequel that would eventually be broadcast in 1980 as *The Further Adventures of Oliver Twist*.

The narrative picks up where the novel finished. Oliver has successfully escaped Fagin but the boy's past is catching up with him. Attempts are being made to trace Oliver's origins but the double-crossing Noah Claypole has stolen the all-important documents. The evil Monks, Oliver's half-brother, is also on the prowl and plants Mr

Bumble, who has previously made life difficult for the boy, at the school he attends. Monks is determined to get rid of Oliver and get at his money. Luckily the Artful Dodger is on hand to help Oliver but will it be enough to see off Monks and Oliver's greatest enemy, Fagin?

Butler developed the series as a novel in the first instance and then broke it down into thirteen parts. Assistance was on hand from his brother Denis, who scripted two episodes while David was overseas. Denis would appear not to have been credited for his efforts in television listings magazines of the time.

The more conventional 1962 BBC adaptation of Dickens's novel was among the first to be made nominally for children by the main Drama Serials department. It was this adaptation that the frustrated Children's Head Owen Reed criticised for being too dark and potentially disturbing to younger viewers.

***Oliver Twist*** (1962)
**BBC**
**13 episodes**
(b&w)
**Broadcast:** Sundays 7/1/62 – 1/4/62

**Main Cast:** Bruce Rochnik (Oliver Twist), Donald Eccles (Mr Sowerby), Barbara Hicks (Mrs Sowerby), Priscilla Morgan (Charlotte), Alec Foster (Carter), Melvyn Hayes (The Artful Dodger), Max Adrian (Fagin), Alan Rothwell (Charley Bates), Carmel McSharry (Nancy), Peter Vaughan (Bill Sykes)

Based on the novel *Oliver Twist or The Parish Boy's Progress* by Charles Dickens (first UK publication c. 1837)
**Dramatised by** Constance Cox

**Music:** Ron Grainer
**Designer:** Stephen Bundy
**Producer:** Eric Tayler

***The Further Adventures of Oliver Twist*** (1980)
**ATV**
**13 episodes** ('Old Acquaintance'; 'The Plot Thickens'; 'Declarations of War'; 'A Awful Example'; 'Runaway'; 'Penny Hang'; 'A Life on the Ocean Wave'; 'The Climbing Boy'; 'Up, Up and Away'; ''Bye, 'Bye Bumble'; 'Three Card and Thimblerig'; 'Old Flat 'At'; 'Ends and Beginnings') (colour)
**Broadcast:** Sundays 2/3/80 – 1/6/80 (no broadcast 6/4/80)

**Main Cast:** Daniel Murray (Oliver Twist), John Fowler (Artful Dodger), David Swift (Fagin), Bryan Coleman (Mr Brownlow), Derek Smith (Mr Grimwig), Harold Innocent (Mr Bumble), Leonard Preston (Noah Claypole), Geoffrey Larder (Monks), Pauline Quirke (Charlotte), Gary Shail (Ned Fingers)

**Written by** David Butler

**Music:** Syd Amos
**Designers:** Anthony Waller and Quentin Chases
**Producer:** Ian Fordyce
**Executive Producer:** David Reid
**Directors:** Ian Fordyce and Paul Harrison

**Tie-in publications:** novelisation by David Butler published in paperback by Futura, 1980

141

## Noah's Castle

An intelligent drama set in the near future at a time when inflation is such that a mere tin of fish costs £200 and food supplies in general are dwindling. The story follows the fortunes of the Mortimer family as they struggle for survival in an uncomfortable vision of the future.

Norman Mortimer, a shoe shop manager, turns his mansion into a giant food store so that he can support his family through the crisis. Norman is pleased with his initiative and expects his family to feel the same way but his actions serve only to distance him from his wife and children. It becomes apparent that the Mortimer home could be in danger from food hijackers and not everyone in the family agrees with Mr Mortimer's tactics. There are those that feel that he should be helping distribute some of the food to the needy.

Norman is driven purely by his desire to create a perfect lifestyle for his family but in doing so cannot see the bigger picture. May Mortimer is devoted to her husband but finds herself torn between him and the children. Nessie, the eldest daughter, is against everything her father stands for and he resents her association with a boy he considers to be a 'layabout'. Norman's son Barry, from whose viewpoint we see the story unfold, has sympathies towards his friends who are struggling to run a food distribution centre and his father's hoarding of food is abhorrent to him.

Series script editor Tony McLaren was primarily responsible for getting the adaptation on screen, bringing what he considered to be a challenging project to the attention of Lewis Rudd. Both felt that the subject matter was within close enough proximity to reality for the audience to take it seriously, especially as inflation rates had been high for four or five years at that point in time.

**Southern**
**7 episodes** ('The Castle'; 'Unwelcome Visitors'; 'Spies'; 'Discoveries and Threats'; 'Pressure'; 'Departures'; 'Conclusions')
(colour)
**Broadcast:** Wednesdays 2/4/80 – 14/5/80

**Main Cast:** David Neal (Mr Mortimer), Simon Gipps-Kent (Barry Mortimer), Marcus Francis (Geoff Mortimer), Louise Olley (Ellen Mortimer), Annette Ekblom (Nessie Mortimer), Jean Rimmer (Mrs Mortimer), Mike Reid (Vince Holloway), Lee MacDonald (Mel Holloway), Alun Lewis (Terry), Chris Fairbank (Cliff)

Based on the novel by John Rowe Townsend (first UK publication 1975, Oxford University Press)
**Adapted by** Nick McCarty

**Designer:** Greg Lawson
**Executive Producer:** Lewis Rudd
**Producer/Director:** Colin Nutley

**Tie-in publications:** editions published in paperback by Puffin, 1980–85

## The Swish of the Curtain

*The Swish of the Curtain* was perhaps unique in that it was the only drama to have been based on a book written by a child. Pamela Brown was only fourteen when she wrote *The Swish of the Curtain* and so logically it might be supposed that the tale should match exactly the preoccupations, hopes and dreams of the child audience. You'd be wrong, of course, as there are always likely to be problems of realisation.

Certainly at face value *The Swish of the Curtain*, the story of a group of children who start their own theatre company in an abandoned church hall, directly taps into the dream of almost every little girl to go onto the stage, be it as a singer, dancer or actress (though note that this virtually cuts out the boys' half of the audience). What counts against the television version is that it made the small screen almost forty years after the book's first publication.

Overwhelmingly, any memory of the TV adaptation of *The Swish of the Curtain* is of nice kids riding round a little town on bikes and drinking ginger beer in the school hols. It's an accurate recollection but only part of the story. The team behind the drama played up the reluctance of the children's parents to back their offspring's bid for stage success but still it can only fail to have the same refreshing impact that the book and 40s' radio play did in their time – a time when children were still seen and not heard and theatre was a most dubious profession. Young Brown's sheer cheek and send-up of stifling authority is diminished by time.

There are some interesting revisions made to Brown's book in an attempt at relevance. Mr Darwin's discomfort at watching his son dressed in ridiculous clothes and prancing around on stage is a small comment on gender roles: 'Why can't he play rugger like a normal boy?' he asks. Some changes had to be made to cover up Brown's naiveté – a 1980 audience would never have believed that a promising dancer whose career is wrecked by a careless driver could then fall in love with that driver and marry him! Here Mrs Halford walks with a stick after polio robbed her of ballet stardom and so is one of the few parents to encourage her children's ambitions.

Several children's dramas have been criticised for casting precocious 'stage school brats' in central roles – an unfortunate necessity of the genre, surely – and here the problem is amplified when young talents are asked to *play* precocious stage school brats. Amanda Kirby was an experienced young actor with considerable experience in children's TV drama but here she seems to have been encouraged to play the lead in as breathlessly gushing a wide-eyed manner as possible. The boys in the gang meanwhile come across as camp luvvies and really only Sarah Greene, at eighteen, gives a mature and considered performance. Greene became a *Blue Peter* presenter just one month after Pamela Brown and the young cast appeared on the programme to promote their serial; this is usually what *Swish* is remembered for.

*The Swish of the Curtain* was a neat little serial in itself and well made but ultimately, as presented, it was rendered outmoded by the class upheavals of the 60s. Its period setting was probably intended to provide balance with the contemporary-set serials airing at the time but, viewed alongside offerings like *Break in the Sun*, *The Swish of the Curtain* couldn't help looking like a museum piece.

**BBC in association with**
**the Australian Broadcasting Commission**
**4 episodes**
(colour)
**Broadcast:** Sundays 13/4/80 – 4/5/80

**Main Cast:** Amanda Kirby (Lynette Darwin), Dominic Savage (Jeremy Darwin), Sarah Greene (Sandra Fayne), Jayne Stevens (Maddy Fayne), Jamie Cowell-Parker (Nigel Halford), Ashley Knight (Percy 'Bulldog' Halford), Sally Jane Jackson (Viccy Halford), Robert Austin (Mr Darwin), Shirley Dixon (Mrs Darwin), Peter Clay (Mr Halford), Marian Diamond (Mrs Halford), Davyd Harries (Mr Fayne), Jane Briers (Mrs Fayne), Mona Bruce (Mrs Potter-Smith)

Based on the novel by Pamela Brown (first UK publication 1941, Thomas Nelson and Sons)
**Dramatised by** Julia Jones
**Script Editor:** Alistair Bell

**Music:** Paul Reade
**Designer:** Martin Collins
**Producer:** Barry Letts
**Director:** Joan Craft

**Tie-in publications:** revised tie-in edition of novel published in paperback by Knight Books, 1979

## The Latchkey Children

As their name would suggest, the Latchkey Children are left to their own devices. When they discover that their favourite meeting place, an old tree in the play area at the centre of their housing estate, is to be removed and replaced with a modern sculpture they realise that it will leave them nowhere to play other than the streets (although it must be pointed out that why this naturally follows, and what their real problem with losing the tree is, are never explained). The kids therefore decide that they will fight the authority's plans to remove the tree. Despite writing letters of protest and taking the issue to the Houses of Parliament and the Greater London Council, they have little success. However, their luck changes when in Battersea Park they stumble across a Thames Television film crew.

The series demonstrated that children of differing backgrounds can unite to defend a common cause. Froggy has no father and has an uneasy relationship with his mother. While she spends all day working, the boy loses himself in fantasies and daydreams. He thinks about his father a lot and tends to alleviate his frustrations through fighting. Ben, on the other hand, is the only one of the gang who doesn't live in a council flat. Instead he stays in a house in Pimlico and is considered to be a little posh but it doesn't stop him fighting alongside the rest of his friends to save their tree.

The majority of filming was carried out in and around the Churchill Gardens Estate in Pimlico, London – the setting detailed in the original novel.

**Thames**
**6 episodes**
(colour)
**Broadcast:** Mondays 2/6/80 – 7/7/80

**Main Cast:** Bobby Collins (Ben), Indra Ové (Etty), Peter Harrison (Froggy), Nigel Hayward (Goggles), Ian Roberts (Duke)

Based on the novel by Eric Allen (first UK publication 1963, Oxford University Press)

**Adapted by** Stephen Wakelam

**Music:** Michael Storey
**Designer:** Anthony Cartledge
**Producer:** Vic Hughes
**Executive Producer:** Pamela Lonsdale
**Director:** Horace Ové

**Tie-in publications:** tie-in editions published by Oxford University Press (hardback) and Magnet (paperback), 1980

## Maggie's Moor

One woman's memories of her childhood living in a remote farmhouse on Dartmoor during the Second World War. Maggie and her father live in relative seclusion but life for the girl certainly isn't dull. Fending off rivalry at the annual gymkhana, a bomber crashing into the reservoir, a rumour of treasure buried on the moor, a young man who flies birds of prey for sport, and prisoners of war helping on the farm are all memories shared with the viewer. Overall it's a very similar format to the earlier World War I drama *Tom Grattan's War*.

It was Tamar le Bailly's familiarity with horseriding on Dartmoor that would eventually play a significant part in winning her the role of Maggie. A multitude of hopeful applicants had already been auditioned and rejected by series writer and director John King. It was decided to postpone filming until such time as a suitable candidate could be found. King then remembered Bailly, whom he had met nine years previously when her mother had helped on another project.

Location filming took place on Dartmoor and significant steps were taken to deliver period realism on the series. The crew went as far as using the country's last flying Lancaster Bomber, maintained by the Battle of Britain Memorial Flight, in the crashed plane episode. The RAF offered to make just one pass over the reservoir, creating pressure for the cameraman to get the shot right first time.

**Westward**
**7 episodes** ('The Wild Dog'; 'The Thoroughbred'; 'The Unexploded Bomb'; 'The Treasure'; 'The Buzzard Boy'; 'The Intruder'; 'The Italians')
(colour)
**Broadcast:** Wednesdays 25/6/80 – 20/8/80*
*Two-week break in broadcast following episode 4 (23/7/80 and 30/7/80) to accommodate Olympic Games.

**Main Cast:** Tamar le Bailly (Maggie), Norman Bowler (Father), Anthony Coaker (David), June Barrie (Narrator)

**Written by** John King

**Designer:** David Drewery (1), Chris Cook (2–7)
**Producer/Director:** John King

## Watch All Night

John Foster took his inspiration from the classic novel *So Long At The Fair* when commissioned to write *Watch All Night*. The story was based on a real-life disappearance and made into a feature film in 1949. The film focuses on an English girl who travels to the Paris World Fair with her 143 brother Johnny. Soon after their arrival, Johnny disappears. There is no evidence to suggest that he ever stayed at the hotel and the staff deny all knowledge of him. It eventually transpires that the authorities believe that Johnny is carrying the bubonic plague and abduct him, conspiring with the hotel staff to cover up his disappearance.

The very similar *Watch All Night* follows seventeen-year-old Tess Eveling as she tries to find her missing father when he vanishes from a London hotel room. The room in which he was staying is suddenly labelled private while hotel staff tell Tess they have no recollection of her father. When Tess reports the incident to the police they are naturally sceptical. The mystery deepens when Ingrid, a young chambermaid, disappears after warning Tess she is in danger.

The bubonic plague aspect of the original novel is missing from *Watch All Night*. Tess' father is a nuclear scientist and is kidnapped by the intelligence service of a foreign nation intent on discovering the latest secrets.

The series was developed under the working title *Thin Air* but producer Pauline Shaw later proposed that they use a title connected with a nursery rhyme, in the same way that *So Long At The Fair* had been taken from the famous rhyme 'Oh Dear What Can the Matter Be'. Shaw eventually settled on *Watch All Night*, taken from the last verse of 'London Bridge is Falling Down'.

### Granada

**7 episodes** ('Night People'; 'Room 13'; 'Cover Up'; 'The Passenetti File'; 'Left Luggage'; 'On the Brink'; 'Web')
(colour)
**Broadcast:** Sundays 10/8/80 – 21/9/80

**Main Cast:** Lucinda Bateson (Tess Eveling), Robert Longden (Max), Paul Ratcliffe (Dr Gerald Buscombe), Ahmed Khalil (Colonel Ferrata), Souad Faress (Xenia), Tony Alleff (Vogler), Alkis Kritikos (Durgnat), Tony Caunter (Det Sgt Coveney), Peter Halliday (Insp Miller), Johnny Shannon (Walters)

**Written by** John Foster

**Music:** Dave Wootton/Doug Wooton (both names given in *TV Times*)
**Designer:** Chris Wilkinson
**Producer:** Pauline Shaw
**Director:** Richard Martin

**Tie-in publications:** novelisation published in paperback by Puffin, 1980

## The Squad

*The Squad* focuses on the trials and tribulations of a group of young cadets making their way through police training college. During the course of their tuition, the cadets are taught many lessons about the society they live in.

Performing some community work opens the eyes of the cadets when they become involved in assisting an elderly lady tackle a confidence trickster. Alan Martin spends some time working in an intermediate treatment centre. His task is to prevent a youngster from committing further offences. Will he have the communication skills he requires to influence the boy round to his way of thinking? Sandra learns the risks of policing when she agrees to act as a decoy in a major crime. George Booker must deal with

the potential consequences when his younger brother is accused of stealing. Jogger Cummins takes on the responsibility of coaching a young five-a-side football team. How will he react when his training methods upset the team's best player before an important match? Before all of that, the cadets are given a taste of real police work, joining the search for a missing child. The series also incorporated sexual equality, following the progress of female cadets.

The recorded view from one real-life police cadet was less than enthusiastic. Seventeen-year-old Ian Black reviewed it, saying that the series 'gives people the impression that the cadets are under a military regime, which they aren't. The staff in the series don't appear to have any sympathy with the cadets and it also makes it look as though there are only twenty or so cadets in the Metropolitan force!'

### Thames

**10 episodes** ('New Boys'; 'Search'; 'Recruits'; 'Rip Off'; 'Elizabeth'; 'Wheels'; 'Decoy'; 'Mates'; 'The Big Match'; 'Hit and Run')
(colour)
**Broadcast:** Wednesdays 1/10/80 – 17/12/80

**Main Cast:** Max Hafler (George Booker), Mark Botham (Alan Martin), Nicholas Cook (Jogger Cummins), Claire Walker (Elizabeth Maxwell), Yvette Harris (Sandra Henley), Tammi Jacobs (Judy Banks), Leon Eagles (Sgt Lewis)

**Written by** John Kershaw (1–4), Paula Milne (5), Roy Russell (6), Simon Masters (7), William Humble (8), Barry Purchese (9), James Follett (10)

**Music:** Ravid Rohl and S. J. Wolstenholme
**Designers:** Jim Nicolson (1, 4, 7), Philip Blowers (2, 3, 5, 6, 8–10)
**Producer:** Pamela Lonsdale
**Directors:** Vic Hughes (1, 7), Paddy Russell (2, 5, 8, 9), Neville Green (3), Brian Lennane (4), Richard Bramall (6), Michael Kent (10)

## A Little Silver Trumpet

When Alison Jessop's father dies, her life changes dramatically. Without an income, she and her mother must relinquish their cottage by the sea and live instead in a dirty London tenement block – a different and difficult life for both of them.

Jim Ashburn, a friend of Mrs Jessop's husband, has entrusted Mrs Jessop with a tin box containing his life savings, fifty pounds. The money is stolen but at the same time Mrs Jessop finds what she believes to be a five pound note stitched into the hem of a petticoat. Her poor eyesight doesn't reveal to her that it is a fifty pound note. When she tries to spend the money at a shop, the shopkeeper becomes suspicious and brings in the police. Mrs Jessop is arrested for theft. Jim speaks up on her behalf but Mr Cleaver, who doesn't like the Jessops, damns her and the judge rules that Mrs Jessop should be put on trial. When Cleaver's son Johnnie discovers his father is responsible for the theft, his loyalties are divided and he is left with a very difficult decision to make.

It is unlikely that *A Little Silver Trumpet* would have been dramatised had it not been for the intervention of an elderly lady from Clitheroe, Lancashire. Helen Garnett wrote to the BBC telling them how much she had enjoyed previous dramas like *The Moon Stallion* and suggested a favourite book she thought would be ideal for adaptation. The book had been out of print for some time but nonetheless Anna Home recognised its potential. The dramatisation that followed led to L. T. Meade's charming novel being revised and reissued. Miss Garnett must have been amazed at what could be achieved with a letter and the price of a stamp.

**BBC**
**5 episodes**
(colour)
**Broadcast:** Wednesday 19/11/80 – 17/12/80

**Main Cast:** Siobhan O'Carroll (Alison Jessop), Ian Land (Johnnie Cleaver), Merelina Kendall (Mrs Jessop), Ron Pember (Mr Cleaver), Patsy Byrne (Mrs Cleaver), Norman Bowler (Jim Ashburn), Peter Clapham (Enoch Jessop), Zoe Cleveland (Bess), Nicholas Davies (Jos), Pamela Mant (Cook)

Based on the novel by L. T. Meade (first UK publication 1885)
**Dramatised by** Julia Jones

**Designer:** Ray London
**Executive Producer:** Anna Home
**Directors:** Dorothea Brooking (1, 3, 5), Michael Kerrigan (2, 4)

**Tie-in publications:** novelisation of Jones' television script by Thea Bennett published in hardback by BBC, 1980. Paperback published by BBC/Knight, 1982.

## The Bells of Astercote

A lost village wiped out by the Black Death centuries earlier, ghostly church bells pealing in the overgrown forest, a ragged man who claims to be from 600 years in the past ... *The Bells of Astercote* sets itself up as a delightful fantasy for the Christmas period.

Mair and Peter Jenkins are two children who have recently moved to the village of Charlton Underwood. One day, out walking in a dense forest, they stumble across Goacher, a man whom the superstitious villagers believe is the guardian of the lost village of Astercote. He holds Astercote's ancient chalice, thought to keep Underwood safe. When one day it goes missing and Goacher himself disappears, the villagers begin to fall ill. District Nurse Evadne Fletcher diagnoses mumps but the villagers believe it to be the bubonic plague returned from Astercote.

The villagers cut themselves off from the nearby towns and villages, barricading themselves in and sealing off through roads. Before long, outsiders try to pass through and the people of Underwood begin to arm themselves against intruders. Mair and Peter realise that the only hope for peace is to find Goacher and the chalice.

This is where the drama takes on an unexpectedly rational turn, most unlike children's fiction. The chalice has been stolen by a member of a motorcycle gang and the children manage to retrieve it and round up the bad guy. The Bells of Astercote are not heard again and we never visit Astercote itself or meet any ghostly villagers. By the end of proceedings we believe Goacher is just a harmless old fruitcake. This is where the piece is strangely out of step with the genre; more usually children's drama will take

fantasy and run with it. The later *Secret World of Polly Flint*, for example, takes the same basic premise and plays it as 'honest' fantasy. *Bells of Astercote* instead trades in plain old superstition and the simmering and more concrete tension of impending violence as the villagers prepare to repel invaders.

The one-off drama was filmed over four weeks in woodland near the seaside town of Porlock, Somerset.

**BBC**
**1 episode**
(colour)
**Broadcast:** Tuesday 23/12/80

**Main Cast:** Siobhan Brooks (Mair Jenkins), Ifor Williams (Peter Jenkins), John Branwell (Goacher), Janis Winters (Evadne Fletcher), Richard Hunter (Luke Tranter), Ivor Roberts (Mr Tranter), Kristine Howarth (Mrs Tranter), Alison Rolfe (Betsy Tranter), David Harries (Mr Jenkins)

Based on the novel by Penelope Lively (first UK publication 1970, William Heinemann Ltd)
**Dramatised by** Valerie Georgeson

**Designer:** John Bone
**Executive Producer:** Anna Home
**Director:** Marilyn Fox

**Tie-in publications:** n/k

## Brendon Chase

This epic period adventure charts the story of the Hensman boys, three brothers spending their summer holiday away from boarding school at the country house of their spinster aunt. To escape the confines of her house, Robin, John and Harold run away to become outlaws in the forest of Brendon Chase. Their aunt enlists the help of the Reverend Whiting and Police Sergeant Bunting to find the children and soon, when news of the missing children spreads, intrepid reporter and aviator Monica Hurling joins the search in her biplane.

The boys' harsh journey lasts for at least a couple of months, with summer passing into autumn towards the end of the story. The children must forage for food from the local village, deal with a bear at large in the forest and avoid their aunt's search parties.

Location filming for the series took place mainly in the New Forest and the scenes set in the village of Brendon were shot in Porchester, Hampshire. The yellow lines on roads were covered with peat, front doors were painted sombre tones and television aerials were removed from roofs to recreate the 1925 setting.

**Southern**
**13 episodes** ('The Getaway'; 'Gone to Ground'; 'The Planet'; 'The Hunt'; 'The Nest'; 'Bang'; 'Brendon'; 'The Blind Pool'; 'The Picnic'; 'The Mighty Caliban'; 'Retreat'; 'The Storm'; 'Run to Earth')
(colour)
**Broadcast:** Wednesdays 31/12/80 – 25/3/81

**Main Cast:** Craig McFarlane (Robin), Howard Taylor (John), Paul Erangey (Harold), Rosalie Crutchley (Aunt Ellen), Christopher Biggins (Reverend Whiting), Michael Robbins (Sgt Bunting), Liza Goddard (Monica Hurling), Paul Curran (Smokoe Joe)

Based on the novel by 'BB' (first UK publication 1944, Hollis and Carter)
**Adapted by** James Andrew Hall

**Title music** composed by Paul Lewis, played by James Galway
**Designer:** Greg Lawson
**Executive Producer:** Lewis Rudd
**Producer/Director:** David Cobham

**Tie-in publications:** edition of novel published in paperback by Magnet, 1980

## Barriers

A convoluted, slightly prolonged conspiracy thriller which followed seventeen-year-old public schoolboy Billy in his quest for identity. Billy's life is turned upside down the day he learns his parents have been killed in a sailing accident. He is taken under the wing of family solicitor Vincent Whitaker who confides to him that the Stanyons were his adoptive parents. Thus begins Billy's search for his real parents – if they are still alive.

Billy's journey and the twisting storyline take in several one-off strands, such as Billy becoming caught up in a student demonstration and befriending a runaway girl, but mostly concerns the hunt for his parents. He travels to London to trace his mother, next on to Scotland on learning that his father was a Hungarian once married to a Scottish heiress and then on to France where he meets Giselle, who played in an orchestra with his mother. By the end of this season, viewers were not much the wiser and the first run ended inconclusively with Billy off to Salzburg, Austria, in an attempt to join Dr Jolland's Academy of Music. Most of the locations visited by Billy were genuine – the series was filmed in North East England, Scotland, Germany and Austria. The first series was thought worthy of a gold medal in the Children's Drama section at the International Television Festival of New York.

Season Two was more of an out-and-out spy caper as Billy got closer to the truth. Mostly filmed in Austria (although returning to Billy's native Northumbria on occasion) this shorter run saw Billy and his girlfriend Julie caught up in intrigue while attending the Music Academy. First, family friend Hilde Gruber is killed in a car crash all too similar to the one which Billy has learned supposedly killed his parents. Next he receives a letter, purporting to be from Gruber herself; then the sinister Konrad tries to sabotage Billy's boat and kill the boy. One day someone turns up at the restaurant where Billy is working as a waiter and asks for Jerri Toth – the name of his dead father ...

**Tyne Tees**
**2 seasons**
(colour)

**Main Cast:** Benedict Taylor (Billy Stanyon), Paul Rogers (Vincent Whitaker), Patricia Lawrence (Miss Price), Laurence Naismith (Dr Jolland), Sian Phillips (Mrs Dalgleish)

**Written by** William Corlett

**Music:** David Haslam
**Designer:** Ashley Wilkinson
**Deviser/Producer:** Margaret Bottomley

**Season One**
**13 episodes**
**Broadcast:** Sundays 4/1/81 – 29/3/81

**Additional Cast:** Brigitt Horney (Elsa Gruber), Ursula Lingen (Hilde Gruber), Jennifer Daniel (Charlotte McIntyre), Robert Urquhart (Stanley McIntyre), Robert Addie (Spike), Natasha Parry (Giselle), Nicholas Courtney (Henri Beauvoir), Alyson Spiro (Mags)

**Directors:** Bob Hird (1–5, 10, 11, 13), Tony Kysh (6–9, 12)

**Season Two**
**7 episodes**
**Broadcast:** Sundays 10/1/82 – 21/2/82

**Additional Cast:** Julia Lewis (Julie Underwood) Christoph Lindert (Gunter Walser), Siegfried Rauch (Konrad Spetz), Robert Coyle (Jim)

**Directors:** Tony Kysh (1, 2, 5), Bob Hird (3, 4, 6, 7)

## Break in the Sun

This serial began life as an idea about the Thames and what a wonderful means of escape it could offer. Writer Bernard Ashley initially thought in terms of a cops and robbers adventure novel but by the time it reached the page the escape had become spiritual as well as physical. A television adaptation appeared the following year.

Patsy Bligh was the girl running away – her stepfather Eddie was a bad-tempered layabout. Sometimes he would hit her and other times she merely lived in fear of the next smack awarded for nothing. Eddie caused her such distress that she would wet the bed. We only glimpse something of Patsy's Deptford tower block life in the first episode but it's enough to shock and get the point across. Patsy dreams of the good times, when she and her mum lived with old Mrs Broadley in Margate, the times before Eddie Green. Margate seems so far away to young Patsy until one day a group of travelling actors arrive on the canal in their barge. She connives to go with them and so begins the search for Mrs Broadley and that safe old house.

The middle passage of *Break in the Sun* is very traditional – several children's adventure stories take place on slow-moving barges in idyllic summers. The action centres around Patsy's efforts to stay one step ahead of her stepfather who is always catching up, with the unwilling aid of her friend Kenny. The travelling theatre company, all very middle-class liberal sorts, diffuse the fear of the earlier episodes but, rather than turn it into a nice, cosy piece, they are there to show Patsy another side of life so far removed from her own. It's the terror of knowing what would happen if Patsy is caught before reaching Margate or her real identity is discovered that powers the middle episodes along.

The climax comes when Patsy, knowing Eddie cannot be far behind, reaches Mrs Broadley's house in Margate, only to discover the brutal truth that the old lady has died. Patsy's nostalgic memories are just that. She keeps running but where is her answer now? Finally cornered at the top of a high fairground ride by Eddie Green, Patsy faces two options. To jump the narrow gap to a nearby ride and risk falling to her death in the process or to go back to Eddie. A remorseful Eddie promises to try again and she climbs back down to him. The subtext: only by facing up to problems can there be real resolution – running away will solve nothing. A break in the sun is all too easily achieved but permanent change takes something more.

An adventure serial essentially, then, but one which dealt in real psychological danger and fear within both of its protagonists. As important as Patsy's own terror is Eddie's trying to come to terms with his own violence and the violent upbringing that caused it. *Break in the Sun* was almost certainly the toughest serial made for children by the BBC up to that point. What makes it so affecting is that the dramatic threat comes not from a bank robber or smuggler but from within an unstable family unit.

**BBC**
**6 episodes**
(colour)
**Broadcast:** Wednesdays 11/2/81 – 18/3/81

Based on the novel by Bernard Ashley (first UK publication 1980, Oxford University Press)
**Dramatised by** Alan England

**Main Cast:** Nicola Cowper (Patsy Bligh), Brian Hall (Eddie Green), Kevin Taffurelli (Kenny Granger), Catherine Chase (Sylvia Green), Brian Peck (Joe), Lindsey Walker (Jenny), Steve Hodson (Pete), Patsy Rowlands (Mrs Granger), Shirley Dixon (Ruth), Bob Mason (Bob)

**Designer:** Peter Blacker
**Executive Producer:** Anna Home
**Director:** Roger Singleton-Turner

**Tie-in publications:** editions of novel published in paperback by Puffin, 1981–88

## Maggie

'She's a rebel of course/ She's a rebel of sorts ...' suggested the theme song to *Maggie* and indeed Glasgow girl Maggie McKinley wasn't your usual surly teenager. While Maggie rebelled against her upbringing it was only in a positive, aspirational way. Her working-class parents expected her to leave school, find a regular job in a shop or factory, get married and settle down with some nice man but Maggie had broader horizons – university, the independent life and a career were the dreams for this modern girl.

'I dislike the label Women's Lib but I suppose it fits,' commented the series' writer, Joan Lingard. Maggie was no selfish proto-Thatcherite however. She loved her Granny and looked after her family and indeed much of the first season centred on Maggie's efforts to convince her father to set up a plumbing business.

Elsewhere, while the series was certainly realistic and plausible, it was never too 'gritty' with a capital 'G' and Maggie's cheerful resourcefulness usually shone through. Maggie's boyfriend troubles involved clashes of class – her posh Edinburgh boyfriend James was an extension of

**Above:** Patsy Bligh (Nicola Cowper) runs away from her stepfather Eddie Green, hoping for a *Break in the Sun* but finds herself pursued to the funfair at Margate.

Maggie's aspirational nature which led to family friction and questions of identity for Maggie. Meanwhile teenage pregnancy became an issue when Maggie's friend Catriona fell pregnant and arranged a shotgun wedding. The latter subject would almost certainly not have been tackled in the usual pre-teatime children's slot but post-6p.m. on BBC2 was now specifically aimed at teenage audiences and *Maggie* was the first drama to air there.

The series had been adapted by Lingard from her own series of four novels; she commented at the time, 'I could never have settled on anyone to translate the words.' Lingard thoroughly reworked her own books as only the original writer would dare, taking a free hand with chronology but retaining all of the central characters and themes.

The series was very much a regional product (despite its English directors) and was one of the first to capture effectively the sights and sounds of Glasgow (this was before STV's detective Taggart began his beat). It seemed part of that new cultural belief and character which had begun in Scottish Fringe Theatre in the 70s and eventually found mainstream success with Bill Forsyth's film *Gregory's Girl* in 1981. Indeed Gregory's Girl herself, Dee Hepburn, played Maggie's friend Isobel. Scots pop success B. A. Robertson meanwhile penned and sung the series' wistful and witty theme song.

The audience were not privy to the outcomes of the big choices that faced Maggie at the end of the second series: to attend university or help with the family business, 147 whether to stay with James or leave him. The show ended there, to be replaced by the adventures of a London teenager in a similar predicament when *Tucker's Luck* aired the following year.

**BBC Scotland**
**2 seasons**
(colour)

**Main Cast:** Kirsty Miller (Maggie McKinley), Mary Riggans (Mrs McKinley), Michael Sheard (Mr McKinley), Ian Michie (James Fraser), Dee Hepburn (Isobel), Maureen Beattie (Cathy), Anne Berry (Jean McKinley), Paul Ferry (Sandy McKinley), Joe Mullaney (Mike Bruce), Ann Scott-Jones (Jessie), Jean Faulds (Granny), David Ashton (Mr Fraser), Margo Croan (Mrs Fraser), Jane Garven (Catriona Fraser), Robin Cameron (Neil – Season Two only)

Based on the four novels by Joan Lingard: *The Clearance*; *The Resettling*; *The Pilgrimage*; *The Reunion* (first UK publication 1974–77, Hamish Hamilton)
**Adapted by** Joan Lingard

**Theme Music:** B. A. Robertson

**Season One**
**9 episodes**
**Broadcast:** Tuesdays and Thursdays 17/2/81 – 17/3/81 BBC2 6.15p.m.

**Designer:** Helen Rae
**Executive Producer:** Anna Home
**Directors:** Renny Rye (1–5, 7), Michael Kerrigan (6, 8, 9)

**Season Two**
**9 episodes**
**Broadcast:** Mondays 8/3/82 – 3/5/82 BBC2 with a variety of starting times between 5.45p.m. and 6.15p.m. (also note that this season was preceded by a full repeat of the first, and *Radio Times* listed the conjoined run as a series of 18 episodes)

**Producer:** Kenny McBain
**Director:** Michael Kerrigan

**Tie-in publications:** editions of Lingard's four novels published in paperback by Beaver, 1981. Omnibus of first three novels *Joan Lingard's Maggie* published in hardback by Hamish Hamilton, 1982.
*Radio Times* cover for 6/3/82 – 12/3/82.

## Echoes of Louisa

In 1876 the Hallam family experience misfortune and are forced to retreat from their socialite life in London to quieter surroundings in the country. Their soldier son Antony has returned from service abroad but having been caught courting a Prince's lady friend his discharge has been less than honourable, bringing what his strict father considers to be shame on the family. Fifteen-year-old Louisa Hallam is however overjoyed to discover that her brother is returning home.

So that Louisa is spared a lonely education, another girl,

Allegra, is brought to Thornaby to be her companion. Despite the fact that Allegra does no wrong, Louisa intensely dislikes the girl. Especially jealous of any time given to Allegra by Antony, she begins to treat the girl in the most callous manner, determined to be rid of her.

More than 100 years later, 1981, and Roger Burr is taking his wife, Fran, and his two children, Allie and Shaun, on an Easter excursion. Their destination is old Rutland, near the historic Thornaby Hall, where he is to engage upon some historical research. While exploring the grounds, Allie hears laughter coming from the deserted stables. It's the first in a series of events that leads Allie to believe that the Hall is haunted. It quickly transpires that the house isn't truly haunted and that Allie, a modern-day double of Allegra, is in fact witnessing real-life events from the Victorian era unfold in front of her. Louisa concocts a plan to sabotage Antony and Allegra's secret assignation but it goes terribly wrong, leaving Allie the unwilling witness to a catastrophe.

The most striking aspect of this drama is the scale and intensity of Louisa's relentless hatred. In the final meeting at the quarry, it is clear that Louisa intends to at least do Allegra some sort of damage, if not kill her. In the end it is Louisa who is killed when she loses her balance and falls into the quarry, bringing to a close a sometimes unsettling take on a familiar story. Its stars were two of the most prolific teenage actresses of the time, Amanda Kirby (*The Clifton House Mystery*, *The Swish of the Curtain*) and Lucinda Bateson (*Metal Mickey*, *Watch All Night*).

**ATV**
**6 episodes** ('The Homecoming'; 'The Meeting'; 'The Secret'; 'The Ride'; 'The Trip'; 'The Quarry')
(colour)
**Broadcast:** Wednesdays 1/4/81 – 6/5/81

**Main Cast:** Amanda Kirby (Louisa Hallam), Lucinda Bateson (Allie Burr/Allegra), Bernard Horsfall (Roger Burr), Judith Bruce (Fran Burr), Simon Sheard (Shaun Burr), Phyllida Hewat (Miss Craddock), Jeremy Nicholas (Antony Hallam)

**Written by** Gail Renard

**Designer:** Jill Oxley
**Executive Producer:** David Reid
**Producer/Director:** David Dunn

**Tie-in publications:** novelisation by Gail Renard published in paperback by Beaver, 1981

## Into the Labyrinth

Broadcast in an early evening timeslot by its parent region, this was intended as a 'family serial' by HTV but for the rest of the ITV network it formed an important part of the early Watch It! schedules. International star Ron Moody took top billing, sounding HTV's intent. A family serial is about more than timeslot, however, and with all the best will in the world the storylines on offer weren't really multi-layered enough for a broader audience.

Rothgo was the immortal sorceror who held the Nidus, Belor the wicked sorceress who tried to wrest it from him. Executive producer Patrick Dromgoole saw this as following in the epic Arthurian tradition of Merlin versus Morgan Le Fay. It was Moody's imposing performance as

**Above:** the original cast of *Into the Labyrinth* take a rare trip out of the Labyrinth for this outdoor publicity shot; (l to r) Belor (Pamela Salem), Helen (Lisa Turner), Phil (Simon Beal), Terry (Simon Henderson) and Rothgo (Ron Moody).

the pale and dark-eyed Rothgo, a seemingly ambivalent goody, that helped make this notion of total good against total evil almost compelling. Pamela Salem, as the sexy Belor (the unmistakable sign of HTV trying to catch the dads of the family) saw herself as a sorceress: 'Sorceress is a much stronger word than witch – witch makes it sound like pantomime.' The black winged costumes, outrageous hand movements and constant cackling laughter, it must be said, meant Belor indeed flew very close to the latter.

In all three of its seasons *Into the Labyrinth* followed a quest or 'Maguffin' structure, with the search for the Nidus (and later the Scarabeus) providing the impetus for as many adventures as required until the last episode hove into view. The format allowed trips to anywhere in time and space but squandered this huge flexibility by being extremely formulaic in episode structure. Each week the young leads would travel through the Labyrinth to a new destination in search of the Nidus, where they would have to find another incarnation of Rothgo. Belor would have tracked them down and, usually heavily disguised, she too would seek the power source. Somewhere in the story there would be a treasure of sorts and among it a shiny object that was the Nidus in disguise. In the closing moments of the episode the Nidus would be uncovered, only for Belor to make her appearance and scream, 'I deny you the Nidus!' – at which point it would shoot off into time and space and another, very similar, episode. To be fair, there was probably some reassuring satisfaction for the young viewer in recognising and 'second-guessing' these motifs.

The repetitive nature of the series was reinforced by the limited resources available. Aside from a few minutes of filmed location material at the very beginning and end of each season, the entire series was made in standing cave sets. Each week the dressers would do their best to disguise this fact but a feeling of *déjà vu* persisted as the

heroes ran up and down the same claustrophobic polystyrene tunnels *ad infinitum*. The end credits proclaimed 'Cave interiors filmed at Cheddar' but this must have been wishful thinking as it in fact only referred to the spooky opening title sequence.

The mighty Labyrinth itself was less than impressive, standing a full six inches high and in clear danger of being trodden on by our young adventurers. If that was the reality, the fantasy was that the Labyrinth was 'a place where fact and fable mingle' allowing Phil, Helen and Terry to meet characters from history, legend and fiction. With the historical pieces there was a strong tendency to accuracy and research, lending an educational aspect to the production. Several stories were at pains not to confuse true historical figures with their mythical counterparts, so that the children met Robin, Earl of Loxley, and not 'Robin Hood' and it is Robert Catesby who is the ringleader of the Gunpowder Plot and not poor Guido Fawkes. The efforts at 'edutainment' are largely foiled however by the maverick approach to mixing the different strands. Sometimes it will be made clear that, for example, Long John Silver is a fictional character, but by and large it is impossible to tell whether the tale of the Alamo has any greater veracity than that of the Minotaur at Knossos.

Having met her ultimate demise a second time, Belor returned with even bigger hair in a 'same but different' third series to face Phil and a new magician fighting for good. Lazlo, played by comic kids' presenter Chris Harris, was always mixing up his spells and calling Phil 'John' for intended comedic effect. A weak attempt at upping the

149

ante saw Phil and Lazlo fighting to retain the Scarabeus gem in order to cure them of a green slime that was spreading through their bodies. The titular Labyrinth itself was in fact absent in this final series – now Phil and Lazlo travelled the vortex of Delta Time, whatever that was, but always ended up in an underground cavern all the same.

The final season is often derided as one of cheap laughs but while there were two initial comic episodes and some inappropriate moments, many other instalments told intelligent tales of well-researched history. What was really lacking was the sense of grandeur often present in the first two series. One never sensed that the destiny of the universe was at stake this time round. When the series went back to its Arthurian source for the final episode it could only succeed in pitting the ravishingly wicked Belor/Morgana against a Lazlo/Merlin rendered as a blundering, silly-voiced wizard in a pointy hat.

'I shall return!' shrieked Belor as she turned into a putrefying corpse at the end of the series but despite her amazing powers of recovery not even she could bring back *Into the Labyrinth* for a fourth run.

**HTV West**
**3 seasons**
(colour)

**Main Cast (Series I and II):** Ron Moody (Rothgo), Pamela Salem (Belor), Simon Beal (Phil), Lisa Turner (Helen), Simon Henderson (Terry)

**Devised by** Bob Baker and Peter Graham Scott
**Story Editor:** Bob Baker

**Series I and II**
**Music:** Sidney Sager
**Designer:** John Reid
**Executive Producer:** Patrick Dromgoole
**Producer and Director:** Peter Graham Scott

**Series I**
**Broadcast:** Wednesdays 13/5/81 – 24/6/81 4.45p.m. (6.30p.m. in HTV West and Wales)

**Episode One**
'Rothgo' by Bob Baker
Terry and sister Helen are out playing near a plain of stones when they bump into another boy called Phil – the three hear a strange voice calling them. In a cavern they find immortal sorcerer Rothgo, trapped in rock by his arch enemy, Belor. They must free him and track down the Nidus, source of his power, by traversing time and space in the Labyrinth. There they will meet Rothgo in a variety of guises down the ages.

**Episode Two**
'The Circle' by Andrew Payne
The children travel back to the time of the Druids where they must find Rothgo and call his name. Only then will he recall his true identity and assume his powers. Belor is there too, disguised as a handmaiden, ready to deny them the Nidus.

**Episode Three**
'Robin' by Anthony Read
The children meet a down-on-his-luck Robin of Loxley, known to them as the legendary Robin Hood.

**Episode Four**
'Masrur' by Andrew Payne
Rothgo is the Grand Vizier in an Arabian adventure. Whose wishes will be granted by the Genie of the Lamp?

**Episode Five**
'Conflict' by Ray Jenkins
Rothgo is now a vagabond player at the time of Oliver Cromwell.

**Episode Six**
'Revolution' by Ray Jenkins
The children find themselves in a subterranean church in Revolutionary France, with Rothgo now a dandified aristocrat.

**Episode Seven**
'Minotaur' by Anthony Read
A return to the very first labyrinth at Knossos built by Daedalus – who, it transpires, was an early incarnation of Rothgo – and a climactic battle for the Nidus. Belor is destroyed and the children returned to their own time, although they will remember nothing of their adventures.

**Series II**
**Broadcast:** Mondays 3/8/81 – 21/9/81 4.45p.m. (Tuesdays 4/8/81 – 22/9/81 at 6.30p.m. in HTV West and Wales)

**Episode One**
'The Calling' by Bob Baker
Belor rises again from a primeval swamp to torment Rothgo. He enlists the three children to try and take hold of Belor's new power source, the Albedo. But instead, following a skirmish in the land of the Norse Gods, Belor scatters the Nidus into five segments which the children must now recover.

**Episode Two**
'Treason' by Christopher Priest
The children discover some of the truth behind Robert Catesby's Gunpowder Plot – Rothgo, as Guido Fawkes, is to be the fall Guy …

**Episode Three**
'Alamo' by John Lucarotti
Senator Davey Crockett and Colonel Jim Bowie try to negotiate with the Mexicans for the recognition of the Lone Star state of the republic of Texas but this may be their last stand …

**Episode Four**
'Cave of Diamonds' by Ivan Benbrook
Forewarned is four-armed as Belor takes the guise of the ancient Indian Goddess Kali. Rothgo meanwhile is an old fakir looking for diamonds and the Nidus among them.

**Episode Five**
'Shadrach' by Robert Holmes
Belor gives Rothgo's face to the Holmesian Victorian detective Thomas Jethro Shadrach as a ploy to confuse the children. The real Rothgo is a beefeater guarding the crown jewels – and another disguised piece of the Nidus – which Belor is trying to steal helped by two Indian bandicoots intent on reclaiming the Koh-i-Noor diamond.

**Episode Six**
'Siege' by John Lucarotti
The children find Rothgo fighting with the French army at the great Siege of Malta in 1565. Despite their best efforts, this time Belor gains possession of four pieces of the Nidus.

**Episode Seven**
'Succession' by Martin Worth
The destination for this final showdown is ancient Egypt and the tomb of the recently deceased Tutankhamen. Belor schemes to make Phil the new King under her command and Rothgo, without the Nidus, is surely powerless to stop her.

**Series III**
**Broadcast:** Wednesdays 28/7/82 – 8/9/82 4.45p.m.
(Thursdays 29/7/82 – 9/9/82 at 5.15p.m. in HTV West and Wales)

**Episode One**
'Lazlo' by Bob Baker
Falling into Delta Time, Phil and his new consort Lazlo come across a rum bunch of piratical coves led by Long John Silver.
**Director:** Peter Graham Scott

**Episode Two**
'Dr Jekyll and Mrs Hyde' by Robert Holmes
When Lazlo mixes a potion to help disguise his features he ends up looking like a hairy Mr Hyde. Belor meanwhile falls in with a gang of rough sorts in Victorian London, disguised as a crone called Mrs Hyde.
**Director:** Peter Graham Scott

**Episode Three**
'Eye of the Sun' by Ivan Benbrook
The Scarabeus may be hidden among Inca gold but can Phil and Lazlo, now a seedy Welsh verger, beat Belor and her Conquistador friends to it as well as save a young girl from being sacrificed to the Sun God?
**Director:** Peter Graham Scott

**Episode Four**
'London's Burning' by Jan McCloskey
Lazlo is Thomas Farriner, the baker who supposedly began the Great Fire of London. In fact Belor is to blame, now in league with a crooked Mayor of London.
**Director:** Ken Price

**Episode Five**
'Phantom' by Gary Hopkins
Phil and Lazlo search for the Scarabeus beneath the Paris Opera, where Augustin the Phantom is said to have his lair.
**Director:** Alex Kirby

**Episode Six**
'Xanadu' by Moris Farhi
Belor persuades the son of the mighty Kublai Khan to assassinate his own father, while framing Marco Polo – Lazlo – for the deed. Khan meditates in front of a wall of fire, behind which is thought to reside the Scarabeus.
**Director:** Peter Graham Scott

**Episode Seven**
'Excalibur' by David Martin
Lazlo makes a rather bumbling Merlin and Belor an evil Morgan Le Fay as the two battle for final possession of the

Scarabeus, now in the shape of King Arthur's sword Excalibur.
**Director:** Peter Graham Scott

**Main Cast:** Pamela Salem (Belor), Chris Harris (Lazlo), Simon Beal (Phil), Howard Goorney (Bram)

**Story Editor:** Bob Baker

**Music:** Sidney Sager
**Designer:** John Reid
**Producer:** Peter Graham Scott
**Executive Producer:** Patrick Dromgoole

**Tie-in publications:** novelisation of Series I by Peter Graham Scott published by Futura (paperback) and Frederick Muller (hardback), 1981. Novelisation of Series II as *Return to the Labyrinth* by Peter Graham Scott published by Frederick Muller (hardback only), 1982.

**Video:** Episodes 1–4 of Series I released complete 1988 by Video Gems. Deleted. 97-minute compilation of episodes 5–7 of Series I released as *Into the Labyrinth II* by Video Gems. Deleted.

## Scarf Jack

A period drama set in rural Ireland during the troubles of 1798. The occupants of a small Irish village face an onslaught from the evil Hunter Gowan and his henchmen but are helped by the mysterious stranger Captain Jack.

P. J. Kavanagh adapted his novel for the small screen and much of the filming took place in the New Forest, Hampshire, which doubled up for windswept Ireland, and Shaftesbury, Dorset, where the famous Hovis bread advert was made. The horses required for the story were provided by a nearby riding stable and weren't thought of very highly by either cast or production crew. Actor Richard Greene, previous star of the 50s production of *Robin Hood*, was injured when thrown from a horse, despite being an experienced rider. Two stuntmen, another actor, a stablehand and the director were all involved in falls from horses.

**Southern**
**6 episodes** ('Captain Moonlight'; 'Rescued'; 'The Interrogation'; 'The Search'; 'The Challenge'; 'The Duel') (colour)
**Broadcast:** Mondays 22/6/81 – 27/7/81

**Main Cast:** Roy Boyd (Scarf Jack), Keith Jayne (Francis), Jo Kendall (Jane), Bernard Kay (Hunter Gowan), Reginald Marsh (Sir William Wynne), Richard Greene (Mr Edward)

Based on the novel by P. J. Kavanagh (first UK publication 1978, Bodley Head)
**Adapted by** P. J. Kavanagh

**Music:** John Mealing
**Designer:** Anna Ridley
**Producer/Director:** Chris McMaster

**Tie-in publications:** edition of novel published by Puffin, 1981

151

## Stig of the Dump

Adapted from the pseudo-autobiographical book by Clive King, *Stig of the Dump* is a rather reflective if Blytonesque affair concerning a small boy called Barney and his imaginary – perhaps not so imaginary – friend, Stig.

Barney's adventures are based on the childhood memories and experiences of both Clive King and his son, Charles. 'I grew up near the original dump and played in it with my brother,' King said, 'so I'm the one who had the adventures. While I was working abroad, years later, my son Charles used to spend holidays at his Granny's house and he went to the dump in his turn.'

Barney is a solitary but happy child on holiday with his big sister Lou at their Granny's house near Sevenoaks in Kent. Uninspired by his surroundings he finds adventure in an old chalk quarry which has since become a dumping ground. At the bottom of the dump he stumbles across a small cave inhabited by a strange vagrant whom he names Stig.

The interaction between Stig and Barney is absolutely enlightening, particularly in the first couple of episodes, detailing the learning processes between two individuals separated by a cultural chasm. Barney is entranced by Stig's tribal instinct, practicality and use of modern technology for rudimentary purposes like digging and excavating. Stig in turn is amazed by the turning of wheels and implements that are of no real use to him, like tin openers.

The conclusion of the second episode unfortunately brings this charming character development to an abrupt halt. The story then veers off into individual, stand-alone episodes and the focal point shifts from the unique relationship that Barney and Stig share to their involvement in comedy escapades. When the BBC later adapted the story for a five-part *Jackanory* they elected to drop what had been Thames' more meandering episodes four to eight.

In the penultimate episode, however, proceedings take a dramatic twist as the plot morphs from an undemanding lark to the utterly fantastical when Barney and Lou find themselves transported back in time to Stig's point in stone-age history. This apparent flight of fantasy in fact represents the first and only attempt to rationalise Stig's anachronistic caveman appearance in contemporary Kent.

Nine-year-old actor Grant Ashley Warnock is more than competent and revels in the role of Barney. 'I'm enjoying it a lot,' he said, when interviewed at the time for *Look-In*. 'Stig does such silly things – like when we go fox hunting he lets the fox go and tries to shoot the horse. He doesn't know so many things you normally would know about and as Barney I have to show him, which is quite good fun.'

Stig, through mimicking Barney, actually only utters one coherent word in the entire adaptation. Rather than hindering Keith Jayne, this served merely to heighten the challenge of the role. 'I have to convey what I mean by facial expression more than anything, and if I'm not careful I tend to overdo that and pull too many faces.'

The plot is simple; the lack of character consolidation and development highlights the fact that *Stig of the Dump* was aimed at a considerably younger audience than many other children's dramas (most are probably aimed at twelve to fifteen-year-olds, but *Stig* seems more suited to those aged eight to ten). The novel is more demanding and the perception of Barney created there is that of an unhappy child. Perhaps it was felt that King's deeper interpretation of Barney existed on a level above that of the target audience. Still, the character of Lou, Barney's sister, is

intriguing because, unlike Barney, she evolves. At the outset she is a rather uppity little madam, uninterested in Barney and highly sceptical of his adventures. As the story progresses, Lou gradually accepts the presence of the mysterious Stig and yearns to be part of Barney's world.

The major difference between the novel and the adaptation is the questionable existence of Stig. Clive King would have us believe that Stig is purely a figment of a small boy's imagination and that every child has a Stig, or a similar imaginary friend in one form or another. The dramatisation leaves us in no doubt that Stig is real. He is clearly seen by children and adults alike and exerts a physical influence over many of the story's major events. These differences should not be allowed to detract from the adaptation's achievements. Children watched it and adored it because of that adamant simplicity, because it was about hideaways and adventure, because it was about a child – one of their kind – and the special friend only he knew about.

Amazingly, almost twenty years later the BBC has adapted the tale again, broadcast from January 2002. This remake uses a more accurate caveman Stig rendered via complex make-up.

### Stig of the Dump (1981)
**Thames**
**10 episodes**
(colour)

### Episode One
'The Ground Gives Way'
Monday 28/9/81 4.45p.m. ITV network
Barney and his big sister, Lou, are staying at their Gran's house for the summer holidays. Barney looks for adventure at a nearby rubbish dump but strays too near to the edge and plunges down a cliff face. He finds himself lying inside a cave and discovers that it is inhabited by a strange-looking boy whom he names Stig.

### Episode Two
'Digging With Stig'
Wednesday 30/9/81 4.45p.m.
Barney helps Stig excavate a new room for his cave. He then decides to modernise Stig's home by installing a window made from jam jars and a chimney made from old tins.

### Episode Three
'The Snargets'
Monday 5/10/81 4.55p.m.
Barney discovers that he and Stig are not the only people inhabiting the dump. The Snargets, three feared local brothers, also have a den of their own.
**With:** Gerry Dolan, John Brewer, Daniel Kipling (The Snargets)

### Episode Four
'It Warms You Twice'
Wednesday 7/10/81 4.55p.m.
It is now winter and Barney and his sister are again staying at their Gran's house for the Christmas holiday. Stig has a cold, so Barney helps him build a fire.

**Above:** caveboy Stig (Keith Jayne) in Thames' 1981 adaptation of Clive King's novel.

**Episode Five**
'Gone A-Hunting'
Monday 12/10/81 4.55p.m.
Lou goes hunting with the local nobility, but Barney would much rather share time hunting with Stig.

**Episode Six**
'Skinned and Buried'
Wednesday 14/10/81 4.55p.m.
Two burglars have infiltrated the village and are intent on relieving Barney's Gran of her jewels and silverware. Barney and Stig work together to foil the robbers' plans.
**With:** Ian Cinderby (Policeman), Ray Roberts, Trevor Harrison (Thieves)

**Episode Seven**
'Stones and Skins'
Monday 19/10/81 4.55p.m.
Barney and Lou have been invited to a local fancy dress party but cannot decide what to wear. Barney barters with Stig to remedy the situation.

**Episode Eight**
'Party Manners'
Wednesday 21/10/81 4.55p.m.
At the fancy dress party, Barney discovers that a leopard has escaped from a nearby circus and is prowling around the grounds of the house.
**With:** Diane Holland (Mrs Fawkham-Greene), Robert Austin (Circus Man), Crispin Mair (Indian Chief), Craig Mair (Cowboy), Lucy Baker (Madame Pompadour), Jonathan Jackson (Superman)

**Episode Nine**
'Midsummer Night'
Monday 26/10/81 4.55p.m.
Barney decides to visit Stig in the middle of the night. Lou decides to go with him, but they soon find themselves lost in

a strange but familiar landscape.
**With:** Kenneth Gilbert (Chief), Peter Ackerman (Singer)

**Episode Ten**
'The Standing Stones'
Wednesday 28/10/81 4.55p.m.
Barney and Lou find themselves somehow transported into the distant past. They stumble across an ancient tribe and finally discover the true origins of Stig and the mysterious stone monument. Returning safely to the present, Barney and Lou begin the journey home to their parents. Stig, however, has one final surprise.
**With:** Kenneth Gilbert (Chief)

**Main Cast:** Keith Jayne (Stig), Grant Ashley Warnock (Barney), Janine Tidman (Lou), Bay White (Gran)

Based on the novel by Clive King (first UK publication 1963, Puffin)
**Adapted by** Maggie Wadey

**Music:** Paul Lewis
**Designer:** Anthony Cartledge
**Producer:** Sheila Kinany
**Executive Producer:** Pamela Lonsdale
**Director:** Richard Handford

**Tie-in publications:** paperback editions of novel published by Puffin 1981–87

**Video:** released in UK as a 120-minute compilation by Thames Video 19/8/91. Deleted 3/11/93.

**Stig of the Dump** (2002)
**Childsplay/BBC**
**6 episodes** ('Over the Edge'; 'The Snargets'; 'The Clean Boot';
'Undercover'; 'Man of the Match'; 'Going Home')
(colour)
**Broadcast:** Sundays 13/1/02 – 17/2/02

**Main Cast:** Thomas Sangster (Barney), Robert Tannion (Stig)

**Adapted by** Peter Tabern
**Producer:** Peter Tabern
**Director:** John Hay

## Vice Versa

It's strange that many adults refer to their days at school as the best of their lives when so few children actually think so at the time. The idea that school could be enjoyable is incomprehensible to Dick Bultitude. He is uncomfortable about returning to school but his father Paul is having none of it, reiterating the cliché and stating that he would love the chance to revisit his schooldays.

Paul Bultitude should be more careful what he wishes for. No sooner has he uttered those words than the Garuda stone, a talisman gifted to Dick by his Uncle Marmaduke, works its magic. Paul is changed from a grown man to a child the spitting image of his son. Paul is horrified but Dick is naturally delighted. Sensing an opportunity for some real fun, Dick immediately wishes that he was a grown-up. As soon as he makes the wish, the stone transforms him, making him the double of his father.

Dick, in the guise of his father, runs amok in the household and at his father's city business, while Paul finds it difficult to adapt to school life. When the two are eventually returned to the correct bodies, there is a considerable mess to clean up. Dick's father has earned him a reputation for being a sneak and a coward. Paul on the other hand finds that discipline in his household and at his business has been all but forgotten. The encounter with the Garuda stone may have created mayhem for both father and son but at the end of their adventure, they at least have a closer relationship.

The most recent screen version was accorded no less an honour than the front cover of *TV Times*, despite airing in a weekday children's slot. This was no doubt due largely to the star billing of Peter Bowles, then at the height of his fame in *To The Manor Born*.

More than a century later Anstey's story is now well-worn as the basis of the body-swap comedy; modern descendants include movies such as *Freaky Friday* and *Big*.

All adaptations based on the novel *Vice Versa or A Lesson to Fathers* by F. Anstey (first UK publication 1882, Smith, Elder)

**Vice Versa or A Lesson to Fathers** (1953)
**BBC**
**2 episodes** ('The Transformation'; 'The Escape')
(b&w)
**Broadcast:** Thursdays 23/7/53 – 30/7/53

**Main Cast:** Anthony Valentine (Dick Bultitude, afterwards his father, Paul), George Benson (Mr Paul Bultitude, afterwards his son, Dick), Raymond Rollett (Dr Grimstone), Bryan Coleman (Marmaduke Paradine), Carole Lorimer (Dulcie Grimstone),

Diana Lambert (Margaret Bultitude), George Bishop (Boaler, the Butler)

**Adapted by** Joy Harington
**Producer:** Joy Harington

**Vice Versa: A lesson to fathers** (1961)
**BBC**
**3 episodes**
(b&w)
**Broadcast:** Sundays 3/12/61 – 17/12/61

**Main Cast:** Graham Aza (Dick Bultitude), William Mervyn (Mr Bultitude), William Devlin (Dr Grimstone), Janina Faye (Barbara Bultitude), Michele Dotrice (Dulcie Grimstone), Richard Caldicot (Marmaduke Paradine), Alban Blakelock (Boaler the butler)

**Adapted by** C. E. Webber
**Producer:** Stephen Harrison

**Vice Versa** (1981)
**ATV**
**7 episodes** ('The Transformation'; 'The Outcast'; 'The Trial'; 'The Fight'; 'The Letter'; 'The Escape'; 'The Reckoning')
(colour)
**Broadcast:** Tuesdays 29/9/81 – 10/11/81

**Main Cast:** Peter Bowles (Paul – later Dick), Paul Spurrier (Dick – later Paul), Iain Cuthbertson (Dr Grimstone), Rebecca Lacey (Dulcie Grimstone), Jeremy Child (Marmaduke), Claire Parker (Barbara Bultitude), Timothy Stark (Roly), Saskia Downes (Rosie), John Blaine (Boaler), Roderick Hart (Coggs), Adam Bass (Coker), Robin Crane (Jolland)

**Adapted by** Jeremy Burnham
**Designer:** Richard Lake
**Executive Producer:** David Reid
**Producer/Director:** Ron Francis

**Tie-in publications:** edition published in paperback by Penguin, 1981

## Marmalade Atkins

Along with *The Young Ones*, it was *Marmalade Atkins* who belatedly brought a punk sensibility to TV, its visual style predating the brash and noisy comic strip of the BBC2 comedy. It was almost literally comic strip, in fact: a TV updating of the likes of Minnie the Minx. The anarchic TV reincarnation of Marmalade was markedly different to the jeans and jumper tomboy of Andrew Davies' first book, written in 1979. It had been the punks who had worn red and black striped mohair jumpers in homage to Dennis the Menace and somewhere in this strange melange was a crossover trash aesthetic which Davies now tapped into.

*Educating Marmalade* sent up the establishment, tackling class, gender and educationalist issues in a manner that was juvenile yet sophisticated. Marmalade is a 'problem child' whom the system believes can be tamed. It's up to the social work department – dubbed by a judge in one episode as 'mealy-mouthed do-gooders' – to place her at a school which will produce an institutionalised good citizen. Attempts range from a nightmarish comprehensive to a

Venetian finishing school and in this way Marmalade encounters every vein of the social strata; at Eton her *nouveau riche* father jumps the twenty-year waiting list with a bundle of used fivers he has swindled from oil sheikhs, while Dartmoor prison is described by its Head Screw as 'a quiet, well-run cesspit of brutality and corruption'. The astounding 'Nanny' episode seems to suggest that the patriarchy running the country was raised by the frightening band of nannies who bring up royalty and prospective MPs, proclaiming them 'nasty little beasts, the lot of them'.

The Catholic Church isn't immune from these comic sideswipes either. At the Convent of the Blessed Limit, 'tough nuns who really put the boot in' rule the roost, whacking their little charges with baseball bats and using them as impromptu coconut shies. One nun is played by the imposing figure of Brian Glover, while the other actor has a moustache! A raffle prize at the Convent's Christmas play is a scale model of the Popemobile made from 'Holy poly-propylene from Galilee'. Another two nuns later form a tag wrestling team. This is madness.

In among this wit is the kind of crudity and toilet humour kids love, with references to snot, vomit, a host of botties and bums and even, on one occasion, 'big jobbies'. As well as this juvenile patter there is plenty of more adult innuendo which must have flown over the kids' heads. Mr Atkins' fixation for the statuesque nanny is truly disturbing; he ends up wearing a babygro and sucking his thumb, hoping for another 'terrible smack on the bot'.

Marmalade is smarter and more adult than her parents of course and the almost iconic character is something of a female role model. When the nanny comes to visit, Marmalade crashes into the room with a burst of machine gun fire, only to be told that guns are a boy's toy. She's less than impressed with nanny's assertion that 'Little girls play with dollies and skipping ropes and that's all they do.' Charlotte Coleman, with her unconventional and liberal upbringing, has a highly developed sense of camp for one so young and her performances are electrifying.

A surreal comic strip world was achieved all in studio with electronic overlay cartoon backdrops, minimal props and black drapes. The production assembled an impressive and varied array of guest performers while giving early breaks to Kathy Burke and Julia Sawalha among others.

The second series sadly saw the biting satire diluted but with an even more militant oddness brought in to replace it. Where else would you find a schoolgirl 'disguised' as a Japanese butler on roller skates? Or playing a pint-size James Bond (007 and a half) spraying a man in a scorpion suit (John Sessions no less) with insect repellent and rendering him blatantly stoned?

The saddest postscript is, of course, to note the death of Charlotte Coleman from an asthma attack in November 2001. The actress was just thirty-three.

**Marmalade Atkins**
**Thames**
**1 pilot** and **2 seasons**
(colour)

**Theatre Box: 'Marmalade Atkins in Space' (1981)**
**Broadcast:** Monday 2/11/81
(Repeated under *Dramarama* banner Monday 20/6/83)

**Above:** Marmalade Atkins (Charlotte Coleman) starts out at another new school in *Educating Marmalade*.

Marmalade Atkins has been expelled from ten schools. Drastic action is called for and Mrs Allgood from social services suggests blasting her into space on an incredibly dull mission.

**Main Cast:** Charlotte Coleman (Marmalade Atkins), John Bird (Mr Atkins/Potsmasher), Lynda Marchal (Mrs Atkins), Gillian Raine (Mrs Allgood/Reeny of Spacehols), Dudley Sutton (Colonel Perry), Dicken Ashworth (Sister Conception/Captain Conch), Freddie Jones (Voice of Nodding Dog)

**Written by** Andrew Davies

**Music:** Andy Roberts
**Designer:** Jan Chane
**Producer:** Sue Birtwistle
**Executive Producer:** Pamela Lonsdale
**Director:** Colin Bucksey

**Educating Marmalade (1982–83)**
**10 episodes** ('Cringe Hill'; 'The Convent of the Blessed Limit'; 'Marmalade at Eton'; 'Walkies'; 'Marmalade at St Cecelia's'; 'Marmalade in Venice'; 'Nanny'; 'A Short Sharp Shock'; 'The Nativity Play' – 20/12/82; 'Marmalade at the Albert Hall' – 3/1/83)
**Broadcast:** Mondays 25/10/82 – 3/1/83

Mrs Allgood tries placing Marmalade at every kind of school there is but each time the bad girl ends up expelled yet again.

**Main Cast:** Charlotte Coleman (Marmalade Atkins), John Bird (Mr Atkins), Lynda Marchal (Mrs Atkins), Gillian Raine (Mrs Allgood)

**Written by** Andrew Davies

**Theme song:** Bad Manners
**Incidental Music:** Andy Roberts
**Designer:** Anthony Cartledge
**Producer:** Sue Birtwistle
**Executive Producer:** Pamela Lonsdale
**Directors:** Colin Bucksey (1, 4, 6, 8, 10),
John Stroud (2, 3, 5, 7, 9)

*Danger: Marmalade at Work* **(1984)**
**10 episodes** ('Social Worker'; 'Marmalade Bravo'; '007½';
'Marmalade and Chef Robo'; 'Private Marmalade'; 'The Cruise
of the Grotty Shark'; 'Marmalade's Masterpiece'; 'What the
Butler Saw'; 'Airplane Atkins'; 'Shame')
**Broadcast:** Mondays 20/2/84 – 30/4/84

Marmalade's new social worker, the liberal Wendy Wooley,
tries to find the bad girl gainful employment on a series of
work experience schemes.

**Main Cast:** Charlotte Coleman (Marmalade Atkins), John Bird
(Mr Atkins), Carol MacReady (Mrs Atkins), Elizabeth Estensen
(Wendy Wooley)

**Written by** Andrew Davies
**Script Editor:** Zanna Beswick

**Theme song:** Richard Harvey, sung by Charlotte Coleman
**Music:** Nigel Hess
**Designer:** Robin Parker
**Producer:** Marjorie L. Sigley
**Executive Producer:** Pamela Lonsdale
**Directors:** Peter Duguid (1, 2, 6, 7, 9), John Stroud (3–5, 8, 10)

**Notable spin-offs:** Coleman, as Marmalade, presents
Children's ITV programmes in April 1983

**Tie-in publications:** *Marmalade Atkins' Dreadful Deeds* by
Andrew Davies, published simultaneously in paperback by
Thames Magnet and hardback by Abelard-Schuman, 1982
(different covers). This is a retitled tie-in reprint of *Marmalade
and Rufus*, first UK publication, 1979, Blackie/Grasshopper
(includes original version of 'The Nativity Play').
*Marmalade Atkins in Space* by Andrew Davies, published
simultaneously by Thames Magnet (paperback) and Abelard-
Schuman (hardback), 1982 (different covers). Novelisation of
'Marmalade Atkins in Space'; 'Eton'; 'Venice'.
*Educating Marmalade* by Andrew Davies, published
simultaneously by Thames Magnet (paperback) and Abelard-
Schuman (hardback), 1983. Novelisation of 'Cringe Hill';
'Blessed Limit'; 'Walkies'; 'St Cecilia's'; 'Nanny'; 'Short Sharp
Shock'; 'Albert Hall'.
*Marmalade Hits the Big Time* by Andrew Davies, published
simultaneously by Thames Magnet (paperback) and Blackie &
Son (hardback), 1984 (different covers). All new material.
*Danger – Marmalade at Work* by Andrew Davies, published
simultaneously by Thames Magnet (paperback) and Abelard-
Schuman (hardback), 1984. Novelisation of all series' episodes
except 'Chef Robo'; '007½'; 'Grotty Shark'.

*Marmalade Atkins Annual 1984*, published by Stafford
Pemberton/Purnell Books, 1983. *Marmalade Atkins Annual*,
published by World International Publishing, 1984.

## Theatre Box

This series of single plays was not just purely intended as
entertainment. The plays were written and selected with
small casts and minimal needs for settings so that they
could be performed by children as part of their drama
classes at school or indeed be tried at home with friends.
A series of published scripts were integral to the series'
ideals, not just mere spin-offs.

The plays tended towards larger than life comedy. The
series opened with 'Marmalade Atkins in Space' – the
success of which probably overshadowed the rest of the
series. Thames must have been pretty sure of the play's
qualities, even taking a full page advert in *Look-In* to
promote it. 'Reasons to be Cheerful' saw former *George and
Mildred* star Brian Murphy as Mr Dibble, a man who takes
his less than enthusiastic family on a camping trip. 'School
for Clowns' was adapted by physical theatre exponent Ken
Campbell from a German play and concerned, as you
might expect, a school for clowns (with Jonathan Pryce as
the mischievous Drippens). Professor Molereasons (Ken
Campbell himself) becomes increasingly frustrated as the
class's interpretations of his scripts tend more and more to
the farcical.

There was a great variety of material on offer elsewhere.
'Death Angel', by actor Brian Glover, was the more serious
story of kids who intend to steal the wrestling takings from
the town hall. 'The Prince and the Demons' was adapted
from traditional Indian legend, while 'You Must Believe
All This' was adapted from *Holiday Romance*, a short story
by Charles Dickens. Patrick Malahide, as Dickens, narrated
the story of four Victorian children sent to their beds for
misbehaving who set about writing a magazine that tells
adults how children really ought to be treated, with much
rendered as fantasy sequence asides.

All of the plays (except 'Reasons to be Cheerful') were
repeated in June and July 1983 under the *Dramarama* title.

**Thames**
**6 episodes**
(colour)
**Broadcast:** Mondays 2/11/81 – 7/12/81 and Thursday
24/12/81

2/11/81 – **'Marmalade Atkins in Space'** by Andrew Davies.
**Dir:** Colin Bucksey
9/11/81 – **'The Prince and the Demons'** by George Moore.
**Dir:** John Stroud
16/11/81 – **'Death Angel'** by Brian Glover. **Dir:** Peter Smith
23/11/81 – **'Reasons to be Cheerful'** by James Andrew Hall.
**Dir:** Neville Green
7/12/81 – **'School for Clowns'** by F. K. Waechter, adapted by
Ken Campbell. 2 parts. **Dir:** Ian McNaughton
24/12/81 – **'You Must Believe All This'** by Adrian Mitchell
from a story by Charles Dickens. **Dir:** Richard Bramall

**Producer:** Sue Birtwistle
**Executive Producer:** Pamela Lonsdale

**Tie-in publications:** scripts published for all plays as separate
books (except 'School for Clowns'), Thames Methuen, 1981

## Codename Icarus

Set in contemporary nuclear-fearing England, *Codename Icarus* takes the theme of manipulation of children by adults and steeps it in political espionage and intrigue. Attempting to engage viewer consideration on the ethics and agendas involved in scientific advance, the moralistic pretensions are obvious, but invariably thought-provoking.

Fourth former Martin Smith is perceived by his teachers as rude, disruptive and stupid – an assessment that completely baffles his parents. In reality Martin is a frustrated prodigy in the fields of applied physics and mathematics. The advanced equations he constructs on the school's computer attract the sinister attentions of the enigmatic John Doll. Representative of Falconleigh High – one of many schools privately funded by the mysterious Icarus Foundation – Doll offers Martin the opportunity to study without hindrance at his institution.

Meanwhile, the British Military have been test-firing their latest developments in missile defence. On both occasions, a powerful, unidentified force has destroyed the rockets. After much speculation, the intelligence service concludes that a foreign power has established laser technology capable of long-range destruction. The viewer is privy to the origin of the laser – an aeroplane manned by two enemy agents, one of whom carries a document bearing the insignia of the Foundation. It is clear that the Icarus Foundation is harnessing the talents of its gifted individuals and their esoteric work to advance science with military application the main motivation.

It's difficult to accept that *Codename Icarus* was initially conceived with a child audience in mind, looking instead like an idea originally designed for mainstream television. Still, it boasts some interesting touches. Particularly bizarre is the almost perverse role reversal at Falconleigh where teachers exist to learn from their genius students, referring to them as sir or ma'am, while the students in turn refer to their tutors by surname. Falconleigh is an oppressive and antisocial place where even the school discotheque is a stilted and uncomfortable affair, clearly demonstrating that childhood has sadly passed the occupants of this unfortunate society by.

*Codename Icarus* strives to make hard-hitting statements about mankind's manipulation of science. Edward Froelich, the scientist at the head of Icarus, has a vision of a controlled utopian society built by the pioneers of modern science. Martin intimates that Froelich's vision is tantamount to that of the Nazis – a regime that Froelich himself tried desperately to escape during the war. Martin tries to explain that science itself isn't evil, only the selfish intentions of mankind make it so.

Despite these thoughtful distractions the drama is elsewhere immersed in stereotypes, two-dimensional ciphers and clichéd dialogue. Heralded primarily as an action thriller, it actually contains very little in the way of action or thrills, spending most of its time on moralistic dialogue and, to a slightly lesser degree, teenage angst. As an illustration of the potential consequences of mankind's obsessive thirst for power, however, it represents at the very least a fascinating concept.

**BBC**
**5 episodes**
(colour)
**Broadcast:** Tuesdays and Wednesdays 8/12/81 – 22/12/81

**Main Cast:** Barry Angel (Martin Smith), Jack Galloway (Andy Rutherford), Peter Cellier (Sir Hugh Francis), Philip Locke (John Doll), Debbie Farrington (Sue Kleiner), Steven Mann (Barry Smith), Geoffrey Collins (Peter Farley), John Malcolm (Edward Froelich), Gorden Kaye (Frank Broadhurst), Ivor Roberts (Sir Roderick)

**Written by** Richard Cooper

**Designer:** Marjorie Pratt
**Producer:** Paul Stone
**Director:** Marilyn Fox

**Tie-in publications:** novelisation by Richard Cooper published in paperback by BBC/Knight Books, 1981

**Video:** released in UK as a 105-minute compilation by BBC Video, 1985. Deleted. Released in US as a 105-minute compilation by CBS/Fox, 1987.

## John Diamond

When the father of young William Jones passes away, the boy is left with a secret so great that he cannot bear it. He knows that his father was a swindler who made his money by embezzling from his ex-business partner, Diamond. William therefore decides to move from the country to London in an effort to find Diamond and try to right the wrongs of his father.

Arriving in London he finds the grimy tenements and dark alleyways less than friendly. There he discovers John, Diamond's son. William attempts to bridge the gap between them but John has been consumed by years of bitterness at the injustice done to his father. He attempts to have William killed but William manages to escape with the help of a friend known as Shot-in-the-Head.

William eventually manages to redeem himself and create an understanding with John when he rescues him from a fire.

*John Diamond* was the first in what would turn out to be many stand-alone one-episode dramas by the BBC, broadcast at sporadic intervals over a nine-year period.

**BBC**
**1 episode**
(colour)
**Broadcast:** Tuesday 29/12/81

**Main Cast:** Tom Hollander (William), Christopher Guard (John Diamond), Robert James (David Jones), Eileen Page (Mrs Jones), Vanessa Paine (Rebecca), Damien Nash (Shot-in-the-Head), David Rappaport (Mr Seed), Patrick Troughton (Joseph K'Nee), Joseph O'Conor (Alfred Diamond), Paul Mari (Jenkins), Charles Lewsen (Uncle Turner), John Colclough (Mr Walker), Steve Fletcher (Liverguts), Geoffrey Collins (Narrator)

Based on the novel by Leon Garfield (first UK publication 1980, Kestrel Books)
**Dramatised by** James Andrew Hall

**Designer:** Derek Dodd
**Producer:** Paul Stone
**Director:** Eric Davidson

**Tie-in publications:** n/k

## The Haunting of Cassie Palmer

The seventh child of a seventh child, thirteen-year-old Cassie Palmer is told by her mother that she will inherit the gift of second sight. A psychic medium herself, Mrs Palmer's powers are now diminishing and she has resorted to delivering false readings and staged séances to her clients just to put food on the table. Cassie is disturbed by the powers she herself may have and is uncomfortable with her mother's practices and expectations of her.

In an attempt to establish if she does indeed possess these powers, Cassie attempts to communicate with the spirit of a harmless child called Charlotte buried at a nearby cemetery but instead raises the sinister black-clad Deverill. Cassie must unlock the secret of Deverill's past, establish his true motives, and help rescue her family from their impoverished existence.

Set in contemporary Southgate suburbia, *The Haunting of Cassie Palmer*, as the title suggests, concerns the haunting of an individual rather than a group of people or specific place. Avoiding the shock tactics of clanking spooks and terrified youngsters that one might expect, the story concentrates instead on creating an air of suspenseful uncertainty through the bizarre relationship shared between Cassie and Deverill. Cassie may not be scared of the apparition, spending periods of time talking to him about her desires and enquiring about his time on Earth, but she questions his motives. Is he there to be her friend or is he using Cassie as a pawn in his game? Is Cassie haunted by a restless spirit desperate to lie in peace or merely the victim of the more rational fears – insecurity and the struggle for individuality – that haunt many children? These questions remain unanswered until the final episode, thus helping to maintain intrigue throughout.

Without any real form of action or frights, *The Haunting of Cassie Palmer* relies heavily on its characters. In one particularly strong scene Mrs Palmer tells Cassie, her sister and brother that they must move house again. The children are distraught, telling Mrs Palmer that they have had to move five times since their father died and complaining that they like the house and can't be expected to do well at school when they keep having to move. In an emotional moment Mrs Palmer breaks down, waving countless bills she cannot pay in their faces. She calls her children selfish and wishes that she had put them into care years ago. We are suddenly aware that Mrs Palmer has been running from town to town, staying in one place until either she is caught ripping off clients or the debts become too high.

With a reasonably small cast, and the story unfolding in a limited number of locations, *The Haunting of Cassie Palmer* wouldn't demand too much of the TVS purse. However, the production doesn't look particularly inexpensive and makes good use of extensive location shooting both in the dusk and darkness. The grainy 16mm film benefits the environment of the narrative perfectly. The scenes shot on the streets surrounding Cassie's school, her home, and the cemetery look suitably bleak. Anna Home brought in Dorothea Brooking to direct and this marked Brooking's retirement after a long career in the director's chair – a fine conclusion to her thirty-year association with children's television.

**TVS**
**6 episodes**
(colour)
**Broadcast:** Fridays 26/2/82 – 2/4/82

**Main Cast:** Helen Probyn (Cassie Palmer), Elizabeth Spriggs (Mrs Palmer), Stephen Bint (Tom Palmer), Ruth Adcock (Mary Palmer), Geoffrey Rose (Deverill)

Based on the novel by Vivien Alcock (first UK publication 1980, William Collins)
**Dramatised by** Alfred Shaughnessy

**Music:** Kenyon Emrys-Roberts
**Designer:** John Newton Clarke
**Executive Producer:** Anna Home
**Director:** Dorothea Brooking

**Tie-in publications:** edition published in paperback by Fontana Lions, 1982

## Murphy's Mob

Dunmore United FC are sitting at the bottom of the fourth division with a serious cash flow problem, woefully inadequate facilities and a ground that has become a meeting point for local vandals and roughnecks.

Rasputin Jones, an ex-pop star with a love of football but an inability to play the game, spots an opportunity to make some money and buys the club. Jones immediately hires Mac Murphy, sacked from his first division job following his team's relegation, to manage Dunmore. This signals the start of a turbulent relationship between owner and manager, especially when Rasputin's answer to the vandalism issue is to ban junior supporters from the ground. Murphy has a better idea and encourages Dunmore's two factions of young tearaway fans to form their own junior supporters' club, believing that it will be an excellent outlet for their energies.

Murphy has other challenges on his hands. Too many of the board members are used to getting their own way and things need to change. The junior supporters' club has its own difficulties. Boys like Terry and Boxer are having a hard time trying to convince those that matter, including the smarmy Dunmore chairman, Cassidy, that they have changed their ways and the kids find themselves blamed for everything that goes wrong, including damage done to the senior supporters' club area.

Season Two sees the beginnings of what could be a success for Dunmore United as they climb towards the top of the fourth division. The club still has its problems, especially the attentions of crooked businessman Charlie Russell. In the third season, Rasputin's eye turns towards the possibility of a Dunmore City FC via a possible merger of United and Dunmore Town. The problem will be bringing the two sets of supporters together. Dunmore United have made it to division three when the fourth season starts. The question is how can a newly promoted team be back in financial crisis? Rasputin's planned merger has gone badly wrong and United's days are numbered.

Although some location shooting took place at Watford FC's ground, Terence Budd was quick to point out that Rasputin wasn't based on Watford Chairman Elton John. To add extra realism to the drama, tapes of genuine Watford matches were intercut with footage of Dunmore's goal-mouth incidents.

Despite these football sequences, this was no *Striker* or *Jossy's Giants* – the United team's activities formed only a partial backdrop to the central topic of wayward young kids kept off the streets by the worthwhile activities of the supporters' club. The show's yobbish theme song, with lyrics about unemployment and 'mindless empty days', speaks volumes about the times in which it was made.

**Central**
**3 seasons**
(colour)

**Main Cast:** Ken Hutchison (Mac Murphy), Terence Budd (Rasputin Jones), Keith Jayne (Boxer), Lewis Stevens (Wurzel), Wayne Norman (Gerry – Seasons 1 and 2), Gary Beadle (Gonk – Seasons 1 and 2), Mandy Mealing (Sheila – Seasons 1 and 2), Tracylynn Stephens (Jean – Seasons 1 and 2), Milton Johns (Derek Cassidy), Robert Austin (Charlie Russell – Seasons 1 and 2), Peter Wells (Bernie – Seasons 1 and 2), Lynda Bellingham (Elaine Murphy – Seasons 1 and 2), Jean Turner (Charlotte – Seasons 3 and 4), Janet Fielding (Caroline – Season 3), Dena Snelgrove (Rose – Seasons 3 and 4), Julian Aubrey (Mugsy – Seasons 3 and 4)

**Written by** Brian Finch
**Producer:** David Foster
**Executive Producer:** Lewis Rudd

**Season One**
**16 episodes**
**Broadcast:** Mondays and Wednesdays 1/3/82 – 26/4/82
No broadcast 12/4/82 due to Easter schedules

**Music:** Mike Moran (theme sung by Gary Holton)
**Designer:** Tony Ferris
**Directors:** David Foster (1–4, 13–16), Chris Menaul (5–8), Pembroke Duttson (9–12)

**Season Two**
**12 episodes**
**Broadcast:** Wednesdays and Thursdays 9/3/83 – 14/4/83

**Designer:** Tony Ferris
**Directors:** David Foster (1–4), Pembroke Duttson (5–8), Ron Francis (9–12)

**Season Three**
**14 episodes**
**Broadcast:** Mondays and Thursdays 29/10/84 – 13/12/84

**Designer:** Michael Perry
**Directors:** David Foster (1–4), Ron Jones (5–8), John Cooper (9–12), Michael Dolenz (13, 14)

**Season Four**
**12 episodes**
**Broadcast:** Mondays and Thursdays 11/11/85 – 19/12/85

**Designers:** Michael Perry and Lynda Harris
**Directors:** Mike Holgate (1–4), David Foster (5–8), John Cooper (9–12)

**Tie-in publications:** *Murphy's Mob* – novelisation of first season by Michael Saunders published in paperback by Puffin, 1982. *Murphy & Co* – novelisation of second season by Anthony Masters published by Puffin, 1983. *The Return of Murphy's Mob* – novelisation of third season by Anthony Masters published by Puffin, 1984.

## Jangles

*Jangles* is the story of a girl trying to find independence and a niche in the world while dealing with the standard obstacles of teenage life. Joanne has been playing truant from school, something of a setback for her parents who have big plans for her future. Joanne is not at one with her parents' aspirations for her. She is determined to become a singer and would rather spend time at the Jangles music venue. This radical difference in ambition leads to relationship difficulties between Joanne and her parents and ultimately leads to the girl leaving home. Other plot strands within the series covered youth concerns such as looking for work and delinquent violence.

The music venue setting gifted the series with the opportunity of including current new music acts within the narrative of the series. After all, a real music venue would have more acts than just one teenage girl. Bands seeking fame and fortune included heavy metal act Tank, reggae group Tallisman, new romantics Our Daughter's Wedding, Slow Twitch Fibres, OK Jive, Streets Ahead and, notably, Fun Boy Three and Bananarama.

More importantly, the character of Joanne was played by real-life singer-songwriter Hazel O'Connor. Her involvement in the project is surprising to say the least, especially as she was at that point in time at the height of her career, having just played another young girl trying to make it in the music biz in the film *Breaking Glass* and enjoying pop chart success.

**HTV in association with Chatsworth Television**
**7 episodes** ('Opportunity'; 'Confrontation'; 'Whose Side You On?'; 'A Home of Your Own'; 'Have A Drink On Me'; 'Gotcha'; 'Getting It Together')
(colour)
**Broadcast:** Sundays 18/4/82 – 30/5/82 HTV and TVS 4.25p.m.; Wednesdays from 28/4/82 Anglia, Grampian 5.15p.m.; Thursdays 29/4/82 – 17/6/82 in regions including STV 4.20p.m. (no broadcast on 13/5/82 due to *Junior Gymnast of the Year*); Tuesdays from 4/5/82 Central, Yorkshire, Tyne Tees, Border 5.15p.m.

**Main Cast:** Hazel O'Connor (Joanne), Jesse Birdsall (Steve), David Delve (Herald), Tony Britts (Gary), Julia Gale (Mary), Brian Croucher (Les)

**Written by** Jack Allen (1–5, 7), Bob Baker (6)
**Story Editor:** Bob Baker

**Designer:** John Reid
**Producer:** Peter Holmans
**Executive Producer:** Patrick Dromgoole
**Directors:** Alex Kirby (1), Ken Price (2, 4–7), (3 n/k)

## Secrets

Without any real friends and unable to communicate with her mother, thirteen-year-old Wendy Ansell feels isolated and alone. Her only confidante is her pet cat, Patty, with whom she shares all her secrets and anxieties. Will her father ever come home? Why does she find it so hard to talk to her mother?

When Mrs Ansell discovers that her daughter has played truant from school to take Patty to the vet, there follows a terrible row in which child and mother discover how big the gap between them has grown and allows them to take steps towards mending their relationship.

This is a moving tale about broken relationships and uncertain futures. The departure of Wendy's father has been an obvious blow to both the girl and her mother. Wendy evidently has serious self-confidence issues and shuts herself away until there comes a point where she is unable, unwilling even, to socialise or put herself in the position where she may have to confront her fears. Both Wendy and her mother have been wrapped up in their own problems rather than sharing their concerns. The realisation of their predicament and the fear of losing each other is enough to make them realise that they need to move on.

**BBC**
**1 episode**
(colour)
**Broadcast:** Wednesday 5/5/82

**Main Cast:** Holly Aird (Wendy Ansell), Kate Binchy (Jean Ansell), Mona Bruce (Fiona Grey), Siobhan O'Carroll (Heather), Ian Thompson (Vet)

**Written by** Roger Parkes

**Music:** David Epps
**Designer:** Susan Spence
**Producer:** Angela Beeching
**Director:** Michael Kerrigan

**Tie-in publications:** n/k

## Andy Robson

Set in 1910, *Andy Robson* tells the story of a young boy uprooted from his life in the pit community of Easington when his father is killed in a mining accident. Sent to stay in remote rural Northumberland, Andy soon upsets the school master following a confrontation with Craggs, the school bully. Andy quickly realises that if he is to settle in his new way of life he has much to learn about the village, its people and their customs.

In Northumberland there are many problems for Andy to overcome. He has a fondness for animals and is soon given his own dog but an outbreak of rabies spells trouble for Andy. Luckily he finds a friend in the upper-class Victoria and village boy Alec, who share in his adventures.

*Andy Robson* returned for a second season when a royal visit to the village of Lilham temporarily prevents Andy's return to Easington, much to the boy's joy. There's further adventure for him while holidaying at the Holy Island, where he becomes involved with a foreign agent and espionage. The children also hunt for buried treasure after assisting a Jamaican sea captain.

**Tyne Tees**
**2 seasons**
(colour)

**Main Cast:** Tom Davidson (Andy Robson), Stephanie Tague (Victoria Dennison), Stevie-Lee Pattinson (Alec Cowen), Jack Watling (Matthew), Richard Wilson (Mr Ridley), Norman Jones (Adam Charlton)

Based on the novel *The Courage of Andy Robson* by Frederick Grice (first UK publication 1969, Oxford University Press)
**Adapted/Written by** Ted Childs

**Designer:** Tim Trout
**Producer:** Michael Westhop

**Season One**
**7 episodes** (n/a – untitled; 'Unwillingly to School'; 'Plague Dogs'; 'Hue and Cry'; 'Flare Up'; 'The Unknown Warrior'; 'Championship')
**Broadcast:** Wednesdays 9/5/82 – 20/6/82

**Directors:** Tony Kysh (1, 2, 4–7), Michael Westhop (3)

**Season Two**
**13 episodes** ('Royal Visit'; 'Time and Tide'; 'Treasure Trove'; 'Lost and Found'; 'Romanichal'; 'New Friends'; 'A Two Horse Race'; 'Masquerade'; 'The Lady from St Petersburg'; 'Capital Crime'; 'Circumstantial Evidence'; 'Ringing the Changes'; 'Pitboy')
**Broadcast:** Sundays 8/5/83 – 31/7/83 (fully networked)

**Director:** Tony Kysh (1, 2, 4–8, 12, 13), Michael Westhop (3, 9, 10, 11)

**Tie-in publications:** edition of *The Courage of Andy Robson* published in paperback by Puffin, 1982

## With My Little Eye

Life becomes complicated for Pete when he is witness to a mugging. Going to the police would be simple but for the fact that the young boy recognises the attacker. Pete therefore faces an awkward and frightening dilemma: turn a blind eye or tell the police and so risk the retribution of the thug. Keeping quiet guarantees his own personal safety but would allow the criminal to escape without punishment and could potentially lead to further attacks on other innocent people.

*With My Little Eye* is a simple but effective story of a young boy wrestling with his own conscience. The story cleverly sets that which is morally right against fear and that which is certainly human nature – self-preservation.

**BBC**
**1 episode**
(colour)
**Broadcast:** Tuesday 28/9/82

**Main Cast:** Liam Flannery (Pete), Margery Mason (Gran), Diana Rayworth (Mum), Robert Austin (Dad), Paul Hargreaves (Reilly), Michael Donelan (Mike), John Colclough (Policeman), Cameron Miller (Old Man)

**Written by** Richard Cooper

**Designer:** Jan Spoczynski
**Producer:** Angela Beeching
**Director:** Marilyn Fox

**Tie-in publications:** n/k

## Jockey School

*Jockey School* tells the story of a teenage girl, Billy, trying to realise a serious ambition within the confines of a predominantly male environment. Following the death of her mother, Billy helped her father look after her brothers, playing the role of a substitute mum. Now that her brothers are old enough to look after themselves, Billy has left home to become a new recruit at Rectory Training Stables, where she is to help the other stablehands, all boys, with the unladylike chores involved in maintaining twenty valuable horses.

Life is hard for the stablehands at Rectory – they work twelve-hour days, stay at a run-down hostel and get little reward for their hard work. On top of all that, Billy must also deal with the prejudices aimed at her, especially if she is to fulfil her ambition of becoming a racing jockey, the real reason she has come to Rectory.

When casting for *Jockey School*, lack of acting experience was less important than the ability to ride a horse. Dana Humphries' familiarity with horses helped to create realistic riding sequences and allowed her to highlight inaccuracies in the script.

*Jockey School* is basically a drama for girls and horse enthusiasts. Nevertheless, the character of Billy, being a bad-tempered and often intolerant girl, is at the very least interesting in another story of a child's quest to have a dream become reality against adversity.

**BBC Bristol**
**6 episodes**
(colour)
**Broadcast:** Wednesdays 29/9/82 – 3/11/82

**Main Cast:** Dana Humphries (Billy), Trevor Wakefield (Titch), Gregory Jones (Phil), David Fry (Pete), Mick Dillon (Jack Harrup), Colin Blumenau (John Harrup), Desmond Maurer (Pat Devlin), Christine Kimberley (Una Devlin), Vince McNamee (Eric)

**Written by** Alan Janes

**Designer:** Chris Robilliard
**Executive Producer:** Paul Stone
**Director:** Colin Cant

**Tie-in publications:** novelisation by Michael Feeney Callan published by BBC/Knight (paperback) and BBC (hardback), 1982

## Young Sherlock
### The Mystery of the Manor House

Following the expiry of the late Sir Arthur Conan Doyle's copyright in 1980, a number of Holmes-related adaptations appeared on television. Granada's *The Adventures of Sherlock Holmes* had been on the slate for a couple of years and was in pre-production by 1982. An adaptation geared towards a younger audience was an inevitable scenario.

The BBC produced the successful *Baker Street Boys* in 1983 but uncharacteristically they had been pipped to the post a year earlier by a little-known serial entitled *Young Sherlock – The Mystery of the Manor House*, produced by none other than Granada. This series also predated Amblin's film adaptation *Young Sherlock and the Pyramid of Fear*, given a cinematic release in 1985.

It is 1871 and seventeen-year-old Sherlock Holmes is returning from boarding school to Pendargh Manor, his family's ancestral home. He discovers that his parents have been forced to flee to France following a financial scandal and that the Manor has been sold. Holmes finds himself in the care of his reluctant and dispassionate Uncle Gideon and Aunt Rachel. While visiting Doctor Sowerbutts, an old family friend, Holmes encounters Natty Dan, a man who earns his living by 'speaking' the news to those who cannot afford papers. He has something to tell Holmes but, when the young detective goes to meet him, he finds him dead with a look of horror frozen on his face. Convinced that the man has been murdered, Holmes begins an investigation that will bring him face to face with his future arch-enemy, Moriarty.

The serial gives an interesting insight into the life of Holmes prior to his partnership with Doctor Watson but is actually told following Holmes' death. The idea was that Holmes had documented his earliest adventures, leaving them in the care of Watson, to be opened after Holmes' death.

**Granada**
**9 episodes** ('The Young Master'; 'The Track of the Three-Legged Dog'; 'The Gipsy Calls Again'; 'The Riddle of the Dummies'; 'A Singular Thorn'; 'The Woman in Black'; 'The Glasscutter's Hand'; 'The Unexpected Visitors'; 'The Eye of the Peacock')
(colour)
**Broadcast:** Sundays 31/10/82 – 19/12/82 (first two episodes broadcast back-to-back 31/10/82)

**Main Cast:** Guy Henry (Sherlock), Tim Brierley (John Whitney), David Ryder-Futcher (Dr Sowerbutts), John Fraser (Uncle Gideon)

**Written by** Gerald Frow
**Designer:** Margaret Coombes
**Producer:** Pieter Rogers
**Director:** Nicholas Ferguson

**Tie-in publications:** novelisation by Gerald Frow published in paperback by Granada, 1982

## Nobody's Hero

Twelve-year-old Billy Austin's life is turned upside down when his family are evicted from the Welsh farmhouse in which they have been squatting. They travel to London and move into a small flat with friends. Billy discovers that life at the local comprehensive school is tough and he soon starts mixing with the wrong crowd.

Billy and his three new 'friends', John, Dominic and Graham, decide to break into an empty house but Billy changes his mind at the last minute and waits outside, leaving the others to get on with it. Inside the house, the

161

boys accidentally start a fire which destroys the house. When they are caught, the three ensure that Billy shares the blame with them. The local authorities step in and have Billy placed in care until the matter is resolved. Billy however escapes and runs away, sleeping rough until such time as he is able to prove his innocence.

It was originally planned that *Nobody's Hero* would be broadcast on Channel Four but it was moved to ITV, where it was screened under the Watch It! banner.

**Thames**
**6 episodes**
(colour)
**Broadcast:** Wednesdays 10/11/82 – 15/12/82

**Main Cast:** Oliver Bradbury (Billy Austin), Kika Marjham (Rachel Austin), Michael Carter (Dodge), Maggie Riley (Dorothy Ellis), Brian Croucher (Mr Hunter), Gary Dolan (John 'Biffo' Morton), Gary Hailes (Dominic Barton), Laurence Hood (Graham Hall)

**Written by** Geoffrey Case

**Music composed by** Nick Bicat
**Designer:** Peter Elliot
**Producer:** Vic Hughes
**Executive Producer:** Pamela Lonsdale
**Co-Producer/Director:** John Goldschmidt

## Billy Boy

Home life is tough for Billy, a fourteen-year-old Protestant boy living in Northern Ireland. He feels that his mother continually moans at him, while his father never pays attention to him. Tired of it all one 12 July holiday, Billy decides to escape to his secret hideaway in an old bombed-out pub. When he arrives there he discovers that he isn't alone; escaped gunman Seamus McCafferty, on the run from the Maze Prison, is taking refuge.

Billy pities Seamus and sets about pilfering the food and drink necessary to sustain the man. When the presence of Seamus is discovered, the two are cornered in the hideaway and Billy soon discovers that he is in real danger from a person he considered a friend.

*Billy Boy* is a story detailing the decaying relationship that Billy has with his parents while examining issues of trust. It also has the distinction of being the first and only play to date on children's television to represent contemporary troubles in Belfast. *Billy Boy* was a cheap to produce, talky two-hander, the majority of which was played out on one set, but a fascinating production nonetheless.

**BBC**
**1 episode**
(colour)
**Broadcast:** Wednesday 10/11/82

**Main Cast:** Peter Breen (Billy), James Ellis (Billy's Father), Valerie Lilley (Billy's Mother), Gerard Murphy (Seamus McCafferty)

**Written by** Samantha Lee

**Designer:** Cecilia Brereton
**Producer:** Angela Beeching
**Director:** Christine Secombe

## Break Point

*Break Point* is an intelligent story of sport versus social class. Barry Grieves has the potential to be an excellent tennis player but has problems both at school and at home. His working-class father perceives the sport as one for snobs and isn't supportive of the boy's talent. Jane Pearson meanwhile has all the comforts of a wealthy middle-class existence but her parents never pay her any attention. She too is good at the sport and desperately hopes that her abilities will impress her parents. Tennis coach Frank Abbott steps in to help Barry develop his skills and Barry finds that he has just as much to learn about himself and others as he does about tennis.

Series creator Jeremy Burnham is an avid fan of the game and plays the part of Frank Abbott, with the then British Davis Cup captain Paul Hutchins playing a behind the scenes role as tennis adviser. Paul Stone must also have enjoyed his involvement in the production, having been a top player during his time in the services. Stone himself auditioned actors in a warehouse where he had a representation of a tennis court marked out on the floor. Location filming took place at courts in Eastbourne and the crew made use of the facilities in their spare time.

Neither Jane Pearson or Ian Barker possessed any substantial previous experience of the game but obviously took their roles seriously, entering real-life competitions. Pearson would go on to become the under-fourteen girls' champion in Hertfordshire.

**BBC**
**6 episodes**
(colour)
**Broadcast:** Wednesdays 17/11/82 – 22/12/82

**Main Cast:** Ian Barker (Barry Grieves), Jane Pearson (Lucy Roberts), Jeremy Burnham (Frank Abbott), Stephen Yardley (Mr Grieves), Christine Hargreaves (Mrs Grieves), Norman Bird (Major Houghton-Jones)

**Written by** Jeremy Burnham

**Designer:** Bill Noble
**Executive Producer:** Paul Stone
**Director:** Roger Singleton-Turner

**Tie-in publications:** novelisation by Jeremy Burnham published by BBC/Knight (paperback) and BBC (hardback), 1982

## Ghost in the Water

A fifty-minute filmed ghost story for Christmas. Teresa and David, two young history fanatics, have been copying inscriptions from gravestones at the local church. At a later meeting of the school history society, Teresa happens to mention that she has in her house an old piece of embroidered cloth signed by an Abigail Parkes, and David immediately connects the name with one he had seen on a grave. They are further intrigued by a part of the inscription that states Abigail died 'Innocent of All Harm'. Together they set out to discover what happened to Abigail Parkes and why she died so young.

Teresa discovers that she is a blood relative of Abigail and, as the story progresses, she seems to become almost possessed by the dead girl's spirit. It's a somewhat tragic tale, depicting Abigail as a girl ruined by the death of her beloved in a mining accident. The poor girl swears after his death that she will wear his ring always but accidentally drops it into a canal. Distraught at the loss she attempts to retrieve the ring but drowns in the process. The coroner incorrectly recorded a verdict of suicide, in those days a sin, and Teresa and David must prove the death was accidental and so free Abigail's troubled spirit.

**BBC**
**1 episode**
(colour)
**Broadcast:** Friday 31/12/82

**Main Cast:** Judith Allchurch (Teresa 'Tess' Willetts), Ian Stevens (David Ray), Jane Freeman (Mrs Willetts), Dave Mitty (Mr Willetts), Joanne James (Jean Willetts/Abigail Parkes)

Based on the novel by Edward Chitham (first UK publication 1973, Longman Young)
**Dramatised by** Geoffrey Case

**Executive Producer:** Paul Stone
**Director:** Renny Rye

**Tie-in publications:** edition published in paperback by Puffin, 1982

## Captain Zep – Space Detective

When former *Morecambe and Wise* writer Dick Hills created space detective Captain Zep, intending him as a kind of TV comic strip hero, it's unlikely he imagined his concept to translate to screen quite so literally. Via the wonders of the CSO bluescreen, the three main cast members interacted within a two-dimensional drawn world of bizarre space creatures and alien planets. The production utilised only one real studio set, that of the bridge of Zep's ship, the *Zep One*.

Similar experiments in mixing live action and animation on TV were tried on BBC2's *Jane* (2/8/82 – 6/8/82), starring Glynis Barber, but *Zep* was still unique in that it was constructed as part drama, part quiz show. In studio, Zep would address an audience of young students from the SOLVE academy (Space Office of Law Verification and Enquiry) and take them through the instalments of one of his famous cases, always advising them to watch carefully for red herrings as they tried to home in on whodunit. Once the final solution to each contrived mystery had been explained by the Poirot of 2095, a supplementary viewer question invited answers on a postcard with a prize of SOLVE academy stickers up for grabs.

There were two cast changes between seasons, so that the actor for Jason Brown remained constant while Zep and his female Professor sidekick saw replacements don the orange jumpsuits for the second run. The original Zep (it's implied that 'Captain Zep' is a codename given to the captain of *Zep One*, rather than an actual name) was a square-jawed comic book hero, the second a rather whimsical buffoon with a predilection for tea and biscuits.

**Above:** Captain Zep (Paul Greenwood, centre) at the controls of Zep One, flanked by Jason Brown (Ben Ellison) and Professor Spiro (Harriet Keevil).

**BBC**
**2 seasons**
(colour)

**Main Cast:** Paul Greenwood (Captain Zep – Season 1), Richard Morant (Captain Zep – Season 2), Ben Ellison (Jason Brown), Harriet Keevil (Professor Spiro – Season 1), Tracey Childs (Professor Vana – Season 2)

**Season One**
**6 episodes** ('Death On Delos'; 'The Lodestone of Synope'; 'The Plague of Santos'; 'The G and R 147 Factor'; 'The Tinmen of Coza'; 'The Warlords of Armageddia')
**Broadcast:** Wednesdays 5/1/83 – 9/2/83

**Written by** Dick Hills

**Designer:** Tom Yardley-Jones
**Graphic Designer:** Ray Ogden
**Producer/Director:** Christopher Pilkington

**Season Two**
**6 episodes** ('Death Under the Sea'; 'The Missing Agent of Ceres'; 'The Small Planet of Secrets'; 'The Sands of Sauria'; 'The Tree of Life'; 'Death by Design')
**Broadcast:** Fridays 9/3/84 – 13/4/84

**Written by** Colin Bennett

**Designer:** Grenville Horner
**Graphic Designer:** Dick Bailey
**Illustrators:** Peter Jones, Trevor Goring, Paul Birkbeck, Peter Clark
**Producer:** Christopher Pilkington
**Assistant Producer:** Michael Forte
**Directors:** Christopher Pilkington (1) and Michael Forte (2–6)

## The Coral Island

Shipwrecked adventure ahoy in this period piece set in 1860. Young Ralph Rover is departing New South Wales, leaving behind him a posh mansion house and an overbearing stepmother. Boarding the sea ship *Arrow* he is heading for England and an Eton education. Friction soon develops between the upper-class youth and Jack Martin, one of the ship's cabin boys. Such differences are put aside when the *Arrow* is ripped apart in a fierce ocean storm.

Jack manages to save a boy by the name of Peterkin and Ralph is rescued by Tod Salter, who perishes in the attempt. The trio find themselves washed up on an unknown coral island. Their immediate concern is to find shelter but the continued animosity between Jack and Ralph could stand in their way.

Soon they have to rescue a Princess, Avatea, from cannibals and find a way to communicate with the girl and her people. They must also tackle pirates and undersea caves while trying to find a way to get off the island and return to their homeland.

The first adaptation of R. M. Ballantyne's novel, by Thames in 1983, was a lavish affair. The cast and crew spent four months filming in Western Samoa and Australia. The desire for authenticity was such that auditions were held among the islanders of Samoa to find someone to play Avatea. The production was a joint venture between Thames and ABC Australia and both worked together to finance the building of a new school as a thank you to the islanders.

Zenith's production in 2000 was filmed on location in South Africa and Liverpool. At four episodes it has clearly been truncated and, as a result, events taking place at the start of the first episode happen too rapidly and are a little confusing.

Based on the novel by R. M. Ballantyne (first UK publication 1858)

***The Coral Island* (1983)**
**Thames/ABC Australia**
**9 episodes**
(colour)
**Broadcast:** Thursdays 6/1/83 – 3/3/83

**Main Cast:** Nicholas Bond-Owen (Peterkin), Richard Gibson (Ralph Rover), Scott McGregor (Jack Martin), Gerard Kennedy (Bloody Bill), Brian McDermott (Captain Carver), Pele Teuila (Avatea)

**Adapted by** James Andrew Hall

**Music composed by** Bruce Smeaton
**Designer:** Quentin Hole
**Producer:** Ray Alchin
**Executive Producer:** John Hambley
**Directors:** Chris Thomson (1, 5, 6), Ray Alchin (2, 7, 9), Ray Alchin and Ray Brown (8), (3, 4 n/k)
**Assistant Director:** Ray Brown

**Tie-in publications:** abridged version of novel adapted by Olive Jones published in paperback by Thames Magnet, 1982

***The Coral Island* (2000)**
**Zenith for ITV**
**4 episodes**
(colour)
**Broadcast:** Wednesdays and Thursdays 7/6/00 – 15/6/00

**Main Cast:** Adam Deacon (Peterkin), William Mannering (Ralph Rover), Ashley Walters (Jack Martin), Trevor Byfield (Bloody Bill), Taryn Joy (Avatea)

**Screenplay by** Barry Purchese

**Music composed by** Joe Campbell and Paul Hart
**Designers:** Pilar Foy and Berrie Le Roux
**Producer:** John Price
**Executive Producer:** Peter Murphy
**Director:** John Gorrie

## Luna

Former Monkees' drummer Mickey Dolenz had begun his career as a TV producer with *Metal Mickey*, a knockabout kids' comedy for LWT. When *Mickey* ended it was directly succeeded the following Saturday by another Dolenz production, something rather more cultured and clever than *Mickey*'s antics. That something was *Luna*, a witty sci-fi comedy which told the story of a dimifemale (teenage girl) living in the Efficiecity, a sealed environment cut off from the polluted Earth of 2040.

The series was co-written by Colin Bennett, the manic handyman who accompanied Tony Hart in his BBC series *Take Hart* for several years, and Bennett also starred as Andy the friendly Android who helps look after Luna. What really set the series apart was its bizarre lingo, known as Technotalk, which most likely took its lead from Anthony Burgess's *A Clockwork Orange*. 'Fingers' became 'dexterous forelimb terminals', while to be down in the dumps meant you were 'as sick as a zygodactyl-footed brilliant plumaged subtropical bird'. Just the episode titles themselves are a joy to behold and decipher.

The series was broadly a sitcom but Bennett saw it as a morality play. The classic science fiction notion at its heart examined how humanity would cope and survive in a technological world. Really this was Alice in Technoland, with the extraordinarily pretty Patsy Kensit, aged fourteen, playing a wide-eyed innocent coming to terms with the oddness of the Efficiecity (the pink pinafore dresses and white Alice hairband were a dead giveaway). A key episode was 'When Did You Last See Your Pater Batch Mix Donor?' in which Luna goes in search of her parents only to find that, like all the younger members of the Efficiecity, she has been grown artificially.

The series also had much to say about bureaucracy, becoming on the surface a much brighter version of *1984*. Every citizen carried an Egothenticity Card which contained all of their personal data, while the personification of bureaucracy was 80H, a fearsome black-clad character who was finally revealed, *Wizard of Oz*-style, to be just an ordinary little man called Sid.

As a comedy there were plenty of wry gags in there too; best of all was the character of Gramps, an old man who dressed punk style and listened to LPs of 'classical music' like Haircut 100 (possibly a sly in-joke, as wild child Kensit was 'stalking' Haircut singer Nick Heyward around this time).

For the second series most of the personnel were retained although the major loss of Kensit as Luna was probably fatal – her replacement Joanna Wyatt possessing little of the ingénue naiveté which had been central to rendering the character as an innocent abroad.

**Central**
**2 seasons**
(colour)

**Main Cast:** Patsy Kensit (Luna – Season 1), Joanna Wyatt (Luna – Season 2), Aaron Brown (Brat), Colin Bennett (Andy), Frank Duncan (Gramps), Roy Macready (80H), Linda Polan (Mother), David Gretton (Mr Efficiecity – Season 1), Russell Wootton (Mr Efficiecity – Season 2), Hugh Spight (Jazzmine – the Habiviron pet), Natalie Forbes (40D – Season 1 only), Vanessa Knox-Mawer (32C – Season 2 only)

**Written by** Colin J. Bennett and Colin Prockter

**Designer:** Tony Ferris
**Producer:** Michael Dolenz
**Executive Producer:** Lewis Rudd

**Season One**
**6 episodes** ('Habiviron Sweet Habiviron'; 'The Clunkman Cometh'; 'All the World's a Teletalk Link Up'; 'Happy Batch Day, Dear Luna'; 'Environmental Ambience Stable, Wish You Were Here'; 'When Did You Last See Your Pater Batch Mix Donor?')
**Broadcast:** Saturdays 22/1/83 – 26/2/83 5.15p.m. in most regions and 6.10/6.15p.m. HTV. TSW Sundays 3.15/4p.m., Tyne Tees Wednesdays 5.15p.m.

**Directors:** Michael Dolenz (1, 6), Chris Tookey (3–5)

**Season Two**
**6 episodes** ('You Can't Judge a Videtalker by its Blurb'; 'Go Forth and Quadruplicate'; 'The Happiest Earth Revolves of Your Span'; 'It Isn't How You Vict or Flunk But How You Co-participate'; 'A Bureaubureau in the Hand is Worth a Pension'; 'You're Only as Multi-Tocked as You Perceive')
**Broadcast:** Wednesdays 15/2/84 – 21/3/84

**Directors:** n/k

## The Boy Who Won the Pools

A strange and rather surreal series that takes a light-hearted look at the pros and cons of winning a large sum of money. Sixteen-year-old Rodney Baverstock finds himself in what most would consider to be an enviable situation when his aunt enters a pools coupon in his name, winning

him £758,000.27. Rodney is an imaginative boy and has many ideas of how he would like to spend the money. There's a red Ferrari for starters, not to mention the tame tiger, a large mansion, and helping his friend Sami to become a rock star.

It's not all plain sailing for Rodney. Money can bring out the worst in people and Rodney's father believes that he should be getting some of the cash. With the assistance of his friend Beazley, Dad sets about trying to prevent his son spending the money.

The series was filmed on location in the South of England and the songs performed by Sami were all written especially for the series.

**TVS**
**10 episodes**
(colour)
**Broadcast:** Sundays 20/2/83 – 1/5/83

**Main Cast:** Michael Waterman (Rodney Baverstock), Vivienne McKone (Sami), Lloyd Peters (Thornton Duff), Don Henderson (Mr Baverstock), Gillian Martell (Mrs Baverstock), Sylvia Sachs (Claudine), David Rippey (Sam Beazley)

**Written by** Gerard MacDonald

**Music Director:** Dennis Bovell
**Designer:** Christine Ruscoe
**Producer:** Brenda Ennis
**Executive Producer:** Anna Home
**Directors:** Roger Tucker (1–4, 10), Christopher King (5–9)

**Tie-in publications:** novelisation published in paperback by Fontana Lions, 1983

## The Machine Gunners

Teachers wishing to show their pupils what life was like for a child during World War II would probably be best advised to pass on *Carrie's War* and plump instead for Robert Westall's *The Machine Gunners*. The former is about an internal 'war' far removed from the trappings of the conflict, but Westall's work is set in among the rubble and carnage of a city under attack. It's a very accurate period piece but one with little place for nostalgia, where the hankered-for Blitz spirit is barely in evidence.

There is far more to the story than the setting, however – crucially the adaptation pulls few punches and shows children as they really are and are always likely to be: by turns confused, selfish and violent. The central character – hero is not the right word – is Chas McGill, a boy who, like many of his friends, collects memorabilia of the war. Status is measured in the number of incendiary fins you own. The instinct of young boys to collect things is married to an irresponsible and unfeeling ghoulishness. While not seen on screen, it's clearly implied that Chas' collecting rival Boddser Brown has even raided the pockets of a dead German pilot to add to his collection.

One scene graphically replays another staple of childhood – the playground scrap. This is a truly vicious fight sequence where, egged on by the braying huddle of screaming kids, the Queensberry-prescribed rabbit punches give way to more basic urges. Chas ends up battering Boddser with his gas mask until he is mercifully pulled off by his friends. There is a lot of on-screen blood in evidence and it is easy to imagine that much careful deliberation went into the editing of the sequence to portray properly the real violence of the situation yet avoid gratuitous sensationalism.

Less visceral, yet potentially even more shocking, is Chas' apparent callousness on learning of the 'death' of his friend Nicky. He stops only momentarily by the debris of the bombed Nichol house. 'We'll give you a cross, Nicky, I promise you,' he says to himself quite matter-of-factly, 'but please let the fortress be all right.' This may well be special to the circumstance, with death something these children experience on a daily basis.

The unrelenting realism has its lighter side too though, to be found in some finely honed dialogue. There's the gawky tomboy Audrey Parton, pausing on the edge of the woods: 'I'm not going to do anything dirty with youse two in there, so you needn't think I am,' before adding, more hopefully, 'I don't mind a bit of kissing but no more.' It's real Northern Gallows' humour for the most part. In a wonderful scene the McGills' neighbour falls screaming into their shelter 'knickers round her ankles': 'I was on the ootside lav – they blew the lavvy door right off,' she screams. In a world where a careful balance must be struck between providing groundbreaking children's drama and not unnecessarily upsetting the letter-writers of Tunbridge Wells, the television adaptation draws the line where language is concerned, substituting 'pig' and 'beggar' for the likes of the 'bastards' and 'buggers' of Westall's novel.

*The Machine Gunners* is a view of the gang mentality of children, but this doesn't mean that characterisation is sacrificed. Nicky is a rather damaged and sensitive boy, more in line with the loners who populate many of the best works of children's fiction. The Nichol household is off-limits to most children in Garmouth but Chas doesn't understand why. His dad just tells him that 'you're too young to understand'. Nicky counters this when he tells Chas, 'They say kids don't understand but I did.' Audrey knows why Mrs Nichol is a subject for gossip: 'It's not just the drinking. It's the, y'know, sailors.' Her assertion that Nichol has been 'living in sin' is as clear a euphemism as is possible. Again, raising these topics in a children's drama is a tricky business. The gin bottles cluttering the kitchen and men wandering around the house in their long johns make the situation clear to those in the audience who are 'old enough to understand'.

As well as making sense of everyday life, *The Machine Gunners* also tackles the bigger issues. War provides not just the period setting but the central question. The children accept Rudi as a friend, with Nicky even seeing him as a substitute for his own dead father. Still this is not enough to overcome their fear and mistrust of a man who is technically 'the enemy' and, in a dreadful misunderstanding, it's the fear that rises to the surface when Clogger shoots Rudi down – probably fatally.

Lavishly if grittily filmed, the production required an extra injection of funding from co-production monies but despite this there were no visible attempts made to 'internationalise' and dull down its fiercely Geordie colour. The working-class setting, more recognisable characters and a real 'blood and snot' style of presentation found an audience who might not usually watch more well-mannered BBC historical dramas. *The Machine Gunners* proved that period drama, be it for children or adults, needn't be all petticoats and prissiness.

**BBC in association with AMC Audiovisual/Monte Carlo Productions/Hatchette Audiovisual**
**6 episodes**
(colour)

### Episode One
Wednesday 23/2/83 5.10p.m.
It's 1941 and the Tyneside town of Garmouth is under the constant threat of bombing by the Nazis. One night a German bomber is shot down and crashes in a forest, only to be found the next day by schoolboy and war memorabilia collector Chas McGill. He returns the next night to steal a fully working machine gun from the wreckage. Before long the authorities realise the gun is missing and know that they must find it before there is a terrible accident.

### Episode Two
Wednesday 2/3/83 5.10p.m.
Chas decides that his gang must do their bit for the war effort by building a fortress on the coast. Nicky Nichol's garden offers the perfect site and so to win Nicky's favour Chas protects him from Boddser's bullying – beating his rival senseless in a playground scrap.

### Episode Three
Wednesday 9/3/83 5.10p.m.
With the help of some trusted friends, Chas oversees the construction of his Fortress Caparetto. When the work is completed, Chas makes the gang swear allegiance on the gun.

### Episode Four
Wednesday 16/3/83 5.10p.m.
Nicky's house is bombed and his mother and her lover killed. The gang agree to look after Nicky. A German bomber is sighted and the Fortress plays its part in bringing it down. The pilot has ejected, however, and hiding out in Garmouth he stumbles across the Fortress.

### Episode Five
Wednesday 23/3/83 5.10p.m.
Rudi, now the kids' prisoner and friend, makes an 'impossible deal' when he agrees to fix the damaged gun in return for a boat to take him back to Germany – but Nicky's dad had a boat …

### Episode Six
Wednesday 30/3/83 5.10p.m.
When the church bells ring out in the middle of a raid, could it be the Germans have invaded? As the townspeople make their attempts to fight or flee it turns out to be a troop of Polish soldiers come to help the British. Come the morning, however, the gang have still not heard so when a line of soldiers approach the Fortress, led by Rudi, they fear he has betrayed them to his Nazi cohorts.

**Main Cast:** Shaun Taylor (Chas McGill), Tony Saint (Cem Jones), Debbie Breen (Audrey Parton), Alastair Craig (Nicky Nichol), Andrew Craig (Clogger Duncan), Raymond Pattison (Boddser Brown), Jurgen Andersen (Rudi Gerlath), Les Wilde (Mr McGill), Pauline Moriarty (Mrs McGill), Lyn Douglas (Nana McGill), Dick Irwin (Granda McGill), Harry Herring (Stan Liddell), John Gannie (Sergeant Green), Steve Evans (John Brownlee)

Based on the novel by Robert Westall (first UK publication 1975, Macmillan)
**Dramatised by** William Corlett

**Designer:** Marjorie Pratt
**Executive Producer:** Paul Stone
**Director:** Colin Cant

**Tie-in publications:** paperback editions of novel published by Puffin, 1983 until c. 1990

## The Baker Street Boys

One could be forgiven for thinking that *The Baker Street Boys* was inspired by Granada's memorable production of *The Adventures of Sherlock Holmes*. Surprisingly though, the first season of the BBC's new detective drama for children was aired a year before Jeremy Brett would make the part of Holmes his own.

*The Baker Street Boys* was an idea derived from Conan Doyle's Baker Street Irregulars, a band of young street urchins who would occasionally assist Holmes by gathering essential information to complete a case. The series carries the premise a stage further with the children actually solving cases that Holmes himself cannot complete for a variety of reasons (work on another case, influenza or being kidnapped by Moriarty). Although Watson appears regularly and Moriarty also features in a story, Holmes is never fully visible and serves only to pass on the occasional piece of written advice, allowing the focus of the series to remain firmly with the children.

Containing a veritable feast of Cockney accents, bushy moustaches and bumbling police officers, *The Baker Street Boys* demonstrates an effective balance of deliberate overacting and straight-faced drama. During the course of their investigations the intrepid young detectives find themselves faced with everything one might expect from a Sherlock Holmes adventure – robbery, conspiracy, murder and disappearing dispatch cases. In one particularly gruesome scene a character is stabbed to death in the back, a clear indication that, although the series didn't entirely take itself seriously, it had ambitions beyond that of a mere lightweight Victorian yarn.

Design-wise it's all very much stereotypical Victoriana with effective street sets depicting the apparent dark and claustrophobic London of the era. On occasions the studio sets can be a little threadbare but the many fine costumes go some way to distracting the critical eye.

The Baker Street Irregulars would undoubtedly have been a more fitting and logical title for the programme, considering that the group of young sleuths was comprised of four boys and two girls. Perhaps, in the 80s, 'irregular' would all too readily suggest that the gang suffered from some sort of unpleasant bowel condition.

**A BBC-TV production in association with Lella Productions PLC and Talbot Television Limited**
**8 episodes**
(colour)
**Broadcast:** Tuesdays and Fridays 8/3/83 – 1/4/83 (BBC1 except episode 3 shown on BBC2 due to Budget coverage)

**Above:** Jay Simpson as Arnie Wiggins, erstwhile leader of *The Baker Street Boys*.

**4 x 2-part stories:**
'The Adventure of the Disappearing Dispatch Case'; 'The Ghost of Julian Midwinter'; 'The Adventure of the Winged Scarab'; 'The Case of the Captive Clairvoyant'

**Main Cast:** Jay Simpson (Arnold Wiggins), Damion Napier (Beaver), Adam Woodyatt (Shiner), David Garlick (Sparrow), Debbie Norris (Queenie), Suzi Ross (Rosie), Roger Ostime (Sherlock Holmes), Hubert Rees (Dr Watson), Colin Jeavons (Professor James Moriarty), Stanley Lebor (Inspector Lestrade)

Series devised by Anthony Read in association with Gatetarn Productions
**Writers:** Anthony Read (1, 2, 7, 8), Richard Carpenter (3–6)

**Music:** Alan Roper (except incidental music for 7 and 8 by David Epps)
**Designer:** Barbara Gosnold
**Producer:** Paul Stone
**Associate Producer for Talbot Television Limited:** Anthony Gruner
**Directors:** Marilyn Fox (1, 2, 5, 6), Michael Kerrigan (3, 4, 7, 8)

**Tie-in publications:** novelisation of the 'Clairvoyant' and 'Dispatch Case' stories by Brian Ball published by the BBC (hardback) and BBC/Knight (paperback), 1983

**Video:** 98-minute compilation containing 'The Adventure of the Disappearing Dispatch Case' and 'The Adventure of the Winged Scarab' released in UK by BBC Video, c. 1985. Deleted.

## Tucker's Luck

*The thing that upset me was hearing that Trisha, Tucker and their mates will not be in the series much any more. As they began the show, they shouldn't be taken out. If they are too old to go to school then surely we can see what happens to them when they leave and how they fight unemployment!*

A reader's letter in the *Grange Hill Annual* published for 1982 may not have been the direct impetus for a spin-off but nonetheless this is almost exactly what transpired. Avid *Grange Hill* viewers had watched Tucker Jenkins develop over a period of five years and the series must have seemed a little empty when the character moved on. Phil Redmond evidently recognised the popularity of the character and the potential for further development, successfully selling the idea of a spin-off series to the BBC. Thus children that had grown up with Tucker could continue to follow the ongoing trials and tribulations of the character as he graduated from secondary school to the big wide world. The result was an often harsh teen drama that addressed the primary concerns of unemployed youth, while still encompassing a degree of comedy that prevented it being overly morose.

It's easy to remember Tucker as being a victim of the Thatcherite government, yet the first season of *Tucker's Luck* clearly highlights that Tucker, Alan and Tommy are victims of nothing other than their own lack of motivation and initiative. They have effectively wasted their school years and left without qualifications. Now, rather than fight to find employment, they are content to take money from the state while selfishly devoting their attentions towards alcohol and romance.

The first season casts a critical eye over certain aspects of youth behaviour. Although heavy going in places, as one

**Above:** Tucker (Todd Carty, left) and Tommy (Paul McCarthy) find girl trouble with Alison (Gillian Freedman, back) and Michelle (Elaine Lordan, front) in the first run of *Tucker's Luck*.

would expect from such subject matter, the narrative is wonderfully tempered by all the skirmishes and comedy escapades the audience expect of Tucker Jenkins. On a number of occasions Tucker and Alan find themselves being pursued through the streets by Ralph Passmore, intent on causing them physical injury for going out with his ex-girlfriend. Passmore bestows upon Tommy black eyes and a bloody nose, yet there's something faintly amusing in watching Alan being chased by a lumbering brute dressed in three-quarter-length trousers, braces and a hat.

There's also much quasi-sitcom fun to be had, although not for Tucker, when he throws a party to take Alan's mind off his failed romance with Susi McMahon. Someone obviously thinks that Arsenal are magic and decides to put their opinions on paper – Mrs Jenkins' wallpaper. Tucker, Alan and Tommy then spend the rest of the episode frantically trying to find the same kind of wallpaper so that they can redecorate before Mrs Jenkins gets home. Having successfully done that, Mrs Jenkins announces that she thinks the place needs redecorating. Cue exasperated look from Tucker and end credits.

There are also moments that border on the ridiculous. Tucker arranges a blind date for Alan with Allison's cousin Anthea. When we first see the girl she is at work wearing overalls, a hat, a pair of thick-rimmed glasses and looks plain to say the least. Tucker thinks Alan's going to be furious. It's obvious what's going to happen and, sure enough, Anthea arrives at the party and is nothing less than stunning. The realism goes out the window, replaced by a *My Guy* photo-story caper.

'No birds, no jobs, no prospects. We seem to be right back where we started,' Tucker says at the end of the season. He's absolutely right. The boys have been through quite a lot for little material gain and the season ends, as it started, on a rather downbeat note.

Whereas the first season examined the impacts of unemployment on a small group of friends, the second season concentrates on the issues of the individual as Tucker, Alan and Tommy begin to react differently to their situation. The death of his father has a massive impact on Alan Humphries. With his father's business affairs left in a less than lucrative state and only his Uncle Vic to look after him, Alan starts to retreat into himself. Rather than accept that he must find a way of supporting himself, he spends his time at Creamy's squat learning to play the guitar. Tommy, on the other hand, is earning good money but from bad people and is soon involved in selling stolen goods at the local market. This could have been an effective thread had more time been devoted to it. Instead the audience is privy to the blossoming but ultimately doomed relationship between Tucker and Sarah, which although interesting shouldn't have been given priority over Tommy's activities. Tucker's character does however continue to develop, gaining a maturity that wasn't present in the first season. This leads to him recognising that to have a secure future he must better himself. To achieve this he takes the step of applying for a college course in printing technology and is successful in his application.

The third season is more internalised. Tommy has moved on and Alan is a virtual bystander, bringing the focus firmly back to Tucker and the Jenkins family. It would appear that Tucker's father has been written into the series with the express purpose of being written out. He is hardly ever referred to in the first two seasons and is never seen. Neither is he seen in the third season. Tucker also seems to have gained an eight-year-old sister that the audience has never set eyes on – contrived writing of the soap opera kind. Nevertheless it is an interesting plot that sees Tucker finally mature and accept responsibility.

There's no doubt that *Tucker's Luck* was watched by children but it's by no means a children's drama. The 6p.m. slot alone signals that this series is intended for older teenagers – although, with its occasional expletives, finger gestures, nights on the tiles and generally more adult content, it's easy to see why teenagers, younger or older, thoroughly enjoyed it.

**BBC**
**3 seasons**
**27 episodes**
(colour)

**Season One**
**9 episodes**
**Broadcast:** Thursdays 10/3/83 – 5/5/83 BBC2
6.00p.m./6.05p.m./6.10p.m.

**Main Cast:** Todd Carty (Tucker Jenkins), Paul McCarthy (Tommy Watson), George Armstrong (Alan Humphries), Gillian Freedman (Allison), Elaine Lordan (Michelle Passmore), Peter Childs (Mr Humphries), Peter McNamara (Ralph Passmore), Hilary Crane (Mrs Jenkins)

Tucker Jenkins and his two friends, Alan Humphries and Tommy Watson, have left Grange Hill without a qualification between them. The prospects of employment are almost as limited as their ambition and all seem to be resigned to a life on the dole. The boys' love lives are no less hassle. Alan hasn't got one, while Tucker and Tommy can't quite decide if they've got it right. Tommy is going out with Allison, ex-girlfriend of local skinhead thug Ralph Passmore. Tucker has started dating Michelle but discovers she's Passmore's sister. This presents a common problem for the two youths: Passmore wants to kick their heads in.

**Devised by** Phil Redmond
**Written by** Phil Redmond (1), Barry Purchese (2, 3, 8), Jane Hollowood (4, 6, 9), Jenny McDade (5, 7)

**Title Music:** Alan Hawkshaw
**Designer:** John Coleman
**Producer:** David Hargreaves
**Director:** Chris Menaul

**Tie-in publications:** *Tucker's Luck* by Jan Needle published by Fontana Lions, 1984

**Season Two**
**9 episodes**
**Broadcast:** Tuesdays 13/3/84 – 8/5/84 BBC2 6.40p.m.

**Main Cast:** Todd Carty (Tucker Jenkins), George Armstrong (Alan Humphries), Paul McCarthy (Tommy Watson), Peter McNamara (Ralph Passmore), Adam Kotz (Chris 'Creamy' Eames), Ray Armstrong (Vic Humphries), Hilary Crane (Mrs Jenkins), Lisa Geoghan (Sarah Gill), Rebecca Calder (Susan Challis)

Tucker, Alan and Tommy are more or less back where they started – unemployed, penniless and without girlfriends. Alan's father has died and Alan is being looked after by his Uncle Vic, who reckons it's time Alan got a job and started behaving like a responsible adult. At least Ralph Passmore is now a reformed character, so that's one less issue to deal with. Tucker gets a temporary job as a motorcycle courier, Passmore takes up a suspicious sales job, Alan buys a guitar and joins runaway Creamy's band but Tommy is falling in with the wrong crowd, relieving trucks of their cargo and selling the goods at the market.

**Developed by** Barry Purchese
**Written by** Barry Purchese

**Designer:** Peter Higgins
**Producer:** Darrol Blake
**Directors:** Darrol Blake (1, 2, 6–9), Margie Barbour (3–5)

**Season Three**
**9 episodes**
**Broadcast:** Tuesdays 22/10/85 – 17/12/85 BBC2 6pm.

**Main Cast:** Todd Carty (Tucker Jenkins), Hilary Crane (Mrs Jenkins), George Armstrong (Alan Humphries), Amanda Waring (Natalia Gordon), Joanne Palmer (Rhona Jenkins), Stephen Persaud (Matthew Clarke), Neil Carrick (Barry Jenkins)

Times are tough for Tucker when his plans to operate a small courier business fall through and his father runs away with another woman. As his mother falls into a state of depression, Tucker must take over the household chores, attend to his little sister Rhona and track down his big brother Barry as quickly as possible. On top of all that, Tucker has been told that he will now have to fight to keep his college place by achieving O-levels in Maths and English.

**Written by** David Angus (1, 2, 8, 9), Trevor Cooper (3, 4), Jim Hawkins (5–7)

**Designer:** Dinah Walker and Paul Haines (episode 2)
**Producer/Director:** Darrol Blake

**Tie-in publications:** *Tucker in Control* by Jan Needle published by Magnet, 1985

**Other tie-in publications:** *Tucker's Luck Annual* published by Fleetway/IPC 1983–84 (covers read Annual 1984–85)

## Dramarama: Spooky
### Season 1A

What's in a name? In the case of this compendium of seven horror stories, rather a lot. While the idea of a weekly plays anthology strand was bandied around at the time this series was launched, the *Dramarama* banner is something of a misnomer. *Dramarama* would come to be known as an umbrella strand covering all sorts of plays, topics and styles from the ITV regions but this very first batch, going out under the subtitle *Spooky*, was obviously far more defined in terms of content and was produced by only one regional centre.

To all intents and purposes this was a resurrection of Thames 70s' strand *Shadows* – *Spooky*'s publicity blurb strongly echoed the outline for the earlier series. 'Seven stories which explore the idea that there is more to our world than we can reliably see. There are other realities which, when conditions are right, affect our own ...' Producer Charles Warren conveyed his intent at the series' outset: 'We don't want to give anybody nightmares but we wouldn't mind if they were watching from behind the sofa.'

*Shadows* was rather clever and witty and just that little bit disturbingly off-kilter while, despite Warren's assurances, *Spooky* seemed to have been designed to scare the viewers out of their wits. *Spooky* didn't really go in for the educational and emotional aspects of most *Shadows* episodes and concentrated on shock effect.

'War Games with Caroline' opened the series and was a straightforward tale of a ghost girl trying to avert past disaster, nonetheless told in an exciting way. Teenager Kevin is kept behind after school to write an essay on why the role-playing war games he enjoys are not the proper way to understand history, when he is disturbed by a strange schoolgirl in old-fashioned uniform. The girl is Caroline, a ghost from World War II, who has come to send Kevin back to her own time to prevent her choir classmates being killed in a doodlebug attack. Amid backwards ticking clocks, eerie singing and weird camera angles, the race is on for Kevin to reach the girls before the bomb drops. There's a message in there too, with Kevin realising how his games and lurid war comics trivialise the real horrors of war as experienced by those who lived through and died in them.

Despite the narrower horror format there was room for some variety. 'The Ghostly Earl' was the light and amusing story of a little girl who befriends the 250-year-old ghost of a foppish Earl and tries to save her stately home from theme park developers. 'The Restless Ghost' was a period tale which saw two young boys set out to scare a curmudgeonly old Sexton by dressing up as a legendary ghostly drummer boy, only to invoke the real thing which then seeks revenge on the old man (Wilfred Brambell in one of his last roles).

Two more episodes were in an updated Gothic vein, set in remote and isolated cottages. Noted children's fantasy writer Alan Garner provided a rather adult tale of two ghost-hunters researching a house supposedly haunted by a malevolent presence. There was also 'In a Dark, Dark Box...' in which a young boy is read an old nonsense poem by his grandmother. 'In a dark, dark forest was a dark, dark house,' it begins, and the boy wonders if the poem is in fact written about the house in which he is staying. If so, what is in 'the dark, dark box' that lies in 'the dark, dark trunk' at the foot of his bed? There's at least one genuine behind-the-sofa moment in which the ghost of the boy's drowned sea captain father appears, soaked and covered in seaweed. The outcome of the story is in fact quite whimsical, something which certainly cannot be said of two further episodes which failed to provide any such reassurance in their closing moments.

'The Exorcism of Amy' and 'The Danny Roberts Show' were truly terrifying in that they failed to send the young viewer off, happy that this week's terrors had been dispelled. In the former we were on fairly familiar territory, with a girl's disruptive and mischievous imaginary friend (or was it a case of split personality?) becoming all too real. Amy's other half, Amelia, was finally dispatched in a form of exorcism ... or so it seemed until in the final moments it's realised that the darker spirit has possessed cousin Elizabeth. 'The Danny Roberts Show' meanwhile was a

very adult tale which featured no child characters among its small cast. This satirical tale saw a smarmy late-night DJ, who milks the misery of his callers, receive his comeuppance from a voice that promises 'Punishment and Retribution' on inane broadcasters such as Roberts (Nicholas Ball). When Roberts is found by the security guard the next morning, frightened out of his wits, he realises that his torture is not over and the voice in his head is still there.

The rest of the twelve-week run was made up of repeated episodes of *Theatre Box*, now recut with the *Dramarama* title sequence. These brought to the strand – albeit by sleight of hand – the variety for which the 'real' *Dramarama* would soon become known.

**Thames**
**7 episodes**
**(colour)**
**Broadcast:** Mondays 18/4/83 – 13/6/83

18/4/83 - **'War Games with Caroline'** by Maggie Wadey.
**Dir:** John Woods
25/4/83 - **'The Exorcism of Amy'** by Paula Milne.
**Dir:** Richard Handford
9/5/83 - **'The Danny Roberts Show'** by David Hopkins.
**Dir:** John Stroud
16/5/83 - **'The Ghostly Earl'** by R. Chetwynd-Hayes.
Dramatised by Alan Seymour. **Dir:** Richard Handford
23/5/83 - **'In a Dark, Dark Box…'** by Jane Hollowood.
**Dir:** Vic Hughes
6/6/83 - **'The Restless Ghost'** by Leon Garfield. Dramatised by James Andrew Hall. **Dir:** Vic Hughes
13/6/83 - **'The Keeper'** by Alan Garner. **Dir:** John Woods

**Designer:** Robert Ide (all seven)
**Producers:** Charles Warren, Vic Hughes
**Executive Producer:** Pamela Lonsdale

Season continues as repeats of episodes from *Theatre Box*, 'rebranded' with the *Dramarama* title. Broadcast Mondays 20/6/83 – 18/7/83: 'Marmalade Atkins in Space'; 'Death Angel'; 'School for Clowns' parts 1 and 2; 'Prince and the Demons'

**Tie-in publications:** *Spooky – Stories of the Supernatural* published by Methuen, 1983 (hardback) and Thames Magnet, 1984 (paperback). Edited by Pamela Lonsdale. Novelisations of all episodes except 'The Keeper' with reprints of 'The Ghostly Earl' and 'The Restless Ghost'.

## Thief

The moral of this play is that money cannot buy happiness and is a poor replacement for parental compassion. Being part of a well-off family, Tony would appear to want for nothing. The boy's need is however greater than material wealth. What he really desires is some attention from his parents, who have very little time for him.

Tony, like many other children deprived of emotional contact, strays from the straight and narrow and is caught shoplifting. This could be seen as a desperate attempt to gain recognition from his parents. Although he is breaking the law, in Tony's mind any reaction from his parents is better than no reaction at all.

Tony's actions are enough for his parents to ask

themselves why their son should be involved in criminal activities. They are naturally shocked when they discover how neglected Tony feels but the incident opens doors to communication and allows the family to sort out their problems and re-evaluate their relationship. Another BBC work of the early 80s to assume that comfortable middle-class upbringings are automatically without affection.

**BBC**
**1 episode**
(colour)
**Broadcast:** Friday 13/5/83

**Main Cast:** James Kelly (Tony Mailor), Roy Boyd (Tony's Father), Kara Wilson (Tony's Mother), Rachel Ffield (Suzanna), James Bateman (Martin Shanks)

**Written by** Roger Parkes

**Designer:** Gillian Howard
**Producer:** Angela Beeching
**Director:** Margie Barbour

**Tie-in publications:** n/k

## Dramarama
### Season 1B
Membership for this first series was open to only three regions, with TVS the nominal head and the large Central and much smaller Tyne Tees franchises also contributing. Within its first nine episodes the series explored the broad genres that would serve it well in the years to come, namely comedy, fantasy and issue-led drama with allowances made

to admit a really weird episode once in a while.

Although the comedy episodes are generally less well remembered or regarded than the fantasy or more serious episodes, it was a comedy that was on offer on the opening night. 'Mighty Mum and the Petnappers' was a comic strip silly about a mum (Judy Cornwell) with a superhero alter ego, a purple leotard and a deadly frying pan. Slightly more earthy was 'The Venchie'. This robust comedy, full of flippings and bog offs, told the story of two gangs of cartoon yobs who get together at the Temple Road adventure playground ('the Venchie' of the title). The Temple Tigers are the boy gang who refuse to let the girls of The Temple Hens join their Sunday football team and it is up to their new 'play worker' Matt to teach them about democracy. While there are flour bombs and exaggerated comic scrapes, the story is grounded in reality. Filmed on a very real and rather grotty Newcastle housing estate, Matt believes that despite the tough reputation of Temple Road kids, every child has a certain innocence at heart and it is his aim to try to 'relate' to them, to use the vernacular. In the end, Matt tricks the kids into believing that the Venchie is to be pulled down to make room for a car park. In the face of this threat Temple Road is united against the common foe of the bogus developers. Writer Adele Rose went on to create Newcastle soap *Byker Grove*.

'The Venchie' demonstrated a grasp on the lives of many of its young viewers from outside the middle classes and

**Below:** in the world over the wall is a bizarre court presided over by the wicked Grand Vamp (Charlotte Cornwell, far left) and the kind-hearted Lovely Rita (Rosemary Martin, far right). Looking on are gangster Fat Cat Malcolm (Martin Cochrane) and Whistle (Robert Putt). From the classic *Dramarama* episode 'A Young Person's Guide to Getting Their Ball Back!'

deployed this in a comedy tale. Other episodes told stories that reflected the concerns of the audience in a more realistic manner. 'Because I Say So' and 'Bully for Cosmo' both dealt with the subject of bullying and school violence, although their being aired in consecutive weeks may have suggested that the formula for balancing output over a run had not yet been perfected. 'Messages' was another modern story about a boy who acts as a go-between carrying messages to and from his estranged parents. Despite their qualities it was easy to see how a run of various gritty, contemporary plays could become dull. *Dramarama*, even this early on, had the capacity to surprise with its choice of subjects. 'Rip It Up' was a spin on the youth club drama, set at the outbreak of rock'n'roll in 1958. *Comic Strip* comedian Stephen Frost was a trendy vicar who tried to chair a debate between the table tennis and Ted factions when some members demand that their Elvis records be played in the club. The episode also marked an early appearance by Nick Berry.

The fantasy strand was not that prominent in this inaugural year. Both sci-fi entries jumped on the 'hackers' bandwagon, viewing computers as things that kids got up to no good with. In 'Jack and the Computer' a boy's electronic friend took on a sinister life of its own and gained almost supernatural powers. Rather less frighteningly, 'Sweet Revenge' saw a class of mischievous computer whizkids get their own back on a curmudgeonly shopkeeper by hacking into stock records and ordering tons of bubblegum on his behalf.

Leagues above these simple fantasies was 'A Young Person's Guide to Getting Their Ball Back!' – an experimental piece, quite possibly typical of fringe/youth theatre but made immediately accessible through the TV medium. When a boy kicks his football over a high wall and goes to retrieve it, he finds himself in a hall full of strange characters who try him on charges of killing a window. There are two sides debating what is 'in the boy's best interest'. The 'white' side is led by a nice woman called Lovely Rita and the 'black' by a flame-haired witch called Grand Vamp (given the time this was made, it is tempting to view the Vamp as a theatrical rendering of Mrs Thatcher). This madhouse of a kangaroo court is clearly a representation of parliament, and 'parliament' conspires to consign the boy to The Vat rather than do what is right, thus maintaining their power base. The boy escapes his fate when he is aided by the sad clown figure of The Instructor, servant of the court (another great turn by Patrick Troughton). The boy rushes past these bizarre buffoons and out back over the wall to what sounds like distorted chants of 'Sieg Heil'. A hard to decipher allegory, it was also one of the most startling twenty-five minutes of children's TV ever and an early classic in the strand.

**Season 1B**
**9 episodes**
(colour)
**Broadcast:** Mondays 12/9/83 – 7/11/83

This is the first all-new season of a variety of plays under this title and so is to all intents and purposes the first season of *Dramarama* as it is remembered.

12/9/83 – **'Mighty Mum and the Petnappers'**, writer n/k. **Dir:** Renny Rye (TVS)
19/9/83 – **'Rip It Up'** by Harry Duffin. **Dir:** Renny Rye (TVS)

26/9/83 – **'The Venchie'** by Adele Rose from an idea by Graeme Rigby. **Dir:** Roger Cheveley (Tyne Tees)
3/10/83 – **'Jack and the Computer'** by Alan England. **Dir:** Diarmuid Lawrence (TVS)
10/10/83 – **'Because I Say So'** by Gerry Huxham. **Dir:** Oliver Horsbrugh (Central)
17/10/83 – **'Bully for Cosmo'** by Gail Renard. **Dir:** Geoff Husson (Central)
24/10/83 – **'Messages'** by Ben Steed. **Dir:** Roger Cheveley (Tyne Tees)
31/10/83 – **'A Young Person's Guide to Getting Their Ball Back!'** by Nigel Baldwin. **Dir:** Diarmuid Lawrence (TVS)
7/11/83 – **'Sweet Revenge'** by David Blake and Alan Banham. **Dir:** Geoff Husson (Central)

**Tie-in publications:** *Dramarama – Four TV Scripts*, edited by Alan England, published by Heinemann Educational, 1986, as part of the Heinemann Spotlights series. Reproduced scripts for 'Because I Say So', 'Bully for Cosmo', 'The Venchie', 'Jack and the Computer'.

**Video:** 'The Venchie' included on 3-episode tape *Dramarama*, released by Video Gems/Tyne Tees c. 1990. Deleted.

## The All Electric Amusement Arcade

Fifteen-year-old Bella Harper dreams of leaving the South Coast of England for Hollywood. To alleviate her boredom in the meantime, she makes an agreement with the owner of a dilapidated amusement arcade. All she has to do is carry out all the required renovations, turning the arcade into a meeting place for young people. If it is successful she will receive a share of the profits, which she hopes will pay her way to Hollywood. The renovation will also solve a problem for Bella's friends, the band Electric Arc, who until now have had no hope of finding a venue to play.

This is the story of a child's ambition to overcome the perceived limitations she has of her quiet seaside town and her turbulent life at home. The arcade is the focus Bella needs while she tries to make sense of her life.

Electric Arc perform in almost every episode of the series and a single containing their series theme tune was released at the time of broadcast.

**Thames**
**7 episodes**
(colour)
**Broadcast:** Wednesdays 14/9/83 – 26/10/83

**Main Cast:** Lorraine Brunning (Bella), Tim Whitnall (Jake), Joanne Campbell (Deshaun), Heather Taylor (Cass), Steven Woodcock (Marcus), Michael Lee Osborn (Dale), Gordon Gostelow (Mr Thomsett)

**Written by** Gerard MacDonald

**Music:** David Rhol
**Designer:** Jane Krall
**Producer:** Sheila Kinany
**Executive Producer:** Pamela Lonsdale
**Directors:** Christopher Hodson (1, 2), John Woods (3, 4, 6), Vic Hughes (5, 7)

**Tie-in publications:** novelisation published in paperback by Fontana Lions, 1983

## Seaview

*'Seaview Guest House, South Shore, Blackpool, Lancashire, Great Britain, Europe, the world, the solar system, the galaxy, the universe. Here.'*

Driven by well-observed character work, *Seaview* was at heart a depiction of that age-old relationship which exists between brother and sister. Older sister Sandy was a teenager with the customary hang-ups about boys and her own identity. George was that couple of years younger, content to drift through life and childishly joke his way out of trouble. They cared for each other really, of course, but George couldn't resist winding up the earnest Sandy and she couldn't help but look down her nose at his immaturity. Sandy, like all teenagers, wanted recognition and control of her own life and decisions. That's why she argues with Mum about saving the seals, even if Mum thinks it's just a phase, and that's why she press-gangs George into joining her dispute over pay at their parents' hotel. Sandy's search for identity usually manifests itself in attempts at fame, so she's angry when, for all her careful planning, her talent audition is upstaged by her little brother's unrehearsed clowning around.

Sandy and George lived with their parents in a Blackpool guest house and the set-up appeared so natural it was tempting to think that writer Chris Barlas had grown up in a similar household. In fact, Barlas had remembered his childhood holidays spent caravanning with his rather adventurous parents – one time they had camped in the middle of a circus in France and the young Barlas wondered what it would be like to grow up in a place that others only see as somewhere to have a holiday.

Some may query *Seaview*'s inclusion here as a drama series – wasn't it a sitcom? Certainly Barlas had not been commissioned to write *Seaview* specifically as either, having just been asked for a children's series. He hoped to write a series which kids would watch because it was funny but which would reward them with something more. Barlas always considered underlying themes when planning his episodes and this to him was the difference between drama and sitcom.

Episodes could look at serious issues but George could always see the funny side. Conversely, comedic scenes could always have some kind of realism or message backing them up. When Sandy tries for a job as a glamorous promotions girl in a Blackpool store she is instead made to dress up in a ludicrous teapot costume. Humiliated, she stumbles around the store in her comedy outfit, tears streaming down her face while she plaintively repeats the words, 'Would you like a leaflet?'

The episode 'In a Good Cause' acts as a soapbox for the fur trade issue but moreover is about Sandy's teenage idealism. She stands in the street with her ecology friends, belting out 'We shall overcome', but her attempts to raise funds for the group are inevitably undermined by George when their charity dog show ends up with seemingly every pooch in Blackpool running wild on the promenade. Only the episode 'Happy Families' doesn't bother to add comedy to balance things out. When James' mother fails to return from a trip to Saudi to visit James' father, the boy is forced to steal to get food.

'In Sickness', by contrast, was *Fawlty Towers*-style farce, with George taking advantage of some indistinct handwriting and ordering seven arcade games instead of one for the hotel. Then, when his friends come to visit the Seaview amusement arcade, they manage to traipse through the wet cement of the new patio. Marilyn Fox was

**Above:** (l to r) George Shelton (Aaron Brown), his sister Sandy (Yvette Fielding) and friend James (Chris Hargreaves) on the seafront at Blackpool's South Shore, home of the Seaview Hotel.

not really a comedy director and this worked in *Seaview*'s favour. Barlas didn't want *Seaview* played for laughs and encouraged the children to play *against* the comedy.

By the second series, the child actors had grown a year older (Aaron Brown's voice had broken too) and Barlas reckoned that it would be silly to pretend they were still the same age. Thus the second run was more teen-orientated, with the focus consciously shifted onto Sandy instead of George as in the first. So *Seaview* grew up with its initial audience. Barlas' view was that girls mature earlier and face relationship problems younger, so there were more tears from Sandy as she fell for a boy called Ian and the course of young love failed to run smooth.

If *Seaview* were to attempt a third series, the leads would be too old for it to continue as a genuine 'children's' serial. There were plans for the series to develop into a more consciously teenage show airing in the BBC2 6p.m. slot once *Tucker's Luck* finished its final run. Discussions were well underway when the powers-that-were at BBC2 decided that the teen dramas were to be phased out.

The two series of *Seaview* that were made stand as excellent examples of true comedy drama for children, where both elements worked together in careful balance. Given what 'comedy drama' has come to mean almost two decades later, it would be a great shame if *Seaview* was retrospectively tarred with the same brush.

**BBC**
**2 seasons**
(colour)

**Main Cast:** Yvette Fielding (Sandy Shelton), Aaron Brown (George Shelton), Chris Hargreaves (James), Maggie Ollerenshaw (Mrs Shelton), David Gooderson (Mr Shelton), Lloyd Peters (Duncan)

**Written by** Chris Barlas

**Music:** Michael Omer
**Executive Producer:** Paul Stone
**Director:** Marilyn Fox

**Season One**
**6 episodes**
**Broadcast:** Wednesdays 5/10/83 – 9/11/83

'First Steps' 5.10p.m.
With the golden handshake he receives from his supermarket redundancy, Mr Shelton decides to open up a guest house in Blackpool. Almost calling it the Ballachulish, he eventually decides on the name Seaview. As the Shelton family muck in to get the hotel open in time, Sandy tries out for a talent audition, while the wise-cracking George almost falls into fame by accident. Bumping into a new friend called James, the lads are almost signed up as a comedy double act.

'In a Good Cause' 5.10p.m.
When Dad gives Mum a real fur coat, Sandy is appalled. Joining an ecology group, Sandy asks George how she can raise some funds to help save the seal. George's bright idea is to have a dog show on the Blackpool beach but has anyone thought to check when the tide comes in?

'In Sickness' 5.10p.m.
Mum and Dad are ill so Sandy and George are run off their feet trying to man Seaview. There's a man coming to lay a new patio and a Space Invaders machine is to be delivered. They really should have known better than to leave George in charge of things …

'In Dispute' 5.10p.m.
Sandy and George decide that they should be paid for the work they do at Seaview but, when Mum and Dad refuse, the pair start a 'go slow' protest and form a picket line.

'Happy Families' 5.10p.m.
James seems to be calling at Seaview rather a lot these days – hasn't he a home of his own to go to? James asks if George can hide him at Seaview. The police are looking for him, which is more than can be said for his mother.

'Band of Hope' 5.05p.m.
'We're tomorrow, we're the brightest thing around!' Sandy gets a chance at stardom when she joins Duncan's heavy metal band. They're pretty awful but maybe she can persuade them to do one of her own songs?

**Designer:** Graham Lough

**Tie-in publications:** first five episodes novelised by Chris Barlas, published by BBC/Knight Books (paperback) and BBC (hardback), 1983

**Season Two**
**6 episodes**
**Broadcast:** Wednesdays 20/2/85 – 27/3/85
'Big Brother' 5.05p.m.
George discovers how looking after his new baby brother, Paul, can be turned to financial advantage when he charges people to have their photograph taken with his bonny brother.

The man with the performing monkey is less than amused by the new competition on his patch. Meanwhile a fortune teller sees love and a broken heart ahead for Sandy.

'The Godfather' 5.05p.m.
Friends and family arrive at Seaview to attend Paul's christening. Jack and Molly's son Ian takes a shine to Sandy.

'Dancin" 5.10p.m.
James is flattered when Sandy asks him to enter a disco-dancing competition. Is James reading too much into the invitation? Sandy only has eyes for Ian.

'Making Up' 5.05p.m.
The Sheltons pursue fame yet again. Sandy manages to drag her friend Petra along to a youth theatre group while George is less enthusiastic when his Nan suggests he enter a make 'em laugh contest.

'Fun Running' 5.10p.m.
The Shelton family are in training for a 'fun run' but Sandy's mind is still on Ian. When the phone rings, she is overjoyed.

'Growing Pains' 5.05p.m.
It's Sandy's sixteenth birthday party and she'll cry if she has to. Duncan has arranged a disco and light show but it's Ian who provides the real floor show when he shows up.

**Additional Cast:** Mark Jordan (Ian), Catherine Pratt (Lisa), Carla Rogerson (Petra)

**Designer:** Mel Bibby

## The Witches and the Grinnygog

The Grinnygog is a small stone figure that once sat in the grounds of St Cuthbert's church. The little statue goes missing, falling from the back of a truck, when the church is dismantled and moved to an alternative location. It is found by a local man and given pride of place on his rockery.

The Grinnygog is less than enchanted with its removal from the church and summons three witches who were charged with its care centuries previously. Rising from the marshes, the witches enlist the assistance of five local children to help them locate the statue. The search that follows leads to some very strange occurrences in their normally quiet village.

*The Witches and the Grinnygog* is a light-hearted story of sorcery and magic set in the countryside around Winchester.

TVS
**6 episodes**
(colour)
**Broadcast:** Mondays 14/11/83 – 19/12/83

**Main Cast:** Paul Curtis (Jimmy Firkettle), Giles Harper (Colin Sogood), Heidi Mayo (Nan Sogood), Adam Woodyatt (Dave Firkettle), Zoe Loftin (Essie Firkettle), Patricia Hayes (Miss Bendybones), Anna Wing (Edie Possett), Hilda Fenemore (Mrs Featherly)

Based on the novel by Dorothy Edwards (first UK publication 1981, Faber & Faber)
**Adapted by** Roy Russell

**Designer:** John Newton Clarke
**Executive Producer:** Anna Home
**Director:** Diarmuid Lawrence

**Tie-in publications:** unconfirmed edition published by
Magnet/Methuen, 1983

## The Winner

Teenager Cheryl Stafford excels at sport, running in
particular, and her parents, sports teacher and friends are
all sure that she has the potential to become a future
Olympic champion. She may well have great athletic
ability but she finds the training boring and time-
consuming. She has a keen interest in fashion design and
isn't at all sure that she wants to pursue a career in sport.
Unfortunately no-one seems to be listening to Cheryl's
doubts and everyone seems to know what's best for her.

Many gifted children experience pressure to fulfil their
ambitions, from both adults and their peer group alike.
This scenario forms the core theme of Roy Russell's play.
Russell got the idea after watching an interview with
athlete Judy Livermore. She had stated that coping with
the pressures wasn't a problem for her but that she found
the training less than interesting. Russell got the
impression that she had never had any doubts about being
an athlete but felt that it would be interesting to examine
the pressures on a child at the point in her development
when she has important decisions to make against the
pressures of expectation.

**BBC**
**1 episode**
(colour)
**Broadcast:** Wednesday 16/11/83

**Main Cast:** Bernadette Bowman (Cheryl Stafford), Angela
Bruce (Mrs Roper), Jan Harvey (Val Stafford), Gary Waldhorn
(Bill Stafford), Helen Newell (Lynsey Dyson), Simon Wilkins
(Martin Ellis)

**Written by** Roy Russell

**Designer:** Graeme Thomson
**Producer:** Angela Beeching
**Director:** Edward Pugh

## Chocky

Twelve-year-old Matthew Gore is an unremarkable child,
excelling in no particular subject at school. When he starts
having conversations with himself, producing wonderful
works of art and counting in binary-code mathematics his
adoptive parents are naturally confused. So Matthew tells
them about Chocky – the voice that lives inside his head.

The adaptation negates certain elements of suspense
present in John Wyndham's novel by giving the character
of Chocky an immediate on-screen realisation. Although it
is only as an energy field of light it leaves the audience in
little doubt that Chocky is real, rather than a figment of
Matthew's imagination. The book delivers no such
description and the reader is given the impression that
Matthew could be suffering from a form of schizophrenia.
The possibility of mental illness is still explored in the
drama as Matthew's parents consult a psychologist in the

hope of identifying the reason for their son's extraordinary
behaviour. While it's interesting to witness the effect that
such pressures can bring to bear on an otherwise stable
family unit, one cannot help but feel that this thread is on
a hiding to nothing when Chocky's existence is absolute.
Special effects were required to give Chocky's screen
presence. This was achieved using a laser and dry-ice
smoke effect, familiar from many an early 80s disco, which
was then transposed over the necessary scenes.

Suspense in the drama is created instead through the
ambivalence of Chocky. Her true intentions are hidden for
quite some time but eventually form the core theme of the
narrative – that of mankind's potential to greed. Chocky
wants to point our race towards a source of infinite power
that will make redundant the use of finite energy sources
like coal and oil. She plans to do this through coaching
Matthew in the field of physics and maths. It is her first
mission and Chocky, seemingly a child herself, becomes
attached to Matthew and tells him too much, thus
endangering his life. When Matthew is kidnapped by
Thorbe and the details of Chocky's theories are extracted
under hypnosis, Chocky recognises that she has failed and
retreats from Matthew to begin again with another child.
What would a child's life be worth to the coal and oil
conglomerates who wish only to protect their profit and
power? This is a valid question that challenges the integrity
of Man and leaves Matthew without his friend.

Published in 1968, Wyndham's novel naturally required
some surface updating to bring it into the 80s. Matthew
completes his friend Colin's Rubik Cube in record time
and, in an almost ridiculous scene, blows up his Atari
games console by shooting aliens at a pace too frenetic for
the machine to handle.

Like other works by Wyndham, *Chocky* is almost
intolerably middle class. This is more predominant in the
novel but invariably survives the transition to the screen.
The Gore family live in a comfortable house, drive the
latest model of car, enjoy picnics in the country and have a
psychologist at hand when their son shows the first sign of
being mentally unstable. This is however a key part of the
narrative, heightening the impact of Matthew's behaviour
when the idyllic lifestyle starts to crumble under the strain.
This is taken to a more extreme level in the book but a step
back seems to have been taken for the adaptation, to
ensure that the on-screen representation wasn't too
upsetting for children. It is worth noting that Wyndham's
novel was not written exclusively for children, being told
from the father's point of view and not Matthew's.

Two sequels quickly followed. *Chocky's Children* is
basically a retelling of *Chocky* and adds very little to the
original story. Matthew, although present throughout, is no
longer the main character, there only to help Albertine
Meyer through everything he himself experienced in
*Chocky*. It does however have a couple of good points, in
particular the character of Albertine's father. Recognising
the importance of his daughter's work and the unwanted
attention it could bring, he tutors her at home. This
controversial move costs him his marriage and very nearly
results in his imprisonment.

For *Chocky's Challenge*, Matthew is phased out altogether
after just a couple of episodes, returning only to help
Albertine rescue one of her peers. Shades of *Codename
Icarus* abound as Albertine, assisted by the three other
Chocky prodigies, strives towards a source of infinite
power. This rather flies in the face of Chocky's statement
in the first story when she tells Matthew's father that the

energy source is an objective that probably won't be developed in his lifetime, yet here we are a mere two years later with the source of power thoroughly tapped.

The sequels demonstrate a progression in the scale of the narrative, if not the depth. There's an excellent continuity in the cast between the three stories with the same actors reprising their roles as and when required. *Chocky's Challenge* was left open-ended, perhaps in anticipation of a sequel which never appeared. It's just as well it didn't, as both sequels failed to recapture the intensity of the original.

### Chocky (1984)
**Thames**
**6 episodes**
(colour)

### Episode One
Monday 9/1/84 4.45p.m.
Matthew starts talking to himself and displays an extraordinary new talent for subjects in school. When he tells his parents about Chocky, a voice that speaks to him inside his head, they believe it to be an imaginary friend.

### Episode Two
Monday 16/1/84 4.45p.m.
Matthew further baffles his parents by asking complex questions about asexual reproduction and starts counting using binary mathematics. When David brings the new family car home Matthew throws a violent tantrum when Chocky tells him the vehicle is stupid.

### Episode Three
Monday 23/1/84 4.45p.m.
Chocky helps Matthew to secure victory for his school's cricket team. Believing that Matthew may be ill, David makes an appointment for Matthew to talk to Roy Landis, a psychologist colleague. Chocky makes herself visible to Matthew.

### Episode Four
Monday 30/1/84 4.45p.m.
Mary is concerned when she finds that Matthew has been creating excellent paintings when he had never previously shown any talent in the area. On holiday Matthew saves his sister from drowning but has never learned to swim.

### Episode Five
Monday 6/2/84 4.45p.m.
The newspapers get hold of Matthew's amazing rescue of his sister and focus on the help he had from his 'guardian angel'. Matthew's parents refer him to another psychologist, Sir William Thorbe, whose questions betray a sinister agenda.

### Episode Six
Monday 13/2/84 4.45p.m.
Matthew is kidnapped on the way home from school and subjected to interrogation by Thorbe's people. He is later released and returns home where Chocky explains to Mr Gore the true reason for her visit.

**Main Cast:** Andrew Ellams (Matthew), James Hazeldine (David), Carol Drinkwater (Mary), Zoe Hart (Polly), Jeremy Bulloch (Landis), John Grillo (Sir William Thorbe), James Greene (Mr Trimble), Devin Stanfield (Colin), Glynis Brooks (Chocky's Voice)

Based on the novel by John Wyndham (first UK publication 1968, Michael Joseph)
**Adapted by** Anthony Read

**Script Consultant:** Richard Bates
**Designer:** David Richens
**Producer:** Vic Hughes
**Executive Producer:** Pamela Lonsdale
**Directors:** Vic Hughes (1, 4, 6) and Christopher Hodson (2, 3, 5)

**Tie-in publications:** editions published in paperback by Penguin, 1984

**Video:** released in UK in edited compilation form by Thames c. 1985. Deleted. Released episodically as Region 2 DVD by Second Sight, October 2002.

### Chocky's Children (1985)
**Thames**
**6 episodes**
(colour)
**Broadcast:** Mondays 7/1/85 – 11/2/85

While on holiday at his Aunt Cissie's house, Matthew meets Albertine Meyer, a child prodigy in maths and physics, who lives like a recluse with her father. They discover that they can read each other's thoughts and move objects using the combined power of their minds. Matthew quickly concludes that Chocky is involved and soon the children find themselves in terrible danger.

**Main Cast:** Andrew Ellams (Matthew), James Hazeldine (David), Carol Drinkwater (Mary), Zoe Hart (Polly), Anabel Worrell (Albertine), Prentis Hancock (Meyer), Jeremy Bulloch (Landis), Ed Bishop (Deacon), Michael Crompton (Luke), Angela Galbraith (Cissie), Glynis Brooks (Chocky's Voice)

**Written by** Anthony Read
**Script Consultant:** Richard Bates

**Designer:** Davis Richens
**Producer:** Vic Hughes
**Executive Producer:** Pamela Lonsdale
**Directors:** Peter Duguid (1, 5, 6), Vic Hughes (2–4)

**Tie-in publications:** none – only season not to be novelised

### Chocky's Challenge (1986)
**Thames**
**6 episodes**
(colour)
**Broadcast:** Mondays 29/9/86 – 16/10/86

Albertine has graduated from university after only a year and now seeks funding to continue her research. She enlists the help of other children recruited by Chocky and together they attempt to discover the source of limitless energy. Very soon they find themselves under threat from a jealous university professor and the British Military.

**Main Cast:** Andrew Ellams (Matthew), James Hazeldine (David), Anabel Worrell (Albertine), Freddie Brooks (Mike), Paul Russell (Paul), Karina Wilsher (Su Lin),

Prentis Hancock (Meyer), Richard Wordsworth (Prof Ferris), Kristine Howarth (Professor Wade), Illona Linthwaite (Dr Liddle), Roy Boyd (Professor Draycott), Leon Eagles (General), Joan Blackham (Mrs Gibson), Glynis Brooks (Chocky's Voice)

**Written by** Anthony Read

**Designer:** Peter Elliot
**Producer:** Richard Bates
**Executive Producer:** Brian Walcroft
**Director:** Bob Blagden

**Tie-in publications:** novelisation by Mark Daniel published in paperback by Thames Magnet, 1986

## The Farm

*The Farm* is an emotional tale of conflicting family interests between generations set in and around the Jenkyns family's Welsh farm. The Jenkyns have maintained the farm for generations and teenager Alun is expected to carry on the tradition when his father retires. Alun however has different ideas. He is diligent in school and farming is not on his career agenda. This leads to heated debates between father and son as Alun tries to convince his father that he should be left alone to make his own decisions and Alun's father struggles to comprehend what he feels is a betrayal.

This is another example of one of the BBC's single episode dramas. Once again exploring the issues of lack of understanding and communication between parent and child, the drama makes good use of a mere half-hour to convey its compelling story.

**BBC**
**1 episode**
(colour)
**Broadcast:** Wednesday 15/2/84

**Main Cast:** Haydn Watkins (Alun Jenkyns), Tim Wylton (John Jenkyns), Elin Jenkins (Gwyneth Jenkyns), Nia Roberts (Menna)

**Written by** Julia Jones

**Designer:** Paul Munting
**Producer:** Angela Beeching
**Director:** Christine Secombe

## Moonfleet

Fifteen-year-old John Trenchard is dissatisfied with life in Moonfleet, a remote village on the Cornish coast. With the exception of attending school or listening to his mother's religious sermons, neither of which he finds appealing, there is little to occupy his time. 'The straight and narrow path. It may be the path of righteousness,' he tells an acquaintance, 'but it seems to me there's little adventure to be had along the way.'

John craves excitement and is intrigued by the legend of Blackbeard, a once famous smuggler of the area. It is said that he left treasure buried somewhere in the local church grounds and that his ghost walks at night. John's inquisitive nature soon delivers the adventure he desires but at a high personal cost. Becoming involved in smuggling activities, he is forced to depart Britain with a price on his head. It

seems to John that there can be no return for him and he must resign himself to a life of slave labour in a foreign country.

The character of John Trenchard is interesting, mainly because he questions the hypocrisy of those upholding the laws of the area. 'His only crime was to be born poor,' he says of a friend certain to hang for smuggling. 'Not all poor people choose to run cargoes,' Grace replies. John however challenges this, saying, 'Not all criminals get caught ... seems to me there are many judges and precious little justice.' His criticism is of those who shout for smugglers to be hanged, while secretly enjoying the fine wines and laces they know to be contraband. It is only the smugglers who are tried, while those that purchase the goods take the moral high ground, remaining untouched by justice.

Grace Maskew's father, the local magistrate, also poses problems for John. A cruel and miserly man responsible for the death of Elzevir Block's smuggler son, he then sets about ensuring that Elzevir loses the tenancy of his tavern, effectively leaving Elzevir and John without a roof over their heads. It's therefore little wonder that John readily joins the smugglers. He doesn't view the act of smuggling as being particularly wrong – not in comparison to the corruption that surrounds him.

*Moonfleet* is an effective adaptation in places. There's much to scare the kiddies, especially in the first couple of episodes when John, stumbling across a hole in the ground at the side of a tomb, ventures down below. There he discovers a smugglers' den but not before he's been confronted with the coffins of the dead, including Blackbeard's. Elsewhere *Moonfleet* is a rather taxing watch. The Cornish dialect is difficult to follow in some instances, even though it has been simplified in the transition from text to screen. The production is dialogue heavy and, although John's trips to the burial chambers create an air of apprehension, there's little else to catch the eye in what is essentially a rather slow-paced drama. The production appears dated and looks like typical Sunday family fare of the early 70s rather than 1984. Shot primarily on location and on 16mm, the film prints look a little rough. There are also clear examples of how not to use a filter lens. Most of the goings-on are indistinguishable, with the filter almost blacking out the entire screen in an attempt to recreate darkness.

*Moonfleet* has actually been adapted for children's television on two occasions. One could be forgiven for failing to immediately associate the first, broadcast in 1964, with J. Meade Falkner's adventure novel. It was aired under the title *Smuggler's Bay*, a likely attempt to avoid children assuming that it was going to be a sci-fi series. It starred both Frazer Hines and Patrick Troughton, a working partnership that would later be reacquainted in *Doctor Who*. The serial was telerecorded and repeated in the summer of 1966 but has since been lost.

Based on the novel by J. Meade Falkner (first UK publication 1898, Edward Arnold)

### Smuggler's Bay (1964)
**BBC**
**6 episodes** ('A Death and a Discovery'; 'In the Vault'; 'The Auction'; 'A Reward of Fifty Pounds'; 'Found – and Lost Again'; 'On the Beach')
(b&w)
**Broadcast:** Sundays 12/7/64 – 16/8/64

**Main Cast:** Frazer Hines (John Trenchard), Patrick Troughton (Ratsey), John Phillips (Elzevir Block), Suzanne Neve (Grace Maskew)

**Adapted by** Bob Stuart

**Designer:** Daphne Shortman
**Producer:** Campbell Logan
**Director:** Christopher Barry

*Moonfleet* (1984)
**BBC**
**6 episodes** (individual titles n/k except 1: 'So sleeps the pride of former days')
(colour)
**Broadcast:** Wednesdays 22/2/84 – 28/3/84

**Main Cast:** Adam Godley (John Trenchard), David Daker (Elzevir Block), Bernard Gallagher (Sexton Ratsey), Ewan Hooper (Magistrate Maskew), Victoria Blake (Grace Maskew), David Gant (Reverend Glennie)

**Adapted by** George Day
**Designer:** Stephen Brownsey
**Producer:** Paul Stone
**Director:** Colin Cant

**Tie-in publications:** edition of novel published by BBC (hardback) and BBC/Knight (paperback), 1984

## Letty

Teenager Letty Boot, born disabled and confined to a wheelchair, has been a resident at Meadowbank Children's Home longer than most of the other children. When it becomes apparent that a thief is at large, Letty, fancying herself as a super-sleuth, decides to form the Letty Bootlace Detective Agency and find out which of the home's occupants is the culprit.

At first her friends are sceptical, asking her who had ever heard of a disabled detective. Letty, never one to let her disability defeat her, acts as the brains of the operation and employs her two friends, Brian and Trevor, to do the legwork. Among her investigations she helps to collar a truckload of illegal immigrants from Pakistan.

*Letty* star Victoria O'Keefe took her part seriously enough to learn what life is like for a teenage girl paralysed from the waist down, travelling to Pinderfields Hospital in Wakefield where three disabled men taught her how to operate a wheelchair.

**TVS**
**6 episodes**
(colour)
**Broadcast:** Wednesdays 28/3/84 – 2/5/84

**Main Cast:** Victoria O'Keefe (Letty Boot), Josh Elwell (Brian), Marc Barfoot (Trevor)

**Written by** Avril Rowlands

**Designer:** Mark Ward
**Executive Producer:** Anna Home
**Director:** Jonathan Wright Miller

**Tie-in publications:** novelisation by Avril Rowlands published in paperback by Puffin, 1984

## Benny

When Jack and Bella discover a maltreated mongrel dog chained to a barge they free him from his cruel master. It is Benny's hope that the children will take him to stay with them on Midsummer Common. That is exactly what the children do and, before they know it, they find themselves in all sorts of adventures.

Benny helps Bella with her paper round and discovers a house on fire but will he be able to save the old man trapped upstairs from certain death? Benny feels that he'd be suited to working on a building site. His abilities as a guard dog come in very useful when some thieves turn up. Benny also involves himself with a jumble sale, a princess and some joggers, to detail but a few of the little fellow's exploits.

The series is designed with the youngest part of the child audience in mind, broadcast both at noon and in the afternoon children's slots, and each episode is narrated by writer Diane Wilmer, who can be seen with Benny at the start of each new programme on Midsummer Common, Cambridge. The series isn't strictly live action but instead uses a mix of still photographs and speech bubbles.

**Yorkshire**
**13 episodes** ('Benny Comes to the Common'; 'Benny and the Jumble Sale'; 'Benny and the Rainbow'; 'Benny and the Allotment'; 'Benny and the Princess'; 'Benny and the RSPCA'; 'Benny Disappears'; 'Benny and the Fire'; 'Benny and the Builders'; 'Benny On the Beat'; 'Benny and the Joggers'; 'Benny and the Dustbins'; 'Benny to the Rescue')
(colour)
**Broadcast:** Thursdays 29/3/84 – 21/6/84

**Main Cast:** Olivia Ward (Bella), Kirk Wilde (Jack), Diane Wilmer (Narrator)

**Written by** Diane Wilmer

**Music:** Gordon Giltrap (tracks 'In Unison' and 'Lucky')
**Associate Producer:** Alan Hydes
**Director:** David Turnbull

**Tie-in publications:** *Benny: the story of a dog* by Diane Wilmer published by Collins, 1985

## Dramarama
### Season Two

Ownership of this run of plays was split between three main regions – TVS, Central and Thames – with just a single entry from Granada. On the whole this season was one of the more thoughtful sets of episodes, with less comedy and fantasy than in subsequent years, no doubt helping the series earn its unwritten epithet of 'a *Play for Today* for children'.

The fantasy genre was represented by just two entries. Cult sci-fi fandom being what it is, one of these is among the more celebrated *Dramarama* episodes. 'Mr Stabs' was another attempt by Trevor Preston to resurrect the *Ace of Wands* villain of the 70s, following 1975's *Shadows* entry 'Dutch Schlitz's Shoes'. Yet again, Mr Stabs and his assistant were recast. David Jason (at that time the voice of cartoon star *Dangermouse* for Thames) now played the evil magician and midget actor David Rappaport was Luko. As it was more than ten years since Stabs had battled Tarot there were no references to the earlier series that had thrilled the previous generation of kids. Disappointingly though, this was a rather grandiose piece of hocus-pocus which saw Stabs attempt to win the Black Glove of Melchisedek and thus gain passage from the Underworld to Earth, in what was clearly a pilot for a possible new series. Very arch and rather over-the-top, there was little to interest younger viewers, though there were some clever design and special effects aspects on show. Patrick Malahide was among Stabs' adversaries.

The run's other fantasy entry, 'Josephine Jo', was an archetypal but entertaining tale of two eras colliding and voices from the past. Jo Wilson, a schoolgirl visiting a former convent on an outward-bound trip, is possessed by Josephine Webb, a dead girl who steps from a mirror. The ghost of a World War I soldier is involved, echoing the present-day Jo's worries that her boyfriend Andy will be sent to Northern Ireland.

There were more comedy entries than fantasy this year, three in all. Christopher Biggins starred as a schoolteacher who entrusts a chess trophy to two boys with the expected 'hilarious consequences' in 'Stalemate'. 'Fowl Pest' was an interestingly strange instalment about a mum who receives four chickens as a present. The chickens proceeded to tell the audience about their lot, played as they were by a strong female cast in chicken outfits: Irene Handl, Joan Sims, Sheila Steafel and Sherrie Hewson were the birds in question. As blatant a pilot episode as any was 'The Old Firm', concerning a run-down detective agency left in a will. Brian Cant was a retired Major, with Tom Watt (later Lofty in *EastEnders*) and Ling Tai his young assistants. Though a series never transpired, similarities could be noted between this and the later comedy series *C.A.B.*

The mainstay of the season was the now-standard batch of challenging, stand-alone dramas. 'Night of the Narrow Boats' concerned two young boys on the run from the police and hiding out on a barge after believing they've killed a gang leader. Leslie Grantham played the boat's owner just prior to his *EastEnders* fame. 'Snoop!', based on a story by George Markstein, co-creator of *The Prisoner*, was the tale of a teenage cub reporter on a local newspaper and an attempted revival of his *Send Foster* series of the mid-60s. An off-the-wall choice of setting cropped up in 'The Purple People Eater' which, like the previous season's 'Rip It Up', was another modern history lesson from the 1950s. Concerning the exploits of a teenage rock'n'roll group, like 'Rip It Up' it again featured Nick Berry.

The most 'difficult' episodes were 'On Your Tod' and 'Rachel and Rosie'. 'On Your Tod' was the story of a self-sufficient and rather indolent eighteen-year-old boy, Ben (Gary Oldman), who spends the money he has come into on endless rounds of parties. Only when a young punk boy gatecrashes one of these does Ben realise what real life is like for others. 'Rachel and Rosie' was this year's issue-led drama, concerning a handicapped girl who befriends a rather haughty – but underneath it all scared – girl who comes into hospital for the first time. Also representing the under-represented was 'Dodger, Bonzo and the Rest', a realistic but never grim drama set in a children's home. 'Dodger' should really be considered the success of the season – it was the only entry in six years of *Dramarama*,

despite a number of pilot-style episodes, to spawn its own series.

**Season Two**
**12 episodes**
(colour)
**Broadcast:** Mondays 14/5/84 – 6/8/84

14/5/84 – **'Night of the Narrow Boats'** by Grazyna Monvid. **Dir:** Geoff Husson (Central).
21/5/84 – **'Fowl Pest'** by James Andrew Hall. **Dir:** Michael Kerrigan (TVS)
(No episode broadcast Bank Holiday 28/5/84)
4/6/84 – **'Dodger, Bonzo and the Rest'** by Geoffrey Case. **Dir:** Richard Bramall (Thames)
11/6/84 – **'Que Sera'** by Ken Robinson and Tony Allen. **Dir:** J. Nigel Pickard (TVS)
18/6/84 – **'Stalemate'** by David Blake and Alan Banham. **Dir:** Geoff Husson (Central)
25/6/84 – **'Snoop!'** by James Doran from an idea by George Markstein. **Dir:** Vic Hughes (Thames)
2/7/84 – **'Mr Stabs'** by Trevor Preston. **Dir:** John Woods (Thames)
9/7/84 – **'Josephine Jo'** by Grazyna Monvid. **Dir:** Andrew Morgan (Central)
16/7/84 – **'The Purple People Eater'** by Harry Duffin. **Dir:** Diarmuid Lawrence (TVS)
23/7/84 – **'On Your Tod'** (aka 'On Yar Tod') by Donald and Polly Churchill. **Dir:** Peter Duguid (Thames)
30/7/84 – **'The Old Firm: Two for Starters'** by Dave Humphries. **Dir:** Patrick Lau (Granada)
6/8/84 – **'Rachel and Rosie'** by Jane Hollowood. **Dir:** Diarmuid Lawrence (TVS)

## The Tripods

'The Tripods are coming,' proclaimed the front cover of *Radio Times*. 'Stand by for the invaders,' it continued in its extensive coverage of the BBC's new science fiction series. *The Tripods*, contrary to popular belief, did not replace *Doctor Who* but merely took its Saturday evening slot between seasons. At the time, fans of the sci-fi genre must have felt they were in for something of a treat. Television adverts teased viewers with tantalising glimpses of giant metal machines towering over villages, a clear attempt by the BBC to impress upon its audience the amount of money lavished on this drama. Regardless of the hype surrounding the launch of the series, inherent flaws would ultimately lead to the programme's premature demise.

In the year 2089 society has been returned to an almost medieval structure. At the age of sixteen all humans are capped by the Tripods – a process which allows them to eradicate illness but also subjugate all creativity and thought of rebellion. Will Parker and his cousin Henry hear of the White Mountains, a far-off place where men are free of the Tripods. Fearing the cap, they run away from home and, joined by a French boy nicknamed Beanpole, set off in search of the White Mountains.

Immediately noticeable is that the ages of the lead characters have been altered for the purposes of the adaptation. John Christopher's first *Tripods* book states that Will is thirteen and that the capping ceremonies take place at fourteen. In the series Will is fifteen and capping occurs at sixteen, widening its audience appeal and allowing exploration of the more adolescent themes of love, friendship and betrayal.

If one wishes to attribute blame for the failure of *The Tripods* then the BBC's publicity machine should accept liability for setting in motion an audience expectation of high sci-fi action that ultimately wasn't met. Even John Christopher didn't consider his books to be science fiction. 'It's an adventure story,' he said. 'It goes right back to my mother reading me to sleep at night with Swiss Family Robinson.' This is apparent in the adaptation and viewers who tuned in to the new series expecting to see metal machines on the rampage soon discovered that the aliens hardly ever appeared.

*The Tripods* was hampered also by the length of its crucial first season. *The White Mountains*, the first novel in Christopher's trilogy, is by no means lacking in content but there simply wasn't enough material to sustain thirteen episodes. Perhaps realising this, Alick Rowe, responsible for adaptation on the first season, added a number of threads absent from Christopher's novel. The most noticeable of these is the presence of the Black Guard, a police force serving the Tripods, that Rowe most likely intended to provide a visual menace in their masters' continued absence. The time spent by the boys at the Vichot family's vineyard and subsequent trial at a local village for stealing food is another noticeable addition. Regardless of these extras the first season is slow in pace and lacking in action. Falling ratings indicated that viewers were becoming bored with the programme. Despite the second season's more frenetic pace, a veritable feast of tripod action and the unveiling of the creatures that control them, the ratings still failed to reach the desired level. The BBC considered the series to be beyond redemption and axed it before work had started on the final season.

Despite its shortcomings *The Tripods* shouldn't be casually dismissed. Had the BBC approached the first season in the same way they adapted John Wyndham's *Day of the Triffids* – as a concise six-part dramatisation – it is entirely plausible the series could have been a major success.

Based on the novels by John Christopher: *The White Mountains* (first UK publication 1967); *The City of Gold and Lead* (first UK publication 1967); *The Pool of Fire* (first UK publication 1968) – all published by Hamish Hamilton

**Season One**
**BBC in association with Fremantle International Inc and The Seven Network, Australia**
**13 episodes**
(colour)
**Broadcast:** Saturdays 15/9/84 – 8/12/84

**Main Cast:** John Shackley (Will Parker), Ceri Seel (Beanpole), Jim Baker (Henry Parker)

**Adapted by** Alick Rowe
**Music:** Ken Freeman
**Designers:** Victor Meredith (1–8), Martin Collins (9–13)
**Producer:** Richard Bates
**Directors:** Graham Theakston (1–8), Christopher Barry (9–13)

**Season Two**
**BBC in association with The Seven Network, Australia**
**12 episodes**
(colour)

**Broadcast:** Saturdays 7/9/85 – 23/11/85

**Main Cast:** John Shackley (Will Parker), Ceri Seel (Beanpole), Jim Baker (Henry Parker – episodes 1 and 2), Robin Hayter (Fritz)

**Adapted by** Christopher Penfold
**Music:** Ken Freeman
**Designers:** Martin Collins (1–4, 11–12), Philip Lindley (5–10)
**Producer:** Richard Bates
**Directors:** Christopher Barry (1–4, 11, 12), Bob Vlagden (5–10)

**Tie-in publications:** editions of *The White Mountains*, *The City of Gold and Lead* and *The Pool of Fire* published separately in paperback by Puffin, 1984. Omnibus edition Puffin, 1984. *Radio Times* cover 15/9/84 – 21/9/84.

**Video:** Season One released in UK as four volumes by BBC Video between 5/4/94 and 4/7/94. Deleted 5/2/96. Reissued 19/3/01 as double cassette pack by Second Sight, also on double disc Region 0 DVD.

## The Box of Delights

Edward Barnes, then Head of Children's Programmes, launched this serial at a press conference in September 1984 and commented: 'We always provide a balanced diet of programmes, but every now and then we serve up a feast. That's how I see *The Box of Delights*.'

While aspects of the drama may well be fondly remembered by those who watched it back in 1984, what really makes this serial one of the key entries in the history of children's drama is its sheer scale. Producer Paul Stone summed it up as springing from 'a desire to cap the ultimate in children's drama – to better the best there's been'. Taking a purely financial measure it was certainly the biggest. Pre-sold to an unprecedented 215 American PBS stations for prime-time viewing (as three one-hour episodes 10/12/84 – 24/12/84 under the WonderWorks banner), the BBC could easily justify the £1 million budget lavished upon it. In the UK, meanwhile, the series made the cover of *Radio Times*, another indicator of its prestige status.

Paul Stone had come across John Masefield's book ten years earlier and sensed then its capacity for what he called 'unsurpassed entertainment' (it had also been a hugely popular Children's Hour serial on radio in 1948). It's unlikely though that it was anything to do with the qualities of the storyline that drew such strong American interest. Instead they were more likely attracted by the 1930s Christmas setting and the BBC's track record in sumptuous period pieces. The carefully constructed atmosphere is a Christmas card set in motion; there are brightly lit shop windows in dark, snowy streets where vendors hawk fresh pheasant. Elsewhere are cosy crackling fires, Vanden Plas coachwork and, as *Radio Times* put it, a helping of 'uniformed housemaids, Fair Isle jumpers and

**Facing page:** enigmatic Punch and Judy man Cole Hawlings (Patrick Troughton) arrives at Seekings House to give a show for Christmas. *The Box of Delights*.

solid, pre-war morality'. It's a world where the bobbies are always friendly and even the villains have lovely diction.

While the setting was paramount, the serial's special effects were also much-trumpeted and much of the budget was spent on these. Stone told *Radio Times* that 'the story calls for feats of animation which television simply couldn't realise five, perhaps even two or three years ago'. Much use was made of the Quantel system which the BBC had utilised since 1980. In conjunction with the long-established colour separation overlay techniques, Quantel could most importantly be used to grow and shrink elements on screen and these capabilities naturally lent themselves to the miniaturising powers of Hawlings' magical box, while also allowing for more dynamic perspectives in the numerous flying sequences.

Stone was unwittingly echoing the sentiments of many producers down the years but, as technology marches on, the best can always be surpassed and it is effects-heavy pieces of television which will date the quickest as a result. *The Box of Delights* was a serial based largely around visual spectacle and so its effects have, naturally, dated the production. Still, there is some excellent work being done – the hand-animated sequences stand up well, including one lasting several minutes that has Kay and Herne transmuted into stags, wild doves and fish.

The problem with all of these magical delights is generally not one of visual realisation but of overpopulation. Every five minutes or so there is something new to stimulate the visual senses and a child's sense of wonder, be it a talking head, winged demons, a flying car, a sword battle in an Arthurian fort, a boat that speeds across the oceans of ancient Greece or a boy who lives in a waterfall. Masefield's yarn seems to have been written as a bedtime story where the events of each night's chapter can be considered self-contained. As a television serial, however, it seems structurally weak, sometimes appearing a directionless ragbag of showy diversions with only Kay's thirst for adventure to drive the story on.

The performances are one of the stronger aspects of the production. Devin Stanfield is full of enthusiasm and really carries the serial in parts in what must have been a very taxing role, particularly given the complex nature of the special effects. His role is all the more important when one realises that the show's billed star, Patrick Troughton, is completely absent for episodes three to five. That Troughton is so well remembered despite little screen time is a tribute to his magnetic portrayal of Hawlings as the child-confidant traditional in children's fiction. The villains, particularly Robert Stephens and Patricia Quinn, supply deliciously camp performances to create an air of sophisticated, adult pantomime in keeping with the season.

Barnes may have described it as a feast; *The Box of Delights* is certainly a feast for the eyes but there's little here to offer real sustenance over the course. It's a superb Christmas dinner at least then, best enjoyed once a year.

**A BBC TV production in association with Lella Productions PLC**
**6 episodes**
(colour)

**Episode One**
'When the Wolves were Running'
Wednesday 21/11/84 5.05p.m.
Young Kay Harker travels to Seekings House for the Christmas

holidays. He meets an old Punch and Judy man who warns him that the wolves are running. In his dreams Kay is visited by the mysterious Herne the Hunter who similarly warns that evil is close at hand.

**Episode Two**
'Where Shall the 'Nighted Showman Go?'
Wednesday 28/12/84 5.00p.m.
Kay meets Hawlings in a dreamworld. Now on the run from 'the wolves' closing in, Hawlings gives Kay a magical box which can make the owner 'go small' or 'go swift'. The next day Kay sees Hawlings 'scrobbled' and bundled into a plane by the bogus clergymen.

**Episode Three**
'In Darkest Cellars Underneath'
Wednesday 5/12/84 4.55p.m.
With the evil Abner Brown and his cronies seeking the box of delights, Kay and his friends are chased while out playing with a toy boat. Kay uses the box to make them go small and they sail away from danger unseen on the boat – but, suddenly, up ahead is what now seems to them huge and raging rapids.

**Episode Four**
'The Spider in the Web'
Wednesday 12/12/84 4.55p.m.
The Bishop of Tatchester has been kidnapped in an attempt by Brown to sabotage the Christmas Eve service. A tiny Kay flies into Brown's castle lair in an attempt to get to the bottom of things. There he sees Brown studying some ancient books which reveal that Hawlings, or Ramon Lully to give him his real name, possesses the elixir of life and must now be 700 years old.

**Episode Five**
'Beware of Yesterday'
Wednesday 19/12/84 4.55p.m.
Kay travels to ancient Greece and meets Arnold of Todi, the inventor of the box, but he cannot help Kay find Hawlings. A miniaturised Kay returns to the castle but, trapped in a jewel box of Brown's loot, he is then thrown to the ground in a discarded rag and knocked out cold.

**Episode Six**
'Leave us not Little, nor yet Dark'
Monday 24/12/84 5.25p.m.
Brown is double-crossed by his gang who take off with his accumulated loot, dropping bags of flour on his head as they fly away. Brown is knocked into the castle moat and drowns. The villain dispatched, Tatchester's 1,000th Christmas Eve service goes ahead as planned ... then Kay wakes up on the train to Seekings and realises that the adventure has all been a fabulous dream.

**Main Cast:** Devin Stanfield (Kay Harker), Patrick Troughton (Cole Hawlings), Robert Stephens (Abner Brown), Patricia Quinn (Sylvia Daisy Pouncer), Jonathan Stephens (Chubby Joe), Geoffrey Larder (Foxy Faced Charles), Glyn Baker (Herne the Hunter), James Grout (Inspector), Carol Frazer (Caroline Louisa), Crispin Mair (Peter), Joanna Dukes (Maria), Heidi Burton (Jemima), Flora Page (Susan), John Horsley (The Bishop of Tatchester), Anne Dyson (The Old Lady)

Based on the novel by John Masefield (first UK publication 1935, William Heinemann)
**Adapted by** Alan Seymour

**Incidental Music:** Roger Limb (BBC Radiophonic Workshop)
**Designers:** Bruce Macadie, David Buckingham
**Animation Sequences:** Ian Emes
**Producer:** Paul Stone
**Associate Producer for Lella:** John Bird
**Director:** Renny Rye

**Repeats:** reshown in US 3-part format 22/12/86 – 24/12/86 BBC1. Episode titles: 'When the Wolves were Running'; 'The Spider in the Web'; 'Fire and Flood'

**Tie-in publications:** editions of novel published in paperback by Fontana Lions, 1984 (numerous reprints of this edition). Hardback by William Heinemann, 1984.
*Radio Times* cover edition 17/11/84 – 23/11/84 issue.
Kay and the box both make cameo appearances on the covers of the 22nd *Blue Peter Book* (published 1985) and there is a two-page article on the series inside.

**Video:** 165-minute compilation as a single tape on Betamax and VHS format released 1985. Deleted. Double tape VHS-only format issued by BBC Video on *Young Classic* label c. 1989. Deleted. Reissued as 165-minute compilation single tape by BBC Video on *Family Classics* label, 3/4/95. Also released in the US as a 120-minute compilation by Simon and Schuster c. 1985. Deleted.

## Jamie Running

Jamie Dodds has an ambition in life – to be a future Steve Cram. If he is to succeed he will need as much help as possible. He gets a break when he becomes acquainted with Ruth Edwards, who then sponsors him for his school run. Better still, she provides moral support, turning up to watch him run and encouraging him to perform to his highest standard.

The play is set on Tyneside, where its writer Ian Renwick worked as a teacher, and the running sequences were shot in Gateshead. The play examines the developing relationship between Jamie and Mrs Edwards and looks closely at their different backgrounds. Jamie comes from a rough area and has had quite a difficult upbringing, whereas Mrs Edwards stays in a richer area. The interest they share in running, the one thing that Jamie truly excels at, is enough for them to establish an understanding and overcome their differing social status.

**BBC**
**1 episode**
(colour)
**Broadcast:** Wednesday 13/2/85

**Main Cast:** Paul Manvell (Jamie Dodds), Stephanie Cole (Ruth Edwards), Ralph Watson (Da Dodds), Michael Yeaman (Roy Dodds)

**Written by** Ian Renwick

**Designer:** Anthony Thorpe
**Executive Producer:** Angela Beeching
**Director:** Edward Pugh

**Tie-in publications:** n/k

## Dodger, Bonzo and the Rest

*Dodger, Bonzo and the Rest* was a realistic comedy based on a *Dramarama* play. Dodger and Bonzo are brother and sister respectively, and the Rest members of Dodger's gang. They all stay at a children's home in the London suburbs.

The series looks at a wide variety of issues experienced by the children while staying at the home. Do they actually want to be fostered? Do children of ethnic minority have the same chance of finding foster parents? Which member of the home is stealing? How do the children cope with the lack of privacy and upset to their routine when a disruptive element arrives at the home?

While these are doubtless challenging questions for a young audience, the character of Dodger, being very like a young Arthur Daley, brings an element of comedy to ensure that the general atmosphere isn't too downbeat.

A second season saw a change of actress for Bonzo. The children have moved house again and Dodger involves himself in the antiques business and has to come up with a scheme for making holiday money.

Dodger's final appearance would be in a seasonal special later the same year which focused on his exploits while holding down a job in a large London store.

**Thames**
**2 seasons plus Christmas Special**
(colour)

**Season One**
**6 episodes**
**Broadcast:** Mondays 18/2/85 – 25/3/85

**Main Cast:** Lee Ross (Dodger), Sophy McCallum (Bonzo), Lyndon Hayes (Brian), Richard Holgate (Delmont), Jenny Jay (Elaine), Stephen Sweeney (Gerry), Mark Fletcher (Ronnie)

**Written by:** Geoffrey Case (1, 3, 5, 6), Johnny Byrne (2, 4)
**Designer:** Alex Clarke
**Producer:** Sheila Kinany
**Director:** Derek Bennett (1, 2, 5, 6), Derek Martinus (3, 4)

**Season Two**
**6 episodes**
**Broadcast:** Mondays and Thursdays 24/2/86 – 24/3/86

**Main Cast:** Lee Ross (Dodger), Jodie Gordon (Bonzo), Jenny Jay (Elaine), Jennie Goossens (Steph), Mark Fletcher (Ronnie)

**Written by** Geoffrey Case
**Designer:** Alex Clarke
**Producer:** Sheila Kinany
**Executive Producer:** Brian Walcroft
**Director:** Derek Martinus (1, 4–6), Peter Tabern (2, 3)

**Christmas Special – broadcast:** Monday 22/12/86

**Main Cast:** Lee Ross (Dodger), Jenny Jay (Elaine), Mark Fletcher (Ronnie), Leesa Williams (Liza), Zeph Ponos (Nikos)

**Written by** Geoffrey Case
**Designers:** Alex Clarke and Jan Chaney
**Executive Producer:** Brian Walcroft
**Director:** Peter Tabern

**Above:** a friendship between a deaf and a hearing boy comes about as a result of an unfortunate accident in Central's award-winning episode of *Dramarama* 'Look At Me'. Ben Mark is Gavin (left) and Hywel Williams-Ellis plays Nick (right).

## Dramarama
### Season Three

While *Dramarama* was ostensibly about endless variety, at least three episodes this season dealt with the same subject of youthful aspirations and a search for identity. 'Easy' was about a football-mad boy forced to take up violin lessons by his pushy father, while in 'The Audition' a budding sports star is pushed into living out the showbiz dreams of a fading dance teacher (Sheila Hancock). A variation on this theme came with 'A Proper Little Nooryeff', with a boy discovering almost by accident that he has a talent for dancing. Needless to say, once his schoolmates learn of his ballet classes he is mercilessly teased and the boy must decide whether to follow this new ambition or allow himself to be bullied out of it.

While there was the usual quota of fantasy episodes, each was of a very different kind. 'The Golden Conch' was a straightforward story of a journey to an undersea world while 'The Universe Downstairs' was a light-hearted sci-fi episode with a little point to make. When Vincent goes to investigate strange noises in the cellar of his new house he falls into a black hole and finds himself in the future world of Cosmo. There he meets the cute Dollbaby (whose 'futuristic' leather outfit actually looks like something out of a Duran Duran video) and her family. Here on Cosmo, Vincent's sensible pullover and National Health glasses are

thought to be the latest thing, home cooking is the new fad and a mangle is thought more advanced than a washing machine. The message is that progress can only go so far before it needs to go into reverse.

The fantasy of dreams was explored in two very different ways. 'Private Eye' was an example of the daydreamer character pieces that would come to be something of a fixture of *Dramarama*. Here a boy sees himself as a Marlowesque gumshoe and indeed this was echoed in the similar 'Just Wild About Harry' a few years later. 'Silver' was a rather more serious piece using metaphor to resolve a boy's inner troubles, in this case overcoming the death of his father in a car accident. Jonathan, himself presently on crutches, meets his father in the ghostly form of his hero Long John Silver (Gareth Thomas) and through this meeting finds the courage to move on from the dreamworld he has retreated into.

'Purple Passion Video' was a surreal piece. Usually remembered for starring Bobby Gee of Bucks Fizz as a reclusive rock star (Gee also scored the soundtrack), this was one of the most daring and audacious episodes of any season of *Dramarama*. At face value this was a tale of a keen fan of pop sensation The Kid who tries to break into his mansion grounds with her brother, only to find herself the unwitting 'star' of The Kid's new video, her every move captured by spy cameras. At this level the drama is a satire of the overblown pop videos typical of the period, featuring a dance troupe of armed soldiers, dry ice and all manner of pretentious imagery. But then things step up – we see The Kid sitting numbly in some kind of control room, reciting banal replies to unheard insipid interview questions. His manager/bodyguard seems to have some control over this 'puppet' pop star. Then all hell breaks loose as the play becomes a meta-narrative intent on savaging the music industry – Gee is seen sitting in front of a studio gallery (with HTV captions visible on the monitors). The play's epilogue suggests that Gee was an actor all along and the two kids were the pop stars who hired him for the show. The spiralling deconstruction may well have alienated many viewers but was equally likely to have thrilled and perplexed the rest.

The season found a political edge in three more entries. There was a sequel to 1983's 'A Young Person's Guide To Getting Their Ball Back!', this time seemingly critical of the acquisitive get-rich-quick attitudes developing at the time. 'Frog' was another allegorical look at 1985 Britain, set in a literal hothouse where a parrot, a lizard and a crocodile were overthrown by a young frog. The three animals represented power brokers of the time: a politician, a nuclear scientist and a newspaper editor respectively. More direct was the stark 'The Coal Princess' which told the story of a community and its folk traditions torn apart by the miner's strike, and a young girl's struggle to understand the conflict that sets friends against each other. Samantha is hoping to be made this year's Coal Princess but with her father a 'scab' this is not likely to happen.

Amid the complex multi-level fantasies and political treatises the simplest episode of the run was perhaps the best. 'Look At Me' was the story of a deaf boy, Nick, and his attempts to get help when his dog is run over in a quiet country lane. When Nick desperately accosts Gavin, passing by on his bike, Gavin has to show patience and understanding to be able to help Nick and his injured dog. The title referred to Nick's need for people to look at him directly when they spoke, so that he could read their lips, but also alluded to his hopes for acknowledgment as a person. The dog dies by the roadside but hearteningly the two boys strike up a new friendship. Less showy than many episodes this year, the tale has the ability to move the viewer over just twenty-five minutes and rightly won a Prix Jeunesse.

**Season Three**
**13 episodes**
(colour)
**Broadcast:** Mondays 1/4/85 – 8/7/85 and Thursday 11/7/85

1/4/85 – **'Easy'** by Dave Sheasby. **Dir:** J. Nigel Pickard (TVS)
(No episode broadcast Easter Monday 8/4/85)
15/4/85 – **'The Coal Princess'**, writer n/k. **Dir:** Alister Hallum (Tyne Tees)
22/4/85 – **'Look At Me'** by David Blake and Alan Banham.
**Dir:** Geoff Husson (Central)
29/4/85 – **'The Young Person's Guide to Going Backwards in the World'** by Nigel Baldwin. **Dir:** Diarmuid Lawrence (TVS)
(No broadcast Bank Holiday 6/5/85)
13/5/85 – **'The Audition'** by Richard Morss.
**Dir:** Alister Hallum (Tyne Tees)
20/5/85 – **'The Universe Downstairs'** by Tessa Krailing.
**Dir:** Michael Kerrigan (TVS)
(No broadcast Bank Holiday 27/5/85)
3/6/85 – **'A Proper Little Nooryeff'** by Jean Ure.
**Dir:** Geoff Husson (Central)
10/6/85 – **'Frog'** by John Fox. **Dir:** Alistair Clark (TVS)
17/6/85 – **'Private Eye'** by Janice Hally. **Dir:** Jim McCann (Scottish)
24/6/85 – **'Emily'** by Linda Hoy. **Dir:** Michael Kerrigan (TVS)

1/7/85 – **'Silver'** by Robert Forrest. **Dir:** Jim McCann (Scottish)
8/7/85 – **'The Golden Conch'** by Peter Cave.
**Dir:** Kenneth Price (HTV)
11/7/85 – **'Purple Passion Video'** by Matthew Bardsley.
**Dir:** Terry Miller (HTV West)

Season backed up with repeats of 'Bully for Cosmo', 'Jack and the Computer', 'Sweet Revenge', 'Stalemate', 'Fowl Pest', 'Snoop!', 'Because I Say So', 'A Young Person's Guide to Getting Their Ball Back!', 'Josephine-Jo', 'Rip It Up', 'Mr Stabs', 'The Venchie'. Mondays and Thursdays 15/7/85 – 22/8/85

## Travellers by Night

News that Peacham's Circus is to close heralds some big problems for two young acrobats, Belle and Charlie. Their days of performing now seem to be at an end and they have nothing to look forward to but the return to dreary school life. Worse still, what is to happen to Rani, the circus's elderly elephant? It's been made quite clear to Belle that you can't keep an elephant in a council flat and no-one can find a zoo able to afford the upkeep.

Terrified that Rani is to be destroyed, Charlie and Belle go on the run taking the elephant with them. A number of obstacles stand in their way. It isn't easy to keep an elephant under cover and the four young thugs they encounter in a forest make life particularly difficult, robbing them of the last of their money. Rani is on hand to help and Charlie and Belle soon find themselves on talking terms with the strange outlaws. Their leader, Flick, tells Charlie that they aren't a gang but drop-outs, sick of civilisation. Having camped in the forest for three months, Flick and his friends assist Charlie and Belle on their journey and also claim they know of an enclosure where Rani can be kept. The question is: can a group of drop-outs content to steal money from two children be trusted?

Young lead Lisa Coleman, sister of Charlotte, would later find fame as Nurse Jude in BBC's *Casualty* and Neil Morrissey was another TV-star-in-waiting who makes an early appearance here.

**TVS**
**6 episodes**
(colour)
**Broadcast:** Sundays 21/4/85 – 26/5/85 (episode 4 broadcast in earlier than usual slot at 1p.m.)

**Main Cast:** Lisa Coleman (Belle), Jake Copard (Charlie), Yvette Byrne (Mrs Thorpe), Ian Gale (Johnny), Neil Morrissey (Flick)

Based on the novel by Vivien Alcock (first UK publication 1983, Methuen)
**Adapted by** Alan England

**Designer:** Brian Ashbrook-Motte
**Executive Producer:** Anna Home
**Director:** Tony Virgo

**Tie-in publications:** edition published in paperback by Fontana Lions, 1985

## Stookie

Siblings Kirsty and David Munro stray into dangerous territory while bird-watching on the banks of the River Clyde in Glasgow. There they encounter 'Big' Harper and his gang, a crowd of punk bullies who don't take kindly to intruders on their patch. Kirsty and David are helped out of trouble by Francis Mungo Doyle, a punk otherwise known as 'Stookie' because of his reputation for putting people in plaster.

Stookie (always willing to take a chance but always the victim of circumstance, according to the series' theme song) has a tendency to end up in trouble with either the law or Harper. He is curious about the two rather posh Munros and agrees to help them build a bird-watching hide. Harper and Eve, a new member of his gang, have other ideas. They want revenge on Stookie and plan to stop the hide from being built.

The situation is further complicated when Stookie discovers a mysterious package in the river, which ultimately leads to their involvement in an art robbery. Stookie now finds himself in the position of having to co-operate with the police in the hope that they will be able to find Kirsty, David and the rest of his friends, now kidnapped by the thieves.

*Stookie* shows children of very different backgrounds working together towards a common goal. There's plenty of local colour on show including a trip to Glasgow's famous Barras market.

**Scottish**
**6 episodes**
(colour)
**Broadcast:** Sundays 15/9/85 – 27/10/85 (no episode broadcast on 6/10/85 due to snooker coverage)

**Main Cast:** David McKay (Stookie Doyle), Melanie McLean (Kirsty Munro), Stephen Cotter (David Munro), Leonard O'Malley ('Big' Harper), Caroline Paterson (Eve Peel), Stuart Hepburn (PC Hendrie)

**Written by** Allan Prior based on the original story by James Graham

**Music:** Maddy Prior and Rick Kemp
**Designer:** Ann Gooch
**Producer:** Leonard White
**Executive Producer:** Robert Love
**Director:** David Andrews

**Tie-in publications:** novelisation by Michael Elder published in paperback by Scottish Television/Mainstream, 1985

## Them and Us

A series of six separate plays, all written by former magistrate Roger Parkes, linked by the central theme of young people at odds with the law. *Them and Us* doesn't only revolve around the police and the 'criminal' but also focuses on the judicial system responsible not only for upholding the law but for determining the fate of the kids who break it. It isn't single-minded, and approaches the theme through different situations.

The disputes between the neighbouring Smith and Ryan families land them both in court in 'Neighbours'. In 'Flash-Point' a chemistry teacher is injured in her class.

Was it an accident or was it deliberate?

Dan and Ron enjoy annoying everyone, particularly the farmer, by riding their noisy motorbikes around the countryside. When the farmer's barn is burnt down, who is responsible? The two boys find themselves under suspicion of arson in the third play 'Firebug'.

Samantha's best friend is her mongrel dog Caesar. The courts have to decide if the dog should be allowed to live following its attack on a local tradesman in 'Caesar's Snarl'. The series also tackles contentious social issues – in final episode 'Wagging It' Mrs Bilton finds herself unable to cope with her three young children when her husband leaves her.

**Central**
**6 episodes** ('Neighbours'; 'Flash-Point'; 'Firebug'; 'Caesar's Snarl'; 'Cannibal'; 'Wagging It')
(colour)
**Broadcast:** Thursdays 26/9/85 – 31/10/85

**Main Cast (Court Officials):** Barry Jackson (Clerk of Court), David Collings, Wendy Gifford, David Neal (Prosecutors), Ralph Nossek (Chairman), Jill Pearson (Chairwoman)

**'Neighbours':** James Coyle (Mr Ryan), Angela Vale (Mrs Ryan), Ron Welling (Mr Smith), Adam Nightingale (Patrick), Fay Maquire (Kate), Mark Nightingale (Shamus), Julia Land (Siobhan), Michael Hutchinson (Michael), Jayne Lawson (Janie), Tim Stanley (Len), Stuart Wattam (Pete)
**'Flash-Point':** Avril Elgar (Miss Frinton), Damien Nash (Trevor), Jessica Radcliffe (Carol), Herman Bailey (Donald), Alison Dury (Jenny)
**'Firebug':** Barry Stanton (Toby Middleton), Leonard Maguire (Freddie Tallis), Jason Curtis (Dave), Lee Rotherham (Ron)
**'Caesar's Snarl':** Gina Kawecka (Samantha), Brian Coburn (Alf Higgins), Gillian Martell (Mrs Mott), Shirley Cain (Mrs Morton), Constance Chapman (Mrs Grey), Curly (Caesar)
**'Cannibal':** Jason Rose (Mr Martin), Jason Smith (Garry), Jo Shotter (Leslie), Ben Mark (Stewart), Mark Wild (Frank), Tom Anderson (Tony)
**'Wagging It':** Lynne Verrall (Mrs Bilton), Lori Wells-Keefe (Mrs Cartwright), Dena Snelgrove (Stephanie), Jason George (Jamie), Patrick George (Rob)

**Written by** Roger Parkes

**Music:** Andrew Harvey
**Designer:** Bryan Holgate
**Producer:** John Cooper
**Directors:** John Cooper (1, 3, 4), David Foster (2, 5, 6)

**Tie-in publications:** script book *Them and Us: five plays adapted from television scripts to read and discuss* by Roger Parkes published by Edward Arnold, 1985

## Jonny Briggs

Produced with younger children in mind, *Jonny Briggs* tells the story of the home and primary school life of a small Yorkshire boy who can't quite keep out of trouble. Jonny is the youngest child in a large family of completely dissimilar personalities and interests.

His eldest brother Humphrey is philosophical, interested in debating societies and the ethics of science. Albert is a layabout who doesn't exactly exude intelligence and is often found pursuing money-making scams. Rita is hot-headed, prone to temper tantrums and a victim of 80s fashion. She also owns an angora beret but is seldom able to find it. Jonny knows more about it than he dares to say. Jonny usually has his hands full, variously with the school rabbit, a haunted living room cupboard, his kite project and a wedding anniversary cake.

Life is just as unpredictable at school. The Twins, Jinny and Josie, do their best to get Jonny in trouble. Jonny's endeavours, innocent or otherwise, tend to lead to the headmaster's office. Nevertheless he's determined to beat Jinny and Josie in the clay modelling competition. In fact, he's determined to beat Jinny and Josie in *every* competition.

Jonny Briggs' adventures had been a mainstay of *Jackanory* for many years, with several of Joan Eadington's stories having been read by Bernard Holley since the 70s. Now as a live action drama the production was realised simply. Almost all of the action takes place in a few standing sets (Jonny's classroom, the Briggs' sitting room, kitchen, back yard, and the boys' bedroom). It's not demanding television by any means but it's nice to be reminded now and then of what one's priorities were at primary school age.

**BBC**
**2 seasons**
(colour)

**Main Cast:** Richard Holian (Jonny), Jane Lowe (Mam), Leslie Schofield (Dad), Sue Devaney (Rita), Jeremy Austin (Humphrey), Tommy Robinson (Albert), Debbie Norris (Mavis), Georgina Lane (Pam), Karen Meagher (Miss Broom), Adele Parry (Jinny), Rachel Powell (Josie)

**Adapted by** Valerie Georgeson
**Designer:** Paul Munting (Season 1), Richard Dupre (Season 2)
**Producer:** Angela Beeching
**Director:** Christine Secombe (OB Director on Season 2: Phillippa Giles)

**Season One**
**13 episodes**
**Broadcast:** Mondays and Tuesdays 11/11/85 – 23/12/85

**Season Two**
**20 episodes**
**Broadcast:** Mondays and Tuesdays 10/11/86 – 20/1/87

**Tie-in publications:** *The World of Jonny Briggs* and *Stand Up Jonny Briggs* by Joan Eadington published by BBC/Knight, 1985 and 1986

## Alice in Wonderland

*Alice in Wonderland* and *Alice Through the Looking Glass* are two of the most famous children's stories ever written. It is therefore strange that neither of them has been adapted for television as full live action, bona fide children's drama.

The BBC's first, and less than straightforward, adaptation of *Alice in Wonderland* was broadcast for an adult audience as part of *The Wednesday Play* (13/10/65). Dennis Potter's take on the story went straight for the subtext and examined the Reverend Dodgson's fascination for innocent youth. Lewis Carroll's real-life alter ego was played by George Baker, with Deborah Watling his Alice.

A slightly more literal but just as curious film was shown 28/12/66. Directed by Jonathan Miller, it is a fantasy for adults and contains monochrome psychedelic imagery, typical of the time, that often borders on the disturbing, further exemplified by Ravi Shankar's then-fashionable soundtrack. Counter-culture meets Oxbridge satire meets BBC costume drama, it is an extremely weird piece of television, almost self-consciously so.

The BBC would later adapt *Alice Through the Looking Glass* in 1973 for BBC2's Christmas evening schedule. Starring Sarah Sutton as Alice and directed by James McTaggart (earlier the producer of Potter's 1965 work), this feature-length play was broadcast at the reasonably late hour of 9.15p.m. (although an afternoon repeat more obviously aimed at children was shown the next year). Photographs taken at Osterly Park suggested that some location filming took place for the adaptation but these were for publicity purposes only and the whole play was in fact recorded in the studio, relying totally on the use of CSO, and all but the first and last scenes were recorded using this method.

Gyles Brandreth had also adapted *Alice Through the Looking Glass* earlier in 1973 for the youngest part of the audience. The lunchtime production of twelve short episodes was largely in the style of the BBC's *Jackanory* stories, with Cyril Fletcher playing the part of Lewis Carroll, narrating the text to Alice and her sister Lorina. This is in keeping with the way in which the Reverend originally narrated to Alice Liddell, the child who inspired his stories.

Two further versions appeared within a year of each other in the mid-80s. Anglia's 1985 production featured Giselle Andrews alongside a puppet cast. The BBC's last adaptation to date was as a 'Sunday Classic' serial in 1986. Although this version could easily have been enjoyed by a younger audience and was certainly the most literal and straightforward produced to date, there was no input from the Children's Department (it was made as usual by the Serials Department) and therefore it cannot be considered true children's drama. Some clever costume and creature make-up and advanced CSO techniques enlivened proceedings.

One cannot help but wonder if one of the greatest children's stories of all time will ever be given a fully live action adaptation for children's television but it may be that animation and technical trickery will always overshadow actors in attempts to recreate the bizarre dreamlike nature of the story. Indeed, two of the big screen versions to come closest have included Disney's Americanised 1951 cartoon feature and the highly inventive 1988 Jan Svankmajer animation.

All adaptations based on the novels *Alice in Wonderland* and *Alice Through the Looking Glass: and what Alice found there* by Lewis Carroll (first UK publication 1865 and 1871)

### *Alice Through the Looking Glass* (1973)
**12 episodes** ('Looking Glass House'; 'The Garden of Live Flowers'; 'The Red Queen's Lesson'; 'Looking Glass Insects'; 'The Walrus and the Carpenter'; 'Tweedledum and Tweedledee'; 'Wool and Water'; 'Humpty Dumpty'; 'The Lion and the Unicorn'; 'The White Knight'; 'Queen Alice'; 'The Banquet')
(colour)
**Broadcast:** Mondays 15/1/73 – 2/4/73 (lunchtime slots)

**Main Cast:** Cyril Fletcher (Lewis Carroll), Carol Hollands (Alice), Fiona Milne (Lorina)

**Adapted by** Gyles Brandreth
**Designer:** Nevil Dickin
**Producer:** Daphne Shadwell

## Alice in Wonderland (1985)
### Anglia
**5 episodes** ('Down the Rabbit Hole and the Pool of Tears'; 'A Long Tail, a Little Bill and Advice from a Caterpillar'; 'Pig and Pepper and Onto a Tea Party'; 'A Mad Tea-Party and The Queen's Croquet-Ground'; 'The Mock Turtle's Story, The Lobster Quadrille and Who Stole the Tarts?')
(colour)
**Broadcast:** Tuesdays 26/3/85 – 23/4/85

**Main Cast:** Giselle Andrews (Alice), Robert Peters (Reverend Charles Dodgson), Kesser Andrews, Kate Tooley (Sisters)
**Puppet voices:** Joan Braban, Paul Eddington, Mary Miller

**Music:** Peter Fenn
**Puppeteers:** Stephen Mottram, Kim Bergsagel, Ray Dasilva, Joan Dasilva, Joe Fane-Gladwin, Richard Marriott, Peter O'Rourke, Gillie Robic
**Designer:** Spencer Chapman
**Producer/Director:** Harry Aldous

## Alice in Wonderland (1986)
### BBC
**4 episodes**
(colour)
**Broadcast:** Sundays 5/1/86 – 26/1/86

**Main Cast:** Kate Dorning (Alice), Jonathan Cecil (White Rabbit), David Leonard (Lewis Carroll), Roy Macready (Caterpillar), Claire Davenport (The Duchess), Michael Wisher (Cheshire Cat), Pip Donaghy (Mad Hatter), Neil Fitzwilliam (March Hare), Janet Henfrey (Queen of Hearts), Elisabeth Sladen (Dormouse), Brian Oulton (King of Hearts)

**Dramatised by** Barry Letts
**Music** composed and conducted by Stephen Deutsch
**Designer:** Kenneth Sharp, John Bristow
**Producer:** Terrance Dicks
**Director:** Barry Letts

**Tie-in publications:** edition published in paperback by Armada, 1985

## Running Scared

A surprisingly grim and frank tale of intimidation, violence and racial tension set in the gritty East End of 80s London. Bernard Ashley's uncompromising script sees teenager Paula Prescott face dire decisions as her life is torn apart by a ruthless criminal.

Paula's grandfather is inadvertently caught up in one of Charlie Elkin's robberies. He hides evidence that could send Elkin down but dies before he can reveal its location. He leaves Paula a clue to its whereabouts and the most difficult decision of her life. Handing the evidence to the police will ensure that Elkin is stopped but will also mean incriminating her family as her cousin Brian is one of the

gang. If she doesn't hand the evidence over, her Asian best friend Narinder, whose family are being extorted and racially abused by Elkin and his men, will have to return to India.

The level of violence in *Running Scared* is immediately noticeable. The majority of this takes place in the first episode, starting with the graphic robbery of a small jewellery outlet. A shotgun is clearly displayed as the vicious ransacking takes place. The thugs even go as far as removing the ring from the inconsolable old shopkeeper's finger. Although the robbery is in itself disturbing, it is the motivation behind it that really sickens. The owner is being persecuted as a result of his failure to pay Elkin protection money. It is worth noting also that the shopkeeper is Jewish, as the persecution of the ethnic minorities forms an integral theme in the narrative.

The most traumatic scene is more subtle and stands out through the intent to harm rather than any real physical violence. Paula is cornered on a river ferry by Leila, Elkin's cruel girlfriend. Clad in black biker leathers, she notices that Paula is going swimming and chillingly suggests that Paula wouldn't last very long in the icy river water. As she manhandles the girl across the railing of the boat and orders her to take a message to her grandfather, Leila's intent is clear should she fail to do so. 'We wouldn't want to overwork the river police, would we?'

Violence on children's television is a particularly contentious issue and one would expect the brutality of some of the scenes in *Running Scared* to be tempered by less threatening moments. The result is an unfortunately ham-fisted scene in episode four when Paula and Narinder recover the musical box from Brian's house. Finding themselves trapped in the kitchen, Narinder throws a pot of oil on the floor, which allows the girls to escape as Brian slips, falls and squirms around on the floor in an unforgivably comedic fashion.

Strong characterisation, a mainstay of Ashley's work, makes *Running Scared* compelling viewing. Charlie Elkin, played fittingly by the imposing Chris Ellison prior to his well-known role as Frank Burnside in *The Bill*, is one of the more memorable villains on children's television. His empire seems to impact on all walks of life, whether it be the working-class Prescotts, the cosy middle-class life of Frank Butler, or across the racial divide where the Sidhu family struggle to make their protection payments. No-one is untouchable. Interestingly Elkin's character is almost an inverse reflection of Detective Inspector McNeil. Both attempt to manipulate Paula using good guy, bad guy techniques. Elkin is the man who ordered the ransacking of Paula's house. He's also the same man that shares a drink and cake with her at Frank's showroom and tells her that he is her friendly uncle. McNeil employs similar tactics, pressuring Paula in one instance and passing himself off as her friend and protector in another.

Paula Prescott is of course the pivotal character in the story. It is upon her shoulders that Elkin's actions and the decision between family or friend lies. Without her grandfather she finds herself without anyone whose motives she can really trust. Her father wants her to lose the evidence and protect the family. Narinder needs her to co-operate with the police. Both make their feelings clear to her, placing her in an almost impossible position.

Clearly there's a strong race angle to the story. The Sidhu family are deeply distrustful of white people and Narinder's parents even go as far as advising their daughter to stay away from Paula, the girl she has grown up with.

Narinder ironically points out to Paula that she was born in Britain before her and has therefore been 'British' longer, yet she is treated as a foreigner by white people. In handing Elkin's glasses to the police, Paula proves that cultural barriers, if they ever existed in her mind at all, can be overcome.

Recording of *Running Scared* took place entirely on location, perfectly capturing the desired urban atmosphere. There are a good couple of frenetic car chases that add an extra visual dynamic. *Running Scared* also stands out as one of the few children's dramas to employ a well-known pop song as a theme tune, in this case Kate Bush's 'Running Up That Hill'.

**BBC Bristol**
**6 parts**
(colour)

**Part One**
Wednesday 15/1/86 5.10p.m.
When Charlie Elkin's getaway car breaks down during a robbery he forces cabbie Sam Butler to drive for him. Elkin's glasses get broken as he makes his getaway and the police later find one half but Sam finds the other half in his cab and keeps it. Elkin knows this could incriminate him so sends his girlfriend Leila to threaten Sam's granddaughter Paula.

**Part Two**
Wednesday 22/1/86 5.10p.m.
Paula tells her grandfather about the threatening woman and he continues to deny knowing the robbers' identities when questioned again by Inspector McNeil. Sam tells Elkin that if he leaves the family alone he will ensure the evidence remains undiscovered by the police. Brian is extorting protection money on behalf of Elkin from Narinder's shopkeeper father, who decides he's had enough and is returning the family to India. Sam falls ill – Paula visits him but as he tries to tell her the whereabouts of the glasses, he passes away.

**Part Three**
Wednesday 29/1/86 5.10p.m.
Sam has left his music box to Paula but Brian thinks it holds the key to the hidden evidence. Narinder refuses to speak to Paula when she finds out that Brian is Paula's cousin. Returning home, Paula discovers that the musical box is missing.

**Part Four**
Wednesday 5/2/86 5.10p.m.
Paula and Narinder manage to escape Brian as they retrieve the musical box from his house. Elkin tells Frank that his son is involved in the gang and has been doing dodgy deals at his father's car business. Elkin tells him if there's any trouble he'll make sure both father and son go down with him and tells Frank to get the musical box. Paula and Narinder have however discovered a secret code contained within it.

**Part Five**
Wednesday 12/2/86 5.10p.m.
Frank brings Paula to meet Elkin. He encourages her to find the glasses and hand them over. Paula's father also thinks she should let Elkin off the hook, telling her to think of the family. Narinder's family will be forced to flee to India unless Elkin's reign is brought to an end. It's Paula's decision.

**Part Six**
Wednesday 19/2/86 5.10p.m.
Paula finally finds the hiding place in which her grandfather placed Elkin's glasses. Pursued by her parents, Narinder, Elkin and the police, she seeks refuge on the river ferry. Should she now cast the glasses into the river, thus saving her family and freeing Elkin? Or should she hand them over and possibly condemn her family?

**Cast**
The Prescott Family: Julia Millbank (Paula), Fred Bryant (Grandad), Desmond McNamara (Mick), Maureen Sweeney (Dolly), Anthony Gorry (Dean)
The Sidhu Family: Amarjit Dhillon (Narinder), Renu Setna (Pratap Singh), Rani Singh (Kamal Kaur)
The Butler Family: Tony Caunter (Frank), Simon Adams (Brian)
The Gang: Chris Ellison (Charlie Elkin), Hetty Baynes (Leila), Alan Ford (Ron Martin), Alan Talbot (Fred Barratt)
The Law: James Cosmo (Detective Inspector McNeil), Catherine Chase (Forensic Officer)
The Community: Cyril Shaps (Wisener), Dimpal Singh (Sikh Shopper), Jason Norman (Tommy), Damon Doyal (Scott)

**Written by** Bernard Ashley

**Designer:** Graeme Thomson
**Executive Producer:** Paul Stone
**Director:** Marilyn Fox

**Tie-in publications:** novelisation published by Julia MacRae Books (hardback) and Puffin (paperback), 1986 (several impressions)

## The Return of the Antelope

Nestling somewhere between *The Box of Delights* and *The Borrowers* on the BBC, ITV had its own tale of little people in a land of human 'giants'.

Two hundred years after adventurer Lemuel Gulliver landed in Lilliput, the land of the little people, three Lilliputians set sail in a boat named the *Antelope* after Gulliver's own vessel. However, a storm at sea wrecks the *Antelope* and washes its crew up on a Victorian beach in 1899. When the three Lilliputians, Brelca, Fistram and Spelbush, hide in a picnic basket they are found and taken home by two holidaying children, Gerald and Philippa Garstanton. The Lilliputians are installed in the nursery's dolls' house until the children can think of a way to get the miniature mariners back home to Lilliput. Eventually finding a splendid model sailing ship in a shop window, the three set off but are shipwrecked again by a tiny weir which seems to them a raging waterfall.

Stuck in England they reside – for a second season – with the Garstanton children. This time the prying eyes of hotel proprietor Harwell Mincing provide a mortal enemy and, in a series of narrow squeaks, Gerald and Philippa manage to keep the shrunken sailors out of his clutches.

When the series reached a third season there were the inevitable cast and character changes. Gerald and Philippa had gone home after their holiday, leaving the Lilliputians stranded in the Garstanton house, but a shoeshine boy called Ernest and an orphan girl named Emily helped to keep them away from Mincing and life in a circus.

A light-hearted adventure serial from *Worzel Gummidge* writer Willis Hall, there was even a Christmas Special told as a high-spirited musical. One other interesting spin-off was an edition of the 'making of television' series *Kellyvision* (17/8/88) which went behind the scenes to demonstrate the TV trickery that had gone into shrinking the Lilliputians for the screen.

**Granada**
**4 seasons and 1 Christmas Special**
(colour)

**Main Cast:** Gail Harrison (Brelca – Seasons 1 and 2), Annie Hulley (Brelca – Seasons 3 and 4), John Quentin (Fistram), John Branwell (Spelbush), Alan Bowyer (Gerald), Claudia Gambold (Philippa), Paul Chapman (Harwell Mincing), Stephanie Cole (Sarah Mincing), Derek Farr (Mr Garstanton – Seasons 1 and 2), Richard Vernon (Mr Garstanton – Seasons 3 and 4), Fiona McArthur (Millie), Erica Sail (Emily Wilkins – Seasons 3 and 4), Garry Halliday (Ernest – Seasons 3 and 4)

**Written by** Willis Hall

**Producer/Director:** Eugene Ferguson

**Season One**
**6 episodes** ('Castaways'; 'Lost and Found'; 'Studio Portraits'; 'Piano Lessons'; 'Everything in the Garden'; 'Where the Heart Is')
**Broadcast:** Sundays 19/1/86 – 23/2/86

**Music:** Wifred Josephs, played by James Galway
**Designer:** Chris Truelove

**Season Two**
**7 episodes** ('Brelca Goes Ballooning'; 'Philippa's Brave Deed'; 'The Temple of Doom'; 'The Lost Park'; 'The Bottle of Amontillado'; 'Mrs Mallarby's Day'; 'Moving On')
**Broadcast:** Sundays 26/10/86 – 7/12/86

**Music:** Wifred Josephs
**Designer:** Chris Truelove

**1 hour Christmas Special:** 'The Antelope Christmas'
**Broadcast:** Sunday 21/12/86

**Music Director:** Tony Britten
**Music:** Wifred Josephs
**Choreographer:** Anthony van Laast
Other credits as Season Two

**Season Three**
**7 episodes** ('Travelling Companions'; 'Home Again'; 'Emily'; 'Back to the Sea'; 'Footprints in the Sand'; 'Sea Fever'; 'That's the Way to Do It!')
**Broadcast:** Sundays 17/1/88 – 28/2/88

**Designer:** Paul Rowan

**Season Four**
**6 episodes** ('Military Manoeuvres'; 'The Secret of the Municipal Museum'; 'Municipal Museum Hide and Seek'; 'Brave Deeds and Gallant Actions'; 'The Stuff that Dreams are Made Of'; 'Bonfire Celebrations')
**Broadcast:** Saturdays 15/10/88 – 19/11/88

**Music:** Wifred Josephs
**Designer:** Paul Rowan
**Executive Producer:** David Plowright

**Tie-in publications:** novelisations by Willis Hall published by The Bodley Head (hardback) and Fontana Lions (paperback). Season One as *The Return of the Antelope*, 1985. Season Two as *The Antelope Company Ashore*, 1986. Season Three as *The Antelope Company at Large*, 1988. Picture book adapted by Mary Hoffman, illustrated by Faith Jaques published by Picture Puffins, 1985

## Sticks and Stones

Alex McNeil is a Glasgow boy with problems, not least of all his temper. He's been in trouble before and it's likely that he will be again as he continually lashes out at those whom he does not like. His problems multiply when his mother opts out of her marriage to Alex's drunken father and flees to London with the boy. There they hope to find more positive opportunities and a fresh start in life.

Instead they find themselves caught up in the racial tensions of London's inner city when Alex takes his frustrations out on Afis, a young black boy. Afis is however part of gang headed by a white bully who sets about Alex. It is up to Afis to come to Alex's rescue and show him the error of his ways.

In his first television play, Adam Delaney draws on his experience of working with teenagers who require special needs tuition to create the character of Alex. Fifteen-year-old Gary Ralston was already planning ahead for a career in journalism and had become, at the age of thirteen, the youngest ever signing for Scottish football club Partick Thistle when he was picked to play the part of Alex.

**BBC**
**1 episode**
(colour)
**Broadcast:** Wednesday 26/2/86 (BBC2; BBC1 in Scotland)

**Main Cast:** Gary Ralston (Alex), Terry Cavers (Mrs McNeil), Tim Bannerman (Social Worker), Sam Smart (Kevin), Mark Whyte (Afis), Stephen Medlin (John)

**Written by** Adam Delaney

**Designer:** Pamela Lambooy
**Executive Producer:** Angela Beeching
**Director:** Margie Barbour

## Seal Morning

An odd choice of novel to adapt for television, this is the story of a girl who takes her pet seal to live with her Aunt Miriam in the Scottish Highlands of the 1930s. The source novel is a blow-by-blow account of each day the young girl narrator (writer Rowena Farre herself) spends with the young seal, which possesses rare musical talents. Very little at all 'happens' in the book and so the teleplay is forced to make so many wholesale changes that the end product is almost unrecognisable.

Young Rowena is an orphan whose parents have been killed in a car crash. As a result she is sent to live with her reclusive aunt in a remote part of Norfolk. Miriam is cold and untrusting, and so essentially the story becomes a

*Secret Garden*-like tale of the adult whose heart is warmed by the company of her niece and the cute seal which Rowena finds on the shore one day. New protagonists had to be written into the script as well with Dr Lacey, a Canadian scientist studying wild geese, and his fiancee Sylvia becoming part of events. For the most part the tone is sentimental (Dr Lacey gives Aunt Miriam a puppy as a present but the dog dies) although there was a late attempt to introduce some action, with a storm almost destroying Miriam's cottage (another addition not in the original book). The airy East Anglian locations and period setting no doubt account for its popularity in the US, where it aired under the PBS Wonderworks banner.

Director David Cobham was no stranger to animal stars, having helmed the 1978 movie *Tarka the Otter*.

**Central in association with Primetime Television**
**6 episodes**
(colour)
**Broadcast:** Sundays 9/3/86 – 13/4/86 (some timing variations in ITV regions)

**Main Cast:** Holly Aird (Rowena Farre), Jane Lapotaire (Miriam Spencer), David Birney (Dr Bernard Lacey), Liza Goddard (Sylvia Beresford)

Based on the novel by Rowena Farre (first UK publication 1957, Hutchinson)
**Dramatised by** Rosemary Anne Sisson; some episodes written by Gerald Kelsey

**Music:** Paul Lewis
**Designer:** Giovanni Guarino
**Producer/Director:** David Cobham
**Nature Photography:** Mike Potts

**Tie-in publications:** editions of novel published by Arrow, 1986

**Video:** feature compilation released in the US by Wonderworks/Questar. Some issues known as *Rowena and the Seal*. Issued in the US on Region 1 DVD, 2000.

## The December Rose

*The December Rose* eschews the normal images of jolly, bustling London that one might expect from a Victorian period drama. Instead the audience are presented with an uncompromising vision of a dark and oppressive environment where trusted members of society steep themselves in conspiracy and stop at nothing, even the murder of children, to safeguard their illicit activities.

When Barnacle, a young sweep's boy, cleans the chimneys of the influential Lord Hobart, he overhears parts of a suspicious conversation between the lord and his two associates, Mr Hastymite and Inspector Creaker. He tries to hear more but falls down the chimney, landing in front of Hobart's gathering. Escaping with a gold locket – an essential ingredient in Hobart's plan – Barnacle is sheltered from the pursuing Creaker by Tom Gosling, the poor captain of an old river barge. As a result of possessing the locket, Barnacle and Gosling along with Gosling's friend Mrs McDipper and her daughter Miranda are soon embroiled in a dangerous world of espionage, murder and a mysterious ship called *The December Rose*.

This is a straightforward adventure story with a Dickensian flavour that relies on sparkling dialogue and a sturdy pace. *The December Rose*'s main strength lies with its many interesting and colourful characters. Courtney Roper-Knight in particular excels in the lead role of Barnacle, bringing a realistic breadth and depth to a part that required a contrasting range of emotions in some wonderful scenes. Barnacle's terror when he finds himself removed from his natural habitat of buildings and chimneys to the barge with its bleak and open surroundings is really well played and equal to his delight when sporting the new outfit bought for him by Tom.

*The December Rose* doesn't shy away from shocking its audience and presents a number of scenes that must surely have been the focal point of long discussions in the production office. Inspector Creaker's murder of Madame Vassilova is nothing short of horrifying. As he casts her dead body into the river we see, from beneath the dark waters, the girl's body silhouetted against the moonlight, sinking into the depths. It is a disturbing image that is returned to on a number of occasions and was edited from the U-certificate video release.

Another piece of realism is surprisingly retained in what is usually a very carefully monitored area. Staggering back at finding a cargo of manure Barnacle bellows, 'It's 'orse shit!' There must have been quite a few parents who put it out of their minds convinced that they didn't hear correctly, although strangely enough the controversial moment was not cut for the video release.

Disturbing also is the way in which children were callously treated by Victorian society. Young boys risked their lives and many died cleaning the chimneys of the well-off. These aren't statistics that seem to bother Mr Roberts, the Master Sweep, or Hobart's housemaid. 'Boys, ma'am – you gotta treat them like animals. They gotta die sometime – so why not up a chimney?'

Filmed entirely on location in Leeds, East Anglia and London, this was the BBC's most ambitious children's drama of 1986 and it's clear to see that a substantial amount of money was spent on its production. The buildings and claustrophobic street geometry of Victorian London were beautifully constructed with a real eye for detail that, coupled with effective lighting, helped to create the Gothic atmosphere so readily associated with Britain in that period. The shots of the barges and scenes set both on and below deck are impressive and benefit greatly from being the real thing rather than studio mock-ups. Use of 16mm film throughout gifts the production a bleak and grainy feeling, which greatly enhances both the grime of the inner city and the desolate river landscapes.

**A BBC TV production in association with**
**Friday Productions Ltd**
**6 episodes**
(colour)

**Episode One**
'Child of Darkness'
Wednesday 12/3/86 5.05p.m.
When Barnacle falls down Lord Hobart's chimney, Hobart and his companion Hastymite believe the boy may have overheard their secret conversation. Barnacle escapes with a locket and a handful of silver spoons – items that could implicate Hobart and his conspirators. Barnacle is rescued by Tom Gosling and is taken to his barge. Hobart, knowing that the locket must be

recovered at all costs, sends Inspector Creaker to locate and silence Barnacle.

### Episode Two
'The Queen and the Lady'
Wednesday 19/3/86 5.05p.m.
Barnacle decides to leave Gosling but is captured in the attempt by Miranda, the young daughter of Gosling's friend, Mrs McDipper. Creaker tells Hastymite that Barnacle has eluded capture and that The December Rose, a ship carrying enemies of the state, will soon dock in London.

### Episode Three
'The Watcher'
Wednesday 26/3/86 5.05p.m.
The December Rose docks, carrying a Russian called Colonel Brodsky. A servant of Lord Stirling hands Brodsky a watch bearing the same design as Barnacle's locket and warns him to be careful of Inspector Creaker. Mrs McDipper visits The December Rose in search of Russian sable for Miranda and on meeting the Colonel, Miranda discovers the watch that Brodsky carries. She tells him she has seen a locket with the same design and he demands that she take him to the owner.

### Episode Four
'What Can The Matter Be?'
Wednesday 2/4/86 5.05p.m.
Miranda takes Brodsky to Barnacle and the locket. Brodsky is surprised, expecting to have found the locket in the hands of a lady. Realising the lady has been murdered, Brodsky persuades Gosling to allow him to travel on the barge. Meanwhile Creaker employs a street youth to deal with Brodsky and Barnacle.

### Episode Five
'The Black Eagle'
Wednesday 9/4/86 5.05p.m.
The Whistling Youth's attempt on Brodsky's life has failed but he promises Creaker that he will return to finish the job and also kill Barnacle. Meanwhile Mr Gosling and Mrs McDipper agree to deliver a letter on behalf of Brodsky to his friend, Lord Stirling. Stirling informs the pair that he is investigating corruption at the heart of the British Secret Service. The Whistling Youth makes another attempt on Barnacle's life but is thwarted when Miranda catches and kills him.

### Episode Six
'The Last Birthday'
Wednesday 16/4/86 5.05p.m.
Lord Stirling's servant arrives at the barge and asks Gosling to accept the dangerous task of delivering Brodsky's bag to Creaker. Barnacle, believing that Gosling has risked his life enough already, steals the bag and takes it to Creaker himself. Barnacle convinces Creaker of Hastymite's deception. Creaker must now confront Hobart and Hastymite …

**Main Cast:** Courtney Roper-Knight (Barnacle), Tony Haygarth (Tom Gosling), Judy Cornwell (Mrs McDipper), Cathy Murphy (Miranda McDipper), Ian Hogg (Inspector Creaker), Michael Poole (Colonel Brodsky), Patrick Malahide (Hastymite), John Quarmby (Lord Hobart), Michael Aldridge (Lord Stirling)

**Written by** Leon Garfield
Based on an idea by James Cellan Jones

**Incidental Music:** Roger Limb (BBC Radiophonic Workshop)
**Designer:** Graeme Story
**Producer:** Paul Stone
**Assistant Producer:** Tony Guyan
**Associate Producer Friday Productions:** Georgina Abrahams
**Director:** Renny Rye

**Tie-in publications:** novelisation written by Leon Garfield and published simultaneously by Puffin Books (paperback) and Viking Kestrel (hardback), 1986

**Video:** 120-minute compilation released in UK by BBC Video, 1989. Deleted 28/4/94.

## Dramarama
### Season Four
With young audiences, stories with one neat hook can stick in the mind much longer than even the best-written and most involving of works. Programmes that deal purely in effect can make an instant impression that persists, even if they forgo well-drawn characterisation and good sense. So it is that many of the fantasy episodes of *Dramarama* are those most clearly recalled.

Such an instalment in this season was the light-hearted 'Flashback', featuring the one note idea of a schoolboy revealed to be trapped in 1940 when a student discovers a piece of old film. The inventiveness is to be applauded although many other aspects of the story – including the ghost of the inventor of the camera that has trapped the boy in time popping up all over the place – mark this out as a clear case of dealing purely in effect.

The run's other fantasy-styled episode was 'The Come-uppance of Captain Katt'. Appearing at first to be the adventures of a rather corny space hero of 3001 (played by Alfred Marks) this was a meta-textual piece which had the camera pull back to reveal that in fact we were watching a TV space series being made. The episode itself was more about the politics behind the series and the grievances of its tired cast.

Just as delightfully odd, if a little more straightforward in the telling, was another entry that demonstrated the range of the umbrella strand. 'Waiting for Elvis' took the true but obscure story of Elvis Presley's only visit to Britain in 1960, a brief stopover made in his flight back to the States from his national service in Germany. Set in the tiny airport of Prestwick on the West Coast of Scotland, this script by Scottish theatre stalwart Alex Norton was a study of teenage obsessions, witnessed through the dialogue of the crowds of girls who wait for a glimpse of their idol. Much of the episode was shot in black and white to emphasise the period setting. The year 1960 must have seemed like ancient history to many young viewers but most Duran and Spandau fans would surely recognise the emotions being played out.

This run examined the customary number of interesting and sensitive topics: 'Flyaway Friend' dealt with the troubles of a girl trying to settle into a new school; 'Maureen Reid, Where Are You?' was the story of a girl looking for real mother; 'Pig Ignorance' was a sympathetic look at an inner city young offender sent to do community service working on a farm. The most contentious episodes were 'Play Acting' and 'A Couple of Charlies'. The former was a look at race – telling the tale of an Indian girl who can't face going on stage in the school play when she realises her parents are in the audience. This is no ordinary case of stage fright – frightened at what her traditionally Asian parents might make of this more Western show she demands that changes be made. Thus the play spoke out on a culture gap and censorship. 'A Couple of Charlies' meanwhile was perhaps the most controversial show in *Dramarama*'s entire run. Opening as the story of a withdrawn boy, teased at school but with an apparent interest in rabbits, the secret behind his unhappiness is slowly revealed – the boy is a victim of child abuse. It could be assumed that parents watching in the background were more upset than their kids at the content of the storyline. The play was written in consultation with the National Society for the Prevention of Cruelty to Children (NSPCC), a sure sign of the care Central took – and had to take – with the controversial episode.

**Season Four**
**14 episodes**
(colour with 1/9/86 episode as b&w/colour mix)
**Broadcast:** Mondays 30/6/86 – 22/9/86 and Thursday 25/9/86 with one episode held over

30/6/86 – **'The Come-uppance of Captain Katt'** by Peter Grimwade. **Dir:** Peter Grimwade (TVS)
7/7/86 – **'A Couple of Charlies'** by Grazyna Monvid. **Dir:** Geoff Husson (Central)
14/7/86 – **'Wayfarers'** by Glenn Chandler. **Dir:** David Andrews (Scottish)
21/7/86 – **'Play Acting'** by Yogesh Asthana. **Dir:** Terry Harding (HTV)
28/7/86 – **'Last Days at Black Bert's'** by Dave Sheasby. **Dir:** Alistair Clark (TVS)
4/8/86 – **'Maureen Reid, Where Are You?'** by James Graham. **Dir:** David Andrews (Scottish)
11/8/86 – **'Flashback'** by Dennis Spooner. **Dir:** Terry Miller (HTV West)
18/8/86 – **'Direct Action'** by Jon Blake. **Dir:** Alistair Clark (TVS)
1/9/86 – **'Waiting for Elvis'** by Alex Norton. **Dir:** Haldane Duncan (Scottish)
8/9/86 – **'Just a Game'** by Michael Bartlett. **Dir:** Alistair Clark (TVS)
15/9/86 – **'Flyaway Friend'** by Nick McCarty. **Dir:** Fiona Cumming (Tyne Tees)
22/9/86 – **'Pig Ignorance'** by Andy Robson. **Dir:** Peter Tabern (Thames)
25/9/86 – **'Jessie's Place'** by Adele Rose. **Dir:** Richard Bramall (Thames)
30/12/86 – **'Frankie's Hat'** by Jan Mark. **Dir:** Peter Tabern (Thames) (held over episode)

## The Cuckoo Sister

Five-year-old Kate overhears a conversation between her parents and discovers that she once had an elder sister called Emma. Snatched from her pram while her mother shopped, Emma has never been found. Seven years later Kate has grown up a spoiled and bitter child who blames her mother for the loss. When tough teenager Rosie arrives with a letter claiming she is the missing Emma, Kate refuses to believe that this common girl could possibly be her sister.

The theft of a child and the subsequent long-term impact on the stability of the family unit is fascinating subject matter and uncharted territory for children's drama. The viewer is given an immediate and personal insight into a family being torn apart by the unknown fate that befell baby Emma. 'Sometimes I think it would be better if we knew she were dead,' Anthony says of his missing daughter. Although his words may seem harsh it's perhaps not too difficult to sympathise with the sentiment of a father desperately trying to remain strong and administer stability. Anthony's wife Margaret is appalled at his suggestion that she should try and forget what has happened: 'Try to forget my own child as if she were a lost umbrella?' Hovering on the brink of a nervous breakdown, Margaret carries the burden that her carelessness led to the loss of Emma and clings to the hope that her daughter may still be alive.

Kate has grown up unable to forgive her mother. 'Mummy lost her. She lost my sister buying dresses. That's hard to forgive.' She is continually frustrated that her parents won't talk to her and feels that they would have preferred it if she had been taken rather than Emma. Even in the early stages of the drama it's all very emotional to watch. The characters have a depth of sorrow that captures the sympathy of the viewer and the conflicts taking place between the three members of the family are more than enough to maintain attention despite the relatively slow pace of the narrative.

The story is based on the classic sociological conundrum. The possibility that the girl might be Kate's missing sister would still have delivered palatable dramatic effect had she been raised in upper-class surroundings like the Seatons. Instead Rosie is a sharp-tongued commoner reared in London's lower class. In doing this, Alcock introduces the main theme of the story, challenging the viewer's perceptions of society and social structure. Over the years Kate has lost herself in hopelessly romantic dreams of what her sister would be like, envisaging a gentle girl who would love and look after her. When she finds Rosie standing on her doorstep she is horrified. As Kate's posh friends would later cruelly say, 'She's weird. Not our sort at all.' Kate rejects Rosie because of what she is and resents her for shattering the fantasy.

It becomes difficult to sympathise with Kate. She is wholeheartedly selfish, deliberately making life difficult for those around her, and destroys the one piece of evidence that could prove Rosie is in fact Emma. It is Rosie that the audience must surely sympathise with. Sent by the woman that she thought was her mother to an almost emotionally sterile environment where people stand on ceremony, she is like a fish out of water. It's actually a pity that the narrative focuses purely on the inner thoughts of Kate as it would perhaps have added another interesting angle had we also been privy to Rosie's.

It's obvious that *The Cuckoo Sister* was written in the first instance as a novel and perhaps without adaptation in mind. Much of the book concerns Kate's private thoughts and reactions to that which happens round about her. It would have been extremely difficult to give these thoughts visual realisation and therefore Julia Jones opted to incorporate a voiceover from Kate.

While there is some reasonably powerful dialogue in the script, with Rosie threatening to do the Seaton's housemaid over and Kate calling Rosie a bitch, Julia Jones decided to spice things up further. In a surprising line, not included in Alcock's novel, Rosie lets fly at Margaret, branding her a 'posh fart.' It's comical despite the serious nature of the scene and an unusual addition.

**Above:** Rosie (Shelley Measures, front) is the cuckoo in the Seaton family nest. Kate (Joanna Joseph) and her Mother (Victoria Fairbrother) wonder if she is Kate's long-lost sister. *The Cuckoo Sister.*

**The Cuckoo Sister**
**BBC**
**4 episodes**
(colour)

**Part One**
Wednesday 29/10/86 5.05p.m.
Repeated Sunday 2/11/86 11.50a.m. (BBC2)
Kate blames her mother for the loss of the big sister she never knew she had. When a strange and tough girl called Rosie shows up with a note claiming that she is the missing sister, Kate's family are thrown into confusion.

**Part Two**
Wednesday 5/11/86 5.05p.m.
Repeated Sunday 9/11/86 11.40a.m. (BBC2)
Anthony makes attempts to trace Rosie's mother but meets with little success. While searching through the family photo album, Kate finds an old picture of a boy called Robbie, one of her father's cousins. When she sees that Robbie looks just like Rosie she destroys the photograph.

**Part Three**
Wednesday 12/11/86 5.05p.m.
Repeated Sunday 16/11/86 11.40a.m. (BBC2)
Kate helps Rosie search for her mother and gains an insight into Rosie's way of life. Rosie cannot find her mother but is given a letter written by her from a friend. It tells her that her mother has run away to be married, leading Kate to believe that she is not her sister.

**Part Four**
Wednesday 19/11/86 5.05p.m.
Repeated Sunday 23/11/86 11.25a.m. (BBC2)
Kate introduces Rosie to her friends but they tease her about her mother and Rosie runs away. Kate and her father find Rosie and bring her back home. They tell Rosie that they want her to stay and she agrees. However, the new husband of Rosie's mother arrives to set the record straight about the cuckoo sister.

**Main Cast:** Joanna Joseph (Kate), Shelley Measures (Rosie), Michael N. Harbour (Anthony), Victoria Fairbrother (Margaret), Jo Kendall (Elizabeth Wait), Toni Palmer (Mrs Trapp)

Based on the novel by Vivien Alcock (first UK publication 1985, Methuen Children's Books Ltd)
**Dramatised by** Julia Jones

**Designer:** Marjorie Pratt
**Executive Producer:** Paul Stone
**Director:** Marilyn Fox

**Tie-in publications:** editions of novel published in paperback by Fontana Lions, 1986

## Running Loose

Children's TV hadn't seen a drama like this since *The Flower of Gloster* in 1967. *Running Loose* was billed as a 'documentary' but was actually a semi-scripted factual series with additional running drama-style plot strands. What this mix of two distinct approaches was meant to achieve is anyone's guess.

The first series saw a gang of eight kids from inner city London taken by two youth leaders on a camping holiday in the countryside. The 'adventures' concerned such everyday events as putting up a tent and cooking your own dinner. The big questions included 'where does your food come from?' and the like. One slightly more racy question was 'who fancies who?' when some of the older kids played spin the bottle. The kids would be presented with a situation and then be asked to improvise what they would do in this situation. One assumes this was meant to produce naturalistic performances but instead the untrained 'actors' did what every kid does when faced with a camera: either look away embarrassed or play up to it. The end result is often nothing short of a rabble, with children showing off, fighting among themselves and screaming at the top of their voices.

Despite what should by now have been obvious drawbacks in the set-up, a second series took the children and their minibus to the Lake District for a week. The series was plotted around visits to various places of interest such as a bobbin factory or Roman ruins, with other character developments helping to link them together. Most famous among these is the day Melissa is in a bad mood, explained at the episode's conclusion by her friend

Eldora: 'Melissa's come on for the first time.' The resulting look of resignation from leader Chris that says 'women's business' is unintentionally hilarious and presumably also unscripted! Chris and fellow youth leader Joy seem to spend the entire series arguing about what is 'best' for the kids, like a couple of social workers (which in a way they are). Would a visit to the Laurel and Hardy Museum or the poet Wordsworth's residence be better for their social development? It's all very politically correct, worthy and, ultimately, a decade later, faintly ridiculous.

The second series' catchy synth reggae music was issued on an album.

**TVS**
**2 seasons**
(colour)

**Season One**
**6 episodes** ('Departure'; 'First Encounters'; 'No Work, No Food!'; 'Natural Feelings'; 'Conflict'; 'Bar-B-Q')
**Broadcast:** Thursdays 13/11/86 – 18/12/86

'Cast' not credited in *TV Times*

**Associate Producer:** Steve Shaw
**Executive Producer:** J. Nigel Pickard
**Director:** Leslie Pitt

**Season Two:** *Running Loose II*
**6 episodes** ('Day One – Day of Arrival'; 'Day Two – The Mountain'; 'Day Three – Discovery'; 'Day Four – In the Woods'; 'Day Five – Water'; 'Day Six – Going Home')
**Broadcast:** Tuesdays 5/1/88 – 9/2/88

**Main Cast:** Tim Munro (Chris), Yvonne French (Joy), Melissa Desbonnes, Eldora Edward, Dwayne Ellis, Oshioma Okomilo, Tania Moore, Michelle Richardson, Selina Richardson, Aaron Thomas (themselves)

**Music:** Errol Reid
**Producer:** J. Nigel Pickard
**Production Associate:** Jonathan Chadwick
**Executive Producer:** Janie Grace
**Directors:** Steve Shaw and Alan Robinson (1, 2, 4, 6), Alan Robinson (3, 5)

**Tie-in publications:** n/k

## The Children of Green Knowe

The first in a series of seven books, and the only one to be adapted for television, *The Children of Green Knowe* is an elegant but disconcerting period fantasy set in mid-50s rural England. The story evokes a strong sense of childhood innocence and magic, while challenging the younger viewers to decipher the borderlines between illusion, memory and reality.

Seven-year-old Toseland, Tolly for short, is travelling from boarding school to spend the Christmas holidays with his great-grandmother Oldknow, whom he has never previously met. His fear that she might be a witch is vanquished when he finds himself confronted by the ancient and gentle woman. She tells him of the three children, Toby, Alexander and Linnet, who previously lived

in the house many generations before her and how they died, together with their mother, during the Great Plague. Tolly is transfixed by the stories of the children, the house and its surroundings. From his point of view the children seem very much alive. He hears snatches of their conversation, laughter and music, yet despite his best efforts he cannot find them. Mrs Oldknow doesn't seem surprised when Tolly speaks of playing hide and seek with the ghosts and his frustrations that they won't reveal themselves to him. 'They're like shy animals,' she tells him. 'You mustn't be impatient.'

Remarkably gentle up to the fourth and final episode, the plot promotes little in the way of dynamic action, but serves instead to combine various subtle and interesting strands. The blossoming relationship between Tolly and Mrs Oldknow is a joy to behold, while the haunting of Tolly by the three children is, for quite some time, almost disturbing. Their benevolence cannot be taken for granted, particularly since they exert physical force against his will, which clearly distresses the boy. When Tolly finally gains their confidence, we are witness to some delightfully subtle scenes and interaction, but their actual presence and purpose remains ambiguous.

Although the adaptation is perceived as being essentially a children's ghost story, the final episode is rich in biblical imagery and steeped in Anglo-Saxon mythology. While these aspects are undoubtedly engaging, it's difficult to establish exactly where they are leading and what possible conclusions will be drawn. The narrative becomes a little clearer when Boggis tells Tolly of the curse placed by gypsy horse thieves on Old Green Noah, the giant tree that stands within the manor grounds, and the poor fortune and disaster it has brought to the men of the family over the years. While Boggis's tale makes sense of the significance placed on Old Green Noah, the final confrontation between Tolly and the evil tree spirit serves only to once again muddy the waters when the stone statue of St Christopher, the patron saint of travellers, intervenes at Linnet's request to defeat Green Noah and rescue Tolly.

With Green Noah destroyed and the curse presumably lifted, it is easy to see what has been achieved, but more difficult to determine the how and the why. Was Tolly destined to be the principal player in the Oldknow legacy? Why did the children help Tolly and not any of the previous victims of Green Noah? While the forces behind the spirit of Green Noah are fathomable, what forces were driving the statue of St Christopher?

*The Children of Green Knowe* relies not on pace or an intricate plot but on complex characterisation and atmosphere. Alec Christie and Daphne Oxenford are excellent in the respective roles of Tolly and Mrs Oldknow. Twelve-year-old Christie copes wonderfully with a varying range of moods and greatly succeeds in creating a definite air of tension in his search for the children and the secrets of Green Noah. Oxenford delivers an exceptionally emotional performance, evoking warmth and compassion through her obvious love for Tolly, and bringing a tear to the eye as she sadly tells the boy of the children's deaths.

While some believe that location shooting took place at Boston's Huntingdon Manor (the book's original setting), a similar manor in Suffolk was in fact used. The production boasts an imaginative use of natural picturesque scenery mixed when necessary with mild use of paintbox technology, in its infancy at the time, to enhance the flooded rural landscapes and the eventual snow-covered grounds of Green Noah. The opening flood scenes are

**Above:** Tolly (Alec Christie) is haunted by the ghosts of three children when he visits his great grandmother Oldknow (l to r); Linnet (Polly Maberly), Toby (Graham McGrath) and Alexander (James Trevelyan).

actually quite stunning, but those shot in the dark as Tolly journeys towards the manor, and later in the story when Toby rides through the night to fetch help for his sick sister, are by far the more daring and effective.

The incidental music is potent and redolent of its period with tender flute music intrinsic in signalling the presence of the children. The story's visual aspect is flavoured with opulent costumes and marvellous sets spanning two separate periods in time. The narrative transition between these periods is seamless, as Mrs Oldknow's stories of family history melt into seventeenth-century set pieces.

While this ornate and lavish drama lacks a fathomable narrative or obvious character motivation, it nonetheless provides enchantment and excitement for children and so deserves to be recognised as one of the principal dramas of the 80s.

**BBC**
**4 episodes**
(colour)

**Episode One**
Wednesday 26/11/86 5.00p.m.
Repeated Sunday 30/11/86 11.20a.m. (BBC2)
With his father and stepmother living abroad, Tolly has a solitary life at boarding school. His father then writes to advise

him that he has located a relative – Tolly's great-grandmother Oldknow – and so Tolly begins the long journey to Mrs Oldknow's dark manor, Green Noah. He quickly discovers that Mrs Oldknow isn't a witch but her house, with its ghostly voices and music, is far from normal.

**Episode Two**
Wednesday 3/12/86 5.05p.m.
Repeated Sunday 7/12/86 11.25a.m. (BBC2)
Tolly is teased by the voices but frustrated that he can't find them. Mrs Oldknow tells him that the children lived in the house hundreds of years ago and are long since dead. As Tolly plays in the grounds of the manor, he discovers what looks like an evil face in the trunk of a tree and is quietly watched by a young girl and boy.

**Episode Three**
Wednesday 10/12/86 5.05p.m.
Repeated Sunday 14/12/86 12.20p.m. (BBC2)
Mrs Oldknow tells Tolly further stories from his family history and explains that he must be patient if he wants to see the children. Journeying through the snow-covered manor grounds, he discovers a gazebo where the children, Toby, Alexander and Linnet, sit with various animals. Toby warns him of Old Green Noah, the demon tree, but Linnet mocks his warning. Returning to the house, Tolly too taunts Green Noah.

**Episode Four**
Wednesday 17/12/86 5.00p.m.
Repeated Sunday 21/12/86 11.20a.m. (BBC2)
Boggis tells Tolly of the curse placed on Green Noah and the danger it apparently represents to the men of the Oldknow family. As a storm breaks, Tolly is confronted in the manor

grounds by the evil tree spirit as Green Noah attempts to claim another Oldknow victim. Linnet begs help from St Christopher and the statue intervenes to rid the Oldknows of Green Noah and the curse.

**Main Cast:** Alec Christie (Tolly), Daphne Oxenford (Mrs Oldknow), Graham McGrath (Toby), Polly Maberly (Linnet), James Trevelyan (Alexander), George Malpas (Boggis)

Based on the novel by Lucy M. Boston (first UK publication 1954, Faber & Faber Ltd)
**Adapted by** John Stadelman

**Music:** Peter Howell (BBC Radiophonic Workshop)
**Designer:** Alan Spalding
**Executive Producer:** Paul Stone
**Director:** Colin Cant

**Tie-in publications:** none although one regular edition has a 'Now on TV' flash in the corner of the cover

# Y-E-S

YES stood for Youth Enquiry Service, the name for a gang of teenagers who set out to help other kids in their city. With the help of the trilby-hatted eccentric Ma Venables they have their headquarters on a barge called *The Rose of Blenheim*, at least until some aggrieved youths sink it.

While YES only want to help people, the nature of the problems they solve can and does aggrieve others who feel their business is being pried into by a bunch of do-gooders. Some of the bored local youths decide to make life hard for YES, making sure they get banned from the youth club before attacking the barge.

Generally *Y-E-S* tackled one problem per episode. There was a girl who wanted to become vegetarian, a boy obsessed with arcade machines and a runaway girl seeking refuge on the *Rose*. There were also problems of racism and cultural understanding in the city – YES-ser Zoe was black, while the group helped to sort out the troubles of their Asian friends. The group had its own internal problems, with Frankie rarely getting on with Dee, whom she thought a bit of a yob and a show-off. The hand of Nick McCarty, writer on *The Siege of Golden Hill* in the 70s, is clear to see on what is to all intents and purposes an 80s update of his earlier Midlands-set series.

**Central**
**12 episodes** ('Accusations'; 'Finders Keepers'; 'King of the Space Invaders'; 'Hot Work'; 'Lies'; 'Kidnapped'; 'Run, Run, Run'; 'Muscle'; 'Bad Luck Man'; 'Hook, Line and Sinker'; 'Dog Rights'; 'Surprises')
(colour)
**Broadcast:** Wednesdays 7/1/87 – 25/3/87

**Main Cast:** Garry Patrick (Terry Gunthorpe), Amanda Loy-Ellis (Frankie Oliver), Melanie Reid (Zoe Green), Richard de Sousa (Dave Oliver), Tamara Williams (Dee Jackson), Sandra Voe (Ma Venables), Vivienne Moore (Aunt Harriet), Michael Lees (Austen), Angela Matthews (Alison), Stuart Bevan (Trevor), Jason George (Mike)

**Written by:** Nick McCarty (1–3, 12), Simon Masters (4, 8–10), Roger Parkes (5–7, 11)

**Music:** Mike Moran
**Designer:** Norman Smith
**Producer:** David Foster
**Executive Producer:** Lewis Rudd
**Directors:** David Foster (1–4, 9), David Dunn (5–8, 11, 12), John Cooper (10)

**Tie-in publications:** novelised in two parts by Roger Parkes: *Y-E-S* and *Y-E-S We'll Crack It!* published in paperback by Dragon Grafton, 1987

# A Little Princess

While staying in India with her wealthy father, Sara Crewe's health enters a decline and the climate is deemed unsuitable for her. Her father sends her to England where she is to attend Miss Minchin's school for young ladies and benefit from a more agreeable environment. For a time Sara enjoys all the luxuries that come with wealth but her idyllic life doesn't last. She is told one day that her father has died, leaving her without a penny. Minchin has the girl banished to the attic and makes her work for the servants that had previously been in her service and envied her.

By pretending that she is a little princess, Sara finds a way to cope with the humiliation. A princess would always give people the perception that she was happy and hide her inner sadness. For Sara, dreams do come true. Returning from an errand she finds her attic has been transformed into a room fit for a princess by a mysterious benefactor.

Having been born into a wealthy family, Sara has no real inclination of what it is like to be poor. When she finds herself fallen upon hard times she witnesses life on the other side of the social divide. It is not the change in fortune itself that lies at the heart of Burnett's novel but is instead the way in which the child deals with the desperate situation that's the real issue.

The first television adaptation of the novel was from the BBC. There was a noticeable theatrical aspect to the production, with the characters framed in a proscenium arch. The BBC adapted the novel again in 1957 and David Aylmer returned to the role of Captain Crewe.

Although the BBC dramatised the story for a third time in the 70s, on that occasion as a 'Sunday Classic', it is LWT's production in the late 80s that is certainly the most lavish, with the production team painstakingly creating realistic Victorian street sets and studio interiors.

Based on the novel *A Little Princess: The story of Sara Crewe* by Frances Hodgson Burnett (first UK publication 1905, Warne)

*Sara Crewe* (1951)
**BBC**
**6 episodes** ('Sara Arrives at Miss Minchin's'; 'The Attic'; 'The Indian Gentleman'; 'The Party'; 'The Transformation'; 'Sara Leaves Miss Minchin's')
(b&w)
**Broadcast:** Tuesdays 6/11/51 – 11/12/51 (South England and Midlands)

**Main Cast:** Patricia Fryer (Sara Crewe), Helen Stirling (Miss Minchin), John Southgate (Mr Carrisford), Mary Lincoln (Miss Amelia), David Aylmer (Captain Crewe)
**Adapted by** Penelope Knox

**Producer:** Naomi Capon

**Above:** Amelia Shankley is the plucky Sara Crewe in LWT's 1987 adaptation of Frances Hodgson Burnett's *A Little Princess*.

---

*Sara Crewe* (1957)
BBC
6 episodes
(b&w)
**Broadcast:** Tuesdays 30/4/57 – 4/6/57

**Main Cast:** Carol Wolveridge (Sara Crewe), Peggy Livesey (Miss Minchin), Rosamund Greenwood (Miss Amelia), David Aylmer (Captain Crewe), Julie Desmond (Lavinia)

**Adapted by** Penelope Knox

**Designer:** Gordon Roland
**Producer:** Naomi Capon

*A Little Princess* (1973)
BBC
6 episodes
(colour)
**Broadcast:** Sundays 18/2/73 – 25/3/73

**Main Cast:** Deborah Makepeace (Sara Crewe), Ruth Dunning (Miss Minchin), Margery Withers (Miss Amelia), Donald Pickering (Captain Crewe), Alison Glennie (Lavinia)

**Dramatised by** Jeremy Paul
**Script Editor:** Alistair Bell

**Incidental Music:** Dudley Simpson
**Designer:** Christine Ruscoe
**Producer:** John McRae
**Director:** Derek Martinus

*A Little Princess* (1987)
LWT
6 episodes
(colour)
**Broadcast:** Sundays 18/1/87 – 22/2/87

**Main Cast:** Amelia Shankley (Sara), Maureen Lipman (Miss Minchin), Miriam Margolyes (Miss Amelia), David Yelland (Capt Crewe), Katrina Heath (Lavinia), Nigel Havers (Carrisford)

**Adapted by** Jeremy Burnham

**Designer:** Gordon Melhuish
**Producer:** Colin Shindler
**Executive Producer:** Nick Elliot
**Director:** Carol Wiseman

**Tie-in publications:** edition published in paperback by Puffin, 1987

**Video:** 150-minute compilation released in UK by Video Collection/WH Smith Exclusive. Deleted 16/4/93. Released in US as 150-minute compilation by Wonderworks Video (EP version only).

## The Secret World of Polly Flint

When Polly Flint's father loses the use of his legs in a mining accident, the family move to the village of Wellow to stay with Polly's Aunt Em, where Polly's father can benefit from better care. The move upsets Polly but she immediately senses that Wellow is a place of magic.

She meets Old Mazy who tells her about a village called Grimstone that once stood on the same location as Wellow but mysteriously vanished – some say swallowed by the earth. He believes the village slipped the net of time and sometimes the church bells of Grimstone can still be heard ringing under the ground. Polly, an unusual girl who sees things that other people don't, soon discovers that the inhabitants of an underground world are calling for help.

Compared to Cresswell's highly successful *Moondial*, at the time just one year away from being screened by the BBC, *The Secret World of Polly Flint* is a comparatively forgotten children's fantasy. It's probably just as well, considering the blatant similarities between the two. Both narratives concern young heroines uprooted from that which is familiar to them, as a result of a serious injury to a parent, and made to stay with difficult aunts. Both Polly and *Moondial*'s Minty are children with a sixth sense and feel the presence of something unusual in particular places and structures. Both learn of legends from mysterious old men and, at a lesser but just as obvious level, the two girls are even given patchwork quilts by their aunts that their mothers can remember from when they were young.

The themes examined within – the circular nature of time, the blurring of fantasy and reality, and the way in which children cope with difficult situations – are also extremely similar. However, the way in which they are handled and the atmospheres created thereafter differ considerably. Whereas *Moondial* would be injected with a strong sense of foreboding incorporating undertones of the occult, thus rendering it a basic story of good versus evil, Cresswell used a less oppressive approach for *The Secret World of Polly Flint*.

*The Secret World of Polly Flint* is an endearing and captivating fantasy, shot entirely on film and location. The special effects requirements are met with great subtlety, particular Polly's vision of the angel in the first episode. The use of narration, used frequently in this case, is vintage Cresswell and enables the thoughts of Polly Flint and the passage of time to be conveyed with relative ease to the audience.

**Central Independent Television (produced in association with Revcom Television and Bayerische Rundfunk)**
**6 episodes**
(colour)
**Broadcast:** Mondays 16/2/87 – 23/3/87

**Main Cast:** Katie Reynolds (Polly Flint), Emily Richard (Alice Flint), Malcolm Storry (Tom Flint), Susan Jameson (Aunt Em), Brenda Bruce (Granny Porter), Don Henderson (Old Mazy), Michael Hordern (Narrator)

**Based on the novel by** Helen Cresswell (first UK publication 1983, Puffin Books Ltd)
**Dramatised by** Helen Cresswell

**Music Composer:** Paul Lewis
**Production Designer:** Giovanni Guarino
**Associate Producer:** Helene Fatou
**Executive Producers:** Lewis Rudd and Michael Noll
**Producer/Director:** David Cobham

**Tie-in publications:** edition of novel published by Puffin (paperback) and Faber & Faber (hardback), 1987

## Dead Entry

Richard Avery, a millionaire who has made his fortune in computers, has turned his attentions towards the fight against world pollution. He is currently funding the refit of an old fishing boat, the *Sea Shepherd*, turning it into a advanced tool for monitoring global pollution.

Teenage computer whizkid Charlie Nelson and his friend Daniel are budding amateur ecologists and find themselves caught up in conspiracy and espionage when they gain illegal entry to the city docks, where the *Sea Shepherd* is moored, and witness the removal of a diver's body.

Charlie's Aunt Melissa, a tough but bored local reporter, suspects that Avery, with his previous left-wing tendencies, is working for foreign agents and is about to defect. Avery is in fact being blackmailed. Foreign spies hold his daughter captive and demand Avery's Centaur program in return. This will give them access to every civilian and government database in Britain.

The serial was shot entirely on location in Bristol, with the production team given permission to film on the *Sea Shepherd*, a genuine anti-pollution campaign vessel which had been involved in quite a few environmental skirmishes.

**BBC**
**3 episodes** ('File 1'; 'File 2'; 'File 3')
(colour)

**Broadcast:** Wednesdays 18/2/87 – 4/3/87

**Main Cast:** Duncan Baizley (Charlie), Lise-Anne McLaughlin (Melissa), Rhett Keen (Daniel), Geoffrey Bateman (Richard Avery)

**Written by** Allan Baker

**Designer:** Graeme Thomson
**Executive Producer:** Paul Stone
**Director:** Margie Barbour

**Tie-in publications:** novelisation published by BBC (hardback) and BBC/Knight (paperback), 1987

## Dramarama
### Season Five

There must have been less to laugh about this year in a season which put the drama back into *Dramarama*. There was only one out-and-out comedy episode, a peculiarly Scottish instalment called 'Stan's First Night'. Another work by Alex Norton, it was set in 1906 and told the story of a sixteen-year-old boy who wants to make it big in music hall. Scots comedy actors Gregor Fisher and Andy Gray were among the cast. Another Rab C. Nesbitt regular to make an early TV appearance was Elaine C. Smith in 'My Mum's a Courgette'. Outwardly a silly episode about a woman who takes on all sorts of daft jobs – the latest being dressing up as a courgette for a supermarket promotion – it was in fact about her daughter's embarrassment at what her mother does for a living. Mum has to convince the girl that she does whatever jobs she can to support the two of them.

This was just one of many episodes with something to say about the lives of modern children. The customary campaigning piece this year was 'Brainwaves', about a girl with epilepsy who has to find the courage to continue with her YTS training course. Jan Wilson and Caroline Paterson starred. In 'Badger on the Barge' (adapted by Janni Howker from her own previously published short story) a troubled girl learns to look beyond her own life to learn something of others when she befriends an old lady (Rosalie Crutchley) who lives on a barge.

Elsewhere, stereotypical representations of contented 2.4 kids family life were dismantled. 'Living Doll', by Kay Mellor, concerned a girl who wishes her squabbling parents could live a life as perfect as those of her favourite dolls. 'Peter' was the tale of a boy coming to terms with the imminent second marriage of his mother (Pam Ferris). The story was given a contemporary twist, in that the boy's father had been killed in action in the Falklands.

Another one-parent family featured in 'Tam'. Tamsin Clark is an attractive but less than outgoing fourteen-year-old girl who still hankers for her father ten years after he walked out on her and her mother. She wonders the reason why, where he is now and what he might be doing. With an interest in yoga and meditation, one night she concentrates on a flickering candle flame and sees her father as a teacher, a chef, a surgeon and a convict. Her reverie is disturbed when a stranger walks into the house – it turns out to be her father come back to see how she is. Now a distinguished journalist whose job pressures led to the break-up of his marriage, he sits for a portrait for his talented painter daughter but when Mother suddenly returns home there is no-one there but Tam. The nice

199

**Above:** Elaine C. Smith plays a mother who'll take any job to support her daughter in Scottish Television's *Dramarama* play 'My Mum's a Courgette'

**Season Five**
**15 episodes**
(colour)
**Broadcast:** Mondays 30/3/87 – 24/8/87

30/3/87 – **'Cannondrum'** by Nigel Baldwin.
**Dir:** Mike Healey (TVS)
6/4/87 – **'Snap'** by Richard Cooper. **Dir:** Michael Kerrigan (TVS)
13/4/87 – **'The Horrible Story'** Adapted by Maggie Wadey from a story by Margaret Mahy. **Dir:** Neville Green (Thames)
(No broadcast Easter Monday 20/4/87)
27/4/87 – **'My Friend Julie'** by John Herriman.
**Dir:** John Michael Phillips (Thames)
(No broadcast Bank Holiday Monday 4/5/87)
11/5/87 – **'The Creature Beyond Torches End'** by Tony Haase and Robin Driscoll. **Dir:** Roger Cheveley (TVS)
18/5/87 – **'My Mum's a Courgette'** by Janice Hally.
**Dir:** Haldane Duncan (Scottish)
(No broadcast 25/5/87 due to athletics coverage. Repeat of 'Flashback' broadcast 1/6/87)
8/6/87 – **'Brainwaves'** by Ann-Marie Di Mambro.
**Dir:** Haldane Duncan (Scottish)
15/6/87 – **'Undertow of the Armada'** Writer n/k.
**Dir:** Stephen Butcher (Ulster)
22/6/87 – **'Stan's First Night'** by Alex Norton.
**Dir:** Haldane Duncan (Scottish)
29/6/87 – **'Living Doll'** by Kay Mellor.
**Dir:** Keith Washington (TVS)
6/7/87 – **'Peter'** by Brian Finch. **Dir:** Geoff Husson (Central)
13/7/87 – **'The Halt'** by Alan England.
**Dir:** Mike Holgate (Central)
(Repeats of 'A Couple of Charlies' and 'Mr Magus is Waiting For You' broadcast 20/7/87 and 27/7/87 )
3/8/87 – **'Tam'** by Claud Holmes. **Dir:** Terry Harding (HTV West)
10/8/87 – **'A Spirited Performance'** by Nigel Crowle.
**Dir:** Pennant Roberts (HTV Wales)
(Repeat of 'Waiting for Elvis' broadcast 17/8/87)
24/8/87 – **'Badger on the Barge'** by Janni Howker.
**Dir:** Kay Patrick (Border)

twist here is that for a moment the audience thinks the whole encounter has been a meditation-induced dream, until Tam turns over the portrait to find a forwarding address from her father. This is another of those entries which sees a self-absorbed child resolve inner troubles, closing the book and moving on.

If 'Tam' was a pseudo-fantasy episode there were many more bona fide entries in that genre. 'Cannondrum', by 'Young Person's Guide' writer Nigel Baldwin, dwelt upon what lies over the wall of a breakers' yard after dark. Similarly, 'The Horrible Story' feared what might lie outside the tent when three boys camp out in the garden. 'A Spirited Performance' had a boy studying Welsh legend for a school project and encountering two knights in a forest near an ancient castle. 'The Halt' was a spooky entry with a message, managing to meld an examination of inner city yobbery with a creepy story of a ghostly and abandoned train station. Four football hooligans cause aggro among a trainful of passengers, spray-painting the windows, tossing drink over people and blasting out their music. When the train goes through a tunnel they emerge the other side as the only occupants of the carriage. Alighting at an eerily quiet station, they find that their misdemeanours are revisited upon them. The timetables have been torn up and they can't phone for help because the phone box has been vandalised. It's the realisation of the effects of their own selfishness and an act of kindness – helping a strange porter when he has a heart attack – that provides their safe passage on the next train away from a station that never existed.

Odder still was the very experimental 'My Friend Julie', the story of two girls who fall out over a boy, told entirely in song. Based on a prize-winning play from the 1986 Edinburgh Fringe, this demonstrated *Dramarama*'s left-field credentials as clearly as any this year.

## Eye of the Dragon

Robin Richards and his younger sister Mari live near the Brecon Beacons with Gwen, their widowed mother. Since the death of her husband, Gwen has devoted her life to the development of the Beacons Mountain Railway and hopes to turn it into a major tourist attraction.

Gwen and Michael, her weak-willed cousin who runs the family business from Hong Kong, are part owners of land that she would like to use to extend the railway. She needs Michael's permission to do so and is shocked when she receives a letter from his assistant, Samuel Chan, reneging on the promise and withdrawing support for her project. Determined to find out what is happening, Gwen travels to Hong Kong, leaving her children in the care of Ianto Rees and his wife.

Robin, Mari and Ianto have discovered a stone tablet inscribed with Chinese writing in the old railway tunnel. They are oblivious to the fact that their every move is being watched by the two oriental monks that have recently moved into the dilapidated old manor house. The stone is a clue to the location of the Eye of the Dragon – one of the largest emeralds in the world – which the children's grandfather, a property developer, took from

Chan's grandfather years previously. Chan is desperate to retrieve the emerald and destroy Gwen and Michael's Morgan Morgan Holdings company, gaining revenge for his grandfather's humiliation. The children are soon caught up in the sinister Chan's plan when he lures them to Hong Kong.

*Eye of the Dragon* is an ambitious and unique children's drama, filmed in both English and Welsh, and was first broadcast earlier the same year on S4C under its Welsh title, *Llygod y Ddraig*. The scenes were shot in both languages one after the other. The crew spent two weeks filming in Hong Kong and six weeks on the Brecon Beacons in Wales.

**BBC Wales**
**5 episodes**
(colour)
**Broadcast:** Wednesday 6/5/87 – 3/6/87

**Main Cast:** Daniel Evans (Robin Richards), Mali Tudno (Mari Richards), Glan Davies (Ianto Rees), Lisabeth Miles (Gwen Richards), Iestyn Garlick (Michael Morgan), Huw Thomas (Sam Chan)

**Written by** Dyfed Glyn Jones

**Designer:** Julian Williams
**Producer/Director:** Allan Cook

**Tie-in publications:** edition by Dyfed Glyn Jones published by BBC/Knight (paperback) and Knight (hardback), 1987

## The Honey Siege

Given the revolutionary past of France, it could only be a French writer who would produce a novel about a group of such anti-authoritarian children. A small and sleepy village on the slopes of the Pyrenees is known only for the nearby moated fort at Bastide and little else. The day the local schoolmaster accuses his pupils of wrecking his precious beehives and refuses the entire school their forthcoming holiday, that all changes, and the town becomes infamous due to the protest of a group of local boys. The gang hole themselves up in the local fort and a siege develops.

The BBC serial was adapted by two close friends of the work's author, Gil Buhet, and production design was informed by a trip to the Pyrenees by producer Kevin Sheldon. Actual production largely took place at Lime Grove, with a minimum of location film inserts shot much closer to home.

The work was adapted almost thirty years later by HTV. Given the growing demand for heritage product, the story was relocated to the local HTV environs of Bristol and Wales and centred around the build-up to the Queen's Coronation in June 1953. The gang of short-trousered rabble rousers similarly laid siege to the nearest castle (in this case Crowker Castle) and found secret passages galore within it. When the boys' red flag is flown over the castle in preference to the Union Jack, with the coronation due to happen, and a local reporter gets hold of the story, the town is threatened with national disgrace. The nostalgic rendering countered the book's initial edge but the serial sold well abroad to countries including Germany, Israel, Spain, Morocco and – a case of coals to Newcastle – France.

Based on the book *Le Chevalier Pierrot* by Gil Buhet (first English translation as *The Honey Siege* by Geoffrey Sainsbury, published 1953, Jonathan Cape)

**The Honey Siege (1959)**
**BBC**
**6 episodes** (first episode title given in *Radio Times* as 'No Surrender! To the Mountains'; others not given) (b&w)
**Broadcast:** Saturdays 17/1/59 – 21/2/59

**Main Cast:** Sam Jephcott (Pierrot), Martin Cox (Tatave), Dudley Singleton (Victor), Nicky Edmett (Cisco), Anthony Richmond (Riquet), Leonard Monaghan (Georget)

**Adapted by** Antonia Ridge and Adrian Thomas
**Designer:** Marilyn Roberts
**Producer:** Kevin Sheldon

**The Honey Siege (1987)**
**HTV**
**7 episodes** ('The Blood Oath'; 'The Traitor'; 'The Disappearance'; 'Defiance'; 'Ghosts'; 'The Battering Ram'; 'Victory!') (colour)
**Broadcast:** Sundays 7/6/87 – 19/7/87

**Main Cast:** Lyndon Davies (Pete Rainbow), Nigel Harman (George Green), Jason Edwards (Gus Belham), Lee Ormsby (Victor Mutch), Martin Eales (Henry Mardilow), John Stilwell (Frank Gattrell), Stephan Chase (Godfrey Green)

**Adapted by** David Martin

**Music:** Paul Lewis
**Designer:** Caroline Smith
**Producer:** Derek Clark
**Director:** John Jacobs

## Shadow of the Stone

Liz Finlay is a lonely girl who yearns to go to sea. Her dreams are realised, it seems, when famous American yachtsman Steve Lamont sails into her home town of Gourock in search of his family roots. However, Liz is troubled by the spirit of the tragic Marie Lamont, a girl who like herself once wished to go to sea but was burned at the stake as a witch in 1662.

On the surface *Shadow of the Stone* seems a very traditional story, with a regional setting, the past and present intermingling and a lonely child haunted by ghosts. Its adolescent concerns are also immediately recognisable. Liz's father left her and mother long ago and now mum's boyfriend Danny is on the verge of moving in to replace him. Slightly conformist as a narrative then; at a subtextual level, however, *Shadow of the Stone* is a bold piece of work.

Liz seems a sullen, angry and spiteful child – her behaviour borders on the anti-social and this cannot simply be explained away by her 'possession' by the spirit of Marie Lamont. We never see the ghost of Marie and there are no on-screen visitations. This suggests that the obsession is going on only in Liz's head; that is to say that she may be mentally ill. By not exploring this avenue sympathetically, thus failing to give some reason for Liz's unruly behaviour, it serves to distance Liz from the audience's affections.

This is unfortunate since the feminist tract that provides the main subtextual thrust of the entire piece is jeopardised by Liz's extreme (split?) personality. Liz – like Marie before her – wants to go to sea and become a sailor. Marie was told it was bad luck to have a woman on a boat and in similar small ways Liz is patronised by some unlikable patriarchs who think her a 'daft wee lassie'. Even the very pleasant Steve, usually very encouraging, sends her home after a day's sailing but invites her boyfriend Tom along to the pub with the boys – but is Steve really being sexist, or just justifiably annoyed with Liz as she has nearly wrecked his boat after another of her 'mad turns'?

This is, at a covert and coded level at least, a serial about burgeoning sexual identity. Several times Liz pushes Tom away when he tries to kiss her, shouting in 'Marie' mode, 'I don't want that!' but in the final episode Liz/Marie wears a red dress (symbolic of lust and 'the wanton whore' since the days of Red Riding Hood) to a beach party where she guzzles cider. As Czerkawska's later novel of the teleplay hints: 'the girl that looked back at her in the mirror could have been any age between 15 and 25'. The vaseline-lensed, *Wicker Man*-style flashbacks to the time of Marie Lamont show a group of women dancing around a plainly phallic stone carving, 'Granny Kempock's Stone'.

**Above:** Liz Finlay (Shirley Henderson) is trapped by her small coastal town and yearns for the freedom of the sea in *The Shadow of the Stone*.

*Shadow of the Stone* was one of the year's largest financial commitments for a small, regional ITV franchise-holder without much track record in drama. Filmed entirely on location in and around Gourock, Glasgow and the Clyde Estuary, the Glasgow scenes in particular have a guided tour quality about them, at a time when Glasgow was rebranding itself as a 'City of Culture'. With the hand of Leonard White at the tiller (hugely experienced in making similar dramas for HTV) the production was an accomplished one.

*Shadow of the Stone* is not as well remembered as it might have been – its surface adventure story isn't always that effective and so is less likely to have left much impression on younger viewers. It is debatable how much of its subtext got through to the target teen audience but at this deeper level it was for its time an undeniably complex and subversive drama.

**Scottish Television**
**6 episodes**
(colour)
**Broadcast:** Sundays 26/7/87 – 30/8/87

**Main Cast:** Shirley Henderson (Elizabeth Finlay*), Nic d'Avirro (Steve Lamont), Alan Cumming (Tom Henderson), Doreen Cameron (Alice Finlay), Charles Kearney (Danny King), Irene Sunters (Rose McKenzie), Louise Goodall (Kate)
* Incorrectly named in on-screen credits as 'Findlay'

**Written by** Catherine Lucy Czerkawska

**Music:** Alan McCusker-Thompson
**Designer:** Ken Smith
**Producer/Director:** Leonard White
**Executive Producer:** Robert Love

**Tie-in publications:** later novelised as *Shadow of the Stone* by Catherine Lucy Czerkawska, Richard Drew Publishing, 1989

## Knights of God

Those parents expecting to sit down with their children and enjoy a typical Sunday family drama like *Little Lord Fauntleroy* or *A Little Princess* must have got a real shock when they tuned into the first episode of *Knights of God*. The title sequence alone, depicting the burning of the Union Jack, menacing helicopters flying through fire and armies of black-clad soldiers carrying machine guns, should have given ample warning of what was to come. Period drama had been firmly thrown out of the window in favour of a harsh futuristic drama where a ragged group of freedom fighters battle for liberty in a decimated Britain buckling under the weight of an oppressive totalitarian militia.

In the year 2000, civil war breaks out in Britain. The government is overthrown, the Royal Family executed and a new order, the tyrannical Knights of God, assumes control of the country. Twenty years later, times are turbulent and the Knights still battle for complete control, fighting a war of attrition against a group of Welsh freedom fighters. Owen Edwards, leader of the resistance, is aware that his son, seventeen-year-old Gervase, will play an essential part in defeating the Knights, locating the one man that can unite Britain and restore democracy. Prior

Modrin, leader of the Knights, captures Gervase and implants orders deep in his mind. When Gervase finds that man, the surviving King of Britain, his instructions are to kill him.

*Knights of God* represented tough talking for Sunday family drama but the message at the heart of the story is simple and clear: love conquers all. When Gervase is taken with other villagers to one of the Knights' prison camps he meets and falls in love with Julia. As the story unfolds it soon becomes clear that her character will be key. Her love for Gervase and his for her is the only force strong enough to overcome Modrin's instructions. In an unexpected plot twist we discover that Gervase himself is the surviving King of Britain. Following Modrin's instructions he attempts to throw himself from the top of a cliff. In an emotional scene it is Julia's love that prevents him and finally breaks Modrin's hold over the young King.

*Knights of God* is more than a mere love story. It's a frenetic adventure story packed with hardware that delivers a number of thrills and a few disturbing scenes. In one particularly strong scene a young boy is shot dead in a gun battle between the Knights and Welsh rebels. The Archbishop of Canterbury is stabbed to death and Julia also suffers her fair share of injury, being shot while escaping from the prison camp and later being punched in the face by one of the freedom fighters.

*Knights of God* unfortunately suffers the same shortfall that previously hampered the progression of *The Tripods*. Although the story at least contains a good degree of action, at thirteen episodes it's just too long. There is a certain element of repetition with much gallivanting across tough country landscapes and battle after battle with the Knights and rogue freedom fighters. Some of these escapades could easily have been sacrificed in favour of a shorter, tighter ten-part story.

**TVS**
**13 episodes**
(colour)
**Broadcast:** Sundays 6/9/87 – 6/12/87

**Main Cast:** George Winter (Gervase), Claire Parker (Julia), John Woodvine (Modrin), Julian Fellowes (Hugo), Gareth Thomas (Owen Edwards), Patrick Troughton (Arthur), Shirley Stelfox (Beth)

**Written by** Richard Cooper

**Composer:** Christopher Gunning
**Production Designer:** Christine Ruscoe
**Producer:** John Dale
**Executive Producer:** Anna Home
**Director:** Andrew Morgan

**Tie-in publications:** novelisation by Richard Cooper published in paperback by Lions, 1987. Also published in hardback.

## The Gemini Factor

Psychic power, telepathy and the apparent ability of children to harness these phenomena are concepts that have been explored on a number of occasions in children's drama. Using complex characters, an uncompromising narrative and unsubtle, hard-hitting subplots, *The Gemini Factor* stands out as an excellent balance of meaty drama and mild, metaphorical fantasy.

Leah, a shy teenage girl abandoned at birth, lives with her well-off adoptive parents, Joy and Dan, and their two biological children, Carla and Dominic. Joy was told that she would never be able to have children of her own, but later fell pregnant after adopting Leah. Carla and Dominic have been spoiled by their parents but Leah, no longer able to communicate with either Joy or Dan and disliked by Carla, feels ostracised and unhappy.

Lee, a disturbed and destructive teenage boy also abandoned at birth, has been given up as a lost cause by previous foster parents who described him as being beyond help with a compulsive urge to destroy. In one final attempt to help Lee, the Department of Social Services hand him over to compassionate foster mother Verity, who lives near Leah and her family.

Despite having children of their own, Verity and her husband Ken have fostered a number of other troubled children. Ken explains that Verity herself fell pregnant at a very early age and had no alternative but to have her child adopted. Ken wants her to stop fostering and concentrate on looking after her own children. Verity, however, sees fostering as the only way to exorcise the ghosts of her past.

It transpires that Leah and Lee are twins and, now that both are in close proximity, a psychic link that neither of them can control or fathom is established. Leah is subjected to terrible nightmares, stark glimpses of near future events, and the image of a strangely familiar boy. Lee in turn is haunted by similar nightmares and influenced by the voice of a girl that only he can hear.

Unbeknown to each other, the twins attend sessions with the same psychiatrist, Oliver. From his gentle investigation we learn much about the strange force – The Gemini Factor – that, in the final episode, brings the two children together. Oliver postulates, 'The sign of Gemini – the notion of twin forces, positive and negative locked in some kind of conflict.' He's right – Lee and Leah are opposites. Calm and co-ordinated Leah exerts some control over the wild and untamed Lee.

Although *The Gemini Factor* benefits from good direction, a frenetic pace and superb character development, the aspects that really make this drama stand out are the close examination of the long-term impact that adoption can have on both children and adults alike, and the unusual but bold step of advocating the expression of anger. As Oliver tells Leah, 'Anger – any emotion – has to have an outlet. Suppress it and it'll turn into something destructive – something you can't control.'

**Thames Television**
**6 episodes** ('The Forerunner'; 'Mirror Image'; 'The Clock Tower'; 'The Ring'; 'Reflection'; 'Electric Storms')
(colour)
**Broadcast:** Mondays 2/11/87 – 7/12/87

**Main Cast:** Louisa Haigh (Leah), Charlie Creed-Miles (Lee), Gabrielle Lloyd (Joy), Andrew Ray (Dan), Cleo Sylvestre (Verity), Doyle Richmond (Ken), David Lyon (Oliver), Alison Groves (Claire), Vicky Murdock (Ruth), Alix McAlister (Carol), Juliette Caton (Carla), Nicholas Grant (Matthew)

**Written by** Paula Milne

**Music:** Richard Harvey
**Designer:** David Richens
**Producer:** Sheila Kinany
**Executive Producer:** Alan Horrox
**Director:** Renny Rye

**Tie-in publications:** novelisation by Thea Bennett published in paperback by Thames Magnet/Methuen, 1987

## Aliens in the Family

Though hardly radical or controversial, *Aliens in the Family* at least attempted to gently rework and subvert some of the more tired-looking staples of the genre. It's worth noting that as we join the story the heroine Jake is, in the traditional manner, setting off to spend her summer holidays with far-flung family. In a twist on the well-worn motif, however, she isn't on her way to visit a cruel stepaunt; instead she is to be reunited with her estranged father and to meet for the first time his new wife and children. Also, Jake travels from the country to the town and not the other way round and, in a rather charming attempt at surface updating, she takes a National Express coach to Bristol. While she was not likely to take the steam train preferred in the worlds of Lewis, Nesbit and Blyton, the point is that the more things change, the more they stay the same.

The serial is an examination of teenage troubles, sympathetic to the changes in the modern family unit, told using a science fiction adventure framework. The sci-fi aspect also permits some degree of metaphor to be utilised – the word 'Alien' in the title is the double meaning key to the serial. As Bond, the visitor from space, asks Jake, 'What's an alien? It's just another word for a fish out of water.' Sometimes, as just demonstrated, the message might be delivered in a way that seems heavy-handed to the seasoned adult viewer but, given the benefit of the doubt and viewed as a primer in metaphor and subplot for a younger audience, it works just fine. It is just complex enough in its character mix and simple enough as an adventure story.

Of these two main elements, the sci-fi aspect perhaps stands up less well. The chase scenario that forms the spine of the story is basic but is weakened by rather shaky plot developments as the serial nears its climax. More serious is a distinct lack of tension in the adventure. When time itself rolls back hundreds of years and the children begin to fear that they will be trapped in the past forever, Bond reassures them that the effect is only temporary, instantly killing the dramatic moment. Then, at the story's end, the evil Wirdegens are revealed to have been the good guys in disguise all along, leaving the viewer feeling rather cheated.

The serial is not overtly sci-fi to look at but the initial scenes on a space station are economically achieved by basic sets and commendably experimental video effects. Best of all is the excellent make-up used to create the foetal but cute Galgonquans, which permits the maximum of bright-eyed expression from the actors to come through.

The character focus is on the two very different teenage girls Jake (Jacqueline) and Dora and the angst they experience in their attempts to compete for the affections of the family unit. The fights are nice and robust – things are thrown around and copies of *Jackie* are torn up as the personalities clash. Dora thinks the androgynous, sullen Jake, who dresses like a cowboy, is weird and accuses her of having nits in her hair. Jake hates the way Dora is obsessed with boys, clothes and hairstyles, calling her 'Miss Teenybop'. In one classic spat she rakes in Dora's drawer and exclaims that 'young ladies shouldn't daub themselves with Gro-Bust!'. The girls shine courtesy of two great performances from the juvenile leads.

The girls' belligerence is countered by the calming influence of Bond, a childlike innocent from outer space with shades of *ET*. Thus, as the story progresses, everyone becomes increasingly nice to each other until before long Dora and Jake are baring their souls, recognising and admitting the insecurities that make them fight like this. At the story's resolution things are taken to almost ludicrous extremes, when the family spend some 'quality time' inside the stone circle. Almost a full five minutes of screen time amounts to nothing more than an extended counselling session and is one of the clearest indicators of the serial's ever-so-reasonable middle-class presentation style. This is an eminently mature, sensible and agreeable family break-up we are talking about here. 'They didn't fight or anything' is how Jake describes the end of David and Pet's marriage. The leafy Bristol suburbs, the Raven family's lovely farmhouse and the Saturday morning pony-trek provide the backdrop to the less than visceral action.

The serial was adapted from the novel by the New Zealand writer Margaret Mahy and, while the original contained much local colour, the only element to suffer in the transition from a New Zealand setting to the UK is a small one – Sebastian Webster was an early settler who lived among the Maoris and his 'bewitched' stone was a gift from the mystical tribespeople, redolent of their spiritual past. Recasting the TV Webster as a Victorian vicar who has lucked upon the charm perhaps makes less sense.

The serial was relocated firmly in the land of Children's BBC 1987 via an overload of fashionable pop references. There's constant name-dropping of such cultural icons as Morten Harket, Curiosity Killed the Cat and Sinitta. These make viewing the serial today rather akin to finding an old copy of *Smash Hits* at the bottom of a drawer. While such ephemera would now limit any present-day repeat or foreign sales potential, they must be considered completely forgivable since at the time they would almost certainly have attracted a young teenage audience to what was, on the whole, a relevant and well-made production.

**BBC**
**6 episodes**
(colour)

### Episode One
Wednesday 18/11/87 5.10p.m.
Repeated Sunday 22/11/87 11.30a.m. (BBC2)
Jake Raven is to spend the summer holidays with her remarried father and his new family. Also preparing to make a journey is Bond, a young Galgonquan who is to undertake an expedition to Earth as part of his training.

**Episode Two**

Wednesday 25/11/87 5.10p.m.
Repeated Sunday 29/11/87 11.30a.m. (BBC2)
Jake and her new stepsister Dora are not getting on, and fights are erupting in the crowded Raven household. Meanwhile Bond is searching for his sister Solita, now disguised as a piece of electrical equipment. He finds Solita in a junk shop within the form of an old radio, but the shopkeepers are Wirdegens in disguise and they try to trap him. Escaping, Bond is pursued by a slow-moving black car until he bumps into Dora and begs for her help.

**Episode Three**

Wednesday 2/12/87 5.10p.m.
Repeated Sunday 6/12/87 11.30a.m. (BBC2)
Dora has hidden Bond in the family's garage. He is grateful but aware that he may be putting the children in danger. Sure enough, the Wirdegen car has tracked him down to the Raven house. Lewis is attacked by a strange alien force and becomes the eyes and ears of the Wirdegen.

**Episode Four**

Wednesday 9/12/87 5.10p.m.
Repeated Sunday 13/12/87 11.30a.m. (BBC2)
Saturday, and the family go on a horse-trekking trip to which Dora 'invites' Bond. The Wirdegens, with the unwitting help of Lewis, are following. There is weird lightning in the sky and Bond, alarmed by this, runs off into the forest, but with Lewis determined to find him.

**Episode Five**

Wednesday 16/12/87 5.10p.m.
Repeated Sunday 20/12/87 11.30a.m. (BBC2)
The Wirdegens materialise out of the air; Bond activates Solita's audio defence mode and although it drives away the Wirdegens – albeit temporarily – it also has the unexpected effect of warping time back as much as 100 years. Before long the Wirdegens return and pursue the children as they run to the stone circle which Bond is so desperate to reach.

**Episode Six**

Wednesday 23/12/87 5.10p.m.
Repeated Sunday 3/1/88 11.30a.m. (BBC2)
Bond surrenders himself to the aliens but quickly senses that something is wrong. He deduces that these are not Wirdegen at all and this is all part of his test. Suddenly there is another time-warping anomaly and the children, bathed in strange light, appear before nineteenth-century Reverend Sebastian Webster who believes them to be ghosts. David and Philippa later find the children safe and well and together the family sit in the stone circle as time rolls forward. Bond has passed his test and becomes a Galgonquan probationer.

**Main Cast:** The Raven Family: Sophie Bold (Jake), Clare Wilkie (Dora), Sebastian Knapp (Lewis), Rob Edwards (David), Clare Clifford (Philippa)
The Galgonquans: Grant Thatcher (Bond), Elizabeth Watkins (Solita), Jon Glover (The Teacher)
**With:** Petra Markham (Pet), Granville Saxon (Wirdegen Leader), Michael Kelligan (Sebastian Webster)

Based on the novel by Margaret Mahy (first UK publication 1986, Ashton Scholastic)
**Dramatised by** Allan Baker

**Music:** Roger Limb (BBC Radiophonic Workshop)
**Designer:** Paul Montague
**Executive Producer:** Paul Stone
**Director:** Christine Secombe

**Tie-in publications:** edition of novel published in paperback by Hippo/Scholastic, 1987

## White Peak Farm

Teenager Jeannie Tanner has led a sheltered but comfortable life with her family on their remote Northumberland sheep farm. Recently it seems to Jeannie that something is happening that she cannot understand. Why does her big sister, who seems so happy, cry when she is alone at night? Why will she not share her thoughts with Jeannie? Why does Jeannie's gran announce that she is to sell her house and move to India? What is her gran's secret? It seems to Jeannie that everyone has secrets and these are breaking the family apart.

The original setting for Berlie Doherty's novel was Derbyshire but for the purposes of the adaptation this was changed to Northumbria. The story was recorded in the autumn previous to its broadcast and the crew spent five weeks on location in and around Hadrian's Wall and the small town of Rothbury. The farmhouse featured in the drama was basic to say the least, with no running water or electricity. This therefore necessitated the presence of a generator to power the production. The farm was devoid even of road access and the cast and crew faced the arduous task of walking a not inconsiderable distance across two fields with all their equipment.

**BBC**

**3 episodes** ('Gran'; 'Kathleen & Martin'; 'Mum & Dad') (colour)
**Broadcast:** Wednesday 13/1/88 – 27/1/88

**Main Cast:** Margery Bone (Jeannie), Jean Heywood (Gran), Annie Raitt (Madge Tanner), John Hallam (John Tanner), Billy Fellows (Martin Tanner), Jan Graveson (Kathleen Tanner), Charlotte Kyle (Marion)

Based on the novel by Berlie Doherty (first UK publication 1984, Methuen)

**Designer:** Marjorie Pratt
**Executive Producer:** Paul Stone
**Director:** Andrew Morgan

**Tie-in publications:** edition of novel published in paperback by Lions, 1988

## Moondial

Written as a teleplay in tandem with her development of the story in book form, Helen Cresswell's *Moondial* is a dark and intricate mood piece mixing supernatural imagery and emotional exploration. The story features stylistic elements typical of Cresswell's work, using real-life settings as the locale for fantasy narratives – so Cresswell adds depth to fantastical happenings by firmly grounding them in the undeniable reality of modern life.

Araminta Cane is staying with her Aunt Mary during the summer holidays when her mother is involved in a serious car accident that leaves her fighting for her life. Minty attempts to fill the long hours between hospital visits by spending time at the nearby mansion where she meets old Mr World. He sadly tells her of the children he has heard crying in the wind for over sixty years and explains she is the one to find the key that will set them free. Minty finds herself drawn to the sundial in the gardens of the house and discovers that it's a gateway to the past and two tortured children whom she must rescue from their respective miserable existences.

Cresswell's harsh treatment of Minty is unrelenting and, as a result of this, she creates one of the stronger heroines in the history of children's drama. Having already coped with the death of her father, Minty now faces the prospect of losing her mother. Her manic reaction when told of the accident – grasping her hair, screaming and eventually laughing uncontrollably – is truly disturbing and a testament to the acting abilities of the young Siri Neal. In Minty's moment of need there is no source of comfort. Aunt Mary's philosophy of 'what cannot be cured must be patiently endured' is desperately out of touch with the younger generation. John Benson wants to help Minty, but his confession of love for her mother leaves her confused and suspicious.

Even when Minty finds herself transported to the past there is little solace for her, only the additional burden of rescuing two children from their own personal torture. Tom, treated appallingly by an oppressive Victorian society, is thin and gaunt. As he coughs up blood Minty knows that he is dying but is powerless to prevent the inevitable. Sarah also leads a wretched life. Despised by everyone because of her facial birthmark, she is threatened with the torment of the Devil if she ever looks in a mirror.

The drama challenges its audience on a number of levels, presenting an ambitious and hard-hitting narrative. To an extent, however, this complexity is *Moondial's* undoing, with many aspects of the story lacking clarity. The concept of moon time and the threads that bind the three children together aren't rationalised, and it remains difficult to ascertain whether Tom and Sarah are actually alive, the spirits of the dead, or indeed both at different points in the story. The resolution of the story is perplexing to say the least. The near genius required to work out that Kronos and Eros – the stone figures supporting the sundial – are in fact tiny clues to the central message that it is time and love that heals all must surely have left most of *Moondial's* younger viewers confounded.

Perhaps the most confusing element in the plot is the ambiguous dual role played by Jacqueline Pearce. In Sarah's time she is Miss Vole – the cruel nanny intent on mentally torturing the poor girl. In Minty's time she is Miss Raven – a sinister ghost hunter whose presence threatens the children Minty is trying to save. Possibly two incarnations of the same evil being, it is subtly but chillingly suggested that Raven is a mere pawn of the Devil itself. Through her despicable treatment of Sarah, the character of Vole is at least ominous. Raven, on the other hand, is completely inconsequential and her disappearance in the resolution feels almost like a cheat. Whereas Vole is vanquished by Minty in a taut, piquant scene, Raven, we discover to our disappointment, simply booked a taxi and caught a train home.

Shot entirely on video in and around the small Lincolnshire village of Belton, the production capitalises on extensive use of Belton House and its impressive grounds. Colin Cant's studious directing provides striking interior shots of the house and lingering journeys through its beautiful gardens. Cresswell had gained stimulus from a prior visit to the house, with the sundial that apparently sits in the gardens providing the inspirational catalyst.

A number of night-time scenes were shot in daylight using filtered lenses and, while the desired effect is not achieved, the use of filters creates by default a foreboding, uneasy atmosphere in keeping with the production as a whole and it could actually be said that the drama benefits from the eerie results.

**BBC**
**6 episodes**
(colour)

### Episode One
Wednesday 10/2/88 5.00p.m.
While spending the summer holidays at her Aunt Mary's house, Minty learns that her mother has been seriously injured in a car accident. Returning from the hospital Minty tries to pass time by visiting the nearby mansion house. There she is drawn to a mysterious sundial standing in the gardens and bumps into a small Victorian kitchen boy called Tom who believes she is a ghost.

### Episode Two
Wednesday 17/2/88 5.05p.m.
Minty and Tom establish that neither of them are ghosts. In fact, it seems that the sundial has transported Minty back to Victorian times. She gains an insight into Tom's tormented world – a world where he is mistreated and beaten by adults. The sundial takes Minty back even further where she meets Sarah – a mysterious hooded child who lives in fear of the foreboding Miss Vole.

### Episode Three
Wednesday 24/2/88 5.05p.m.
Aunt Mary excitedly tells Minty that she is going to take on a lodger, Miss Raven – a woman who'll be researching a book on ghosts. The sundial brings Tom to Minty's time where she warns him of Miss Raven. Escaping Aunt Mary's house at night, Minty returns to the sundial in search of Sarah. She finds the girl wandering through the gardens unaware that she is being followed by mysterious hooded figures.

### Episode Four
Wednesday 2/3/88 5.05p.m.
Minty discovers that the hooded figures are in fact children. They trap Sarah, calling her a devil's child. Minty scares them away but before she is able to comfort the girl, Vole drags Sarah back to the house. Returning to Aunt Mary's, Minty meets Raven – a suspect woman who bears a resemblance to Vole. Minty and Tom search for Sarah and, when they find her, they discover the child's secret.

### Episode Five
Wednesday 9/3/88 5.00p.m.
Terrified that Minty and Tom have seen her facial birthmark, Sarah runs for the safety of the house. Following her, Minty and Tom witness Sarah's horrendous treatment at the hands of Vole. Raven makes Aunt Mary hide the key to the house, preventing Minty from getting to the sundial after dark. She then informs Minty and Aunt Mary that she will be travelling to the mansion that night on a ghost hunting expedition.

### Episode Six
Wednesday 16/3/88 5.05p.m.
Minty manages to get to the sundial after dark where she meets Tom. Together they rescue Sarah from her tormentors and vanquish the evil Miss Vole. With the children at last free, Minty returns to Aunt Mary's, where she is told that Miss Raven has left and her mother has regained consciousness.

**Main Cast:** Siri Neal (Minty), Tony Sands (Tom), Helena Avellano (Sarah), Valerie Lush (Aunt Mary), Jacqueline Pearce (Miss Vole and Miss Raven), Martin Sadler (John), Joanna Dunham (Kate), Arthur Hewlett (World)

**Written by** Helen Cresswell
Novel by Helen Cresswell (first UK publication 1987, Faber & Faber Limited)

Location shooting at Belton House, Lincolnshire by kind permission of the National Trust

**Music** composed by David Ferguson
**Designer:** Malcolm Thornton
**Executive Producer:** Paul Stone
**Director:** Colin Cant

**Tie-in publications:** editions published in paperback by Puffin Books, 1988 (earlier editions by association with the National Trust)

**Video:** first released in UK as a 113-minute compilation by BBC Video, 1990. Deleted. Re-released as a 113-minute compilation by Paradox Films, 1996. Compilation re-issued on Region 2 DVD by Revelation, 2001.

## City Tails
A comedy drama addressing serious, leftish concerns. The Brick Alley city farm is under threat from the developers – Clinton Lewis at the Borough Council wants to demolish it and build a profitable office block in its place. In order to run the farm down he decides that he must appoint the most useless candidate possible in charge. To this end he appoints 'a complete idiot' called Ronnie Merganser.

The 'little man' begins to win through against the avarice of big business, however, and soon Merganser's unconventional management begins to pay off. The farm has never been so well run, much to the particular delight of three kids who go there, Ben, Janet and Flop.

As well as alternative comic Alexei Sayle appearing as Merganser, Tony Robinson played a Baldrick-like lackey suggesting cunning plans to Mr Lewis. In doing so, Robinson again fulfilled his vocal commitment to quality children's television – he had presented *Tales from Fat Tulip's Garden* and starred in the long-running comedy *Maid Marian and Her Merry Men*.

**Thames**
**3 episodes** ('Fowl Play'; 'Sheep's Clothing'; 'Trough Justice') (colour)
**Broadcast:** Mondays 11/4/88 – 25/4/88

**Main Cast:** Alexei Sayle (Ronnie Merganser), Anton Rodgers (Lewis), Tony Robinson (Gerry), Jason Forrester (Ben), Alessia Gwyther (Janet), Daniel Steel (Flop)

**Above:** the three 'ghosts' brought together in moontime by the *Moondial* - Minty (Siri Neal, top), Tom (Tony Sands, left) and Sarah (Helena Avellano, right).

**Written by** David Stafford

**Music:** Jim Parker
**Designer:** Peter Elliott
**Producer:** Carol Wiseman
**Executive Producer:** Alan Horrocks
**Director:** Carol Wiseman

## Dramarama
### Season Six
This season billed itself as 'children's drama that's a little out of the ordinary' and while that may have hinted at a bias towards fantasy episodes, of the six or so presented in that category most preferred a light-hearted vein to spooky shocks or a hard science fiction edge.

Satire stalwarts John Bird and John Fortune starred in 'Forever Young', a body-swap comedy set in a storm-lashed Gothic folly where teachers attending a seminar in understanding their young charges got more than they bargained for. A pre-Raquel Sarah Lancashire also guested in this, one of three contributions this year from the previously quiet Granada region. Another of Granada's efforts, 'Bubbles', was surely inspired by the then recent A-ha video for 'Take On Me' since it saw kids step inside the pages of a comic after finding a mystic stone in the attic. 'Now You See Them' was a little more sinister, with Don Henderson as a fairground magician who teaches two 207 naughty children a lesson. 'The Alien' was another fantasy-tinged episode to utilise a theme recurrent in *Dramarama* – that of the over-imaginative child unable to distinguish between the real world and the child's own land of make believe (in this case a world of sci-fi comic strip).

The comedy-fantasy vein is probably best exemplified by 'The Wrong Button'. Christopher Biggins camped it up as a second-class novice Devil who could only be seen by those in a mischievous frame of mind. When an art class of wise-cracking teens visits Alton Towers on a school drawing trip, hoping to bunk off to the theme park but finding it closed, Arnold the Devil goes to work with a magical device that looks like an ordinary personal stereo. Chaos breaks out as he rewinds the park owner, Lord Towers, back to his youth as a 50s Teddy Boy and fast-forwards the art teacher into a pond.

The only 'straight' fantasy instalment of the run was 'The Secret of Croftmore' from Scottish Television. Two city kids from Edinburgh go to visit their cousin Callum, who faces having to leave behind the coastal idyll of Croftmore when his mother's business fails. Cousin Neil is the cynical townie, only silenced by the appearance of three ghosts from the time of the Highland clearances, seen leaving Croftmore for the New World. Having something to say about the breakdown of the rural lifestyle as well as providing a little history lesson, 'The Secret of Croftmore' was very much a product of the regional model of ITV broadcasting which was slowly solidifying into a more homogenous network whole by this time.

The lighter feel was prevalent this year with a number of overt comedy episodes. 'Big T for Trouble' centred on the tribulations of a typically naughty twelve-year-old girl forced to be a bridesmaid to her pushy older cousin (in a dress the colour of 'a monkey's bum'). The boring wedding of snotty aunts and dippy grooms was enlivened as she boogied up the aisle while listening to her personal stereo. Former *Screen Test* host Brian Trueman penned the tale of an eccentric fisherman, played by Jim Broadbent, in 'Making Waves', while former Goodie Bill Oddie provided the daftest episode of the run with the zany 'Bubblegum Brigade', about kids who run an agency mending broken hearts.

There had to be some balance and this came in the shape of a handful of more serious pieces. 'Blackbird Singing in the Dead of Night', an early work by *Band of Gold* writer Kay Mellor, examined the fears of a girl about to undergo an operation that could restore her hearing after an accident. 'Room for One More' studied the problems that arose when a white Scottish family fostered an Asian boy (with Dorothy Paul playing mother). Another submission from Scottish, 'The Macrame Man', concerned a girl trying to help her unemployed father (*Taggart* star Mark McManus) find work. The most controversial entry this season had to be the bold and awkward 'Just a Normal Girl'. This told the story of a girl left paraplegic after a car accident in which her mother had been killed but who finds new hope and purpose after coming to know other disabled youngsters in hospital. The real talking point of the episode was the use of handicapped actors from the Lord Mayor Trelow College for the Disabled. A held over episode also centred on the disabled; 'Snap Decision' was about a tennis-playing boy who becomes jealous of the attention his girlfriend pays to his wheelchair-bound brother. There may have been less real drama in *Dramarama* this season but on these occasions at least it showed it was still capable of taking risks.

**Season Six**
**14 episodes (plus 1 held over)**
(colour)
**Broadcast:** Mondays 9/5/88 – 15/8/88

9/5/88 – **'Forever Young'** by Gary Hopkins.
**Dir:** Gareth Morgan (Granada)
16/5/88 – **'The Macrame Man'** by Stuart Hepburn.
**Dir:** Haldane Duncan (Scottish)
23/5/88 – **'The Wrong Button'** by Anthony Horowitz.
**Dir:** Geoff Husson (Central)
6/6/88 – **'Bubbles'** by Janey Preger.
**Dir:** Rod Natkiel (Granada)
13/6/88 – **'Blackbird Singing in the Dead of Night'** by Paul Abbott and Kay Mellor. **Dir:** Spencer Campbell (Granada)
20/6/88 – **'Big T for Trouble'** by Janey Preger.
**Dir:** Tony Kysh (Tyne Tees)
27/6/88 – **'Room for One More'** by Ann-Marie Di Mambro.
**Dir:** Andrew Gardner (Scottish)
4/7/88 – **'Making Waves'** by Brian Trueman.
**Dir:** John Darnell (TVS)
11/7/88 – **'Just a Normal Girl'** by Grazyna Monvid.
**Dir:** Geoff Husson (Husson Production for Central)
18/7/88 – **'Now You See Them'** by Nick McCarty.
**Dir:** Alistair Clark (TVS)
25/7/88 – **'Bogeymen'** by Jan Needle. **Dir:** John Darnell (TVS)
1/8/88 – **'The Alien'** by John Chambers.
**Dir:** Kay Patrick (Border)
8/8/88 – **'The Secret of Croftmore'** by James Graham.
**Dir:** Haldane Duncan (Scottish)
15/8/88 – **'The Bubblegum Brigade'** by Bill Oddie and Laura Beaumont. **Dir:** Roger Cheveley (HTV)
22/8/88 – **'Playing for Wales'** by Nigel Crowle.
**Dir:** Pennant Roberts (HTV)
Episode held over:
4/1/89 – **'Snap Decision'** by Grazyna Monvid.
**Dir:** Geoff Husson (Husson Production for Central)

**Video:** 'Big T for Trouble' included on 3-episode tape *Dramarama*, released by Video Gems, 1990. Deleted.

## The Chronicles of Narnia

The adaptation of several instalments of C. S. Lewis' *Chronicles of Narnia* represents the BBC's most ambitious undertaking in terms of scope and finance for children's television to date. *The Lion, the Witch and the Wardrobe* was the only Chronicle previously adapted for the small screen in Britain. ABC's 1967 production was limited visually by budget constraints and available technology. Advances in the video effects and computer animation key to the successful adaptation of complex fantasy stories had reached the point two decades later where Paul Stone's production team felt that full on-screen representation could be given to the characters and images conveyed by Lewis through his novels.

The BBC had already proven their technical prowess four years earlier in *The Box of Delights*. It is therefore little surprise that the visual effects displayed in *The Lion, the Witch and the Wardrobe* are of a high standard. Paintbox technology is put to good use and is especially effective, primarily in the scenes where the White Witch turns characters to stone. Video computer imaging is also in evidence, giving Aslan the ability to fly. Animation is used against live action in many areas, usually to recreate Narnia's more complex animals like flying horses and also for creatures, like birds, which would have been impossible to control whether in the studio or on location.

The main animal characters like Mr and Mrs Beaver were handled in a naturalistic manner with actors. The fact that the animals don't look like they would in the real world is largely irrelevant. Fantasy is about suspending disbelief and if the characters are written in such a way that they display human traits, it is not difficult to believe that they would be more human in aspect. The use of simple but effective make-up allowed the actors' faces to remain uncovered, unlike the half-masks used in the ABC production.

The money lavished on *The Lion, the Witch and the Wardrobe* is apparent even in the wonderful locations used. Recording for the forest scenes took place in the Cairngorm Mountains near Aviemore in Scotland, where the BBC's scenic production team had already spent three weeks constructing the Beavers' house. There the actors and crew endured harsh terrain and sub-zero temperatures for much of the duration of the shoot. Minor delays in production occurred when weather conditions became so poor that the safety of those involved in the production couldn't be guaranteed. The vast impressive expanse of Manivere Castle, situated in coastal Wales, features as the home of the White Witch, although, thankfully for those involved, recording here took place in the warmer climate of spring.

Despite this ostentatious display of effects, locations and costumes, the audience must not lose focus on the characters. The actions, responsibilities and individual traits of the four children remain true to the novel. Ironically Peter, Susan, Edmund and Lucy are sent to the country to escape the atrocities of a war they can have no impact on. What they find at the Professor's strange mansion is a gateway that ultimately leads them into another war, which this time they can influence.

The characters of the White Witch Jadis and Aslan do differ noticeably from those in the novel. Lewis wrote Jadis as a cruel and disturbing creature perhaps considered too strong for children's television. While Barbara Kellermann is excellent in the role, her portrayal is of a rather camp villain, with all the wild arm movements and booming voice in keeping with that which one might expect of a pantomime. Aslan's character is different for technical reasons. Paul Stone wanted to avoid the traditional method of an actor standing on two legs wearing a mask and felt that Aslan should have the majesty of a real lion. A third-party company was employed to design a lion that would look visually realistic and could be operated without the need for actors. The final realisation has both its good and bad aspects. The body of the lion may look like that of a big cuddly toy but facially the model is stunning, built in a way that allows the mouth to move electronically. This presents obvious problems because the mouth, although mobile, is very slow. Obviously Aslan's voice must match the movement of the lion's face and this necessitated a very slow voice. This clearly defeats Stone's desire that the animal be majestic, presenting instead a rather subdued animal.

The BBC's plan was to adapt four of the seven Chronicles. The second season was represented by *Prince Caspian* and *The Voyage of the Dawn Treader*, while *The Silver Chair* was dramatised for the third season.

At a mere two episodes in length, *Prince Caspian* is reduced to basic narrative. It may well be tight and well

**Above:** Aslan the lion is flanked by his brave young disciples; (l to r) Susan (Sophie Cook), Lucy (Sophie Wilcox), Peter (Richard Dempsey, seated) and Edmund (Jonathan R. Scott) in *The Lion, the Witch and the Wardrobe*. The Satyrs were played by Garfield Brown (left) and Keith Hodiak (right).

paced but the audience is given little time to establish a rapport with the characters. Peter, Susan, Edmund and Lucy find themselves returned to Narnia but function as little more than mere bystanders in a subplot, only joining Caspian to save Narnia in the latter stages of the story. It's debatable if *Prince Caspian* was adapted through choice or out of necessity because it sets up the two stories that follow.

*The Voyage of the Dawn Treader* and *The Silver Chair* are two very similar stories. The first concerns a voyage by sea to try and discover the whereabouts of seven missing Narnian lords. The second revolves around a quest by land to locate King Caspian's missing son, Prince Rilian. Although the central characters in each story face many dangers during their intrepid journeys, both stories lack the feeling of possible impending doom so wonderfully captured in *The Lion, the Witch and the Wardrobe*. The audience is never led to believe, in either *Treader* or *The Silver Chair*, that Narnia is in any danger should our heroes fail to complete their missions. *The Silver Chair* feels more like the work of J. R. R. Tolkien than C. S. Lewis.

Three of the Chronicles remain unadapted. Reading the books chronologically, the first should be *The Magician's Nephew*. Naturally the BBC had to start with the most recognised novel, which is certainly *The Lion, the Witch and the Wardrobe*. *The Horse and his Boy* is a story within a story, set during events in *The Lion, the Witch and the Wardrobe*. This would therefore pose the problem of splitting *The Lion, the Witch and the Wardrobe* in two. Although the budget for the series was considerable, it would not have stretched as far as being able to realise *The Last Battle* on screen.

The BBC were both brave and original in adapting Chronicles other than *The Lion, the Witch and the Wardrobe*. In doing so, though, they confirmed its status as the superior Chronicle. Any one of the Narnia stories would make adequate viewing for children but *The Lion, the Witch and the Wardrobe* is a more personal battle involving four children in the fight between good and evil. It has the perfect Christmas card setting that entrances children and adults alike and was of course transmitted at a time of year associated with magic and the togetherness of families.

**The Chronicles of Narnia**
**BBC in association with Wonderworks**
**3 seasons**
(colour)

***The Lion, the Witch and the Wardrobe* (1988)**
**6 episodes**
**Broadcast:** Sundays 13/11/88 – 18/12/88

Siblings Peter, Susan, Edmund and Lucy Pevensie have been evacuated from war-torn London to stay in a country mansion owned by an old professor. Exploring the house, they find a room containing nothing but an old wardrobe. It is the gateway to a magical land called Narnia, dominated by the evil White Witch. She holds Narnia in a state of perpetual winter but never allows the arrival of Christmas. The children must play their part in ancient prophecy and help the mighty lion Lord Aslan free Narnia.

**Main Cast:** Richard Dempsey (Peter), Sophie Cook (Susan), Jonathan R. Scott (Edmund), Sophie Wilcox (Lucy), Barbara Kellermann (The White Witch), Kerry Shale (Mr Beaver), Lesley Nicol (Mrs Beaver), Jeffrey Perry (Mr Tumnus), Michael Aldridge (The Professor)

Based on the novel *The Lion, the Witch and the Wardrobe* by C. S. Lewis (first UK publication 1950, Geoffrey Bles)
**Dramatised by** Alan Seymour

**Music** composed and conducted by Geoffrey Burgon
**Designer:** Alan Spalding
**Producer:** Paul Stone
**Executive Producer for Wonderworks:** Colin Shindler
**Director:** Marilyn Fox

**Tie-in publications:** tie-in edition of novel published in paperback by Lions, 1988. Second tie-in edition by Lions, 1990.

**Video:** Released in UK as 165-minute compilation on double cassette by BBC, 1990. Reissued on single cassette by BBC, 1995. Various US releases also available.

***Prince Caspian* and *The Voyage of the Dawn Treader* (1989)**
**2 episodes** and **4 episodes**
**Broadcast:** Sundays 19/11/89 – 24/12/89

Summoned by the young Prince Caspian, the Pevensie children return to Narnia. Arriving near the ruins of their once glorious castle Cair Paravel, they find Narnia in a state of civil war. Caspian, the rightful heir to the throne, is being pursued by his evil uncle, King Miraz. Having already murdered

Caspian's father, Miraz now intends to put his own son on the throne but first he must also kill Caspian.
Edmund and Lucy are staying with their horrible cousin Eustace during the school holidays. While looking at a painting of a distinctly Narnian sailing ship, the three children are drawn into Narnia where they eventually find themselves aboard King Caspian's ship, the Dawn Treader. Caspian has set sail on a quest to find seven lost lords of Narnia, friends of his dead father.

**Main Cast**
'Prince Caspian': Richard Dempsey (Peter), Sophie Cook (Susan), Jonathan R. Scott (Edmund), Sophie Wilcox (Lucy), Jean Marc Perret (Prince Caspian), Robert Lang (King Miraz), Henry Woolf (Dr Cornelius), Warwick Davis (Reepicheep)
'The Voyage of the Dawn Treader': Jonathan R. Scott (Edmund), Sophie Wilcox (Lucy), David Thwaites (Eustace), Samuel West (King Caspian), Warwick Davis (Reepicheep)

Based on the novels *Prince Caspian* and *The Voyage of the Dawn Treader* by C. S. Lewis (first UK publication 1951 and 1955 respectively, Geoffrey Bles)
**Dramatised by** Alan Seymour

**Music** composed and conducted by Geoffrey Burgon
**Designers:** Alan Spalding, Sarah Greenwood, Adrian Uwalaa
**Executive Producer for Wonderworks:** Colin Shindler
**Producer:** Paul Stone
**Director:** Alex Kirby

**Tie-in publications:** compilation paperback edition of novels published as *Prince Caspian and The Voyage of the Dawn Treader* by Lions, 1989. Second tie-in editions as separate novels in paperback by Lions, 1990.

**Video:** *Prince Caspian* released in UK as 57-minute compilation by BBC, 1990. *The Voyage of the Dawn Treader* released in UK as 109-minute compilation by BBC, 1990. Both reissued by BBC, 1995. Various US releases also available.

***The Silver Chair* (1990)**
**6 episodes**
**Broadcast:** Sundays 18/11/90 – 23/12/90

Eustace tells Jill Pole about his previous adventure in Narnia as the two of them take shelter from school bullies. Jill is of the opinion that their only chance of escape is to transport themselves to Narnia. Somehow they manage it but it may not be entirely their own doing. Aslan has a dangerous mission for them. Assisted by Puddleglum the Marsh-wiggle, they search through the dangerous underground layers of Narnia in the hope that Prince Rilian can be found before old King Caspian passes away.

**Main Cast:** David Thwaites (Eustace), Camilla Power (Jill), Tom Baker (Puddleglum), Richard Henders (Prince Rilian), Barbara Kellermann (Green Lady), Warwick Davis (Glimfeather)

Based on the novel *The Silver Chair* by C. S. Lewis (first UK publication 1953, Geoffrey Bles)
**Dramatised by** Alan Seymour

Music composed and conducted by Geoffrey Burgon
Designers: Alan Spalding, Sarah Greenwood, Adrian Uwalaka
Producer: Paul Stone
Executive Producer for Wonderworks: Colin Shindler
Director: Alex Kirby

Tie-in publications: tie-in edition published in paperback by
Lions, 1990

Video: released in UK as 158-minute compilation on double
cassette by BBC, 1991. Reissued on single cassette by BBC,
1995. Various US releases also available.

## The Snow Spider Trilogy

The time of 4.15 on a Saturday afternoon was surely a slot
more associated with imports such as *Knight Rider* or
*Airwolf* than the screening of a brand new home-grown
children's drama. For those children lucky enough to be
watching *The Snow Spider*, a powerful and challenging tale
of regret, betrayal and resentment immersed in ancient
Welsh magic lay in store.

Gwyn Griffiths' ninth birthday is a sad affair. On his
birthday four years previously he asked his big sister
Bethan to look for his black ewe lost on a nearby mountain
during a storm. Bethan never returned and Gwyn's father
Ivor has never forgiven him. In one particularly powerful
scene Ivor gives a clear demonstration of his resentment
when he ruins Gwyn's birthday party, ranting, 'He's the
one. My Bethan is lost because of him ... it's his fault she
never came back.'

Gwyn's subsequent discovery that he is a magician
serves only to confuse the boy at first. The Snow Spider
Arianwen shows him a world of ice where Bethan appears
to exist happily and she calls to him. The meaning of this
is ambiguous to Gwyn but his Nain tells him that he is
getting nearer to his heart's desire. At this point it seems
inevitable that Gwyn will be reunited with Bethan –
particularly when, after a savage beating at school (where a
child can clearly be heard gleefully shouting, 'Kick his head
in'), he is helped home by Eirlys, a new girl in his class who
bears a striking resemblance to Bethan.

Eirlys spends time with Gwyn's family and is the key to
the entire mystery. Following her rescue from a storm,
Gwyn refers to her as Bethan but she tells him, 'I'm not
Bethan. I might have been once but now I'm Eirlys. I'll
never be Bethan again.' Is her purpose a benevolent one?
Did she return as a result of her family's unhappiness and
a desire to give them the opportunity to say a final
farewell? Or is she in fact trying to lure Gwyn to the same
fate that once befell Bethan? Whatever her motives, her
brief return heals the emotional chasm between Gwyn and
his father and allows the Griffiths family to move on with
their lives. That much is surely magic.

Much acclaimed, the novel of *The Snow Spider* won the
Smarties Grand Prix in 1986 and was awarded the Tir na n-
Og by the Welsh Arts Council in 1987. Although the
resolution left little in the way of an obvious path to a
sequel, Nimmo enjoyed writing about magic and felt
unable to let go of the characters she had created. *Emlyn's
Moon* (published in America as *The Orchard of the Crescent
Moon*) and *The Chestnut Soldier* quickly followed, both of
which were adapted for television.

*Emlyn's Moon* is in essence a repetition of *The Snow
Spider*, except with a greater breadth in narrative created
through a shift in locale and the introduction of two new

characters. Events are no longer confined to Gwyn, Nain
and the mountain as Nia, sister of Gwyn's best friend Alun,
moves with her family from the mountain to the valley,
where she encounters Gwyn's strange outcast cousin
Emlyn Llewelyn. Like *The Snow Spider*, *Emlyn's Moon* also
explores a mysterious disappearance, in this instance that
of Emlyn's mother, sister of Gwyn's mother.

Emlyn has hopelessly romantic notions of his mother,
envisaging her face looking down at him from the moon.
He may be romantic but he certainly isn't deluded,
realising full well that there are more earthly explanations
for his mother's absence. He recounts to Nia the terrible
fights he remembers between his mother and his
struggling artist father Idris. He tells her also of the last
night he saw his mother, when she burned her husband's
paintings and fled with Emlyn's baby brother in Gwyn's
father's car, an involvement that has divided the two
families and led Emlyn to hate Gwyn.

This is the major difference between the two stories. In
*The Snow Spider* something truly fantastical took place.
Bethan was transported to another world and her very
being transformed into something new. In *Emlyn's Moon*
there is nothing so magical about the mother's departure.
Forced to the point of a nervous breakdown by her
husband's drinking, his obsession for his work and their
woeful poverty, she has fled the family home in a deeply
depressed state.

The character of Emlyn is not the focal point of the
story, a mantle that instead lies with Nia, the clumsy
middle child of a large family who desperately wants to
establish her own identity. She does so with the help of
Idris, who encourages her to express herself through art.
Meanwhile she discovers her own power and importance
when she helps the magician Gwyn to rescue Emlyn from
the same beings who captured Bethan, thus reuniting the
two estranged families.

The problem with trilogies is that they tend to run out
of steam by the third segment. *The Snow Spider* is
unfortunately no exception. Now aged thirteen, Gwyn has
become frustrated with his powers. He must call upon
them once more when Nia's cousin Evan Llyr comes to stay
and becomes entangled in the struggle between Gwyn and
the enraged spirit of a Celtic prince – a spirit that Gwyn
has kept trapped but now desperately wants to free.

*The Chestnut Soldier* loses the subtlety of its predecessors,
opting instead for a more teen angst approach. The main
issues lie in the characterisation. Despite Gwyn being the
pivotal character he is reduced to a mere bystander while
Evan Llyr seduces Nia's beautiful sister Catrin with walks
in the forest and trips to the beach. Catrin however is
bland and it's difficult to establish any kind of empathy for
the girl and her peril. In the same respect it's far from easy
to form sympathy for the sneering Evan Llyr.

Children unfamiliar with Welsh mythology may have
found much of the Trilogy confusing. The general premise
at work behind each narrative is explained throughout, the
basis being that the central characters in each story are
playing out roles in tragic tales destined to repeat
themselves throughout the generations. The most subtle
of these is in *Emlyn's Moon* where the triangular relationship
between Gwyn, Nia and Emlyn reflects, to a degree, a
modern-day interpretation of the ancient Celtic legend of
the Mabinogion, a legend that was explored in more depth
in Alan Garner's *The Owl Service*.

All three productions, recorded on video and largely on
location, are of a generally very high standard and cost a 211

considerable amount. Special effects included Arianwen, the Snow Spider herself, represented by a small silver model when she is still and computer animatronics when she is required to move.

***The Snow Spider*** **(1988)**
**4 episodes**
**HTV Wales**
(colour)
Broadcast: Saturdays 26/11/88 – 17/12/88

**Main Cast:** Osian Roberts (Gwyn), Sian Phillips (Nain), Robert Blythe (Ivor), Sharon Morgan (Glenys), Rossilyn Killick (Bethan/Eirlys), Gareth Pritchard (Alun)

Based on the novel by Jenny Nimmo (first UK publication 1986, Methuen Children's Books Ltd)
**Adapted by** Julia Jones

**Music:** Danny Chang
**Designer:** Phil Williams
**Executive Producer:** Peter Elias Jones and Peter Murphy
**Producer/Director:** Pennant Roberts

**Tie-in publications:** published in paperback by Mammoth, 1989

**Video:** released as a 90-minute compilation by Video Gems, c. 1990. Deleted.

***Emlyn's Moon*** **(1990)**
**HTV Cymru/Wales**
**5 episodes** ('The Move'; 'A Fight'; 'Cold Flowers'; 'The Wrong Reflection'; 'The Orchard of the Moon')
(colour)
**Broadcast:** 6/9/90 – 4/10/90

**Main Cast:** Lucy Donovan (Nia), Steffan Morris (Emlyn), Osian Roberts (Gwyn), Sian Phillips (Nain), Gareth Thomas (Idris)

Based on the novel by Jenny Nimmo (first UK publication 1987, Methuen Children's Books Ltd)
**Adapted by** Julia Jones

**Music:** Danny Chang
**Designer:** Phil Williams
**Executive Producer:** Peter Murphy
**Producer/Director:** Pennant Roberts

**Tie-in publications:** published in paperback by Mammoth, 1989

***The Chestnut Soldier*** **(1991)**
**HTV Cymru/Wales**
**4 episodes** ('A Prince Returns'; 'Broken Horses'; 'Fiery Dreams'; 'Out of the Forest')
(colour)
**Broadcast:** Wednesdays 20/11/91 – 11/12/91

**Facing page:** Gwyn Griffiths (Osian Roberts) learns of magic and the old legends from his Nain (Sian Phillips) in the first instalment of *The Snow Spider* trilogy.

**Main Cast:** Sian Phillips (Nain), Osian Roberts (Gwyn Griffiths), Lucy Donovan (Nia Lloyd), Steffan Morris (Emlyn Llewelyn), Cal Macaninch (Evan Llyr), Stephanie Hull (Catrin Lloyd)

Based on the novel by Jenny Nimmo (first UK publication 1989, Methuen Children's Books Ltd)
**Adapted by** Julia Jones

**Music:** Danny Chang
**Designer:** Phil Williams
**Executive Producer:** Peter Murphy
**Producer/Director:** Pennant Roberts

**Tie-in publications:** published in paperback by Mammoth, 1990

## The Watch House

Teenager Anne is left in the care of Prudie, an old family friend, while her mother tries to sort out her own personal problems. Prudie lives next to the mysterious Watch House, the now redundant headquarters of the Garmouth Volunteer Life Brigade.

Arthur, Prudie's brother, is the caretaker of the Watch House and is pleased by Anne's interest in its history. Anne discovers that the Watch House is haunted by the ghost of its founder, Henry Cookson. Cookson's spirit begs for help and it is up to Anne and two local teenagers, Pat and Timmo, to solve the riddle of the Watch House and free the spirit of 'the Old Feller'.

In writing *The Watch House* Robert Westall wanted to author a ghost story where the haunting takes place as a result of specific happenings and motivations, rather than for the mere sake of it. In doing so he produced a thought-provoking novel worthy of adaptation for the small screen. However, people familiar with the novel may well have wondered how Westall's carefully crafted characters and detailed narrative could be fully explored in a comparatively short drama. In the event they couldn't and a number of in-depth aspects from the book were either omitted or substantially reduced.

*The Watch House* was one of the last children's dramas to be produced by a provincial programme-maker, in this case BBC North East – Newcastle. Despite co-production with Television New Zealand, it is entirely possible that financial resources limited the production to three parts, thus necessitating that sections of the book be removed. Additionallly, cuts were made to avoid potentially contentious issues deemed unsuitable for broadcast on children's television.

The most noticeable absences in the drama are Westall's two wonderful clergymen. Father Fletcher's allegiance lies with the Church of England, while Father da Souza works for the Catholic Church. There's a wonderful conversation between the two as they flippantly discuss Garmouth's lack of interesting sin. Missing also is the disturbing exorcism that they carry out on the beach and the séance that takes place between Anne, Pat and Timmo. Although Timmo is present in the adaptation, the representation of the character is completely different. In the book he is a flamboyant figure and it is hinted that he may have a strong anti-establishment point of view. In the drama he is reduced to a tanned, well-groomed but faceless character.

Production took place in and around the seaside town of Tynemouth, with chunks of the town's geography used to represent Garmouth – the story's fictional locale. Despite 213

**Above:** Anne (Diana Morrison) finds her holiday on the Tynemouth coast is far from dull when ghosts haunt *The Watch House*.

co-funding, the drama remains faithful to its Geordie roots and retains its delightful local characters and dialect. There's even a character called Charles McGill, whom we must assume is the adult version of the central character from Westall's first novel *The Machine Gunners*. The Watch House building was in reality home to Britain's first Volunteer Life Brigade and is a museum open to the public. In some of the drama's flashbacks we are witness to how such a building and service would have worked – adding the interesting element of historical education.

Considered separately from Westall's novel the serial still works as an effective ghost story. The concept of the dual haunting – that of Anne by the benevolent Old Feller, and that of the Old Feller both in life and death by the malevolent Scobie Hague – is fascinating, gifting the audience not one but two mysteries to solve.

**BBC North East – Newcastle**
**3 episodes**
(colour)
**Broadcast:** Wednesdays 7/12/88 – 21/12/88

**Main Cast:** Diana Morrison (Anne), Lynette Davies (Fiona), Sheri Shepstone (Prudie), James Garbutt (Arthur), Linda Huntley (Pat), Michael Nicholson (Timmo), Ying Tong John (Scobie Hague), Allen Dale (Old Feller)

Based on the novel by Robert Westall (first UK publication 1977, Macmillan)
**Dramatised by** William Corlett

**Music:** Rodney Newton
**Designer:** Bob Hutton
**Producer:** Brenda Ennis
**Executive Producer:** Paul Stone
**Director:** Ian Keill

## Billy's Christmas Angels

Billy idolises his guitar-playing brother Dave, whom he believes has moved out of the family home to take up a recording contract. His mother relies on Valium to steady her nerves and his father casts aspersions on his dream of being a drummer in his brother's band. 'This music lark. I know it's good fun but there's no future in it,' he tells Billy. 'Dreams. Bloody dreams. That's all he was ever good for,' he says with regards to Dave.

Billy gathers his savings and runs away to join his brother. He soon finds himself a victim of Mr Big, a street gangster, who takes his money and leaves him with nothing but the knowledge that his brother is a busker outside a cinema. Billy is devastated but finds himself guided by three mysterious strangers. Faith helps him escape from Mr Big and Hope helps him get his money back. Charlie, a crippled emporium owner, helps Billy to understand his brother's motives and heal the gap between them.

*Billy's Christmas Angels* is a wonderful tale of Christmas magic. 'You turn your back on me and you turn on your brother,' Faith tells him. In other words, if Billy loses his faith he loses everything. Hope shows him that there's always a way to conquer obstruction. Charlie (Charity) consolidates the lesson. In his emporium he has a beautiful drum kit, something that Billy has always wanted. He also has Dave's old guitar. Billy can only afford one. Billy's choice isn't simply one of drum kit and/or guitar but one between selfishness and his brother. Realising that all Dave has done is try to protect him and sustain his faith, Billy buys the guitar and reunites himself with his brother.

Recorded in Bristol, the play benefits from an excellent music score courtesy of female chorus group The Mint Juleps, who play Billy's invisible angels. Their repertoire includes a cappella renditions of U2's 'I Still Haven't Found What I'm Looking For' and Springsteen's 'Dancing in the Dark'.

*Billy's Christmas Angels* was the last of the BBC's sporadic series of plays for children to be made during the 80s.

**BBC Bristol**
**1 episode**
(colour)
**Broadcast:** Friday 23/12/88

**Main Cast:** Jeremy Stuart (Billy), John Shackley (Dave), Daniel Peacock (Mr Big), The Mint Juleps (Billy's Angels), Nabil Shaban (Charlie), Fay Masterton (Hope), Victor Romero Evans (Faith), Christopher Quinn (Dad), Deborah Manship (Mum)

**Written by** Sheila Fox

**Music** arranged and produced by The Mint Juleps, Griff Fender and Rita Ray
**Designer:** Stephen Brownsey
**Producer:** Brenda Ennis
**Executive Producer:** Paul Stone
**Director:** Christopher Baker

## Tom's Midnight Garden

All of us are time travellers. It's only because we pass through it in a strictly linear path from one day to the next that makes it less than obvious to us. This fact is revealed to young Tom Long when he is given a sideways glimpse into the passage of time, in the fascinating and touching novel from Philippa Pearce. Noted commentator John Rowe Townsend declared the book 'one of the tiny handful of masterpieces of English children's literature'. Adapted three times by the BBC down the years, has it produced any small screen masterpieces?

The first adaptation was tucked away in the daytime schedules, made and transmitted as part of the BBC Schools output. This is a shame since it was eminently worthy of an after-school timeslot. With the need to keep close to the original written text no doubt foremost in the makers' minds, a lot of the book ends up being read verbatim courtesy of a voiceover from Tom. Intentionally or otherwise, the end result thus appears very much influenced by Jonathan Miller's surreal 1966 film of *Alice in Wonderland*. Refreshingly for this time, all of the garden sequences are made on location giving a surprisingly slick edge to a schools broadcast.

Where the production suffers is in its truncation of the novel; three episodes is simply not enough time to get across the nuances of the book. This is forgivable in this case, however, since the programme was intended as a primer and aid to study of the full text. The same reasoning cannot be applied to the 'present day' remake of the same script, shown as regular teatime viewing in 1974. Now considered as a stand-alone drama, the rushed nature of the compressed story is all too obvious. What this time travel story needs is time to *tell* the story. The viewer must be allowed to come gradually to the realisation that each time Tom meets Hatty, time is moving forward faster for her than for him. Time is also needed for their emotional attachment to come across – likewise the way their relationship gradually fades as Hatty grows up.

It is unfair of course to complain that Tom has a ridiculous pudding bowl haircut in this 70s update, but some logistical production flaws are a fair target. Most of the dialogue scenes in the titular garden are shot in studio on a walled garden mock-up. The black and white version had clearly divided the allotted film time so that the interior sets conveyed the cramped conditions Tom experiences in the flats and the airy garden location work his boundless escape. One of the serial's finest moments meanwhile would have been lost on the audience; as an in-joke, Barty, the love of Hatty's life, is played by Simon Turner – Tom in the 1968 version.

The rejection of a contemporary backdrop for the 80s update, in favour of a return to the original late-50s period of the novel, does not bode well. With the BBC as a whole keen to sell 'heritage television' overseas at this time you could be forgiven for expecting a rather safe and cosy

packaging of the tale. In fact, this is its definitive telling, superbly made.

This version reinstates all of the small but essential points that make up the satisfying whole of the original work. Most importantly there is at last the luxury of time. We are introduced properly to the cruel Aunt Grace, who has had the orphan Hatty foist upon her and wants rid of her at the first opportunity. Tom has always believed that by his own time Hatty is dead. The uncertainty of her life under Aunt Grace's guardianship and the abruptness of Tom's separation from her means that she is lost to him forever. Through these details we share Tom's anguish when the garden is finally closed off to him. He will never know what happened to her after that last day they spent together.

It's only the presentation of this background that can make the final revelation truly touching, when Tom realises that old Mrs Bartholomew who lives upstairs is Hatty. His friend didn't die after all and he learns of the full and happy life she shared with Barty. These details turn the intriguing if basic time travel tale told in the earlier three-part adaptations into a metaphor for life, love and friendship.

Thankfully, the bigger budget available this time round, lavish but never gaudy, allows Christine Secombe to restore one of the book's vital sequences. Hatty hides her ice skates in a secret place many years earlier and when Tom finds them safe in his own time he is able to return them to Hatty and an Edwardian winter. The barrier of time between Tom and Hatty collapses as they share an impossibly romantic journey down the frozen river, both of them wearing the same pair of skates courtesy of a beautiful paradox. There's also an almost cinematic sweep that at last captures the novel's key moment. When Tom first opens the door of the dingy hallway that fateful midnight he is almost blinded by the glow of a summer's day.

Based on the novel by Philippa Pearce (first UK publication 1958, Oxford University Press)

**Merry-Go-Round: Tom's Midnight Garden** (1968)
**BBC Schools**
**3 parts** ('The Clock Strikes Thirteen'; 'Are You a Ghost?'; 'Time No Longer')
(b&w)
**Broadcast:** Mondays 18/11/68 – 2/12/68

**Main Cast:** Simon Turner (Tom Long), Verna Harvey (Hatty Melbourne), Myvanwy Jenn (Aunt Gwen), Geoffrey Denton (Uncle Alan), Enid Lindsey (Mrs Bartholomew), John Line (Abel), Martin Baker (Barty), Jean Hulness (Aunt Melbourne)

**Script by** John Tully

**Designer:** Gordon Roland
**Producer:** Dorothea Brooking
*Merry-Go-Round* series edited by Claire Chovil

**Above:** Tom Long (Jeremy Rampling) travels from the 1950s to meet Victorian girl Hatty (Caroline Waldron) in his Midnight Garden – a still from the 1989 BBC adaptation of *Tom's Midnight Garden*.

***Tom's Midnight Garden*** (1974)
**BBC Birmingham**
**3 episodes** ('The Clock Strikes Thirteen'; 'Are You a Ghost?'; 'Time No Longer')
(colour)
**Broadcast:** Mondays 7/1/74 – 21/1/74

**Main Cast:** Nicky Bridge (Tom Long), Adrienne Byrne (Hatty Melbourne), Myvanwy Jenn (Aunt Gwen), Charles West (Uncle Alan), Margot MacAlaster (Mrs Bartholomew), John Franklyn (Abel), Stephen Hawkins (Barty as a child), Simon Turner (Barty grown up), Anne Ridler (Aunt Grace Melbourne)

**Dramatised by** John Tully

**Designer:** Myles Lang
**Producer:** Dorothea Brooking

***Tom's Midnight Garden*** (1989)
**BBC**
**6 episodes**
(colour)

**Episode One**
Wednesday 4/1/89 5.05p.m.
Tom Long is sent to stay with his uncle and aunt in their small flat, while his brother convalesces with a dose of measles. Tom is cooped up and bored until one night old Mrs Bartholomew's grandfather clock at the foot of the stairs chimes thirteen o'clock. Going downstairs to investigate he opens the back door to find not the small yard he expected but a huge garden in bright sunshine.

**Episode Two**
Wednesday 11/1/89 5.10p.m.
The next day Tom wakes and immediately goes to the back door once again but the garden has gone. A few nights later however he is able to return to the garden, where he finds he can pass through solid doors. Is he a ghost in the garden? He seems invisible to everyone he meets there except possibly a little girl called Hatty.

**Episode Three**
Wednesday 18/1/89 5.10p.m.
Hatty can indeed see Tom and the two explore the garden together. On their trip, Hatty accidentally lets some wild ducks into the garden, wreaking havoc in the flowerbeds. Aunt Grace scolds Hatty, branding her a shame and an expense. Tom begs for the cruel aunt to stop …

**Episode Four**
Wednesday 25/1/89 5.10p.m.
Tom finds himself alone in the garden except for a very small girl dressed in mourning black. This is a 'little Hatty' grieving for her dead parents. Back in his own time, Tom sees Victorian costumes in a museum and realises that the Hatty he meets must have lived more than half a century ago. On his next trip to the garden Tom and Hatty are playing in their treehouse when she falls to the ground and is badly hurt.

**Episode Five**
Wednesday 1/2/89 5.10p.m.
When Tom next visits the garden it is winter. A recovered Hatty remarks that Tom is 'thinner through' and occasionally she has trouble seeing him. He urges her that if she should ever leave the house she should leave her ice skates behind in a secret place for him to find. When he returns to the flat he finds the skates are waiting there for him. Now both of them can skate on the frozen river, sharing the same pair of skates existing in different times.

**Episode Six**
Wednesday 8/2/89 5.10p.m.
On Tom's next visit to the past, Hatty is a grown-up woman. Making their way home, Hatty is offered a lift by the amorous Barty of whom she has grown fond. Tom, unnoticed in her excitement, disappears from sight. The next night Tom discovers that the garden has disappeared forever and he screams out for Hatty. The following morning old Mrs Bartholomew introduces herself to him – she is his Hatty. Time is no longer.

**Main Cast:** Jeremy Rampling (Tom), Caroline Waldron (Hatty), Isabelle Amyes (Aunt Gwen), Shaughan Seymour (Uncle Alan), Renee Asherson (Mrs Bartholomew), Richard Garnett (Abel), Gareth Kirkland (Barty), Simon Fenton (Peter), Sarah Jane McKechnie (Mrs Long), Katherine Schofield (Aunt Grace)

**Adapted by** Julia Jones

**Music:** Paul Reade
**Designer:** Gwen Evans
**Producer:** Paul Stone
**Director:** Christine Secombe

**Tie-in publications:** editions published in paperback by Puffin, 1989

Video:** 141-minute compilation released by BBC Video 4/7/94. Deleted 18/1/96.

Also told on
*Jackanory* 14/8/67 – 18/8/67
**5 episodes** ('The Clock That Struck 13'; 'Hatty'; 'Time in the Garden'; 'A Pair of Skates'; 'A Cry in the Dark')
**BBC**
(b&w)
**Read by** Martin Jarvis

## Press Gang

*Press Gang* was the result of a chance meeting in 1984 between a Scottish headmaster and an executive producer working for ITV. Harry Secombe's religious magazine programme *Highway* was recording an edition in a school in Paisley, Scotland, where headmaster Bill Moffat had been working on an environmental studies pack based around a newspaper for young people. He approached Bill Ward, *Highway*'s executive producer, believing that his idea, then called *The Norbridge Files*, could be successfully developed for children's television. Ward contacted Sandra Hastie, an American producer based in Britain, with the idea and although she was initially interested, it would be 1986 before she would follow the idea up.

Bill Moffat's son Steven, a secondary school teacher and spare-time writer, converted his father's idea into a script which led to a commission in 1987. The end result was *Press Gang*, a fast-paced, bittersweet children's drama balancing high volume humour against the stark realities of life.

Highly rated journalist Matt Kerr has taken over the reins at the *Norbridge Gazette* and is eager to set up a companion junior newspaper. He receives help from Mr Sullivan, a teacher at Norbridge High, who assigns his top pupils to the project. Acidic, headstrong sixteen-year-old Lynda Day, a highly intelligent girl who has skipped a year at school, is given the job of editing the paper. Unfortunately it won't be staffed completely by top performers. The teachers see the project as a way of positively challenging the energies of wayward pupils and, although Lynda has the support of reliable people like Kenny, Sarah and Julie, she must also try to make use of the intellectually challenged Frazz and a tearaway American boy called Spike Thomson. Lynda's bizarre relationship with Spike would become legendary over the course of the drama's run, as the two of them go out, break up and then do it all again while exchanging a veritable artillery of crippling one-liners at the other's expense.

*Press Gang*'s hook was its unique equilibrium between humour and dramatic content. It was not unusual for the comedic idiosyncrasies of the *Gazette*'s maverick accountant, Colin Mathews, and the sparkling dialogue between Lynda and Spike, to be played against a number of daring and challenging stories without interfering or taking anything away from the tough themes they were exploring.

The humour is often cutting edge for a children's drama, particularly the self-mocking tetraplegic, Billy Homer. 'You'll understand if I don't get up,' he says on first meeting everyone. When Chrissie Stuart starts firing questions at the boy about how he manages day-to-day life, he fends her off, saying, 'Why did the tetraplegic cross the road? He was pushed. Why did the tetraplegic cross back again? He was pushed.' While such humour may be considered lacking in

taste, these jokes are Billy's jokes and it is clear that he's at ease with his existence, thus the audience doesn't need to feel overly guilty at laughing with him.

The first season certainly pulls no punches as far as the examination of difficult issues is concerned. 'How To Make A Killing' encompassed the dangers of solvent abuse but, rather than moral high-horsing, the story concentrates on one of the sources of the problem, the shopkeepers who disregard the law and sell dangerous substances to youngsters. 'Monday-Tuesday' is by far the most controversial episode of the season. David Jefford, son of an important local businessman, blackmails Lynda, threatening to expose certain secrets about her running of the paper when his efforts for the *Gazette* are largely ignored. Lynda, along with the rest of the team, confronts David, telling him exactly what she thinks of him. The following day they discover that David has taken his own life with a shotgun. This taboo subject was again handled with great care as the news team spend a follow-up episode trying to piece together what went wrong.

The show's examination of difficult themes reached a definite epoch in the show's second season with 'Something Terrible'. Colin meets Cindy Watkins, a schoolgirl who seems to have an in-depth knowledge of him. After spending time with her he realises that Cindy has a desperate secret to tell him – that she is being abused by her father. Moffat's decision that she should confide in Colin is ingenious. Children who suffer often keep their abuse secret, certain that no-one will believe them. Colin is basically a con man, so why should anyone believe a word he says? This is the difficulty he faces when trying to convince people of Cindy's predicament. The speech he eventually uses when 'selling' the truth to the news team is inspiring and Paul Reynolds' greatest moment in the show. The story sends out a clear message to children that they have to confide in someone, that they are not alone and that they have nothing to be ashamed of.

The season also included the touching 'Rest of My Life', which saw Spike trapped beneath a record shop caught in a gas explosion, and the sweetly nostalgic 'Going Back to Jasper Street', which showed Kenny and Lynda in flashback as childhood friends. It seemed that *Press Gang* could tell any story it wanted, brilliantly.

Steven Moffat and Sandra Hastie won a BAFTA Award for Best Children's Programme and Richmond received a Royal Television Society Award, once again for Season Two, for Best Children's Programme.

For Season Three, Central decided to reduce *Press Gang*'s allowance to six episodes per season in a bid to support other projects. Steven Moffat was more than happy with this, feeling that it would be a struggle for him to deliver another twelve scripts in the desired time. The team have now left school and taken on the paper as a full-time commercial exercise. The cast were growing older and, with their characters now independent of the school, the vital connection that kept *Press Gang* in check as a programme for children was lost. The effervescent 'brat pack' ensemble feel matured in a run of even more sophisticated stories. 'The Last Word' opens with the revelation that a member of the team has been killed by a crazed gunman and slowly reveals just who has survived, one by one. It's nerve-shredding stuff with a stunning conclusion. 'Love and War', a truly moving episode centring on Spike's antagonistic relationship with his father, also packs a sickening kick to the guts in its final scenes.

**Above:** (l to r) Spike (Dexter Fletcher), Lynda (Julia Sawalha) and Kenny (Lee Ross) take a look at the first edition of the *Norbridge Junior Gazette* in the award-winning *Press Gang*.

**Written by** Steve Moffat
Based on an idea by Bill Moffat
**Producer:** Sandra C. Hastie
**Executive Producer for Central Television:** Lewis Rudd

*Press Gang*'s real strength was its ability to be laugh-out-loud funny one moment and almost tearfully intimate the next. As well as the issues and emotions there was the bizarre (70s TV hero Colonel X haunts a concussed Frazz) and the slapstick (Colin's murder of Julie's pet goldfish, bird and cat in ten seconds is fabulous farce). All were told with inventive direction and deceptive plot twists.

That *Press Gang* was perhaps above the expectations and interests of its target audience after Season Two might count against it. It matured from being brilliant children's television to become brilliant television, pure and simple. The pinnacle of ITV children's output of the 80s and 90s? The best children's series ever made? Just maybe.

**Richmond Films & Television Production
in association with Central
5 seasons
43 episodes**
(colour)

**Main Cast:** Julia Sawalha (Lynda Day), Dexter Fletcher (James 'Spike' Thomson), Lee Ross (Kenny Phillips – Seasons 1–3), Paul Reynolds (Colin Mathews), Kelda Holmes (Sarah Jackson), Mmoloki Chrystie (Frazz Davis), Lucy Benjamin (Julie Craig – Seasons 1, 4, 5), Joanna Dukes (Tiddler), Andy Crowe (Billy Homer – Seasons 1 and 2), Charlie Creed-Miles (Danny McColl – Season 1), Gabrielle Anwar (Sam Black – Season 2)

**Season One**
**12 episodes** ('Page One'; 'Photo Finish'; 'One Easy Lesson'; 'Deadline'; 'A Night In'; 'Interface'; 'How To Make A Killing' (part 1); 'How To Make A Killing' (part 2); 'Both Sides of the Paper'; 'Money, Love and Birdseed'; 'Monday-Tuesday'; 'Shouldn't I Be Taller?')
**Broadcast:** Mondays 16/1/89 – 10/4/89 (no broadcast 27/3/89 due to Easter schedules)

**With:** Nick Stringer (Mr Sullivan), Clive Wood (Matt Kerr), Angela Bruce (Chrissie Stuart), David Collings (Mr Winters), Miranda Forbes (Miss Hessope), Penelope Nice (Mrs Day)

**Music:** Peter Davis, John Mealing and John G. Perry
**Designer:** Chris Edwards
**Directors:** Bob Spiers (3, 4, 6, 9, 11, 12), Lorne Magory (5, 7, 8, 10), uncredited (1, 2)*
*The director on episodes 1 and 2 was dissatisfied with editing carried out on his episodes and requested his name be removed

**Season Two**
**13 episodes** ('Breakfast At Czar's'; 'Picking Up the Pieces'; 'Going Back to Jasper Street'; 'The Week and Pizza'; 'Love and the Junior Gazette'; 'At Last A Dragon'; 'Something Terrible' (part 1); 'Something Terrible' (part 2); 'Friends Like These'; 'The Rest of My Life'; 'Yesterday's News'; 'Rock Solid'; 'The Big Finish?')
**Broadcast:** Thursdays 18/1/90 – 12/4/90

**With:** Rosie Marcel (Sophie Jenkins), Claire Hearnden (Laura Wilmot), Nick Stringer (Mr Sullivan), Clive Wood (Matt Kerr), Angela Bruce (Chrissie Stuart), Penelope Nice (Mrs Day)

**Music:** Peter Davis, John Mealing and John G. Perry
**Designer:** Alan Cassie
**Directors:** Bob Spiers (1, 5–8, 10, 12, 13), Gerry O'Hara (2), Bren Simson (3, 4), John Hall (9), Lorne Magory (11)

**Season Three**
**6 episodes** ('The Big Hello'; 'Killer On the Line'; 'Chance Is A Fine Thing'; 'The Last Word' (part 1); 'The Last Word' (part 2); 'Holding On')
**Broadcast:** Tuesdays 7/5/91 – 11/6/91

**Music:** Peter Davis
**Designer:** Martin Childs
**Directors:** Bob Spiers (1, 3, 6), Lorne Magory (2, 4, 5)

**Season Four**
**6 episodes** ('Bad News'; 'UnXpected'; 'She's Got It Taped'; 'Love and War'; 'In the Picture'; 'Day Dreams')
**Broadcast:** Tuesdays 7/1/92 – 11/2/92

**With:** Clive Wood (Matt Kerr)

**Music:** Peter Davis
**Designer:** Martin Childs
**Directors:** Bob Spiers (1, 3, 6), Lorne Magory (2), Bill Ward (4, 5)

**Season Five**
**6 episodes** ('Head and Heart'; 'Friendly Fire'; 'A Quarter to Midnight'; 'Food, Love and Insecurity'; 'Windfall'; 'There Are Crocodiles')
**Broadcast:** Fridays 16/4/93 – 21/5/93

**With:** David Collings (Mr Winters), Clive Wood (Matt Kerr), Lee Ross (Kenny Phillips)

**Music:** Peter Davis
**Designer:** Julian Fullalove
**Directors:** Bill Ward (1, 3), Bob Spiers (2, 4, 6), James Devis (5)

**Tie-in publications:** novelisations from Seasons 1 and 2 by Bill Moffat published in paperback as *Press Gang 1 – First Edition*, *2 – Public Exposure*, *3 – The Date* and *4 – Checkmate* by Hippo Scholastic, 1989, 1989, 1990 and 1990 respectively

**Video:** four episodes released in episodic format in UK as 95-minute single cassette ('Page One', 'Photo Finish', 'One Easy Lesson', 'Deadline') by Central Video 1990. Deleted 14/12/94.

## The Country Boy
Ben Westcott isn't particularly interested in school and would rather spend his time competing in sheepdog trials with his beloved collie, Duke. When a canister of chemicals from a nearby chemical plant ends up in the river inlet near Ben's home, both Ben and his dog are poisoned following a swim. Duke dies and such is Ben's

illness he is admitted to a hospital in London.

It soon transpires that dangerous chemicals are being smuggled from the plant and sold abroad for huge profits. Ben, his nurse, a local reporter and a worker from the plant are soon caught up in a struggle to prevent further smuggling and environmental pollution.

Following dramas like *Break In the Sun* and *Running Scared*, Bernard Ashley's name had become synonymous with hard-hitting urban narratives addressing contentious social issues. *The Country Boy*, with its Kent marshes setting and less visceral themes, is quite different.

Although the issue of environmental pollution had previously been covered in *The Battle of Billy's Pond*, a 70s production by the Children's Film Foundation, *The Country Boy* was the first children's TV serial to cover the subject.

Pollution, though, serves only to introduce the main theme of the drama: that of the old versus the new and the cultural gap between supposedly simple life in the country and the perceived complex rat race of the city. It is the corporate machine that has poisoned Ben but will it be modern medicine or his grandmother's folk cures that save him? When Ben is admitted to hospital in London he finds himself in an unfamiliar, uncomfortable environment. Tall buildings dominate his surroundings, the air smells and he finds himself taunted and bullied as a simpleton by the tough city boy in the next bed.

Ben's dad Dave keeps his mother's herbal practices and opinions at arm's length, treating them almost with suspicion yet maintaining an obvious respect for them. Mum is more outspoken, even referring angrily on one occasion to her mother-in-law as a witch. Grandmother Alice is at least a realist, an example of an older generation who believe that adversity must be faced. She makes no attempt, against the wishes of Ben's parents, to hide the fact that Duke is dead.

In children's drama it is usually the child that rights the wrongs, conquers adversity and generally deals with the menace of self-serving and often villainous adults. Ashley operated with a different agenda in *The Country Boy*, establishing two almost completely separate plot elements: that of the country boy struggling to adapt in difficult surroundings, and the thriller aspect of industrial espionage and smuggling. In doing this the central character of Ben is distanced from some of the more frenetic goings-on in and around J.M. Chemicals, leaving it up to the adults to deal with the villains. It doesn't make Ben's life any easier though. The poison inside him, unseen and without antidote, is just as effective a menace, if not more so, than thuggish chemical smugglers.

Bernard Ashley was inspired to write *The Country Boy* while enjoying a holiday with his wife in the countryside of the Auvergne in France. Ashley considered the impact that an enforced change in the opposite direction, from country to town, might have on a person and how they would cope in new surroundings. He approached Paul Stone with the idea but Stone made it clear that, due to financial constraints, filming in France wouldn't be an option. Ashley relocated the drama to the Cliffe Marshes, a remote and moody landscape where he once lived, incorporating some of its landmarks into the story.

The unique barn-like design of Boatrick House became the Westcotts' farm and a line of disused coastguards' houses became the villains' lair. Alice's shack didn't exist and the BBC production team stepped in to construct this on a small estuary island, with everything fitted out inside for interior recording.

*The Country Boy*
**BBC**
**6 episodes**
(colour)

## Episode One

Wednesday 15/2/89 5.10p.m.
A canister of dangerous chemicals finds its way to the bottom of a river inlet and releases its contents into the water while at J.M. Chemicals a lab assistant discovers that missing canisters cannot be accounted for … Against his father's instructions, Ben Westcott swims in the river with his beloved sheepdog Duke. When his father drives past, Ben pulls Duke under the water to avoid being caught. When Ben surfaces he discovers Duke has disappeared.

## Episode Two

Wednesday 22/2/89 5.10p.m.
Charmaine discusses the missing insecticide with Doctor Skellman, postulating that the canisters have been stolen and smuggled abroad for a price. The owner of J.M. Chemicals is involved in a plot and a journalist holds a secret meeting with an embassy official who advises him that chemicals are indeed being smuggled. Duke is missing and Ben feels unable to tell his father what has happened but soon the boy falls ill.

## Episode Three

Wednesday 1/3/89 5.10p.m.
Ben is taken to a London hospital where they diagnose poisoning. Believing that she can cure him with natural medicines, Ben's grandmother wants him returned home. While walking with her boyfriend, Ben's sister Sally finds Duke's body floating in the water.

## Episode Four

Wednesday 8/3/89 5.10p.m.
Ben's father brings in an analyst to check for poisonous substances at the inlet. The owner of J.M. Chemicals comes under increasing pressure to supply more chemicals to his foreign contacts. A local reporter tricks hospital staff into giving him information about Ben's predicament and prints the story.

## Episode Five

Wednesday 15/3/89 5.10p.m.
Skellman and Charmaine work to find an antidote to Ben's condition but when Barbara and Ben's parents take him out for the day he runs away to his grandmother's.

## Episode Six

Wednesday 22/3/89 5.10p.m.
The herbal cure prepared for Ben by his grandmother appears to work and his health returns. Barbara arrives at Ben's grandmother's house and tells him that an antidote has been found and that he must return to hospital to ensure he is fully cured. Skellman discovers that the company director is involved in the smuggling while Ben, Charmaine and the reporter attempt to put a stop to the criminal activity.

**Main Cast:** Jeremy Sweetland (Ben), Siobhan Burke (Sally), Nigel Humphreys (Dave), Helen Duvall (Lyn), Mary Wimbush (Alice), Bronwyn Baud (Dr Skellman), Claire Callaghan (Charmaine), Marc Sinden (West), Janet Palmer (Barbara), Mark Burdis (Adam)

**Written by** Bernard Ashley

**Music:** David Ferguson
**Designer:** Malcolm Thornton
**Producer:** Brenda Ennis
**Executive Producer:** Paul Stone
**Director:** Colin Cant

**Tie-in publications:** reproduction of script published in paperback by Julia MacRae Books, 1989

## Children's Ward/
## Why Can't I Go Home?
### The story of a children's ward

ITV's longest-running drama series for children is *Children's Ward*, on air since 1989. The format is a simple one – the children's ward of a busy city hospital is where all kinds of kids come with all their attendant ailments and personalities. While children come to the ward to get better, they may also just learn a few life lessons in the meantime.

The series of the past decade or so was preceded by a largely forgotten entry from 1979. *Why Can't I Go Home?* was subtitled as 'the story of a children's ward' and shared an identical format to its better-known successor.

In St Catherine's Ward, play leader Mrs Lever and two new student nurses oversaw kids like Robert, in for a broken leg and sullen and frustrated with his incarceration, Rosalie, a Cockney runaway constantly seeking attention, and Adrian, who has both his real father and stepfather coming at visiting hours. Various plots and issues can be aired within a limited number of standing sets, with no limit to the patients who can come through the ward doors. The flexibility of this format and suitability for soap has been proven by the longevity of *Children's Ward* and in the adult arena with *General Hospital*, *Casualty* and *ER*.

That *Why Can't I Go Home?* failed is no doubt entirely due to the ITV strike of 1979. Coverage in strike-bound *TV Times* was limited, an episode was rescheduled and finally transmissions stopped altogether. Remaining episodes were shown after ITV came back on air but all impetus had surely been lost.

While there are no apparent hard and fast links between the ATV series and Granada's series of a decade later, Russell T. Davies, one of the producers of *Children's Ward*, echoed exactly the tenets of *Why Can't I Go Home?*, even if unconsciously. 'One of the show's great strengths is that we're not restricted by age,' Davies told *Radio Times*. Add to this other aspects such as class and ethnicity and you see the melting pot the convenient format provides. 'Children of all ages are on an equal footing in hospital so all the barriers come down,' Davies qualified.

One of the key examples of this was written by Davies himself, in a Season Seven storyline that saw a bunch of thoughtless joyriders placed on the Southpark ward alongside the victims of their stupidity, with resulting electrifying tension. As with most 'soaps' *Children's Ward* is often issue-led and topics have included teenage pregnancy, alcoholism (patient Billy, in the role that established Tim Vincent, later of *Blue Peter* and *Emmerdale*), anorexia, Ecstasy misuse and sexual abuse. More 'mundane' plots have included, several times, thieves abroad on the ward – this recycled plot examines the abuse of trust and respect, with the thieves always eventually realising that they are stealing from their own friends.

**Above:** Nurse Keely Johnson (Jenny Luckcraft, left) welcomes Tiffany Kendall (Kate Emma Davies), another patient on the *Children's Ward.*

As in all hospital drama, much mileage is derived from the life or death dramas you expect of the setting. What this series has in advantage over its grown-up rivals such as *Casualty* is that TV death – and not all of the *Ward*'s patients go home safely at the end of their stay – is still an affecting subject of great import for the target audience, though with this 'dramatic benefit' comes added responsibility for its makers. Patients have suffered from cancer, leukaemia, cystic fibrosis and AIDS.

The kids have come into the ward for a variety of reasons. Often this is not as a result of a medical condition but by unexpected accident. There's been a footballer felled by a kidney injury, kids hurt rock climbing, a boy brought in after a stabbing. Recently, while it has meant opportunities to venture outside the ward walls, the show has tended towards the kind of contrived melodramatic incidents favoured by *Casualty* – a gas explosion or fire, for example. Showing either ingenuity or desperation, a particular favourite had boys shooting a home-made pop video fall into a grain hopper! Among the most interesting admissions has been Delli, a twelve-year-old war victim from Eastern Europe, crushed by rubble after a bomb attack on her home in the opening scenes of Season Eleven.

There's sometimes a lighter side to the series, most notably Scott's attempts to set up a hospital radio station in Season Ten which leads to a visit from Radio One DJ Mark Radcliffe. In the first season there had been a similar appearance by superstar DJ Bruno Brookes. In a slightly different vein was footballer Robbie Fowler's visit to see Davey, a boy dying of cancer. For someone like Fowler, who no doubt gives what comfort he can to real kids dying in hospitals, it must be a strange experience.

***Children's Ward/The Ward*** (1989–ongoing)
**Granada**
**12 seasons** (at spring 2000)
(colour)

**Season One**
**13 episodes**
**Broadcast:** Wednesdays 15/3/89 – 7/6/89

**Main Cast:** Carol Harvey (Dr Charlotte Woods), Ian McCulloch (Dr McKeown), Janette Beverley (Nurse Diane Meadows), Tim Stanley (Nurse Gary Miller), Jenny Luckcraft (Keely Johnson), Rita May (Nurse Mags), Alan Rothwell (Dr Davies), Nina Baden-Semper (Jan Stevens), Tim Vincent (Billy Ryan), Rebecca Sowden (Fiona Brett), Andrew Hall (Dave Spencer), William Ash (Darren Walsh), Laurence Porter (George), Kate Emma Davies (Tiffany Kendall), Leyla Nejad (Dawn Khatir), Kim Burton (Ben Croft), Paul Varney (Dean)

**Written by** Paul Abbott and Kay Mellor
**Designer:** Nick King
**Producer:** Rod Natkiel
**Executive Producer:** Nick Wilson
**Directors:** Rod Natkiel, Nicholas Mallett, Alistair Clark

**Season Two**
**14 episodes**
**Broadcast:** Mondays 8/1/90 – 9/4/90

**Main Cast:** Carol Harvey (Dr Charlotte Woods), Janette Beverley (Nurse Diane Meadows), Tom Higgins (Dr Kiernan Gallacher), Tim Stanley (Nurse Gary Miller), Jenny Luckcraft (Keely), Rita May (Mags), Leyla Nejad (Dawn), Judy Holt (Nurse Mitchell), Dean Gatiss (Mathew McCann), Paul Lally (Dr Strickland), Alistair McGowan (Casualty Doctor), Mark Hamer (Spida), Mark Dixon (Cal Spicer), Kirsty Skelhorn (Gaynor), Adam Sunderland (Sean), Darren Brennan (Lob), Tony Bamforth (Terry), Chris Bisson (J. J.), Nichola Stephenson (Amanda), Maxine Ruth-Suter (Sarah), Rachel Egan (Lisa), Abbie Choyce (Melanie), Ben Sowden (Thomas Hogarth), Eddie Otoo (Dominic Richardson), Jo Otoo (Richie Richardson)

**Written by** Paul Abbott, Kay Mellor, Martin Riley
**Designer:** James Weatherup
**Producer:** Gareth Morgan
**Executive Producer:** David Liddiment
**Directors:** Alan Bell, Julian Jarrold, Gareth Morgan

**Season Three**
**13 episodes**
**Broadcast:** Tuesdays 23/10/90 – 18/12/90 and 8/1/91

**Main Cast:** Carol Harvey (Dr Charlotte Woods), Janette Beverley (Nurse Diane Meadows), Tom Higgins (Dr Kiernan Gallacher), Tim Stanley (Nurse Gary Miller), Jenny Luckcraft (Keely), Rita May (Mags), Leyla Nejad (Dawn Khatir), Judy Holt (Nurse Mitchell), Kiran Hocking (Dr Tanya Davies), Margery Bone (Nurse Katie Grahams), Mark Dixon (Cal), Natalie Wiblin (Helen Jordan), Emily Aston (Sally Jordan), Martin Corrigan (Colin Jordan), Kieran O'Brien (Lee Jones), Daile Endicott (Marcus Jones), Michael Friel (Danny Phillips), Sarah Cooper (Bryony Shaeffer), Tim Vincent (Billy), Catherine Grimes (Rowena Easson), William Mellor (Ben Rowlingson), Gillian Waugh (Gail Bevan)
**Written by** Paul Abbott, Kay Mellor, Martin Riley, John Chambers
**Producer:** Gareth Morgan
**Directors:** Alan Bell, Julian Jarrold, David Richards

**Season Four**
**10 episodes** and **1 special**
**Broadcast:** Tuesdays 15/10/91 – 17/12/91
**Christmas Special:** 25/12/91 (12.15p.m.)

**Main Cast:** Janette Beverley (Sister Diane Meadows), Tom Higgins (Dr Kiernan Gallacher), Jenny Luckcraft (Keely), Rita May (Mags), Matthew Marsh (Dr Brian Stoker), Mark Dixon (Cal), Natalie Wiblin (Helen Jordan), Emily Aston (Sally Jordan), Martin Corrigan (Colin Jordan), Adam Durham (Lenny), Zoe Owen (Donna), Judy Brooke (Bev), Clinton Blake (Rob), Emily Oldfield (Lucy), Jonathan Sassen (Joey Palmer)

**Written by** Paul Abbott, Kay Mellor, Martin Riley, John Chambers

**Season Five**
**10 episodes**
**Broadcast:** Tuesdays 13/10/92 – 15/12/92

**Cast includes:** Janette Beverley (Sister Diane Meadows), Tom Higgins (Dr Kiernan Gallacher), Jenny Luckcraft (Keely), Matthew Marsh (Dr Brian Stoker), Ronnie McCann (Gary)

**Written by** Paul Abbott, Kay Mellor, John Chambers, Garry Lyons, Sally Wainwright
**Producer:** Russell T. Davies

**Season Six**
**10 episodes**
**Broadcast:** Tuesdays 12/10/93 – 21/12/93 (no broadcast 30/11/93 due to Budget coverage)

**Cast includes:** Janette Beverley (Sister Diane Meadows), Tom Higgins (Dr Kiernan Gallacher), Jenny Luckcraft (Keely), Judy Holt (Sister Mitchell)

**Written by** John Chambers, Sally Wainwright, Russell T. Davies
**Producer:** Russell T. Davies

**Season Seven**
**10 episodes**
**Broadcast:** Tuesdays 11/10/94 – 20/12/94 (no broadcast 29/11/93 due to Budget coverage)

**Cast includes:** Janette Beverley (Sister Diane Meadows), Tom Higgins (Dr Kiernan Gallacher), Jenny Luckcraft (Keely), Judy Holt (Sister Mitchell), Rita May (Mags), Ben Hull (Martin)

**Writers** include Sally Wainwright, Russell T. Davies

**Season Eight (*The Ward*)**
**12 episodes**
**Broadcast:** Tuesdays 5/9/95 – 28/11/95 (no broadcast 17/10/95 due to ITV 40th birthday special programmes)

**Cast includes:** Jenny Luckcraft (Keely), Rita May (Mags), Patrick Connolly (Swifty), Jane Danson (Paula)

**Written by** Russell T. Davies, Paul Abbott, Sally Wainwright, Julian Preston, Jan McVerry, Catherine Hayes

***Inside The Ward*** was a behind the scenes special shown Monday 16/10/95

**Season Nine (*The Ward*)**
**12 episodes**
**Broadcast:** Tuesdays 10/9/96 – 26/11/96

**Main Cast:** Janette Beverley (Sister Diane Gallagher), Jenny Luckcraft (Keely), Rita May (Mags), David Elliot (Dr Adam Sullivan), Phillip King (Charge Nurse Nick Williams), Patrick Connolly (Swifty), Jane Danson (Paula), Chris Cooke (Chas), Steven Nuttall (Martin), Alison Darling (Rachel), Frank Lauder (Ritchie), Jamie Harrison (Gareth), Leanne Burrows (Sophie), Michelle Totton (Anne Marie), Sarah Dubery

(Jessica), Jenny Humphries (Mandy), Oliver Furness (David), Matthew Littler (Patrick),
Andrea Young (Trish), Paul Fox (Tim), Lucy Bradburn (Katie), Sharon Muircroft (Fiona), Benedict Sandiford (Joe), Frances Cox (Grace), Samantha Hilton (Skye), Sebastian Thompson (Billy), Gregg Baines (Greg), Sally Walsh (Denise), Anthony Lewis (Scott)

**Written by** Catherine Hayes, Jan McVerry, Joe Turner, Julian Preston, Tom Elliot, Paul Cornell

**Season Ten (*The Ward*)**
**12 episodes**
**Broadcast:** Tuesdays 11/11/97 – 16/12/97 and 6/1/98 – 10/2/98

**Main Cast:** Rita May (Mags), Phillip King (Nick), Brigit Forsyth (Sylvia Dickinson), Trevor Cooper (Big Bob), Sharon Muircroft (Fiona), Anthony Lewis (Scott), Chris Cooke (Chas), Victoria Finney (Julie Barrow), Kirk Smith (Tony), Elliott Tiney (Cal), Tina O'Brien (Claire), Kelly Greenwood (Geri), Gus Gallagher (Phoenix), Micaiah Dring (Lisa), Hayley Fairclough (Shona), Ralf Little (Robbie), Vicky Binns (Tash Naylor), Emma McGrane (Ruthie), Gregg Baines (Greg), Jane Danson (Paula)

**Written by** Jan McVerry, Joe Turner, Martin Jameson, Tony Basgallop, Lee Pressman, Paul Cornell

**Season Eleven (title reverts to *Children's Ward*)**
**13 episodes**
**Broadcast:** Thursdays 4/2/99 – 29/4/99

**Main Cast:** Rita May (Mags), Phillip King (Nick), Victoria Finney (Julie), Anthony Lewis (Scott), Gregg Baines (Greg), Vicky Binns (Tash), Sharon Muircroft (Fiona), Kauren Huckerby (Amy), John Catterall (Davey Pearson), Jonathan Taylor (Si), Ben Sherriff (Richard), Ben Stapleton (Sam), Heston Aniteye (Louie), Kirsty Elsby (Sophie), Corinne Coward (Jacqueline), Daniel-Thomas Lloyd (Jimmy), Tara Pendergast (Lizzie), Alexandra Gilbreath (Geena), Kate West (Vicky), Pauline Jefferson (Sheila), Louise Bromilow (Kate), Vinette Robinson (Joy), Ciaran Griffiths (Jack), Hayley Elliott (Alice)

**Written by** Joe Turner, Peter Kerry, Patrea Smallacombe, Paul Cornell, Martin Jameson, John Chambers, Bill Taylor, Karin Young

**Season Twelve (*Children's Ward*)**
**13 episodes**
**Broadcast:** Thursdays 10/2/00 – 4/5/00

**Main Cast:** Rita May (Mags), Danny Edwards (Charge Nurse Marcus Oliver), Victoria Finney (Julie), Gregg Baines (Greg), Sharon Muircroft (Fiona), John Catterall (Davey), Jonathan Taylor (Si), Miranda Hutcheon (Delli), Josh Maguire (Auni), Sadie Pickering (Sarah), Holly Scourfield (Becky), Claude Close (Big Bob), Matthew Booth (Joe Ellis), Oliver Hamilton (Adam), Rebecca Norris (Zoe), Richard Cadman (Rick), Charlie Ryan (Tommy), Joe Fairbrother (Damon), Martin Anderson (Kieran), Rhea Bailey (Emma), Fine Time Fontayne (Gordon), Ellie Paskell (Tilly), Hannah King (Alex), Sarah Hirst (Jenny), Louise Hirst (Laura)

**Written by** Martin Jameson, Patrea Smallacombe, John Chambers, Chris Thompson, Peter Kerry, Julie Wilkinson, Janys Chambers, Bill Taylor, Matt Jones

**Tie-in publications:** five paperbacks written by Helen White and published by Network/BBC Books. *Children's Ward*, 1990. *Children's Ward: Deadly Enemies*, 1991. *Children's Ward: Make or Break*, 1991. *Children's Ward: Lost and Found*, 1992. *Children's Ward: On The Run*, 1993. Also *Children's Ward: The Crash* by Helen White published by Puffin, 1994.
Script book edited by Lawrence Till (contains scripts by Paul Abbott, Kay Mellor, John Chambers), published by Heinemann Plays/Oxford, 1992.

**Why Can't I Go Home?** (1979)
**ATV**
**12 episodes**
(colour)
Broadcast: Mondays 18/6/79 – 26/11/79*

**Main Cast:** Craig McFarlane (Robert Evans), Steven O'Shea (Adrian Foster), Susan Tully (Rosalie), Vivienne Avramoff (Nurse Sandy Scoular), Pat Wainwright (Nurse Patricia Ross), Finnuala O'Shannon (Sister O'Neill), Sue Nicholls (Mrs Lever), Gordon Case (Dr Martin)

**Written by** David Fisher (1, 2, 9, 12), Dick Sharples (3, 4, 8), Christopher Bond (5), Allan Prior (6), Max Marquis (7, 8), Frank Moore (11), 10 n/k due to *TV Times* strike
**Script Editor:** David Fisher

**Designer:** Su Chases (1–4), Don Fisher (5, 6), Su Chases and Don Fisher (7–12)
**Producer:** Royston Morley
**Directors:** Royston Morley (1, 9, 12), Pembroke Duttson (3, 8), Paul Harrison (2, 5, 6, 11), Chris Tookey (4, 7), 10 n/k.

* Episode 7 was postponed from 30/7/79 and shown on 6/8/79. Broadcasts were then interrupted by the ITV blackout of autumn 1979. The series went off the air after episode 9 on 20/8/79. It returned with a repeat of episode 1 on 29/10/79. After one further repeat, episodes 10–12 were broadcast 12/11/79 – 26/11/79.

# Dramarama
## Season Seven

It was in its final run that *Dramarama* reached what had seemed its aim all along, with as many companies as possible contributing to the season. There were just two spooky offerings this time. 'Ghost Story' was as simple as its title suggests, a tale of teenage army cadets lost on a foggy moor. Their leader was haunted by a boy he had left to die on an earlier expedition when teaching him a lesson in discipline. Glossily made all on location, the director even went as far as to shoot in faux widescreen.

'Back to Front' was the other fantasy episode. David Powers receives a mirror from Mr Rolyat's antique shop and begins to notice that his reflection is taking on a life of its own. His friend realises just too late that Mr Rolyat is the extra-dimensional alter ego of the previous owner Mr Taylor (Rolyat backwards, you see) and David ends up trapped behind the mirror, replaced by a reversed double. It provided some nice shocks but was a bit of a one note

---


tale. Its most inventive touch was the use of a reversed Yorkshire caption graphic at the end.

A back-to-basics adventure story came in the shape of 'The Pisces Connection'. A gang of four kids investigate goings-on in a supposedly radioactive area to find a group of drug smugglers (you even got to see cocaine being wrapped in foil) using the fish from the local river as a cover. An updating of Blyton/CFF-styled adventure to all intents and purposes, it contained the great line from one of the kids despairing of his mate's enthusiasm: 'He thinks we're the flippin' Famous Five!' The villains were a good deal rougher than in Blyton's day but were outwitted nonetheless. Geoffrey Bayldon enlivened proceedings as a mad old poacher.

Issues-based scripts were 'Badger', about a girl discovering the horrors of badger-baiting, and 'In the Pink', which looked at the prejudice encountered by an albino girl when she arrives at a new school. Another of the more thoughtful episodes was 'Mitchin'' (the title coming from a Devonshire term for truanting). This told the story of two boys – one from a comprehensive and the other from public school – and the strange friendship that is formed when both decide to play truant. The play was written by a drama teacher from Plymouth who fully intended it to act as a pilot although a series never appeared.

Almost half of the final run were comedies. 'Rosie the Great' was a nicely satirical tale of the little people on a remote island in the Atlantic overcoming the big world outside. Very much *Local Hero* in style with a curious Scots/Welsh flavour, the story concerns various superpowers dispatching their ambassadors to Longsea, aiming to build a military airbase in the little haven. All are ridiculous stereotypes; there's the bumbling Brit (Peter Capaldi), a Russian looking for 'Mickey the Mouse' and a loud-mouthed American asking where her stretch limo has got to. When papers are uncovered revealing that the island is not part of Britain, the islanders outwit a councillor with aims of presidency by appointing twelve-year-old Rosie as monarch. 'Just Wild About Harry' was an amiable submission from Geordieland. Harry was Harriet, a girl who reads too many cheap detective novels and sees herself as Tina Topps, private eye, via black and white noir pastiche and her ham American voiceover. Finding a foot poking out from a tarpaulin in her hockey teacher's garage, her wild imagination means that she sees everything around her as incriminating evidence. The foot, of course, turns out to be a shop dummy the teacher needs for an amateur dramatics show.

Some more pronouncedly low comedy entries were rather at odds with the *Dramarama* monicker. 'Monstrous' was set in a Welsh funfair with a very special ghost train and had people changing into werewolves among other comedy business. 'Codzmorf' was probably the silliest *Dramarama* of all, with an amateur magician turning himself into a blobby blue alien and encountering incredulous double-taking policemen and two glaziers carrying a patented slapstick sheet of glass. As varied as ever in its final season, it may be that the series had admitted to rather too broad a church when it allowed in 'Codzmorf'.

**Season Seven**
**11 episodes**
(colour)
**Broadcast:** Mondays 12/6/89 – 21/8/89
12/6/89 – **'Codzmorf'** by Mark Everest. **Dir:** David Crozier (TVS)
19/6/89 – **'Ghost Story'** by Colin Davis.
**Dir:** Julian Jarrold (Granada)
26/6/89 – **'Badger'** by Charlotte Keatley.
**Dir:** Gareth Morgan (Granada)
3/7/89 – **'Back to Front'** by Anthony Horowitz.
**Dir:** Patrick Titley (Yorkshire)
10/7/89 – **'Monstrous'** by Nigel Crowle. **Dir:** Pennant Roberts (HTV Wales)
17/7/89 – **'The Pisces Connection'** by Peter Corey.
**Dir:** Kenneth Price (HTV West)
24/7/89 – **'Rosie the Great'** by David Stafford.
**Dir:** Michael Winterbottom (Teliesyn Production for Thames)
31/7/89 – **'Snakes and Loofahs'** by Valerie Georgeson.
**Dir:** Kay Patrick (KPO Ltd/Border)
7/8/89 – **'Just Wild About Harry'** by Jenny McDade.
**Dir:** Mike Connor (Tyne Tees)
14/8/89 – **'Mitchin''** by Richard Marsh.
**Dir:** Christopher Barry (TSW)
21/8/89 – **'In the Pink'** by Andy Smith from a story by Annah Fitch. **Dir:** Geoff Husson (Husson Productions for Central)

**Video:** 'Just Wild About Harry' included on 3-episode tape *Dramarama*, released by Video Gems, c. 1990. Deleted.

## Streetwise

This series focuses on the teenage cyclists who risk their lives on the busy streets of London delivering packages for a courier company called Streetwise. While there's much in the way of pedal-powered dynamics, the narrative is quick to highlight the dangers faced by the intrepid youngsters when one of the couriers, Dave, is seriously injured by a speeding ambulance in a hit-and-run incident. This forms two of the main threads for the rest of the series, following Dave's difficult road to recovery and the private investigations carried out by Dave's colleagues as they try to track down the ambulance involved in the incident.

The character of Billie introduces the theme of sexual equality as she tries to make the grade in a profession dominated by men. Owen eventually takes the girl under his wing but with some reluctance and, from there on, it is up to Billie to prove herself.

As one would expect of a series geared towards older children, the teenage employees of Streetwise must deal with turbulent love lives hand in hand with the company's uncertain future.

**TVS/Childsplay for ITV**
**3 seasons**
(colour)

**Season One**
**13 episodes** ('Running Scared'; 'Moving In'; 'On the Circuit'; 'Breaking In'; 'Homecoming'; 'Mixed Feelings'; 'Blowing It'; 'Teamwork'; 'Stakeout'; 'Home Truths'; 'Love & Money'; 'Blood, Sweat and Tears'; 'Money Talks')
**Broadcast:** Mondays 25/9/89 – 18/12/89

**Main Cast:** Sorcha McMahon (Billie), Stephen McGann (Bob), Paterson Joseph (Dave), Andy Serkis (Owen), Garry Roost (Troop), Gerard Logan (Big Bang), Sara Sugarman (Angel), Suzanne Hamilton (Diana), Russell Gold (Zonker), Zoot Money (Marty), Janet Palmer (Cindy), Nicola Cowper (Gina)
**Written by** Peter Tabern and Jon Hardy (1–8), Al Hunter (9, 13), Al Hunter and Brendan J. Cassin (10), Simon Moss (11, 12)

**Design:** Art Effects
**Producers:** Peter Tabern and Valerie Farron
**Executive Producer:** J. Nigel Pickard
**Directors:** Ian Emes (1–4, 9–11), Andrew Body (5, 6), Peter Tabern (7, 8, 12, 13)

**Season Two**
**10 episodes**
**Broadcast:** Thursdays 11/4/91 – 13/6/91

**Cast includes:** Garry Roost (Troop), Sara Sugarman (Angel), Andy Serkis (Owen), Joanne Ridley (Natasha), Toby Cockerell (Toby)

**Season Three:** 'Double Take'
**4 episodes**
**Broadcast:** Tuesdays 19/5/92 – 9/6/92

**Cast includes:** Stephen McGann (Bob), Andy Serkis (Owen), Colin Teague (Tim), Joanne Ridley (Natasha)

**Written by** Matthew Graham and Peter Tabern

## Byker Grove

The seemingly never-ending soap opera began life as a six-part serial from *Coronation Street* writer Adele Rose, albeit one that is usually referred to as a pilot series. This told the story of Julie Warner, a girl forced to move from London to the Byker housing estate in Newcastle. She hates it there until she visits Byker Grove, a sprawling old house that's been converted to a youth club. Soon Julie begins to make new friends although she finds bad company when she falls for local bad boy Gill.

The first series was certainly realistic, often grimly so. Many of the kids who went to Byker Grove after school simply had nowhere else to go. Many came from very poor backgrounds and broken homes; some lived in a local foster home. Most found a sense of belonging at the Grove and a surrogate family with Geoff Keegan as the father figure at its heart.

The second series saw the show expand to become almost a fully fledged soap, with a greatly enlarged cast and an extension to a regular quota of around twenty episodes a year. The Grove itself became a production centre, not just acting as the main location but also including sets, offices and production facilities. Such investment usually requires return and this set-up confirmed *Byker Grove* was here to stay.

Indicators of the programme's hard-hitting style first came in the second run, when a joyriding craze went out of control and ended up with Gill dead under the wheels of a truck. Since then all manner of topics have been tackled including drug dealing, disability, ram-raiding, gang warfare between the Grove and the Denton Burners, shoplifting

and homosexuality. It was the latter that really put *Byker Grove* on the map. Season Six's major storyline focused on Noddy, a confused boy who never could quite express his feelings with girls. In this season it becomes clear that Noddy is struggling to come to terms with his sexual identity and the plot hinges on one electrifying key scene in which Noddy leans over to his friend Gary in a cinema and kisses him on the cheek. 'That did not just happen, right?!' is Gary's immediate furious response and from then on he shuns his long-standing friend. The scene drew howls of protest but the storyline was a strong one which finally reached its conclusion when it is Noddy and not Gary who proves his macho credentials by saving Geoff from a fire at the Grove.

As in *Grange Hill*, *Byker Grove*'s most controversial subjects are usually given validity by their moral coda. The series' first producer, Matthew Robinson, used to keep all viewer complaints in a folder he called his red book and always returned to this moral backbone when called to justify his show's subject matter. 'One theme I am particularly fond of is that consequences do follow actions,' he explained. 'Life has a way of paying back evil in one form or another even if it's not in an obvious way. We can't and don't want to tell a story without moral guidelines.' The emphasis should probably be placed upon the 'can't' in this statement – *Byker Grove* is only allowed its indulgences if it functions as a morality play else it could be seen as deliberately provocative. Thus Gill's irresponsible enjoyment of joyriding is punished by his violent death and Barney ends up in prison for mugging an old woman (and was beaten up once inside). Even if it's just a very bad hangover for Karen after a night's drinking on her trip to Spain, each naughty action reaps suitable punishment.

The high death rate at the Grove has not always come about through reward for misdemeanour – there was the tragic loss of Flora in Season Nine from a cancerous brain tumour and the sudden death in an explosion of Grove leader Geoff marking the end of an era in Season Twelve (past alumni PJ and Duncan attended his funeral). These stories outwardly function as lessons in bereavement – the balloon release after Flora's funeral is particularly well remembered.

As Matthew Robinson was often keen to point out, 'it's not all doom and gloom on the Grove'. There were many traditional plots incidental to the big issues, such as the story of ghosts on the loose or the comic escapades of young Spuggie in its earlier years. The series has also always had an obsession with the media, which often seemingly provided validity and an apparent way out for many of its wannabe characters. Many formed groups or became DJs; Charlie tried modelling; others dabbled in video projects and film-making. This may seem like navel-gazing from the production team but in the modern world such dreams are probably just an updating of the aspirational tales of old, such as *Ballet Shoes*.

The most famous pop progeny of the Grove were of course PJ and Duncan, aka Ant McPartlin and Dec Donnelly, and their pop duo characters crossed over into reality with a stream of shiny, happy, rappy hits. Their cheeky chappie style has persisted, leading to phenomenally successful presenting careers for Ant and Dec. Oddly though, this has since come to represent the popular image of *Byker Grove* outside of its core audience, few realising that PJ spent an entire series coming to terms with being blind after a jilted girlfriend, Debbie, shot him with a paintball gun. Duncan joined a religious cult in order to come to terms with his friend's disability. Returning for Geoff's funeral, the pair explained that they now worked for blind charities.

More contrived humour has crept into the Grove in recent years. One of the worst examples came when the Grove girls created a fabulously over-the-top gaudy coat for bighead Jake, emblazoned with the 'designer label' of Imazillipoza. You have to ask whether any kid would really go to such lengths for a cheap laugh.

For all its worthwhile issues and exciting escapades, the problem with *Byker Grove* appears to be its format. Excellent writers such as Wally K. Daly, Chris Barlas and Mallorie Blackman have found themselves pressed into service and shackled to the soap format. One is tempted to think of the old line about Shakespeare writing soaps if he were alive today. It's likely he would starve if he didn't, since the format, whether in children's or adult TV, seems almost the only option open to a jobbing writer.

The soap format is an inherently poor one for drama – themes and ideas are compressed and forced to jostle for position with other storylines vying for the viewer attention until everything is wound up to increasing levels of overwrought melodrama. Imagine the 'Noddy is gay' storyline told in a self-contained six-part drama and think of the impact it could have had then. Like the adult soaps, *Byker Grove* also demonstrates the revolving doors approach to on/off relationships. Oddly, this probably very realistically portrays the confusion of teenage romance but does not make for good drama.

With children's controllers from both BBC and ITV coming out with positive noises about all-year-round shows, and *SM:tv Live*, *Blue Peter* and the finally cancelled *Live and Kicking* all having made moves in this direction, it can surely only be a matter of time before a genuine soap opera (i.e. unbroken run serial) for children hits the screen. So will it be *Byker Grove* or Mersey TV's *Grange Hill* that does it? And who then will remember that both began life as short-run serials?

**Zenith North for BBC**
**12 seasons by end of 2000 – ongoing in autumn 2002**
(colour)

**Season One**
**6 episodes**
Broadcast: Wednesdays 8/11/89 – 13/12/89

**Main Cast:** Lucy Walsh (Julie Warner), Caspar Berry (Martin 'Gill' Gillespie), Lyndyann Barrass (Spuggie), Steven Bradley (Speedy), Craig Reilly (Winston), Sally McQuillan (Donna), Niall Shearer (Cas), Amanda Webster (Hayley), Louise Towers (Kelly), Declan Donnelly (Duncan), Colin MacLachlan (Jim), Vicky Murray (Alison), Billy Fane (Geoff Keegan), Jenny Twigge (Clare)

**Written by** Adele Rose (1–3, 5, 6), Carrie Rose (4)

**Designer:** Bob Hutton
**Producer:** Matthew Robinson
**Executive Producer:** Andrea Wonfor
**Director:** Matthew Robinson

**Season Two**
**20 episodes**
Broadcast: Wednesdays and Fridays 17/10/90 – 21/12/90

**Main Cast:** Lyndyann Barrass (Spuggie), Lucy Walsh (Julie), Caspar Berry (Gill), Sally McQuillan (Donna), Steven Bradley (Speedy), Craig Reilly (Winston), Colin MacLachlan (Jim), Vicky Murray (Alison), Amanda Webster (Hayley), Declan Donnelly (Duncan), Jill Halfpenny (Nicola), Morten Lind (Jan), Michael Nicholson (Brad), Michelle Charles (Charley), Anthony McPartlin (PJ), Denise Welch (Polly), Billy Fane (Geoff Keegan)

**Written by** Adele Rose, Don Webb, Carrie Rose

**Producer:** Matthew Robinson
**Executive Producer:** Ian Squires
**Directors:** Frank W. Smith, Matthew Robinson, Peter Boisseau

**Season Three**
**18 episodes**
Broadcast: Wednesdays and Fridays 23/10/91 – 20/12/91

**Main Cast:** Lucy Walsh (Julie), Lyndyann Barrass (Spuggie), Sally McQuillan (Donna), Steven Bradley (Speedy), Craig Reilly (Winston), Colin MacLachlan (Jim), Amanda Webster (Hayley), Jill Halfpenny (Nicola), Morten Lind (Jan), Michael Nicholson (Brad), Michelle Charles (Charley), Anthony McPartlin (PJ), Declan Donnelly (Duncan), Nicola Ewart (Jemma), Michelle Warden (Joanne), Vicky Taylor (Angel), Christopher Hardy (Robert), Rory Gibson (Lee), John Jefferson (Fraser), Nicola Bell (Debbie), Scott Patty (Bill), Joe Caffrey (Paul), Vicky Murray (Alison), Billy Fane (Geoff Keegan)

**Written by** Adele Rose, Don Webb, Wally K. Daly
**Producer:** Matthew Robinson

**Season Four**
**20 episodes**
Broadcast: Tuesdays and Fridays 13/10/92 – 18/12/92

**Main Cast:** Lyndyann Barrass (Spuggie), Anthony McPartlin (PJ), Declan Donnelly (Duncan), Ford Prefect (Speedy), Craig Reilly (Winston), Jill Halfpenny (Nicola), Michelle Charles (Charley)*, Donna Air (Charlie Charlton)*, Nicola Ewart (Jemma), Michelle Warden (Joanne), Vicky Taylor (Angel), Rory Gibson (Lee), John Jefferson (Fraser), Nicola Bell (Debbie), Scott Patty (Bill), Joe Caffrey (Paul), Luke Dale (Frew), Lesley Saint John (Kath), Gemma Graham (Amanda), Tony Hodge (Alan), Sean Gorman (Kevin), Olive Simbo (Tessa), David Oliver (Marcus), Gavin Kitchen (Dexter), Jayni Hoy (Leah), Brett Adams (Noddy), Kevin Silberman (Matt), Stephen Carr (Barney Hardy), Justine McKenzie (Patsy), Victoria Murray (Alison), Billy Fane (Geoff Keegan)
* Confusingly these characters are indeed two different people and not a recasting – Charlie was Charley's younger cousin

**Written by** Don Webb, Wally K. Daly, Chris Barlas, Matthew Graham
**Producer:** Matthew Robinson

**Season Five**
**20 episodes**
**Broadcast:** Tuesdays and Fridays 12/10/93 – 17/12/93

**Main Cast:** Anthony McPartlin (PJ), Declan Donnelly (Duncan), Brett Adams (Noddy), George Trotter (Gary Hendrix), Nicola Bell (Debbie), Nicola Ewart (Jemma), Louise Mostyn (Marie), Oliver Stone (Marcus), Donna Air (Charlie), Clare Graham (Anna), Justine McKenzie (Patsy), Jayni Hoy (Leah), Vicky Taylor (Angel), Andrew Smith (Alfie), Kerry-Ann Christiansen (Flora), Tracy Dempster (Morph), Gemma Graham (Amanda), Neil Blackstone (Arran), Rory Gibson (Lee), Luke Dale (Frew), Stephen Carr (Barney), Leslie Baines (Dale), Grant Adams (Ed), Victoria Murray (Alison), Billy Fane (Geoff Keegan)

**Written by** Matthew Graham, Judy Forshaw, Fred Kerins, Roy Apps

**Season Six**
**20 episodes**
**Broadcast:** Tuesdays and Fridays 18/10/94 – 23/12/94

**Main Cast:** Declan Donnelly (Duncan), Donna Air (Charlie), Brett Adams (Noddy), George Trotter (Gary), Nicola Bell (Debbie), Nicola Ewart (Jemma), Gemma Graham (Amanda), Louise Mostyn (Marie), Clare Graham (Anna), Justine McKenzie (Patsy), Vicky Taylor (Angel), Jayni Hoy (Leah), Andrew Smith (Alfie), Kerry-Ann Christiansen (Flora), Neil Blackstone (Arran), Rory Gibson (Lee), Luke Dale (Frew), Stephen Carr (Barney), Leslie Baines (Dale), Grant Adams (Ed), Jason Roberts (Kit), Chloe Annett (Janey), Billy Fane (Geoff Keegan)

**Written by** Matthew Graham, Judy Forshaw, Roy Apps, Fred Kerins, Lizzie Mickery

**Season Seven**
**20 episodes**
**Broadcast:** Tuesdays and Thursdays 26/9/95 – 30/11/95

**Main Cast:** Donna Air (Charlie), Brett Adams (Noddy), George Trotter (Gary), Gemma Graham (Amanda), Louise Mostyn (Marie), Clare Graham (Anna), Justine McKenzie (Patsy), Vicky Taylor (Angel), Jayni Hoy (Leah), Andrew Smith (Alfie), Kerry-Ann Christiansen (Flora), Neil Blackstone (Arran), Luke Dale (Frew), Stephen Carr (Barney), Leslie Baines (Dale), Grant Adams (Ed), Emma Brierly (Laura), Jonathan Brooke (Andy), Kimberly Dunbar (Karen), Joanne McIntosh (Brigid), Shaun Mechen (Ashley), Chris Woodger (Terry), Gauri Vedhara (Sita), Ingrid Hagemann (Jasmine), Gayle Winlow (Jane), Victoria Murray (Alison), Billy Fane (Geoff Keegan)

**Written by** Matthew Graham, Judy Forshaw, Roy Apps, Lizzie Mickery, Kolton Lee, Brian B. Thompson

**Season Eight**
**20 episodes**
**Broadcast:** Tuesdays and Thursdays 24/9/96 – 28/11/96

**Main Cast:** Vicky Taylor (Angel), George Trotter (Gary), Louise Mostyn (Marie), Clare Graham (Anna), Andrew Smith (Alfie/Ben), Kerry-Ann Christiansen (Flora), Luke Dale (Frew), Stephen Carr (Barney), Grant Adams (Ed), Kimberly Dunbar (Karen), Joanne McIntosh (Brigid), Chris Woodger (Terry), Gauri Vedhara (Sita), Edward Scott (Jack), Adele Taylor (Teraise), Libby Davison (Gloria), Leah Jones (Harry), Jody Baldwin (Cher), John Bowler (Carl), Gavin Makel (Rob), Philip Miller (Philip), Victoria Murray (Alison), Billy Fane (Geoff Keegan)

**Written by** Matthew Graham, Judy Forshaw, Roy Apps, Lizzie Mickery, Kolton Lee, Brian B. Thompson, Barry Simner, Simon Heath

**Season Nine**
**20 episodes**
**Broadcast:** Tuesdays and Thursdays 23/9/97 – 27/11/97

**Main Cast:** Kerry-Ann Christiansen (Flora), Andrew Smith (Alfie/Ben), Grant Adams (Ed), Kimberly Dunbar (Karen), Joanne McIntosh (Brigid), Chris Woodger (Terry), Gauri Vedhara (Sita), Adele Taylor (Teraise), Leah Jones (Harry), Jody Baldwin (Cher), Gavin Makel (Rob), Philip Miller (Philip), Vikki Spensley (Leanne), Louis Watson (Ollie), Alexa Gibb (Nat), Sharon Percy (Jill), Patricia Jones (Jean), John Rogers (Tony), Holly Wilkinson (Emma), Billy Fane (Geoff Keegan)

**Written by** Brian B. Thompson, Simon Heath, Catherine Johnson, Nick Reed, Mark Holloway, Julian Perkins

**Season Ten**
**20 episodes**
**Broadcast:** Tuesdays and Thursdays 22/9/98 – 26/11/98

**Main Cast:** Andrew Smith (Ben), Kimberly Dunbar (Karen), Joanne McIntosh (Brigid), Chris Woodger (Terry), Gauri Vedhara (Sita), Adele Taylor (Teraise), Leah Jones (Harry), Jody Baldwin (Cher), Gavin Makel (Rob), Louis Watson (Ollie), Alexa Gibb (Nat), Holly Wilkinson (Emma), Nick Figgis (Jake), Edward Scott (Jack), Anne Orwin (Lou), Charlie Hardwick (Sian), Gary Crawford (Greg), Siobhan Hanratty (Nikki), Jade Turnbull (Regina), Steven Douglass (Barry), Janine Birkett (Maggie), Billy Fane (Geoff Keegan)

**Written by** Brian B. Thompson, Stephen McAteer, Michael Ennis, Tilly Black, Steven Chambers, Roy Apps, Philip Gerard

**Season Eleven**
**19 episodes**
**Broadcast:** Tuesdays and Thursdays 30/9/99 – 2/12/99

**Main Cast:** Andrew Smith (Ben), Kimberly Dunbar (Karen), Gauri Vedhara (Sita), Adele Taylor (Teraise), Leah Jones (Harry), Jody Baldwin (Cher), Gavin Makel (Rob), Louis Watson (Ollie), Alexa Gibb (Nat), Holly Wilkinson (Emma), Nick Figgis (Jake), Edward Scott (Jack), Gary Crawford (Greg), Siobhan Hanratty (Nikki), Jade Turnbull (Regina), Victoria Hawkins (Claire), Nicholas Nancarrow (Bradley), Steven Douglass (Barry), Pete Hepple (Liam), Adam Scott (Matt), Louise Henderson (Laura), Paul Meynell (Stumpy), Billy Fane (Geoff Keegan)

**Written by** Brian B. Thompson, Steven Chambers, Roy Apps, Philip Gerard, Chris Fewtrell, Zeddy Lawrence, Rachel Dawson

**Season Twelve**
**16 episodes**
**Broadcast:** Tuesdays and Thursdays 10/10/00 – 30/11/00

**Main Cast:** Andrew Smith (Ben), Gauri Vedhara (Sita), Adele
Taylor (Teraise), Leah Jones (Harry), Jody Baldwin (Cher),
Louis Watson (Ollie), Alexa Gibb (Nat), Holly Wilkinson
(Emma), Gary Crawford (Greg), Siobhan Hanratty (Nikki), Jade
Turnbull (Regina), Steven Douglass (Barry), Victoria Hawkins
(Claire), Nicholas Nancarrow (Bradley), Pete Hepple (Liam),
Adam Scott (Matt), Louise Henderson (Laura), Paul Meynell
(Stumpy), Adam Ironside (Ben), Chris Beattie (Joe), Patrick
Miller (Akili), Alex Beebe (Adam), Dominic Beebe (Luke), Rory
Lewis (Eve), Patrice Etienne (Paul), Billy Fane (Geoff Keegan)

**Written by** Brian B. Thompson, Roy Apps, Philip Gerard,
Chris Fewtrell, Rachel Dawson, Malcolm Campbell, Malorie
Blackman, Caspar Berry, Andrew S. Walsh

**Tie-in publications:** numerous novelisations published in
paperback by BBC. *Byker Grove* by Adele Rose, 1989.
*Heartbreak for Donna* by Carrie Rose, 1990. *Turning On,
Tuning In* by Don Webb, 1990. *Odd Ones Out* by James Weir,
1990. *Love Without Hope* by Wally K. Daly, 1990. *Fighting
Back* by Wally K. Daly, 1991. *Green for Danger* by Don Webb,
1991. *Temptation* by Wally K. Daly, 1992. *The Dark House* by
Don Webb, 1992.
*Byker Grove Annual* published by Grandreams, 1989

# 1990s

It is difficult to look back over this decade in television without coming away with a somewhat gloomy prognosis. More than ten years of Conservative rule meant that the television service was almost totally subject to market forces. Commercial television had always operated under a need to produce ratings successes in order to gain advertising revenue but now the BBC was running scared and constantly required to deliver audiences lest it lose its right to a licence fee as 1996's charter renewal approached.

A clear sign of the increased importance of hard cash came with the 1991 ITV franchise 'sell-off', as it was often referred to. Prospective franchise-holders had to make a financial bid in addition to setting out their programming aims, meaning that in many cases the process was reduced to an auction. In 1993 TVS lost its franchise and was replaced by Meridian. HTV was forced to cut costs and its children's drama output was cut to virtually nil. Children's television had lost two great servants.

The model of production had changed. The in-house overseeing of all aspects of production by the Children's Department which had served the BBC well for so many years was now replaced by the era of producer choice. A quota of output was to come from outside production houses although the BBC Department (with Anna Home as its head from 1986–97) still obviously retained executive control. The Children's Film Foundation, which changed its name to the Children's Film Unit in this decade, often acted as a negotiator between outside contractors and the BBC and the ITV companies, helping to develop children's projects and scripts. The Unit no longer produced its own material however, due to falling levy funds, and acted in this consulting role only.

In *Children's Television in Britain*, Buckingham *et al.* provided a statistical analysis of drama output through the decades. Drama for children appeared at first to have increased in the 90s but once repeats were removed from the equation it was revealed to have stayed at a fairly consistent level compared with the 80s. However, this quantitative analysis tells only part of the story. A qualitative survey highlights many other issues. Forty of the year's twenty-five-minute drama slots on the BBC were automatically block-booked by *Grange Hill* and *Byker Grove* for most of the 90s. Both series were written around one large standing 'set' (*Grange Hill* moving to a purpose-built backlot at BBC Elstree in this decade in preference to filming at a real school location), enabling economies of scale if enough episodes were made.

Soap, with all its attendant faults, particularly in the discipline of storytelling, was the dominant genre of the 90s. Simplified 'issues' and on-off romances took their lead from two of the series most watched by children since the mid-80s, the Australian imports *Neighbours* and *Home and Away*. Both sunny soaps aired directly following the designated children's programmes and also drew in parents just home from work, delivering huge audiences

**Above:** the 90s saw the birth of several long-running children's drama 'franchises'. *The Queen's Nose* was one of these. A tie-in edition of the original novel and a video of the first two episodes were released.

**Above:** there were three series of *The Demon Headmaster* produced in the 90s – the first series was issued as a tie-in book (top) and also released on video.

(although *Home and Away* aired at 6.30p.m. in some regions for some years until finally being dropped by ITV in 2000, whereupon it moved to Channel Five). ITV had much shorter runs of ten or twelve episodes of Granada's *Children's Ward/The Ward* but overlapping storylines in a soap style still dominated. *three seven eleven*, also from Granada, was in the same mould. *Press Gang* had the looseness of format that would have extended to soap but in the 90s its later runs actually shortened, with the accent remaining on the quality of the writing rather than the quantity of episodes. The shorter runs of ITV's soap-style programmes only reflected the apparent lack of drama slots overall.

The growth of the children's soap genre squeezed out the serial format. What the serial did, rather like a novel, was create a world in six or seven weeks and cover one topic in as much depth as possible. Now the opportunities to explore new worlds and meet new characters were greatly reduced. When this erosion of the short-run, self-contained serial is considered alongside the virtual elimination of the one-off play at the end of the 80s, it is hard to see the bright side of children's drama in the 90s.

The most successful serials of the 90s would enjoy an extended run. *The Demon Headmaster* and *The Queen's Nose* both returned several times, despite few artistic reasons for doing so. *The Queen's Nose* in particular stood alone as the adaptation of Dick King-Smith's book and, when its popularity begat further runs into the next decade, the concept seemed stretched. For the fourth and fifth series, aired in 2001, the original heroine was phased out in favour of a new generation of child leads. The aim here has clearly been to create franchises of recognisable properties and to build up a significant number of episodes for packaged syndication sale abroad and on satellite. This seems to be done whether the source material can sustain the additional runs or not. Again, what the recommissioning of series does is create fewer opportunities for new one-run only serials and leads to a poverty of difference.

Glossy co-productions followed the lead provided by *The Box of Delights* and *The Chronicles of Narnia* in the 80s. Now the British TV companies no longer saw their rivals as 'the other side' but as the likes of global players like Disney. A small number of expensively made, pre-sold international productions such as *The Borrowers* and *Phoenix and the Carpet* came to define the decade. As expected, the pre-selling of series and the need to be certain of recouping outlay led to the remaking of familiar serials and properties. The practice of remaking had been commonplace in the 70s too, but back then it was forced by the pressing need to move into colour and the destruction of many series from the 60s. Many of the 90s remakes already existed in the archives of the BBC and ITV companies in colour or as feature films but were remade nonetheless with added gloss, greater pace and better special effects. While several improved on their more primitive predecessors in many respects, it was again the capacity for innovation which was lost.

One of the biggest trends in children's drama was in fact little to do with drama at all and more to do with marketing spin. The so-called 'comedy drama' which proliferated on both channels in the 90s is something of a misnomer. The template for 'comedy drama' in the 90s ought have been the superb *Dark Season*. There was comic strip action interspersed with witty dialogue exchanges but these were underpinned by an emotional realism and the struggle for identity of its central heroine. The first season of *The Queen's Nose* was another sweet example of a realistically portrayed girl living in a world of comic fantasy.

The 'comedy drama' retained its sub-genre tag as the decade progressed but eventually possessed about as much emotional depth or genuinely dramatic content as an episode of *Rentaghost* or *Chucklevision*. The 'comedy drama' became comedy with a vague plotline in increasingly silly series of *The Queen's Nose* or such slapstick efforts as *The Worst Witch, Barmy Aunt Boomerang, Bernard's Watch, Adam's Family Tree* or any number of similar entries – anywhere else these would be referred to purely and simply as hyperactive sitcom. This is not to do down comedy – it is as valid a genre as drama and should of course be produced for children. The difference in the 90s was that it seemed to be made to the exclusion of everything else.

The tag seems to have been most useful when making up end of year reports. Series marketed and classed as 'comedy drama' can be usefully counted at a surface level as 'drama' and thus help bolster your drama index. This became increasingly important as the debate on perceived declining standards in children's television grew towards the end of the decade. The controversy over *Teletubbies* put the topic of children's television firmly into the spotlight and in the resulting discussion a commitment to 'drama' of any sort was seen as a good thing. Drama, particularly of the home-grown variety, has always stood for 'quality', no matter how bad or good it actually is! Its polar opposite has always been seen as American animation. You only need posit a below-average episode of *Byker Grove* against any instalment of *The Simpsons* to see what a nonsensical generalisation this can be but, nonetheless, a promise of a 'firm commitment to children's drama' is a key phrase in any broadcaster's manifesto.

The wave of 'American trash' which threatens to do away with British 'quality' is all too obvious in the satellite arena. The various dedicated children's channels broadcasting on satellite in the 90s, such as Nickelodeon, The Cartoon Network and Disney Channel, have shown barely any British programming, depending instead on a heavily recycled diet of American cartoons and teen/tweenie series like *Sabrina the Teenage Witch* and *Kenan and Kel*. In almost a decade, *no* satellite broadcaster has made one single new British children's drama. It will be a bizarre miracle if one does – most are American-owned and these low maintenance operations simply do not presently have the revenue available to make any new shows. They probably never will.

Although heavily outweighed by the negatives, the one positive aspect of satellite has been a small number of opportunities to view again some archive repeats of children's drama. The first dedicated children's satellite channel was The Children's Channel (TCC) which began airing to Sky subscribers in 1992. In its first few years of operation, at a time of fairly low satellite and cable penetration, it broadcast many classic ITV drama series of the past. *Freewheelers, The Black Arrow, Dominic, Shadows, The Flockton Flyer, The Clifton House Mystery* and *Into the Labyrinth* all received airings.

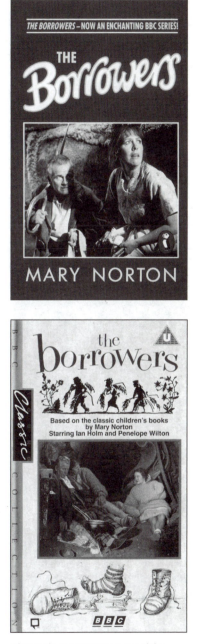

**Above:** *The Borrowers* was one of the BBC's biggest children's drama successes of the decade.

Copies of home tapings made at the time now circulate among avid collectors. In the mid-90s, however, TCC's programme policy changed and more recent American fare overtook the schedules. The channel eventually became self-conscious about having the word 'children's' in its name and later rebranded as Trouble. UK Gold also showed several archive serials on Sunday mornings in the early 90s including *The Secret Garden*, *Carrie's War* and *The Changes*, The Sci-Fi Channel ran repeats of the 70s *Tomorrow People* and the *Chocky* trilogy, while Nickelodeon managed an incomplete rerun of *Press Gang*.

There were certainly some excellent 'small scale' serial dramas of the kind that had typified the 70s and 80s in among the co-produced blockbusters and never-ending soaps. *Dark Season*, *Dodgem*, *A Likely Lad*, *Century Falls*, *Earthfasts* and *Elidor* were definite highlights of the 90s.

It was a decade of wide-ranging change for television as a whole but that change didn't really seem to be for the better as far as children's drama was concerned.

**Above:** period drama for children fell from fashion in the 1990s – successful exceptions were the E. Nesbit Psammead tales. These period fantasies were issued on video in the UK (pictured here) and in the US.

## Little Sir Nicholas

Nicholas Tremaine is the heir to the Tremaine fortune. The family, which resides in Trecastle, Cornwall, has delivered an unbroken succession of naval heroes since the days of the Armada. The end of the dynasty seems inevitable when Nicholas is shipwrecked along with his mother and father, Captain Walter Tremaine.

Nicholas survives and is brought up in Brittany. In Cornwall, the Dowager Lady Tremaine, unaware of the child's safety and left without an heir, is forced to advertise. This brings a remarkable change of fortunes for Joanna Tremaine and her children, all of whom live in squalor in London. The elder of the children, ten-year-old Gerald, becomes the new baronet. His newly established wealth is quickly threatened when Nicholas is found to be alive. Will Gerald and his mother accept that they may soon have to return to London? While the rivalry grows between Nicholas and Gerald, differing factions of the Tremaine family begin the battle for supremacy.

Brothers Stephan and Max Beazley obtained their parts in the drama in quite a unique way. They were watching *Going Live!* and responded to a request for French-speaking children for the up-and-coming production. Excerpts of their auditions were screened on a later edition of *Going Live!* Max, at least, went on to find fame as a member of the 'Brit Pack' of young UK actors.

The drama is loosely based on a novel by C. A. Jones and considerable changes were made in adapting it for television – so many that the tie-in book which accompanied the series was actually a reworked novelisation.

**BBC**
**6 episodes**
(colour)
**Broadcast:** Wednesdays 3/1/90 – 7/2/90

**Main Cast:** Max Beazley (Nicholas), Jonathan Norris (Sir Gerald Tremaine), Louisa Haigh (Margaret Tremaine), Rachel Gurney (Lady Tremaine), Jack Watson (Robinson)

Based on the novel by Cecilia Anne Jones (first UK publication 1890, Warne)
**Adapted by** David Benedictus

**Music** composed and conducted by Ian Hughes
**Designer:** Humphrey Jaeger
**Producer:** Richard Callanan
**Director:** Andrew Morgan

**Tie-in publications:** newly adapted novelisation by David Benedictus published in paperback by BBC Books, 1990

## The Gift

While staying with his grandparents in Wales, young Davy Price discovers that he has 'the gift' – an ability passed down through his family that allows him to read the thoughts of others. His grandmother begs him not to use the gift, telling him that it brings only grief. When Davy does use it, however, he discovers there are those only too willing to try and exploit him and that his father is involved in planning a robbery.

For generations the gift has driven a wedge between various members of the Price family. It is the reason that

John Price, Davy's father, has avoided his parents for years and is also responsible for his insecurity, inability to hold down a job and the endless arguments with his wife. The use of the gift as a metaphor for the unfathomable arguments that some children witness driving their family apart may not be wholly original but is, in this instance, more than effective.

A sizeable crew was involved in bringing *The Gift* to the screen as a high-powered, dynamic production. There is a massive explosion set in a quarry, skilfully directed in what surely had by necessity to be a one-shot take. A further explosion was filmed later in the drama when, in a scene that utterly convinces, the Price house is destroyed in a bomb blast. Davy's visions are far from the run-of-the-mill, hazy-edged effect one might expect, presented instead in a surreal and often disturbing manner.

Some surface updating has taken place, bringing the setting from the early 70s depicted in Peter Dickinson's novel to the early 90s. In an obvious bid to entice young viewers to watch, Peter O'Brien (previously responsible for the role of Shane in teen soap opera *Neighbours*) was cast in the role of Jack Venn. In an almost inexcusable line of dialogue, schoolgirl Sonia describes him as 'like Jason Donovan, only more mature'.

The adaptation differs from the novel in a number of other areas. Davy is the elder of two children in the series, whereas he is the youngest of three in the novel. For reasons of content, some of Davy's family history has also been altered. When Davy's grandmother illustrates the power of the gift, the novel describes how she cheated on her husband many years previously. Possessing the gift, her husband discovered her betrayal through her thoughts and killed both himself and her lover. On screen the grandmother's illustration is somewhat different, detailing how Davy's father went missing in a quarry and her husband's brother was killed while using the gift to find him. Sonia's meddlesome Uncle Palozzi is an addition to the serial, functioning as a secondary villain attempting to exploit Davy's abilities as a theatre act.

**A Red Rooster Films Production for BBC Wales**
**6 episodes** ('The Warning'; 'Wolf'; 'Black Hat and Monkey'; 'Man of Fire'; 'Count-down'; 'Full Circle')
(colour)
**Broadcast:** Wednesdays 28/3/90 – 2/5/90

**Main Cast:** Tat Whalley (Davy Price), Jeff Rawle (John Price), Jacqueline Tong (Rita Price), Emma-Louise Harrington (Penny Price), Cynthia Grenville (Nain), Dafydd Edmwnd (Dadda), Jodhi May (Sonia Parsons), John Levitt (George Palozzi), Gary Whelan (Wolf), Peter O'Brien (Jack Venn)

Based on the novel by Peter Dickinson (first UK publication 1973, Victor Gollancz Ltd)
**Adaptation by** Anthony Horowitz

**Music:** Michael Storey
**Production Designer:** Steve Hardie
**Producer:** Linda James
**Executive Producer for BBC Wales:** Geraint Evans
**Directors:** Marc Evans and Red Saunders

## Enid Blyton's Castle of Adventure

While spending their holidays at Spring Cottage, Philip, Dinah, Jack and Lucy-Ann learn from Sam, the old rag-and-bone-man, of a nearby ruined castle. He tells them of its dark history and that it's believed to be haunted. Philip and Jack notice a golden eagle in flight around the castle and surmise that it must be nesting there.

Later the gang meet a gypsy girl called Tassie and she too tells them a similar story of an old man that haunts the castle. When Jack goes to the castle to photograph the eagle, he later discovers that there is a mysterious figure in some of the pictures. Is it a man or a ghost?

The narrative has everything one would expect of an Enid Blyton story. Young children roaming around the country while on holiday, ruined castles thought to be haunted, mysterious happenings and secret underground passages are all present and correct and only the omission of a dog stops this story from being a carbon copy of a typical *Famous Five* story.

The series is shot entirely on film and one might have expected an adaptation of a Blyton story in 1990 to be adapted as a period piece. Surprisingly, the production crew opted for a contemporary setting which, with Blyton's wholesome, posh, bird-watching children, looks strangely out of its time.

**TVS**
**8 episodes**
(colour)
**Broadcast:** Thursdays 19/4/90 – 7/6/90

**Main Cast:** Richard Hanson (Philip), Rosie Marcel (Dinah), Hugo Guthrie (Jack), Bethany Greenwood (Lucy-Ann), Eileen Hawkes (Tassie), Gareth Hunt (Bill Cunningham), Brian Blessed (Sam)

Based on the novel by Enid Blyton (first UK publication 1946, Macmillan)
**Screenplay by** Lionel Augustus and Edward Francis

**Music:** Toney Kinsay
**Designer:** Bob Cartwright
**Producer:** Edward Francis
**Co-Producer:** John Price
**Executive Producer:** J. Nigel Pickard
**Director:** Terry Marcel

**Tie-in publications:** edition was published; details n/k

**Video:** 118-minute compilation released by Tempo Video. Deleted. Reissued by Abbey Home Entertainment as a W. H. Smith Exclusive. Deleted 19/9/96.

## Sea Dragon

Following his capture by a group of marauding Vikings, twelve-year-old English boy Jestyn is taken to Dublin where he is sold as a slave to Viking Lord Thormod. Jestyn gets on well with his new master and, after rescuing Thormod from a band of murderous Irishmen, he is granted his freedom. He elects however to remain with Thormod and accompanies him back to his homeland of Denmark.

Once there, Thormod discovers that his father has been murdered and is determined to avenge the death. Jestyn

offers to help Thormod and the two perform a ritual mingling of blood so that Jestyn now shares Thormod's blood feud with his father's killers. Joining the crew of *The Red Witch*, they sail the Baltic and the Russian rivers to Kiev where they join Prince Vladimir's war host, helping to defend Miklagard (the Viking name for Constantinople) from the Bulgars.

Rosemary Sutcliff was one of Britain's foremost historical fiction writers and the majority of her books were essentially adventure stories, written with a younger readership in mind. Here she uses the setting of eleventh-century Russia and the Byzantine empire to explore the theme of self-discovery and coming of age. The journey made by Jestyn as he accompanies his friend into danger is a metaphoric reflection of the boy's progression from child to adult.

Sutcliff's novel was published as *Blood Feud* but adapted as *Sea Dragon*. It's likely that *Blood Feud* was considered too strong a title for a children's drama and was therefore given a less 'offensive' name for its broadcast.

**Thames**
**4 episodes** ('Raiders from the Sea'; 'The Journey Home'; 'The Pursuit'; 'The Blood Feud')
(colour)
**Broadcast:** Thursdays 22/11/90 – 13/12/90

**Main Cast:** Graham McGrath (Jestyn), Baard Owe (Haki), Janek Lesniak (Thormod), Holly Aird (Ffion), Pat Roach (Aslak), Anna Massey (Prioress)

Based on the novel *Blood Feud* by Rosemary Sutcliff (first UK publication 1976, Oxford University Press)
**Written by** David Joss Buckley

**Producer:** Alan Horrox
**Director:** August Gudmundsson

**Tie-in publications:** n/k

## Five Children and It

E. Nesbit's novel was already over half a century old by the time public television came along. The first production was basic to say the least and most indicative of this was the realisation of its magical little star, the Psammead, here played by a grown man dressed in what can only be described as a carpet with ping-pong-ball eyes stuck on.

Nearly another half century later, the Psammead was now a cute but grumpy glove puppet with a range of endearing animatronic expressions. While the original BBC serial no longer exists, making direct comparison impossible, it's unlikely that, bar the technology, little else had changed except the potential for overseas sales.

*Five Children and It*, 1991 style, is a straightforward retelling of Nesbit's slight and comedic novel about nice Victorian children being ever so slightly naughty on meeting a mythical sand fairy who grants wishes. The serial was not as lavish as those that paved the way for these 'classic' remakes, such as *Box of Delights*, and its production values suggest an exercise in book balancing after the rather more expensive *Silver Chair* in the previous quarter. Most of the action seems to take place in the house and grounds where the four children and their baby brother are staying. One bigger budget wish sees them trapped in a besieged castle under attack from a medieval army, but another which would have called for a whole tribe of Red Indians was dropped from the adaptation. Then again, this may just have been on grounds of dubious racial taste. One more addition which provided a little work for the special effects staff was the new coda to the story which has the children make one last sensible wish to grow wings and fly.

The story, like the original novel/serial, is rather bitty with little in the way of a running thread except for constant reiteration that you should be careful what you wish for as you may get it. Helen Cresswell's sequel, *Return of the Psammead*, greatly improves on the first serial by adding a running storyline. This all-new sequel was preferred to Nesbit's own sequel of 1906, *The Story of the Amulet*, in which the five children had gained the ability to travel into the past in a bid to reunite the two halves of a broken magic amulet.

*Return of the Psammead* sees a new family of four children – indistinguishable from those of the first story – coming across the sand fairy much as before. They have been sent to stay with their cold-hearted Aunt Constance, who is about to throw her employee Sam Dawkins out of his home along with his daughter, the sickly Lil, despite his wife having died not long ago.

The difference this time is that the Psammead's wishes really do have a magical quality, almost all of them furthering the ongoing storyline. The key event occurs when Aunt Constance unwittingly wishes to remember what it was like to be a child and as a result spends a day running around the village being extrememly rude to people. Most importantly, the magic stays with her and her icy heart melts, leading to a happy ending for all concerned. The wishes still have a comic edge to them, including a brilliant scene where these middle-class children in petticoats and plus-fours find themselves at a teenage rave party in the 1990s and, in an odd way, finally meet their TV audience. The sequel also benefits from the more direct involvement of the Psammead in the adventure – in the previous tale the irascible little chap had spent most of his time hidden under the sand pit, which had been a terrible waste of a good character.

*Five Children and It* based on the novel by E. Nesbit (first UK publication 1902, T. Fisher Unwin)

### Five Children and It (1951)
**2 episodes** ('The Beginning of "It"'; 'The End of "It"')
**BBC**
(b&w)
**Broadcast:** Sundays 17/6/51 – 24/6/51 (South England and Midlands only)

**Dramatised by** Dorothea Brooking

### Five Children and It (1991)
**BBC**
**6 episodes**
(colour)
**Broadcast:** Wednesdays 9/1/91 – 13/2/91

**Main Cast:** Simon Godwin (Cyril), Nicole Mowat (Anthea), Charlie Richards (Robert), Tamzen Audas (Jane), Laura Brattan (Martha), Francis Wright (Voice of the Psammead)

**Above:** four children and 'It' – the children meet the Psammead in his sand pit; (l to r) Jane (Tamzen Audas), Cyril (Simon Godwin), Robert (Charlie Richards) and Anthea (Nicole Mowat) in *Five Children and It.*

**Dramatised by** Helen Cresswell

**Music:** Michael Omer
**Designer:** Humphrey Jaeger
**Producer:** Richard Callanan
**Director:** Marilyn Fox

**Tie-in publications:** edition of novel published in paperback by Puffin, 1990

**Video:** 139-minute double tape compilation released in UK by BBC Video, 1/6/92. Released in the US c. 1992 as *The Sand Fairy.*

### Return of the Psammead (1993)
**BBC**
**6 episodes**
(colour)
**Broadcast:** Wednesdays 6/1/93 – 10/2/93

**Main Cast:** Anna Massey (Aunt Marchmont), Laura Clarke (Ellie), Toby Uffindell-Phillips (George), Leonard Kirby (Pip), Nicci Avery (Lucy), Polly Kemp (Bessie), Simon Slater (Sam Dawkins), Joanna Barrett (Lil Dawkins), Francis Wright (Voice of the Psammead)

**Written by** Helen Cresswell

Main credits same as *Five Children and It*

**Tie-in publications:** novelisation by Helen Cresswell published in paperback, 1993. Large format illustrated storybook published by BBC, 1993.

**Video:** 137-minute compilation by BBC Video, released 4/7/94. Deleted 5/2/96. Released in the US c. 1994 as *Return of the Sand Fairy.*

## Dodgem

*Dodgem* is an uncompromising drama which further demonstrates Bernard Ashley's willingness to address delicate and emotional social issues without the safety net of fantasy metaphor used by many children's writers. Since the death of his mother, Simon Leighton has been playing truant from school for sustained periods of time in a desperate bid to help his deeply depressed father. The local social services, concerned by Simon's poor attendance, feel that his father is unfit to look after him and have the young boy taken into care.

Rose Penfold also refuses to attend school, opting instead to work the fairgrounds with her uncle. When she too is taken into care she meets Simon and the two of them plan an escape that will return them to their loved ones and discover the truth behind the death of Simon's mother.

While the death of a child's parent is undoubtedly tragic, and an emotional topic to convey to a young audience, Ashley bravely pushed the boundaries further by intimating at an early stage in the narrative that Simon's mother may in fact have been murdered by her husband. In a particularly brutal scene Simon is cornered in the playground and taunted by the inevitable school bullies. They tell him that they've heard his mother was a tart, that she deserved to be run over by his father, and that Simon's dad is now only putting on an act to avoid punishment. When Simon reacts he is beaten up and forced to flee the school. Although it's unlikely that the majority of viewers would be able to relate to the true feelings involved in losing a parent, it is very possible that a good few could reflect on their own experiences of similar peer cruelty.

Although *Dodgem* tackles a number of difficult topics – death, mental illness, children taken into care – the central theme of the drama is clearly that of bullying. It's an unfortunate happening that many associate purely with the school playground but Simon quickly discovers that it exists in one form or another wherever he goes. As soon as he arrives at the children's home, he finds himself harassed by an older boy, and when he is reunited with his father and both find work at a fairground, Simon once again finds that there is someone only too willing to bully him. 'There's always one of you lot,' Simon says. 'Doesn't matter where you go. Your sort's all over the rotten place.'

Simon and Rose are two very different central characters brought together by circumstance and the interaction between them is a key ingredient of *Dodgem*. The only thing they have in common is their desire to be back with what family they have but this is enough to create an immediate bond between them. Prior to his mother's death, Simon would appear to have led a rather sheltered, middle-class existence. Rose is resolutely working class, having spent much of her time skipping school and struggling to earn a living with her uncle at various fairgrounds. Streetwise and cunning, she masterminds the escape from the children's home. In a daring scene, Simon and Rose roll almost naked in nettles to develop a convincing rash designed to fool everyone into believing they are unwell.

From a visual point of view, *Dodgem* possesses a stark realism, primarily a result of being shot on video. This aspect is further enhanced by being recorded entirely on location. Fresh from his role as Tegs in *Grange Hill*, Sean Maguire copes admirably in the not entirely dissimilar part of Simon. Indeed, some viewers tuning in during the early school scenes during the first episode could have been forgiven for believing that they had switched on during an episode of *Grange Hill*.

It is perhaps strange, or even telling, that the difficult and dark *Dodgem* was the last Ashley drama to be adapted by the BBC.

**BBC**
**6 episodes**
(colour)

**Episode One**
Wednesday 20/2/91 5.10p.m.
Following the death of his mother, Simon has been skipping school to care for his depressed father, Alex. The social services decide that Simon is not being looked after properly and decree that he should be taken into care.

**Episode Two**
Wednesday 27/2/91 5.10p.m.
Simon arrives at the children's home and finds it difficult to settle. He dreams of happier times when his mother was still alive. He soon makes friends with Rose who has also been taken into care but finds himself being picked upon by an older boy.

**Episode Three**
Wednesday 6/3/91 5.10p.m.
Simon escapes from the home but when he gets to his house he discovers Alex is no longer there. He visits his grandparents and discovers that his father is now in a home for the mentally ill. Simon returns to the lodge and his father is brought to see him.

**Episode Four**
Wednesday 13/3/91 5.10p.m.
Simon tells Rose about his mother and together they plan their escape from the children's home. Charlie, Rose's grandfather, arranges to smuggle Alex from the mental home and finds sign-painting work for him at Charlie Tucker's fairground.

**Episode Five**
Wednesday 20/3/91 5.10p.m.
The police arrive at the fair looking for Simon and Alex. Rose comes to the rescue and convinces the police that nobody has seen either Simon or his father. Simon demands the truth about his mother from Alex. Breaking down, his father tells him what happened.

**Episode Six**
Wednesday 27/3/91 5.10p.m.
Simon and Rose travel to his grandparents where they recover a portrait of Simon's mother once painted by Alex. Simon is caught by Rick Bayne but, rather than return him to the home, Rick takes him to Alex in order to assess if his father is fit enough to have his son returned to him.

**Main Cast:** Sean Maguire (Simon Leighton), Lucy Speed (Rose Penfold), John Telfer (Alex Leighton), Trevor Peacock (Charlie Penfold), Richard Bonneville (Rick Bayne), Alan Thompson (Grandfather), Doreen Anderson (Grandmother), Erin Geraghty (Linda Leighton)

Based on the novel by Bernard Ashley (first UK publication 1981, Julia MacRae Books)

**Adapted for television by** Bernard Ashley

**Music:** John Drinkwater
**Designer:** Robert Foster
**Producer:** Richard Callanan
**Director:** Christine Secombe

**Tie-in publications:** edition of novel published in paperback by Penguin, 1991

## Dark Season

A writer for the kids' comedy series *Chucklevision* went on to write the controversial and groundbreaking gay drama *Queer as Folk*; in between he managed to script two superb dramas for children, *Dark Season* and *Century Falls*. Russell T. Davies was working as a producer in children's television at the BBC, despairing of the quality of children's drama then being made. Deciding to do something about it, he wrote episode one of *Dark Season* in full and sent it to Anna Home, Head of Children's, who immediately commissioned the series.

*Dark Season* was the first children's drama to have obviously been written by a member of the generation who grew up with the genre. Inspired by vivid memories of the likes of fantasy serials for children such as *Timeslip*, *Children of the Stones* and *Sky*, but determined to improve upon their odd disappointments (in particular what Davies recalled as weak endings), *Dark Season* and *Century Falls* were the work of a fan trying to surpass what had gone before. The work of a colourful and outspoken writer, *Dark Season* is pure comic strip where a love for the fantasy genre is matched by disdain for its clichés. In some places, it's high camp; in others, gripping high drama.

Since Davies considered six parts too long, the 'serial' in fact consisted of two three-part serials with a central villain linking the otherwise self-contained stories (shades of *Freewheelers*) while big, bold cliffhangers ended each episode (shades of *Doctor Who*). The first story sees a bleach-blond, chisel-jawed baddie in black leather coat and ray-bans try to take over the planet using technobabble and the fledgling internet (at a time when Mosaic was exciting for a small number of academic users). The second tale concerns a band of neo-Nazis, led by Servalan from *Blake's 7* (in other words the baroquely camp actress Jacqueline Pearce), trying to locate a bloody huge talking super-computer buried thirty years earlier by the Ministry of Defence. It's larger than life, noisy and colourful, grabbing the youngsters and giving the older viewer or sci-fi buff a good laugh. Which audience Davies thought was more important matters not and it could be appreciated hugely on both levels. It's the kind of pure self-indulgence that comes from a writer who just knows he's right (Davies dismisses much children's TV drama as having been put through 'all that focus-group market-testing bollocks').

The three child heroes are cynical and sharp, with a fine array of one-liners to hand. Certainly no child ever talked like this, but this isn't realism. Davies even takes the mickey out his own dialogue, Marcie dismissing Thomas and Reet's wry conversations as 'quoting Garfield T-shirts'. It's all part of the comic strip style, with everything taken to extremes. Olivia is the school swot with the big glasses that make her look like Velma from *Scooby Doo*, the Hitler-youth-style Nazis all have cropped blond hair and ze ridiculose accentz, and Reet and Thomas wear ludicrous, brightly coloured outfits that make them look as if they'd stepped from one of the funkier strips in *2000AD* comic. Colin Cant understands the script perfectly and gets into the spirit of things, ditching his usual heavy mood aesthetics for a brash, over-the-top, dynamic style. Added to the cartoon punch is Davies' post-modern humour – clearly signposted in the opening scene where Eldritch declares with relish, 'Nothing in the world can stop me now!' Most memorably, Marcie finds herself trying to escape via a ventilation shaft and mutters, 'Marvellous, I'm a cliche' – you can't get more blatant than that.

Davies wanted to create a heroine who was 'cleverer, ahead of the game', sick as he was of children's' drama where the lead would 'oh-so accidentally' overhear the villains making their plans. Marcie is a wonderfully bizarre, inquisitive, tangential girl who runs rings round her teacher. While never in any way 'real', Marcie manages to impart the Behemoth computer a piece of life advice in individuality when she tells it that she won't be a nurse even if that's what her mother wants for her. And when Eldritch asks her how it is that she knows so much, she replies, 'I watch a lot of TV.' While Marcie is the real star of the piece, it's Reet who is its best-remembered character, played as she is by a pre-*Titanic* Kate Winslet.

Like Marcie, Davies had watched a lot of TV and set out to rid children's drama of the perceived failing of weak endings, wanting 'good, explosive and logical climaxes'. It was certainly explosive in this case, with a spectacularly cacophonous blowing up and submerging of the Behemoth courtesy of some enthusiastic work on the part of the special effects crew. Most of all, Davies wanted 'to scare kids and take risks' to make the kind of show he wanted to see as a kid. In both aims he definitely succeeded. Striking a great balance between fun and dramatic adventure, this could have formed the blueprint for BBC children's comedy drama in the 90s.

**Above:** Reet (Kate Winslet), Marcie (Victoria Lambert) and Thomas (Ben Chandler) investigate the strange computers gifted by Mr Eldritch in *Dark Season*.

*Dark Season*
**BBC**
**6 episodes**
(colour)

### Episode One

Thursday 14/11/91 4.35p.m.
Repeated Sunday 17/11/91 10.40a.m. BBC2
When a fleet of vans and an Aryan stranger called Eldritch arrive at school and announce that they will distribute an Abyss computer to every pupil free of charge, Marcie Hatter smells trouble. School swot Olivia is invited to visit the Abyss facility but when she returns to school she is no longer her usual self.

### Episode Two

Thursday 21/11/91 4.35p.m.
Repeated Sunday 24/11/91 10.40a.m.
The computers seem to have mind-altering capability – Thomas says that using it you feel like Eldritch is inside your head. Using a network link, the kids manage to hack into government files which reveal that Marcie's neighbour Mr Polzinski was once a prominent scientist called Becjinski, working on a top secret computer–human symbiosis project – but Eldritch is monitoring the transmission and tries to get to Polzinski before Marcie and friends can.

### Episode Three

Thursday 28/11/91 4.35p.m.
Repeated Sunday 1/12/91 10.40a.m.
The countdown to Eldritch's plan to enslave the world – by linking all its computers and their users to his will – is underway when Mr Polzinski's wife sends an interrupter signal to the Eldritch master computer, causing the program to stall and mayhem to ensue. She has been Professor Becjinski all along, not her husband. She then destroys Eldritch's computer by ordering it to cleanse the program.

### Episode Four

Thursday 5/12/91 4.35p.m.
Repeated Sunday 8/12/91 10.40a.m.
Three months after their first adventure, the children find Miss Pendragon and her curiously Aryan group of archaeologists digging up the school sports field supposedly in search of Celtic artefacts. In fact Pendragon is searching for her Behemoth. There is an explosion and a tunnel into the ground is blown open. Stealing inside, Thomas and Marcie open up a doorway underground and Behemoth calls out …

### Episode Five

Thursday 12/12/91 4.35p.m.
Repeated Sunday 15/12/91 10.40a.m.
Thomas and Marcie find themselves in what thirty years before had been a Ministry of Defence research base. Pendragon has come to reclaim the Behemoth war computer she helped build before her right-wing politics led to the project's closure. Behemoth needs a human mind to be reactivated – Thomas is chosen but he pushes Pendragon into the pilot's chair. As Behemoth wakes and crashes up through the floor of the gym hall, Mr Eldritch arrives to claim Behemoth for himself.

### Episode Six

Thursday 19/12/91 4.35p.m.
Repeated Sunday 22/12/91 10.30a.m.
Rejecting Pendragon, the computer must be persuaded by Marcie not to execute its final destruct program as Eldritch intends.

**Main Cast:** Victoria Lambert (Marcie Hatter), Kate Winslet (Reet), Ben Chandler (Thomas), Brigit Forsyth (Miss Maitland), Grant Parsons (Mr Eldritch)
**With:** (1–3) Samantha Cahill (Olivia), Cyril Shaps (Mr Polzinski), Rosalie Crutchley (Mrs Polzinski), Tim Barker (Dr Osley), Roger Milner (Headmaster)
(4–6), Jacqueline Pearce (Miss Pendragon), Martina Berne (Inga), Stephen Tredre (Luke), Marsha Fitzalan (Voice of Behemoth)

**Written by** Russell T. Davies

**Music:** David Ferguson
**Designer:** Michael Trevor
**Executive Producer:** Richard Callanan
**Director:** Colin Cant

**Tie-in publications:** novelisation by Russell T. Davies published in paperback by BBC, 1991

## Merlin of the Crystal Cave

Having overseen Arthur's succession to the throne, Merlin returns to his homeland in the hills accompanied by his trusted servant Ralf. As they travel, Merlin tells Ralf of his childhood adventures.

One hundred years after the last Romans have departed Britain's shores, the country is in the throes of a civil war. Allying himself with Saxon invaders, King Vortigern of North Wales seizes the high throne, deposing the rightful heir Ambrosius, who then flees the country with his brother, Uther Pendragon. Merlin, a disrespected 'bastard child', lives with his disgraced mother in Vortigern's court. While exploring, the child discovers a cave of crystals inhabited by a strange vagrant called Galapas. It is the beginning of a long journey of discovery that will reunite Merlin with the father he never knew, bring Uther to power and move Britain closer to stability.

Nine weeks were spent recording on location in Snowdonia and complicated sets included a recreation of tribal Britain and Stonehenge. The producers (note that this was Shaun Sutton's final children's drama before his retirement after he virtually invented the genre in the 50s) hoped that this screen adaptation would have as big an impact as *The Chronicles of Narnia* three years previously. However, Mary Stewart's novels hadn't benefited from the years of high profile exposure enjoyed by *The Chronicles of Narnia* and, ultimately, *Merlin of the Crystal Cave* failed to scale those dizzy heights.

**Noel Gay Television for BBC**
**6 episodes** ('The Cave'; 'The Flight'; 'Ambrosius'; 'The Return'; 'Reckoning'; 'The Raising of the Stones')
(colour)
**Broadcast:** Sundays 17/11/91 – 22/12/91

**Main Cast:** George Winter (Merlin), Robert Powell (Ambrosius), Trevor Peacock (Ralf), Kim Thomson (Ninianne), Don Henderson (Galapas), John Finch (Vortigern), Roger Alborough (Uther), Thomas Lambert (Merlin as a child), Jody David (Merlin as a boy)

Based on the novels by Mary Stewart: *The Crystal Cave* (first UK publication 1970, Hodder and Stoughton) and *The Hollow Hills* (first UK publication 1973, Hodder and Stoughton)
**Adapted by** Steve Bescoby

**Music:** Francis Shaw
**Designer:** James Dillon
**Producer:** Shaun Sutton
**Executive Producers:** Bill Cotton and Maurice Taylor
**Director:** Michael Darlow

**Tie-in publications:** edition of novel published in paperback as *Merlin of the Crystal Cave* by Coronet, 1991

**Video:** 166-minute two-part compilation released on double cassette by BBC Video, 5/5/92. Deleted 28/4/94.

## Archer's Goon

Initially it all seems very simple. Howard Sykes returns from school with his little sister Awful and discovers the Goon sitting at the kitchen table. Quentin, Howard's father, has fallen behind with his payments. He owes Archer two thousand and Archer wants payment pronto. The Goon has come to collect.

Thing is, it's not that simple at all. Quentin doesn't owe 2,000 pounds but 2,000 *words*. He didn't even know that his words were going to Archer. Quentin thought he was making payments to Mountjoy. Mountjoy, it would appear, is just a middle man. Who is Archer? Howard is determined to find out and, in doing so, stumbles across a dastardly plot to rule the world.

*Archer's Goon* is, up to a point, a reasonably straightforward whodunit. Or, to be more precise, a who-is-it. Thirteen years previously Quentin, a writer by profession, was suffering from a severe bout of writer's block. Mountjoy proposed a unique solution: that Quentin would submit to him 2,000 words per quarter or suffer the consequences, the idea being that Quentin's fear would be sufficient to overcome his ailment. Now it would appear that Mountjoy is an agent of Archer, one of seven siblings, each of whom controls different aspects of the town in which the Sykes family live. After some investigations Howard discovers that Archer isn't the recipient of Quentin's words and that the words possess a power preventing Archer and his family from expanding their empire outside the town. With many of the siblings fighting among themselves for power, Howard must figure out which one is the true recipient of Quentin's work and prevent the world from falling under the control of a megalomaniac.

Few children's dramas successfully achieve dynamic equilibrium between comedy and drama. There are a number of potentially serious issues within *Archer's Goon*: the Sykes are hounded on a continual basis – their power is cut off, bank account frozen and Quentin's wife Catriona is forced out of her job. The situation is undoubtedly serious for the Sykes family but the impact is lost in the surreal and overtly comedic narrative.

There are a couple of interesting plot twists, the best of these centring around Howard. Adopted as a baby by Quentin when found lying abandoned, it transpires that Howard is actually Venturis, the seventh and youngest of the warring siblings. Venturis is the key to the mystery and the one person capable of vanquishing Archer and his

destructive sisters, Dillian and Torquil. The plot becomes complicated to the point of confusion.

It's improbable that there's much in the way of metaphor and that Diana Wynne Jones fully intended surreal comedy rather than fully realised allegory. It is interesting to note however that Hathaway, brother of Archer and controller of public transport, is stuck in the past. It would also be reasonable to assume that Archer, Dillian *et al.* are personifications of the mundane bureaucratic forces appeased by form filling and bill paying. Amusingly it is Archer, Dillian and Shine, those responsible for banking, police and crime – in other words, those that enforce rigid structure on chaos – that are vanquished.

*Archer's Goon* is very much a no-expense-spent drama. The constraints of budget prevented the adaptation from fully representing the grandeur of some the scenes from the novel. Torquil's appearance in the third episode suffers in particular. In the novel his appearance is an ostentatious affair, accompanied by a multitude of choirboys and dancers. On screen the crowd is rather thin on the ground and fails to convey the immensity of Torquil's power.

Although *Archer's Goon* is in essence an inexpensively made comedy escapade, its rather flippant approach to a number of potentially serious issues makes it something of a curate's egg.

**BBC**
**6 episodes**
**(colour)**
**Broadcast:** Wednesdays 8/1/92 – 12/2/92

**Main Cast:** Jamie De Courcey (Howard), Angela Forry (Awful), Roger Lloyd Pack (Quentin), Susan Jameson (Catriona), Morgan Jones (Goon), Victoria Worsley (Fifi), Thomas Lockyer (Archer), Michelle Newell (Dillian), Andrew Normington (Torquil), Annette Badland (Shine), Clive Merrison (Hathaway)

Based on the novel by Diana Wynne Jones (first UK publication 1984, Methuen Children's Books Ltd)
**Dramatised by** Jenny McDade

**Designer:** Chris Robilliard
**Producer:** Richard Callanan
**Director:** Marilyn Fox

**Tie-in publications:** paperback edition of novel published by Mammoth, 1992

## Runaway Bay

*Runaway Bay* is a little more exotic than one might normally expect of a home-grown children's drama. Focusing on the adventures of a group of children staying on a Caribbean island, this series of stand-alone adventures sees the children investigating a haunted chateau, an old shipwreck, unexplained accidents in the local farming community, fraud and an assassin determined to make an impact at the Liberation Day celebrations.

A second season introduced some new characters, while retaining some of the old, and launched the children into a new set of adventures, among them yacht thieves and an on-the-run prisoner.

Each season was shot on location over a ten-week period on the Caribbean island of Martinique. Jeremy Burnham, well known for his 70s children's drama *Children of the Stones*, made a welcome – if unlikely – return to co-write a number of episodes in the first season.

**Yorkshire**
**2 seasons**
(colour)

**Main Cast includes:** Diana Eskell (Alex), Eric Fried (Dion), Jude Magri (Zoe), Jason Smith (Ziggy)

**Season One**
**13 episodes** ('Into the Heat'; 'Rotten Fish'; 'Lonely is the Brave'; 'Taking the Rap'; 'Fool's Gold'; 'You Only Live Once'; 'Treasure Hunt'; 'Curse of the Monkey's Skull'; 'All that Glitters'; 'Fast Forward'; 'The Venture'; 'History Revisited'; 'All in the Mine')
Broadcast: Thursdays 9/1/92 – 2/4/92

**Written by** Jeremy Burnham and Lucy Wagner (1–6), Ben Steed (7–10), Sylvie Dervin and Fabrice Ziolowski (11), Aaron Barzman and Sylvie Dervin (12), Lucy Wagner (13)

**Season Two**
**13 episodes** ('Going for Gold'; 'Race Like the Wind'; 'Sink or Swim'; 'The Escape'; 'Heartbreak Hotel'; 'The Secret Garden'; 'The Robbery'; 'Turtles Role'; 'Music to my Ears'; 'Bombs Away'; 'Deadline'; 'Masquerade'; 'Radio Daze')
**Broadcast:** Mondays 15/2/93 – 24/5/93 (no transmission 12/4/93 and 3/5/93 due to Easter and Bank Holiday schedules)

**Writers include:** Elizabeth Baxter and Martin Brossolet (1–4), (others n/k)

**Tie-in publications:** n/k

## A Likely Lad

There is only a subtle semantic difference between having genuine aspirations and being merely aspirational but where Willy Overs and his father are concerned the gap between the two is a chasm. Mr Overs tries to force his own self-made values on his son and is never slow to lecture on how he has worked hard to get to where he is now, owning a corner shop in Victorian Manchester. He has mapped out a career for Willy in the imposing Northern Star Insurance building in town but the question is how much of this is for Willy's benefit and how much for his own?

Mr Overs places burdensome expectations on Willy, always quick to tell anyone who'll listen what a 'thruster' the boy is going to be in the insurance world. Mr Overs takes his son to the Town Hall to look at the statues of the City Fathers and, pointing to an empty plinth, tells the boy, 'This one is reserved for you, my lad.'

The serial is an essay in class. Mr Overs who claims to be 'salt of the earth', and is proud of his achievement in becoming lower middle class, but obviously considers anything higher to be a betrayal based on ideas above one's station. This is evidenced by his refusal to let Willy, a studious boy keen on books, apply for

a scholarship to the grammar school. Mr Overs ignores his boy's true talents and believes that university is for the bourgeois, the wasteful occupation of parasitic aristocrats.

Willy doesn't know what he wants, aside from thinking that the Northern Star seems like a prison. The story takes in various points along his meandering journey to a decision; on the way he discovers that in England there are both poor old ladies eking out a living and Earls and Lords who own vast tracts of the countryside. He meets by chance the aunt whom no-one talks about. Aunt Maggie disowned her daughter, Willy's mother, for marrying into the lower classes and is the chief reason for Mr Overs' resentment. While there are no real big incidents or turning points to the storyline, the subtle elements that provoke the class issues are well paced over the six episodes of the serial, each informing Willy's final and personal decision. Rejecting an offer of a cut of Aunt Maggie's will, by recognising it as a proposal made only to spite his father, Willy shows loyalty to his own family and is rewarded in kind when his father allows Willy to apply for the grammar scholarship. Aunt Maggie meanwhile is literally scared to death by the slavering dogs which guard her life savings of banknotes.

For a young audience it's a thoughtful work of little obvious brawn and, while one hesitates to underestimate them, one ponders what the attraction might be to the child viewers of 1992. Most children today would not really consider the questions that face Willy at thirteen until they are sixteen, which renders its arguments quite pointless to a lot of the audience. With virtually nothing in the way of visible action, it's hard to imagine that the serial would hook an audience early in its run. *A Likely Lad* was another typically well-made BBC costume drama, with the customary redressed Victorian streets, excellent VT location work in the older parts of Manchester and a couple of steam trains thrown in for good measure. Nonetheless it also has the distinction of being thus far the last true period drama for children to be shown outside of the Sunday teatime slot, where more sedate works such as this are more readily accepted.

**BBC**
**6 episodes**
(colour)
**Broadcast:** 19/2/92 – 25/3/92

**Main Cast:** Lee Brennan (Willy Overs), Robert Curley (George Overs), John Flanagan (Mr Overs), Alice Martin (Mrs Overs), Christopher Benjamin (Harold Sowter), Paul Sarginson (Stan Sowter), Sue Wallace (Kitty Sowter), Pauline Letts (Aunt Maggie Chaffey), Linda Polan (Hannah Rafferty), Ann Way (Nancy Price), Robert Swann (The Earl), Richard Huw (Mr Church), David King (Mr Ramsbottom)

Based on the novel by Gillian Avery (first UK publication 1971, William Collins Ltd)
**Adapted by** Julia Jones

**Pianist:** Jonathan Cohen
**Designer:** Robert Foster
**Producer:** Richard Callanan
**Director:** Christine Secombe

**Tie-in publications:** edition of novel published in paperback by Red Fox, 1992

## Torch

This futuristic drama takes the audience to a Europe of the future where the survivors of an environmental disaster live in isolated communities and lead a pre-industrial lifestyle. When a small group of teenagers find a dying man on a beach, they discover that he is the Guardian of a mysterious treasure, the legendary Olympic torch. Before he dies, the stranger convinces the children to assume his role and pleads with them to take the treasure from where he has hidden it and 'find the Games'.

They set out to fulfil the old man's request and are joined along the way by the Nikathlon, a young man who has trained as a runner. Together they encounter many different cultures – intellectual, materialistic, fanatically religious – while using their wits to avoid enslavement and incarceration.

*Torch* was something of an event for Dame Judi Dench, starring alongside her husband and daughter, Michael and Finty Williams. The production took the cast and crew to various areas in Europe including Spain, Czechoslovakia, Croatia and Greece in the search for the perfect locations in which to create an environmentally damaged Europe of the future and, no doubt, also in search of financial backers, as the lengthy production credit attests.

**Children's Film and TV Foundation Production for BBC/ETB/TVG/TVam/TV3/NSN**
**6 episodes** ('The Guardian'; 'The Nikathlon'; 'The Poseidon'; 'The Raft'; 'The Slave State'; 'The End of the World')
(colour)
**Broadcast:** Fridays 24/4/92 – 29/5/92

**Main Cast:** Judi Dench (Aba), Michael Williams (Sage), Altay Lawrence (Nikathlon), Graham McGrath (Peri), Finty Williams (Cal), Lyndon Davies (Dio), Kate McGrath (Cassie), Taylor Scipio (Ekow), John Carney (Guardian), Juan Jose Parrilla (Tinker), Borivoj Navratil (Tandor)

Based on the novel by Jill Paton Walsh (first UK publication 1987, Viking Kestrel)
**Adapted by** William Corlett

**Producer/Director:** Robin Crichton

**Tie-in publications:** n/k

## Wilderness Edge

'People's personalities change dramatically when faced with the challenge of abseiling, canoeing and assault courses,' explained *Wilderness Edge* co-author John Coombes. 'A different set of rules apply when you're stranded in the middle of a lake or clinging to a vertical rock face.' Together with Martin Riley he devised a children's drama series where teenagers of varying backgrounds are thrown together at an outdoor activity centre situated in the Lake District. The idea is that in difficult circumstances the background or class you come from becomes irrelevant and that all must work together to protect the group. Basically it's a lesson in teamwork and co-operation with others.

Gareth Morgan, series producer, ideally wanted twelve children from the North of England to fulfil the required characters in the plot. Finding himself short in available stage schools, he took the unusual step of casting ordinary schoolchildren. After watching thousands of children from local schools and youth groups perform various scenarios, those selected were tested for the ability to carry out essentials such as remembering lines. Those that remained were then asked to complete the assault course in order to ensure that the production crew didn't later discover that any of the children were too scared to participate.

**Granada**
**6 episodes**
(colour)
**Broadcast:** Fridays 8/5/92 – 5/6/92 ITV (all episodes broadcast Friday except episode 5, which was broadcast Thursday 4/6/92)

**Main Cast:** Jemma Thompson (Debby Trout), Hilary MacLean (Liz), Jason Salkey (Feasty), Daniel Brown (Jazzy)

**Written by** John Coombes and Martin Riley

**Producer:** Gareth Morgan

**Tie-in publications:** novelisation published in paperback by Network Books (imprint of BBC Books), 1992

## The Borrowers

Mary Norton had grown up in a large house in Leighton Buzzard and passed the time playing on the floor with her dolls. She imagined what it would be like if her dolls were real 'little people', leading a life of their own. How would they survive and what would our world look like from their point of view? This idea would form the basis for her series of classic *Borrower* novels, which tell the tale of a group of vertically challenged beings measuring no more than seven inches in height. They are known as Borrowers, due to their 'borrowing' of items from the unsuspecting 'human beans'.

The large house of George's bedridden Aunt Sophy had been home to a number of Borrower families. Now that the Harpsichords and the Mantles were gone, only the Clock family – Pod, his wife Homily and their young daughter Arrietty – remain, living under the floor at the grandfather clock. It isn't usual practice for a girl to go borrowing but Pod is getting old and realises that, if they are to survive, his only child Arrietty must be able to gather the things they need. Things go wrong when Arrietty breaks the number one rule, befriending the human boy George and accidentally telling him where in the house the family lives. They soon discover that George can be trusted when he brings them many presents for their house. Things change when the evil housemaid Mrs Driver discovers the Borrowers' presence. Having destroyed the 'nest', she then brings in the rat-catchers, signalling an end for the Clocks' safe existence in the house and the beginning of a dangerous quest to find another home.

The story unfolds primarily through the eyes of young Arrietty. She is an intelligent girl and, unlike her parents, she can read and write. Being naturally curious she is starting to ask them difficult questions about upstairs. It's a clever metaphor for growing up where 'upstairs' could be seen as the 'adult' world. Arrietty's impending graduation from child to young adult and all the difficult questions that are asked along the way will inevitably lead to the facts  241 of life conversation that many parents dread, hence Homily and Pod's reluctance to start the discussion.

Such a story obviously relies on a number of technical tricks to create the illusion of tiny people living in a world of giants. 'It's not just a matter of scaling things down or up,' set designer Sophie Becher commented. 'Wood takes on a grainier, knottier character when you increase its scale. You have to work everything out logically and mathematically.' Regardless of the obviously difficult tasks faced by the production team, the end result is very good. Using a combination of large props, mixed with some basic computer animation and CSO backgrounds, the world of the Borrowers is brought to the viewer in a pleasing and realistic manner. Advice came from Mary Norton herself on how to adapt her work, although sadly the author would never see the finished production. She passed away the same day that recording on the first season finished.

*The Borrowers* became one of the BBC's greatest successes of the decade. It won two Baftas (best children's series and best photography) and an award for best children's drama from the Royal Television Society. A second season followed one year later, detailing the further adventures of the Clock family as they settle in a new home and have to find a way to avoid being put on display when they are again discovered by humans. An unrelated Hollywood movie version, starring John Goodman, followed the series' lead.

*The Borrowers* is a fine example of well-produced children's televsion, well paced and with many pleasing effects to catch the eye. It was also the second highest placed children's drama to make the BFI's all-time Top 100 of Television list published in 2000, making number 79 (*Grange Hill* was highest at 43) and coming in ninth in the children's genre section.

**Working Title for BBC/Turner Pictures in association with BBC Children's International, The Children's Film and Television Foundation, The deFaria Company**
2 seasons
(colour)

**Main Cast:** Ian Holm (Pod), Penelope Wilton (Homily), Rebecca Callard (Arrietty), Paul Cross (George), Sian Phillips (Mrs Driver), Daniel Newman (Spiller)

**Screenplay by** Richard Carpenter

**Music:** Howard Goodall
**Designer:** Sophie Becher
**Producer:** Grainne Marmion
**Executive Producers:** Walt deFaria and Tim Bevan
**Executive Producer BBC:** Paul Stone
**Director:** John Henderson

**Season One**
**6 episodes**
**Broadcast:** Sundays 8/11/92 – 13/12/92

Based on the novels *The Borrowers* and *The Borrowers Afield* by Mary Norton (first UK publication 1952 and 1955, J. M. Dent & Sons)

**Season Two**
**6 episodes**
**Broadcast:** Sundays 14/11/93 – 19/12/93

Based on the novels *The Borrowers Afloat* and *The Borrowers Aloft* by Mary Norton (first UK publication 1959 and 1961, J. M. Dent & Sons)

**Tie-in publications:** paperback editions of all Borrowers novels (including *Borrowers Avenged*) published by Puffin, 1992

**Video:** *The Borrowers* (Season One) released in UK as 166-minute compilation on double cassette by BBC, 8/3/93. *The Borrowers II* (Season Two) released in UK as 166-minute compilation on double cassette by BBC, 7/3/94. *The Borrowers* (containing Seasons 1 and 2) released in UK as 332-minute compilation on double cassette by BBC, 19/10/1994. Deleted 12/2/1998.

## Oasis

Ecological messages abound as we see a group of children trying to turn the 'Jungle', a South London wasteland area on the banks of the Thames, into an inner city farm, complete with a variety of animals.

Peter McNamara puts his bullying days as Ralph Passmore in *Tucker's Luck* behind him to play the hero of the story, drifter Jimmy Cadogan. Jimmy is determined to save the wasteland from development, a continual threat from local authorities. Cadogan has a number of supporters on hand to help him, including a public-school drop-out.

Series creator Barry Purchese felt that children had little to occupy their time in the concrete sprawl of the city and that prospects for education and employment can be bleak. The farm at least gives the children the opportunity to contribute to a worthwhile project, be creative and show people what they are capable of doing.

**Carlton**
**10 episodes**
**(colour)**
**Broadcast:** Tuesdays 5/1/93 – 9/3/93

**Main Cast:** Peter McNamara (Jimmy Cadogan), Lily Souza (Carmel), Samantha Hammond (Bronwyn), Anthony Lee (Marc), Clare Matthews (Mivvy), Kelly Forest (Skates)

**Written by** Barry Purchese

## Eye of the Storm

Written specifically for television by Richard Cooper, *Eye of the Storm* was part of a growing 'green movement' of children's drama. The twist here was that the issues were now dressed in fantasy trappings.

Tom Frewen – a former pop star turned ecologist – and his daughter Nell have docked their ship, *Eye of the Storm*, just off Montliskeard Bay in Devon intent on investigating the potential environmental impact of an incident that took place during the storms of 1987. A ship bound for Felixstowe shed five barrels of highly toxic material and, although four barrels were successfully recovered, one remains lost. Tom believes this could pose a major hazard to marine life and is intent on discovering its whereabouts.

Meanwhile, at nearby Montliskeard House, young Luke Montliskeard is being drugged and manipulated by his evil guardian, Martha. Gilbert Montliskeard, one of Luke's forefathers, was a practising alchemist and believed that five family jewels could deliver him great power when brought together. The other men of the house recognised Gilbert's evil intentions and scattered the stones. Martha traces the other descendants of Montliskeard, intending to bring the four stones back together, and uses Luke's apparent clairvoyant abilities in an attempt to find the fifth. Soon the Frewens are embroiled in a desperate struggle to rescue Luke while fighting a government cover-up of an ecological disaster waiting to happen.

What starts as a straightforward, topical drama, geared around the Frewens' search for that which threatens the environment, soon immerses itself in fantasy. Although these two components work reasonably well in their own right, they fail to gel convincingly and the eventual climax that brings the two strands together seems almost contrived. One could easily be forgiven for thinking that *Eye of the Storm* is in fact an amalgamation of two entirely separate projects.

*Eye of the Storm* relies on action and suspense rather than strong characters, which is a great shame because there is definite potential for character development. By far the most interesting characters are the Frewens but little is explained about their strange lifestyle and desire to care for the planet's ecosystem. This makes it difficult for the audience to establish a rapport or empathy with their characters. At Montliskeard House we are presented with stereotyped henchmen and the token over-the-top megalomaniac. The character of Martha is simply a mad professor with a strong desire, like many before her, to conquer and destroy. What led her to such an obsessed and sorry state is, once again, a more than valid question that wasn't explored.

From a production point of view, *Eye of the Storm* looks good. The crew makes good use of the scenic coastline and a reasonable amount of money would appear to have been spent supporting the many action scenes that take place in the water. To safeguard the people involved and to ensure realism, a diving consultant was used to choreograph the underwater scenes. The sequences that take place in the claustrophobic subterranean tunnels are particularly effective and it is difficult to tell if they are taking place in a pool or in the sea itself.

*Eye of the Storm* fails to realise that which it was capable of achieving, being at best an uneasy balance between ecological issues and sci-fi adventure. Childsplay would however go on to create a series more successfully combining both of these elements with *Life Force* in 2000.

**A Childsplay production for Meridian**
**6 episodes**
(colour)
**Broadcast:** Fridays 8/1/93 – 12/2/93

**Main Cast:** Cordelia Bugeja (Nell Frewen), Kristopher Milnes (Luke Montliskeard), Bill Nighy (Tom Frewen), Judy Parfitt (Martha), Deborah Poplett (Fran Tuett), Felipe Izquierdo (Rob Appleton), Philip McGough (Henry Pryce)

**Written by** Richard Cooper

**Music:** Henry Marsh
**Production Designer:** Lizzy Ashard
**Executive Producer for Meridian:** Janie Grace
**Producer and Director:** Peter Tabern

## three seven eleven

*three seven eleven* is as close as the commercial channels have come to directly rivalling *Grange Hill*. Set in a primary school rather than a comprehensive, Barton Wood was a modern, purpose-built school including its own nursery. This provided the series' title, 'three seven eleven' referring to the age range of children the episodes focused upon.

While the Barton Wood children were younger than the *Hill* regulars, some were no less tough. Perhaps the main character of the series – and certainly its most interesting – was Miranda, the uncommunicative, borderline mentalcase progeny of shell-suited scrap-dealers. The first episode sees her break into the school before it has opened, causing wilful damage without a care. Given the careful guidance and patience of the school's liberal, modern-thinking Head, Mrs Sherry, Miranda finally finds purpose and contentment helping out in the nursery and with the pets corner. Most of the kids have been around a bit (Barton Wood is clearly an estate with something of a reputation) but the writers attempted to create a mix, with the odd well-off kid like footballer David working beside Nicky, a boy whose dad was regularly in and out of prison. Various ethnic backgrounds were also represented by Ghanaian girl Esi and Kompel, an Asian shopkeeper's son.

Despite the realism of the background and characters, the series was aimed at a generally younger audience than most children's drama and so there was a lot of humour in the stories. In one episode the girls and boys – all eighteen of them – take on another team's schoolboy side and have the game abandoned by throwing a dog onto the field. By the second run the series' plots were already beginning to appear derivative of *Grange Hill*. These included a trip to an outdoor centre and stories of the ghost of a Roman centurion abroad. More serious issues were examined when Nicky began shoplifting.

The series was created and for the most part written by skilled children's writer Bernard Ashley with his son Chris. Both were headteachers and so didn't lack experience – their own teaching ideals shone through, with special attention and understanding usually given to the 'problem kids'. While he has continued to write for print, this was Bernard Ashley's last credit to date for television. He has since bemoaned that despite a proliferation of channel outlets there is a decided shortage of opportunity for serious drama aimed at young people.

**Granada**
**2 seasons**
(colour)

**Season One**
**10 episodes**
**Broadcast:** Wednesdays 17/2/93 – 21/4/93

**Main Cast:** Nicola Redmond (Mrs Sherry), Ray Ashcroft (Jack Higgins), Julia Haworth (Miranda Pudsey), Gavin Gallimore (David Kent), Marion Reid (Jordan), Don Henderson (Empire Sam), Michael Ford (Nicky Power), Paul Hanley (Lee Rayner), Dionne Sandiford (Esi Mensah)

Written by Chris and Bernard Ashley

Producer: Edward Pugh
Directors: Michael Kerrigan and John Darnell

Tie-in publications: first four Season One episodes novelised by Chris and Bernard Ashley, published by Puffin, 1993

Season Two
10 episodes
Broadcast: Wednesdays 13/4/94 – 15/6/94

Main Cast: Nicola Redmond (Mrs Sherry), Shirley Stelfox (Mrs Clegg), Ray Ashcroft (Jack Higgins), Nick Bartlett (Joe Kerton), Avril Clark (Mrs Swainsgate), Owain Shaw (Mr Skellern), Julia Haworth (Miranda Pudsey), Michael Ford (Nicky Power), Paul Hanley (Lee Rayner), Dionne Sandiford (Esi Mensah)

Written by Bernard Ashley (1, 4, 5, 10), Chris Ashley (2, 7, 8), Marvin Close (3, 6, 9)

Producer: Sue Pritchard
Executive Producer: Edward Pugh

Tie-in publications: Season Two novelised as *three seven eleven: Barton Wood For Ever* by Nigel Robinson, published by Puffin, 1994

**Above:** Tess Hunter (Catherine Sanderson, left) comes to Century Falls, a village curiously devoid of children but for two exceptions – Ben (Simon Fenton) and Carey (Emma Jane Lavin).

# Century Falls

*Dark Season*, Russell T. Davies' previous entry to the children's drama canon, may have been post-modern, self-aware sci-fi comedy but without a doubt *Century Falls* is based on pre-modern values. The belief in the supernatural drama that unfolds is total and through this conviction it draws the viewer into a make-believe world.

Like *Dark Season*, *Century Falls* draws on Davies' own recollections of fondly remembered spooky children's drama from years gone by but in this case he goes to great lengths to hide rather than expose the joins. Davies fuses familiar elements together to provide a fresh and invigorating take on this strand. It is the perfect distillation of every children's fantasy drama that had gone before.

Despite this, *Century Falls* began life as a story veering perilously close to pastiche if not outright plagiarism – Davies' original drafts concerned a Professor Llewellyn researching an ancient stone circle. The idea seems almost a carbon copy of 1977's *Children of the Stones* but thankfully the idea progressed, the circle became a waterfall, the Professor was dropped and the more complex and original storyline that made it to our screens began to evolve.

The well-worn idea of psychic power is central to the story. While this would certainly be enough to hold the interest of a young audience who had not seen the earlier dramas which influenced Davies, even those older viewers familiar with the likes of *Children of the Stones* and who were lucky enough to have caught this serial would have been hooked by the near perfect execution and exploitation of such a well-used theme.

To run through a synopsis of the basic plot of *Century Falls* is to do it a disservice; no such potted plotline can do justice to the way the twists are slowly teased out to the increasing surprise of the viewer. Tess Hunter and her mother have come to live in a remote village called Century Falls. Mrs Hunter hopes that her daughter, an overweight and lonely girl, will make friends here.

The first episode establishes its characters and location as obliquely as possible and continually hints at something in its enigmatic dialogue exchanges and it is this style which persists throughout the serial. Little revelations constantly turn events on their head in the serial – Davies' beautifully constructed script seems to be built on an underlying 'slow reveal' principle. He gives away just enough to keep the viewer's interest piqued. For example, it is utterly indicative of the serial's nature that the names given in the end credits to the first episode hide the true identities of at least three of its characters.

The horrific central premise of an evil force created in the unformed mind of Mrs Hunter's unborn baby was one that triggered nervous objections from some connected with the production, but the producer and director firmly believed that 'there ought to be more of this *Rosemary's Baby* stuff'. This was a sure sign that the team intended to stretch the boundaries of what was acceptable in children's drama, even given that it was within a fantastical framework.

Davies injects more than mere clever sci-fi narrative into the script via some interesting character work, an area where earlier genre examples may not have been as strong. Tess Hunter is the classic 'loner' figure, indecisive and self-absorbed for much of the time but with some great lines to show that she has some spark about her. The one where she comes crashing into the post office to demand 'Two Mars bars, three first class stamps and one explanation – fast!' is a bit of a classic. Perhaps Tess' most fascinating scene occurs when her mother turns against her in desperation, determined not to believe that her baby's life is threatened: 'You're a lonely fat girl who fills her days with stories instead of friends because life's easier like that.'

Elsewhere we find engaging and original characters. Ben Naismith is an anti-hero figure – at best his motives and (lack of) ideals can be seen as ambivalent, at worst utterly inhuman. Together with his sister and the mysterious Julia, the three form a triumvirate psychic mind based on the Freudian collective consciousness. The enigmatic Julia is a fascinating riddle with tragic origins which are revealed, like everything else in this story, only a bit at a time. Esme Harkness meanwhile is a fascinating novelty – 65-year-old psychic heroines tend to be a rare sight in television!

Century Falls was in reality the village of Langthwaite in Yorkshire – *Radio Times* likewise located the fictional village within Yorkshire but there is no evidence on screen to confirm this and no-one speaks with a Yorkshire accent! Director Colin Cant taped enough material for a seven-part story but at the editing stage felt that the serial would be tighter if reduced to six episodes. Cant creates a palpable air of menace with his meticulously constructed style and eye for detail.

Perhaps indicative of how the BBC viewed its audience was the way in which *Radio Times* promoted the serial. Rather than publicise it as a tale of a fat girl caught up in spooky goings-on, it was sold on the possibilities of Simon Fenton as a pin-up for pubescents.

**BBC**
**6 episodes**
(colour)

### Episode One
Wednesday 17/2/93 5.10p.m.
Repeated Sunday 21/2/93 10.30a.m. (BBC2)
Tess Hunter and her mother have moved house to live in the remote village of Century Falls. Tess meets the only two children in the village, twins Ben and Carey Naismith, who are staying with their Uncle Richard. Ben has psychic powers which enable him to revisit the terrible past of Century Falls and the fateful day of 17 July 1953.

### Episode Two
Wednesday 24/2/93 5.05p.m.
Repeated Sunday 28/2/93 10.30a.m. (BBC2)
The villagers hold a psychic gathering and discover that Mrs Hunter is pregnant. Esme Harkness tries to tell Mrs Hunter that no children have been born in Century Falls since 1953 and urges her to leave the village. Ben meanwhile conjures up a golden figure from the local waterfall – it is the past of Century Falls and it is coming back …

### Episode Three
Wednesday 3/3/93 5.05p.m.
Repeated Sunday 7/3/93 10.30a.m. (BBC2)
Richard Naismith is a man of many secrets; he has a badly scarred 'patient' hidden in the house and also knows that Ben gets closer to dying every time he uses his psychic powers. Even so, Richard Naismith serves a greater power …

### Episode Four
Wednesday 10/3/93 5.10p.m.
Repeated Sunday 14/3/93 10.30a.m. (BBC2)
Esme reveals the origin of the figure known as Century – she is an image of the village's shared psychic power, conjured up at the ceremony in 1953. Tess learns that she is psychic too and that her mother is one of the 'scattered children' of Century Falls, brought back to the village by Naismith for a sinister purpose.

### Episode Five
Wednesday 17/3/93 5.10p.m.
Repeated Sunday 21/3/93 10.30a.m. (BBC2)
Carey, Tess and Esme rescue Ben from the clutches of Naismith and his sinister charge Julia who intend that Ben use his power one last time to take them back to 1953. Julia tricks May into returning Ben to them and, similarly, when the villagers confront Julia and Naismith they are taken into her power.

### Episode Six
Wednesday 24/3/93 5.10p.m.
Repeated Sunday 28/3/93 10.30a.m. (BBC2)
Ben takes the villagers back to a time before the 1953 ceremony and the fire. They intend to use their psychic abilities to create a new Century in the unformed mind of Mrs Hunter's unborn baby and only Tess and Esme, with their protected minds, can possibly stop them …

**Main Cast:** Catherine Sanderson (Tess Hunter), Heather Baskerville (Mrs Hunter), Simon Fenton (Ben Naismith), Emma Jane Lavin (Carey Naismith), Bernard Kay (Richard Naismith), Mary Wimbush (Esme Harkness), Georgine Anderson (May Harkness), Eileen Way (Alice Harkness), Tatiana Strauss (Julia)

**Written by** Russell T. Davies

**Music:** David Ferguson
**Designer:** Robert Foster
**Producer:** Richard Callanan
**Director:** Colin Cant

## The Lodge
The lodge of the title is Birnham Lodge, a home for deprived children. The story focuses on the situations they face throughout the duration of their stay in care. The scenario had previously been explored in dramas like *Dodger, Bonzo and the Rest* and, more recently, *Dodgem*.

Although there are some interesting episodes, examining the motives behind a child's decision to steal or the dangers of alcohol, *The Lodge*, like *Dodger, Bonzo and the Rest*, shies away slightly from examining the full extent of life within a children's home. The home also functions as a convenient basis for a format which goes on to explore narratives such as the children telling each other spooky stories during a dark and scary night when, as one might expect, a power cut occurs.

There were occasional flights into fantasy – in one episode daydreamer Lawrence imagines he is Indiana Jones.

*The Lodge*
**Richmond Films and TV Productions for Central**
**10 episodes** ('Top of the World'; 'New Blood'; 'Breakout';
4 n/k; 'Best Intentions'; 6 n/k; 'Dates and Video Tapes';
8–10 n/k)
(colour)
**Broadcast:** Wednesdays 7/4/93 – 16/6/93 (no broadcast
28/4/93)

**Main Cast:** Nancy Lodder (Zoe), Benjamin Rennis (Martin),
Martino Lazzeri (Lawrence)

**Written by** Victor Gialanella (episodes 1–3 and 10),
(others n/k)

## Smokescreen

Set in the summer of 1907, *Smokescreen* tells the tale of a
determined girl called Chrissie Gallant whose father often
leaves her and her brothers home alone in the pursuit of
work. Chrissie and her siblings stay in a cramped house in
the smoky town of Fenbury and, with no mother to take
care of them, they rely on their grandmother for support
in their father's continued absence. Chrissie finally decides
that she will find a job and support her brothers by herself
while awaiting her father's return.

One day Chrissie stumbles across the enigmatic Frank
Sherringham. She fears that the rumours she has heard
about Sherringham must be true when his door is
answered by a pale woman with a garrotted neck. Chrissie
soon discovers however that there is nothing sinister at all
in the house and that the inhabitants are actually motion
picture actors.

Sherringham invites Chrissie to be the lead actor in his
latest picture. Unfortunately it's not a straightforward
situation and Chrissie soon finds herself the go-between in
a secret affair involving Sherringham's stunning daughter.
Worse still, Chrissie becomes entangled in the long-
standing rivalry between Sherringham and the manager of
Fenbury's picture house, Albert Gold.

Shot entirely on film, *Smokescreen* is a lavish production
typical of the few Sunday family dramas made at the time.
Similar too is the message it carries – adversity can always
be overcome.

**Red Rooster Film & TV Entertainment Production for BBC**
**6 episodes**
(colour)
**Broadcast:** Sundays 2/1/94 – 6/2/94

**Main Cast:** Sally Walsh (Chrissie Gallant), Timothy West
(Mr Sherringham), Kate Hardie (Vicky Sherringham),
Paula Wilcox (Sara Bean), Anita Dobson (Gertie the Cashier),
Joan Sims (Mrs Nash), Peter Guinness (Albert Gold), Annette
Badland (Big Smithy), Michael Sanderson (Harry Gallant)

**Based on** the novel by Elsie McCutcheon (first UK publication
1986, J. M. Dent)
**Dramatised by** James Andrew Hall

**Music:** Robert Lockhart
**Designer:** Bruce Grimes
**Producer:** Jill Green
**Executive Producers:** Anna Home and Linda James
**Director:** Giancarlo Gemin

**Tie-in publications:** edition of novel published in paperback
by J. M. Dent, 1993

**Video:** 155-minute compilation released in UK by BBC
Worldwide 4/7/94. Deleted 5/2/96.

## Earthfasts

While walking on the Yorkshire Hills, teenagers David and
Keith hear a strange noise reverberating round them.
When the hills open up and a strange boy from another
time appears, it signals the start of a sequence of bizarre
events that lead to the disappearance of David. With
standing stones beginning to move and giants roaming the
countryside, Keith is left to solve the mystery of the
earthfasts and journey through time to locate his friend.

Author William Mayne lived in the small Yorkshire
village of Thornton Rust and gained inspiration for his
story from his locale and Yorkshire Arthurian folklore.
'Earthfasts' is the name given to large stones in the fields
surrounding Thornton Rust which rise from the ground
during the dry season. Mayne cleverly drew parallels
between the earthfasts and local legends suggesting that
Arthur of the Britons and his army lie asleep in caverns
below nearby Richmond Castle and will rise from their
resting place to defend England in its time of greatest
need.

Although Arthurian fantasy is a tried and tested route in
children's drama, the more localised aspect used in
*Earthfasts* is nevertheless intriguing. It's also highly
complex and viewers may well have been forgiven for
wondering exactly what was happening. It would appear
Mayne designed this with a specific purpose in mind. 'If
you can make the whole story look as if it hasn't a logical
explanation and then provide one,' Mayne stated in an
interview, 'you've given the reader a surprise without
causing incredulity.' The desired effect is certainly
achieved. The significance of Nellie Jack John's
reappearance after 200 years is far from clear. His
disappearance at the end of episode one back into the
hillside from which he emerged, leaving nothing other
than a burning candle, is unexpected. It is obvious that the
candle, which burns without heat and doesn't run down, is
key but it's up to Keith and David – and the viewer – to
solve the riddle.

It isn't all Arthurian legend though. David's apparent
death when struck by lightning on the Yorkshire Hills
opens the drama to the ever-emotive feelings surrounding
the loss of someone close to us but takes the situation a
stage further by confronting the viewers with the loss of
one of their own – a child. Some of the scenes that follow,
particularly when Keith is informed of his friend's death
and the subsequent announcement to David's school
friends, are truly upsetting.

It is the very nature of children's drama to offer its
young audience hope. Keith never gives up hope that
David is alive and when he unlocks the secret of the candle
and its importance to the ambivalent Arthur figure he is
reunited with his lost friend. The climax is remarkably
simple but, as Mayne desired, doesn't fail to surprise.

Although Keith's fear of the events in which he is
involved and the anguish he faces when dealing with the
loss of his friend are visually realised more than adequately,
Marilyn Fox incorporated mild use of narration in the
adaptation. Delivered as a voiceover from Keith, this
served to further realise the character's inner turmoil and

distress. Recorded on video, the production was shot entirely on location in Yorkshire. The barren moors are suitably bleak and quite in keeping with the overall feeling of this delicate drama.

Mayne's story has been furthered in print in recent years with the publication of *Candlefasts* and *Cradlefasts*, two sequels to the original novel.

**BBC**
**5 episodes**
(colour)
**Broadcast:** Wednesdays 27/2/94 – 23/3/94

**Main Cast:** Chris Downs (Keith), Paul Nicholls (David), Bryan Dick (Nellie Jack John), David Hargreaves (Dr Wix), Bobby Knutt (Frank Watson), Ruth Holden (Eileen Watson)

Based on the novel by William Mayne (first UK publication 1966, Hamish Hamilton)
**Dramatised by** Marilyn Fox

**Music:** Ilona Sekacz
**Designer:** Humphrey Jaeger
**Producer:** Richard Callanan
**Director:** Marilyn Fox

## Moonacre

Horses, magic, mansions, period frocks and side whiskers. Haven't we been here before? *Moonacre* is based on the classic children's novel *The Little White Horse*, a childhood favourite of J. K. Rowling, no less, and itself an influence on TV dramas such as *The Moon Stallion*. So, consciously or subconsciously, this fantasy-tinged period piece harks back to typical BBC fare of the 70s but adds a 90s co-production sheen to the proceedings.

The pan-European funding for the drama (made by a Czech company but with largely British personnel) meant *Moonacre* was lovingly shot on film and on location with an excellent cast of British thespians. These were the plusses but as usual the deal comes with strings attached. The drama was shot in the impressive mountains and forests of Slovenia, a whitewashed villa doubling up as Moonacre Manor and a foreboding hillside castle playing the lair of the Blackheart family. Stunning as the scenarios appear, by being shot in Slovenia the drama loses any real sense of setting. The actors, their accents and costumes are at odds with backdrops intended to represent West Country England in the mid-19th century.

The nature of the production's financial backing also brings about its only tatty moments, by badly dubbing local actors in small background parts. In one unintentionally hilarious scene, a pair of villagers share a two shot – one is a Czech trying a West Country accent and the other is dubbed by an over-enthusiastic English voice artist. Worse still, the villainess Lady Blackheart is played, undubbed, by a Czech actress so that we have the nonsense situation of an East European/Germanic-sounding villain residing in the mountains of the West Country with a son who speaks received BBC English.

*The Little White Horse* is the tale of an orphaned girl called Maria who travels with her governess to the remote Moonacre Valley, where her Uncle Benjamin is caught up in an ancient feud. When she arrives, Maria catches a glimpse of an ethereal white horse and later discovers that she is

this generation's 'Moon Princess', a legendary figure who can fulfil a centuries-old prophecy and reunite the warring families.

William Corlett's adaptation retains only these main tenets from the source novel but creates his own narrative to weave around them. The Blackhearts are a politically correct renaming of the original evil Black Men, with their chief antagonist becoming a woman in place of the extremely exaggerated Monsieur Coq de Noir. Noir had been a piratical cove with a black cockerel permanently residing on his shoulder whose name must have been thought to veer too close to *double entendre*. Maria is aged upwards into her late teens and so too is the boy she meets, Robin Loveday, now a blond hunk and a source of romantic interest. Corlett's best work is done in making Maria a heroine for the 90s audience; she is far more proactive, brave and outspoken than her passive novel counterpart. Maria now also carries the caring 90s message of tolerance and understanding, missing from Goudge's more black and white tale of good against evil. To provide identification for the younger age group, a brother is invented – Peter thinks kissing is yuk and indulges in comedy escapades. Broadly, Corlett injects more action into the piece, restructuring it as adventure melodrama.

The little white horse, it's worth noting, does very little in the story – no doubt the reason for the serial's retitling. This is more a straight period romp than it is a fantasy effort. When the horse and Wrolf, a dog possessed with the spirit of an ancient knight, do appear, it's unfortunately only to act as plot devices that further events via coincidence.

**Television Slovenija/Ceska Television/**
**S4C Wales/Grampian/ARD/BBC/ORTF/RTE/TV Aqui**
**6 episodes**
(colour)
**Broadcast:** Wednesdays 6/4/94 – 11/5/94 BBC1

**Main Cast:** Camilla Power (Maria), Noah Huntley (Robin), Thomas Szekeres (Peter), Philip Madoc (Sir Benjamin), Jean Anderson (Miss Heliotrope), Alannah O'Sullivan (Loveday), Richard Elfyn (Simon Blackheart), Polona Vetrih (Lady Blackheart), Big Mick (Marmaduke Scarlet), Miriam Margolyes (Old Elspeth), Iain Cuthbertson (Father Francis)

Based on the novel *The Little White Horse* by Elizabeth Goudge (first UK publication 1946, University of London Press)
**Screenplay by** William Corlett

**Music:** John Moore (played by the Czech National Theatre Orchestra)
**Producer/Director:** Robin Crichton

**Tie-in publications:** none – some copies stickered as 'Now on TV as Moonacre'

## Emily's Ghost

This period ghost story is an involved and complicated retelling of the well-worn ghost-girl trope begun by *Charlotte Sometimes*, *Echoes of Louisa* and the like.

Emily, a headstrong Victorian girl with an interest in chemistry, is moving from London to a large house in the country. Her family is by no means wealthy and must confine themselves to as few rooms as possible to save on running costs. Shortly after their arrival, Emily begins to hear strange noises, including the laughter and whispering of children in the empty rooms and deserted grounds of the house. She also falls victim to terrible nightmares during the night and quickly decides that the house is haunted. Her suspicions are seemingly confirmed when she meets the ghost, another girl called Emily.

The twist in the narrative, and a good one at that, is that it isn't exactly a ghost story but more to do with time travel, the other Emily being from 1992. Both of the girls are alive in their own time but when the Victorian Emily finds herself in the modern age of computers and cars, she cannot be seen. She is however aware of what she must do. She has had a premonition of the later Emily's drowning and knows that somehow she must prevent it from happening.

Shot completely on film, the production on *Emily's Ghost* is absolutely sumptuous and wouldn't have been out of place on the big screen where, one expects, its producers hoped to sell it. It is without doubt a drama for older children and some of the content is rather risqué, especially a scene which has Emily catching her brother looking at what would in Victorian times have been considered pornographic pictures.

There are some terrifying moments, including Emily's nightmare visions that are enhanced through excellent directing and musical scores. By far the most horrifying moment has Emily rowing on the river only to see the drowned body of the later Emily floating in the water. As the boat passes, the body raises its head from the water and glowers at her.

The explanation for this 'haunting' is rather confusing and is best left in the hands of the modern-day Emily: 'We're sort of time twins. People born at exactly the same time at different places. Have linked lives even if they never meet. We were born in different years but somehow we kept getting mixed up ... we met because we were both unhappy in our time. We didn't belong. Now we can change place.' With that, the two girls change places, exchange lives. A somewhat confusing ending to a nevertheless extremely enjoyable drama. Interestingly, many of the crew members on the production were fourteen to sixteen year olds.

**Children's Film Unit production for Channel Four**
**1 hour single drama**
(colour)
**Broadcast:** Saturday 9/4/94

**Main Cast:** Anna Jones (Emily), Emily Howes (Ghost Girl), Rosalind Ayres (Mama), Martin Jarvis (Papa), Toby Gregory (James), Hannah Fleur Fitzgibbon (Charlotte), Blanche Schofield (Louise), Tom Beeby (Edward), Anna Massey (Miss Rabstock), James Hobbs (Will), Ron Moody (Dawson), Patsy Byrne (Mrs Crabtree), Gillian Hawser (Polly)

**Written by** Colin Finbow

**Original music** written and performed by Dave Hewson
**Art Director:** Diana Johnstone
**Producer:** Brianne Perkins
**Director:** Colin Finbow

## Little Lord Fauntleroy

New York 1879 and twelve-year-old Cedric Errol leads a humble but happy life with his widowed mother. Times change for Cedric when a lawyer arrives from London with news that the boy is in fact the grandson of the Earl of Dorincourt and the heir to his lands and fortunes.

Cedric moves with his mother to England where he takes residence in the Earl's castle as Little Lord Fauntleroy. The Earl is a bitter man, refusing to acknowledge his subjects and barring Cedric's mother from his estate. It's up to Cedric to change the old man's point of view but his right to succeed the present Earl is soon brought into question.

There really is very little that could be described as subtext in Frances Hodgson Burnett's overly sentimental story of the philanthropic boy. Her examination of class, social structure and all the assumptions that go with them are up-front and often less than subtle. Lord Dorincourt ostracised his son for marrying an American woman he considered to be of inappropriate social stature. With his son now dead, Dorincourt wants his grandson Cedric returned to Britain. He assumes that the boy will be unruly and unkempt, a product of his common upbringing, but believes if Cedric can be separated from his mother he can be made of a suitable class to inherit Dorincourt's riches.

Lord Dorincourt is of course wrong in his assumptions, as is Cedric's American friend Mr Hobbs. A grocer by trade, Hobbs is a strong supporter of the Democratic movement, a belief that has rubbed off on Cedric. Hobbs considers the Republicans, whom he perceives to be at the heart of everything aristocratic, to be the enemy. It is therefore something of a shock for Hobbs to discover that his young friend is to be a rich Earl and so become one of the enemy. Hobbs knows enough of Cedric though not to alter his feelings towards the boy. He knows that he is kind at heart. This is one of the messages that Burnett strives to push forward and a recurring theme in many of her novels.

The story contains much dialogue with little in the way of action. Cedric must accept his elevation to Earl-in-waiting and deal with the responsibilities that wealth and stature bring. Apart from suggesting that some of his grandfather's subjects get a little extra money, he doesn't actually do anything. Yes, his innocence and kindness unearth the compassion in his grandfather but Cedric is so innocent that he doesn't see the cold and bitter side of the man. Therefore Cedric doesn't actually knowingly do anything to change him. Cedric is sickeningly good; Lord Dorincourt is predictably pompous.

The production is slick and looks reasonably expensive, as one would expect of a drama made with the purpose of being touted for mass syndication across the Atlantic. Shot on film mainly in and around Eastnor Castle in scenic Herefordshire, there's much to be seen in the way of detailed costumes and authentic village squalor. The scenes that are supposed to be set in New York fool nobody, however.

**BBC**
**6 episodes**
(colour)
**Broadcast:** Sundays 1/1/95 – 5/2/95

**Main Cast:** Michael Benz (Cedric), George Baker (The Earl of Dorincourt), Betsy Brantley (Mrs Errol), David Healy (Hobbs), Truan Munro (Dick)

Based on the novel by Frances Hodgson Burnett (first UK publication n/k)
**Adapted by** Julian Fellowes

**Music** composed and conducted by Michael Omer
**Designer:** Robert Foster
**Art Director:** Rachel Heady
**Producer:** Richard Callanan
**Associate Producer:** Alison Law
**Director:** Andrew Morgan

**Tie-in publications:** paperback edition published 1995

**Video:** 158-minute two-part compilation released on double cassette by BBC Video, 1995

## Elidor

Alan Garner recalls that this was the sixth time of trying for a film or TV adaptation of his classic book. The BBC themselves had floated the idea many times but with only a *Jackanory* reading by John Stride ever making it to the screen (broadcast 10/6/68 – 14/6/68, now sadly destroyed). It was to be the 90s before they were fully confident that a small screen dramatised adaptation was viable, in the main due to the now affordable capabilities of digital special effects technology (it is worth noting that Garner's other best-known book, *Red Shift*, had earlier been superbly adapted for an adult audience as part of BBC2's *Play For Today* strand, shown 17/1/78).

Screenwriter Don Webb was given a free hand by Alan Garner, who instructed Webb to 'get to the heart of the book' – without telling him what that was – and to then 'throw it away and make the story his own'. Garner was so pleased with the end result that he joked that if there were complaints from purists he would write back to them and tell them this version was better than his own.

Certainly *Elidor* is not an easy novel to adapt directly for television. Much of the book consists of Garner's rather poetical descriptions of the 'shadows' that threaten to break through from another dimension into our own (harsher critics have commented that very little happens in the novel). The book is about a not quite palpable if tangible air of menace but fighting shadows was never likely to be visually stimulating TV fodder. Webb had little option but to try and make concrete the vague threat of Garner's novel, and so the Warrior and Sniffer characters were invented to provide rather more flesh and blood mortal enemies. A narrator (a ploughboy of Webb's invention) was also to have been used to provide further explanation but was dropped shortly before transmission.

Webb's adaptation also opts to show us more of Elidor itself, so that the split between our world and theirs is fairly even, as compared with fleeting glimpses in Garner's novel. Elidor is now realisable via computer-captured imagery; the landscape is a collage of footage shot by various units compositing castles, shoreline and barren hills. This world is only seen as a dying land in black and white, with the inhabitants in pale colours. Here Roland is trapped by stones that move and he and his siblings are attacked by flying lizard creatures. Webb also invents a witch-like mentor character who encourages Elidor's deposed King Malebron in his efforts to take back his crown.

Despite this, much of the Elidor footage is still quite static. Most of it is rendered without dialogue and when

**Above:** Malebron (Stevan Rimkus) the deposed ruler of *Elidor*, a world in another dimension.

there is dialogue it can tend towards the rather portentous. Doubtless more immediate and exciting to the young audience was the action set in the familiar environs of Manchester city centre, where a backstreet video games shop is not all it seems and where you have to jump on a double-decker bus to avoid inter-dimensional warriors. In its way this resembles the games played by any imaginative child, where the extraordinary can easily break through and co-exist with the ordinary. The 'ordinary' is still given a digital helping hand, such as in the scene where a ruined church is spectacularly destroyed.

The adaptation chooses to retain from Garner's novel the run-down backstreets of the inner city. In the 60s, when *Elidor* was originally written, these parts of town had suffered bomb damage in the war and were being pulled down and transformed into the tower block schemes of a supposedly bright new future. This echoed the time of change and promise of a new dawn in Elidor. In its 90s context, however, this twilight world – 'Day of the Dead,' Nick calls it – can surely only be read as a comment on a country ravaged by a decade or more of Thatcherite excess.

Webb also addresses a perceived need to update the action and attitudes of a thirty-year-old book to communicate better with a supposedly sussed 90s audience. Some of it is easily done – now Malebron uses a computer monitor to send a message to Roland and there are many contemporary references (including the kids chanting 'Ooh-ah-Cantona' when Roland kicks his football through the church window). There's also a more adolescent angle here, Webb even going as far as to include a teenage house party, its staircase filled with snogging couples, to appeal to the widest possible young audience. 249

Perhaps most telling of all, Webb develops the world-weary cynicism of these 90s kids – even young David remarks that a lot of what Roland tries to tell them is really happening is just 'Cobblers!' It's Nicholas, the eldest of the Watson children, who is almost unceasingly cynical though. He calls his younger brother David 'a computer-driven retard' and remarks that patchouli 'smells like the lav in a rave club'. Even as far on as episode five he still persists with his rational explanations for all the weird experiences they have been through.

This is a plain attempt to match the cynicism of an older element of the audience and thus bring them into the story. It's the more imaginative Roland who tells it like it is when David complains that Malebron is a lunatic for asking four kids their age to help him: 'Only people our age'd believe him,' Roland argues. 'That's why you won't believe him. You're getting too old and that's sad.' It's a key quote that sums up a central theme of *Elidor* and indeed pretty much all of children's fantasy.

**Screen First Production for BBC**
**6 episodes**
(colour)

**Episode 1**
Wednesday 4/1/95 5.10p.m.
Repeated Sunday 8/1/95 10.55a.m.
The four Watson children take a walk round Manchester one day but find themselves in a rather run-down part of town. When Roland accidentally kicks his football through the window of a ruined church and goes in to retrieve it, he meets a ragged stranger. This is Malebron – deposed ruler of a world called Elidor. He tells Roland that he is the chosen one, born to save Elidor in this, its darkest hour.

**Episode 2**
Wednesday 11/1/95 5.05p.m.
Repeated Sunday 15/1/95 10.55a.m.
Transported to Elidor, Nick, Helen and David are trapped inside a mountain. Aided by Malebron, Roland creates a mental doorway in the hillside and frees his brothers and sister. In the mountain are the four treasures of Elidor: a sword, a spear, a stone and a cauldron. Whoever holds the treasures rules Elidor and Malebron instructs the children to keep them safe in their world from the evil overrunning his own.

**Episode 3**
Wednesday 18/1/95 5.10p.m.
Repeated Sunday 22/1/95 10.55a.m.
Returning to Manchester, the Watson family are moving to a new house. On their arrival the treasures play havoc with the household electrics. Roland reckons he is being followed by 'shadows' from the other world.

**Episode 4**
Wednesday 25/1/95 5.10p.m.
Repeated Sunday 29/1/95 10.55a.m.
The children bury the treasures in the back garden and the static fades. There is a constant rattling at the letterbox meanwhile – but when the family go to see who is there, no-one is around. When Roland peers through, he can see the evil army massing in Elidor. By the power of his will, Roland can both summon and hold back the other dimension but for how much longer can he resist?

**Episode 5**
Wednesday 1/2/95 5.10p.m.
Repeated Sunday 5/2/95 10.55a.m.
Returning home at night from a party, the children have a brush with Findhorn, the unicorn of Elidor. Malebron contacts Roland via the computer and tells him that he must find Findhorn again and make him sing. Then one night, while Mum and Dad are out, the Warrior and his 'Sniffer' break through to this world and mark the house with a hex.

**Episode 6**
Wednesday 8/2/95 5.05p.m.
Repeated Sunday 12/2/95 10.55a.m.
At the Manchester docks, the Watson kids find Findhorn but so too do the Warrior and Sniffer. Using the sword of Elidor, Roland tries to fight them both and is joined by Malebron, now also broken through. The shadow warriors defeated in battle, the children must now make Findhorn sing. But the unicorn only sings when it dies and so Roland slays it with the spear. The treasures returned to him, Malebron and Elidor are safe.

**Main Cast:** Damian Zuk (Roland), Alexander Trippier (David), Suzanne Crowshaw* (Helen), Gavin J. Morris (Nicholas), Stevan Rimkus (Malebron), Noreen Kershaw (Gwen Watson), David Beckett (Frank Watson), Renny Krupinski (Lead Warrior), Abi Eniola (Sniffer), Valerie Lilley (The Sibyl)
* Later to become known by stage name of Suzanne Shaw in pop group Hear'Say

Based on the novel by Alan Garner (first UK publication 1965, William Collins & Son)
**Adapted by** Don Webb

**Music** composed by Ilona Sekacz
**Production Designer:** Paul Laugier
**Art Director:** Rod Gorwood
**Producers:** Paul Madden and Mairede Thomas
**Associate Producer:** Christopher Sutton
**Director:** John Reardon

**Tie-in publications:** edition of novel published in paperback by Fontana Lions, 1995

## The Biz!
At the Markov School of Dance and Drama, a group of budding young actors try to make a name for themselves while coping with gruelling training and auditions. A new group of hopefuls have arrived at the school and while they adapt to the strict regime the older students battle their way through auditions for a job on television. Paul Nicholls, who would soon become a star in *EastEnders*, plays Tim, a character already coming to terms with the downside of stardom.

*The Biz!* was likened to 80s American hit show *Fame*, with *Radio Times* stating that it was breathing new life into the old format of talented kids at stage school trying to make it big. The truth is that the two are completely dissimilar. Despite its often sickly sweet scripts, *Fame* had a dynamic (an often unrealistic one at that) that *The Biz!* certainly lacks. One can put up with *Fame*'s insistence that the righteous will prevail when watching Valerie Landsburg belting out 'High Fidelity' in the middle of a New York music store. What the audience is faced with in *The Biz!* is a noticeably less frenetic group of melodramatic, moody children who are either infuriatingly sweet, annoyingly egotistical or petulant attention seekers.

The second season saw the majority of the cast unchanged and concentrated on Tim's relationship with Sasha, while Nick, Chris and Luke are still struggling to launch their careers. The third, considerably longer, season introduced quite a few new characters, but not so much in the way of fresh ideas, as *The Biz!* retrod old ground and moved from borderline drama into the soap genre.

**BBC**
**3 seasons**
(colour)

**Main Cast:** Paul Nicholls (Tim), Nathan Constance (Luke), Lindsey Wise (Emma), Sacha Pitimson (Chris), Marie Wevill (Pippa), Stephanie Bagshaw (Sasha), Craig Stein (Mark), Mahommed George (Ben), Hilja Lindsay-Parkinson (Natalie), Hannah Lawrence (Jules – Seasons 1 and 2), Keeley Forsyth (Nicky – Seasons 1 and 2), Lydia Hrela (Miranda – Season 1), Rhys Moore (Huw – Seasons 2 and 3), Vanessa Cavanagh (Amber – Seasons 2 and 3), Kelly Reilly (Laura – Season 2), Natalie Anderson (Francesca – Season 3), Ania Sowinski (Kerry – Season 3), Sarah French (Zara – Season 3), Delia Lindsay (Gaby – Season 3), Sally Spencer-Harris (Caro – Season 3), Geoffrey Bayldon (Markov – Season 1)

**Season One**
**6 episodes**
**Broadcast:** Wednesdays 15/2/95 – 22/3/95

**Written by** Chris Ellis (1, 3), Jeremy Front (2, 4, 6), Matthew Graham (5)

**Season Two**
**6 episodes**
**Broadcast:** Tuesdays and Thursdays 4/12/95 – 21/1/96

**Written by** Chris Ellis (1, 2), Jeremy Front (3, 4), Matthew Graham (5, 6)

**Season Three**
**12 episodes**
**Broadcast:** Tuesdays and Thursdays 3/12/96 – 16/1/97

**Written by** Chris Ellis (1, 2, 9, 10), Sarah Louise Hawkins (3, 4, 7, 8), Jeremy Front (5, 6, 11, 12)

**Tie-in publications:** n/k

## The Queen's Nose

Thirteen-year-old Harmony Parker enjoys football with the boys, mercilessly ridicules her vain older sister and plays her electric guitar very loudly. This tomboy is one of the most engaging characters to be found in children's drama of recent years. Her pre-pubescent lack of preoccupation with boys and make-up makes her the ideal individualist heroine for younger viewers of both genders in a high-spirited serial that, for once, actually fits the tag of 'comedy drama'.

When Harmony is given a magical fifty pence coin and ten wishes, she gets into more silly scrapes and japes than usual. The comedy usually manages to make a point,

however, with most of it centring around the family unit. Most of the wishes made in haste teach Harmony that however much her family annoy her, they love her really and she loves them back. Mother is always having headaches brought on by Harmony's boisterous behaviour, Father far too often acquiesces to whatever Mother says and Melody is always busy hunting boys and preening herself. One of the silliest wishes sees this nice middle-class family turned into a bunch of smelly slobs, eating fry-ups and riding motorbikes. Harmony has to waste another wish to get them back to normal and, further, she has to truly mean the wish when she makes it.

It's an updating of Nesbit's *Five Children and It* in essence, with the Psammead replaced by the magical coin known as the Queen's Nose. Like its predecessor, *The Queen's Nose* carries a central message of being careful in what you wish for. The mentor who guides Harmony in her journey of discovery is the eccentric Uncle Ginger who, in giving Harmony the Queen's Nose, is presenting her with a test and not a gift. Ginger is a fascinating presence as Harmony's confidant. 'Dad says you're a bit childish,' Harmony tells him. 'I hope so' is his answer. Ginger lends a fantasy element to the production when Harmony glimpses him on his travels (hunting the Yeti or talking to wild bears) in mirrors, paintings or a snowshaker. Donald Sumpter effortlessly conveys the impish wisdom required of the part.

It's this test for Harmony that provides the dramatic spine of the story. Not only does she learn more about herself and her family but finally she must learn of 'real magic'. In a coda (an addition to the original novel by adaptor Steve Attridge) she helps organise a charity football match for her friend Tom without the aid of the coin's powers.

The second series lacks this kind of dramatic core. While it would have been ridiculous to repeat the original storyline and have Harmony learn the same lesson all over again, there is nothing put in to replace it. The main plot concerns Mr Parker's upcoming court case on fraud charges but this doesn't sustain throughout the six episodes. Instead this idea opens and closes the 'serial' in the first and last instalments, with unconnected episodic interludes in between. One such diversion sees the family go on a haunted house treasure hunt in order to win the £10,000 needed to mount their court case – by such tenuous means is a storyline almost put together. The serial is notably more comedic, including an appearance by Gran on a TV dating game with a cameo role for DJ Tony Blackburn as the host.

The serial also suffers from some large plot holes of the kind that children would immediately spot. Initially Ginger tells Harmony that the coin is not hers to wish on this time round and yet before long she is clearly doing so. More crucially, what's to stop the first wish being that the family could be out of their current predicament and Mr Parker found innocent? Plus points include the fleeting appearances of Donald Sumpter as Ginger, and Stephen Moore is excellent as the decent father out of work who feels he has let his family down. There's a beautiful scene which has Dad and Harmony share a moment together on the rooftops; wondering where the case will take them, they end up baying at the moon like wolves. This provides some nice emotional realism which counters some increasingly caricatured playing elsewhere.

Mum and Dad were absent for the third series and so too, sadly, was any attempt at a dramatic subplot. With the

**Above:** Harmony (Victoria Shalet) and furry chum contemplate the power of the magical fifty pence known as *The Queen's Nose.*

Thirteen-year-old animal-mad tomboy Harmony Parker is given a magic fifty pence coin by her mystical Uncle Ginger. By rubbing the 'queen's nose' on the coin, she can be granted ten wishes, but she must use them wisely …

**Main Cast:** Victoria Shalet (Harmony Parker), Anthony Hamblin (Tom Williams), Paula Wilcox (Mrs Parker), Stephen Moore (Mr Parker), Heather Jones (Melody Parker), Donald Sumpter (Uncle Ginger)

Based on the novel by Dick King-Smith (first UK publication 1983, Victor Gollancz)
**Screenplay by** Steve Attridge
**Script Editor:** Gillian Gordon
**Script Supervisor:** Vivianne Royal
Developed in association with the Children's Film and Television Foundation

**Music:** Carl Davis
**Production Designer:** Gordon Melhuish
**Art Director:** Richard Elton
**Producer:** Clive Parsons
**Director:** Carol Wiseman

**Tie-in publications:** edition of novel published in paperback by Puffin, 1995

**Video:** first two episodes only released unedited by Carlton Home Entertainment, 15/9/97

series now billed in *Radio Times* as 'a six-part comedy', the exaggerated caricatures of the family were replaced by out-and-out cartoon figures in what was now pure slapstick sitcom. Within just a couple of years, Victoria Shalet had become an elegant teenager and this couldn't help but dilute the sparky tomboy Harmony whom the earlier series centred on. Without Harmony causing disharmony, there was little genuinely delinquent fun about the second sequel, replaced by the likes of giant puppet thistles shouting, 'Och Aye the noo!'

The fourth season seemed to take most of the third's shortcomings into account. Harmony set off on holiday for most of the series but not before passing on the secret of the Queen's Nose to three foster children – Sam, Pansy and Jordan. The usual shenanigans ensued, usually accompanied by a little moral lesson. These ranged from 'You can have too much ice cream' to 'Don't search for your real mother when there's a perfectly good one here.' When Jordan wishes real life was more like TV, the episode becomes a TV series within a TV series (*The Fifty Pence Tip*). Certainly a little wittier and with more credible backbone to the comedy than in the previous year, it seemed unlikely the fourth season would be the last in *The Queen's Nose* franchise. To nobody's surprise, the series returned for a fifth season in autumn 2001 and a sixth has just begun as this book went to press in Autumn 2002.

**Film and General Productions for BBC**

**Season One**
**6 episodes**
(colour)
**Broadcast:** Wednesdays 15/11/95 – 20/12/95

**Season Two:** *Harmony's Return*
**6 episodes**
(colour)
**Broadcast:** Wednesdays 13/11/96 – 18/12/96 (repeated Sunday mornings 17/11/96 – 22/12/96)

Mr Parker is suspected of embezzling money from the company where he works. The family are forced to move out of their home and go to stay in their Gran's chaotic flat. Uncle Ginger gives Harmony back the Queen's Nose with another ten wishes restored. She hopes to use the coin to get the family out of their predicament but it seems she can't help losing it …

**Main Cast:** Victoria Shalet (Harmony Parker), Paula Wilcox (Mrs Parker), Stephen Moore (Mr Parker), Heather Jay-Jones (Melody Parker), Callum Dixon (Gregory), Liz Smith (Grandma), Max Digby (Jeremy Trelawn), Donald Sumpter (Uncle Ginger)

**Written by Steve Attridge** based on characters created by Dick King-Smith
**Developed by** Steve Attridge and Carol Wiseman
**Script Executive:** Gillian Gordon
**Script Supervisor:** Gillian Wood

**Music:** Carl Davis
**Production Designer:** Gordon Melhuish
**Producers:** Clive Parsons and Davina Belling
**Director:** Carol Wiseman

**Tie-in publications:** novelisation *The Queen's Nose: Harmony's Return* published in paperback by Puffin, 1996

**Season Three: *Harmony's Holiday***
**6 episodes**
(colour)
**Broadcast:** Wednesdays 18/11/98 – 23/12/98 (repeated Sunday mornings 22/11/98 – 27/12/98)

Harmony and Melody are spending their summer holidays on their Aunt Glenda's houseboat when their vacation is disturbed by the arrival of a young tearaway called Dino. It seems that this time round Dino is to be the guardian of the coin and she has a lot to learn about the wise use of its magic …

**Main Cast:** Victoria Shalet (Harmony Parker), Heather Jay-Jones (Melody Parker), Callum Dixon (Gregory), Nerys Hughes (Aunt Glenda), Vicky Lee Taylor (Dino), Donald Sumpter (Uncle Ginger), Ian Reddington (Grobbler), Gary Moreline (Gus)

**Written by** Steve Attridge based on characters created by Dick King-Smith
**Script Executive:** Gillian Gordon

**Music:** Carl Davis
**Production Designer:** Gordon Melhuish
**Producers:** Clive Parsons and Davina Belling
**Director:** Carol Wiseman

**Tie-in publications**: tie-in novelisation *The Queen's Nose: Harmony's Holiday* published in paperback by Puffin, 1998

**Season Four**
**6 episodes**
(colour)
**Broadcast:** Mondays 13/11/00 – 18/12/00 (episodes 1–5 repeated Sunday mornings BBC2 19/11/00 – 17/12/00)

Mr and Mrs Parker have returned from Australia and set up a foster home. As they prepare for a crucial funding review, three of their young charges find the Queen's Nose. Harmony leaves for a world trip but, before she goes, warns the children of the coin's power.

**Main Cast:** Ella Jones (Sam), Grace Atherton (Pansy), Scott Charles (Jordan), Paula Wilcox (Mrs Parker), Stephen Moore (Mr Parker), Heather Jay-Jones (Melody Parker), Victoria Shalet (Harmony Parker), Judith Jacob (Sabrina Kitts)

**Written by:** Graham Alborough (1, 3, 5, 6) and Emma Frost (2 and 4)
**Development:** Gillian Gordon

**Music:** Carl Davis
**Production Designer:** Gordon Melhuish
**Producers:** Davina Belling and Clive Parsons
**Director:** Carol Wiseman

**Season Five**
**6 episodes**
(colour)
**Broadcast:** Mondays 24/9/01 – 29/10/01

**Season Six**
**6 episodes**
(colour)
**Broadcast:** Monday 23/9/02 – 28/10/02

## Black Hearts In Battersea

A period drama set in a fictional 1830s and the time of the reign of King James III, concerning the adventures of a young orphan farmboy by the name of Simon. The boy only has one friend, Dr Field, whom he follows to the back streets of London. Once there he finds himself involved in the criminal antics of the Twite family and is soon uncomfortably close to high treason and an anti-royalist plot to depose the King. Simon soon learns the truth of his own identity – that he is the heir of a titled family and his parents were killed in a highway ambush when he was a baby.

It's typical period skullduggery and Simon must help to prevent the assassination of a Duke and Duchess, avoid a watery grave, pilot a hot-air balloon and triumph over murderous villains in a tale described by director David Bell as 'more Dickens than Dickens'.

**BBC**
**6 episodes**
(colour)
**Broadcast:** Sundays 31/12/95 – 28/1/96

**Main Cast:** William Mannering (Simon), Jade Williams (Dido), Stephen Moore (Abednego Twite), Tilly Vosburgh (Ella Twite), Jay Villiers (Dr Gabriel Field), Philip Jackson (Eustace Buckle), Annette Badland (Dolly Buckle), John Altman (Midwink), Barry Ewart (John Daggett), Celia Imrie (Duchess of Battersea), Ronald Pickup (Duke of Battersea)

Based on the novel by Joan Aiken (first UK publication 1965, Jonathan Cape)
**Adapted by** James Andrew Hall

**Producer:** Angela Beeching
**Director:** David Bell

**Tie-in publications:** n/k

## Delta Wave

Dr Ruby Munro, a scientist at DELTA – the Department for Experimental Linked Thought Activity – recruits two youngsters, Ania and Jason, with strong psychic abilities. Together they form the Delta Gang, and travel back through time solving crimes ranging from crop circles to vanishing villages.

The series is comprised of five stories that see the Delta Gang fight off the evil Doctor Weevil, who plans to use them in his experiments, and then travel back to Victorian times where they help to prevent Olga Crick from swindling millions of pounds from Sheldon Hubble. In their next adventure they become involved with two ruthless gangsters, Rex and Roy Valentine. Former Tetra *Tomorrow People* scribe Grant Cathro, writer of the fourth *Delta* story, takes the opportunity to appear on screen, playing the part of Mr McClurg. The Gang also come up against Doctor Zeckler, who is determined to transform the human race.

**Delta Wave**
**Meridian/Tetra Films**
**10 episodes** (5 x 2-part stories)
('A Twist of Lemming'; 'A Glitch in Time'; 'Dodgy Jammers';
'The Light Fantastic'; 'Something Fishy')
(colour)
**Broadcast:** Wednesdays 3/1/96 – 6/3/96

**Main Cast:** Robin McCaffrey (Dr Ruby Munro), Ania Sowinski
(Julia Stone), Jason Stracey (Ed Curtis)
**With:** Graham Crowden, Una Stubbs, Peter Capaldi,
Leslie Grantham

**Written by** Lee Pressman (1–4), Ken Allen Jones (5, 6),
Grant Cathro and Alex Bartlette (7, 8), Alex Shearer (9, 10)

**Producer:** Alan Horrox
**Directors:** Roger Gartland (1, 2), Niall Leonard (3, 4),
A. J. Quinn (5, 6), Juliet May (7, 8), Rita Leena Lynn (9, 10)

## The Demon Headmaster

Eleven-year-old Dinah Glass lost both her parents when she was only a year old and has lived in various children's homes ever since. Arriving at her new foster home, she meets the Hunter brothers, Lloyd and Harvey. They are friendly but strangely reluctant to discuss the school that Dinah is to attend with them.

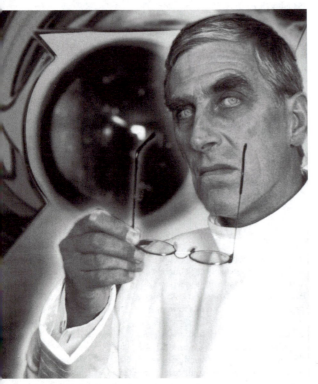

**Above:** a clone of *The Demon Headmaster* returns to wreak havoc with his new Hyperbrain project in the third run of the popular BBC series.

She soon finds herself in a playground where the children all stand in small circles memorising such topics as dates in history and world capitals. The prefects, who act as the voice of the headmaster, rule the children with military precision. Dinah isn't particularly enamoured with them or the sinister headmaster but nonetheless she feels oddly compelled to say that the Head is a marvellous man and this is the best school she's ever been to, whenever asked how she's getting on.

The series of *Demon Headmaster* books may never have been written had it not been for the intervention of the daughter of author Gillian Cross. Elizabeth Cross had particularly enjoyed a section of one of her mother's other novels, *Save Our School*, in which a character called Clipper writes about a wicked headmaster. She considered it much better than anything else her mother had written and begged her to write a story about a nasty headmaster.

It was perhaps felt that there wasn't sufficient material in *The Demon Headmaster* to warrant a six-part drama – the first series on television comprises *The Demon Headmaster* and its sequel, *The Prime Minister's Brain*. It is however the first story that is undoubtedly the more interesting. Gillian Cross was initially concerned about how she could write a book about a villainous headmaster in the kind of school that ordinary children would attend. A fantasy narrative was therefore developed where the headmaster has the strange ability to hypnotise people using only his eyes, which has the impact of reducing the realism of the situation and creating an altogether more alien character.

The hold that the headmaster has over his pupils is just one of the many ways that the story examines the recurring theme of bullying. On one occasion the prefects make Dinah, Harvey and Lloyd sweep the freezing playground clear of snow without jackets or gloves. Once they have completed their task, the three children are pushed into the pile of snow by the prefects. Dinah is a child prodigy but keeps her intelligence hidden for the fear of being alienated by her peers.

While these instances represent an obvious form of bullying, the author's criticism of the medium of television and the role it plays in the lives of children is more subtle. Lloyd and Harvey are transfixed by the *Eddy Hair Show*, in which two school teams compete against each other, with the headmaster of the winning school being given camera time to make a speech at the end of the show. The Demon Headmaster hatches a scheme to win this competition and so hypnotise the children of the nation. This is a clear statement by Cross that not all hypnotism or 'bullying' is obvious and that the things we see and hear on television can also colour our opinions and actions. The nation of young and impressionable television viewers are hypnotised every day by colourful images, trends and smart marketing jargon.

From a technological point of view, *The Prime Minister's Brain* carries the theme a stage further, examining the power that computers have to transfix youngsters with fast moving games and colourful graphics. The Demon Headmaster is now the demon computer company owner but, other than that, the sequel adds very little of consequence to the original story. *The Demon Headmaster* would return to children's television for two further seasons and, although this provided further entertainment for followers of the series, both stories ultimately amounted to mere retreads of the first story.

Not content with his villainous antics on the small screen, the evil headmaster also wreaked havoc on the stage when Terrence Hardiman reprised his role in *The Demon Headmaster Musical*. It is unusual for a contemporary children's drama to be adapted in this manner, the only previous examples being *Grange Hill* and *The Famous Five*.

The subject matter at the heart of the drama may appear rather disturbing but Cross' novel is handled in a light-hearted way which is carried across to the small screen, pushing *The Demon Headmaster* into the domain of the comedy drama. The SPLAT! team (the Society for the Protection of our Lives Against Them), formed by Dinah and other children beyond the control of the Headmaster, wouldn't look out of place in an Enid Blyton adventure. The group, operating from the garden shed HQ, mount a number of no-adult-included offensives against the headmaster. While scenarios like these deliver a more cheerful aspect to the narrative, *The Demon Headmaster* is unfortunately pantomime on a number of occasions, none more so than at the end of the first story when the headmaster is defeated by Dinah and some Noel Edmonds-esque gunge.

Although the character of the headmaster lacks the on-screen menace he exudes in the original novel, this shouldn't detract from the fact that the first season of *The Demon Headmaster* is actually a pleasing adventure yarn. It has been said that the best villain is one that keeps coming back. This isn't true in the case of *The Demon Headmaster* – that which followed was unnecessary overkill and the BBC could and should have moved on to a new and original project instead.

**BBC**
**3 seasons**
(colour)

**Main Cast:** Terrence Hardiman (Demon Headmaster), Frances Amey (Dinah Glass/Hunter*), Gunnar Cauthery (Lloyd Hunter), Thomas Szekeres (Harvey Hunter), Tessa Peake-Jones (Mrs Hunter)
**Season One and Two only:** Katey Crawford Kastin (Rose Carter), Anthony Cumber (Ian), Rachael Goodyer (Mandy), Kirsty Bruce (Ingrid)
**Season Two only:** James Richard (Simon James)
*Dinah Glass became Dinah Hunter when she was adopted

**Adapted by** Helen Cresswell
**Script Editor:** Marilyn Fox (Season One)

**Music** composed by Richard Attree (BBC Radiophonic Workshop)
**Designer:** Paul Munting
**Producer:** Richard Callanan (Season One), Roger Singleton-Turner (Season Three)
**Executive Producer:** Richard Langbridge (Season Three)
**Director:** Roger Singleton-Turner

**Season One**
**6 episodes** (episodes 1–3: 'Look Into My Eyes'; episodes 4–6: 'The Prime Minister's Brain')
**Broadcast:** Tuesdays and Thursdays 1/2/96 – 18/2/96

Dinah Glass discovers that her new headmaster is hypnotising the school to bow to his every command. If his school team are successful on TV's Eddy Hair Show, the headmaster will use his televised winning speech to hypnotise a nation of children. It's up to Dinah and SPLAT!, a small group of unaffected children, to stop him. Even if they can, he has another plan and a powerful supercomputer up his sleeve.

Based on the novels *The Demon Headmaster* and *The Prime Minister's Brain* by Gillian Cross (first UK publication 1982, Oxford University Press)

**Season Two**
**7 episodes**
**Broadcast:** Wednesdays 25/9/96 – 6/11/96

Dinah's father has a new job at the Biogenetic Research Centre (BRC) and the Hunter family move to a small village near the plant. It would appear that the BRC is a wonderful thing to have in the village. A really good neighbour. It doesn't take Dinah long to figure out that the Demon Headmaster is back. This time he's assumed the role of the BRC Director and is now tampering with evolution …

Based on the novel *The Demon Headmaster Strikes Again* by Gillian Cross (first UK publication 1996, Oxford University Press)

**Season Three**
**6 episodes**
**Broadcast:** Tuesdays and Thursdays 6/1/98 – 22/1/98

While clearing up following the BRC incident, the army inadvertently trigger the cloning of the Demon Headmaster. Determined to avenge his previous defeats, he sets out to track down Dinah Hunter. His latest cunning device is the Hyperbrain – a living supercomputer.

Based on the novel *The Demon Headmaster Takes Over* by Gillian Cross (first UK publication 1997, Oxford University Press)

**Tie-in publications:** paperback editions of *The Demon Headmaster and The Prime Minister's Brain*, *The Demon Headmaster Strikes Again* and *The Demon Headmaster Takes Over* published by Puffin, 1995, 1996 and 1998 respectively

**Video:** Season One released in UK as a 139-minute two-part compilation (containing 'Look Into My Eyes' and 'The Prime Minister's Brain') by BBC Worldwide 5/1/98. Deleted 31/10/00.

# Island

'They're young, they're glamorous,' said *Radio Times* of the characters in ITV's latest children's drama, *Island*. The series focuses on a group of teenagers working during the summer on the scenic Channel Island of Jersey. *Island*, created by *Byker Grove* scribes Adele and Carrie Rose, was planned as a response to the big Australian soaps like *Neighbours* and *Home and Away*, promising to be 'bright, fresh, peppered with teenage issues'.

Such issues included cabaret dancing, unexpected visitors in hotel rooms, Danny and Philip's love life and Dominic's encounter with the police. In the show's second season, Philip is told he could be the next Jason Donovan. He goes into the recording studio, sings for a record company talent scout and eventually gets a contract.

*Island* was planned as a soap and certainly displays the expected characteristics. The story interweaves the activities of a number of people and situations rather than focusing on just the one and the issues covered are distinctly more in line with soap than drama. The problem is that for a programme to establish itself as a successful soap, it really has to run over a longer period of time than six weeks. *Radio Times* surmised that *Island* 'could make babes and hunks of its stars'. It didn't, although Matthew Marsden went on to *Coronation Street*.

Uniquely, this is the only children's drama ever made by the tiny Channel Television franchise.

**Channel Television**
**2 seasons**
(colour)

**Main Cast:** Matthew Marsden (Philip), Suzanne Maddock (Sandra), Desmond Askew (Danny), David Blair (Stuart), Juliet Caton (Louise – Season 1), Aoife Kavanagh (Theresa – Season 1), Tom Ward (Dominic – Season 1), Daisy Bates (Zoe – Season 2), Milly Gregory (Cathy – Season 2), Guy Leverton (Chris – Season 2), Adam James (Ross – Season 2)

**Season One**
**(6 episodes)**
**Broadcast:** Tuesdays 19/3/96 – 23/4/96

**Written by:** Adele Rose (1–4), Carrie Rose (5), Adele and Carrie Rose (6)

**Season Two**
**(6 episodes)**
**Broadcast:** Tuesdays 29/4/97 – 3/6/97

**Written by** Carrie Rose

## Retrace

When the three Fisher children, Harry, Zillah and Joe, return from school one day to discover that their father has mysteriously vanished, it signals the start of a terrifying adventure. Could their father have been involved in armed robbery? Hard-faced men arrive to search the boatyard and the children decide to head for Bamburgh where they believe they will find their father. When the police take Mr Fisher into custody, the children are taken to a secret hiding place. What will happen to the children and what fate awaits their father?

A further shorter season of *Retrace* detailed the kids' return to Britain to continue the search for their mother. Once again they find themselves unable to determine whom they can trust as they become embroiled in conspiracy at a company called Terrachem. Joe is kidnapped and Terrachem's agents try to prevent the children from discovering what happened to their mother.

The first season of *Retrace* was awarded Best Children's Drama 1996 by The Royal Television Society and scored highly in the ratings with a 51% audience share.

**Perx Production for Yorkshire**
**2 seasons**
(colour)

**Season One**
**6 episodes**
**Broadcast:** Wednesdays 11/9/96 – 16/10/96

**Season Two**
**4 episodes**
**Broadcast:** Thursdays 6/8/98 – 27/8/98

**Main Cast:** Michael Jowett (Harry Fisher), Kim Brearley (Zillah Fisher), Adam Scourfield (Joe Fisher), Ralph Arliss (John Fisher), Michael Troughton (Dirk French)

**Written by** Tom Needham

**Producer:** Angela Silvester

## Frighteners

*Frighteners* first appeared in 1996 as a one-off play for Hallowe'en that told the tale of a family holidaying in France whose lives are endangered by dark secrets linked to the past.

A series of four plays the following year meant a welcome if brief return for the anthology series format. In the first instalment, Nickki has an arrangement to meet her friend Ruth at the tomb of a seventeenth-century witch at midnight. Instead of finding Ruth, she is confronted instead by a young rector. In the second play, a pensioner in a coma needs an individual to take care of her cottage. In the third, Angela's mother has recently remarried. Unhappy at this, Angela decides to come between the two of them. The last episode saw a girl called Daphne make a strange discovery – are there really fairies at the bottom of her garden?

The title *Frighteners* was rather misleading – although supernatural happenings formed the basis of each play, more reassuring scares were the order of the day.

**Myrddin for Anglia**
**1 pilot and 1 season**
(colour)

**Pilot episode: 'Guillame'**
**Broadcast:** Thursday 31/10/96
**Written by** Andrew Buchanan

**Season One**
**4 episodes** ('The Promise'; 'Rose Cottage'; 'Jevan'; 'If You Meet a Fairy...')
**Broadcast:** Tuesdays 25/2/97 – 18/3/97

**Main Cast**
'The Promise': n/k
'Rose Cottage': Paul Shelley (Bill Turner), Derek Benfield (Jack Hammond), Andrew Falvey (Greg Turner), Dominic Taylor (John Appleby), Kathleen Byron (Bessie Hammond), Simon Denny (Rex), Sophia Langmead (Carole)
'Jevan': Joanne Campbell (Flick), Joe Dixon (Jack), Nathan Constance (Jevan), Hannah Lawrence (Angela), Michelle Wesson (Jo), Nancy Lodder (Michele)

'If You Meet a Fairy': Rosemary Leach (Nursie), Lucy Robinson (Mother), Thea O'Hear (Daphne), Thomas Elliot (Henry), James Elliot (Edward), Tamsin Weaver (Elsie)

**Written by** Charles Buchanan (2), Malorie Blackman (3), Jan Mark (4), (episode 1 n/k)

## The Prince and the Pauper

With the health of King Henry VIII in steady decline, the young Prince Edward prepares to take his place on the throne. One day, however, Edward meets Tom Canty, a pauper's son who is in every aspect the Prince's double. The two boys decide to swap places for an hour but the stunt quickly backfires.

Mistaken for the Prince, Tom is taken to the royal palace where he is expected at an audience with the King. Edward, wearing Tom's clothing, experiences first-hand the brutality of Tom's father, John Canty. Fleeing London to avoid being arrested for murder, Canty forces Edward into going with him. With Henry on his deathbed, Tom finds himself a pawn in the political scheming of the palace's powerful nobles. When the King dies, it seems that Tom is about to be crowned the new King of England. Edward, having learned of his father's death, must escape Canty and find a way back to his rightful destiny.

The first adaptation for children's television was in 1955 and this early production cast twins in the parts of Tom and Edward. This was a necessity in the early days of television when it would have been impossible to direct the scenes where the two characters appear together. In 1976, television techniques had reached the point where the production could support the one actor, in this case Nicholas Lyndhurst, playing both roles.

The third and last adaptation to date was certainly the most lavish. Location filming took place against a variety of stunning backdrops and stately Elizabethan houses, including Parham Park in West Sussex, Haddon Hall in Derbyshire, Arundel Castle in West Sussex and Christchurch Priory in Dorset.

Producer and adaptor Julian Fellowes felt that the story required enhancement in certain areas:

I felt Twain wasn't much interested in the prince so we've developed a storyline following his experiences as a commoner. On the other hand, Tom didn't have a good enough reason to stop protesting he wasn't the real prince so I've introduced a plot revolving around the ambitious Seymour family, who warn Tom that if he continues to say he's not the prince he'll be declared insane.

Securing Keith Michell to once again play the part of King Henry VIII was a major coup. Both Julian Fellowes and director Andrew Morgan returned from holiday, each having independently reached the idea of asking the man who made the part his own in the BBC's 70s mini-series to step into the costume once more.

All adaptations based on the novel by Mark Twain (first UK publication 1881)

### The Prince and the Pauper (1955)
**BBC**
**6 episodes** ('Exchange'; 'Miles Hendon'; 'The Beggars'; 'Hendon Hall'; 'Prison'; 'The Coronation')
(b&w)
**Broadcast:** Sundays 21/8/55 – 25/9/55

**Main Cast:** Tegid Wyn Jones (Prince Edward), Dwyryd Wyn Jones (Tom Canty), Colin Douglas (John Canty), Vera Cook (Mistress Canty), Leslie Kyle (Henry VIII), Anneke Willys (Lady Jane Grey), Alan Edwards (Miles Hendon), Seymour Green (Lord St John)

**Adapted by** Rhoda Power

**Designer:** Gordon Roland
**Producer:** Dorothea Brooking

### The Prince and the Pauper (1976)
**BBC**
**6 episodes**
(colour)
**Broadcast:** Sundays 4/1/76 – 8/2/76

**Main Cast:** Nicholas Lyndhurst (Tom Canty/Edward, Prince of Wales), Ronald Herdman (John Canty), June Brown (Mother Canty), Ronald Radd (King Henry), Barry Stokes (Miles Hendon), Martin Friend (Lord Sudbroke), Ronald Lacey (Lord Rushden)

**Adapted by** Richard Harris
**Script Editor:** Alistair Bell

**Designer:** Kenneth Sharp
**Director:** Barry Letts

**Tie-in publications:** edition published in paperback by J. M. Dent & Sons, 1976

### The Prince and the Pauper (1996)
**BBC**
**6 episodes**
(colour)
**Broadcast:** Sundays 10/11/96 – 15/12/96

**Main Cast:** Philip Sarson (Tom/Edward), John Judd (John Canty), Jenny McCracken (Mother Canty), Keith Michell (King Henry VIII), James Purefoy (Miles Hendon), Elizabeth Ann O'Brien (Lady Elizabeth), Sophia Myles (Lady Jane Grey), Rupert Frazer (Lord Seymour), Peter Jeffrey (Duke of Norfolk)

**Adapted by** Julian Fellowes

**Producer:** Julian Fellowes
**Director:** Andrew Morgan

## Wavelength

Paul Cornell once penned a glowing epitaph to *Press Gang* in the excellent book *Classic British TV* and Cornell's own subsequent kids' drama *Wavelength* was a similar tribute. Made by the same production company as his inspiration, it borrowed the series' format of teenagers running their own media base but substituted a radio station for a junior newspaper.

With *Wavelength*, Cornell tried to replicate his own favourite aspects of *Press Gang* and often succeeded. The kids spoke the sort of finely honed witty dialogue which only comes from the pen of a scriptwriter on his fifth draft, in preference to more functional but dull patois. Like *Press Gang*, *Wavelength* often liked to play little tricks with televisual diagesis, admitting dream sequences and the like. In one, idealistic head of the young City Beat FM crew James foresees his future as a homeless vagrant, mocked by the itinerant and long-suffering boss of the station, Tony Horton. Horton is always the villain of the piece, forced to accede to the stupid notion of having these children overrun his airwaves at weekends but always looking for a way of catching them out.

What's most interesting about *Wavelength* is how its core message aimed at the misfit outsider kids goes hand in hand with an imposed, more crowd-pleasing presentation style for the 'cool' tweenie audience. Among the City Beat crew is Rudyard Boswell ('named after Kipling, who makes exceedingly good books about tigers'), a tweedy sci-fi geek who plays pan-pipe music on his shows. Predictably he gets called 'a poof' by two tormentors in his introductory episode. There's also Annie Kumar, a mousey Asian girl from an overprotective family (Meera Syal playing her mother), who is transformed into a supremely loud heavy metal DJ when on air.

The pair work alongside the cool kids: floppy-fringed Jacks, clean-cut hunk James and self-assured pouting blonde Kyla Kane. In the audition episode 'Rough Mix', which brings the team together, James tells Boswell to be proud of who he is: 'You get bullied at school because you're different but once you've left school it's the thing that makes you different that's the best thing about you.' Rudyard has doubts in the episode 'Out of Luck', when he tells Matty that he's tired of being different. Matty tells him how to be cool – or more like everyone else basically – and Rudyard is forced to betray his duffle-coat-wearing, *Star Trek*-fan chum when in the company of the United-loving, monosyllabic lads before he decides to stand up for his friend and his own identity. Matty concedes that this is what's really 'cool'. The tendency towards conformist surface style – witness the pandering to the *Neighbours* and *Home and Away* teen audience by casting Aussie soap starlet Isla Fisher as a rather too pert and pretty runaway in one episode – is never allowed to undercut the series' true ethos.

The second season suffered a little through enforced cast inconsistencies – James' partner in crime Jacks leaving for Australia (no doubt to star in a soap) and three handsome new stars introduced, upsetting the cool/nerd balance. One cast change worked brilliantly within the ongoing serial format, providing the shock exit of James in the second episode after he accidentally swears on air (no, we don't hear what he says). As Boz puts it, 'so sometimes the bad guys do win'.

Indeed – *Wavelength* never seemed to enjoy the same kind of support from the network as *Press Gang* and thus, with just two short series transmitted, was unlikely to build a similar cult following.

**Richmond Films and Television for Yorkshire**
**2 seasons**
(colour)

**Story Editor:** Victor Gialanella

**Music:** Peter Davis
**Designer:** Steve Clark
**Producer:** Sandra Hastie

**Season One**
6 episodes ('Chase the Fade'; 'Rough Mix'; 'Swag and Swagger'; 'Truth Game'; 'The X-DJ'; 'The Butterfly Effect')
**Broadcast:** Wednesdays 4/6/97 – 9/7/97

**Main Cast:** Daniel Bennett (James Derry), Kristopher Milnes (Terry Jacks), Ellie Beaven (Kyla Kane), Ruby Visaria (Annie Kumar), Oliver Grig (Steven Price), Philip Wright (Rudyard Boswell), Kate Harper (Kathy Kane), David Roper (Tony Horton)

**Created and written by** Paul Cornell
**Script Supervisor:** Sian Prosser

**Art Director:** Dick Lunn
**Directors:** Diana Patrick, Bill Ward, Kfir Yefet

**Season Two**
6 episodes ('Mixed Messages'; 'Video Nasty'; 'Out of Luck'; 'Cartoon Boyfriend'; 'Boys in Black'; 'Sound and Vision')
**Broadcast:** Tuesdays 24/3/98 – 28/4/98 (scheduled episode 1 postponed from 10/3/98 due to forthcoming Budget coverage the following week – repeats shown)

**Main Cast:** Daniel Bennett (James Derry), Ellie Beaven (Kyla Kane), Ruby Visaria (Annie Kumar), Oliver Grig (Steven Price), Philip Wright (Rudyard Boswell), Caroline Hayes (Siobhan O'Riordan), Benjamin Waters (Kev Wright), Junior Laniyan (Matt Jenkins), David Roper (Tony Horton)

**Written by** Paul Cornell (1–3, 6), Philip Gerard (4), Brian Finch (5)

**Art Director:** Andy Hamilton
**Designer:** Steve Clark
**Producer:** Sandra Hastie
**Directors:** Diana Patrick (episode 1), Bill Ward (5), Lorne Magory, Peter Mulryan

## Aquila

Two school friends, Tom Baxter and Geoff Reynolds, are attending a geography field trip when the ground gives way beneath their feet. Under the earth they find a cave containing a mysterious vehicle-like object. Climbing inside, they discover the mechanism is still operational and they are soon travelling in a 6,000-year-old flying machine known as Aquila (meaning 'eagle'). While this is very exciting for the boys, it also poses problems. How are they going to get Aquila home without being caught?

The boys soon discover that Aquila not only has the ability to become invisible but also carries a powerful weapon in the shape of a laser-cannon, which brings its own problems. The boys soon have to cope with a nosey next-door neighbour, some very suspicious school teachers and the overhaul of a 6,000-year-old machine.

Andrew Norriss had previously worked on *Woof!* and felt that the most popular episodes were the ones where the dog was put in a car. He realised, however, that you couldn't portray a child doing this in case of real-life imitation. So he devised the idea of Aquila, something that wasn't quite a recognisable car but that would still encompass a common fantasy of young children – having their own vehicle and thus independence.

*Aquila* seemed to take its statutory 'comedy drama' label a little too literally with the two elements failing to gel. 'Serious' plots, such as one of the boys' distrust of his mother's new boyfriend, seemed completely separate and almost at odds with the undermining comedy capers going on elsewhere.

**BBC**
**2 seasons**
(colour)

**Main Cast:** Ben Brooks (Tom Baxter), Craig Vye (Geoff Reynolds), Sallyanne Law (Mrs Baxter), Vivien Parry (Mrs Reynolds)

**Written by** Andrew Norriss

**Script Development:** Marilyn Fox
**Music:** David Chilton and Nick Russell
**Producer/Director:** David Bell

**Season One**
**7 episodes** ('The Eagle Has Landed'; 'Homeward Bound'; 'Losing Sight'; 'Manual Control'; n/k; n/k; 'The Eagle's Eyrie')
**Broadcast:** Tuesdays and Thursdays 2/12/97 – 23/12/97

**Season Two**
**6 episodes** ('The Birthday Surprise'; 'Battling Bobby'; 'An Elephant Surrounded by Blind Men'; 'The Gooseberry'; 'End of an Eyrie'; 'On Second Thoughts, Let's Panic…')
**Broadcast:** Tuesdays and Thursdays 1/12/98 – 17/12/98

**Tie-in publications:** novelisation of first season by Andrew Norriss published in paperback by Puffin, 1997

## The Children of the New Forest

When the Beverley children's mansion is burnt to the ground by Cromwell's Roundheads and their father is killed in battle defending King Charles, the four orphans are hidden deep within the New Forest by Jacob Armitage – a retired forester and loyal servant of the family. He teaches the children the arts of hunting, housekeeping and living off the land. When Jacob suddenly dies, the children must fend for themselves while evading the marauding Roundheads. Edward, the eldest of the children, is intent on restoring the King to the throne and regaining his rightful inheritance.

In a coming of age story, Edward takes on the responsibility of safeguarding his three siblings while dealing also with his growing feelings for Patience, the young daughter of one of Cromwell's men. With little else in the way of characterisation or themes, however, *Children of the New Forest* is primarily an adventure story, focusing instead on loyalty, heroism and swashbuckling action.

Captain Marryat's novel has so far been adapted for children's television on four occasions, the first two being produced in black and white by the BBC in 1955 and 1964. The latter made use of location filming in the New Forest, where Marryat's story is actually set.

The first colour adaptation of the story was produced in 1977. It was recorded entirely on location on video, a process still in its infancy at the time. This unfortunately nullified the dynamics of the action, rendering even the most frenetic horse-riding and battle scenes slow and ineffective. And could it be that the budget could not stretch as far as hiring a stuntwoman? It seems so. In one truly appalling scene Edward's aunt is captured by Roundheads and slung across the back of a horse. The actor involved is then substituted for an obvious dressed-up dummy and the horse runs off, throwing rider and floppy dummy to their deaths. One rather more gritty scene has a man seen coughing up blood as he dies after being stabbed by a Roundhead.

The fourth and most recent adaptation to date is a demonstration in the advance of co-funding and television production. Shot completely on film, it is slick, benefits from a liberal budget, deploys booming incidental music, has reasonable panache and is directed in a more adventurous manner than its predecessors. On this occasion Edward's aunt is spared the indignity of being replaced by a dummy and instead dies in the family mansion when it is set alight – a clear deviation from Marryat's novel.

Back in the 50s and 60s, *Children of the New Forest* may well have been an exciting experience for those youngsters fortunate enough to have a television in their house but, by the 90s, further adaptation appeared simply fodder for relentless sale across the Atlantic.

Based on the novel by Captain Marryat (first UK publication 1847)

### The Children of the New Forest (1955)
**6 episodes** ('The Flight'; 'A New Life'; 'Alone'; 'Hunted'; 'The Attack'; 'Back to Armwood')
**BBC**
(b&w)
**Broadcast:** Tuesdays 5/4/55 – 10/5/55

**Main Cast:** John Charlesworth (Edward Beverley), Shirley Watson (Patience Heatherstone), Clement Lister (Ned Corbould), Shirley Cooklin (Alice Beverley), Harold Scott (Jacob Armitage), Anthony Valentine (Humphrey Beverley)

**Adapted by** Tom Twigge (1, 3, 6) and Douglas Hurn (2, 4, 5)
**Designer:** Stephen Bundy
**Producer:** Douglas Hurn

### The Children of the New Forest (1964)
**6 episodes** ('The King's Messenger'; 'A Rescue'; 'Sword and Pistol'; 'A Common Enemy'; 'Into Battle'; 'The Name of Beverley')
**BBC**
(b&w)
**Broadcast:** Sundays 23/8/64 – 27/9/64

**Main Cast:** Richard Arthure (Edward), Kara Wilson (Patience), Melanie Parr (Edith Beverley), Norman Tyrrell (Jacob Armitage), Brendan Collins (Humphrey Beverley)

**Dramatised by** Anthony Coburn
**Script Editor:** Betty Willingale
**Designer:** Desmond Chinn
**Director:** Brandon Acton-Bond

**The Children of the New Forest** (1977)
BBC
5 episodes
(colour)
**Broadcast:** Sundays 13/11/77 – 11/12/77

**Main Cast:** Richard Gibson (Edward Beverley), Rebecca Croft (Patience Heatherstone), Donald Sumpter (Corbould), Timandra Alwyn (Edith Beverley), Edwina Ashton (Alice Beverley), Kendrick Owen (Jacob Armitage), Arthur Campbell (Humphrey Beverley)

**Adaptation by** William Pointer
**Script Editor:** Alistair Bell
**Designer:** Oliver Bayldon
**Producer:** Barry Letts
**Director:** John Frankau

**Tie-in publications:** abridged novel published in paperback by Armada/Fontana Paperbacks, 1977

**The Children of the New Forest** (1998)
A Childsplay Production for the BBC
6 episodes
(colour)
**Broadcast:** Sundays 15/11/98 – 20/12/98

**Main Cast:** Tom Wisdom (Edward Beverley), Kelly Reilly (Patience Heatherstone), Craig Kelly (Reverend Abel Corbould), Emily Ruck-Keene (Edith Beverley), Joanna Kirkland (Alice Beverley), Malcolm Storry (Jacob Armitage), Danny Worters (Humphrey Beverley)

**Screenplay by** Richard Cooper and Peter Tabern
**Original Music:** Ian Hughes
**Production Designer:** Robert Foster
**Executive Producer for the BBC:** Anna Home
**Producer:** Peter Tabern
**Director:** Andrew Morgan

**Tie-in publications:** published 1998, details not known

**Video:** released unedited as 6 episodes (168 minutes) by Columbia Tristar Home Video, 2000

## See How They Run

When the BBC and the Australian broadcaster ABC pooled their resources to produce a children's drama suitable for both home audiences, it must have seemed highly unlikely that they would find a suitable script set half in the UK and half in Australia. Amazingly, there was such a storyline to hand in the shape of a children's novel from Australian writer David McRobbie.

*See How They Run* concerned the dangers encountered by a family placed on a witness protection programme. Father of the household, accountant Don Cassidy, steps forward to give evidence against a big-time drug dealer whose money laundering Don has uncovered. The basic central idea was retained but in the hands of five script adaptors and four producers (two from each continent) McRobbie's story was torn apart and restructured to match the rather neatly prescribed needs of a global television drama.

'A new name ... a new home ... is it enough?' Even the BBC adverts for the drama were adrenalised, movie-style trailers. This was the serial that brought children's drama crash-bang up to date, with a glossy action style at the end of a decade characterised by period remakes and dowdily efficient soaps. Graeme Harper's direction is the star here, never letting up in the paciest BBC children's drama ever made. An example of Harper's energetic style is his removal of the traditional title sequence in favour of running the opening credits over the non-stop action. Added to this, the co-production budget allows for a vast amount of hardware, car chases and even a helicopter escape.

The mechanics of the book's adaptation for television are at least as interesting as what's on screen. First off, the producers noted the lack of romantic interest and, surely sensing that's what's required to hold a 90s teenage audience, the drama's emphasis changed to become that of a love affair dashed by circumstance. Emma's boyfriend Sam is invented to this end – now we have two incredibly good-looking star-crossed lovers to focus on and it's worth noting that we first meet them cavorting in a swimming pool. It's Emma's attempts to contact Sam and explain her sudden disappearance that get the family into trouble via another of the TV version's inventions. Here Sam's father is the head of the drugs ring – Emma's attempts to reach Sam unwittingly leading his gang of hired hoods closer all the time. This does open up a big plot hole though – in McRobbie's novel, the villainous 'Gorgon' is in custody as a suspect and this makes far more sense than his being at large as he is here.

The first four episodes of the serial deal with the Cassidys' attempts to go to ground and the tension that lurks for them around every corner. There's usually one point per episode where the baddies get to them, forcing them to flee once more. Obviously this format cannot be repeated indefinitely and so, in episodes five and six, things step up a gear when Emma and younger sister Nicola are abducted by Nina and Roy, the Gorgon's hired hands. While there's a great surface of thrills and spills thanks to Harper, this is where the serial loses its adult sense of menace and falls into a trap of more traditional juvenile fiction, coming across like an Enid Blyton or Children's Film Foundation effort on steroids.

In McRobbie's book only Nicola is abducted and there follow some harrowing moments as, privy only to Emma's point of view, we are left to dwell on what treatment she might be suffering at the kidnapper's hands. Here both girls are snatched together, leading to some predictable 'I've got a plan' escapes by the plucky youngsters. The baddies are rather bungling – Roy is knocked out when Emma accidentally reverses a van's wing mirror into him – and, ludicrously, don't carry guns. The (again invented) climax, where Nina and Nicola struggle on the roof of a dilapidated old house, is made similarly unlikely when police marksmen don't open fire on Nina given a window of a full five seconds for a clear shot. Also, in the source novel Don's business partner Alec is a witness and placed under police protection but dies in suspicious circumstances, demonstrating the seriousness of the gang's threats. Alec is completely absent from the TV adaptation. Hinted-at threat seems fine but direct violence not so. In fact, the police who forcibly take Don back to Britain to testify while his daughters are still missing are more threatening than the bad guys, particularly the ambivalent and taciturn Grayson (played by one of the serial's script consultants, no less).

Elsewhere, one small moment of possible controversy passed seemingly unnoticed. Emma argues with Sam and exclaims unmistakably, 'That's crap!' You can call it realism but it comes across as gratuitous, particularly when the supposedly hard-bitten gang members never say a word out of turn. Still, the *Radio Times* wasn't inundated with complaints and the nation failed to grind to a halt, while it's conceivable that it would have, had this happened twenty years earlier.

The drama's resolution is its most mature moment over all the on-screen histrionics. Emma reflects on events, on how the family will never again be truly safe and on how she knows that when she waves Sam goodbye at the airport it's the last time she will ever see him. Happy endings are for kids.

**Above:** the Cassidy family, on the run to Australia in a witness protection programme; (l to r) Dad (Peter O'Brien), Nicola (Becky Simpson), Emma (Katie Blake) and Mum (Anne Looby). From the BBC/ABC co-production *See How They Run.*

**A BBC production in association with ABC Australia**
**6 episodes**
(colour)

**Episode One**
Tuesday 5/1/99 5.10p.m.
Emma Cassidy returns home one day to be bundled into a car with her family and driven away to a hotel. The family are now under a witness protection programme until Emma's father can give evidence against a drug baron whom younger sister Nicola nicknames The Gorgon. The family are discovered in their hideaway and so move on to start a new life in Stoke-on-Trent.

**Episode Two**
Thursday 7/1/99 5.10p.m.
Though life is tense the family return to some kind of normality when the girls start at a new school. Emma lies about going to visit a new schoolfriend, running off with Nicola to see boyfriend Sam play cricket. Passing their old house on the way back to Stoke, they discover that it has been burnt to the ground.

**Episode Three**
Tuesday 12/1/99 5.10p.m.
The Gorgon's hired hands track the girls down to the school and manage to kill the family's dog. The family must flee again – the girls are taken out of school and their parents smuggled out of the house in the bins. The family are picked up in a helicopter and are now headed for Australia …

**Episode Four**
Thursday 14/1/99 5.10p.m.
The family begin to settle on the other side of the world but by sending a letter to Sam, postmarked in Sydney, Emma places the family in mortal danger once again. Don reveals that the Gorgon is Graham Foster, Sam's father. Emma's new friend Greg leaves a birthday present on the Cassidy doorstep and the bomb squad move in to defuse the suspect package. The event makes the TV news and gives the family away. That night, as the Cassidys prepare to move on yet again, the girls are kidnapped.

**Episode Five**
Tuesday 19/1/99 5.10p.m.
The girls are held in an old Dormobile somewhere in Australian scrubland. Don is forced to fly back to Britain to give evidence and, escaping his hotel, he tries to get to Foster. He finds Sam at home and tells him the truth of his father's business. After confronting his father, Sam flies out to Australia to help get the girls back but finds himself captured too. With the help of Nicola's pet spider, the three escape their captors momentarily. As Nina grabs back Nicola, Emma crashes the van she is driving.

**Episode Six**
Thursday 21/1/99 5.10p.m.
Emma and the wounded Sam trek across the outback with their captors after them with dogs. Emma finds an abandoned house, only to be discovered by the gang and tied up in the attic with Nicola. The police track down Sam in hiding and with his help round up the gang. Roy and Nina are inside the house, surrounded. The girls get out onto the roof, pursued by Nina. Nina grapples with Nicola but they fall through the dilapidated roof, Nina and Roy breaking Nicola's fall. With the girls rescued, Don gives evidence back in Britain and Foster goes to prison.

**Main Cast:** Katie Blake (Emma Cassidy), Becky Simpson (Nicola Cassidy), Peter O'Brien (Don Cassidy), Anne Looby (Lily Cassidy), Vaughan Sivelle (Sam Foster), Christopher Scoular (Graham Foster), Shelley King (Nina), Adam Ray (Roy), Al Hunter Ashton (Inspector Grayson), Lucy Maria Hopkins (WDC Arnott), Juliette Grassby (WDC Gillian Lawrence), Julia Haworth (Christine), Brendan Donaghue (Greg), Judith Wright (Rogue Policewoman), Ritchie Gugeon (Rogue Sidekick)

Based on the novel by David McRobbie (first UK publication 1996, Puffin)
**Adapted for television by** Al Hunter Ashton and Tim O'Mara
**Script Development:** Marilyn Fox and Steven Andrew
**Script Editor:** Tammy Burnstock

**Music Composer:** Mario Millo
**Art Director:** Clara Morland
**Production Designer:** Jonathan Taylor
**Producer:** Josephine Ward
**Associate Producers:** Giles Ridge (BBC), Annette Gover (ABC)
**Executive Producers:** Richard Langridge (BBC),
Claire Henderson (ABC)
**Director:** Graeme Harper

**Tie-in publications:** edition of novel published in paperback in UK by Puffin and Australia by Penguin Australia, 1999

## The Magician's House

*The Magician's House* brought an idealised notion of the 'classic' Sunday teatime drama somewhere close to the present day. Bringing things up to date oddly equals dysfunctional families, and broadly this is the story of Canadian girl Mary Green and her efforts to adjust to a new family set-up. Mary's father Jack now has his girlfriend Phoebe living with him and expecting a baby. Mary's jealousy towards the new partner and forthcoming baby makes her a convenient ally for Matthew Morden, a similarly resentful young apprentice to an Elizabethan magician called Stephen Tyler.

While written by William Corlett based upon his own books, he himself added Mary's jealous motivations for television – Mary had been sister to Jack's niece and nephew Alice and Will Constant in the printed version, not his daughter.

If it updates the images of family, elsewhere the first run of *The Magician's House* is as traditional as possible: a Christmas holiday in the mystical Welsh countryside, magic and time travel are the staple elements. Tyler entrusts Mary and her cousins to save the rare badgers that live in the Golden Valley and to fulfil the valley's future destiny by ensuring that Phoebe's baby is born safely in Golden House, the mansion Uncle Jack has bought intending to turn it into a hotel.

The two plots aren't really enough to sustain over six episodes, however. Even with the additional threat of Morden and his attempts to gain hold of the magic he feels Tyler withholds from him, the production suffers from a lack of interstitial interaction and direct incident, with Tyler and Morden only occasionally warping through to today from the 16th century. A talking owl and rat flit between the two eras but there is never quite enough concrete conflict as a result. The story lacks a solid villain – misguided sorcerer's apprentice Morden falls short. A slightly older character in Corlett's original novel, here he's deployed as a misunderstood, foolish boy used to illustrate

the adolescent frustrations that can lead to anger. It's left to a gang of two-dimensional badger-trappers to try and provide a suitable foe. To be fair, almost all of these criticisms are answered in a far more visceral final episode which puts right these faults, if a little too late in the day.

The second season has a far bigger threat to the valley, that of property developers wanting to take it over, and this is a firm basis for the script to build on. The message is slightly less didactically put across than in Corlett's book, which was a clear call for retaining tradition in the face of globalisation. Corlett mentions Disneyfication in the book and such forces are probably represented by PlayCo. On screen, MordWorld is the development company run by Matthew Morden's descendants – he had been unrelated to the Crawdens who ran PlayCo in the book. It is maybe worth pausing to consider the globalised nature of the serial's production and whether this counters its argument.

There is a subplot allied to this that helps to raise the stakes yet further. Morden is again easily led, this time by the lure of Black Gold, accidentally created by Tyler in his laboratory. The Black Gold – the opposite of the pure gold that produces Tyler's magic – is a metaphor for temptation (for power and control) which both Morden and Will must resist. What's more, it also allows for much more visual and 'zappy' magic on screen than we saw first time round. A fragment of this black rock is now embedded into the standing stone that has resided by the Golden Water for thousands of years, thus poisoning the valley and its wildlife. The stone is part of the valley's delicate balance which also takes in the lake, a waterfall and a ley line. The Black Gold is not only a manifestation of evil and corruption but also echoes the greedy developers' plans to 'poison' the valley. Yet again Tyler finds himself prevented from taking full part in the action, when he is trapped in the cave behind the waterfall, but this stands true to the ethos of the serial, which is that the kids must take matters into their own hands and not rely on the omnipotence of Tyler's magic.

In all, the second serial is far more exciting than the first and bodes well for any sequel. With a fourth Corlett book still to be adapted (*The Bridge in the Clouds*), and a franchise gathering momentum, it seems inevitable that we'll be taking at least one more trip to the Golden Valley, although the series was conspicuous by its abscence from the seasonal 2001 schedules.

The production was largely funded by Canadian tax breaks and state funding incentives, resulting in perhaps the most ludicrous location shoot ever undertaken. BBC Wales shot this entirely Welsh-based drama in British Columbia, Canada, with its imposing redwood forests and rather flat valleys. While a BBC executive insisted that 'this offered the perfect setting' it's difficult to imagine a more perfect location than Wales itself. What this really means is that without a Canadian shoot, the same level of budget would not have been available. A letter to *Radio Times* also complained about the unrecognisably indigenous Canadian species of talking animals in the first series. Elsewhere there was some obvious dubbing of Welsh accents onto Canadian actors which also annoyed. Most worrying is the number of producers involved – the rather bloodless aggregate of a story to Season One is what might be expected of a committee.

A Kudos Productions/Forefront Entertainment Group/
BBC Wales co-production
2 seasons
(colour)

**Main Cast:** Ian Richardson (Stephen Tyler), Neil Pearson
(Jack Green), Sian Phillips (Meg Lewis), Katie Stuart
(Mary Green), Steven Webb (William Constant), Olivia Coles
(Alice Constant), Christopher Redman (Matthew Morden),
Stephen Fry (Voice of Jasper the Owl)

**Season One**
**6 episodes**
**Broadcast:** Sundays 31/10/99 – 5/12/99 BBC1

William and Alice Constant visit their Uncle Jack and his
girlfriend Phoebe in the Golden Valley in Wales. Also staying
for the Christmas holidays is Jack's estranged daughter Mary,
who has flown in from Canada. Uncle Jack is living in the 500-
year-old Golden House which he plans to open as a hotel. The
house and the valley have a lot of history, including time-
travelling magician Stephen Tyler who wants the children to
help him save the valley and its rare badger population. He
also tells the children that Phoebe's baby, due soon, is central
to the valley's destiny. Matthew Morden, the magician's
inexperienced and headstrong young apprentice, steals Tyler's
golden pendulum – the source of his magic powers – and
sends his familiar, the rat, to the future where it convinces the
jealous Mary that Phoebe is a witch and her baby will bring
evil to the valley.

**Additional Cast:** Kate Greenhouse (Phoebe Taylor), Jennifer
Saunders (Voice of the Rat), Martin Evans (Kev), Matthew
Walker (Arthur)

Based on the novels by William Corlett: *The Steps Up the
Chimney: Being the First Book of The Magician's House*
(first UK publication 1990, The Bodley Head) and *The Door in
the Tree: Being the Second Book of The Magician's House*
(first UK publication 1991, The Bodley Head)

**Screenplay by** William Corlett
**Script Supervisor:** Lucy MacLeod
**Script Supervisor for BBC Wales:** Sophie Fante
**Executive Story Editor:** Elizabeth Stewart

**Music:** Ken Williams
**Production Designer:** Glen Pearson
**Associate Producers:** William Corlett and Jana Edelbaun
**Production Executive:** Deborah S. Patz
**Associate Producer for BBC Wales:** Helen Vallis
**Executive Producers for BBC Wales:** Maggie Russell,
Pedr James
**Executive Producer (Canada):** Forefront Entertainment Group
**Executive Producer (UK):** Stephen Garrett
**Creative Producer:** Karen Troubetzkoy
**Director:** Paul Lynch

**Developed for TV** by Elizabeth Stewart

**Season Two**
**6 episodes**
**Broadcast:** Sundays 12/11/00 – 17/12/00

Greedy developer Charles Morden plans to open a theme park
called MordWorld on the shores of Golden Water and claims
to own most of the land. Stephen Tyler, meanwhile, has been
experimenting with electricity and has accidentally created
Black Gold, which falls into the curious hands of Matthew
Morden. Tyler visits Will, Alice and Mary in the present day but
while on the lake they are almost capsized by the current of
an underwater river and Tyler, suddenly returned to his own
time, loses his power source, the golden pendulum. Mary later
discovers she has the pendulum. Will takes charge of it but
misuses it to converse with Matthew in Elizabethan times.
Using the chunk of Black Gold that the apprentice has
snapped free from the ancient standing stone, Matthew is
blasted into the present day. Soon trees are dying and the
Golden Water is slowly being poisoned – the effects of the
Black Gold.

**Right:** 'I'm a mystic …
and here's me stick!'
Ian Richardson as
Stephen Tyler, resident of
*The Magician's House.*

**Additional Cast:** Kendall Cross (Phoebe Taylor),
Robert Wisden (Charles Morden), Jesse Moss (Mark),
Ken Pogue (Sir Henry Morden)

Based on the novel *The Tunnel Behind the Waterfall: Being
the Third Book of The Magician's House* by William Corlett
(first UK publication 1991, The Bodley Head)
**Screenplay by** William Corlett
**Script Supervisor:** Ingrid Kenning
**Story Editor:** Karen Troubetzkoy
**Script Editor:** Howard Burch
**Script Editor for BBC Wales:** Sophie Fante
**Executive Story Editor:** Elizabeth Stewart

**Music:** Ken Williams
**Production Designer:** Glen Pearson
**Associate Producer:** William Corlett
**Production Executive:** Deborah S. Patz
**Associate Producer for BBC Wales:** Helen Vallis
**Executive Producer for BBC Wales:** Maggie Russell
**Executive Producer (Canada):** Mickey Rogers
**Executive Producer (UK):** Stephen Garrett
**Producer:** Karen Troubetzkoy
**Director:** Graeme Lynch

**Developed for TV by** Karen Troubetzkoy

**Tie-in publications:** editions of all four Corlett novels
published in paperback by Red Fox, 1999

**Video:** Season One issued as a double tape pack by Acorn
Video 30/10/00. Season Two also released as a double tape
pack by Acorn 28/12/00.

## Pig Heart Boy

*Pig Heart Boy* may at first appear like a strange choice of
novel to adapt for the small screen, with its subject matter
the ethics and impact of xenotransplantation.

With a terminal heart condition, thirteen-year-old
Cameron Kelsey's life depends on a heart transplant.
When the possibility of an operation falls through for the
third time, Cameron's father contacts a leading professor
in the field of xenotransplants – the use of organs from
genetically modified animals for human transplant.
Cameron reluctantly accepts this as his one remaining
chance of survival but neither he nor his family are
prepared for the attention this will bring.

*Pig Heart Boy* is a far-reaching drama that doesn't rest
solely on Cameron's plight but moves also to examine the
impact of his operation on family and friends. From the
outset, even before the narrative introduces the notion of
xenotransplantation, the atmosphere in the Kelsey
household is one of extreme tension. In what is essentially
a sad and vicious circle, Cameron is piggy in the middle as
his parents, crumbling under the stress of his illness,
frequently argue over what is best for him. Cameron craves
normality in his life yet at the same time cannot help but
hold himself responsible for his parents' problems, telling
his Nan, 'I just want them to be happy. The way they were
before.' Rather than offering a positive way forward, the
possibility of a transplant using the heart of a pig only
serves in the short term to throw the family into further
conflict. Cameron's father, responsible for initiating
contact with Professor Rae, is desperate in his pursuit of

any option that could save his son's life. Cameron's mother,
unhappy at the ethics of using animals for such a purpose,
is resolutely against the idea regardless that it offers
Cameron his only remaining hope of life. The arguments
that ensue merely serve to frustrate Cameron further.

As important as the ethical questions asked of science
and medicine are those put to a tabloid-dependent society
and people's reactions to sensationalist headlines. When
news of Cameron's operation is leaked to the press, he is
made to feel like a freak by some of Fleet Street's less
tactful journalists and Blackman carries this theme of
isolation and suspicion further when Cameron is
ostracised by his friends. Unable to break the
psychological barrier of what has happened to Cameron,
most of his friends behave in the same manner and in time
Cameron comes to treat them with the same disregard.
The extent of Cameron's alienation is summed up
perfectly when Julie, who previously had a crush on
Cameron, will no longer go near him because her mother
has told her Cameron is different and might be carrying
pig germs.

*Pig Heart Boy*'s most immediate talking point,
commented upon by Mark Lawson in his *Guardian* TV
column, is that the narrative is centred on a black family.
Not that this should be considered unusual, of course; after
all, black actors had been cast previously in children's
dramas including *The Tomorrow People* and *Grange Hill*. *Pig
Heart Boy* stands out, however, as the first children's drama
to present an Afro-Caribbean family as the focal point.
Black writer Malorie Blackman was inspired to start
writing when she couldn't find any books that featured
black children as the protagonists.

It's difficult to determine whether *Pig Heart Boy* should
be treated as realist or sci-fi. As xenotransplantation on
the scale of that witnessed in *Pig Heart Boy* is not yet used
in contemporary medicine, it would perhaps be most
useful to class it as plausible science fiction. As a drama it
is slick and seamless. *The Literary Review* described the
book as 'a novel so relentless in its realism that parts of it
read like the transcript of a fly-on-the-wall documentary'.
It's an aspect not lost in the adaptation. The serial is very
much faithful to the novel except that the ending in the
dramatisation is slightly more upbeat. At the end of the
dramatisation Cameron's mother has her baby, symbolic of
the fact that life goes on, and Cameron returns to full
strength following his second transplant. The novel
finishes before the baby is born, with Cameron still very
weak and a long way from recovery and with the discovery
that Professor Rae's other pig heart patient has died, thus
casting doubt over Cameron's long-term prospects. It's
worth noting, given the different endings, that while
Malorie Blackman wrote the first four episodes, the final
two were credited to Carolyn Sally Jones.

**BBC**
**6 episodes**
(colour)

### Episode One
'The D Word'
Tuesday 7/12/99 5.10p.m.
Cameron's life depends on a heart transplant. With three
failed attempts already, he's all but given up hope before a
professor offers him the transplant he needs. However, the
heart would be that of a genetically modified pig.

### Episode Two
'Trudy'

Thursday 9/12/99 5.10p.m.

Cameron's father is all for the operation but Cameron's mother doesn't feel the same and arguments become more frequent. When Cameron discovers that his mother is pregnant he begins a video diary for his future sibling. Cameron's health is deteriorating rapidly, however, and he decides that he wants to go ahead with the transplant.

### Episode Three
'Betrayal'

Tuesday 14/12/99 5.10p.m.

Cameron arrives at hospital for his operation. The transplant is a success but Cameron's best friend's father has found out that it involved a pig's heart. Desperate to save his family from financial ruin, he sells the story to the tabloid newspapers.

### Episode Four
'Consequences'

Thursday 16/12/99 5.10p.m.

The Kelseys return home to find it besieged by journalists. They hold a press conference and discover that not everyone is sympathetic with their situation. At school Cameron finds that his friends treat him differently and some are too scared to come near him.

### Episode Five
'Losing It'

Tuesday 21/12/99 5.10p.m.

Cameron is finding it difficult to cope with the intense media pressure and reaction from his friends. The Bainbridges apologise for leaking the story to the paper but Cameron cannot forgive Marion, his best friend, for telling his father in the first place. Cameron starts to swim again but is attacked at the pool by an animal rights activist.

### Episode Six
'End of the Line'

Thursday 23/12/99 5.10p.m.

Cameron passes out when swimming and is saved by Marion. It is discovered that Cameron's body has rejected his new heart and that he must have another transplant. Cameron however has given up hope but his Nan tells him that he must never give up. When Cameron later finds her dead, he changes his mind and prepares for the second transplant.

**Main Cast:** Marlon Yearwood (Cameron Kelsey), Patrick Robinson (Tyler Kelsey), Clare Perkins (Cathy Kelsey), Mona Hammond (Nan Preston), Simon Williams (Professor Rae), Jonathan De Herit (Marion Bainbridge), Jermaine Desmarais (Nathan)

Based on the novel by Malorie Blackman (first UK publication 1997, Doubleday)

**Adapted by** Malorie Blackman (1–4) and Carolyn Sally Jones (5, 6)
**Script Editor:** Barbara Cox

**Music:** Nick Bicât
**Production Designer:** George Kyriakides
**Producer:** Diana Kyle
**Associate Producer:** Elizabeth Binns
**Executive Producer:** Elaine Sperber
**Director:** Kate Cheeseman

**Tie-in publications:** edition published in paperback by Corgi, 1999

## The Ghost Hunter

With 3.1 million child viewers recorded for the first series of *The Ghost Hunter* it would seem that ghost stories for children are still as popular as ever. The series was the highest-rated children's programme on either channel for the year.

Ivan Jones helped adapt his original novel for TV. 'Usually it seems that we must get rid of the ghost or kill the ghost,' he said. 'I thought it would be quite nice if he could make friends with the ghost who was being hunted. I think that gave it a kind of unusual twist.' Clearly then, Jones was blissfully unaware of the almost identical premise to the 1976 Tyne Tees comedy drama *Nobody's House* which also had a Victorian urchin ghost boy befriend two modern-day siblings.

*Ghost Hunter* lacked its predecessor's sense of pathos. When Roddy first meets William, the shoeshine boy explains that he was run over by a hansom cab: 'Still 'ere I am, no 'arm done!' There is some kind of hint at the tragedy of the young deaths of the ghost children in the sequel series but it's rather glossed over and less than central.

The mysterious Ghost Hunter turns out to be Mrs Croker, masquerading as the village shopkeeper, although an actor of Jean Marsh's calibre is wasted here as the pantomime villain of the piece. For the most part the series rather predictably indulges in 'William is invisible and gets up to larks at Roddy's school' schtick, where Roddy and Co. are chased about by the grumpy janitor, Old Nosey.

The first series' conclusion confirms suspicions that this is just surface drama, when Mrs Croker accidentally falls to her death in the castle moat. There's a missed opportunity here – if Croker inexplicably hates ghosts, wouldn't it be an interesting irony if she died and *became* a ghost? The easy resurrection of Croker for a second run marks *The Ghost Hunter* down as a comedy franchise-in-waiting.

The second series saw Croker and her assistant De Sniff take on the ghosts with her even more obviously comic strip ghost hoover, the Ghost Guzzler. There's no internal logic to this fantasy, it seems. Where did Croker get all this hi-tech equipment and why does she now plan to live forever by distilling the ghosts' psychic energy via the Spectryka machine (whereas last year she just hated them)? Croker mistakenly opens up a time portal and ends up in Victorian London at the series' conclusion and, while that's rather ludicrous, the thought of William and his new ghost friend Flora travelling back to join them for a third series was more interesting than proceedings so far. In fact the run was as before, while lacking the attention to period detail one expects from the BBC.

While it's difficult to predict nostalgia, some excellent visuals will probably stay long in the minds of its young audience, in particular the sight of dozens of shrunken ghosts trapped in jars or the spirits from down the ages gathering for their annual ghosts meeting at the solstice. Its visual aspect is the series' biggest plus but at a reputed cost of £160,000 an episode you would certainly expect some sort of televisual gloss. If *The Ghost Hunter* is to be considered as drama, and it has been sold as such, there's been very little genuine substance to go with that gloss as yet.

**A Zenith North Production for BBC**
**3 seasons**
(colour)

**Main Cast:** Lee Goodwin (William Povey), William Theakston
(Roddy Oliver), Verity-Jane Dearsley (Tessa Oliver), Jean Marsh
(Mrs Croker), Richard Hanson (De Sniff), Trevor Byfield
(Old Nosey), Terry Crow (Wally Crabbe), Tracey Brabin
(Mrs Oliver), John McAndrew (Mr Oliver), Angela Bruce
(Mrs Justin), Peter Stockbridge (Eric), Rachel Hudson
(Flora – Seasons 2 and 3), Andrew Havill
(Professor Darcy – Season 3)

Based on the novel *The Ghost Hunter* by Ivan Jones (first UK
publication 1997, Young Hippo Spooky)

**Script Consultant:** Jim Eldridge
**Script Supervisor:** Susannah Binding (Season One),
Elaine Matthews (Season Two)
**Music:** David Chilton, Nick Russell-Pavier
**Art Director:** Teresa Kay (Season One), Alex Evans
(Season Two)
**Production Designer:** Pilar Foy
**Producer:** David Bell
**Production Executive:** Alan Fairholm
**Programme Associate:** David Hallam
**BBC Executive:** Christine Secombe
**Executive Producer for Zenith:** Peter Murphy
**Director:** David Bell

**Season One**
**6 episodes** ('The Ghost in the Bedroom'; 'Who is The Ghost
Hunter?'; 'Caught!'; 'The Hunt for Mrs Croker'; 'Chillwood
Castle'; 'Showdown!')
**Broadcast:** Tuesdays and Thursdays 4/1/00 – 20/1/00

**Written by:** Ivan Jones (1, 5), Roy Apps (2, 4),
Jim Eldridge (3, 6)

**Season Two**
**6 episodes** ('The Secret of Deadlock Hall'; 'The Ghost in the
Machine'; 'The Trap is Set'; 'Ghost Children'; 'A Brush With
Terror'; 'The Final Countdown')
**Broadcast:** Tuesdays and Thursdays 2/1/01 – 18/1/01

**Written by:** Roy Apps (1, 3), Ivan Jones (2, 4),
Jim Eldridge (5, 6)

**Season Three**
**6 episodes**
**Broadcast:** Mondays 18/2/02 – 25/3/02

**Written by** Roy Apps (1, 4), Ivan Jones (2, 5),
Jim Eldridge (3, 6)

**Tie-in publications:** edition of original novel published in
paperback by Scholastic Hippo, 2000. Novelisation of Season
One episodes 5 and 6 as *The Ghost Hunter at Chillwood
Castle* written by Ivan Jones, published in paperback by
Scholastic Hippo, 2000. Novelisation of Season Two material
as *The Ghost Hunter's House of Horror* published by
Scholastic Hippo, 2001.

# Life Force

For Childsplay and its head Peter Tabern, *Life Force* was an
opportunity to pursue and develop the ideas first explored
in 1992's *Eye of the Storm*. That serial had aired ecological
concerns using a fantasy framework and *Life Force* shared
the same ethos, this time choosing the inescapable truth of
global warming as its major topic.

The future Britain was strikingly presented to us in the
opening episode – a map of the UK in 2025 appeared as a
collection of small islands. Even more immediate was a
throwaway visual gag in the fourth episode which had the
very top of the Blackpool Tower jutting from the sea. The
finer points might not have been exactly watertight but
the future world of our children and grandchildren was
sweepingly painted. Petrol for boats and trucks is in short
supply, people buy goods from vast junk markets in Euros
or by bartering and the internet is no more, replaced by
intermittently available satellite link-ups.

The key episodes were broadly drawn adventure stories
which sprung naturally from the situation: one week the
crew meet a weird sun cult while searching for a rare plant
needed to provide the ingredients for making sunblock,
vital in the new British climate; in another, our young
heroes stumble across dog-like mutants while searching a
vast scrapyard island for an all-important antique car
engine part desperately needed for their electric generator.

The series wisely followed a self-contained 'story of the
week' route after launching with a linked serial format for
the first few weeks. Remembering long plods like *The
Tripods* and *Knights of God*, it seems that continuous 'epic'
serials rarely sustain over twelve or thirteen-week runs.
Indeed this was the first truly 'episodic' British series
aimed at children in many years. With this format came a
great variety of stories. Several tackled a different cause for
green concern, touching on industrial pollution of the food
chain and toxic farming chemicals among other subjects.
Some used the well-mined, fashionable tropes of virtual
reality and computer viruses, but always to good effect.
What could have come across as didactic, but was well
executed in the adventure format, was the series' drugs
episode 'No Quick Fix' which saw young Ash using
sticking patches sold by a shady dealer to heighten his
psychic abilities while leading him perilously close to burn-
out.

There was even room for a comedy episode among the
more hard-hitting fare, though even this was not without a
message. In 'Yesterday Island' a demented robot killer
granny tries to trap the youngsters in a virtual world of
late-twentieth-century video games but they fight to
escape back to their 'real' lives with all its attendant
hardships. The central performance from Pauline McLynn
(*Father Ted*'s Mrs Doyle, no less) was a comic joy and the
scene where she plugged a power lead into her eye 'socket'
(groan!) was sure to have equally horrified and delighted
that section of the target audience that reads Roald Dahl
with glee.

As well as the inventive scripts, everything else about
the series oozed class – expansive video location work and
sailing excursions on the waters of the globally warmed
world of 2025 (the Lake District doubling up), superb video
effects and effective action sequences.

The final episode, which saw the reactivation of the
early serial threads, didn't answer all of the series'
questions. For instance, who was the shadowy boss of the
Commission and what were their aims? It may be that in
the hope of a second series these matters were intentionally

left unanswered. The episode and the series were open-ended and showed the young Greenwatchers full of the hope for the future. This was bittersweet in the event, considering the series' disgraceful treatment at the hands of the ITV bosses.

*Life Force* had threat, conflict, imminent danger, cruelty, mystery and tension and it would seem that, as far as ITV are concerned, that is not suitable for children. The series was pulled from its 'prime time' Monday afternoon slot after four episodes and, without warning, thereafter relegated to one showing a week in its Sunday morning slot. First it leaked out that the series was pulled after a few parents complained about some of the more scary sequences. Then a semi-official statement recorded on Childsplay's website suggested that it might have been due to poorer than expected ratings. Are either of these reasons really acceptable?

**A Childsplay Production in association with ITEL**
**13 episodes**
(colour)

**Episode 1**
'The Girl Who Flipped'
Monday 10/1/00 4.35p.m.
Repeated Sunday 16/1/00 9.50a.m.
Mai-Li, a teenage girl at school on one of the North West islands in the submerged UK of 2025, discovers she has strange psychic powers. Amy Webber runs a series of tests and realises that, like herself, Mai-Li's powers are extremely well-developed. She also knows too well the danger Mai-Li will be in the next time Kurt Glemser comes harvesting senders for the mysterious Commission.

**Episode 2**
'Greenwatch'
Monday 17/1/00 4.35p.m.
Repeated Sunday 23/1/00 9.50a.m.
When Greg and Karen's mother and father are taken away by Glemser, Goodman becomes their guardian. A scientist from the time before science was outlawed, he tells them about Greenwatch, a group of ecologists who tried to save the world from global warming but with catastrophic results.

**Episode 3**
'On the Run'
Monday 24/1/00 4.35p.m.
Repeated Sunday 30/1/00 9.50a.m.
Learning of Mai-Li's powers, Glemser sets out to find her. Goodman will be forced to betray her unless she can alter his memories ...

**Episode 4**
'Greenhouse Effect'
Monday 31/1/00 4.35p.m.
Repeated Sunday 6/2/00 9.50a.m.
The French Climies – climate refugees – are taken in by an exploitative farmer who uses banned and highly toxic chemicals to promote the growth of his crops.

**Episode 5**
'The Village That Dreamed Itself to Death'
Sunday 13/2/00 9.50a.m.
The children come across a totally deserted village – they can find only one little girl, who appears not to have slept for a week. The villagers have come under a shared hallucination caused by contaminated gull eggs.

**Episode 6**
'Yesterday Island'
Sunday 20/2/00 9.50a.m.
The gang find themselves on a remote island and are met by an old woman who tends an abandoned virtual reality theme park. She is very keen for them to stay ...

**Episode 7**
'Beware of the Dog'
Sunday 27/2/00 9.50a.m.
Searching for an old car motor to salvage for their generator, the gang travel to an island that is a huge scrapyard – but they find dog-like feral mutant children among the junk.

**Episode 8**
'Return to Sender'
Sunday 5/3/00 9.50a.m.
The Greenwatch computer is attacked by a form of psychic virus.

**Episode 9**
'Siren Song'
Sunday 12/3/00 9.50a.m.
The kids search for a rare plant needed as a vital ingredient in sunblock. When they find one, it is in the possession of a strange cult of sun worshippers.

**Episode 10**
'Paradise Island'
Sunday 19/3/00 9.50a.m.
The gang discover a woman continuing her father's research into cold fusion.

**Episode 11**
'Age Before Beauty'
Sunday 26/3/00 9.50a.m.
Greg is trapped by an eccentric scientist and looked after by his young daughter ... but what – or who – is he experimenting with?

**Episode 12**
'No Quick Fix'
Sunday 2/4/00 9.50a.m.
Ash gets involved with a boy who is stealing from the market to feed his habit for a stimulant that can take a sender's powers to new heights, but which also has dangerous side effects.

**Episode 13**
'The Thought Fish'
Sunday 9/4/00 9.50a.m.
Amy Webber has escaped from Glemser's clutches and returns to Greg and Karen – but something's not quite right ...

**Main Cast:** Paul Fox (Greg Webber), Julia Haworth (Karen Webber), Sarah Hollis (Mai-Li Cheung), Pablo Duarte (Ash Karnak), David Mallinson (Goodman), Damian Lewis (Kurt Glemser), Kelly Hunter (Amy Webber), Helen Griffin (Gwyneth, The Refuge Lady), Sarah Lam (Sally Cheung)

**Devised by** Peter Tabern
**Writers:** Peter Tabern, Rik Carmichael, John Hay, Greg McQueen

**Music** Composed by Ian Hughes and Krystian Hughes
**Art Director:** Chris Coldwell
**Assistant Art Director:** Elizabeth Craig
**Production Design:** Jim Holloway
**Producer:** Peter Tabern
**Directors:** Justin Chadwick, Lorne Magory, Peter Tabern

## Hero To Zero

Football personalities including Brian Robson and Bobby Charlton had previously made guest cameos as themselves in children's series like *Jossy's Giants* but in *Hero to Zero* the Liverpool and England striker Michael Owen plays a major role throughout the narrative, existing in the imagination of a troubled child.

Following the separation of his parents, life isn't easy for young Charlie Brice. His school work is suffering and whenever his parents meet all they do is argue. Charlie desperately wants to play for a local youth football team but his father, wary of the manager's bullying tactics, refuses to let him. Charlie is upset with his father, blaming him for ruining everything. When Jimmy gets the chance to manage struggling Hope Rangers, Charlie – with the help of his idol Michael Owen – has the opportunity to rebuild his confidence and try to reunite his family.

The drama doesn't centre purely on Charlie's difficulties but focuses also on his father Jimmy. Once a professional footballer, Jimmy's career was destroyed when an opposing team's manager ordered one of his players to deliberately injure him. Stuck in a dead-end sales job, Jimmy's life has fallen apart, leading ultimately to the separation from his wife. Once a hero, he now considers himself a nothing, thus it is Jimmy to whom the title of the drama actually refers.

Series creator John Salthouse, formerly a lead actor in *The Bill*, uses an in-depth knowledge of youth football to present a particularly realistic and gritty portrayal of what happens both on and off the pitch. It isn't just the football matches, striking though they are, that capture the eye. Salthouse's depiction of the often childish, almost animalistic behaviour of the parents involved in the game is an eye-opener. Vic Morrish, manager of the Eagles, is a bully who will stop at nothing to win, even ordering his son to injure other players. Even Jimmy finds himself momentarily behaving in the same fashion when a cup match between the two teams spirals into a brawl between the competitive parents.

Salthouse uses the character of Kelly, Hope Rangers' only female player, to introduce the harsh and uncomfortable theme of domestic abuse. When Kelly fails to turn up for an important match, Jimmy and Charlie visit her house. When she reluctantly lets them in, they find her mother sitting battered and bruised, clutching her baby. It's a sad sign of the times when such issues need to be addressed on children's television but a brave decision nonetheless. It also serves to reinforce the importance that something as simple as a local football team can have for some children. As Kelly explains to Charlie, it's the only time she feels good about herself.

Michael Owen fulfils the role of an imaginary agony uncle. With his father living away from home, Charlie lacks confidence and a role model and so turns to his idol for help. Owen is Charlie's positive side and the conversations between the two represent Charlie's inner struggle to assert himself and give reason to events happening round about him. When Charlie's parents get back together and Hope Rangers triumph over the Eagles, Charlie no longer needs Owen. Delivering one last piece of advice to Charlie, his idol spells out the message at the heart of the drama: 'Trust in yourself and you can do anything.'

The story had previously aired on Radio Five (Tuesdays and Wednesdays 30/11/93 – 15/12/93) with Gary Lineker as Charlie's hero. In this medium it was not much of a stretch of the imagination to think of Lineker's voice inside the boy's head but on television not only was the manifestation required to be more visual but the guest footballer was required to do much more in the way of acting. Michael Owen may be a gifted footballer but it's clear to see that giving up his Saturday job in the pursuit of an acting career would be foolhardy. *Hero To Zero* didn't require the presence of Owen or any other real-life footballer. It wouldn't be unreasonably cynical to assume that this was designed with viewing figures firmly in mind. A fictitious idol along the lines of *Roy of the Rovers* might have improved this drama yet further.

**BBC**
**6 episodes**
(colour)
**Broadcast:** Wednesdays 23/2/00 – 29/3/00

**Main Cast:** Huw Procter (Charlie Brice), Ian Burfield (Jimmy Brice), Angela Simpson (Rachel Brice), Michael Owen (as himself), Alan Ford (Ron Warley), Cliff Parisi (Vic Morrish)

**Written by** John Salthouse and Michael Cook

**Music:** Simon Whiteside
**Designer:** David Hitchcock
**Producer:** Cas Lester
**Executive Producer:** Elaine Sperber
**Director:** Bob Tomson

# Conclusion

It seems inevitable that any retrospective will hark back to a supposed 'golden era' while presiding over a perceived decline in current output. Much of this often stems from insecurity and indefinites – in the maelstrom of the present the future always looks uncertain. In this book we have tried to see things as they were – let's not forget that children's drama died altogether in the 60s on the BBC, and the production values, budgets and pacing of much early 70s programming left a lot to be desired. Nonetheless, from a 2001/2 viewpoint we seem to be mourning the death of the one-off play and witnessing the slow extermination of the serial in favour of the continuous soap, just as other commentators are doing when they look back at mainstream adult television.

One ray of light appears to be a continued commitment to drama from the BBC. No doubt much of this stems from the extremely high ratings earned by *See How They Run* and *The Ghost Hunter* in 1999 (the latter was the highest-rated children's programme of all for that year). The most positive aspect of all was the broadcast of the excellent play *Out of the Ashes*, the story of a young girl living on a farm during the foot-and-mouth outbreak. This was the first one-off drama to be shown by the BBC in over a decade.

Only time will tell if the trend continues. October 2002 has seen Children's Controller Nigel Pickard announce he is set to leave the post to become ITV's Director of Programmes from early 2003. Pickard's track record in drama for children was a notable one; working with Anna Home at TVS in the mid-80s and later scheduling many ITV archive classics on satellite station The Children's Channel before becoming head of Children's at ITV and launching *SM:tv Live* among other shows. If proof were needed that Pickard is of 'the old school', a fresh adaptation of *Stig of the Dump* appeared in early 2002 but Pickard's stay has turned out much shorter than perhaps expected. Compared with the years of service put in by predecessors such as Monica Sims, Edward Barnes and Anna Home it appears positively fleeting. This raises fresh questions of the BBC children's service, currently running junior tie-ins of the BBC's adult *Fame Academy* 'reality' game show.

Much of the BBC's resources, time and thought currently seems to be diverted towards Saturday mornings where for the first time in years they lost ground, deservedly, to ITV's *SM:tv Live*, presented by Ant and Dec for three years until December 2001. *Grange Hill* and *Byker Grove* are hogging the limited drama slots available and innovation is being stifled by this. Curtailing or, heaven forbid, axing of these series in favour of something new seems unthinkable at the BBC. An all-year-round (and thus genuine) soap for children now seems increasingly likely, with the news in early 2002 that Phil Redmond has taken back control of his 'baby', *Grange Hill*. The series airing from January 2003 will be made in Liverpool by Redmond's Mersey TV, producers of *Brookside* and *Hollyoaks*.

Pressure from the government and the broadcasting regulators will hopefully force assurances that both the BBC and ITV will continue to invest in drama. In November 2000, Broadcasting Minister Janet Anderson voiced concerns that 'while many children's programmes such as *Art Attack*, *The Worst Witch* and *See How They Run* were clearly in the tradition of the best, the Government shared parents' concerns that some fell well short'. She also agreed with the regulators' assessment that it was unacceptable for either BBC or ITV to take a lead from the unregulated satellite and cable channels who had 'dumbed down' children's programming to 'the lowest common denominator' by relying on a diet of cartoons.

These seem very real concerns and there is persistent loose talk in the industry to suggest that ITV wants to drop all drama for children. The cowardly treatment of the superb *Life Force* at the hands of the ITV controllers appeared to support such rumours when the series was suddenly pulled from the afternoon schedules and dumped in an early Sunday morning shift.

Amid complaints (from parents naturally) that the series was too frightening, the controllers seemed unable to comprehend that perhaps children like to be scared within the fantasy settings of a television programme and ceded to what surely amounted to no more than a handful of parental rantings. More importantly, should the rumblings that poorer-than-expected ratings have been the real reason for its 'axing' then this is final admission that, for ITV at least, Children's is another sector of programming where public service policies no longer matter. Children's ITV (CITV) needs to have a good look at its attitudes to drama if it is pulling a fine series like this from its schedules instead of recommissioning it immediately. Tellingly, when the Monday showing was dropped, it was replaced with the comedy import *Sabrina the Teenage Witch*, seemingly into eternity.

There are still vague stirrings from ITV in the genre. *The Gypsy Girl*, shown in 2001, was an excellent seven-episode series that harked back to seemingly lost values. Though it was roundly marketed as a British *Sabrina*, and probably only commissioned in the hope that it would be, the reality was that the stories it told were rather more thoughtful. The broadcast of *The Gypsy Girl* marked another shift in children's programming when it became the first drama to air on consecutive days, Mondays to Fridays, and this 'stripped' schedule experiment is up for review at the beginning of 2002. A second run of the drama *24 Seven* has since aired in the more familiar weekly pattern.

On the negative side again, ITV has recently shorn off another five to ten minutes from the back end of children's afternoon broadcasting so that it ends at 5.00 p.m. The axing of the banal *Home and Away* from the ITV schedules gave way to Carlton's revival of *Crossroads*, itself pandering to a child/teenage audience with a preponderance of young characters within it.

In November 2001, CITV Controller Janie Grace addressed a conference with a speech that outwardly seemed to throw in the towel and admit defeat when faced with the BBC's spend on Children's. No doubt her speech was politically motivated and aimed at persuading Network Centre to give CITV a greater share of the ITV budget but it nonetheless threw a spotlight on the very real problems the commercial broadcaster currently faces in addressing what is a not so commercial area. To cut the CITV budget would surely mean that the ITV chiefs had abandoned any notion of public service broadcasting.

A downturn in advertising revenues of 17 per cent for ITV as a whole had resulted in a 25 per cent drop in the yearly CITV budget, from £40 million to £30 million, and this situation can only exacerbated by the collapse in spring 2002 of the ITV Digital platform. Grace failed to see how new drama in particular could be made in Britain with such reduced departmental income. Grace could only suggest a centralising of CITV revenues so that earnings from CITV-related merchandise could be ploughed back directly into CITV's production budgets. All of this seems to indicate that children's television on ITV, and drama in particular, is in a parlous state if not quite on its knees. CITV ended 2001 with a promising new thirteen-part series, *24 Seven* from Granada but a second run airing at time of going to press appears glossy but vapid.

The BBC meanwhile is at yet another crossroads as it tries to become a digital broadcaster. There are criticisms from its commercial rivals that such quasi-commercial activities are tantamount to an abuse of a licence fee which gives the BBC unfair advantage at a time of dwindling advertising revenues. Children's television looks set to become a main battlefield on which this digital war will be waged.

On 2 February 2002, the BBC launched two new free-to-air digital channels, catering for 'younger' and 'older' children (CBeebies for the under-sixes, CBBC Digital for six to thirteen-year-olds). Promises are being made that there will be 250 hours of new programming, to come from the indie sector, and that 75 per cent of programmes on the 'older' channel will be home-grown.

Still, there are questions over these bold claims made by Nigel Pickard at the time of launch. Pickard talked of 'economies of scale' in longer-running dramas, which suggests to cynics more conveyor-belt soap. Given the track record of BBC Choice it appears likely that any programmes funded by the BBC will be shown on both the regular BBC service and the digital children's channels, meaning output is likely to be shared (i.e. recycled) rather than doubled. Pickard also hinted in an interview given to the *Financial Times* in October 2001 that 'there are always opportunities for co-production' with other nations like Australia and Canada. Obviously, Pickard's ideas may well never see fruition, given his defection to ITV.

Utopia still seems a long way off but by the first half of 2002 the digital future of children's drama had begun to take shape. While much play has been made of the live and interactive presentation approach taken by *Xchange*, drama has been limited to around an hour per day on Children's BBC (CBBC). Archive material shown has included repeats of the S Club 7 series, *The Ghost Hunter*, *Hero To Zero* and *See How They Run*. Perhaps more surprisingly, CBBC has also aired reruns of *Dark Season*, *The Biz!*, the Nesbit Psammead tales and *Just William*, although some of these have been spoiled by cropping of 4:3 source material to fit the 16:9 widescreen format. A comedy drama series *Cave Girl* has premiered on CBBC Digital before airing on BBC1 – is this merely a case of the quickness of the hand deceiving the eye?

The continuing debate into children's drama and children's television is just part of a growing concern that we are somehow witnessing the death of childhood itself. It is easy to see children today as Gareth-loving tweenies, eight-year-old girls who want to wear make-up and spend money on clothes, or as the kids hanging around outside off-licences in shellsuits, when they're not nicking violent computer games or downloading Eminem and porn from the internet. Children's television meanwhile can seem something of a procession of hyperactive presenters shouting in-between sexed-up pop videos, while drama consists merely of the exploits of the uber-race of cloned models which populate the teensoap of *Hollyoaks*. Probably much of this has more to do with people now distanced from their own childhoods, wallowing in out-of-context nostalgia and left feeling a bit bewildered by it all. Maybe the modern face of drama in 2002 is, perfectly legitimately, the global pop adventures of S Club 7?

Thank God, then, for the phenomenal success of *Harry Potter*. These simple tales of magic and wonder – actually written down on paper in words that have to be read and everything – have taken over the globe despite following in traditions some felt were lost forever. Essentially this is the story of a boy who discovers powers previously unknown to him and must make a journey of self-discovery and a series of difficult choices before he can learn to truly use them – a theme at the core of most children's fiction and drama, whether fantasy or no.

One regret, however, is that Harry and his friends won't be making the transition to their own British-made television series. In today's global village an instant hit can quickly be converted to mega-budget blockbusters. Free McDonald's toys didn't appear in this case but only because of objections from J. K. Rowling. Harry now comes to a cinema near you but not, we're afraid, to that pernicious box in the corner of the living room. Still, perhaps the mega-success of Potter can act as the catalyst to a new golden age of children's television drama. Children's television may once again take its cue from the printed page.

# Select Bibliography

## Books

Baker, Simon and Olwen Terris, *A for Andromeda to Z for Zoo Time – the TV holdings of the National Film and Television Archive 1936–1979* (London: BFI, 1994).

Baskin, Ellen, *Serials on British Television, 1950–1994* (Aldershot: Scolar Press, 1996).

Baxter, Biddy and Edward Barnes, *Blue Peter – The Inside Story* (Hertfordshire: Ringpress, 1989).

Buckingham, David *et al.*, *Children's Television in Britain – History, Discourse and Policy* (London: BFI Publishing, 1999).

Cornell, Paul, Martin Day and Keith Topping, *The Guinness Book of Classic British TV* (Middlesex: Guinness Publishing, 1993); first edition.

Corrie, Andrew and John McCready, *Phil Redmond's Grange Hill – The Official Companion* (London: Weidenfeld and Nicolson, 1988).

Down, Richard, Richard Marson and Christopher Perry, *The British Children's Television Research Guide 1950–1998* (Dudley: Kaleidoscope Publishing, 1999); revised edition.

Fulton, Roger, *The Encyclopedia of TV Science Fiction* (London: Independent Television Books/Boxtree, 1990–2000); various editions.

Home, Anna, *Into the Box of Delights – A History of Children's Television* (London: BBC Books, 1993).

Rogers, Dave, *The ITV Encyclopedia of Adventure* (London: Boxtree/TV Times, 1988).

Sangster, Jim (ed.), *The Press Gang Programme Guide* (Leomac Publishing, 1995).

Sutton, Shaun, *The Largest Theatre in the World – Thirty Years of Television Drama* (London: BBC, 1982).

Townsend, John Rowe, *Written for Children – An Outline of English-Language Children's Literature* (London: Penguin, 1987); third edition.

Vahimagi, Tise, *British Television – An Illustrated Guide* (London: BFI/Oxford University Press, 1994); first edition.

## Periodicals

*BBC Handbook*, BBC, various years

*ITV – Guide to Independent Television*, IBA, various years

*Look-In: the Junior TV Times,* Independent Television Publications, 1971 onwards (ended c. 1995)

*Radio Times*, BBC Publications

*Time Screen*, revised editions, Engale Marketing, 1987–95

*TV Times*, TV Publications/Independent Television Publications/EMAP

## Web

(All web addresses current at 1/4/01)

Blackstar: http://www.blackstar.co.uk

TV Chronicles: http://www.tvchronicles.com

TV Cream: http://tv.cream.org/archive.htm

Watched It!: http://www.geocities.com/TelevisionCity/1011/

Simon Luxton's *Grange Hill* Online: http://www.grangehill.contactbox.co.uk/index.htm

Unofficial *Byker Grove* Fan Site: http://www.users.globalnet.co.uk/-rprice/introduction.htm

# Archive Access

Readers of this book will no doubt wish to see again many of the series contained within. Repeats, be they on terrestrial or satellite channels, and DVD and video releases are of course the most readily accessible ways of viewing archive television but obviously depend on what is selected for such output. Viewers can help influence these selection decisions by writing or emailing to the TV stations and video companies – hopefully this book will bring many series back to the reader's attention and help in some way to motivate calls for repeat screenings. Access to archive television of this kind can prove difficult but there are various approaches the researcher can take.

## Public Access

True public access to children's series, as with any part of the UK's television heritage, is limited but there are occasional opportunities. The British Film Institute is instrumental in the preservation of television history and among its activities regularly provides screenings of archive television at the National Film Theatre on London's South Bank. Recovered black and white episodes of *Freewheelers* have been among the offerings of their annual Missing, Believed Wiped events for instance.

Similar screening events are held by a fan organisation called Kaleidoscope. Based in the Midlands this team of enthusiasts, headed by Richard Down and Chris Perry, have published several excellent archive holdings guides and also hold an annual screening day named The Main Event. Usually held annually in Birmingham, the event screens rare archive material and welcomes guests who worked on the shows. Previous guests have include Alfred Burke, Irene Shubik, Leonard White and Tony Hatch. Screenings cater to all tastes, ranging from restored *Til Death Us Do Part* to *Big Breadwinner Hog*. Children's television is always catered for and screenings have included episodes of *Freewheelers*, *Smith* and *The Feathered Serpent*.

Even wider access can be found at The National Museum of Photography, Film and Television in Bradford. Uniquely, the museum offers free on site viewing access to all, with more than two hundred programmes stored in their *TV Heaven* archive. This is probably Britain's most accessible television archive – a huge variety of items includes representative episodes of such children's classics as *Blue Peter*, *The Basil Brush Show*, *Crackerjack*, *Play School* and *Pipkins*. Of programmes covered in this book, highlights available to view include the first episode of *Follyfoot*, an episode of *Ace of Wands*: 'The Meddlers', *Just William*: 'Violet Elizabeth Wins', the *Flaxton Boys* first season episode 'The Witches' and other sample episodes of *Catweazle*, *Murphy's Mob* and *Press Gang*.

While the collection at Bradford is wide-ranging and begins to address the issue of free public access to the television heritage, academic and commercial researchers will often have more specific needs.

## Commercial Access

The BBC's vast archive holds something like over a million separate items and while thousands of programmes were sadly lost in the short-sighted archive purges of the 1960s and 70s, since 1978 the archive has actively sought the return of missing items. It was at that time the BBC realised the potential commercial worth of their television back catalogue – restoration and clean up of the more commercial items (e.g. *Dad's Army*, *Doctor Who*) with a view to DVD release are among current activities. It should be obvious from this that the BBC's archive is run along commercial lines. The division is run to service BBC repeat schedulers, programme-makers and merchandisers and is not geared up to deal with private enquiries for viewings. The BBC will deal with a small number of requests to view archive material but these are usually only handled if the caller or a close family member took a significant part in the making of the original production.

Private researchers will also find it difficult to access material produced by the independent television companies. The federal nature of ITV, with its regional production centres and a variety of franchise holders down the years since 1955, has often made archiving problematic. Researchers today may not quite face a wild goose chase but will often need to follow fairly lengthy trails to track down certain programmes, requiring efforts and contact networks beyond the means of all but professional TV researchers.

In many cases, ownership of ITV programmes has been bought up and passed on down the years, particularly since satellite television increased the industry's appetite for back-catalogue programming. For example the international sales catalogue from ATV (mostly the Lew Grade productions made and distributed under the ITC banner) passed through various owners before being bought by Carlton. The Thames archive meanwhile is now part of media giant FremantleMedia (formerly Pearson International).

This picture is seemingly ever-changing but most material seems to be working its way slowly into the hands of Carlton and Granada Media. If the two merge a central ITV archive could become a reality. Wales and West broadcaster HTV was recently taken over by Granada Media and its complete programme runs have passed into Granada's hands (their incomplete and thus unsaleable items have been generously and thoughtfully deposited with the National Film and Television Archive). This means that many notable children's dramas of the 70s – including *Sky* and *The Clifton House Mystery* – now reside in Granada archives while episodes of incomplete HTV works such as *King of the Castle* and *The Georgian House* reside in the NFTVA store, the J Paul Getty Jr Conservation Centre at Berkamsted (with regard to *King of the Castle*, the master tape of episode three of this 1977 serial is missing but as we went to press it appeared that a fan VHS copy of the lost segment was to be made available to the NFTVA).

Granada Media have long owned the output of 'rival' broadcasters Yorkshire and Tyne Tees, which means Granada also hold the rights to many children's dramas such as *Follyfoot*. Rights are not the whole story however – when Tyne Tees moved from using 2" videotape to 1" in the 1980s, its 2" facilities were discontinued. Subsequently the entire Tyne Tees 2" tape collection has been transferred to digital tape for Granada, with the originals remaining at the NFTVA for safekeeping. This means the BFI now holds the master tapes for series such as *Nobody's House* and *The Paper Lads* (by accident or design the NFTVA even holds ten minutes or so of audition footage for the latter). Granada now also own London Weekend Television (LWT) and thus their archive, which includes ITV Sunday serials from *Jamie* to *Just William*.

Perhaps the biggest archive casualty resulted from the enforced merger of London broadcasters Rediffusion and ABC to form Thames in 1968. The tape archive seemed to have slipped the net when the two came together and has largely been junked. Losses include eight out of ten episodes of ABC's 1967 version of *The Lion, The Witch and The Wardrobe* and the vast majority of the long-running Rediffusion series *Sexton Blake* and *Orlando*. The only hope now is to find 16mm film recordings of this material, marketed abroad by a company called Global Television in the 1960s and 70s. The NFTVA has acquired a handful of *Orlando* episodes – it held episodes One and Three of the 1966 adventure 'Dangerous Waters' for some years and recently added episodes Two and Four.

All of the above illustrates some of the difficulties for individuals in obtaining and viewing archive material from both the BBC and ITV which, after all, are commercial concerns. Not least of all there is the matter of cost – several ITV companies will happily sell copies of material to inviduals but at prices of several hundred pounds per hour, well beyond the means of most.

## Access to The National Film and Television Archive

The only real alternative to commercial business-to-business research is of course via the BFI and the access it offers to the contents of the NFTVA. The BFI is open to bona fide researchers – both academic and commercial – and to industry professionals, with preferential treatment given to those donors who have deposited their material with the NFTVA over the years. All viewing is on site and must be made by prior appointment.

There can be occasional problems with accessing all of the NFTVA material – many items are held as VHS viewing copies for almost immediate use but some are held on other archive formats and must be converted to viewable cassette formats before viewing is possible.

2" videotape can be transferred to VHS relatively easily but 'telecine' transfers from film to tape are far more difficult. Preservation issues can be a stumbling block here – if the BFI holds a rare or master film copy of a programme it may refuse to transfer it for fear of damaging the original. In these instances transfers will only be made to professional DigiBeta tape – the cost of such transfers can run into several thousands of pounds and so is restricted to commercial requests.

Despite such occasional limitations, the BFI undoubtedly offers the UK's most accessible, comprehensive and inexpensive source of archive television. The NFTVA (formerly the NFA) has been acquiring and preserving examples of television output since 1959 although technical concerns over the longevity of videotape and severe financial restrictions meant acquisition in the 1960s was mostly restricted to film recordings of high profile one-off plays and coverage of cultural events. Some 'ephemeral' material was preserved including episodes of *Doctor Who* and *Z Cars*. This was just as well, as in many cases the BBC destroyed their own copies in the mid-70s. Two 1950s drama depictions of World War Two seem to have been preserved as a result of this policy, *The Silver Sword* (1957) and *The Watch Tower* (1956).

More recently the NFTVA's store has swelled dramatically as a result of donation of 2" videotape material from television companies who have been converting to digital formats since the 1990s. There is a wealth of children's drama in among this superb resource obtained from the BBC and various ITV companies and much of it can easily be made available to researchers due to its tape format. In certain circumstances, agreements in place mean that it may be possible for the NFTVA to acquire any other BBC material on loan.

In addition to collections mentioned previously, such as the HTV and Tyne Tees donations, the acquisition of copies of most of the vast Thames collection means the NFTVA now has extensive runs of *The Tomorrow People* and *Marmalade Atkins* as well as obscurities such as *Horse in the House*. LWT has donated many episodes of *Just William* among other highlights. Yorkshire tape material includes a full run of all four seasons of *The Flaxton Boys* while film series such as *Boy Dominic* are also well represented. Such acquisitions form a centralised, accessible collection unrivalled for research users.

Alistair D. McGown with thanks to Steve Bryant and Ian Potter

## Missing, Believed Wiped

Should you believe you might have videotape recordings or films of programmes that may be missing from official archives, please get in touch with Dick Fiddy via the BFI to see if lost material can be recovered.

Dick Fiddy, National Film Theatre, London, SE1 8XT
e-mail: dick.fiddy@bfi.org.uk

On the facing page is a list of just some of the missing children's drama material currently sought after:

The majority of 1950 and 60s BBC material is missing – black and white material known to have been film recorded at the time but later lost includes *Queen's Champion*, *The Gordon Honour* and *Quick Before They Catch Us*, as well as location footage shot for the 1950s versions of *The Railway Children*. Much of the early 50s BBC output went out live and is lost forever.

Southern's adventure serials of the mid-60s including *Mystery Hall* and *Danger Island*

Virtually all episodes of Rediffusion videotape serials are missing including *Orlando* (four exist) and *Sexton Blake* (the first episode exists). 16mm film telerecordings sold around the world may have survived.

Episodes 1 and 8 of ABC's 1967 version of *The Lion, The Witch and The Wardrobe* have survived as 16mm film recordings – the other eight are missing, junked perhaps as recently as 1978.

The first two seasons of Thames' *Ace of Wands* were wiped in their entirety. Only a handful of audio recordings are known to exist while thankfully the third and final season exists in full.

While black and white film copies of ATV fantasies *Timeslip* and *Escape Into Night* have survived, virtually all of the colour tapes have disappeared.

Episodes 2–6 of HTV time travel fantasy *The Georgian House* were wiped. The NFTVA holds Episodes 1 and 7 only.

## Further reading on the preservation of television

Baker, Simon and Olwen Terris. *A for Andromeda to Z for Zoo Time - The TV holdings of the NFTVA 1936–1979* (London: BFI, 1994)

Ballantyne, James (Ed). *Researcher's Guide to British Film and Television Collections* (London: British Universities Film and Video Council, 1993, 4th edition)

Bryant, Steve. *The Television Heritage – Television archiving now and in an uncertain future* (London: BFI, 1989)

Fiddy, Dick. *Missing, Believed Wiped – Searching for the lost treasures of British television* (London: BFI, 2001)

# Index

This index provides an alphabetical reference to titles of television programmes covered in the book as well as contextual titles of books, films and other television programmes mentioned in the text. It also indexes all credited actors, writers, producers and directors. Relevant names and titles mentioned in the decade overview articles are also indexed.